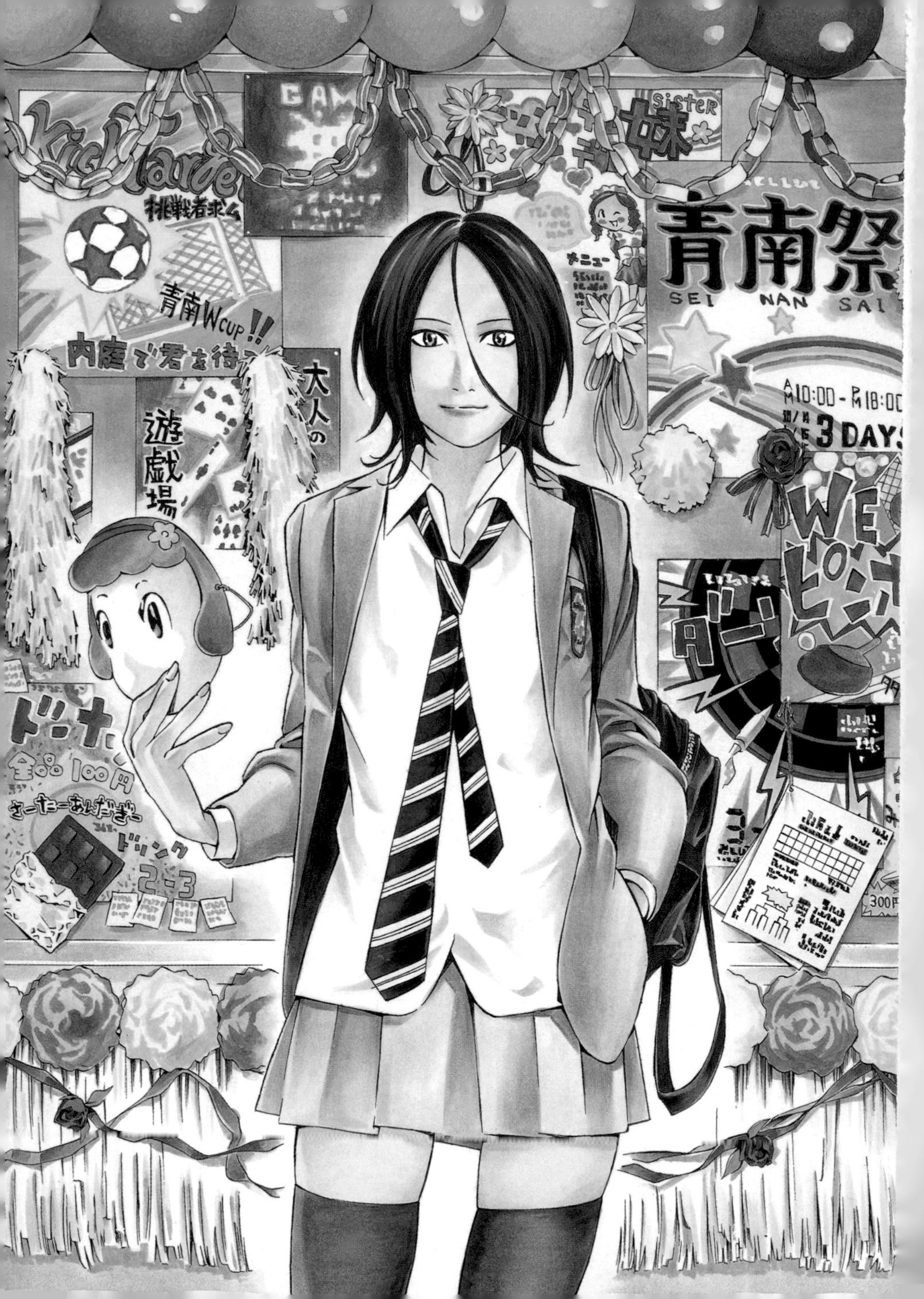

挑戦者求ム
青南Wcup!!
大人の遊戯場
sister
妹
メニュー
青南祭
SEI NAN SAI
AM10:00-PM18:00
3 DAYS
全品100円
さーたーあんだぎー
ドリンク

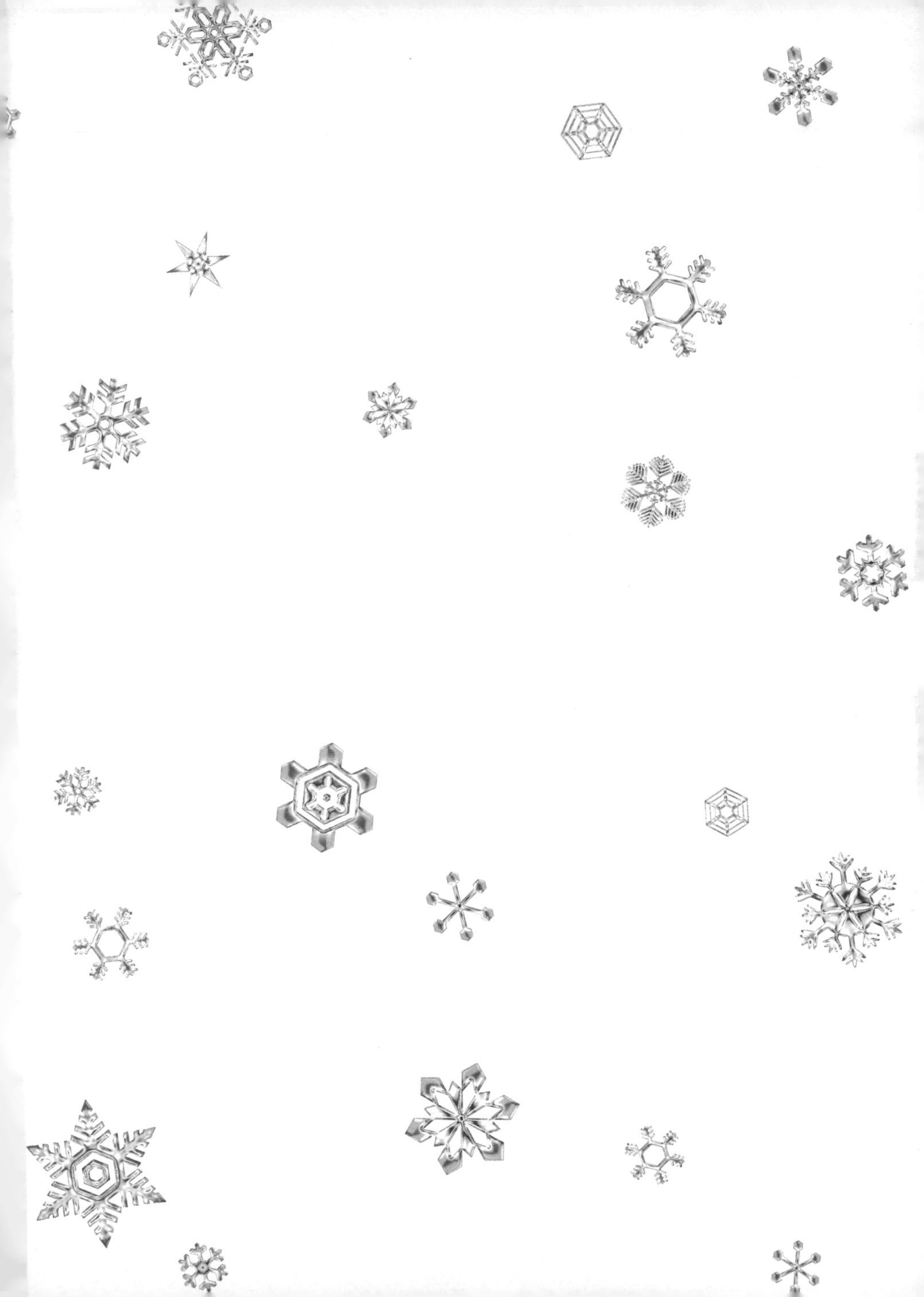

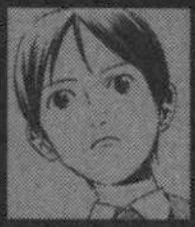

Mitsuru
Third-year at Seinan Gakuin.
Has a somewhat timid personality, which makes him an easy target for bullies.
He has feelings for Rika.

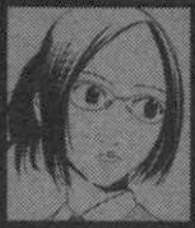

Shimizu
Third-year at Seinan Gakuin.
A hardworking model student who gets the highest scores in her grade.

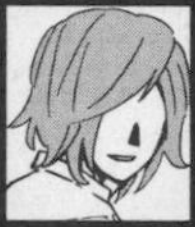

Sakaki
Homeroom teacher to Mizuki and the others. Despite being Takano's cousin, his personality is not even remotely close to Takano's.

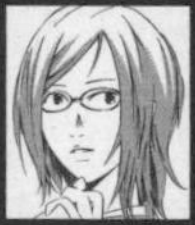

Haruko
Third-year at Seinan Gakuin.
She was Mizuki's best friend until she abruptly started to give Mizuki the cold shoulder.

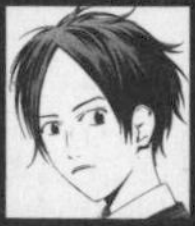

Suwa
Third-year at Seinan Gakuin and the student council president.
He's a popular guy with a cheeky personality.

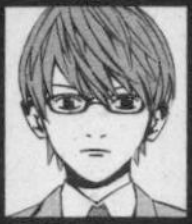

Takano
Third-year at Seinan Gakuin.
A popular guy with a sharp mind and outstanding athletic abilities.

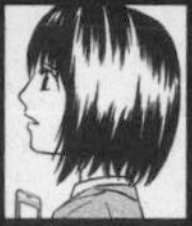

Mizuki
Third-year at Seinan Gakuin.
A bright and kindhearted girl. She is childhood friends with Takano.

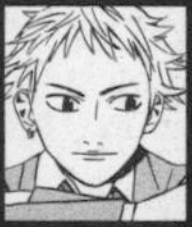

Sugawara
Third-year at Seinan Gakuin.
A mischievous brat who was suspended from school for gambling with mahjong.

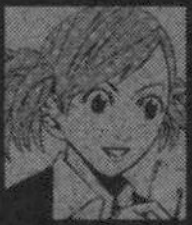

Rika
Third-year at Seinan Gakuin.
An energetic girl who's so talkative that some could find her annoying. She is in love with her homeroom teacher, Sakaki.

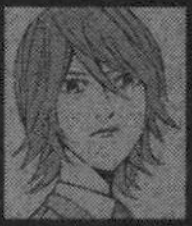

Akihiko
Third-year at Seinan Gakuin.
A cool and collected realist. But he actually has a softhearted side.

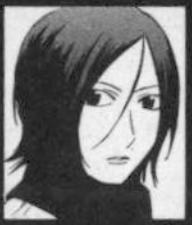

Keiko
Third-year at Seinan Gakuin.
A calm girl with a strangely intimidating air.

Story

On a snowy school day, Takano gets trapped inside his school building with seven friends. Their phones don't work, the clocks have stopped running—and then Takano's beloved friends start disappearing one by one...

"What if we're trapped inside the mental world of the person who took their own life on the last day of the school festival?"

This theory is proposed by Shimizu, but then she, too, vanishes. Now, Takano, Mizuki, Keiko, and Sugawara are the only ones who remain. Could the "perpetrator" who created this frozen reality be amongst them? And what is that person's aim?

As the school chime echoes through the building once again, they know what awaits them is more judgment and danger...

Will they be able to solve all these mysteries and return to their normal lives?!

A School Frozen in Time

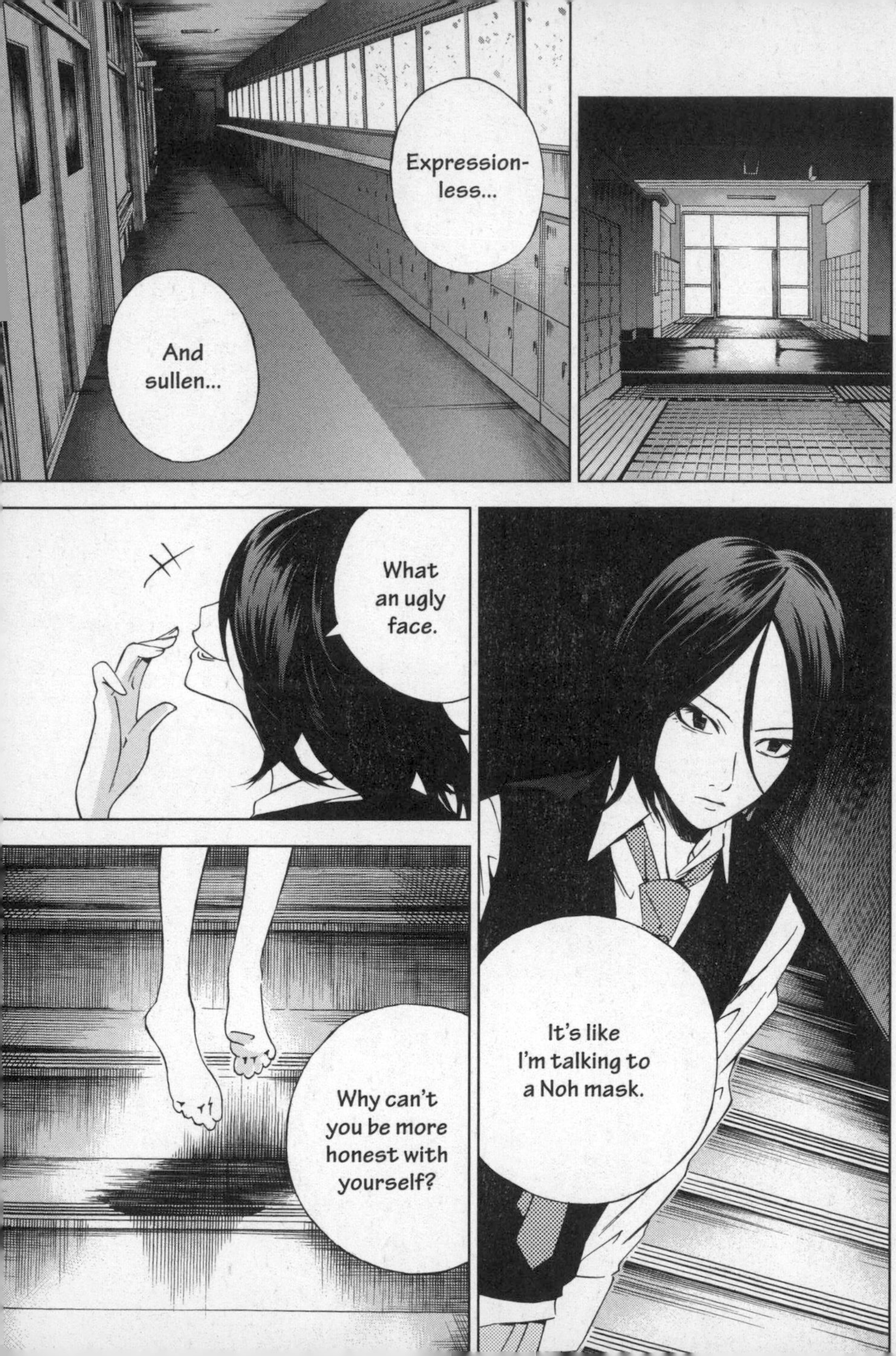
Expression-less...
And sullen...
It's like I'm talking to a Noh mask.
What an ugly face.
Why can't you be more honest with yourself?

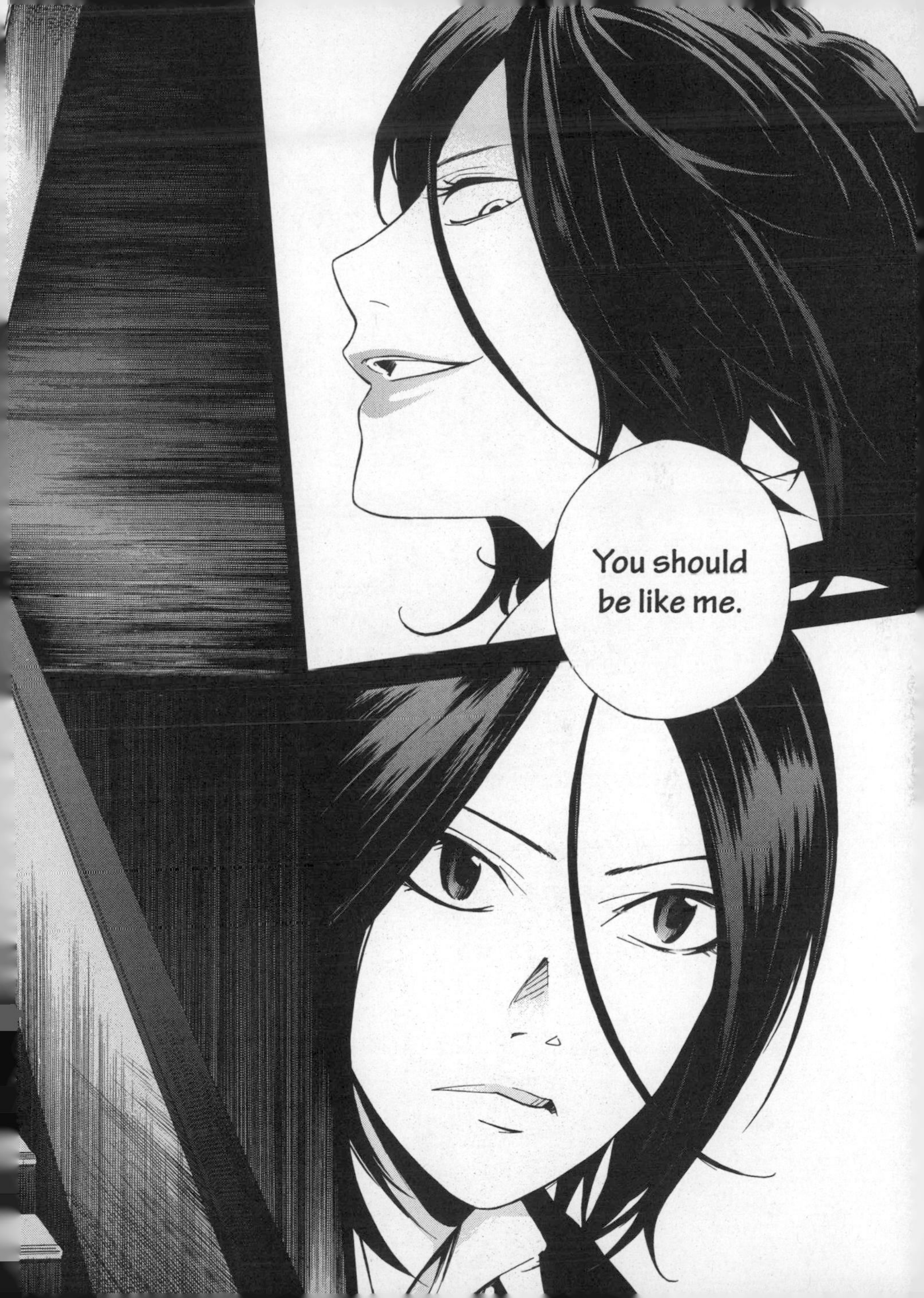
You should be like me.

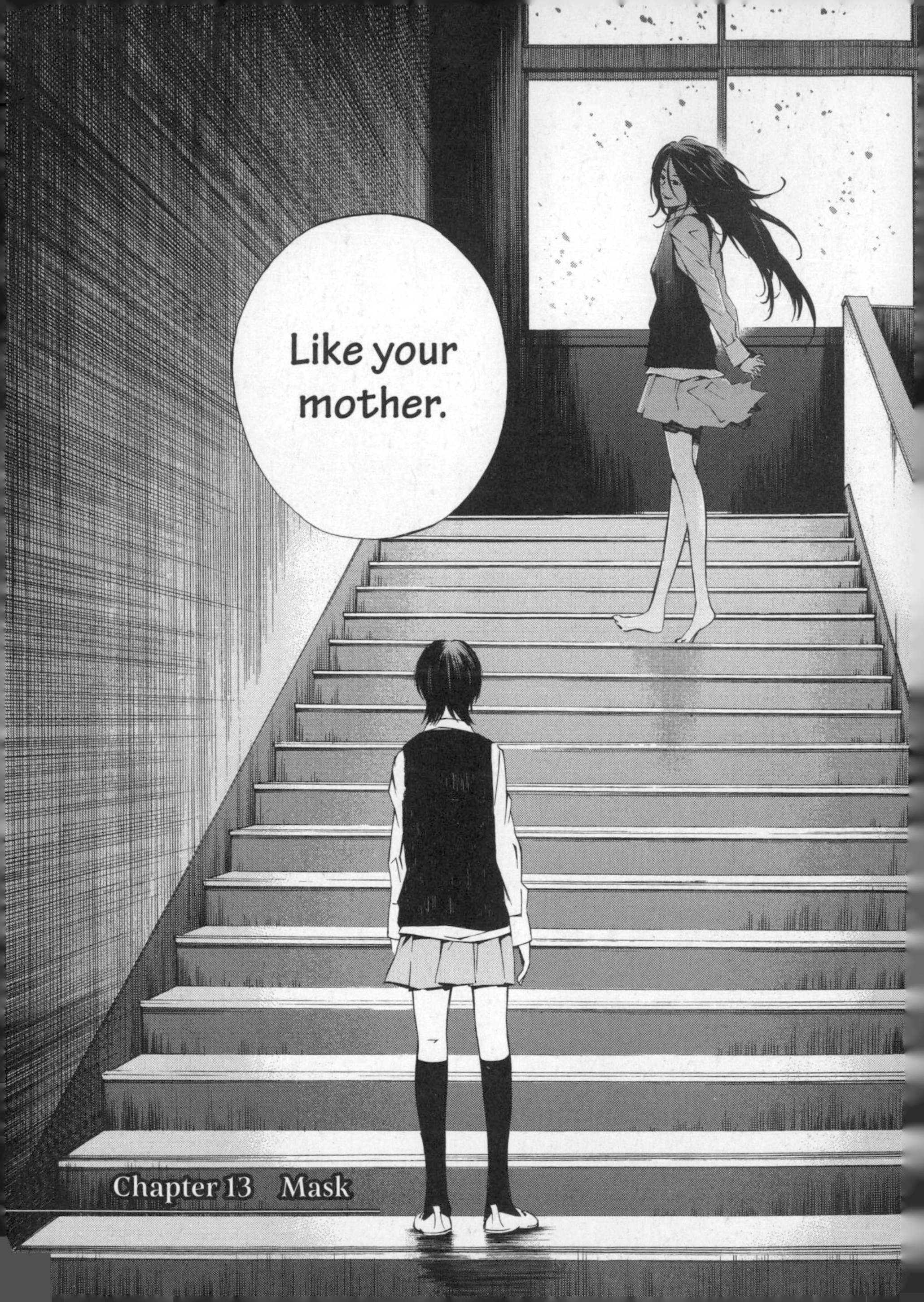
Like your mother.
Chapter 13 Mask

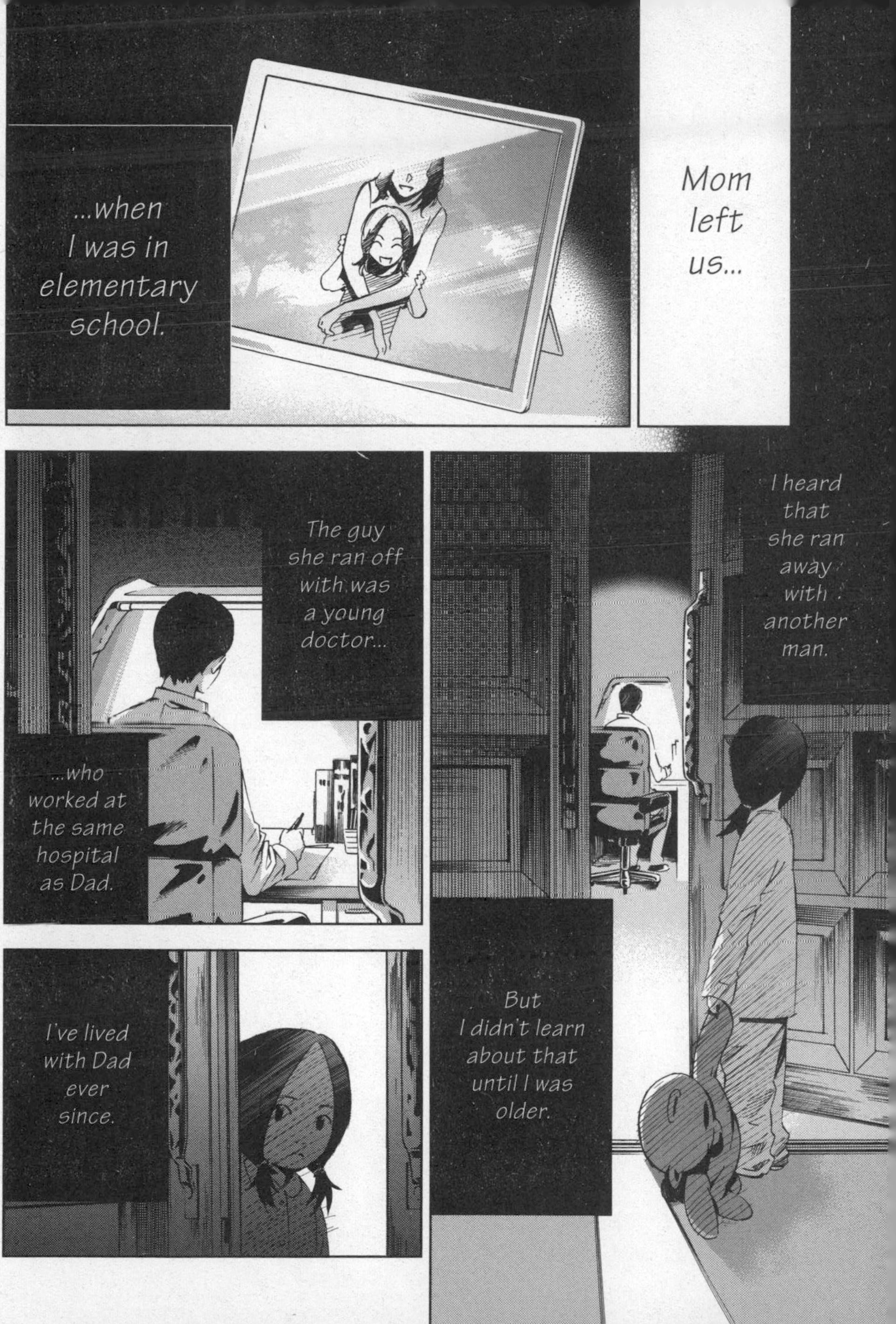
Mom left us...
...when I was in elementary school.
I heard that she ran away with another man.
But I didn't learn about that until I was older.
The guy she ran off with was a young doctor...
...who worked at the same hospital as Dad.
I've lived with Dad ever since.

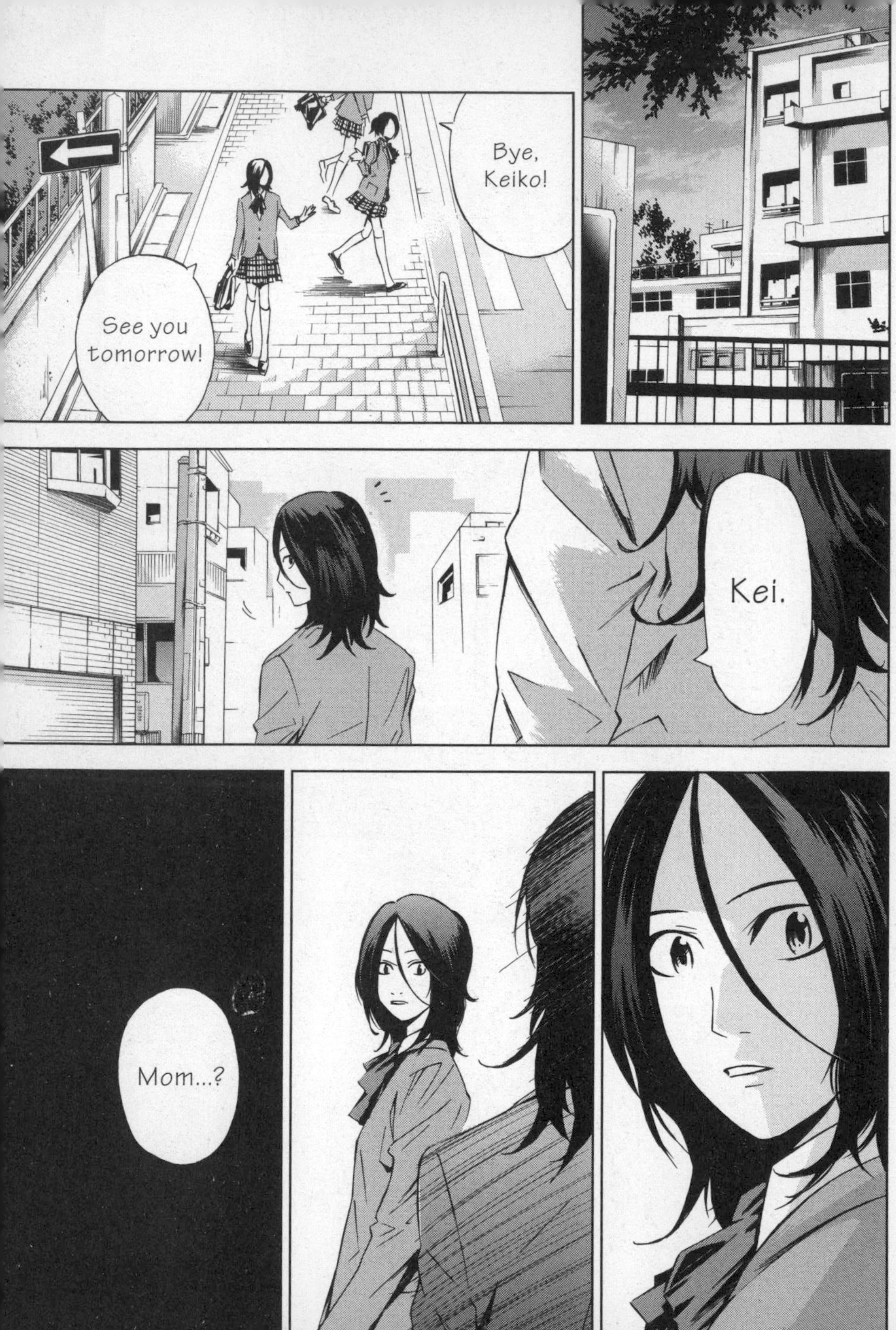
Bye, Keiko!
See you tomorrow!
Kei.
Mom...?

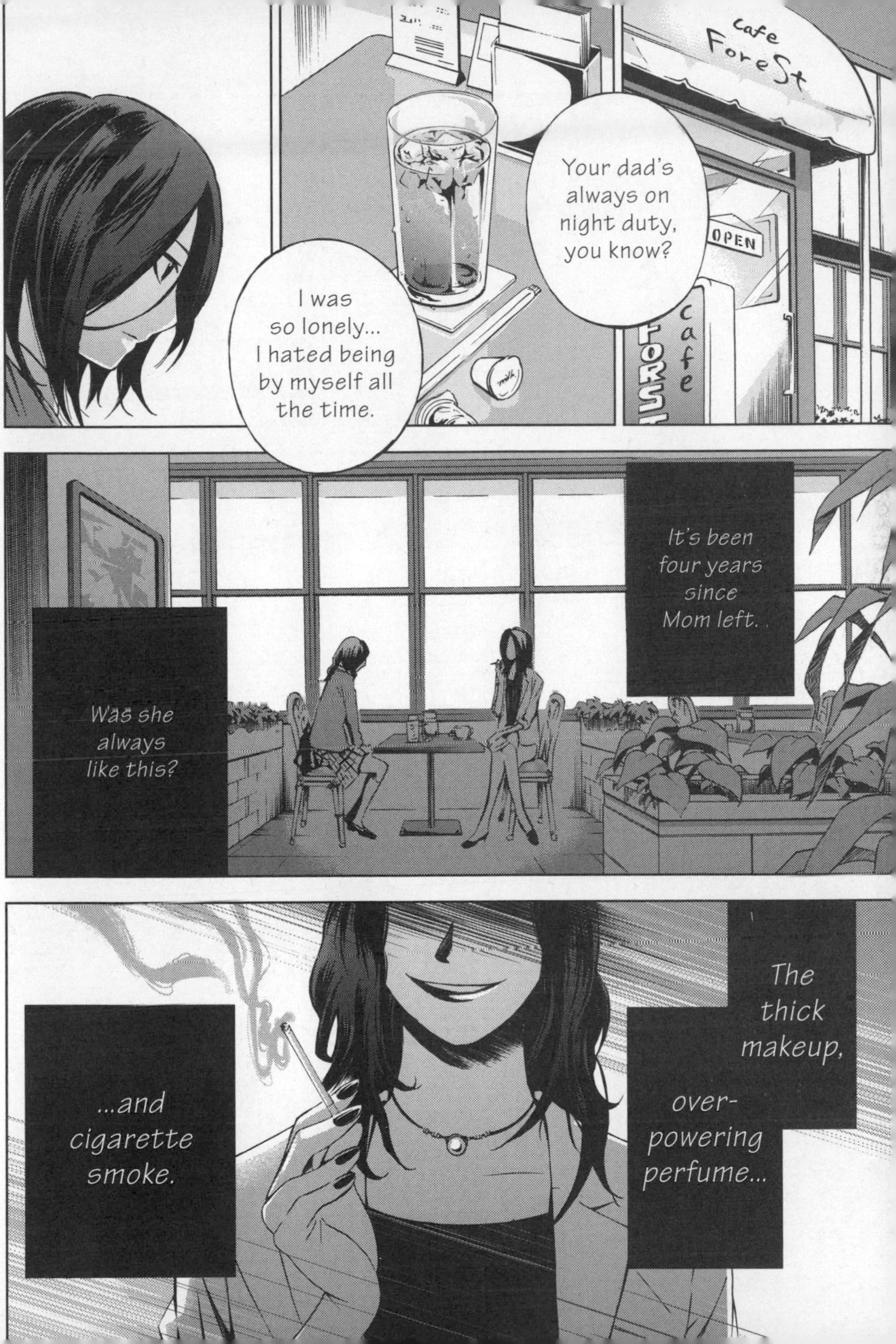
cafe ForeSt
Your dad's always on night duty, you know?
OPEN
I was so lonely... I hated being by myself all the time.
It's been four years since Mom left. .
Was she always like this?
The thick makeup,
over-powering perfume...
...and cigarette smoke.

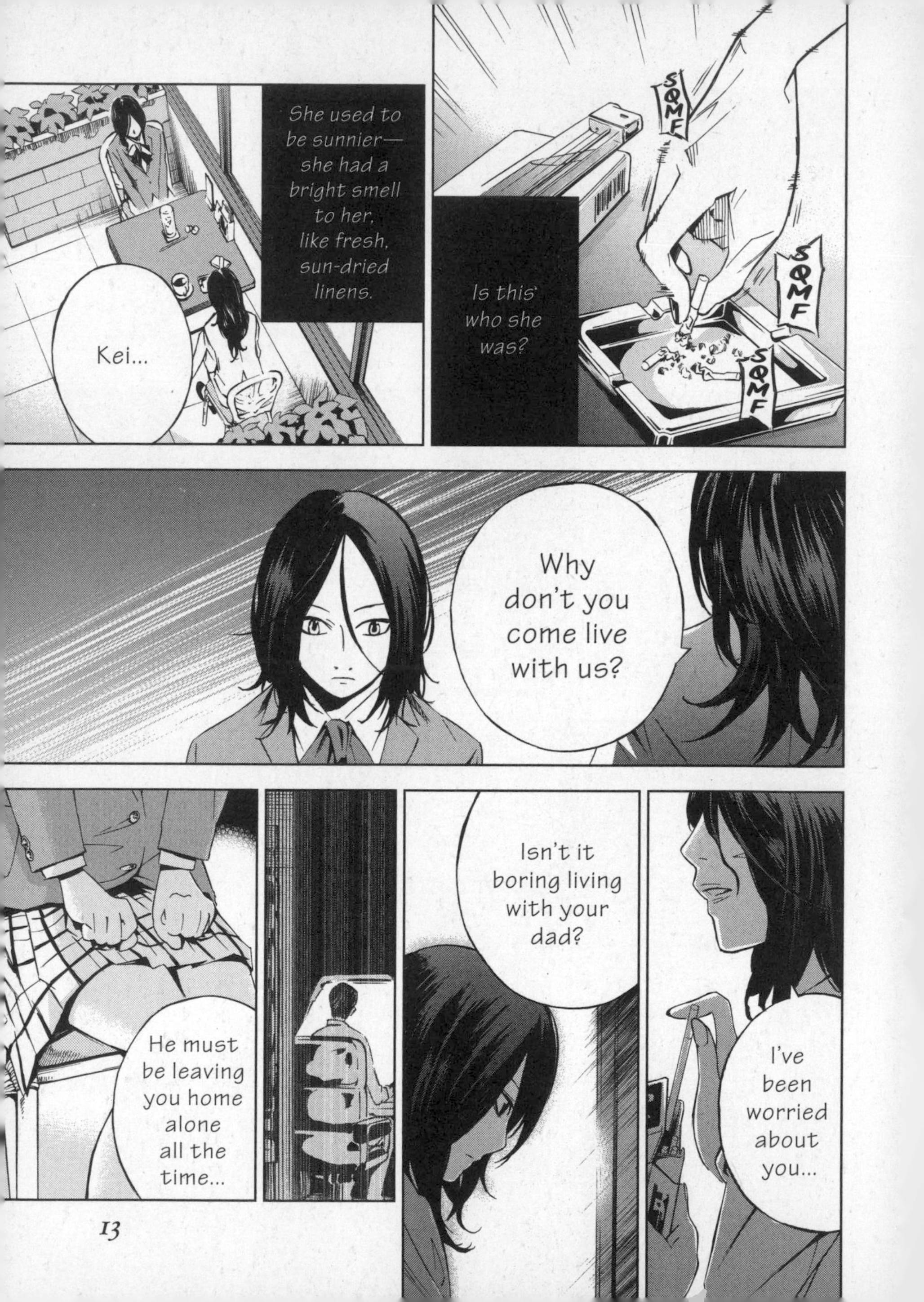
SQMF
SQMF
SQMF
Is this who she was?
She used to be sunnier— she had a bright smell to her, like fresh, sun-dried linens.
Kei...
Why don't you come live with us?
I've been worried about you...
Isn't it boring living with your dad?
He must be leaving you home alone all the time...

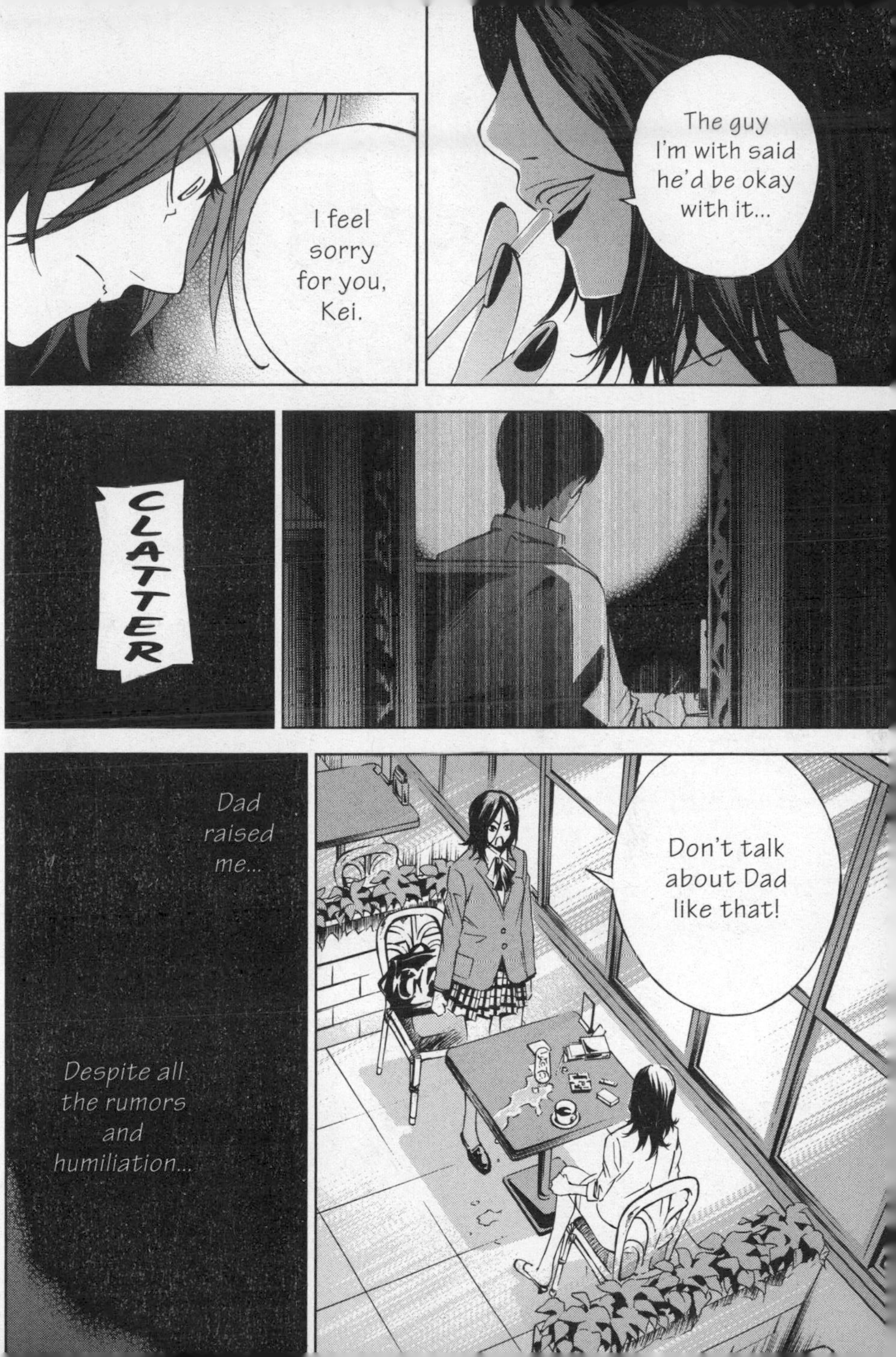
The guy I'm with said he'd be okay with it...
I feel sorry for you, Kei.
CLATTER
Don't talk about Dad like that!
Dad raised me...
Despite all the rumors and humiliation...

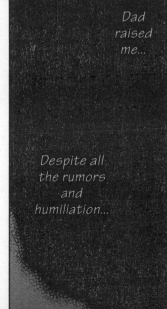

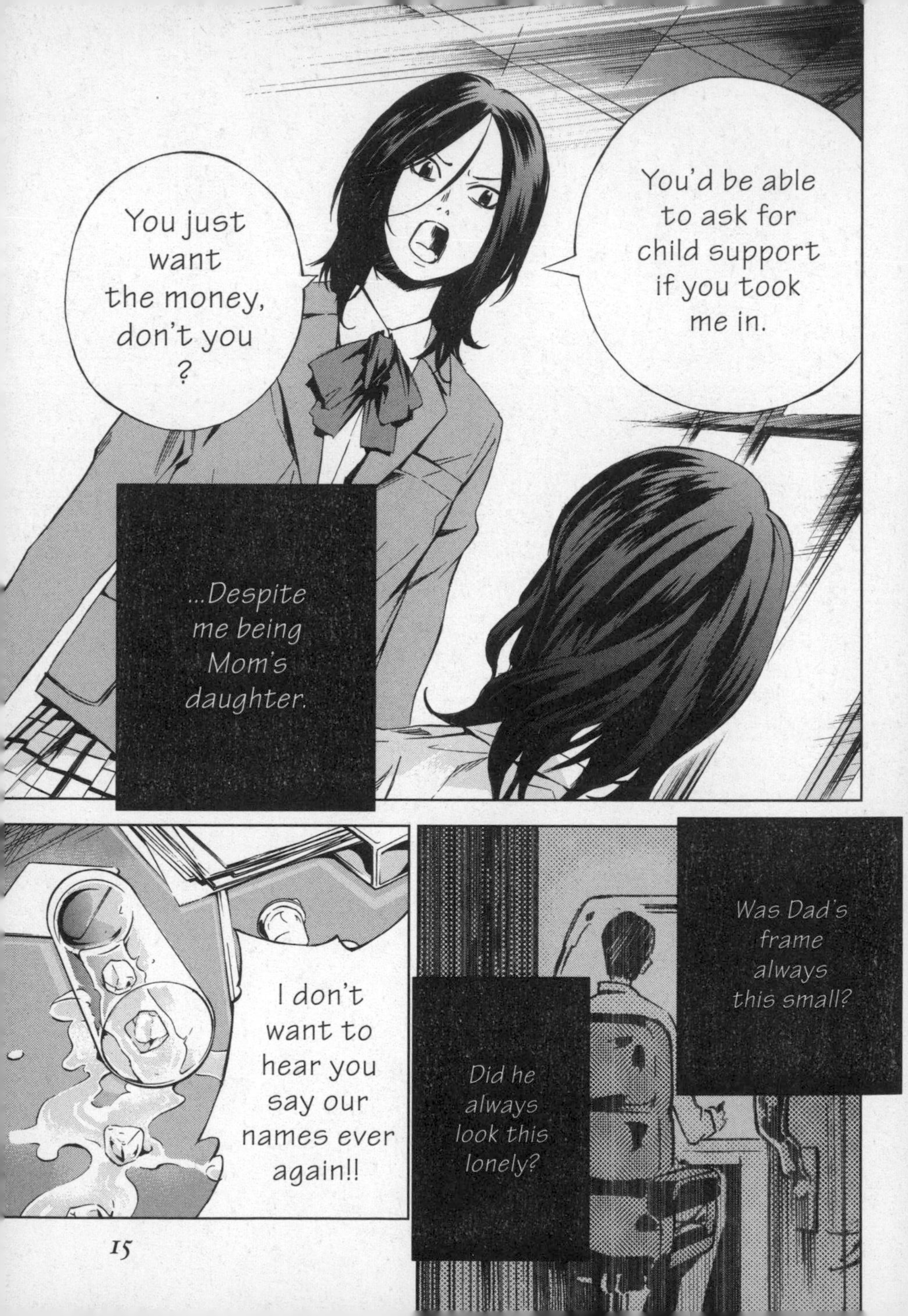
You'd be able to ask for child support if you took me in.
You just want the money, don't you ?
...Despite me being Mom's daughter.
Was Dad's frame always this small?
Did he always look this lonely?
I don't want to hear you say our names ever again!!

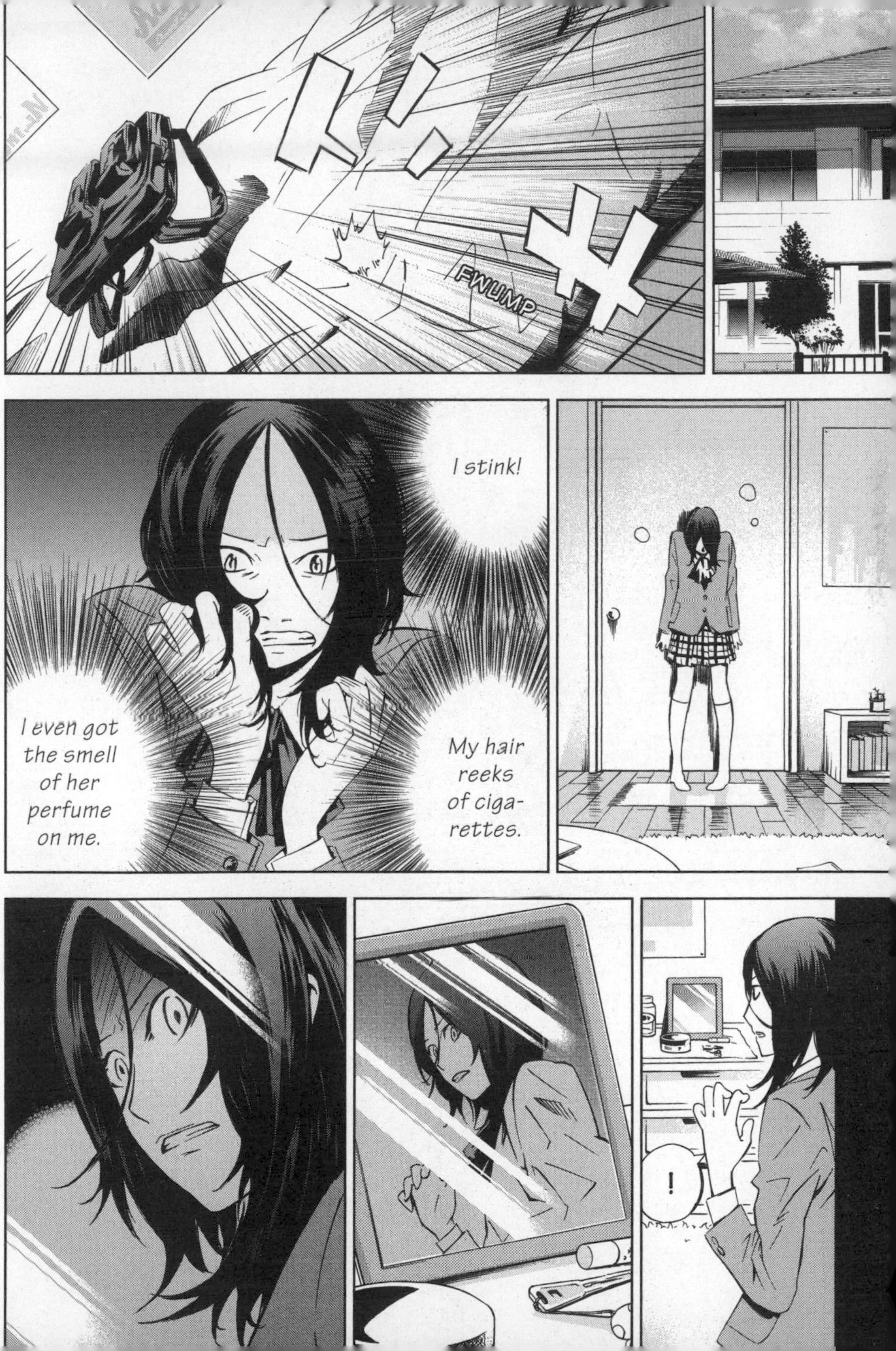
FWUMP
I stink!
My hair reeks of ciga-rettes.
I even got the smell of her perfume on me.
!

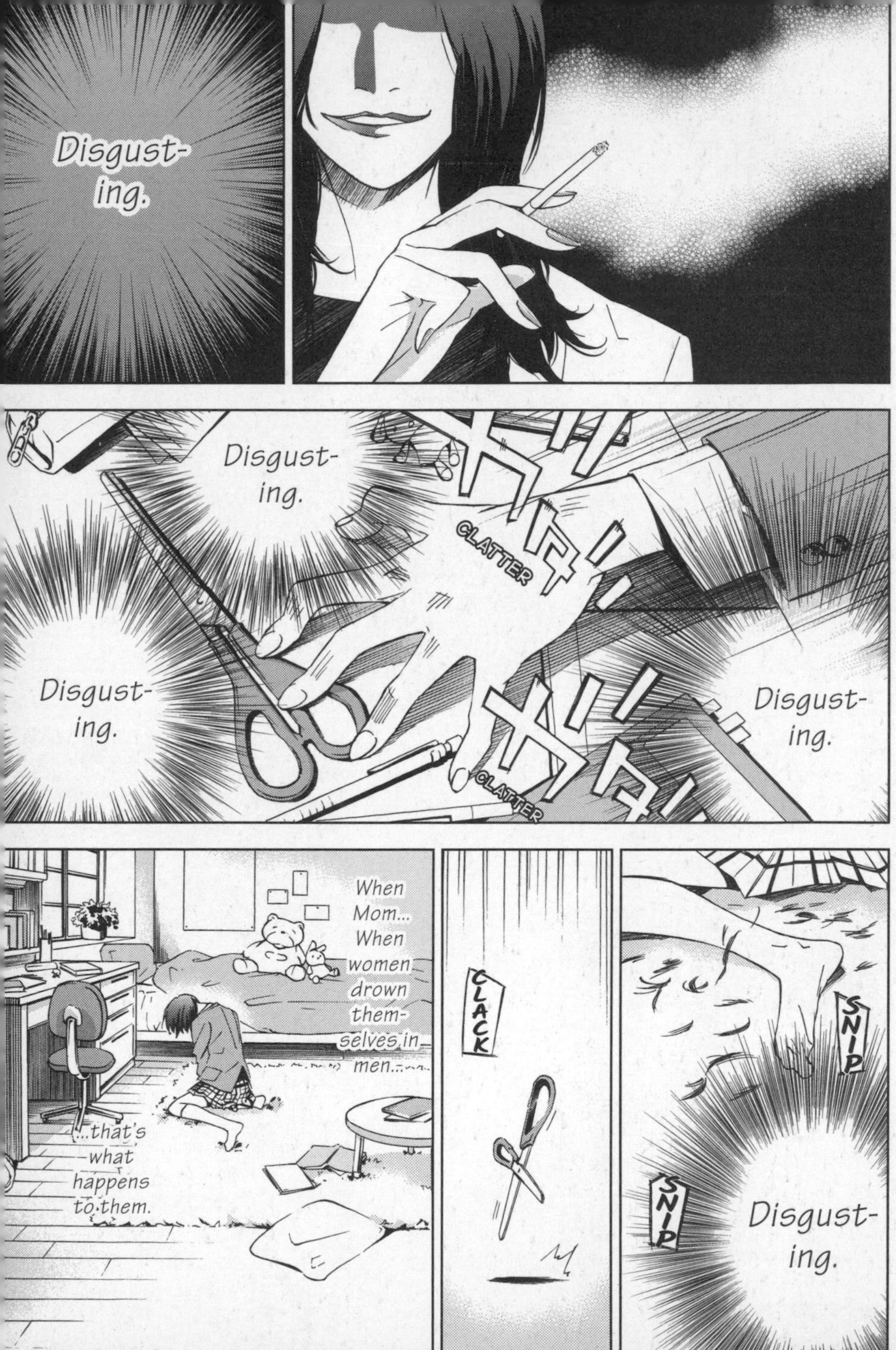
Disgust-ing.
Disgust-ing.
CLATTER
Disgust-ing.
CLATTER
Disgust-ing.
SNIP
SNIP
Disgust-ing.
CLACK
When Mom... When women drown them-selves in men...
...that's what happens to them.

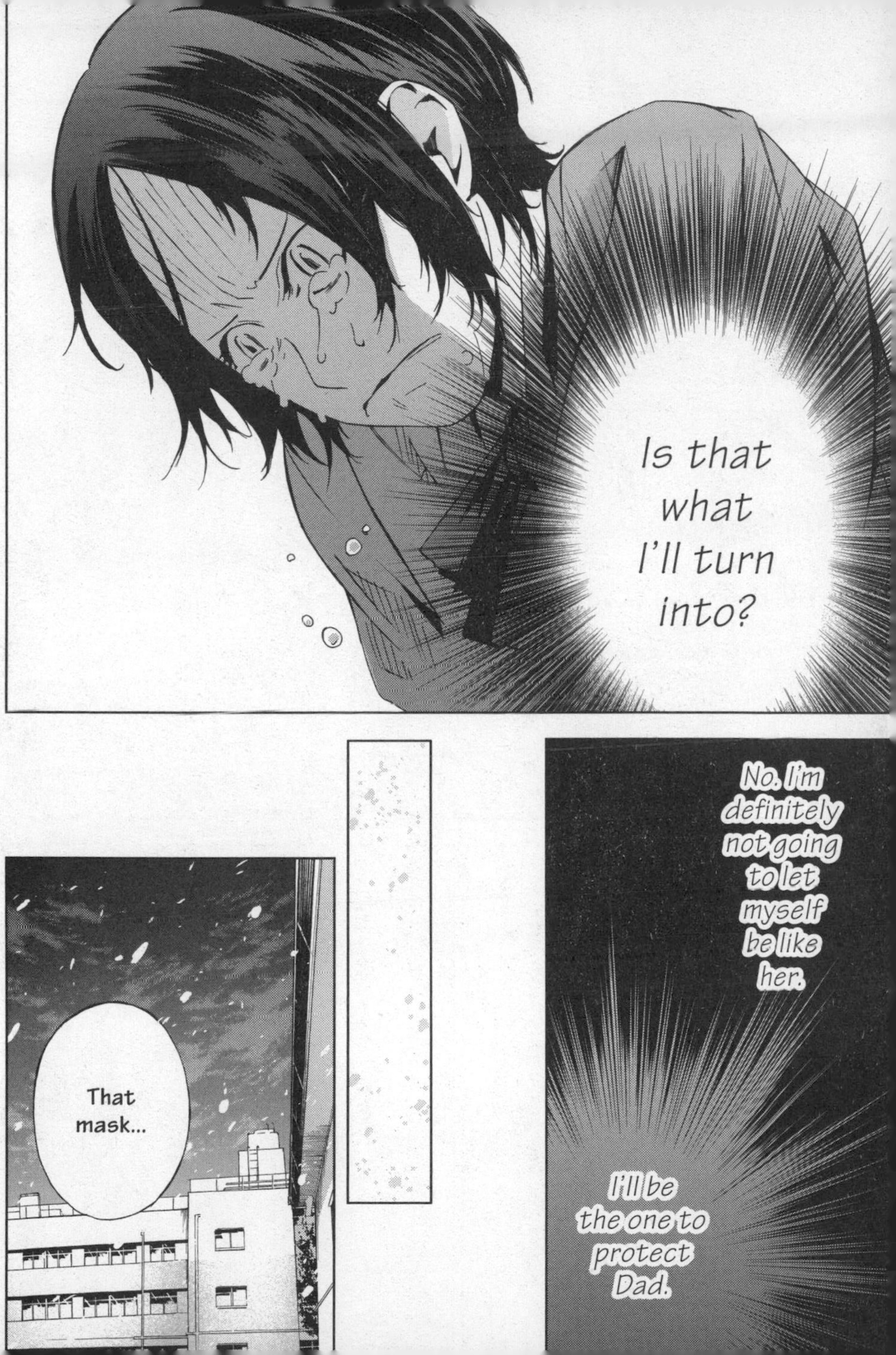
Is that what I'll turn into?
No. I'm definitely not going to let myself be like her.
I'll be the one to protect Dad.
That mask...

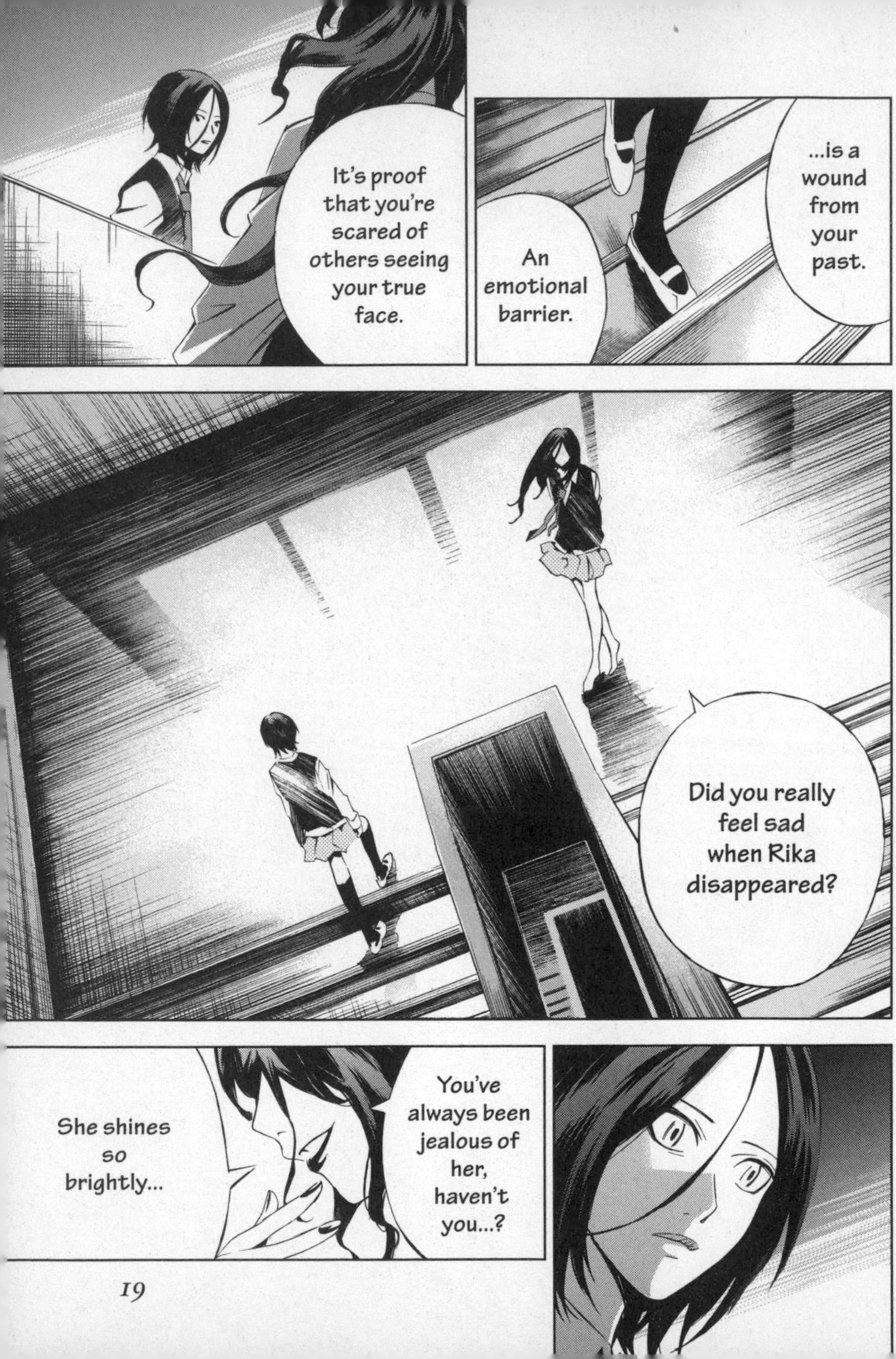
...is a wound from your past.
An emotional barrier.
It's proof that you're scared of others seeing your true face.
Did you really feel sad when Rika disappeared?
You've always been jealous of her, haven't you...?
She shines so brightly...

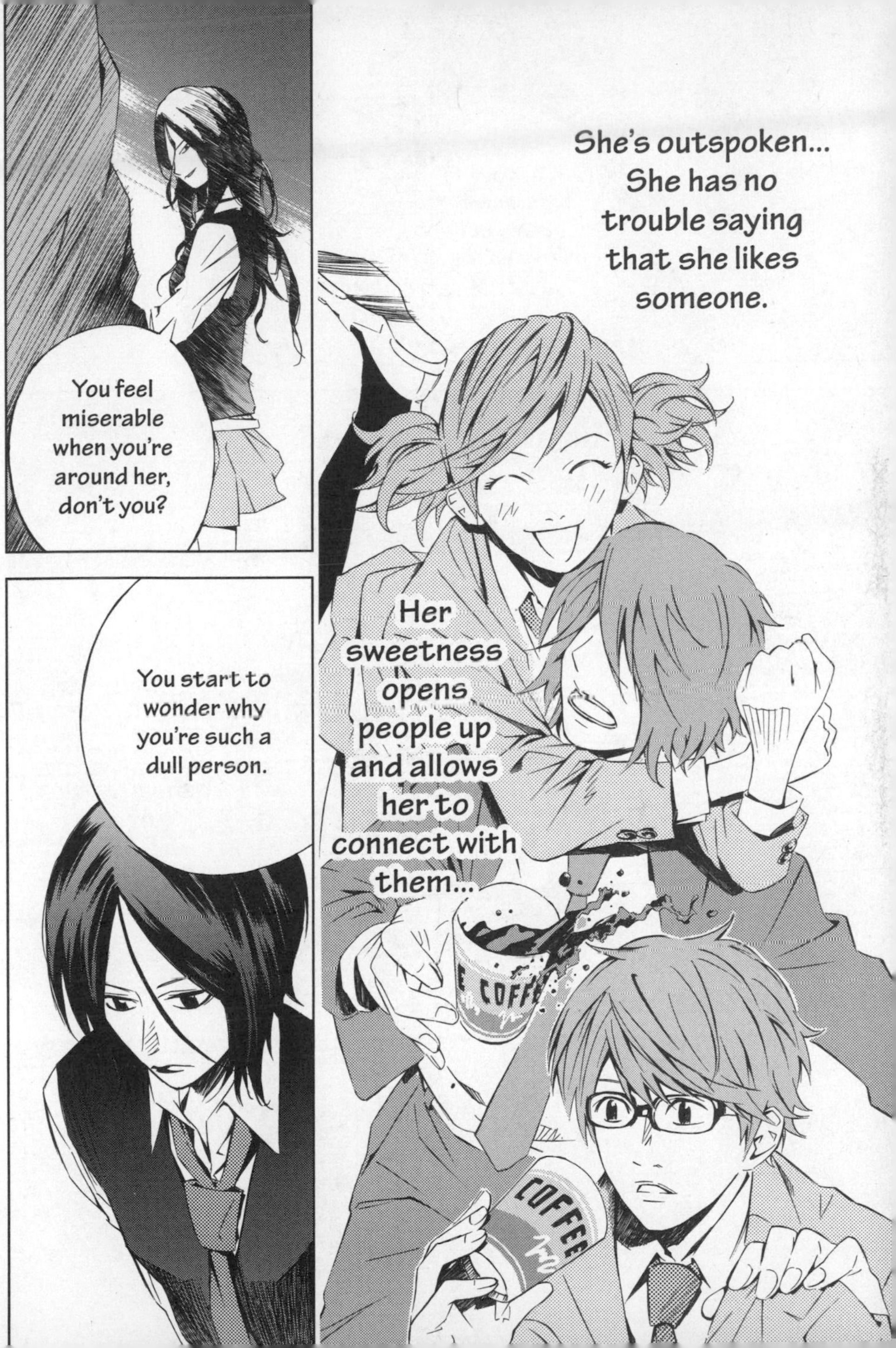
She's outspoken... She has no trouble saying that she likes someone.
Her sweetness opens people up and allows her to connect with them...
COFFEE
You feel miserable when you're around her, don't you?
You start to wonder why you're such a dull person.

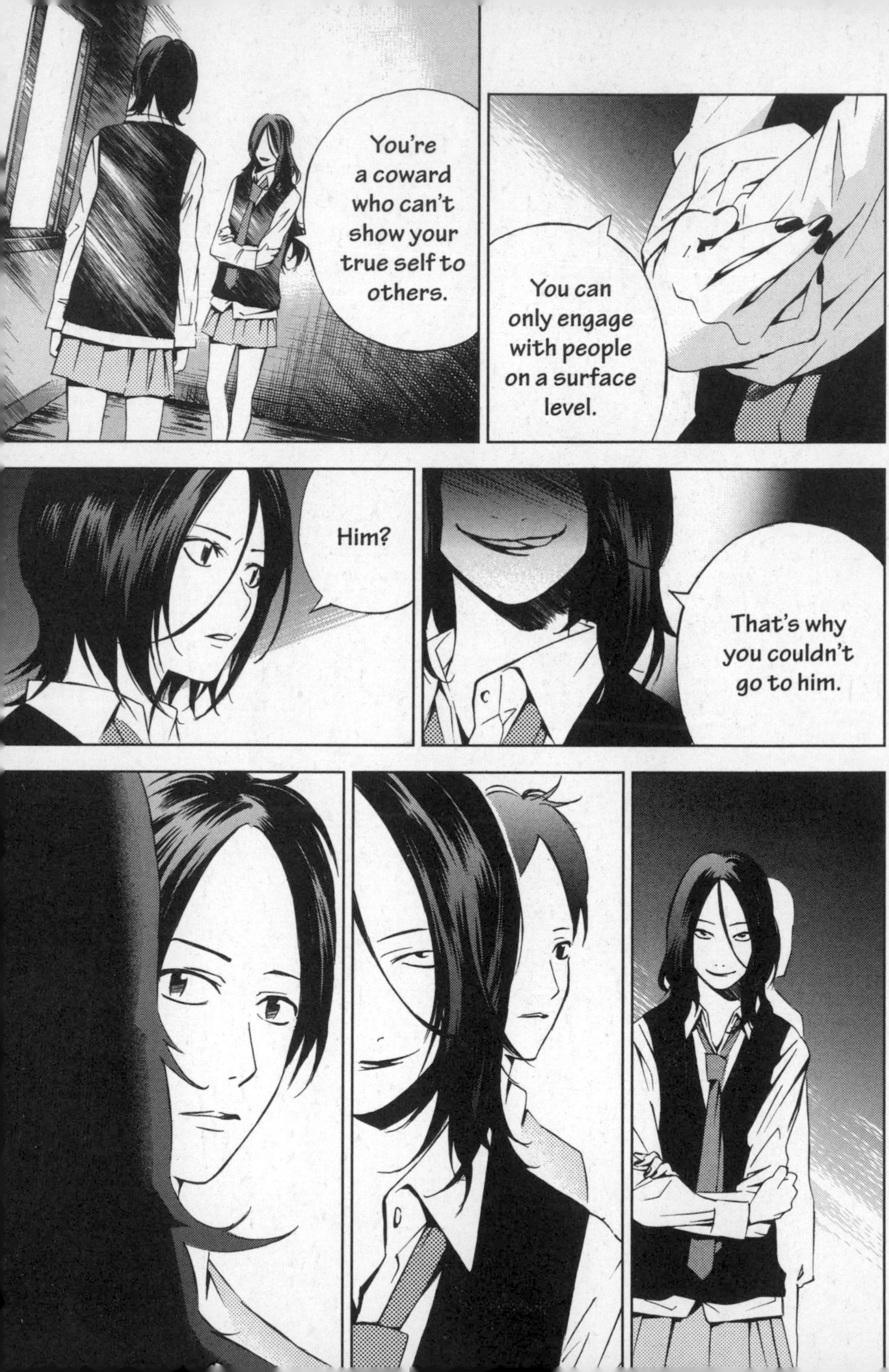
You can only engage with people on a surface level.
You're a coward who can't show your true self to others.
That's why you couldn't go to him.
Him?

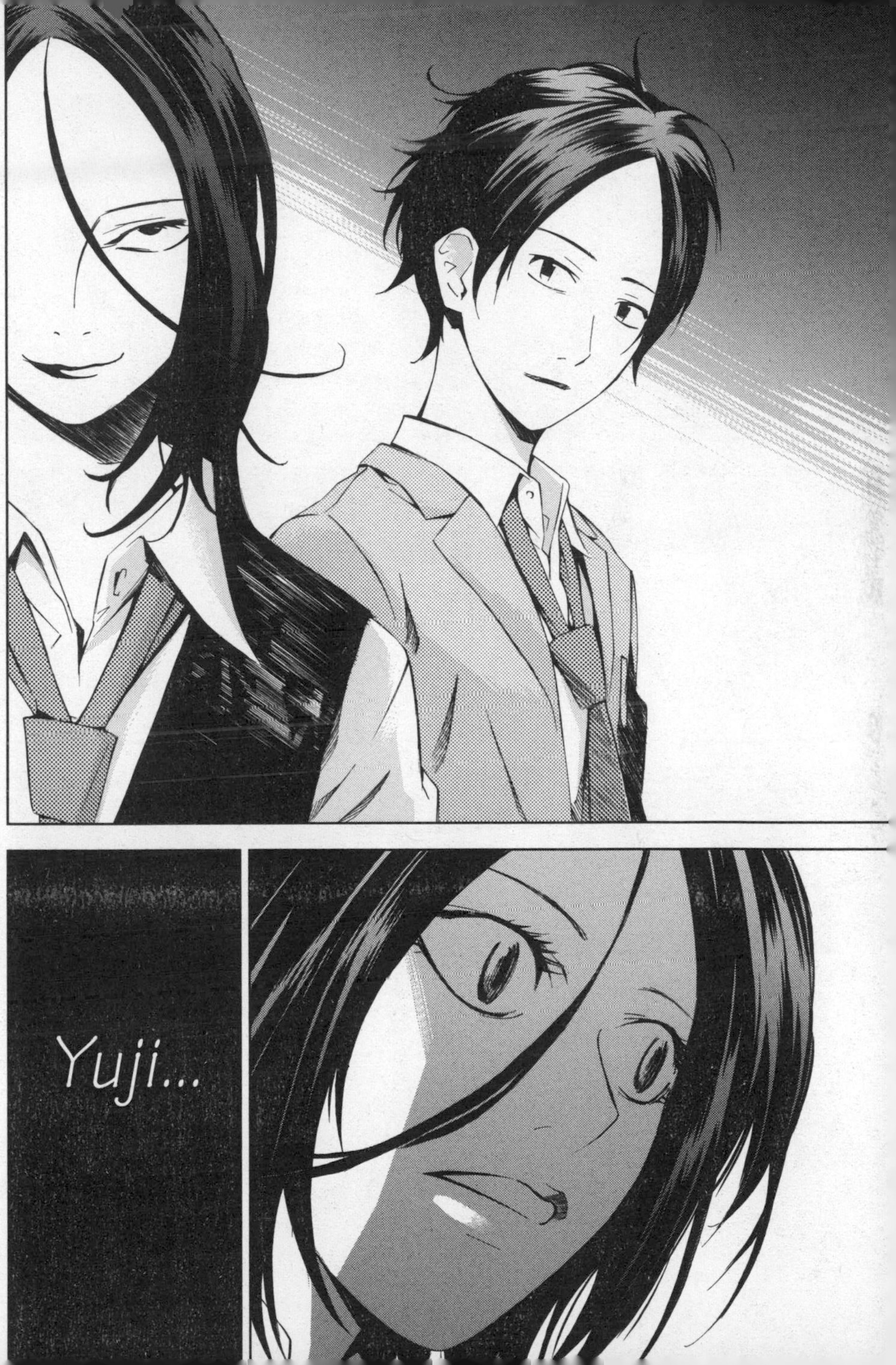
Yuji...

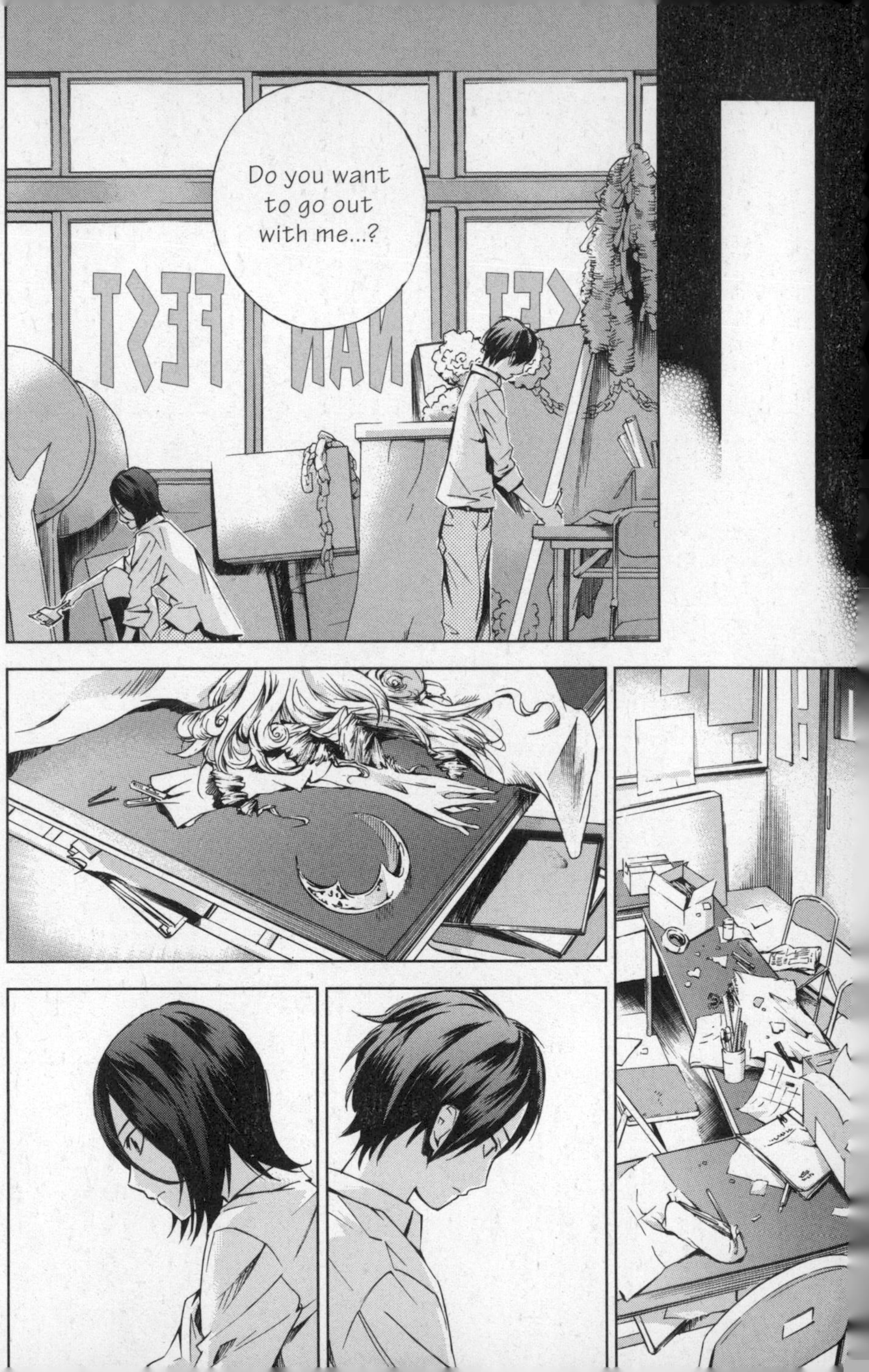
Do you want to go out with me...?

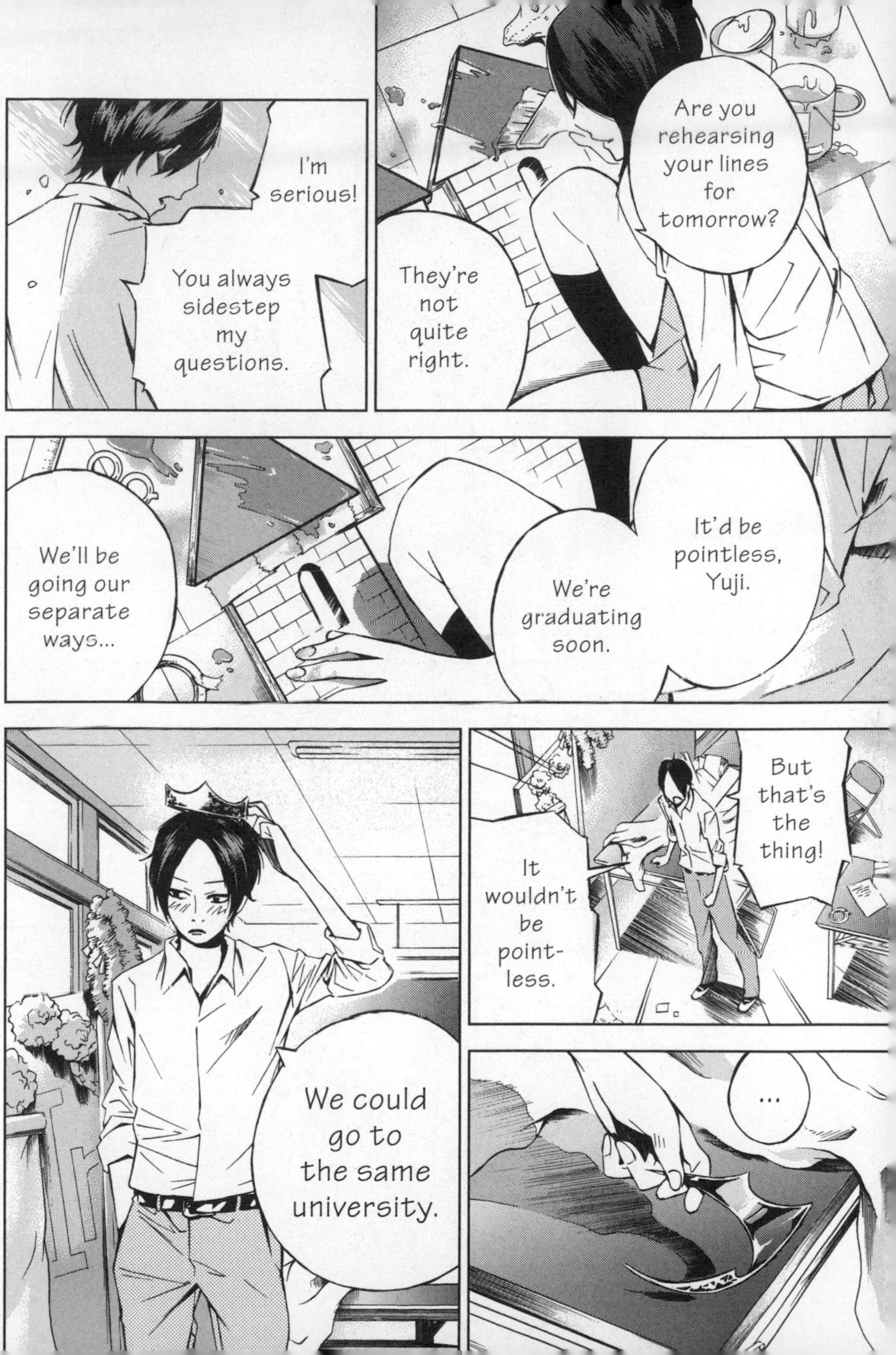
Are you rehearsing your lines for tomorrow?
They're not quite right.
I'm serious!
You always sidestep my questions.
It'd be pointless, Yuji.
We're graduating soon.
We'll be going our separate ways...
But that's the thing!
It wouldn't be pointless.
...
We could go to the same university.

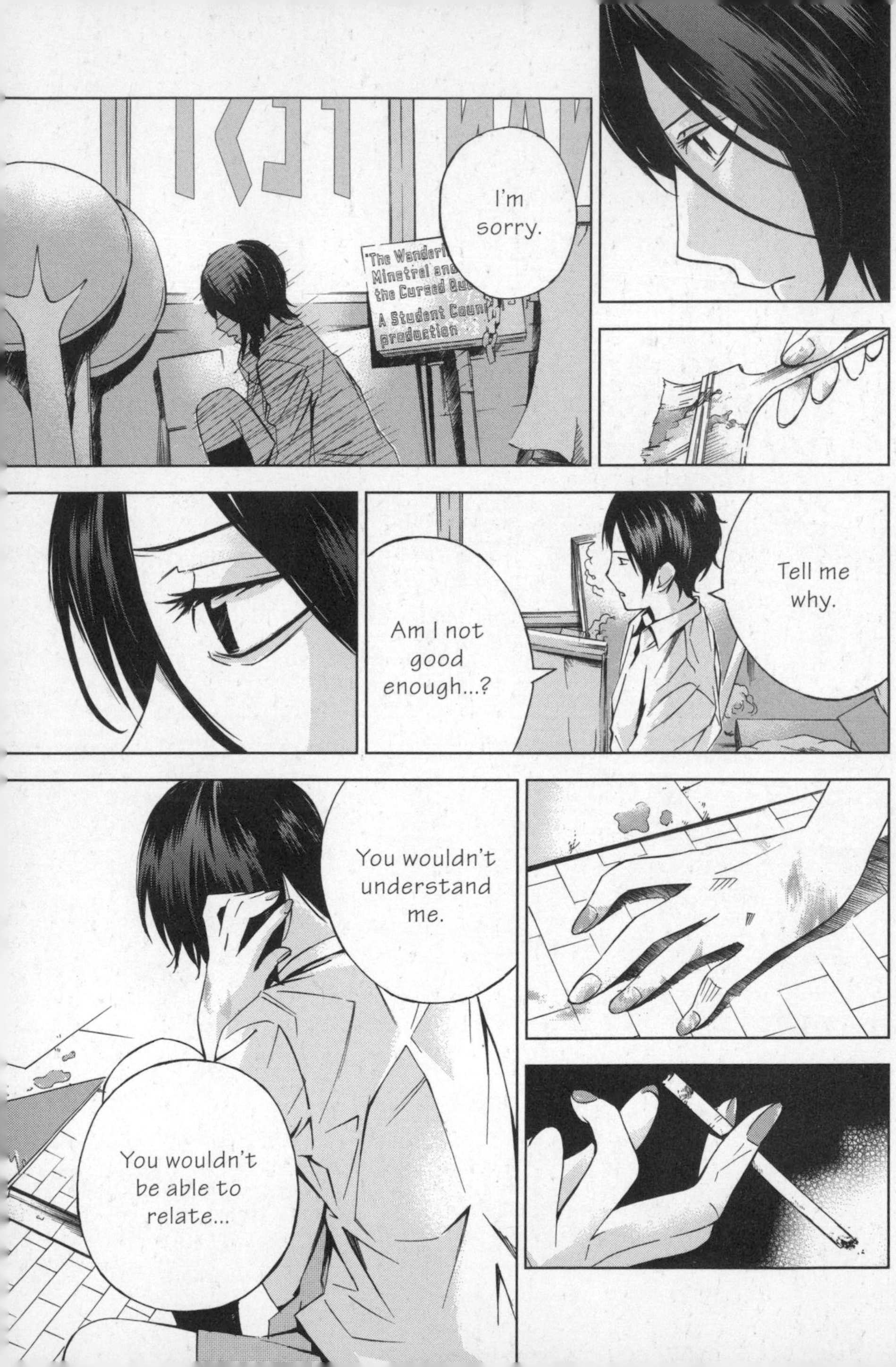
I'm sorry.
"The Wanderi
Minstrel and
the Cursed Que
A Student Coun
production
Tell me why.
Am I not good enough...?
You wouldn't understand me.
You wouldn't be able to relate...

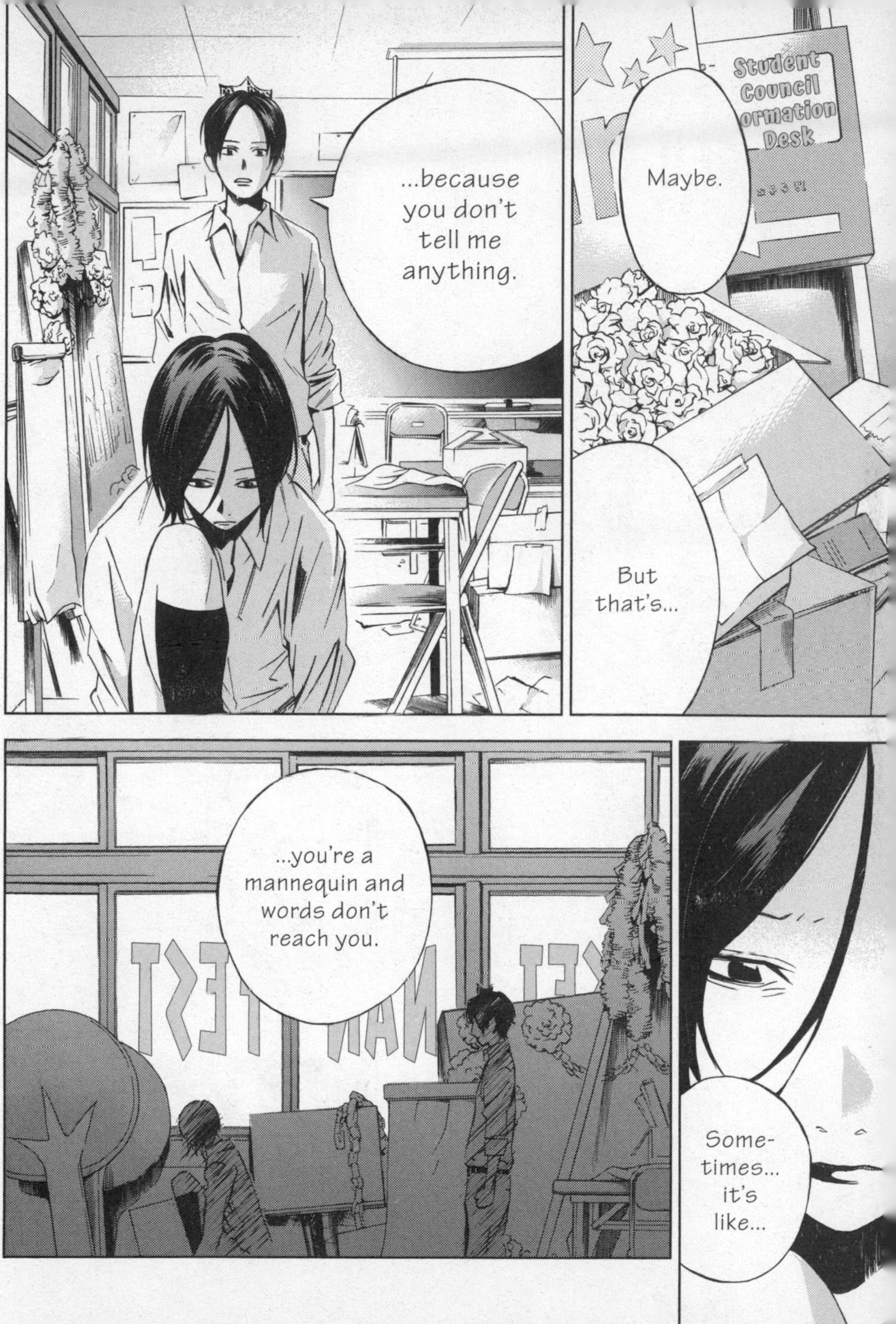
Student Council ormation Desk
Maybe.
But that's...
...because you don't tell me anything.
Some- times... it's like...
...you're a mannequin and words don't reach you.

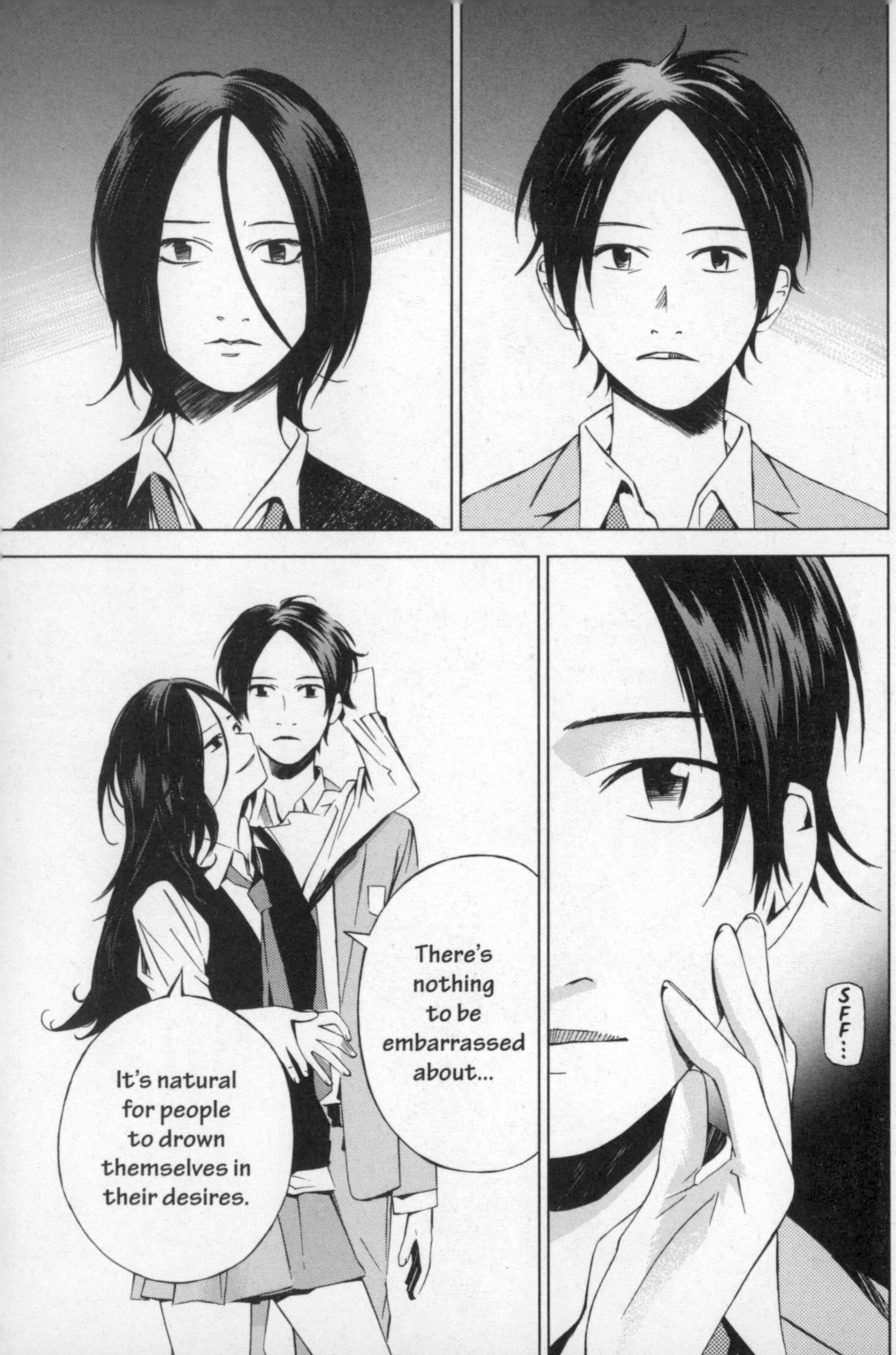
SFF...
There's nothing to be embarrassed about...
It's natural for people to drown themselves in their desires.

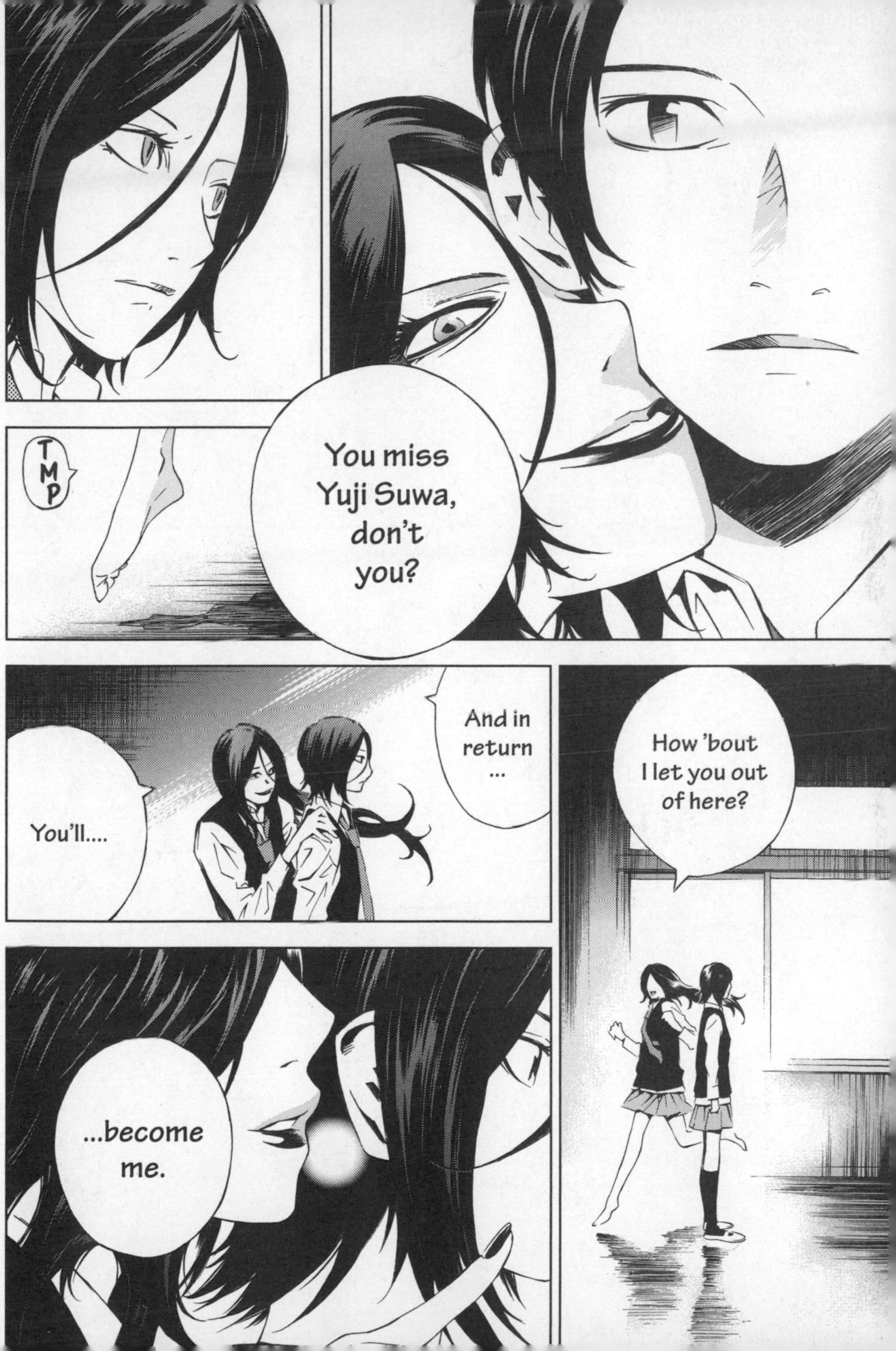
You miss Yuji Suwa, don't you?
TMP
How 'bout I let you out of here?
And in return ...
You'll....
...become me.

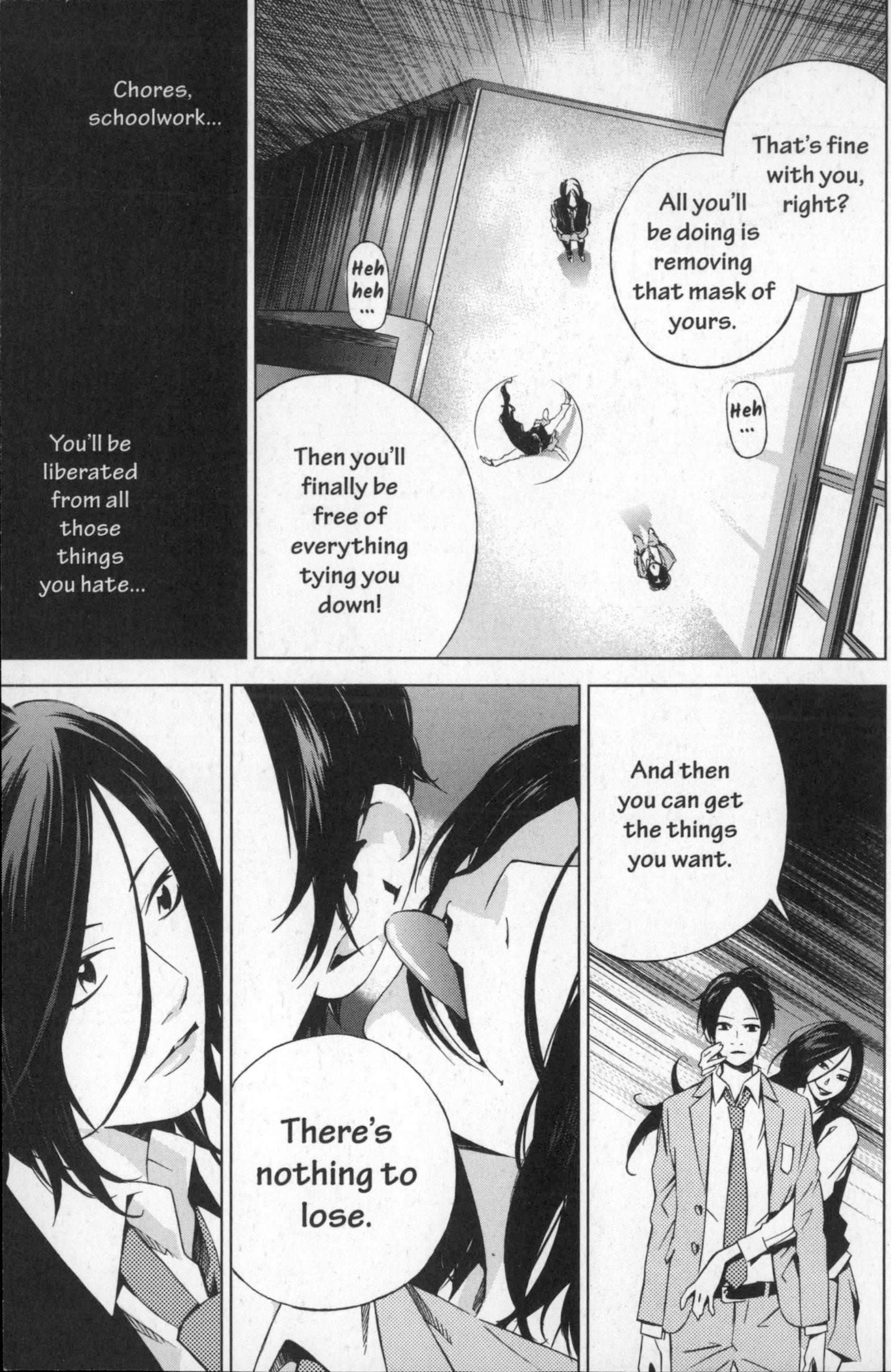

That's fine with you, right?
All you'll be doing is removing that mask of yours.
Heh heh...
Heh...
Then you'll finally be free of everything tying you down!
Chores, schoolwork...
You'll be liberated from all those things you hate...
And then you can get the things you want.
There's nothing to lose.

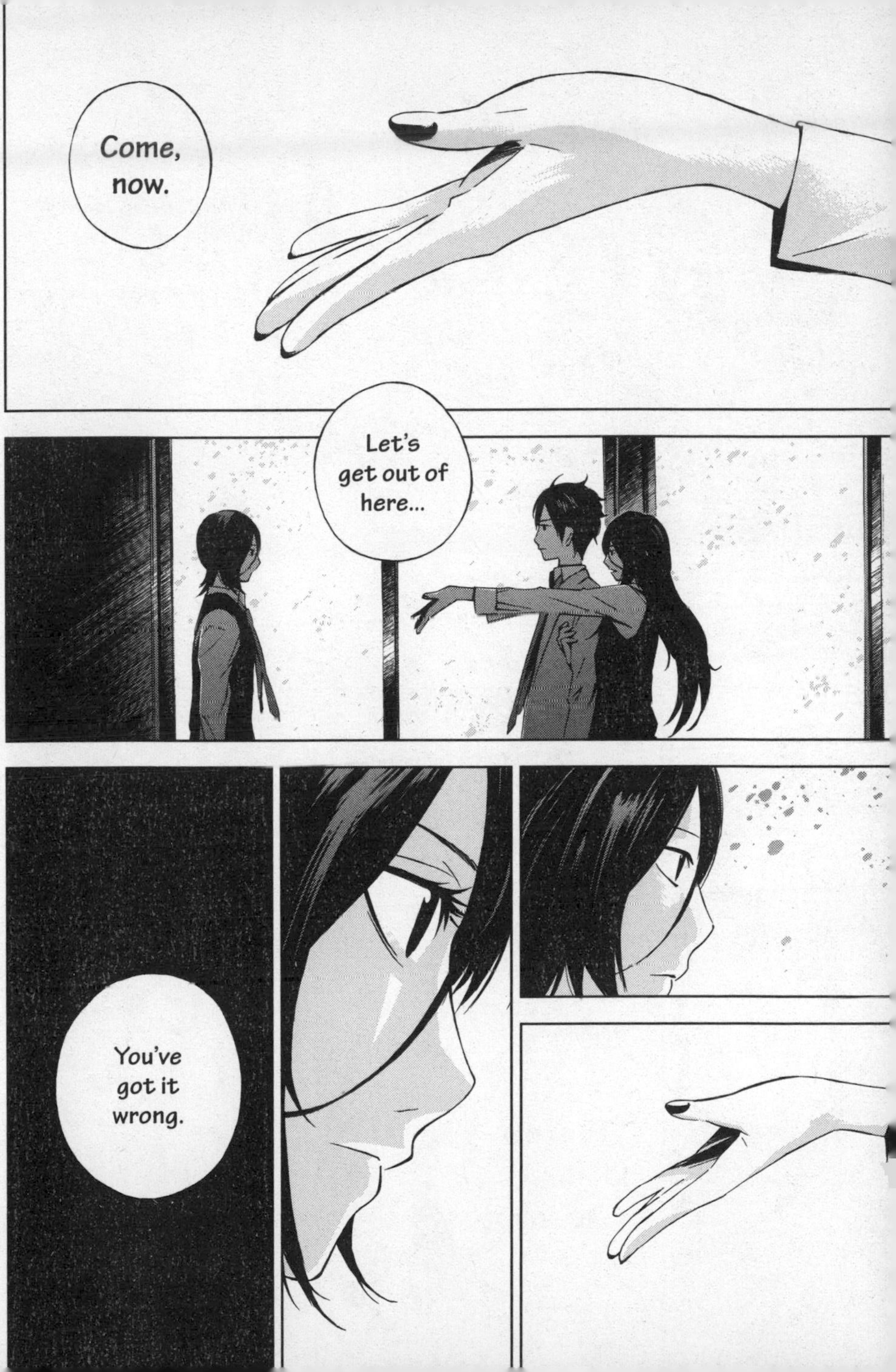
Come, now.
Let's get out of here...
You've got it wrong.

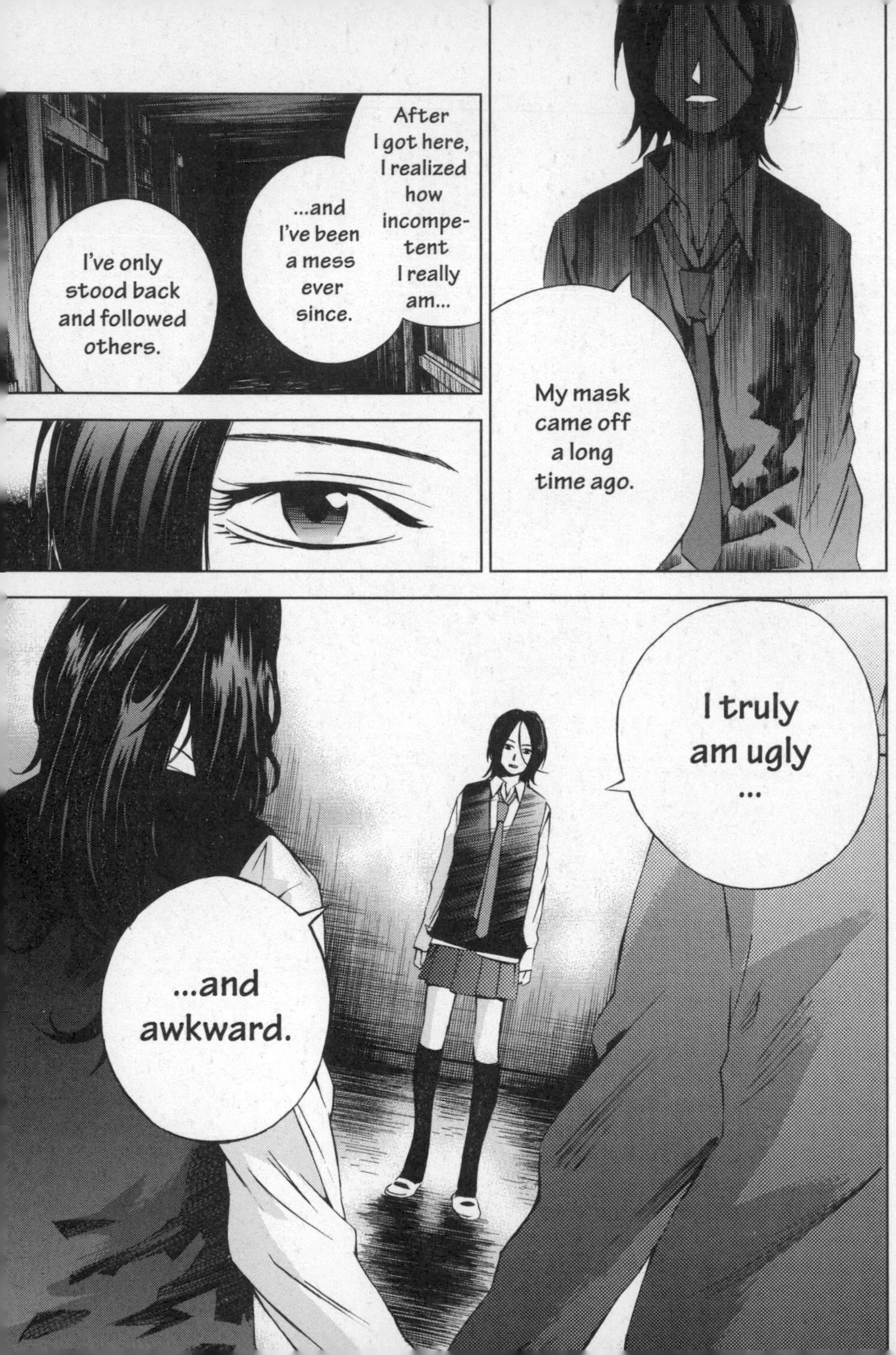
My mask came off a long time ago.
After I got here, I realized how incompete-tent I really am...
...and I've been a mess ever since.
I've only stood back and followed others.
I truly am ugly ...
...and awkward.

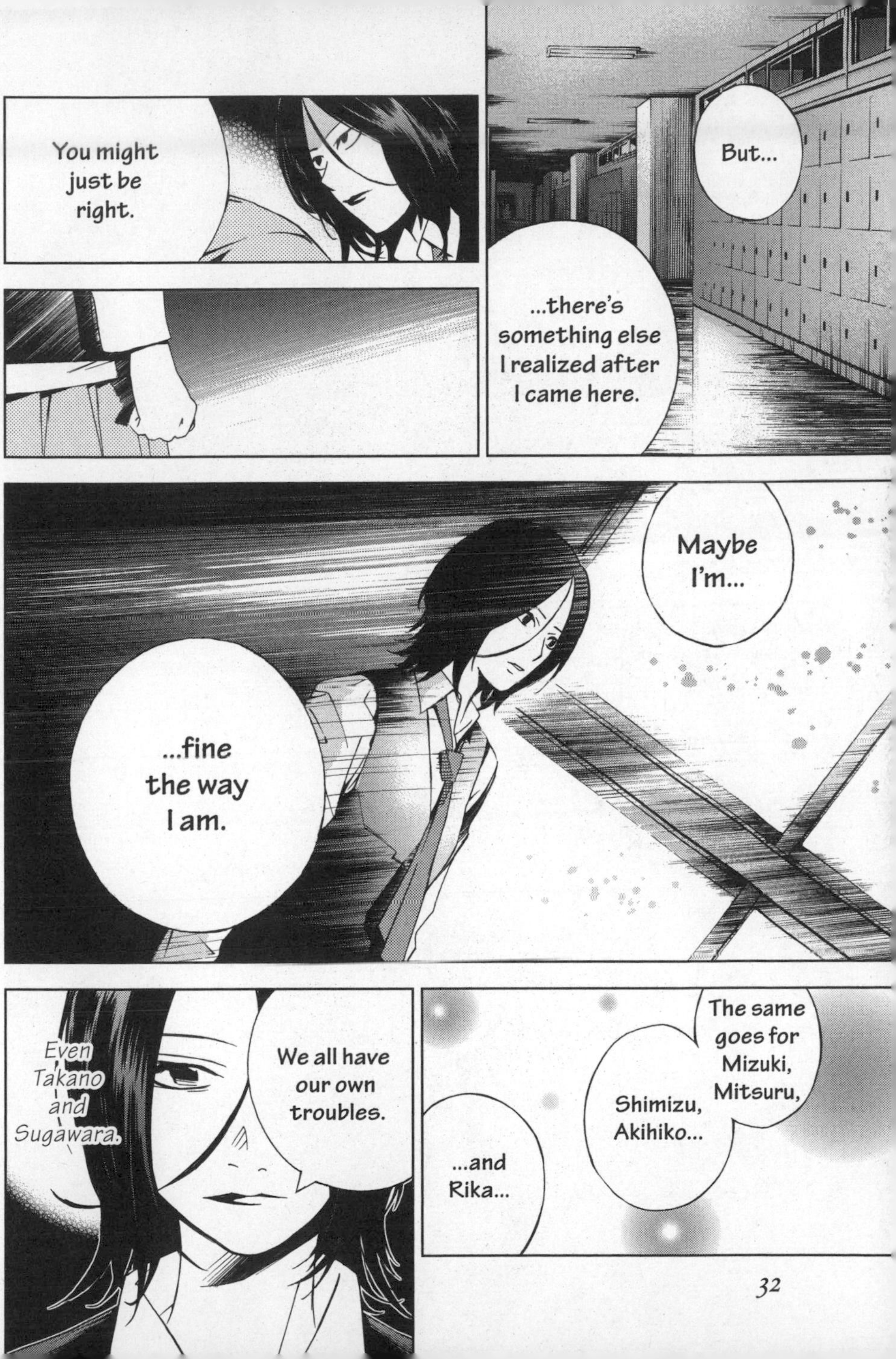
But...
...there's something else I realized after I came here.
You might just be right.
Maybe I'm...
...fine the way I am.
The same goes for Mizuki, Mitsuru,
Shimizu, Akihiko...
...and Rika...
We all have our own troubles.
Even Takano and Sugawara.

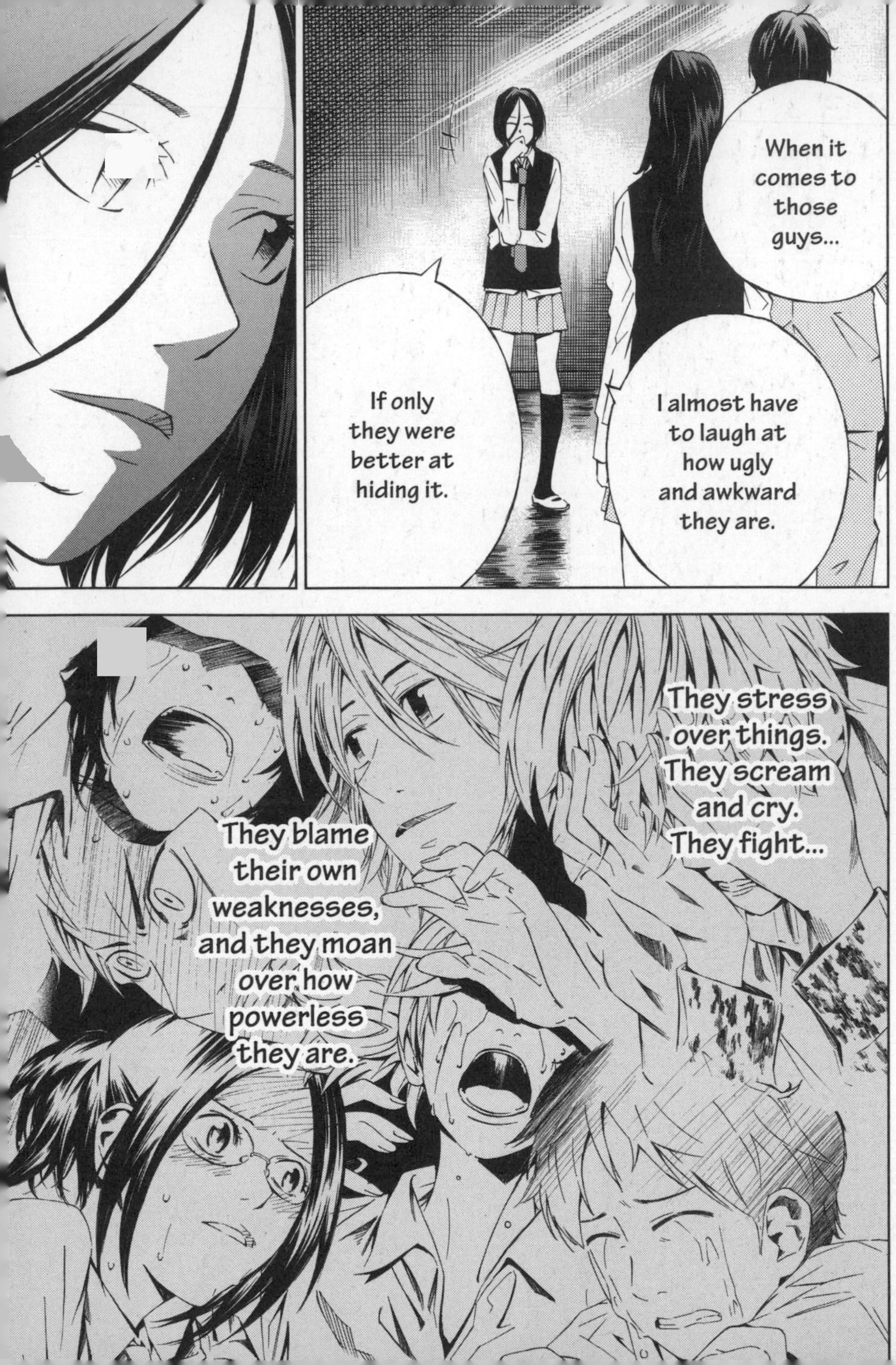
When it comes to those guys...
I almost have to laugh at how ugly and awkward they are.
If only they were better at hiding it.
They stress over things. They scream and cry. They fight...
They blame their own weaknesses, and they moan over how powerless they are.

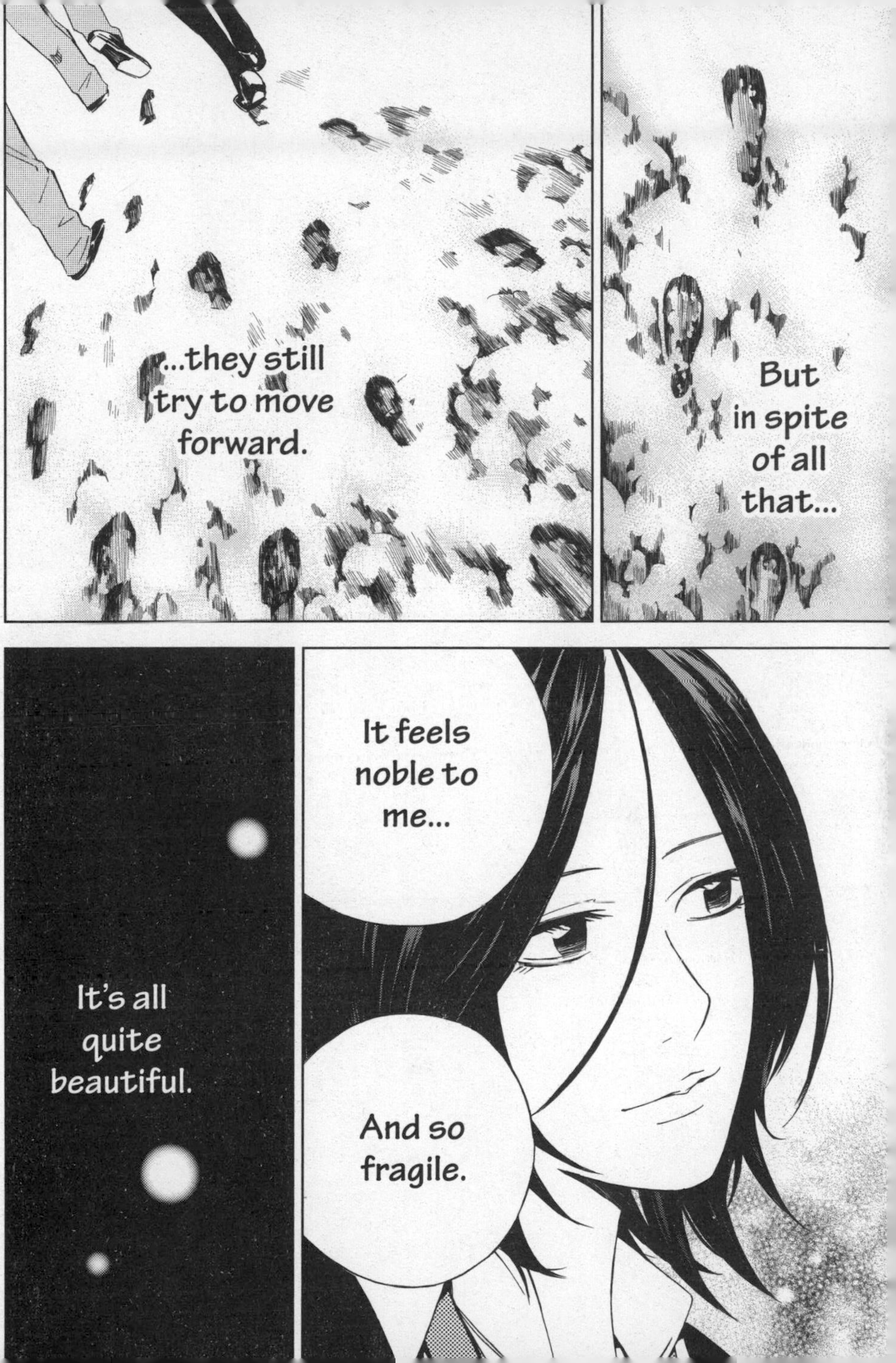
But in spite of all that...
...they still try to move forward.
It feels noble to me...
And so fragile.
It's all quite beautiful.

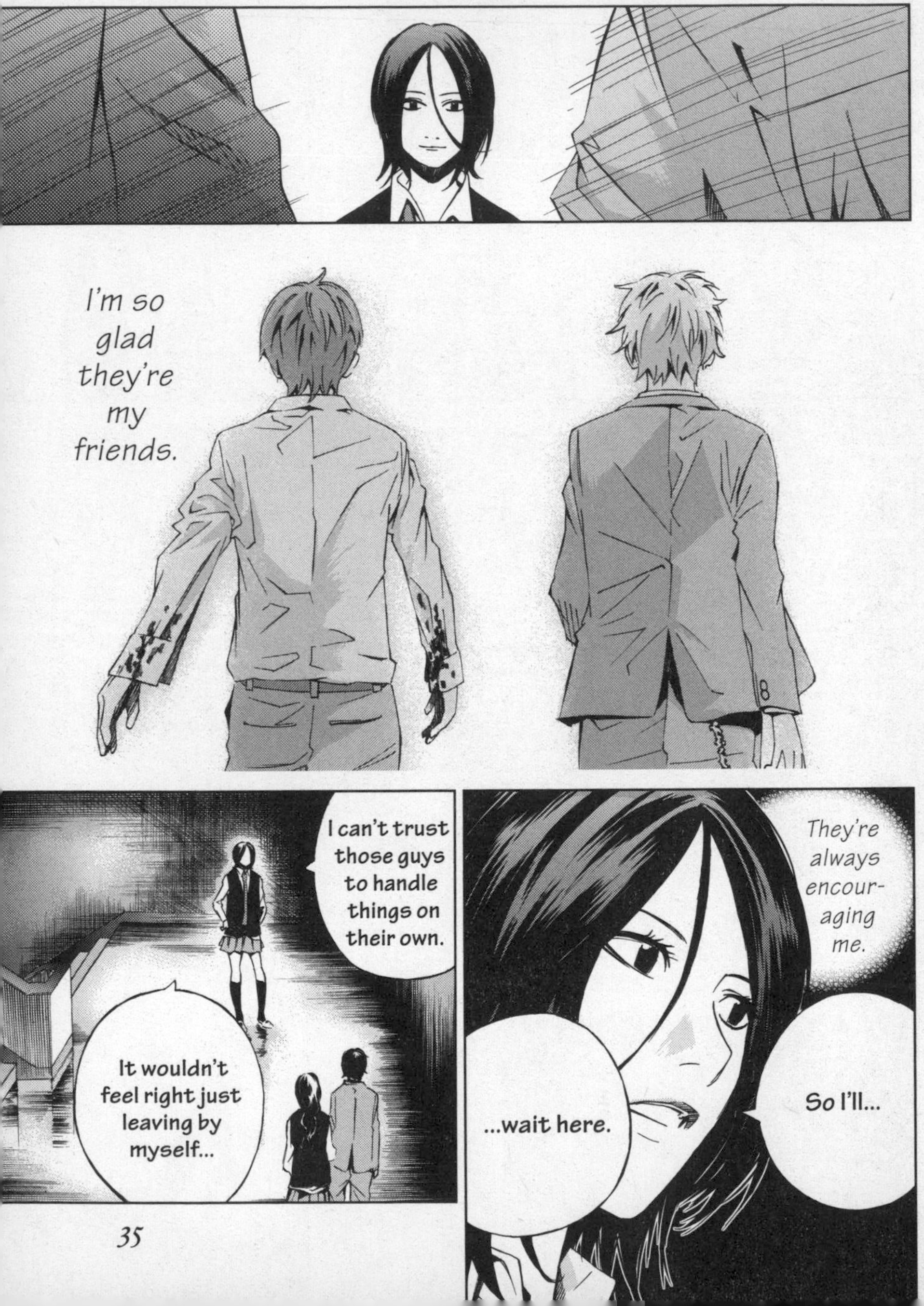
I'm so glad they're my friends.
They're always encouraging me.
So I'll...
...wait here.
I can't trust those guys to handle things on their own.
It wouldn't feel right just leaving by myself...

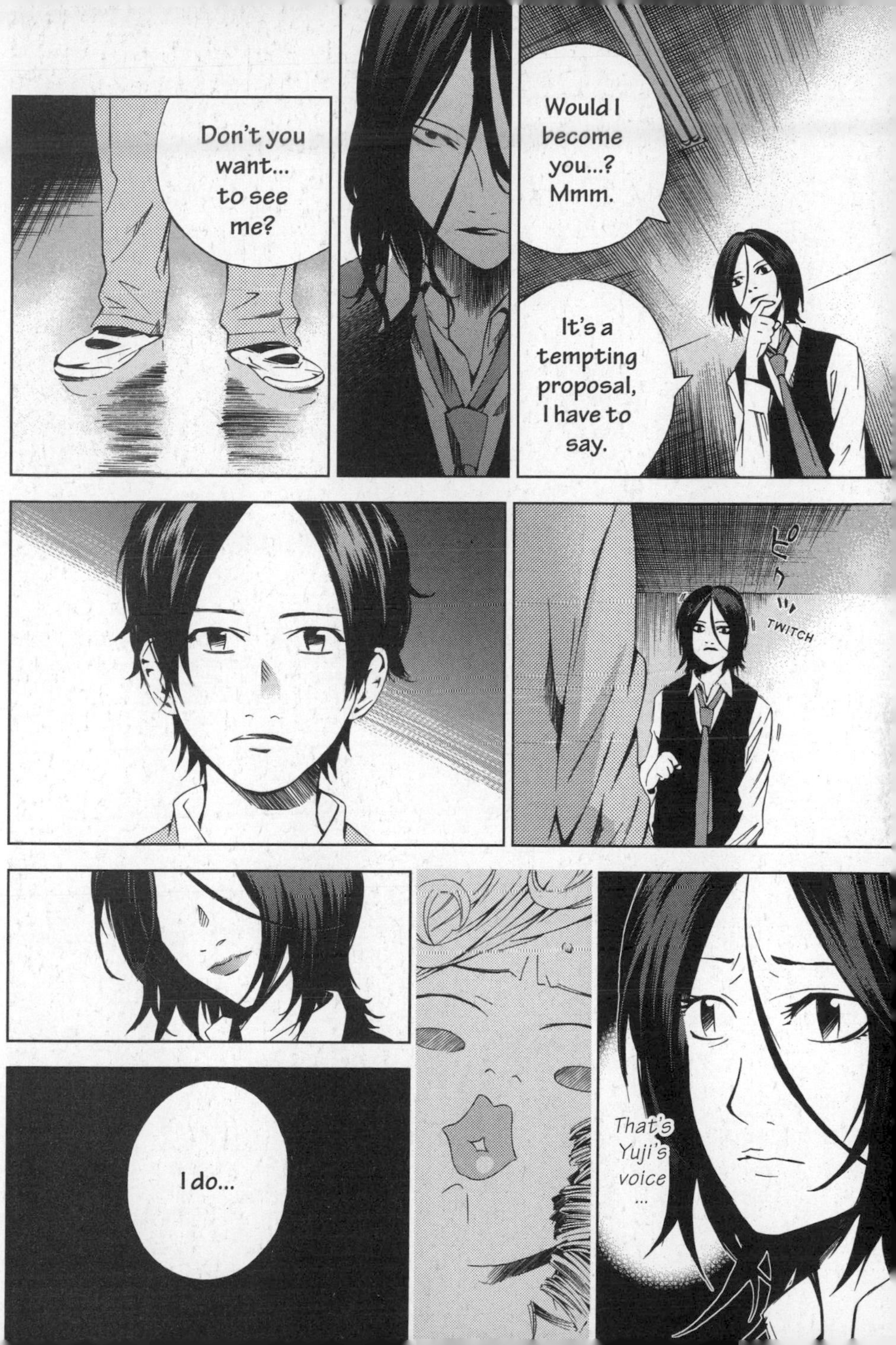

Would I become you...? Mmm.
It's a tempting proposal, I have to say.
Don't you want... to see me?
ピク
TWITCH
That's Yuji's voice ...
I do...

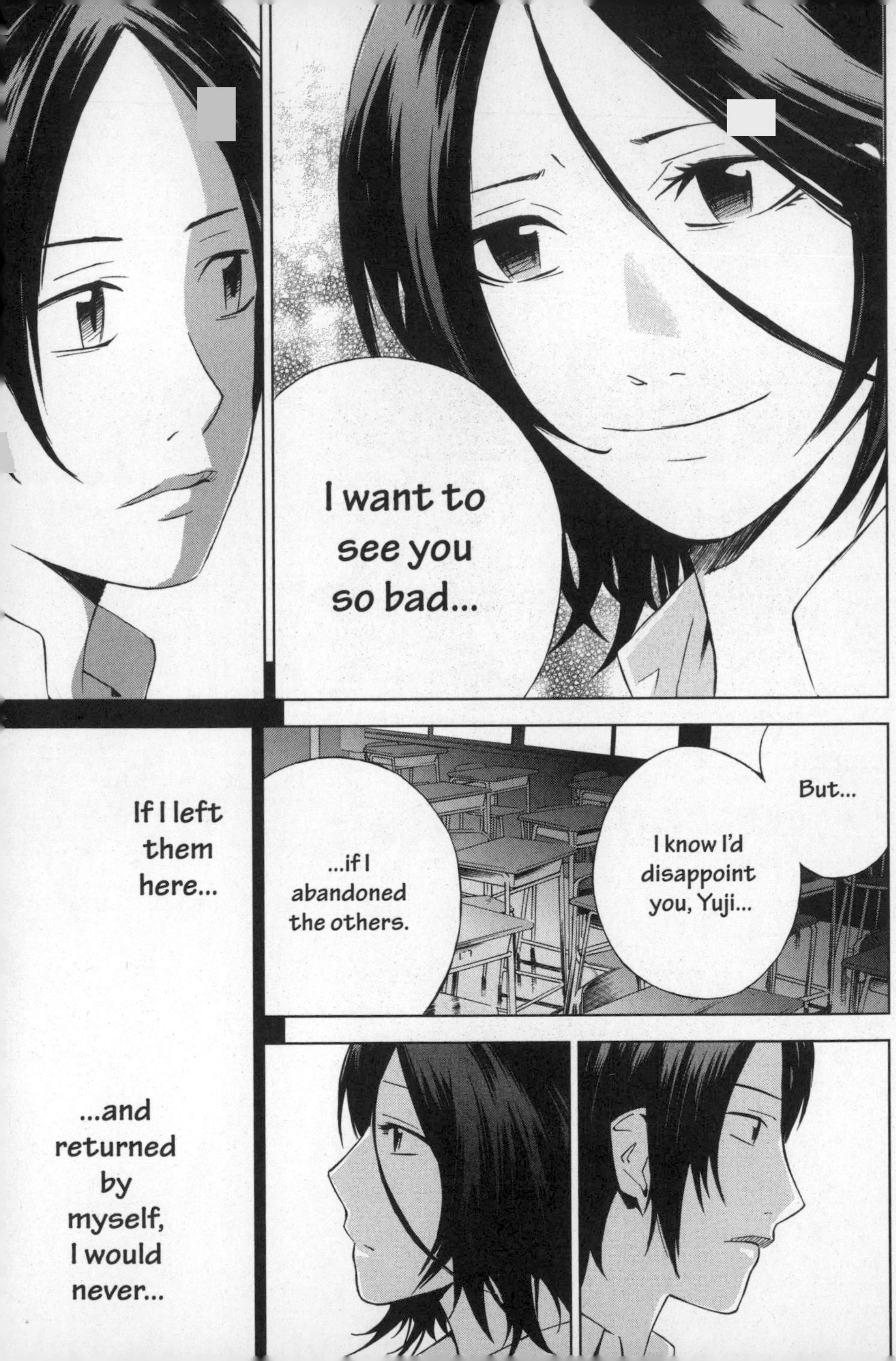
I want to see you so bad...
But...
I know I'd disappoint you, Yuji...
...if I abandoned the others.
If I left them here...
...and returned by myself, I would never...

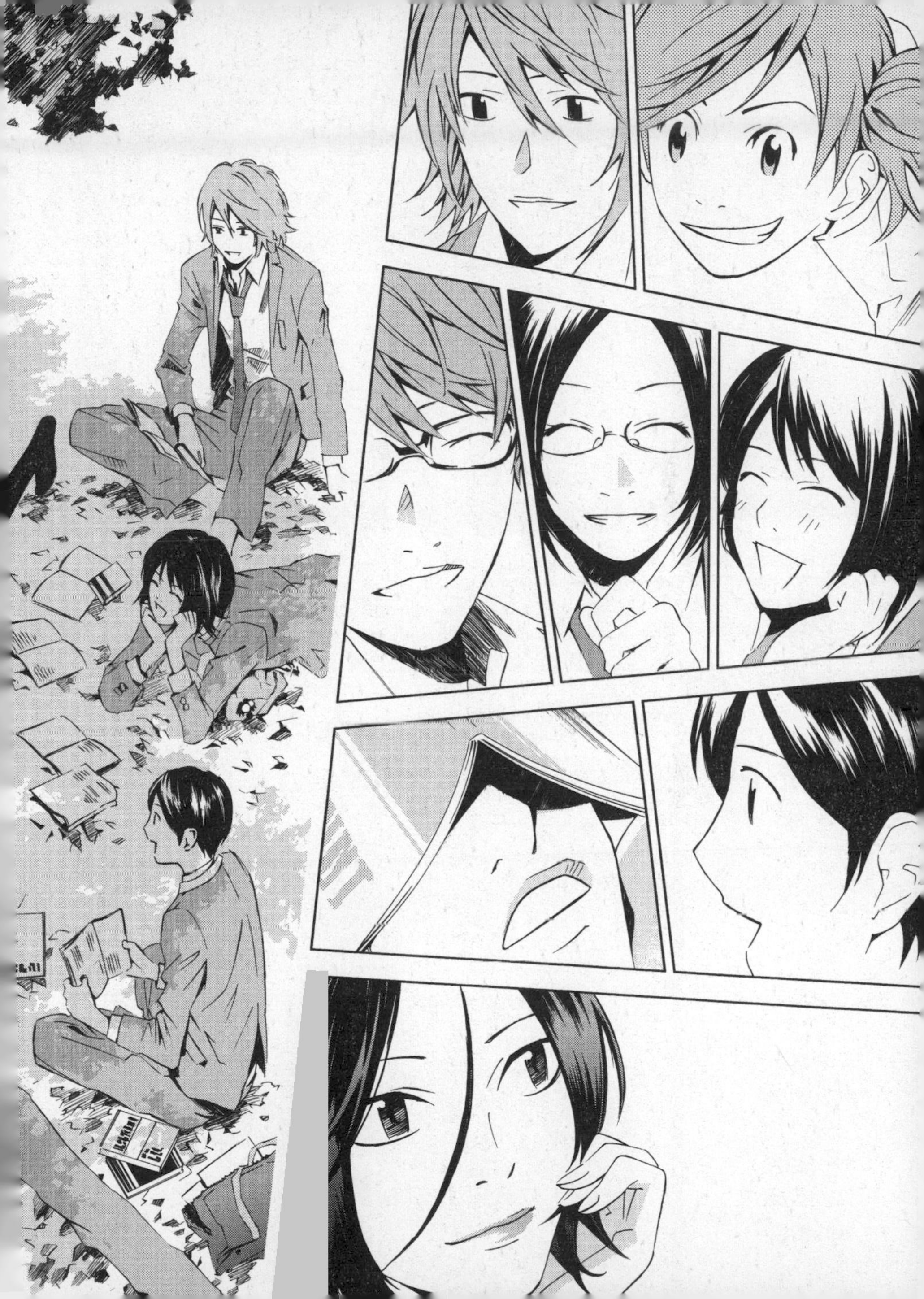

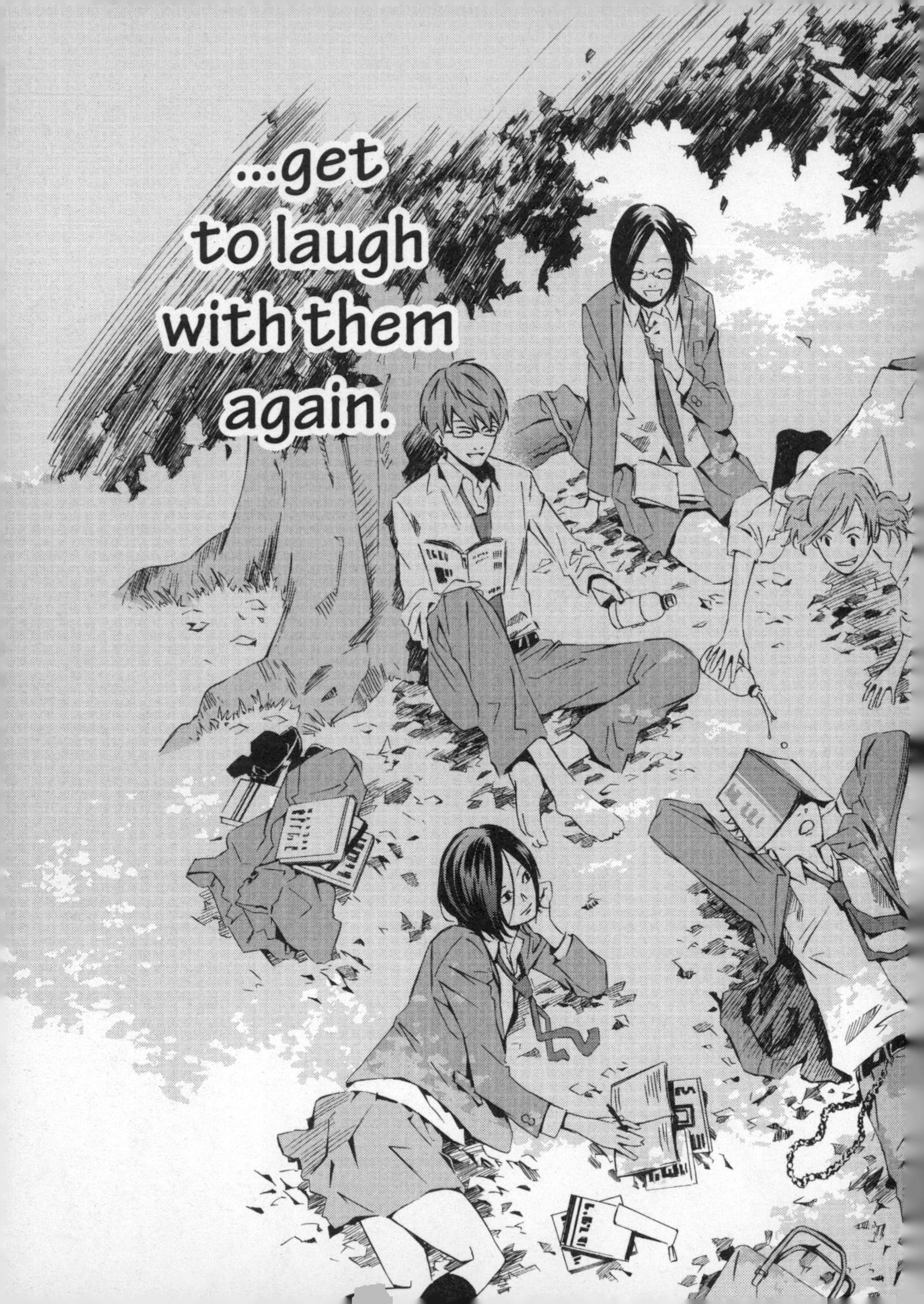
...get to laugh with them again.

I'd hate that.

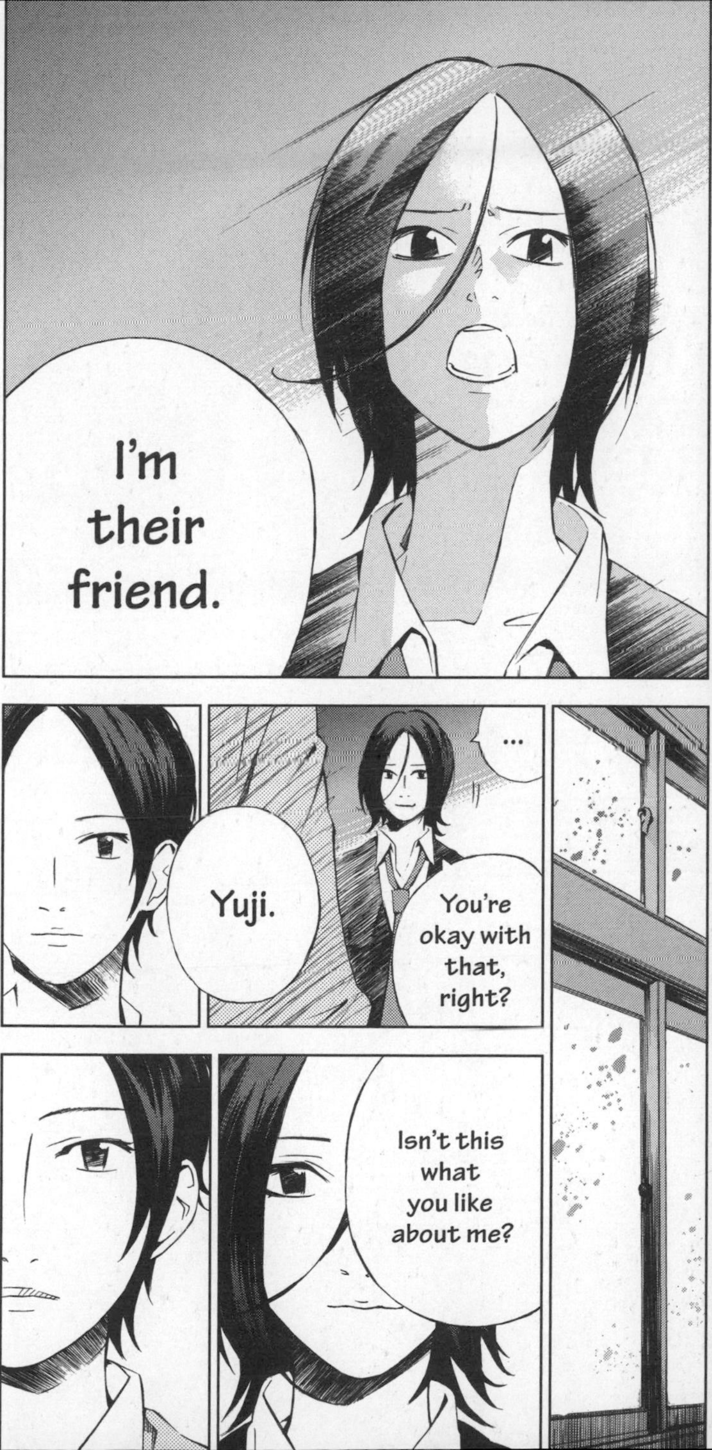
I'm their friend.
...
Yuji.
You're okay with that, right?
Isn't this what you like about me?

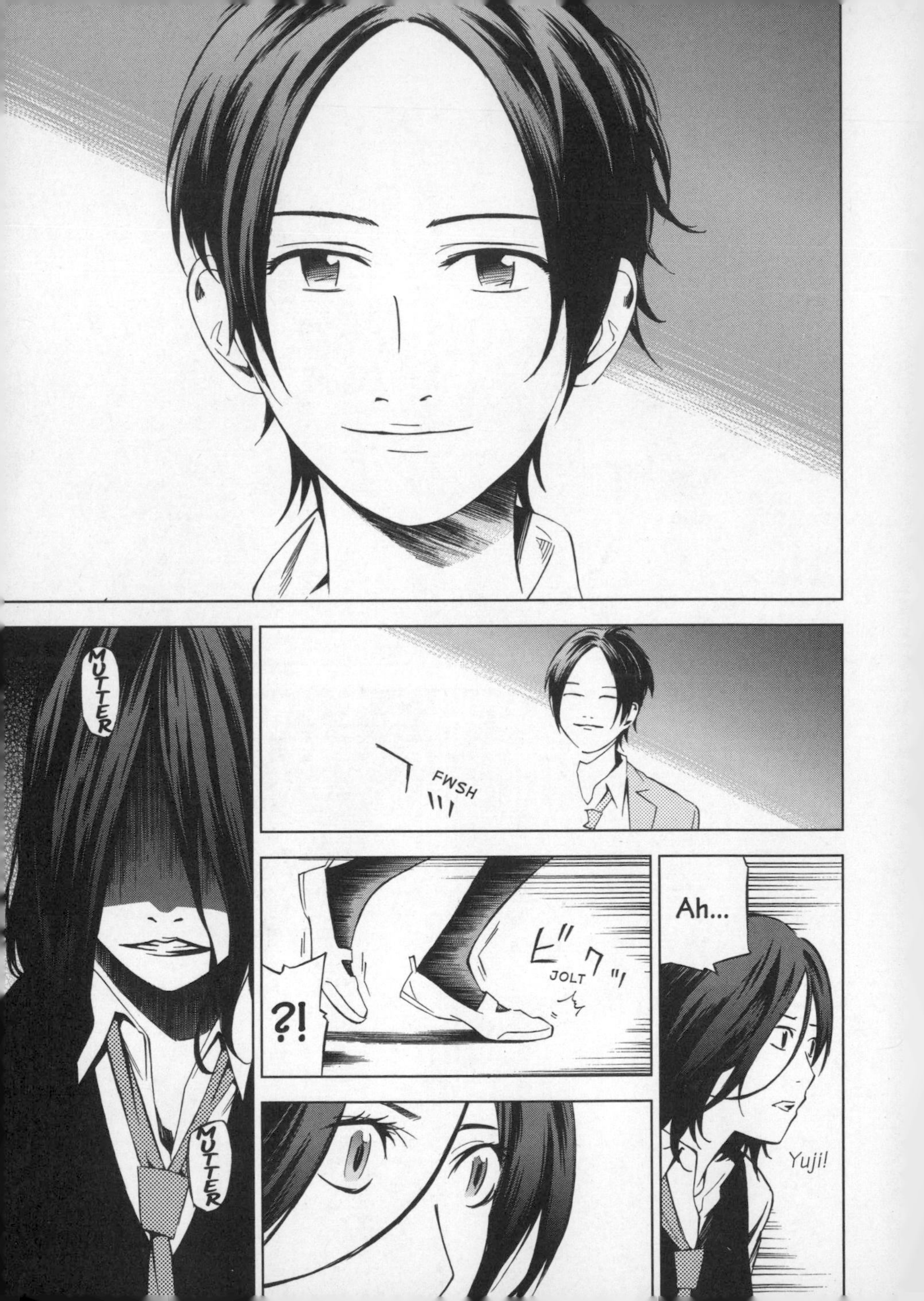
FWSH
Ah...
Yuji!
ビクッ
JOLT
?!
MUTTER
MUTTER

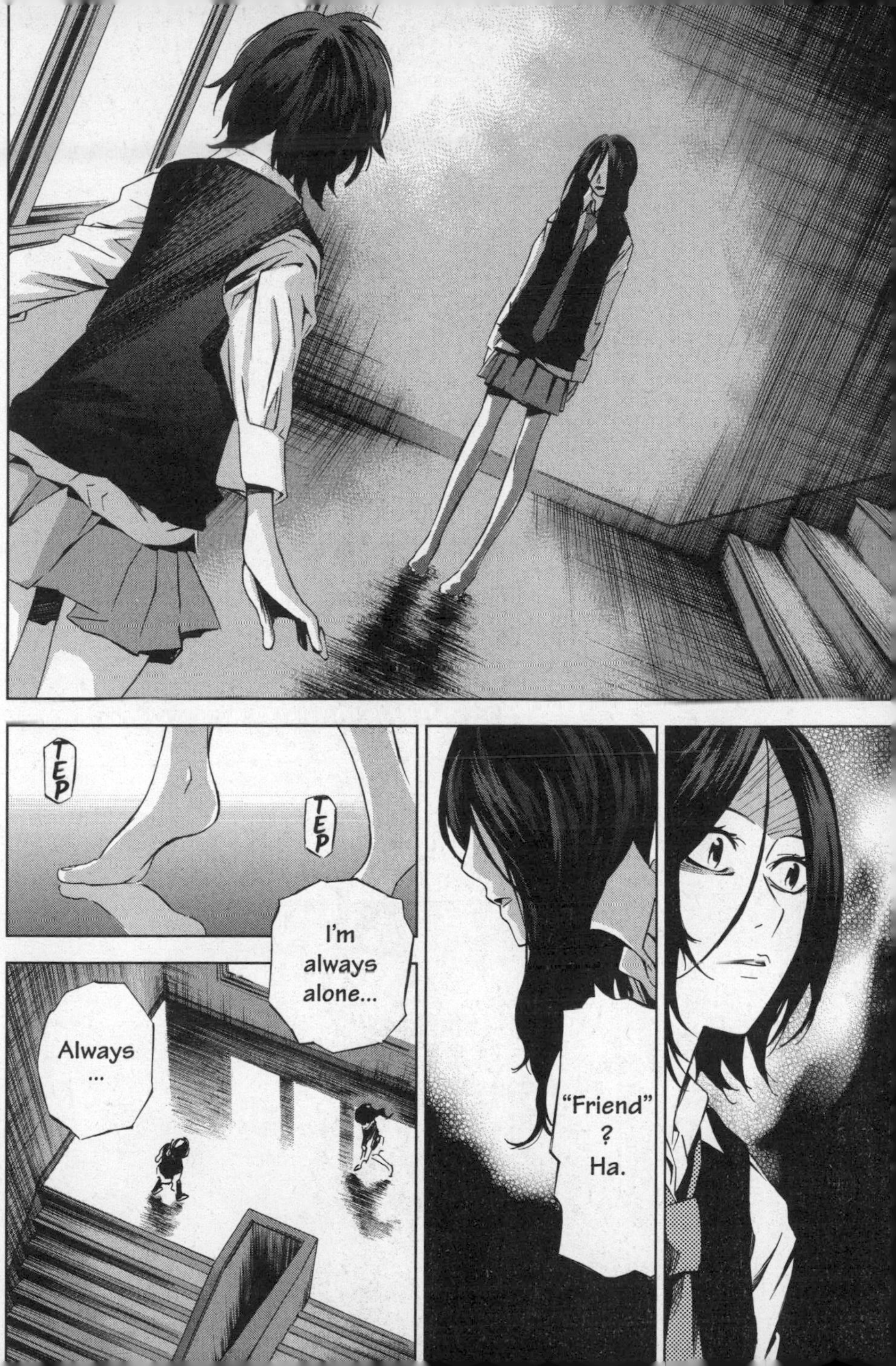
"Friend"?
Ha.
TEP
TEP
I'm always alone...
Always ...

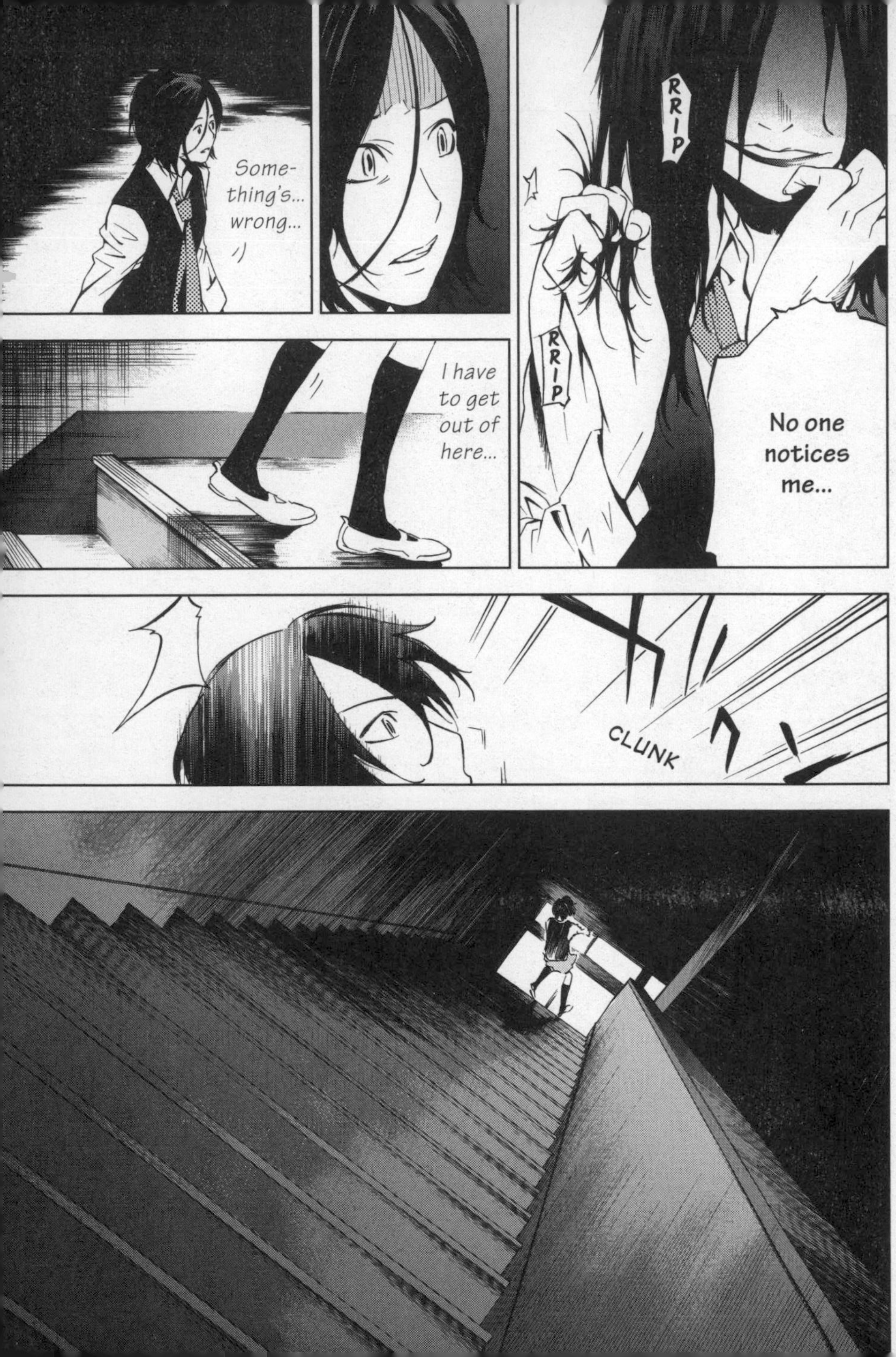
RRIP
RRIP
No one notices me...
Something's... wrong...
I have to get out of here...
CLUNK

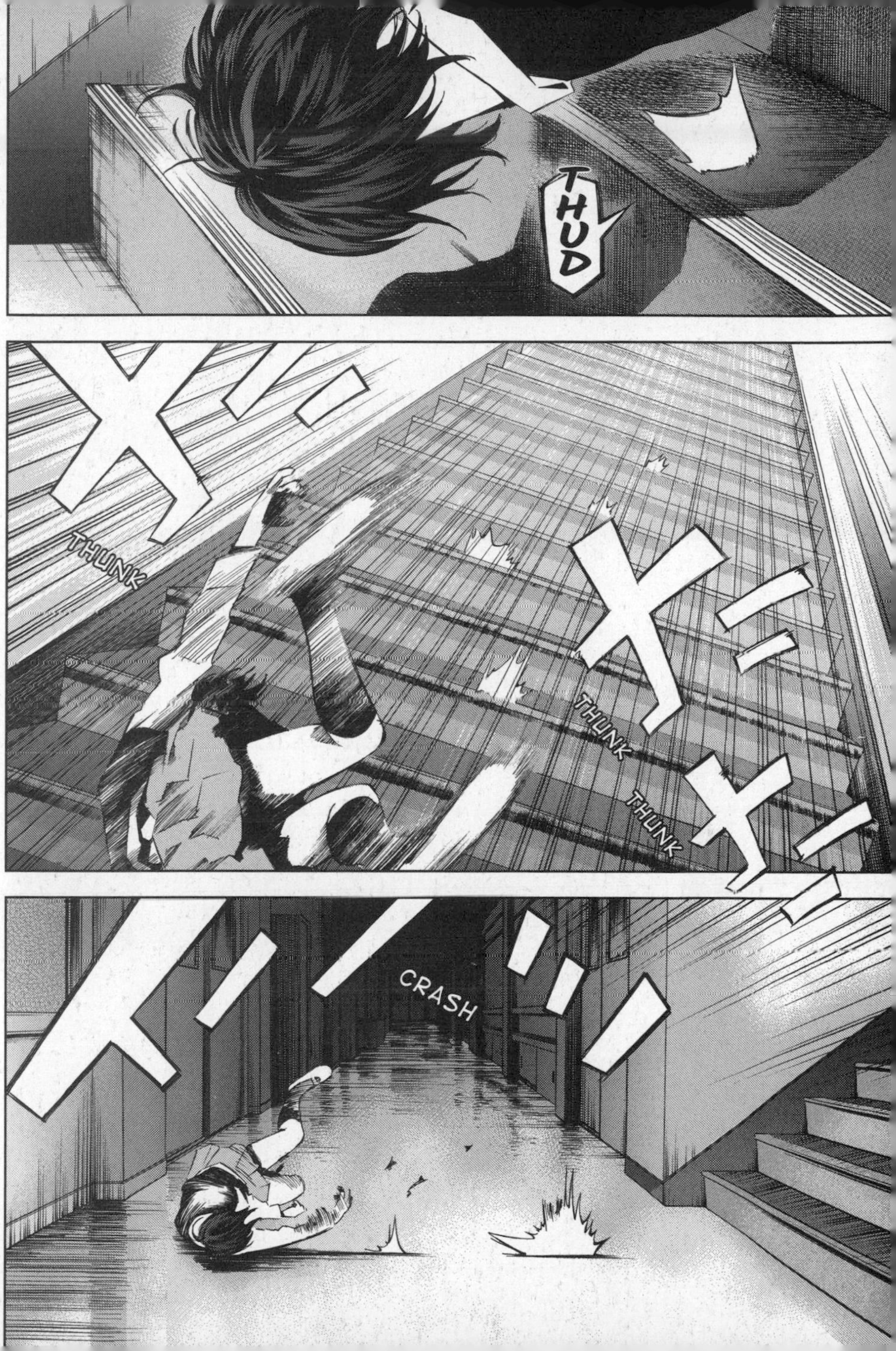
THUD
THUNK
THUNK
THUNK
CRASH

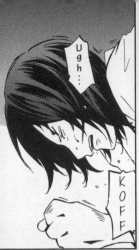

Ugh
...

KOFF

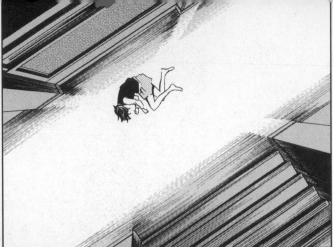

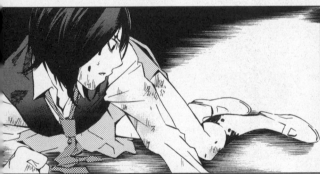

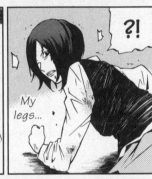

?!

My
legs...

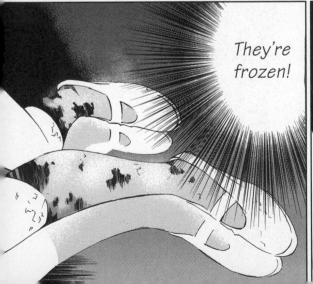

They're
frozen!

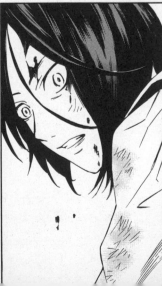

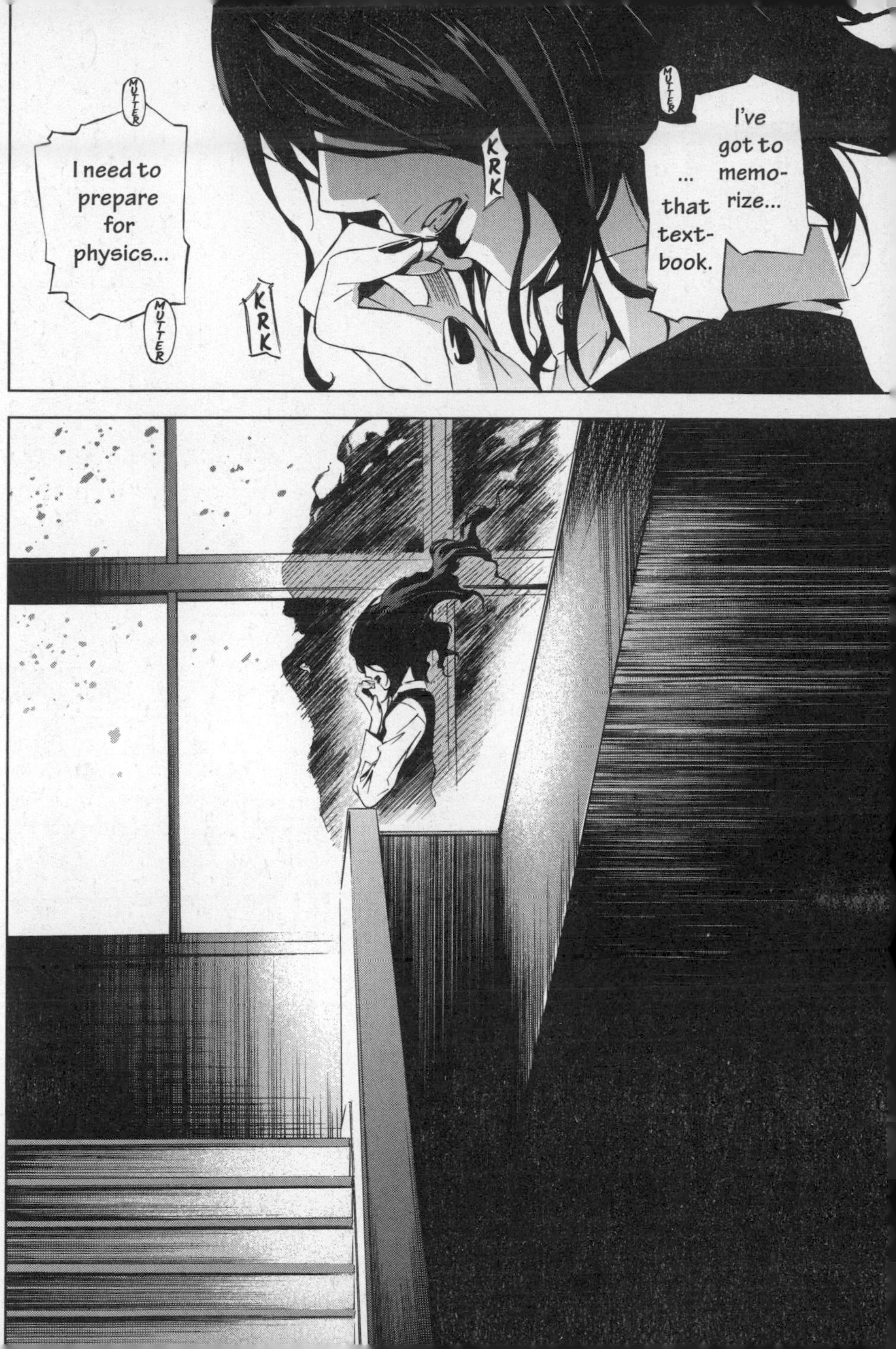
MUTTER
I've got to memo-rize...
... that text-book.
KRK
MUTTER
I need to prepare for physics...
MUTTER
KRK

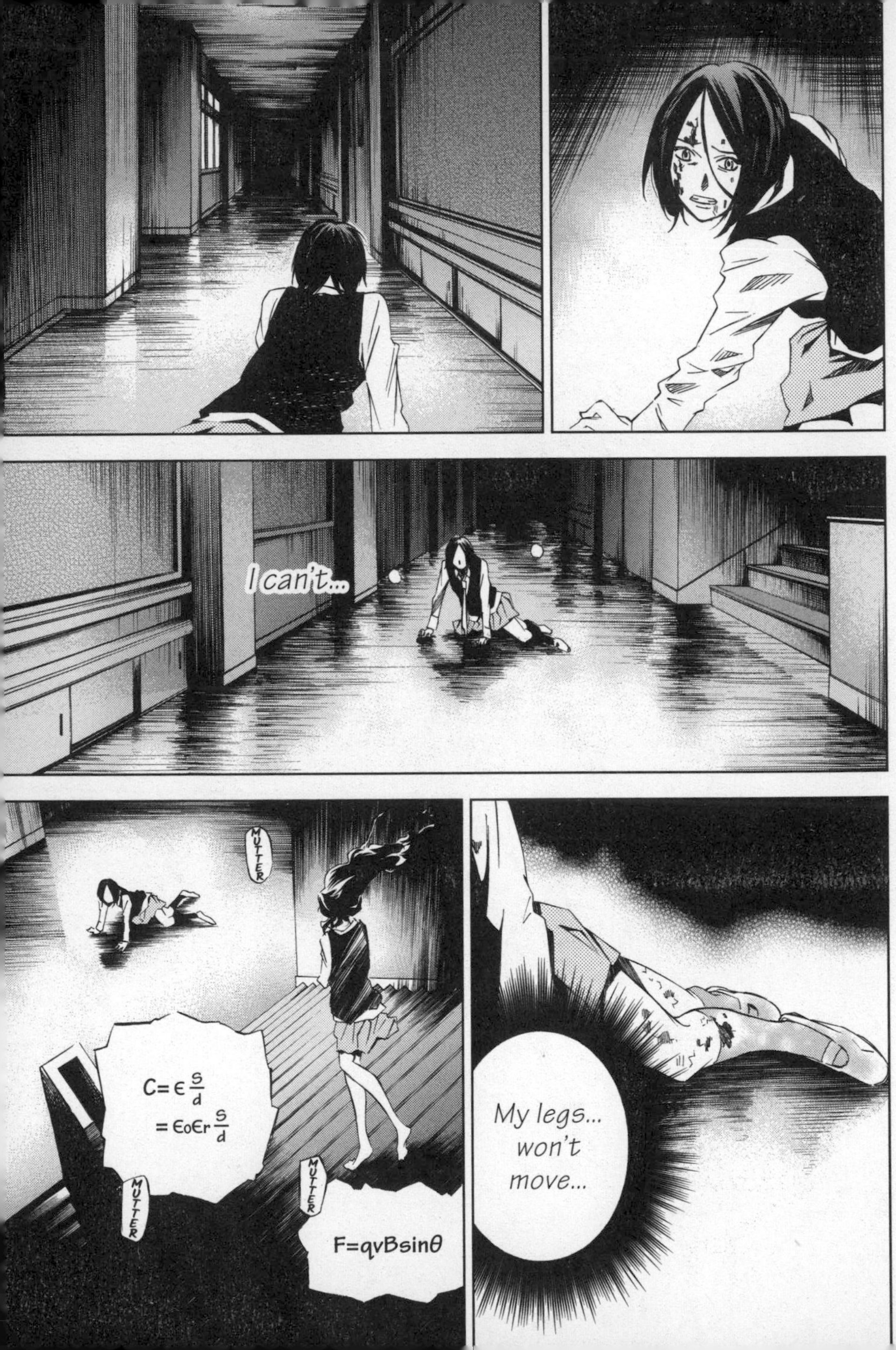
I can't...
My legs... won't move...
MUTTER
$C=\epsilon\frac{S}{d}$
$=\epsilon_0\epsilon_r\frac{S}{d}$
MUTTER
MUTTER
$F=qvB\sin\theta$

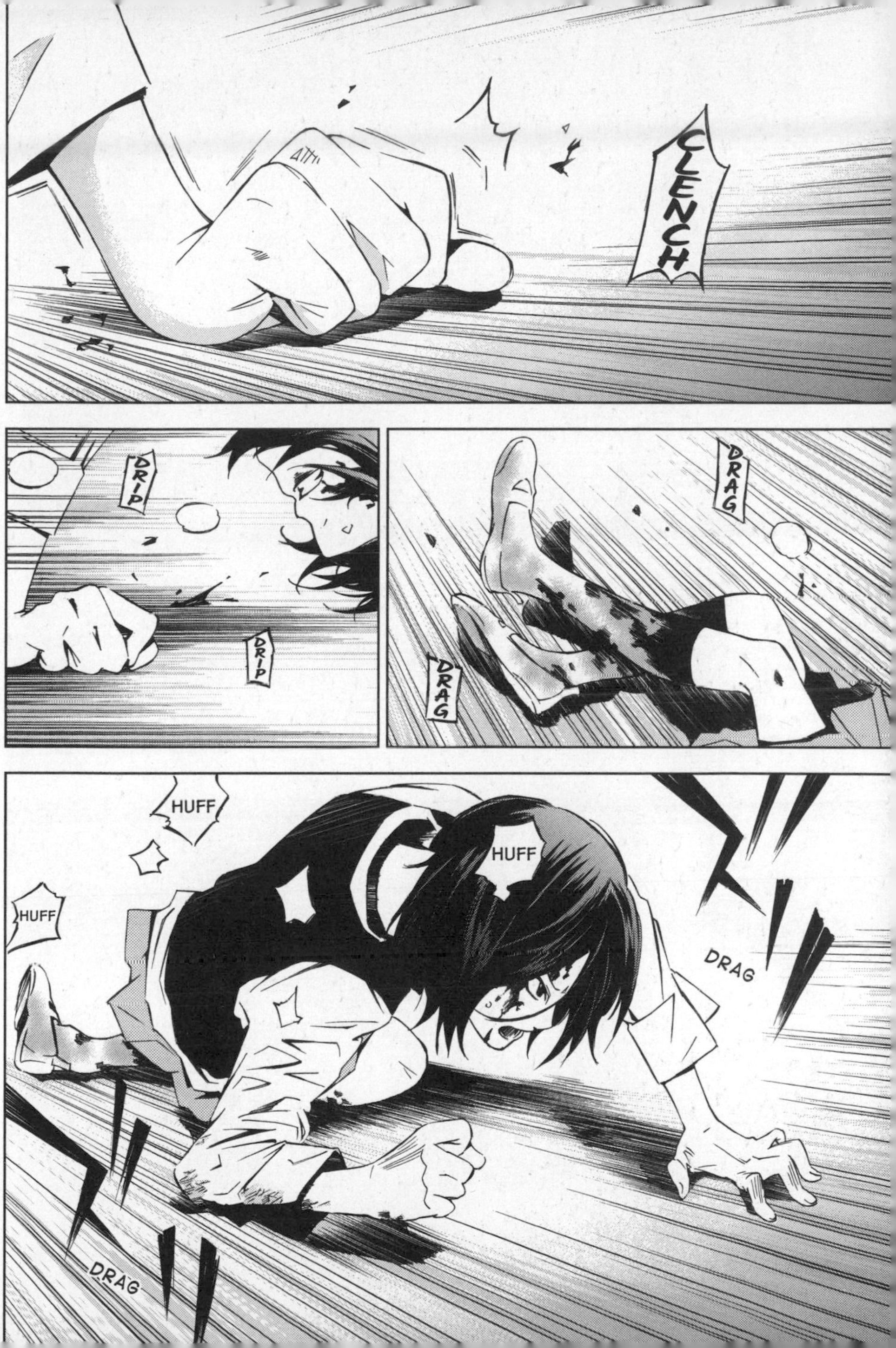
CLENCH
DRAG
DRAG
DRIP
DRIP
HUFF
HUFF
HUFF
DRAG
DRAG

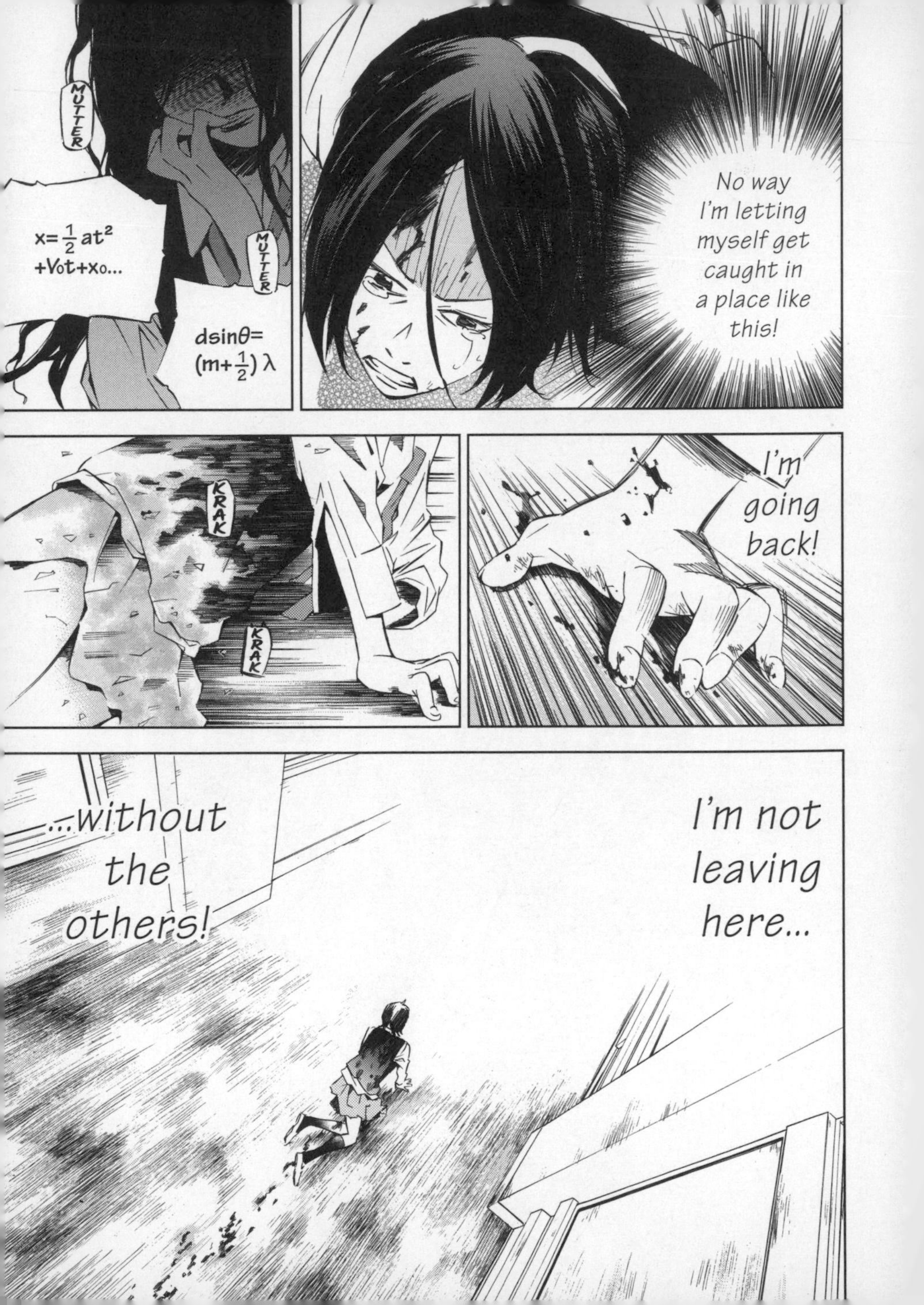
No way I'm letting myself get caught in a place like this!
MUTTER
MUTTER
$x=\frac{1}{2}at^2+V_0t+x_0$...
$d\sin\theta=(m+\frac{1}{2})\lambda$
I'm going back!
KRAK
KRAK
I'm not leaving here...
...without the others!

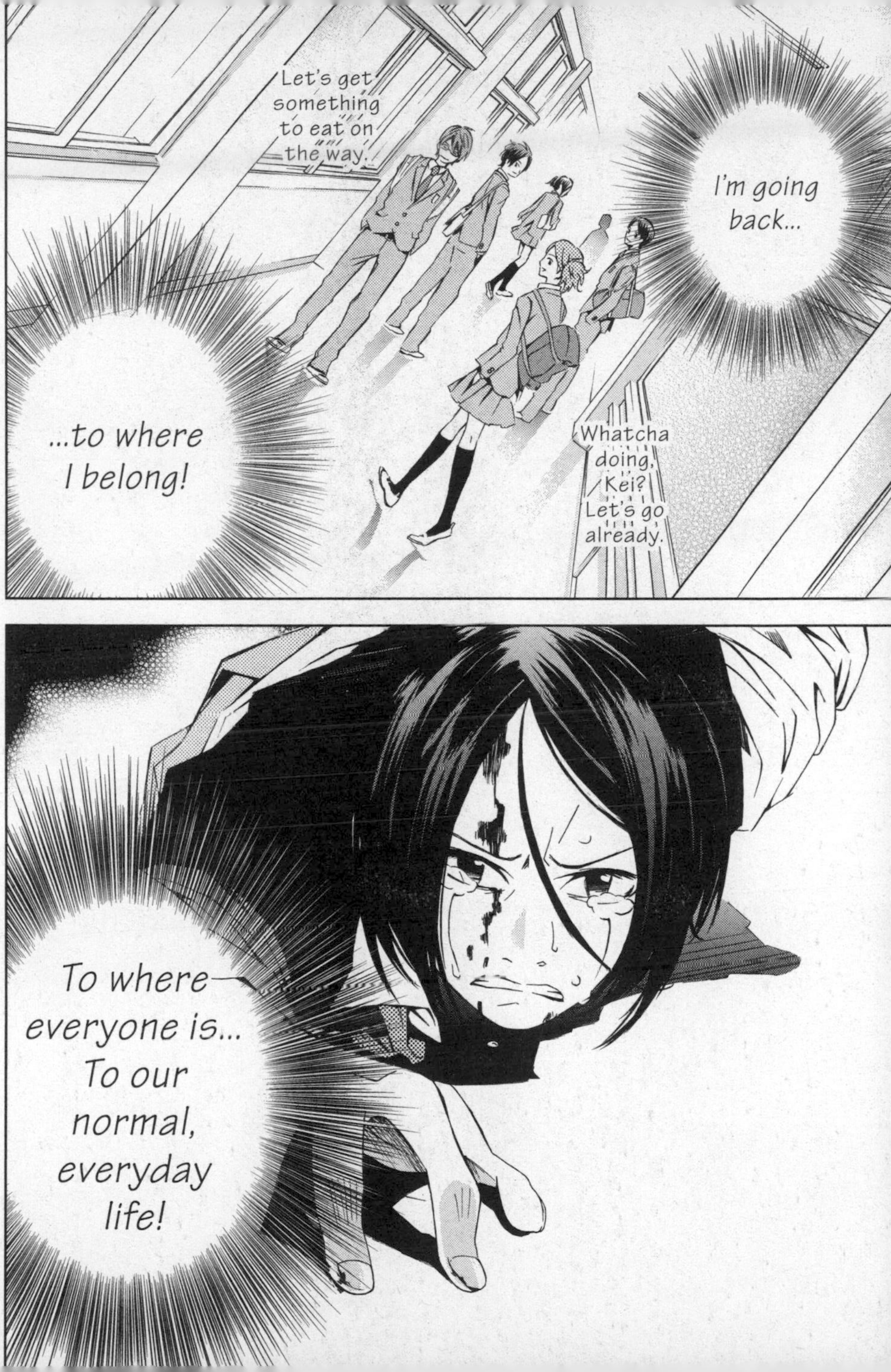
I'm going back...
Let's get something to eat on the way.
Whatcha doing, Kei? Let's go already.
...to where I belong!
To where everyone is... To our normal, everyday life!

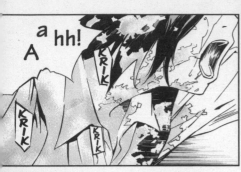

KRIK
KRIK
I'm going back.
Aahh!
KRIK
KRIK
KRIK
Aahh!
I'm going... back...
To everyone ...
キン
PLINK

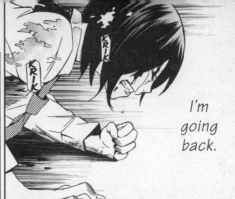

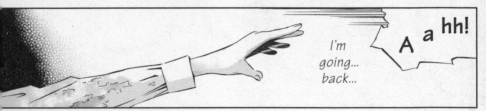

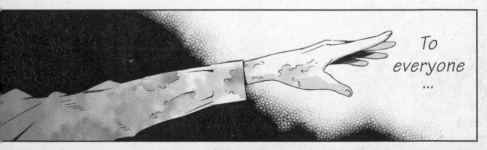

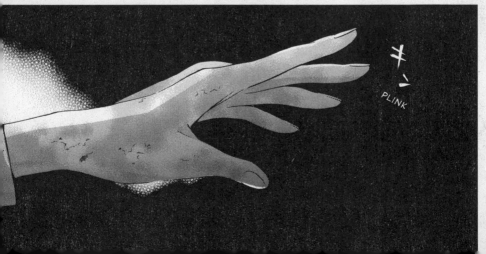

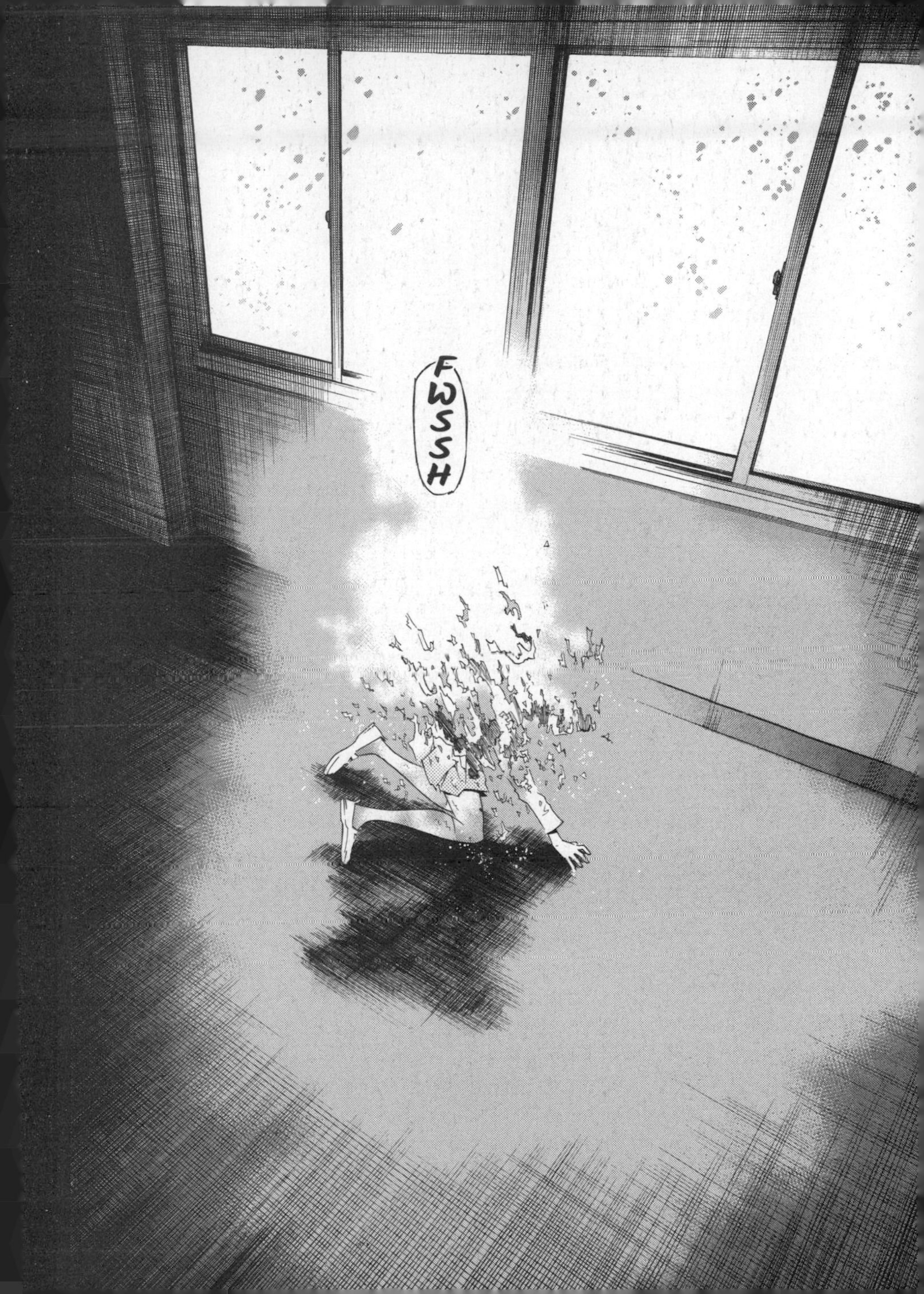
FWSSH

A School
Frozen
in Time

A School
Frozen
in Time

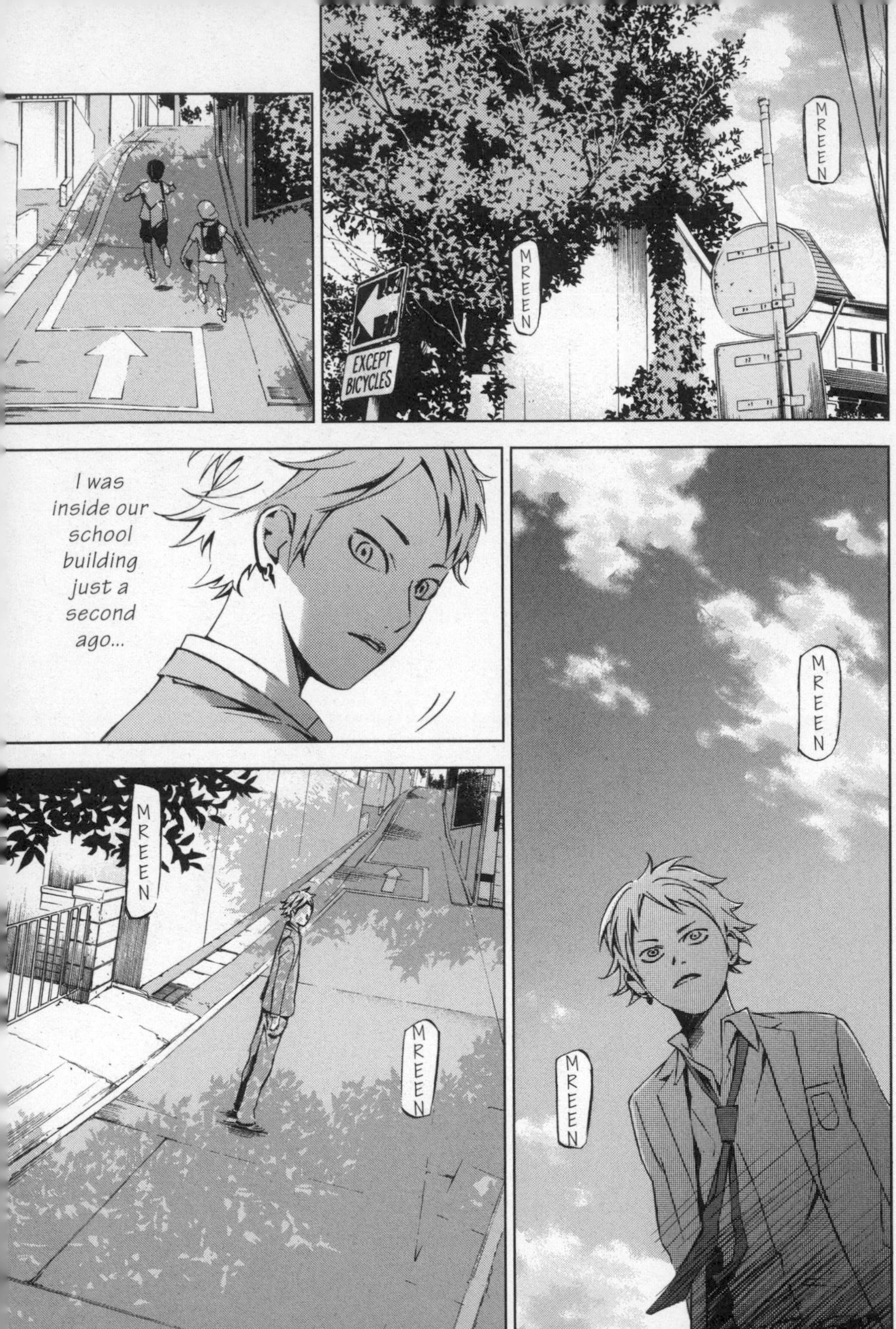
MREEN
EXCEPT BICYCLES
MREEN
MREEN
I was inside our school building just a second ago...
MREEN
MREEN
MREEN

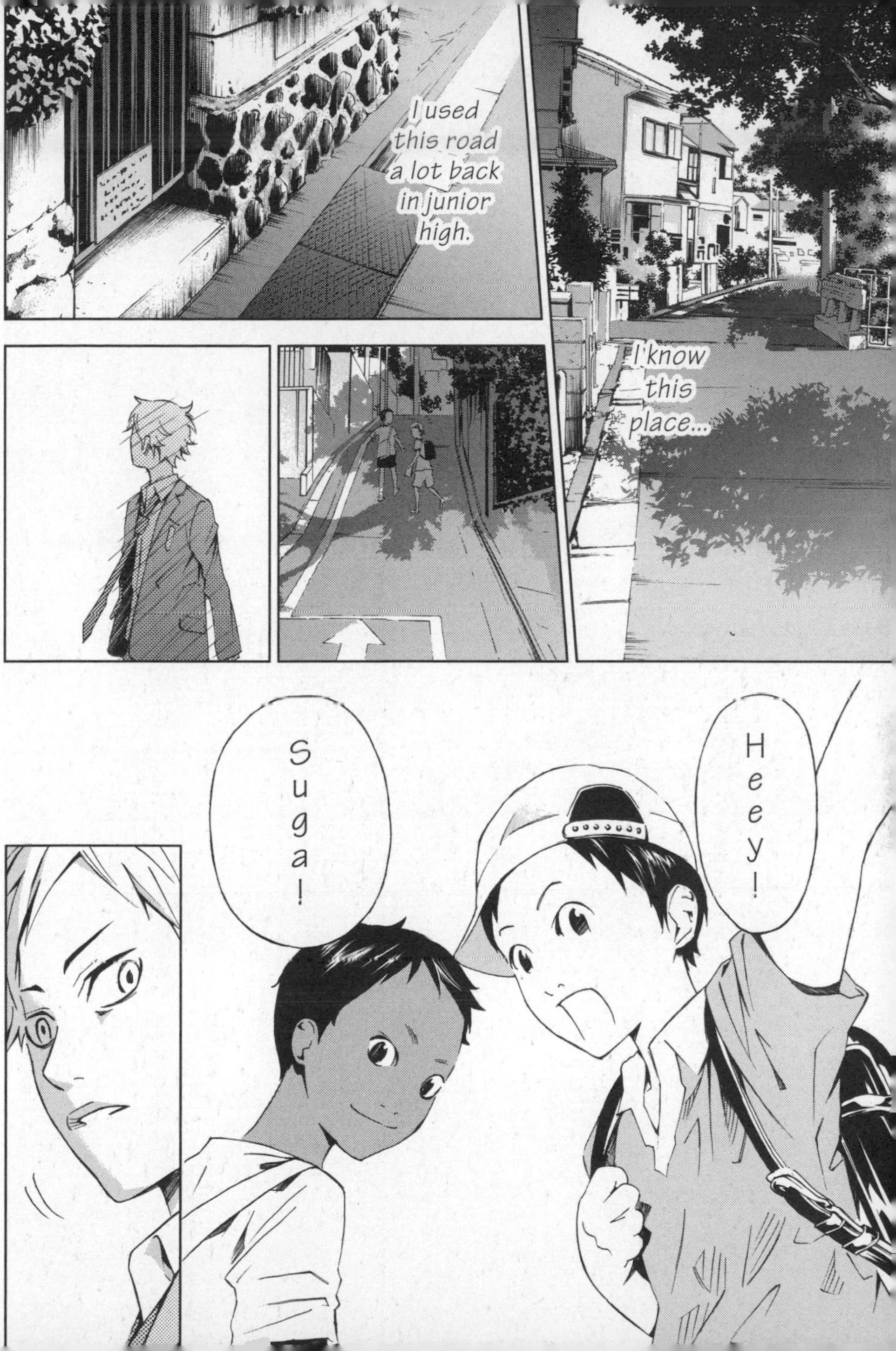
I know this place...
I used this road a lot back in junior high.
Heey!
Suga!

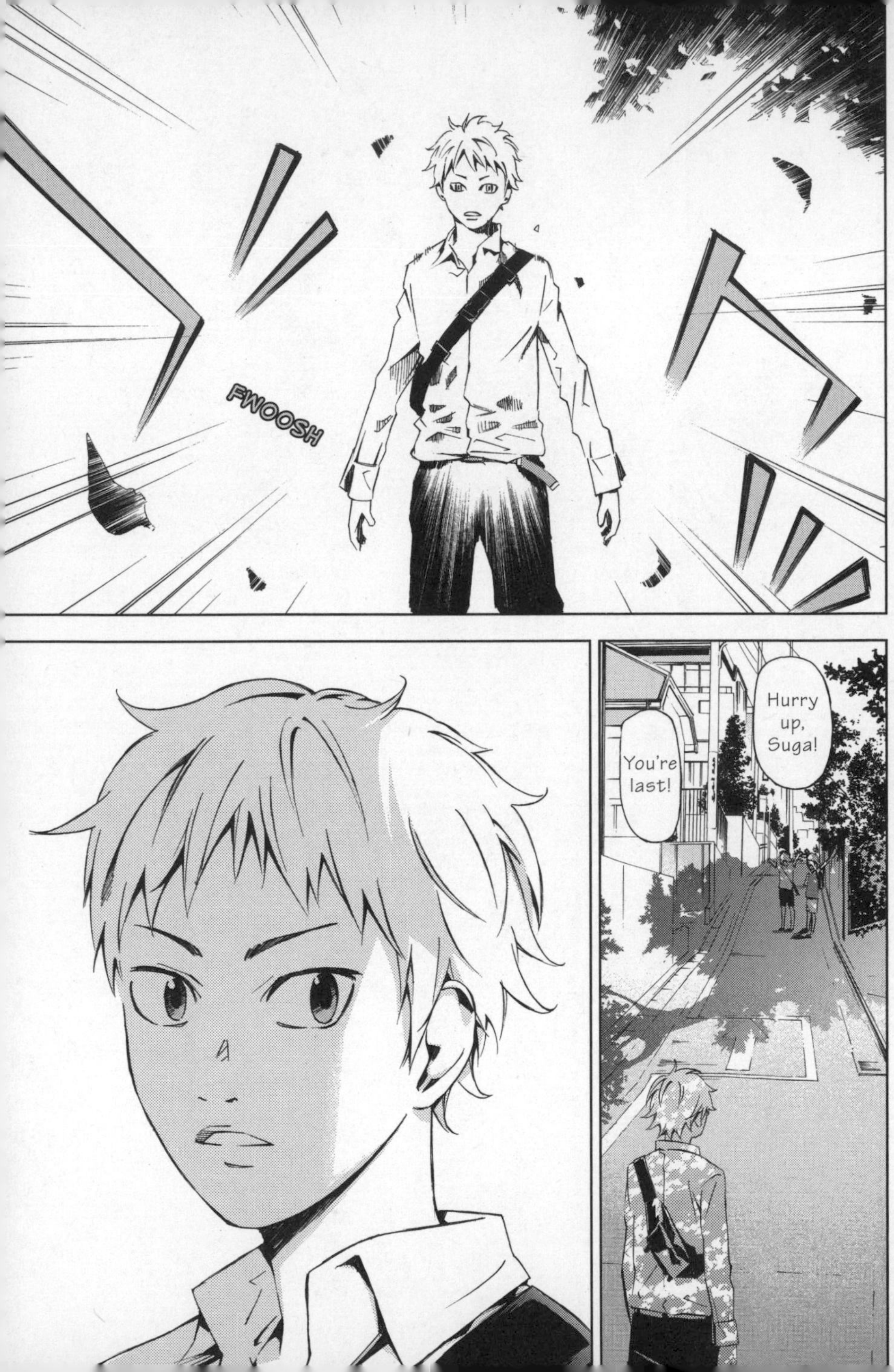
FWOOSH
Hurry up, Suga!
You're last!

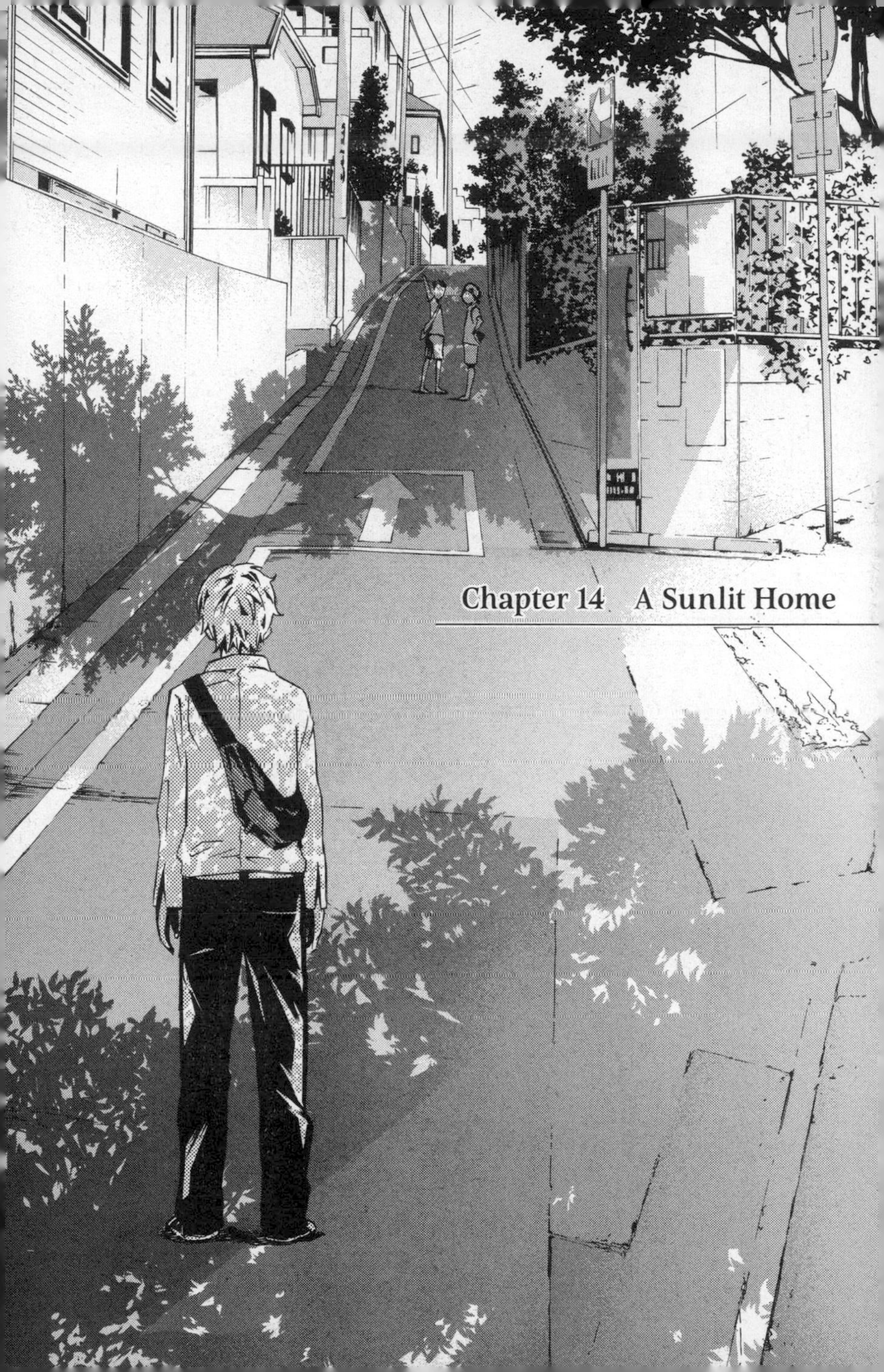
Chapter 14 A Sunlit Home

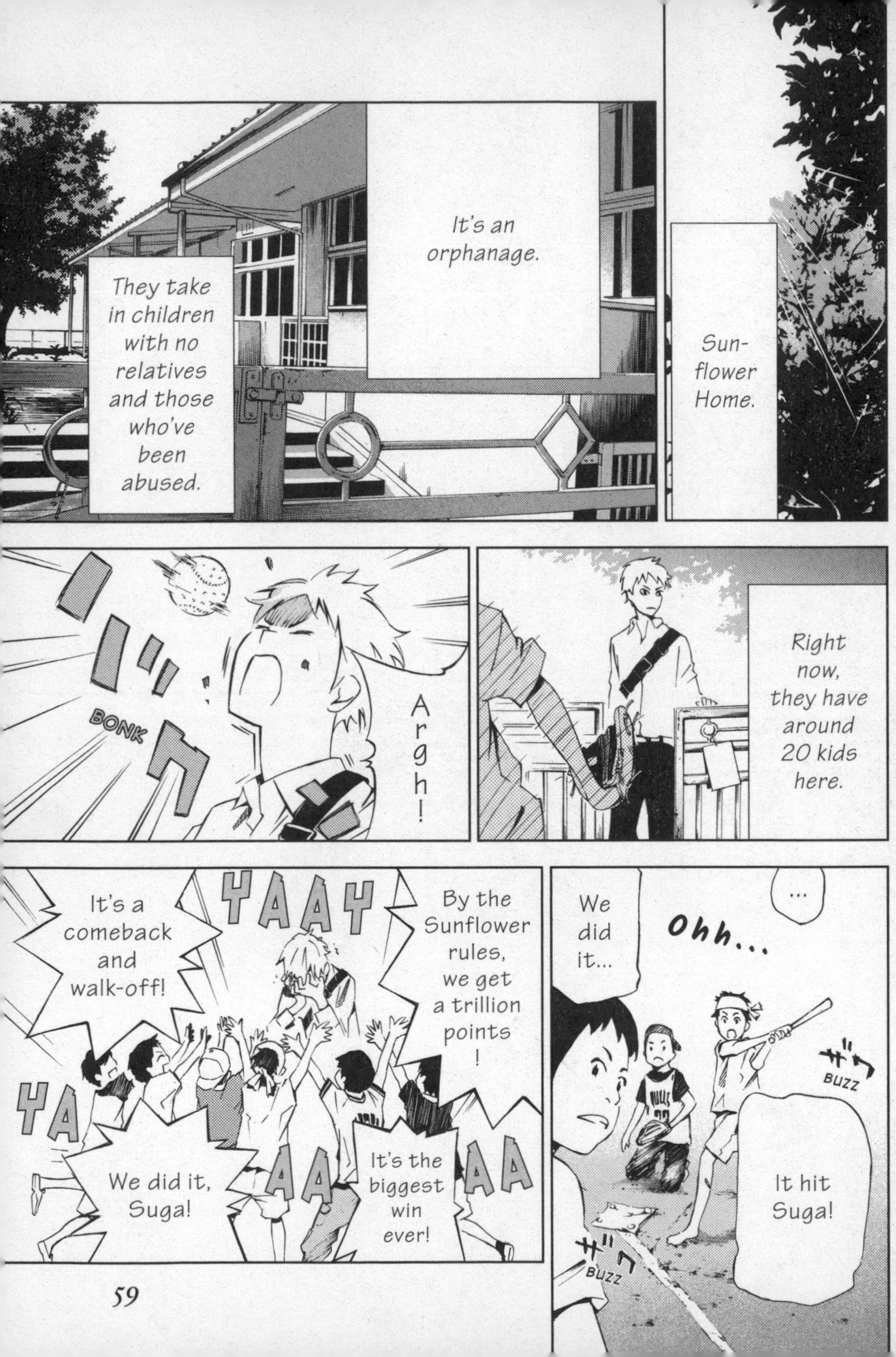
Sun-flower Home.
It's an orphanage.
They take in children with no relatives and those who've been abused.
Right now, they have around 20 kids here.
Argh!
BONK
...
We did it...
Ohh...
BUZZ
It hit Suga!
BUZZ
By the Sunflower rules, we get a trillion points!
YAAAY
It's a comeback and walk-off!
It's the biggest win ever!
AA
We did it, Suga!
YA
AA

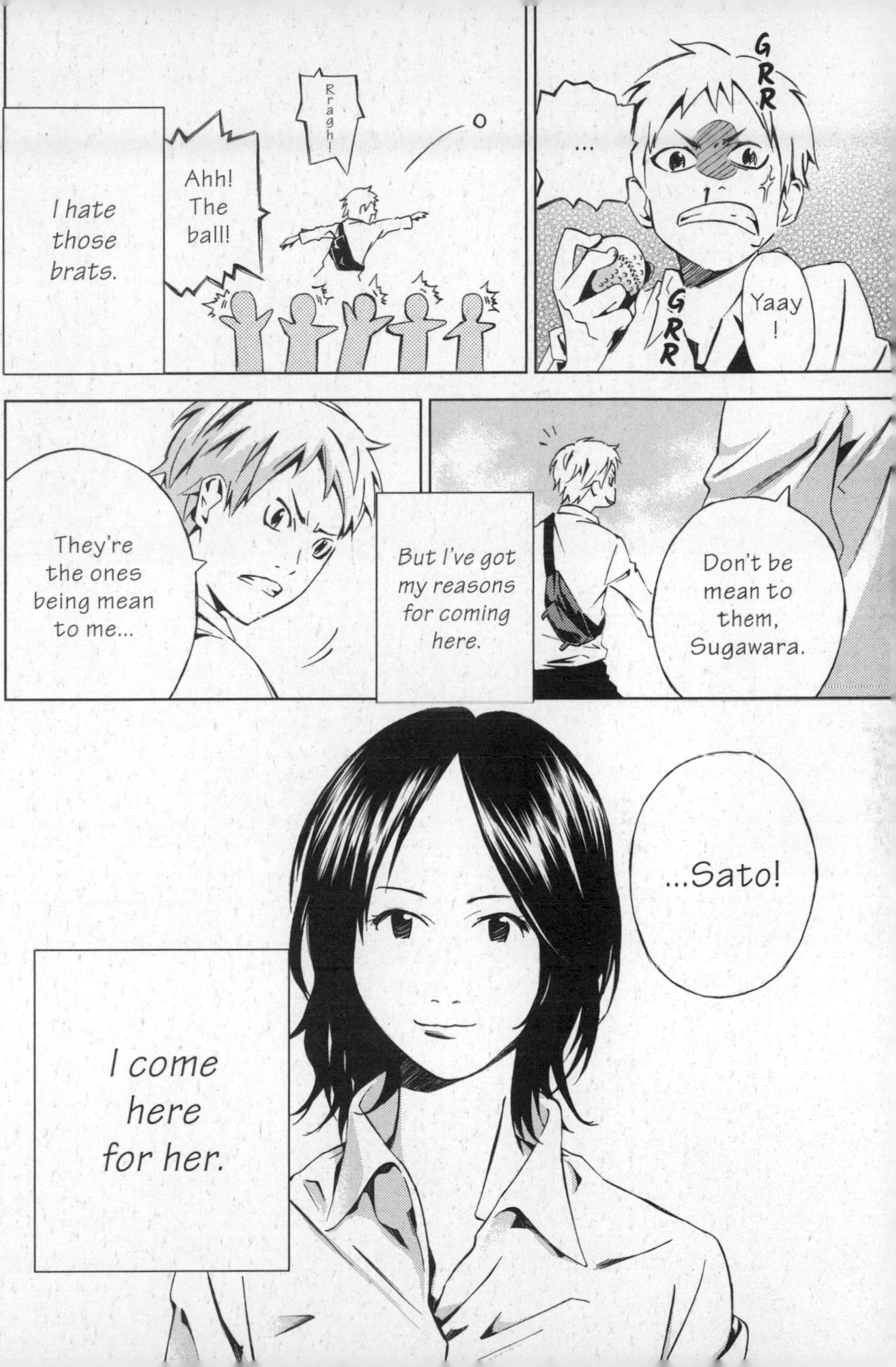
GRR
...
Yaay!
GRR
Rragh!
Ahh! The ball!
I hate those brats.
Don't be mean to them, Sugawara.
But I've got my reasons for coming here.
They're the ones being mean to me...
...Sato!
I come here for her.

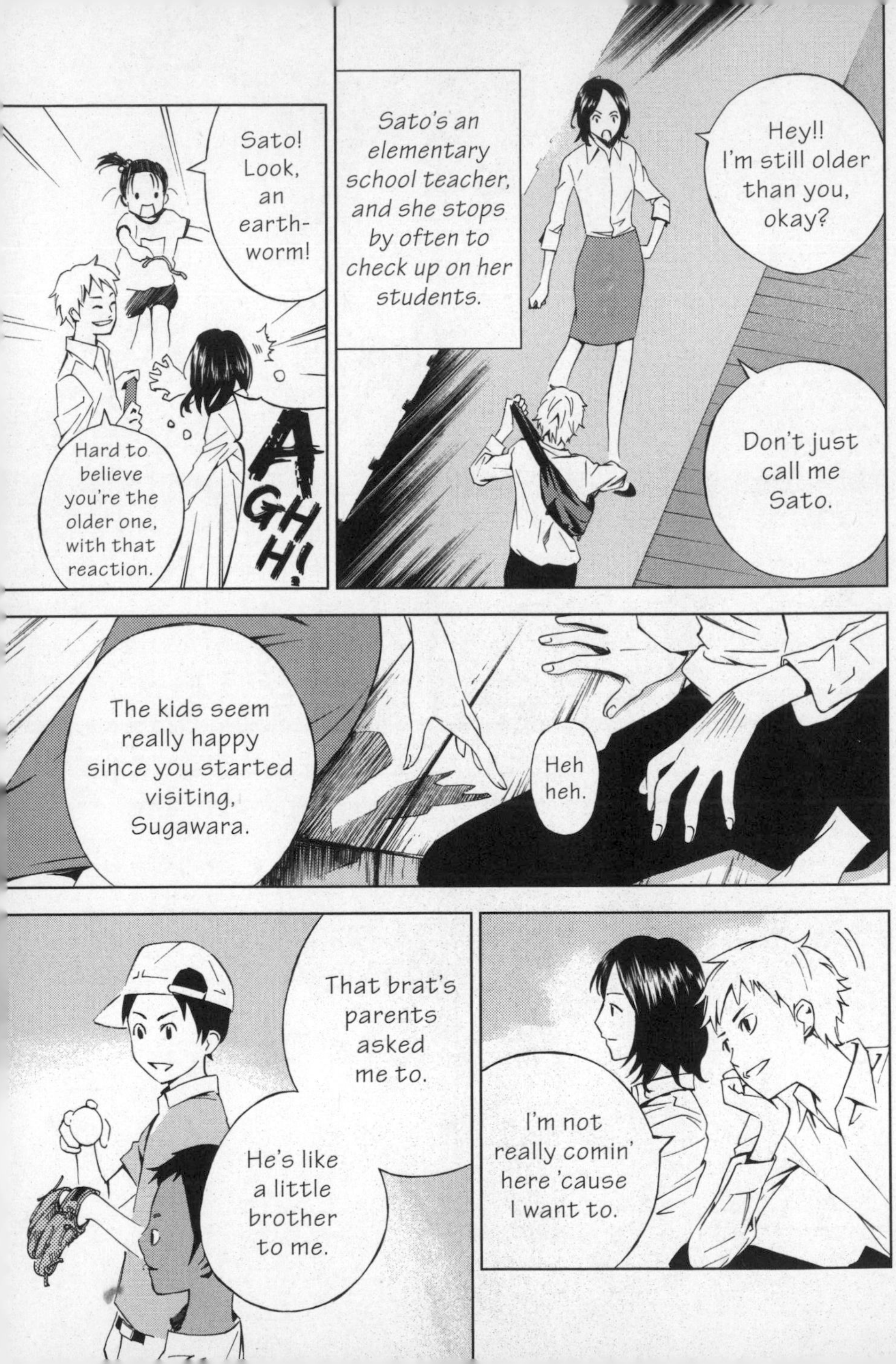
Sato's an elementary school teacher, and she stops by often to check up on her students.
Hey!! I'm still older than you, okay?
Don't just call me Sato.
Sato! Look, an earthworm!
AGHH!
Hard to believe you're the older one, with that reaction.
The kids seem really happy since you started visiting, Sugawara.
Heh heh.
I'm not really comin' here 'cause I want to.
That brat's parents asked me to.
He's like a little brother to me.

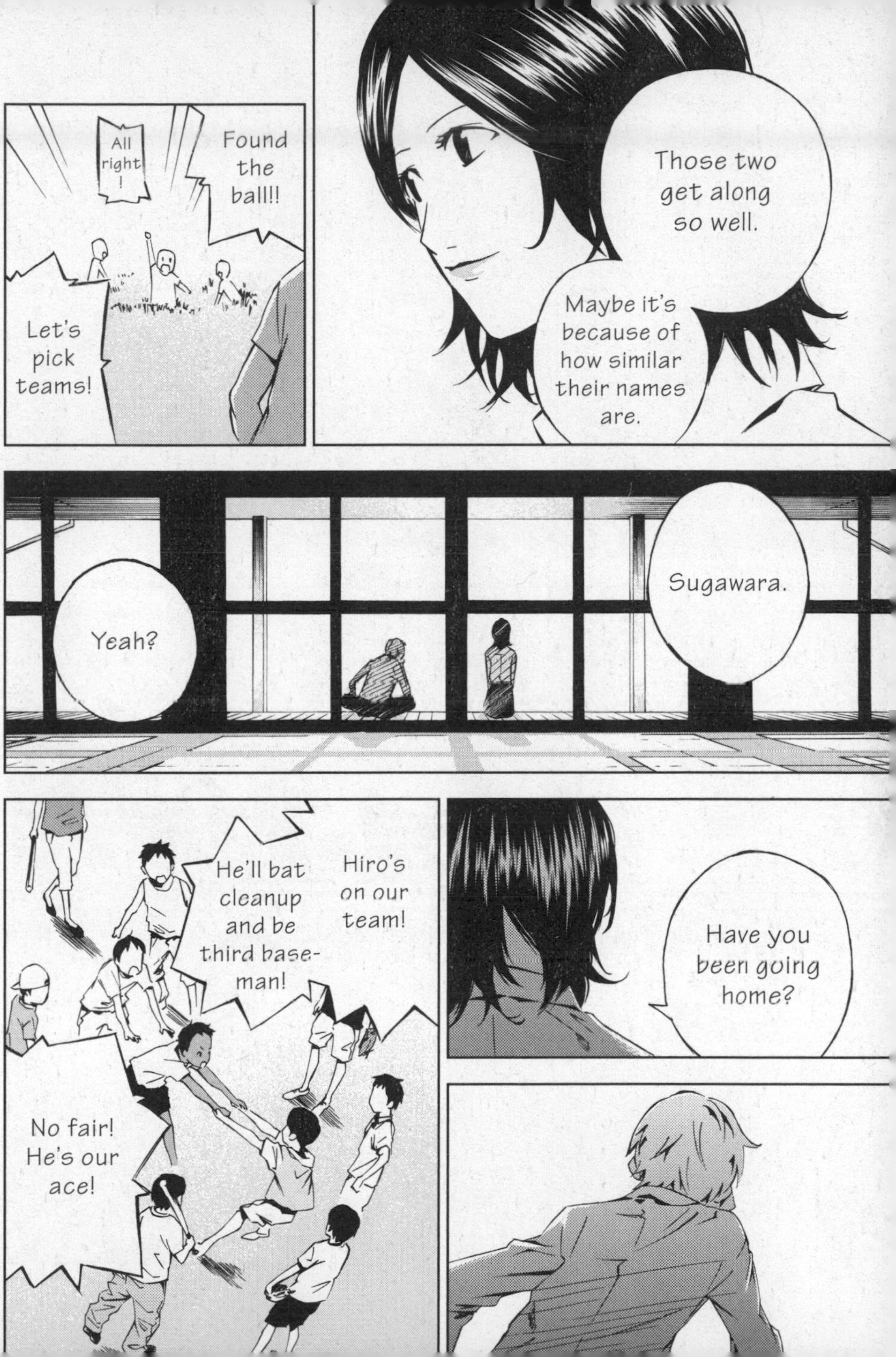
Those two get along so well.
Maybe it's because of how similar their names are.
Found the ball!!
All right!
Let's pick teams!
Sugawara.
Yeah?
Have you been going home?
Hiro's on our team!
He'll bat cleanup and be third baseman!
No fair! He's our ace!

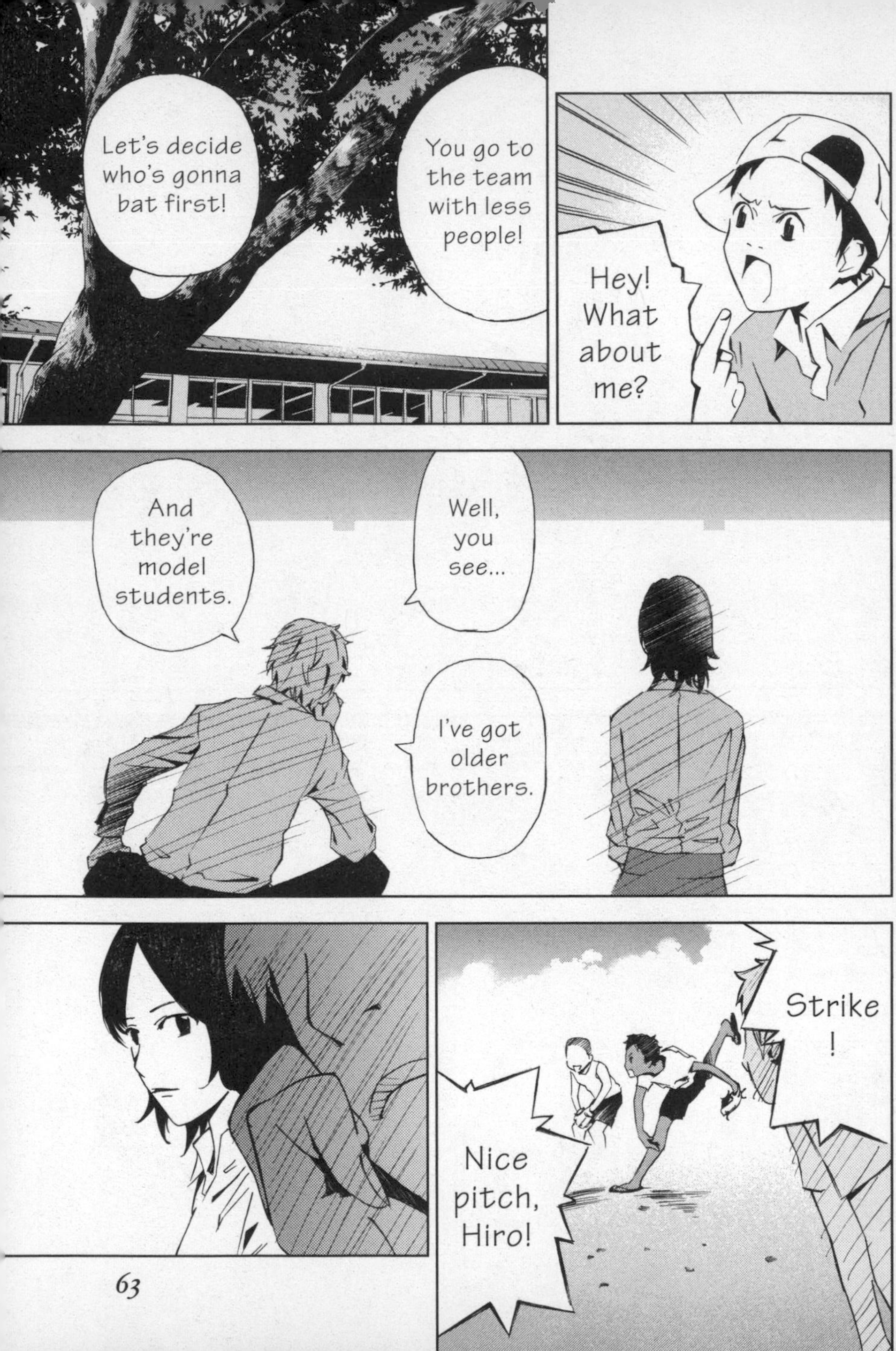
Hey! What about me?
You go to the team with less people!
Let's decide who's gonna bat first!
Well, you see...
And they're model students.
I've got older brothers.
Strike!
Nice pitch, Hiro!

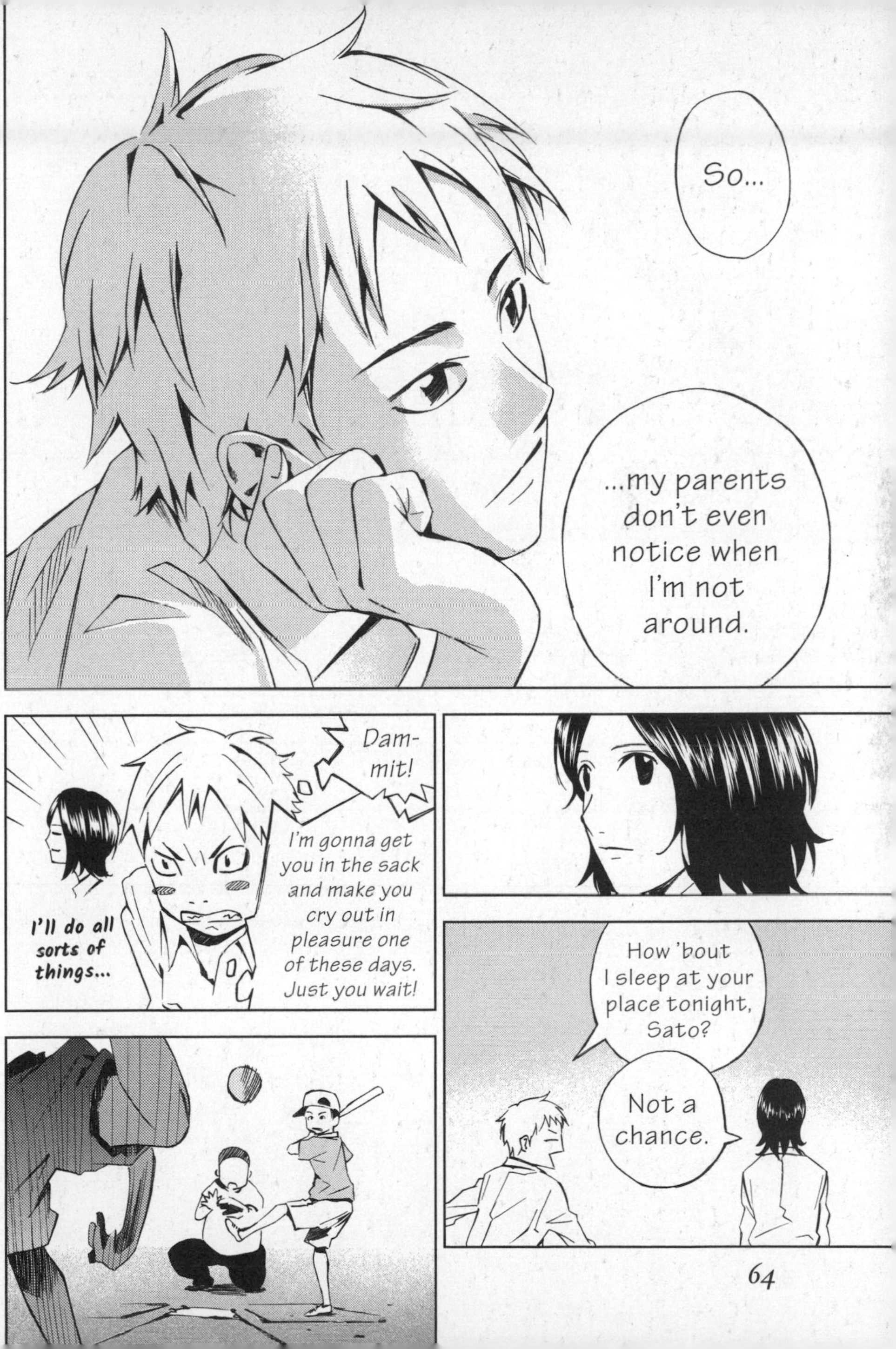
So...
...my parents don't even notice when I'm not around.
Dam-mit!
I'm gonna get you in the sack and make you cry out in pleasure one of these days. Just you wait!
I'll do all sorts of things...
How 'bout I sleep at your place tonight, Sato?
Not a chance.

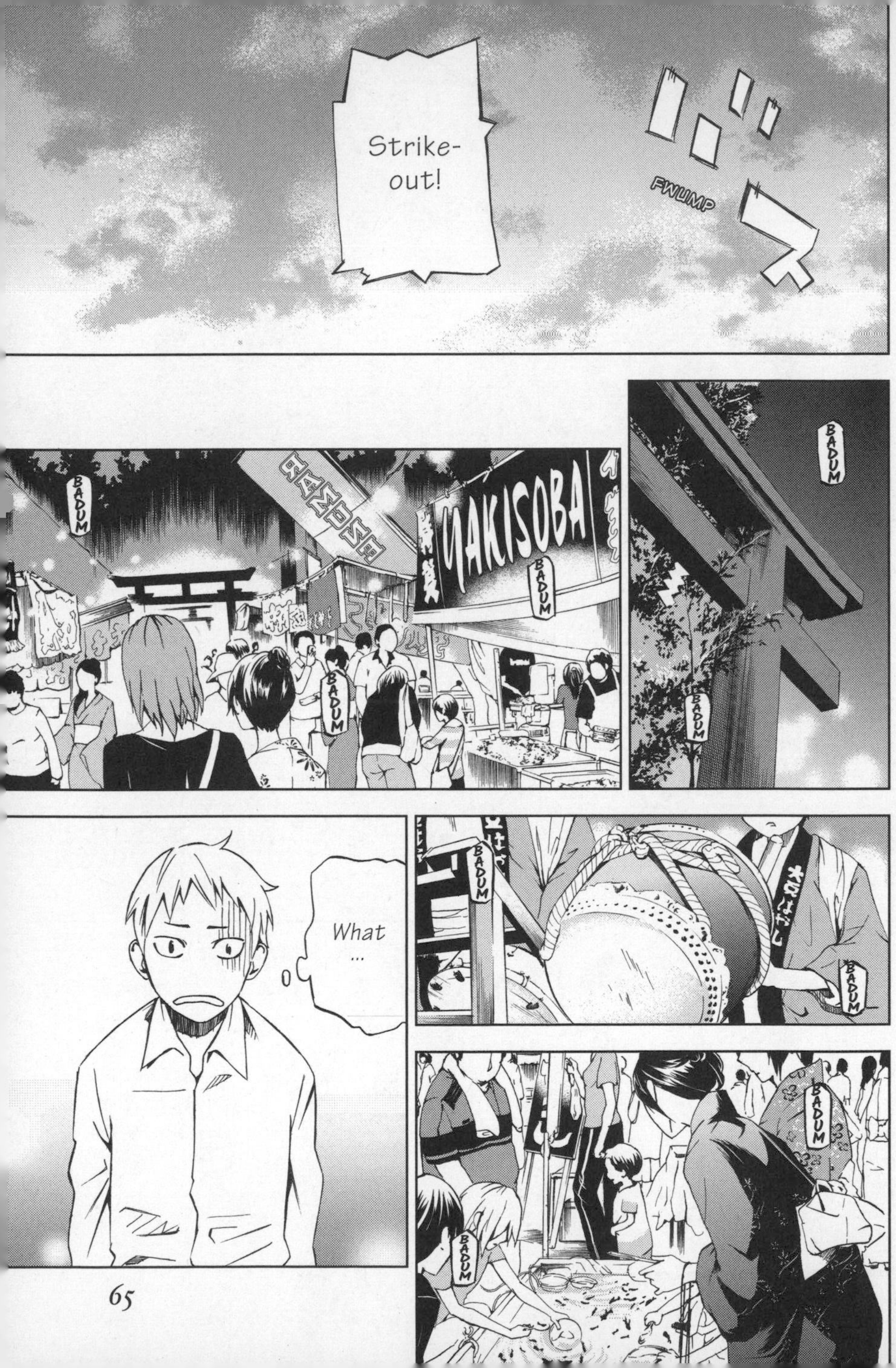

Strike-out!
FWUMP
BADUM
BADUM
BADUM
YAKISOBA
BADUM
BADUM
BADUM
BADUM
BADUM
BADUM
What ...

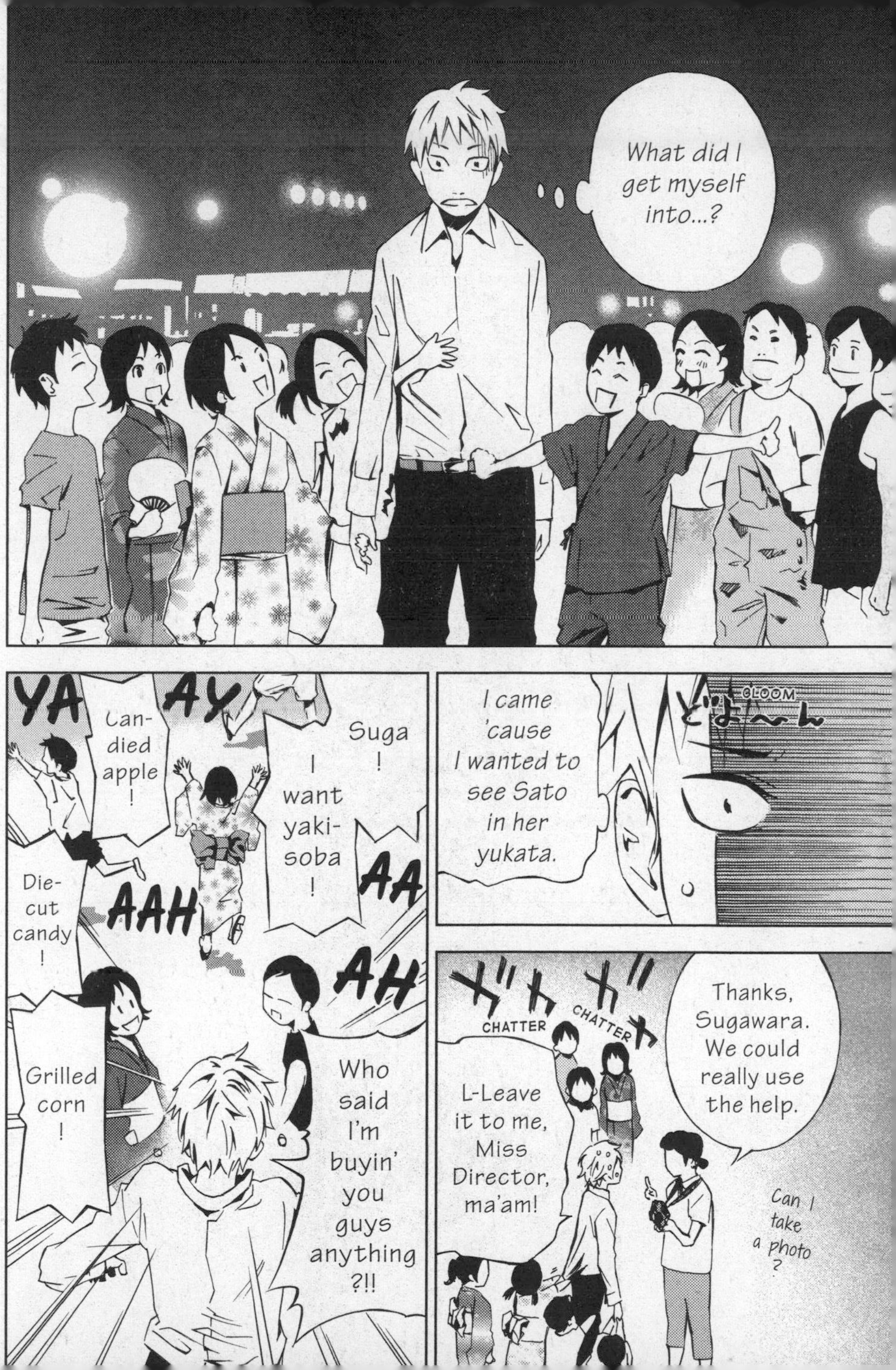
What did I get myself into...?
どよ〜ん
GLOOM
I came 'cause I wanted to see Sato in her yukata.
ザワ ザワ
CHATTER CHATTER
Thanks, Sugawara. We could really use the help.
L-Leave it to me, Miss Director, ma'am!
Can I take a photo?
YA AY AA AAH AH
Suga! I want yakisoba!
Candied apple!
Die-cut candy!
Grilled corn!
Who said I'm buyin' you guys anything?!!

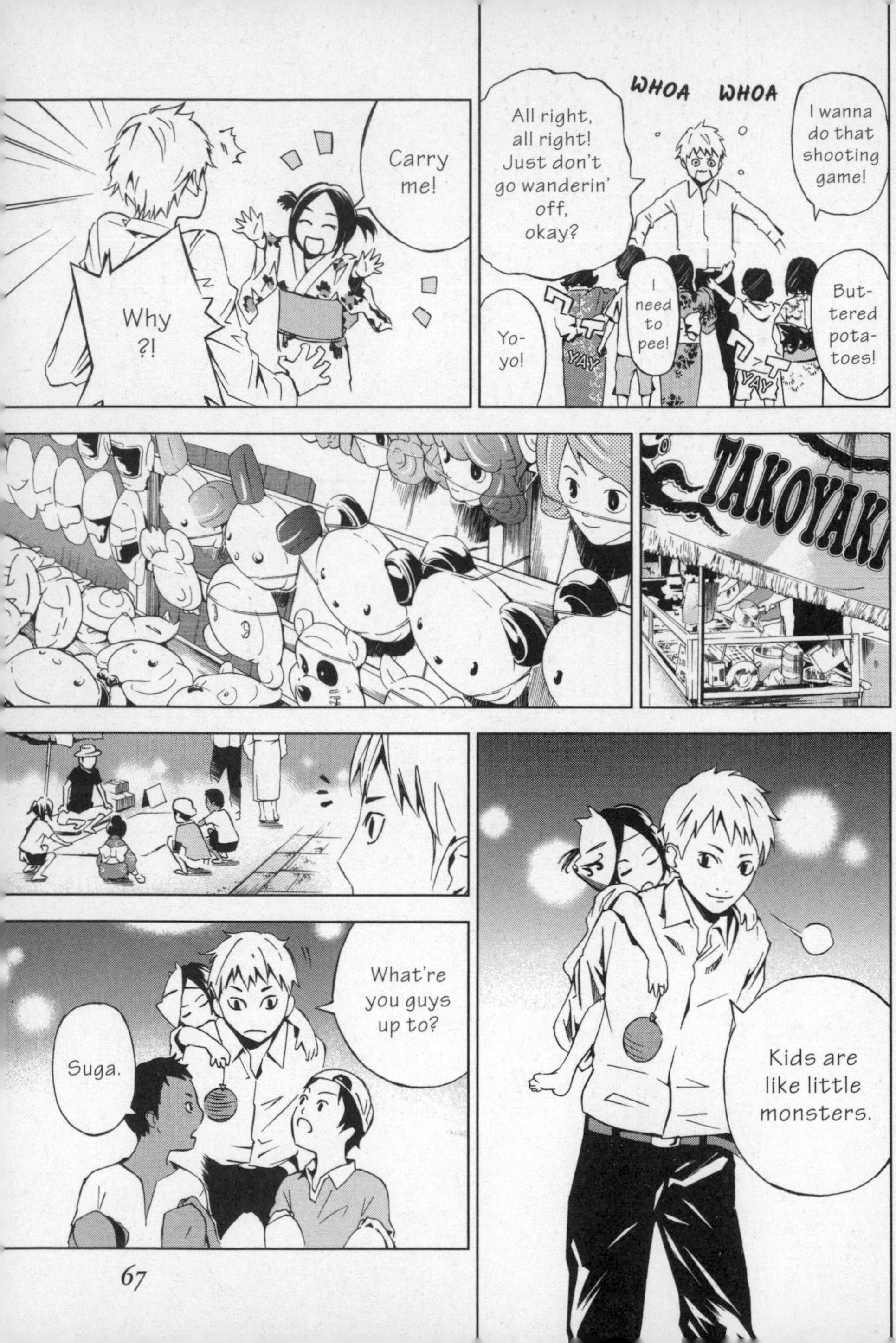
WHOA WHOA
I wanna do that shooting game!
All right, all right! Just don't go wanderin' off, okay?
But-tered pota-toes!
YAY
I need to pee!
YAY
Yo-yo!
Carry me!
Why?!
TAKOYAKI
Kids are like little monsters.
What're you guys up to?
Suga.

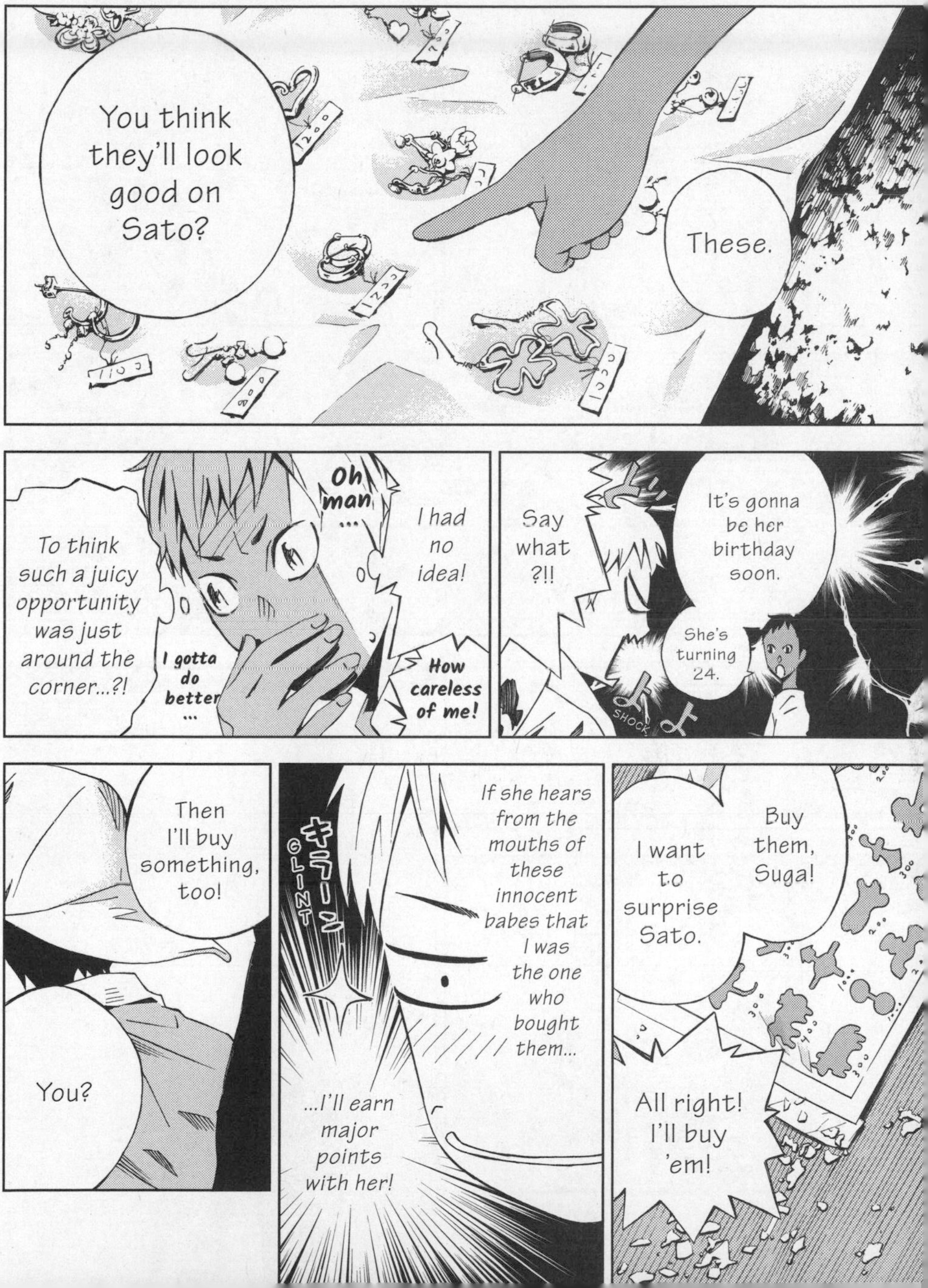
These.
You think they'll look good on Sato?
It's gonna be her birthday soon.
She's turning 24.
Say what?!!
SHOCK
I had no idea!
Oh man...
How careless of me!
I gotta do better...
To think such a juicy opportunity was just around the corner...?!
Buy them, Suga!
I want to surprise Sato.
All right! I'll buy 'em!
If she hears from the mouths of these innocent babes that I was the one who bought them...
GLINT
...I'll earn major points with her!
Then I'll buy something, too!
You?

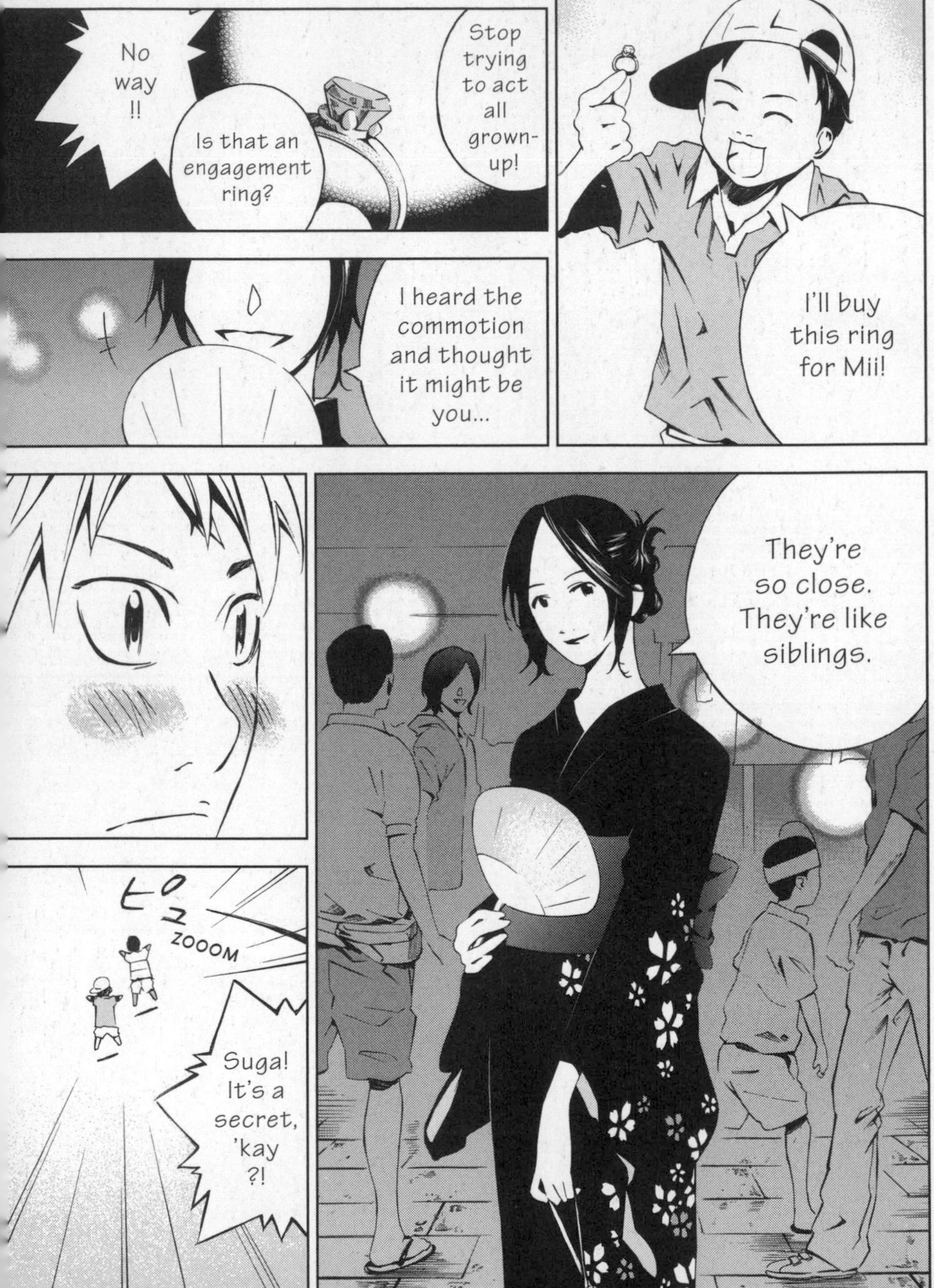
I'll buy this ring for Mii!
Stop trying to act all grown-up!
No way!!
Is that an engagement ring?
I heard the commotion and thought it might be you...
They're so close. They're like siblings.
ピュ
ZOOOM
Suga! It's a secret, 'kay?!

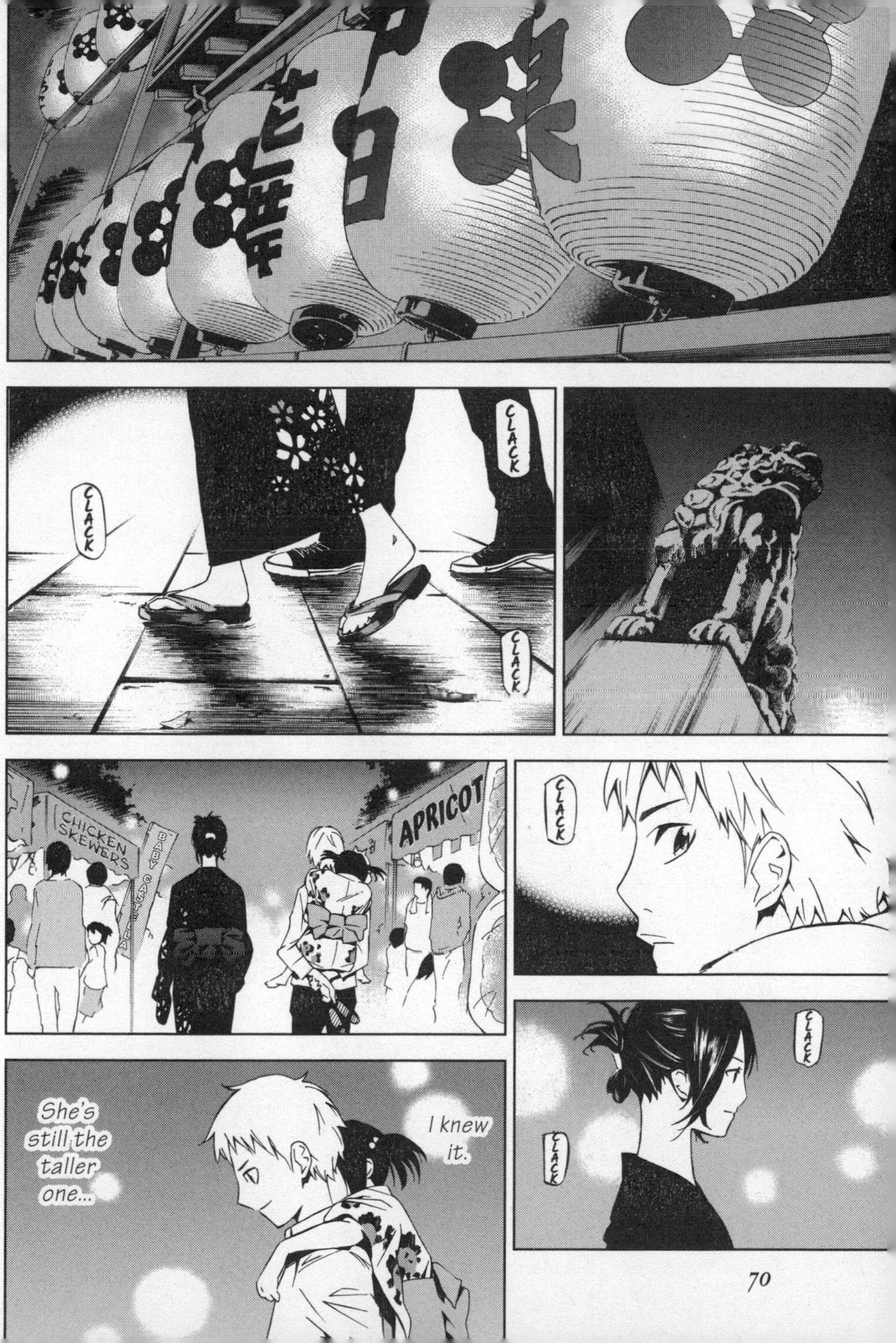
CLACK
CLACK
CLACK
CLACK
APRICOT
CHICKEN SKEWERS
BABY CASTELLA
CLACK
CLACK
I knew it.
She's still the taller one...

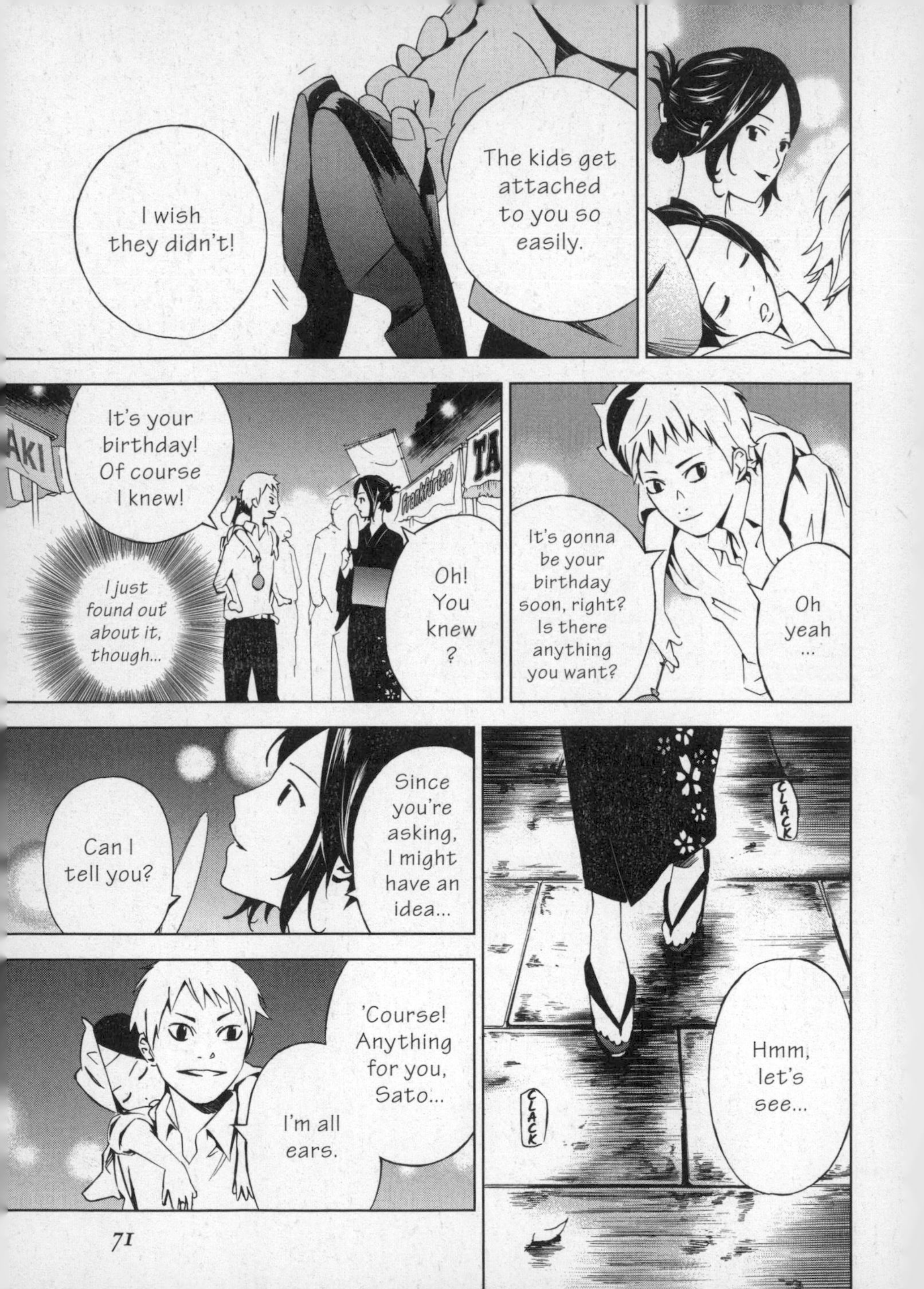
The kids get attached to you so easily.
I wish they didn't!
Oh yeah...
It's gonna be your birthday soon, right? Is there anything you want?
Oh! You knew?
It's your birthday! Of course I knew!
I just found out about it, though...
AKI
TA
Frankfurters
Hmm, let's see...
CLACK
CLACK
Since you're asking, I might have an idea...
Can I tell you?
'Course! Anything for you, Sato...
I'm all ears.

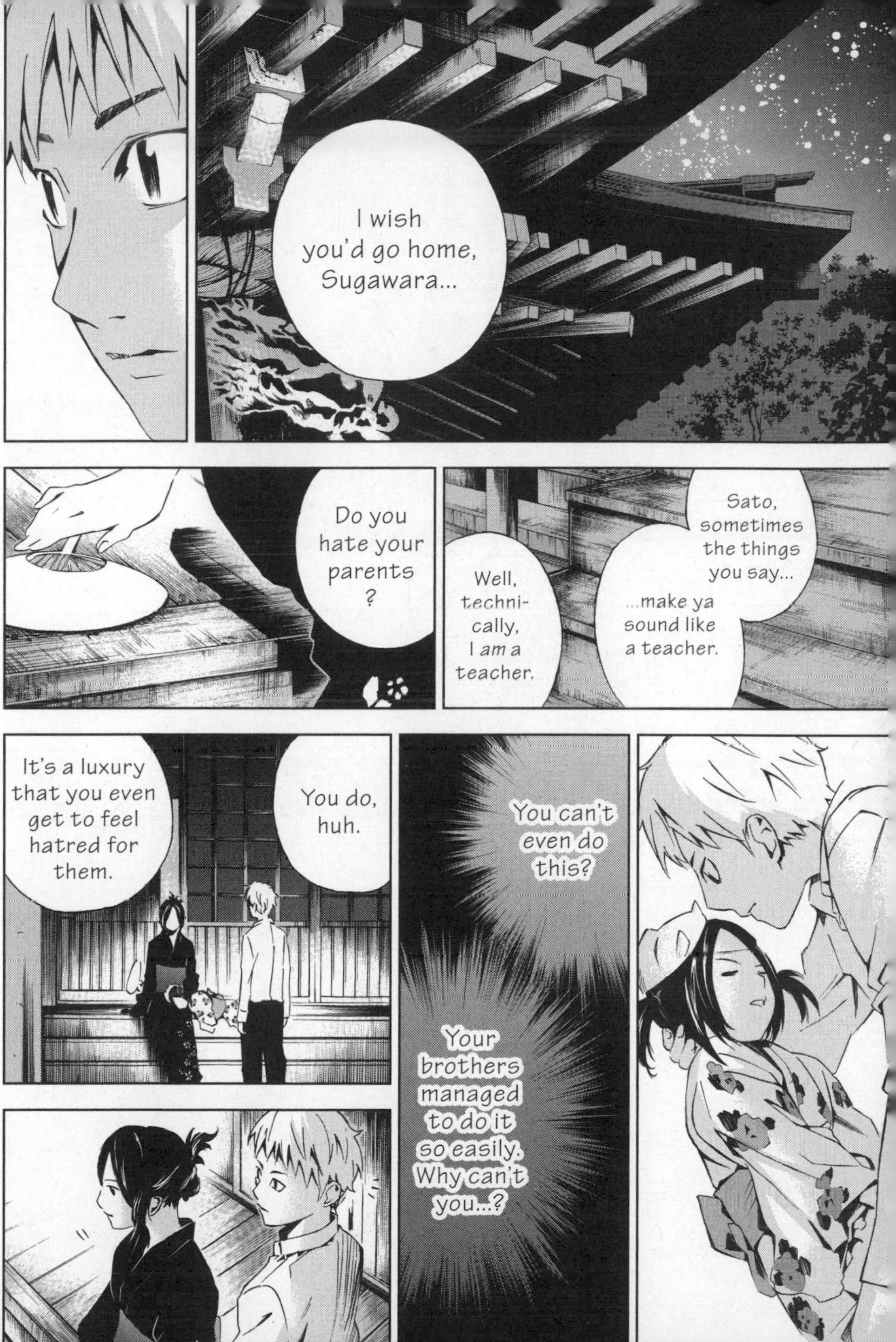
I wish you'd go home, Sugawara...
Sato, sometimes the things you say...
...make ya sound like a teacher.
Well, technically, I *am* a teacher.
Do you hate your parents?
You can't even do this?
Your brothers managed to do it so easily. Why can't you...?
You do, huh.
It's a luxury that you even get to feel hatred for them.

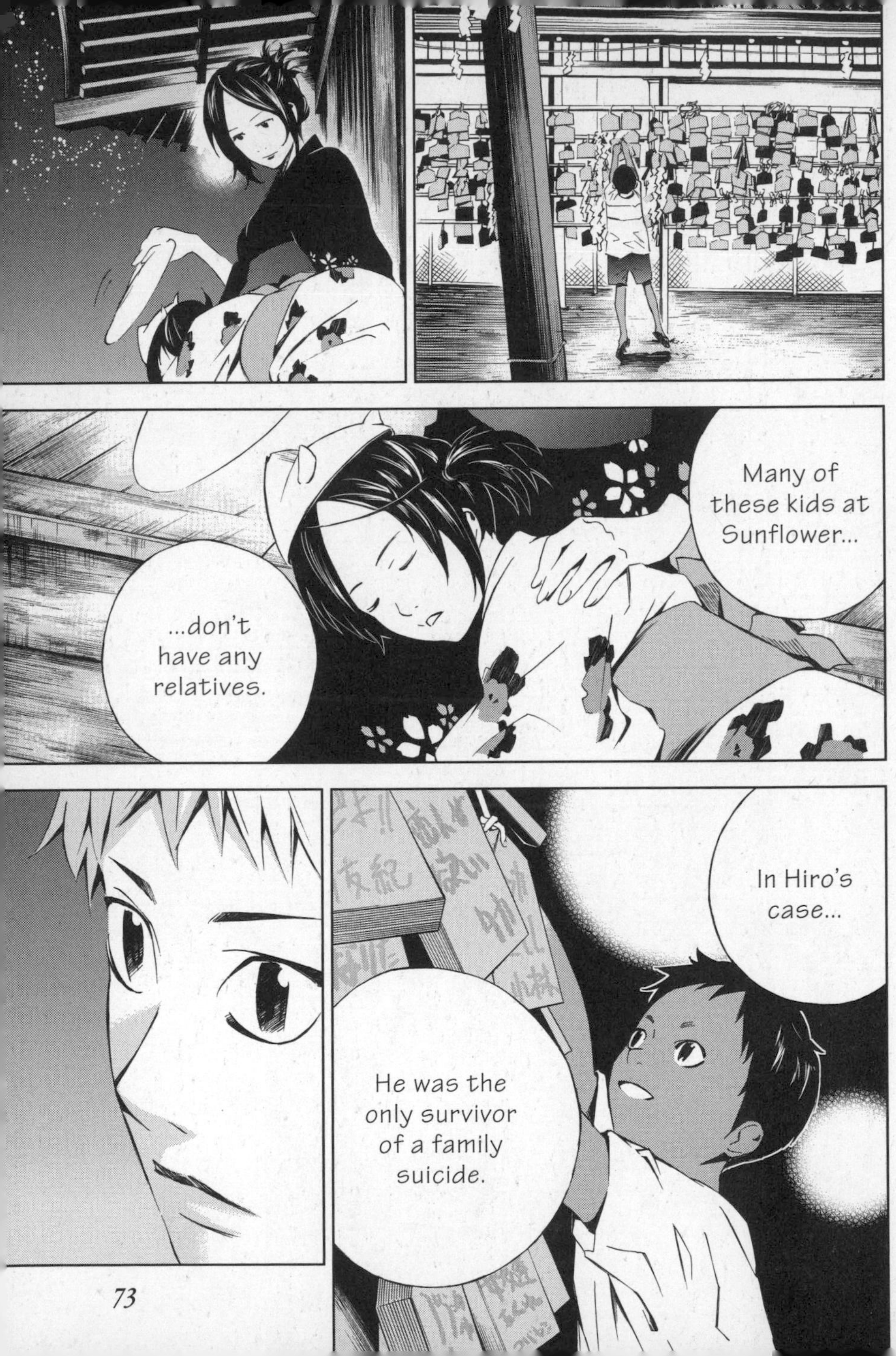
Many of these kids at Sunflower...
...don't have any relatives.
In Hiro's case...
He was the only survivor of a family suicide.

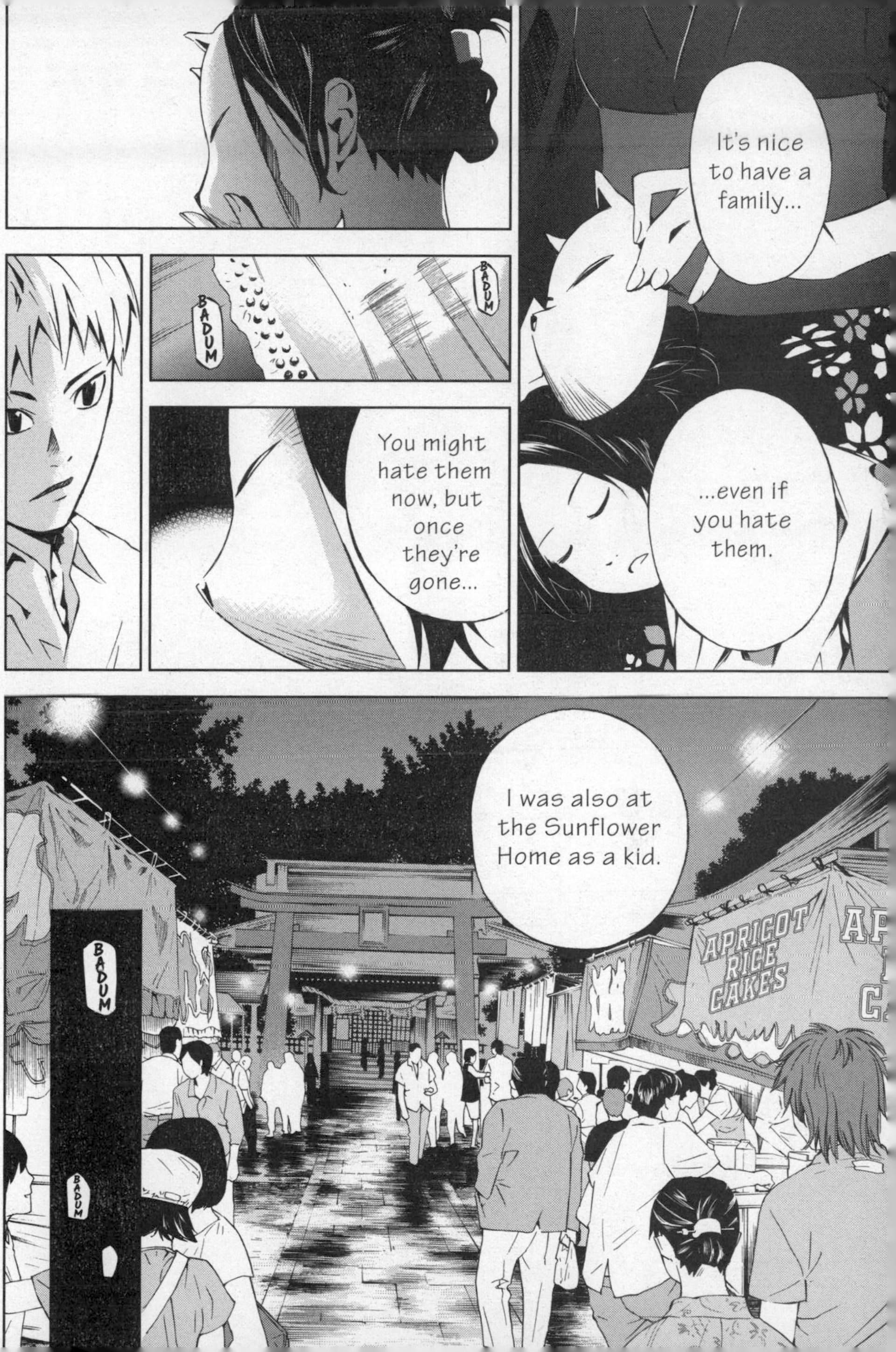
It's nice to have a family...
...even if you hate them.
BADUM
BADUM
You might hate them now, but once they're gone...
I was also at the Sunflower Home as a kid.
APRICOT RICE CAKES
BADUM
BADUM

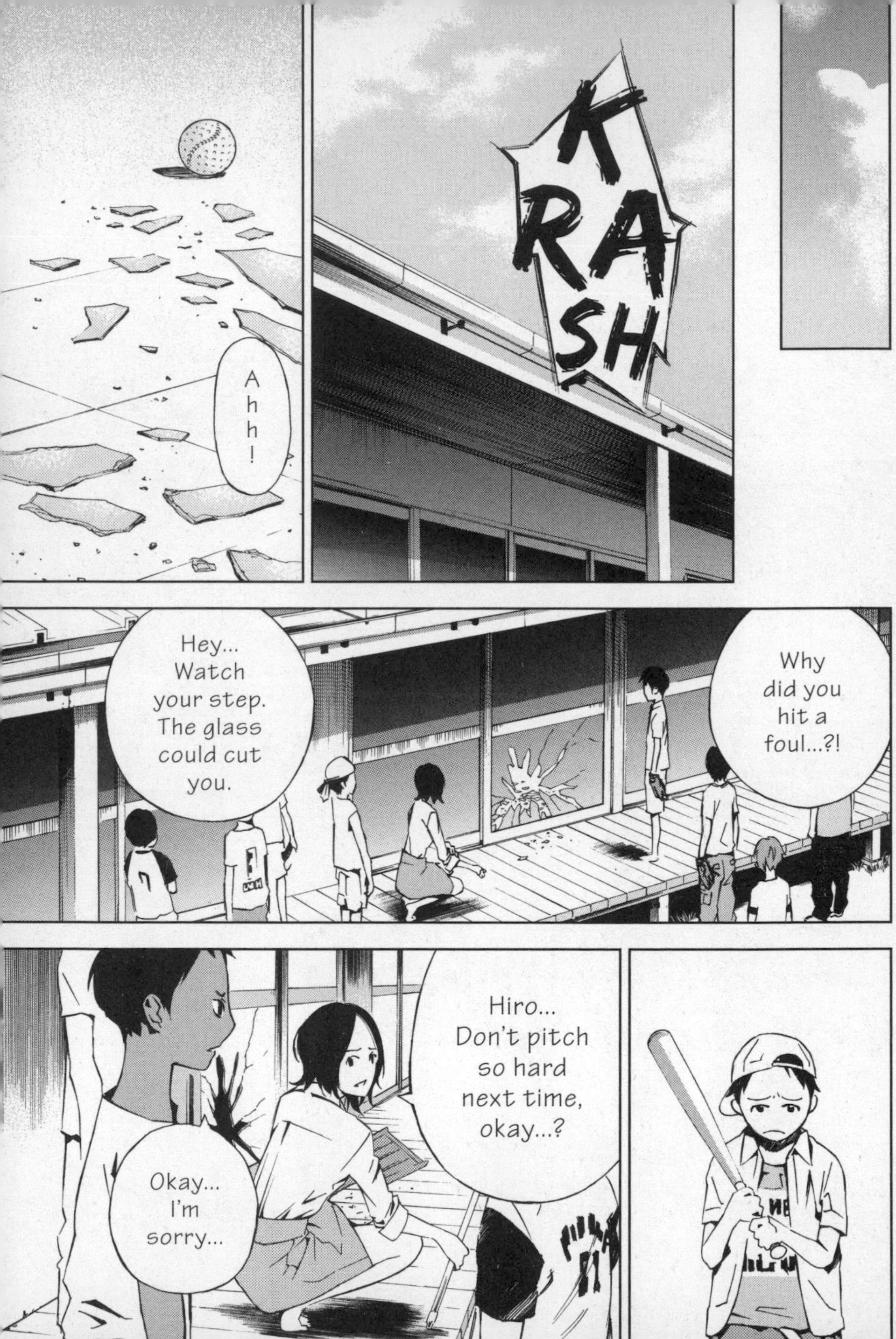
KRASH
Ahh!
Why did you hit a foul...?!
Hey... Watch your step. The glass could cut you.
Hiro... Don't pitch so hard next time, okay...?
Okay... I'm sorry...

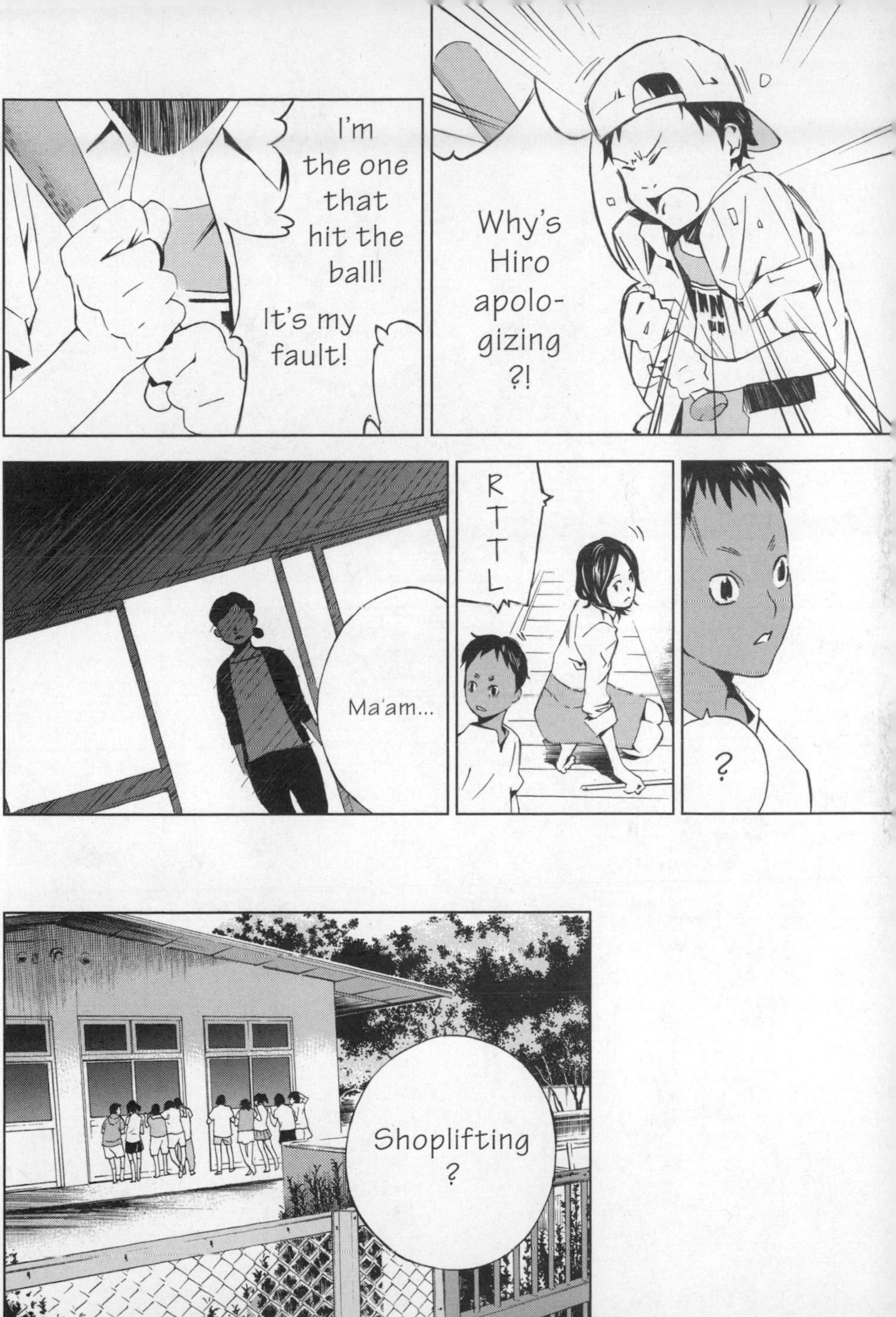
Why's Hiro apologizing?!
I'm the one that hit the ball!
It's my fault!
?
RTTL
Ma'am...
Shoplifting?

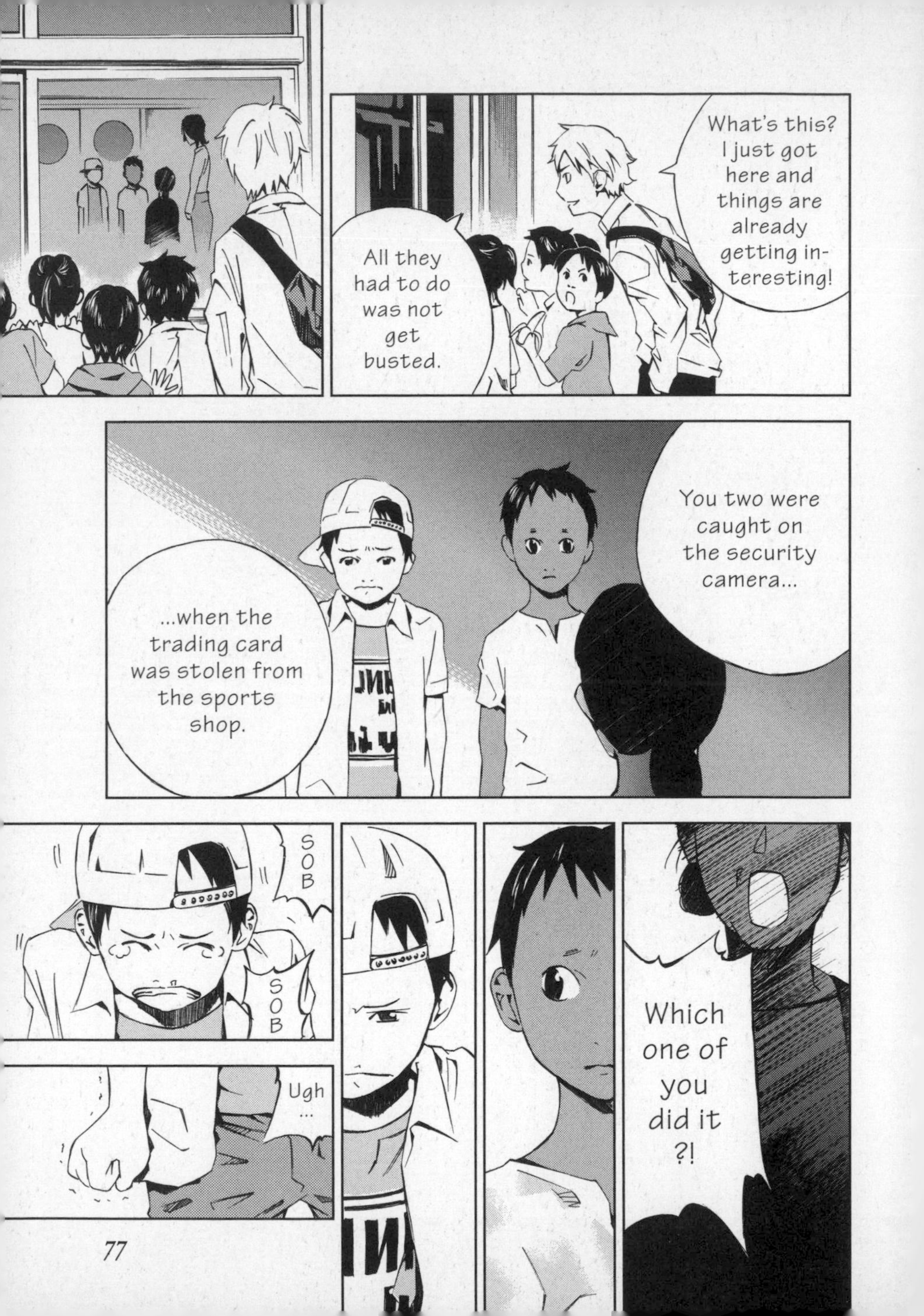
What's this? I just got here and things are already getting in-teresting!
All they had to do was not get busted.
You two were caught on the security camera...
...when the trading card was stolen from the sports shop.
Which one of you did it ?!
SOB
SOB
Ugh ...

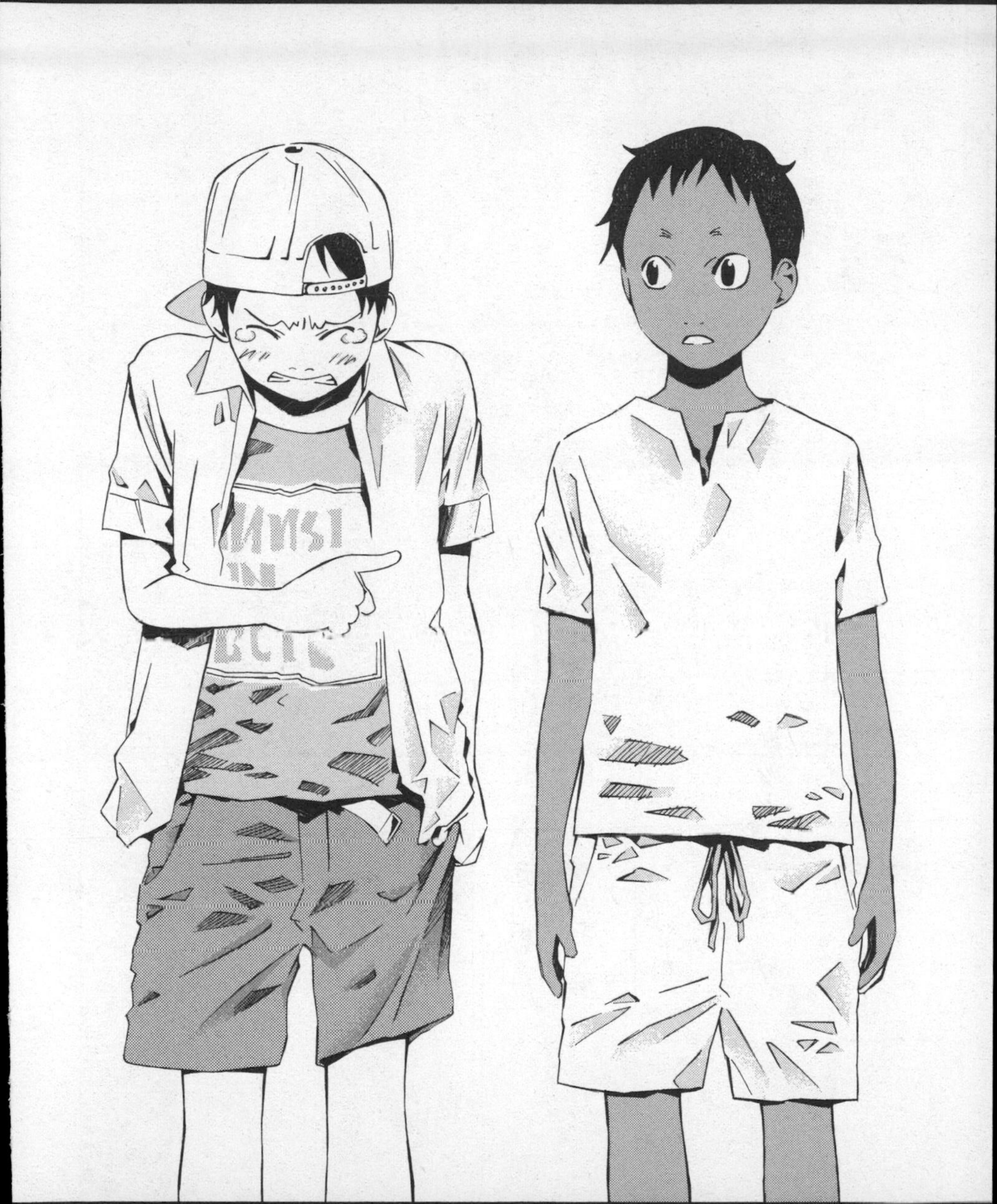

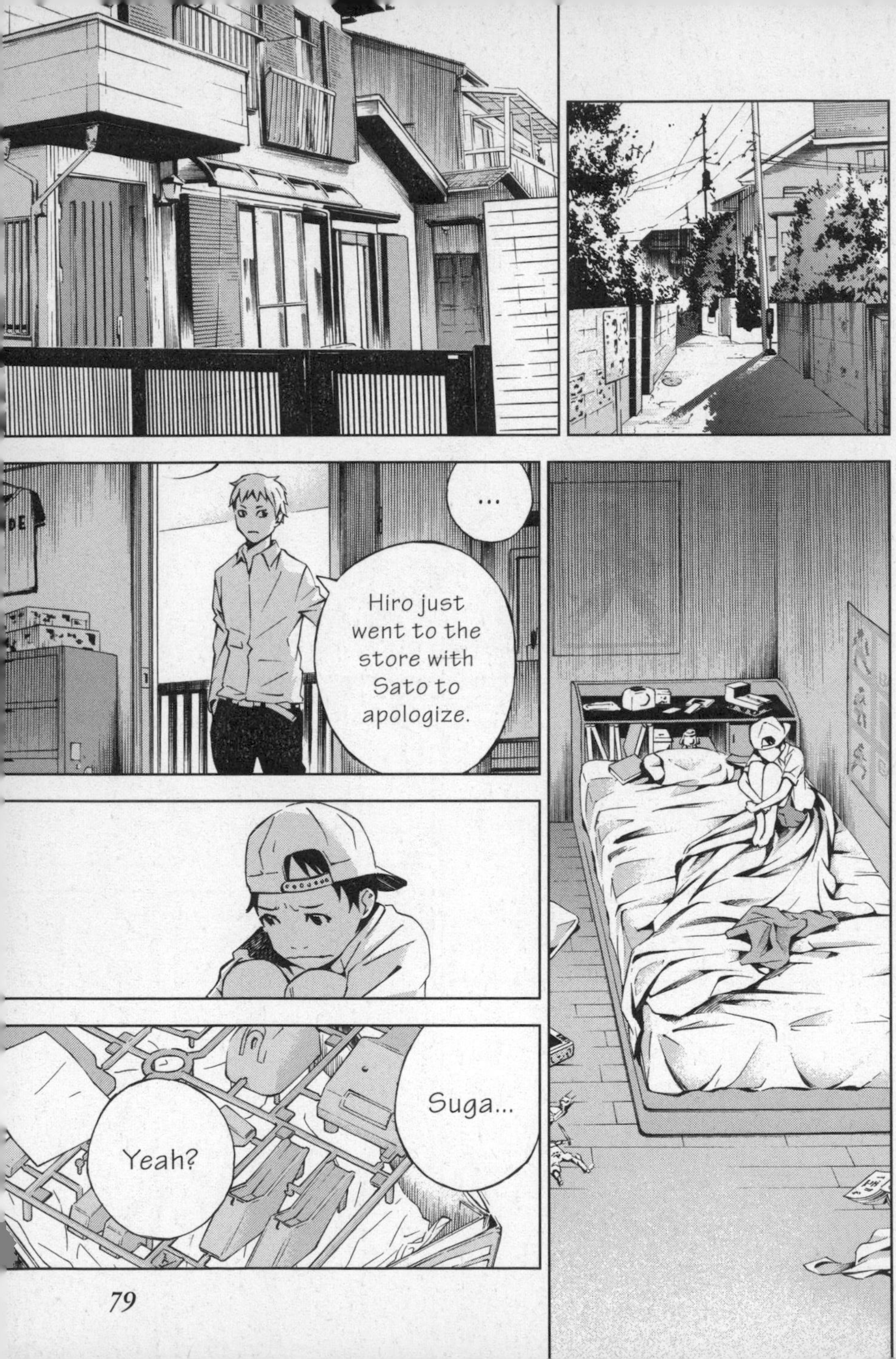
...
Hiro just went to the store with Sato to apologize.
Suga...
Yeah?

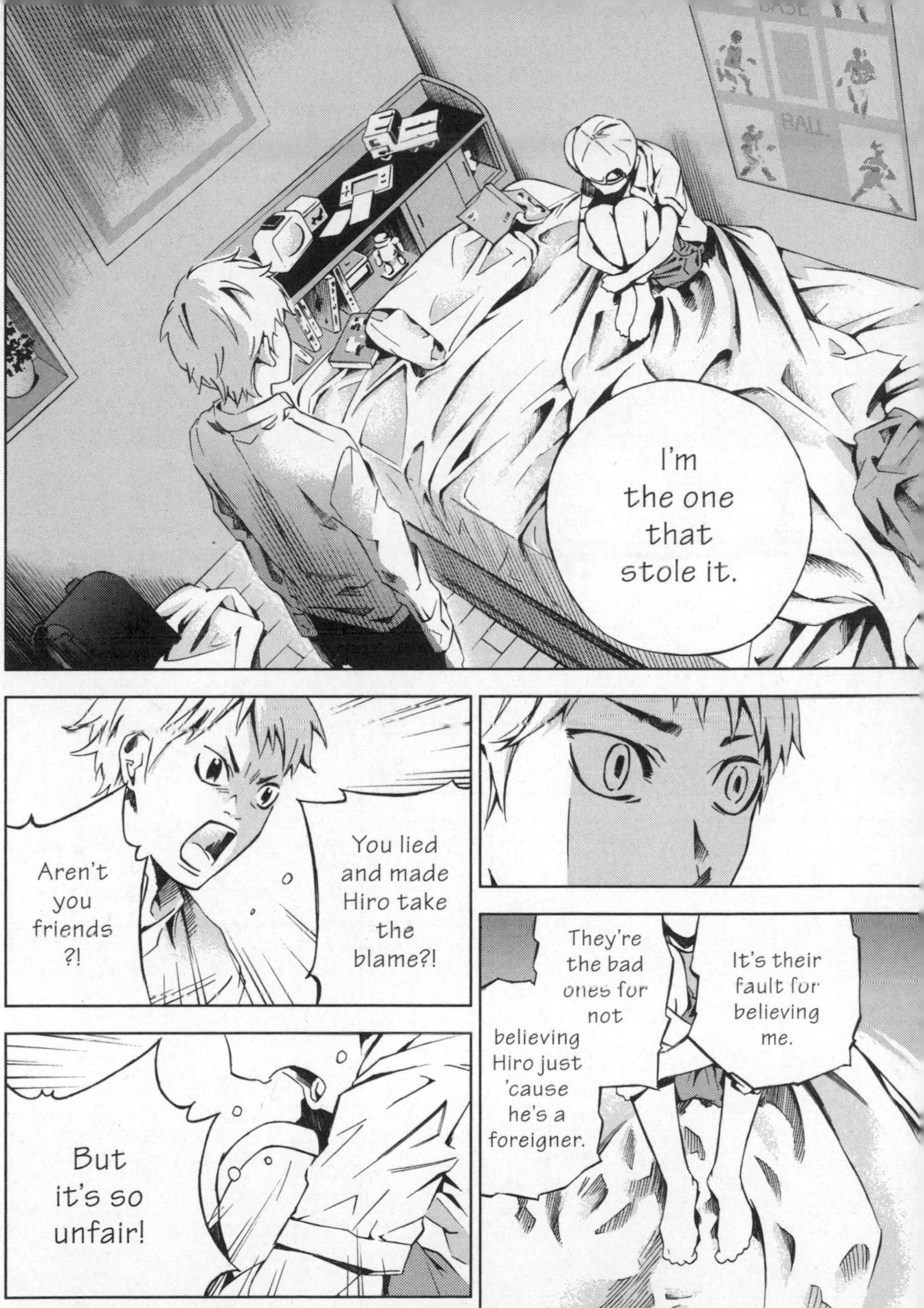
I'm the one that stole it.
You lied and made Hiro take the blame?!
Aren't you friends?!
It's their fault for believing me.
They're the bad ones for not believing Hiro just 'cause he's a foreigner.
But it's so unfair!

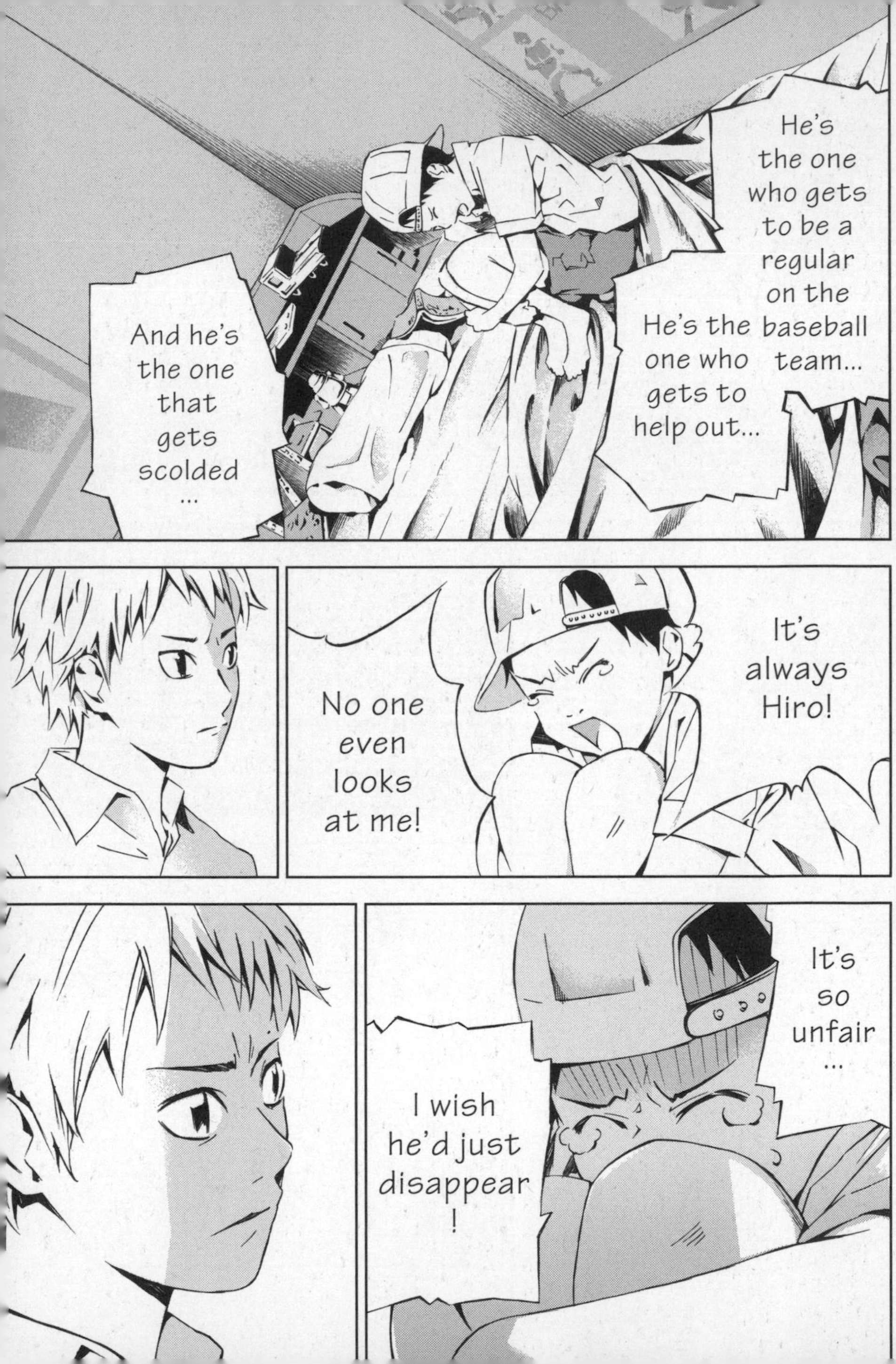
He's the one who gets to be a regular on the baseball team...
He's the one who gets to help out...
And he's the one that gets scolded...
It's always Hiro!
No one even looks at me!
It's so unfair...
I wish he'd just disappear!

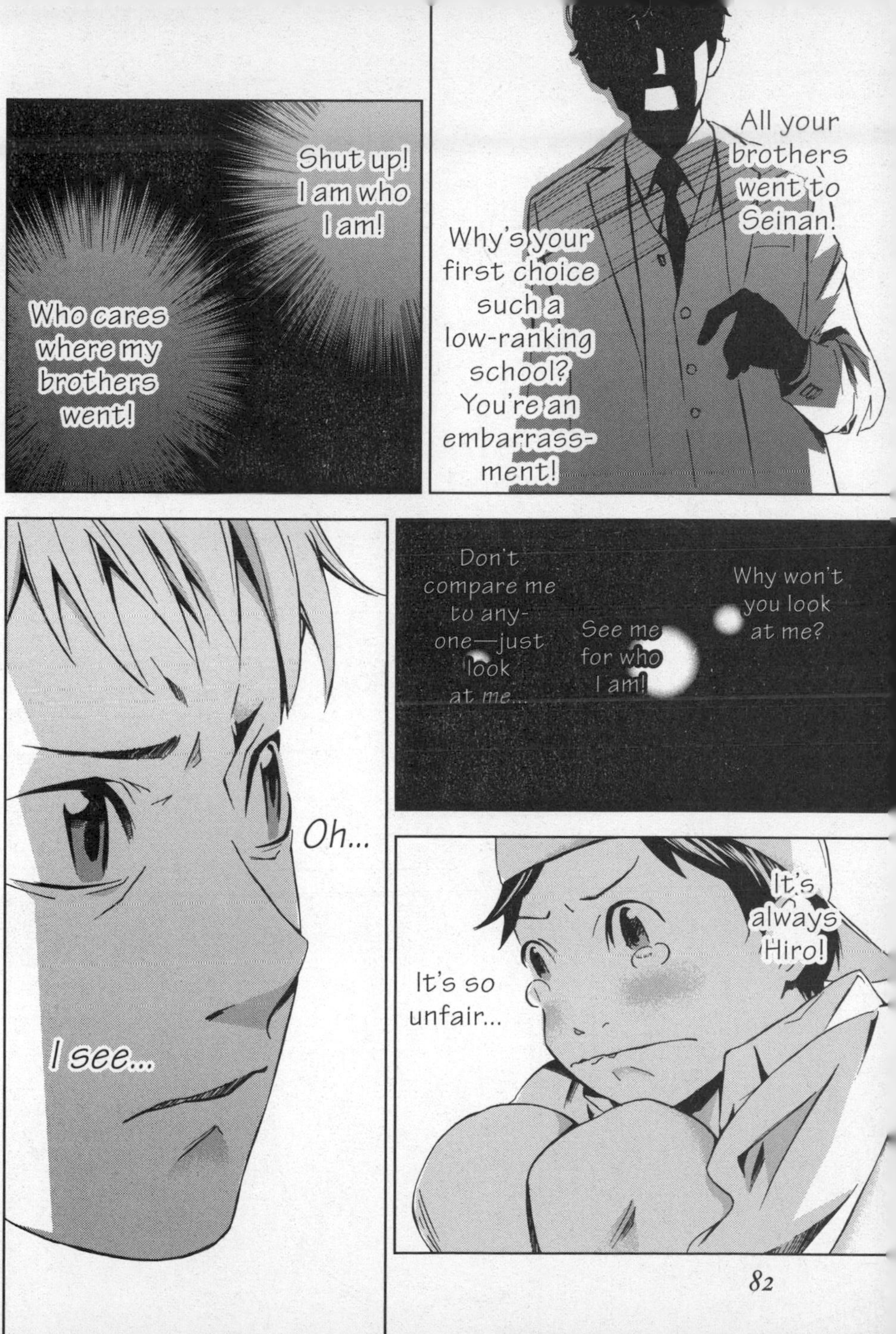
All your brothers went to Seinan!
Why's your first choice such a low-ranking school? You're an embarrass-ment!
Shut up! I am who I am!
Who cares where my brothers went!
Why won't you look at me?
See me for who I am!
Don't compare me to any-one—just look at me...
It's always Hiro!
It's so unfair...
Oh...
I see...

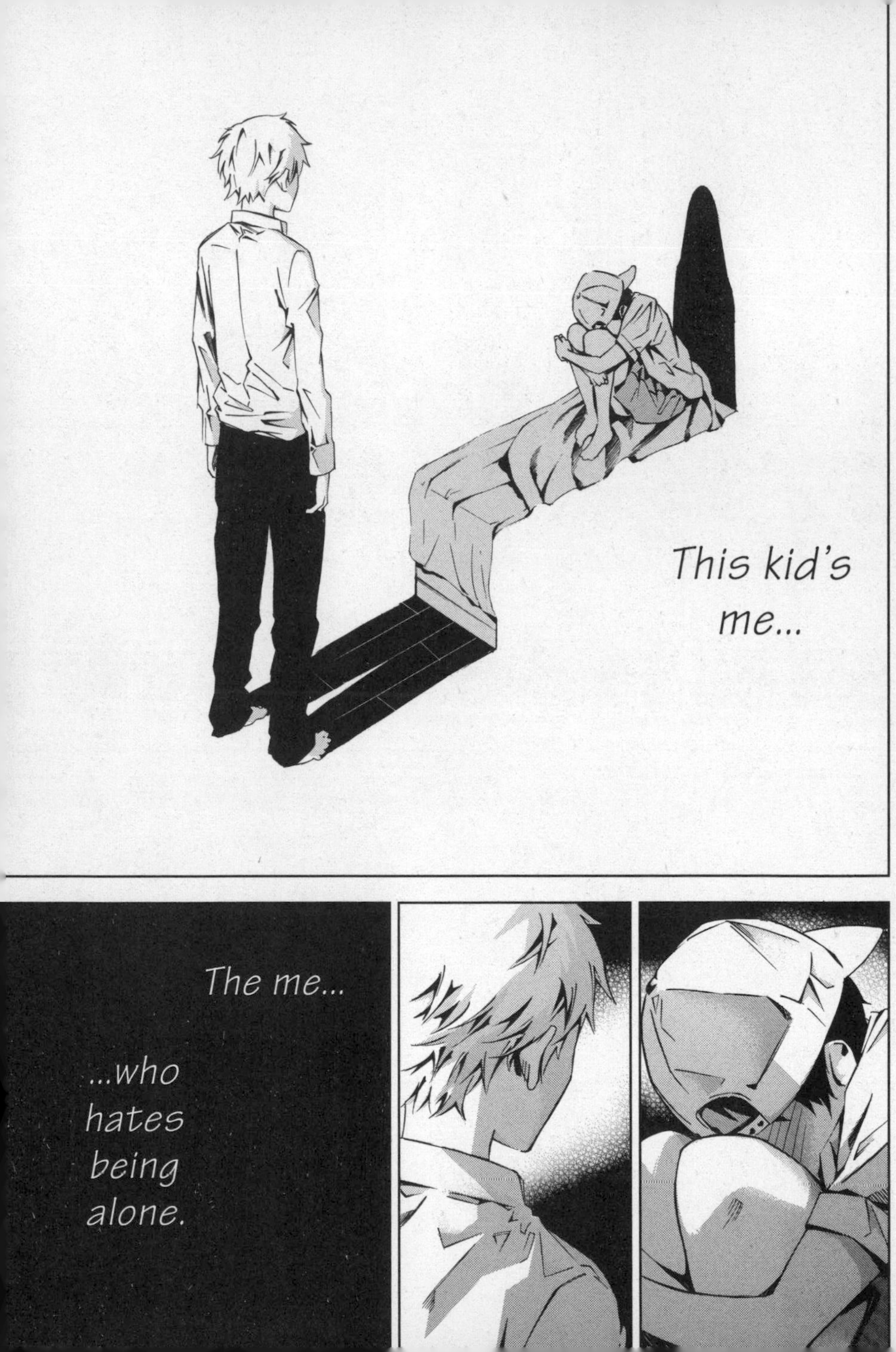
This kid's me...
The me...
...who hates being alone.

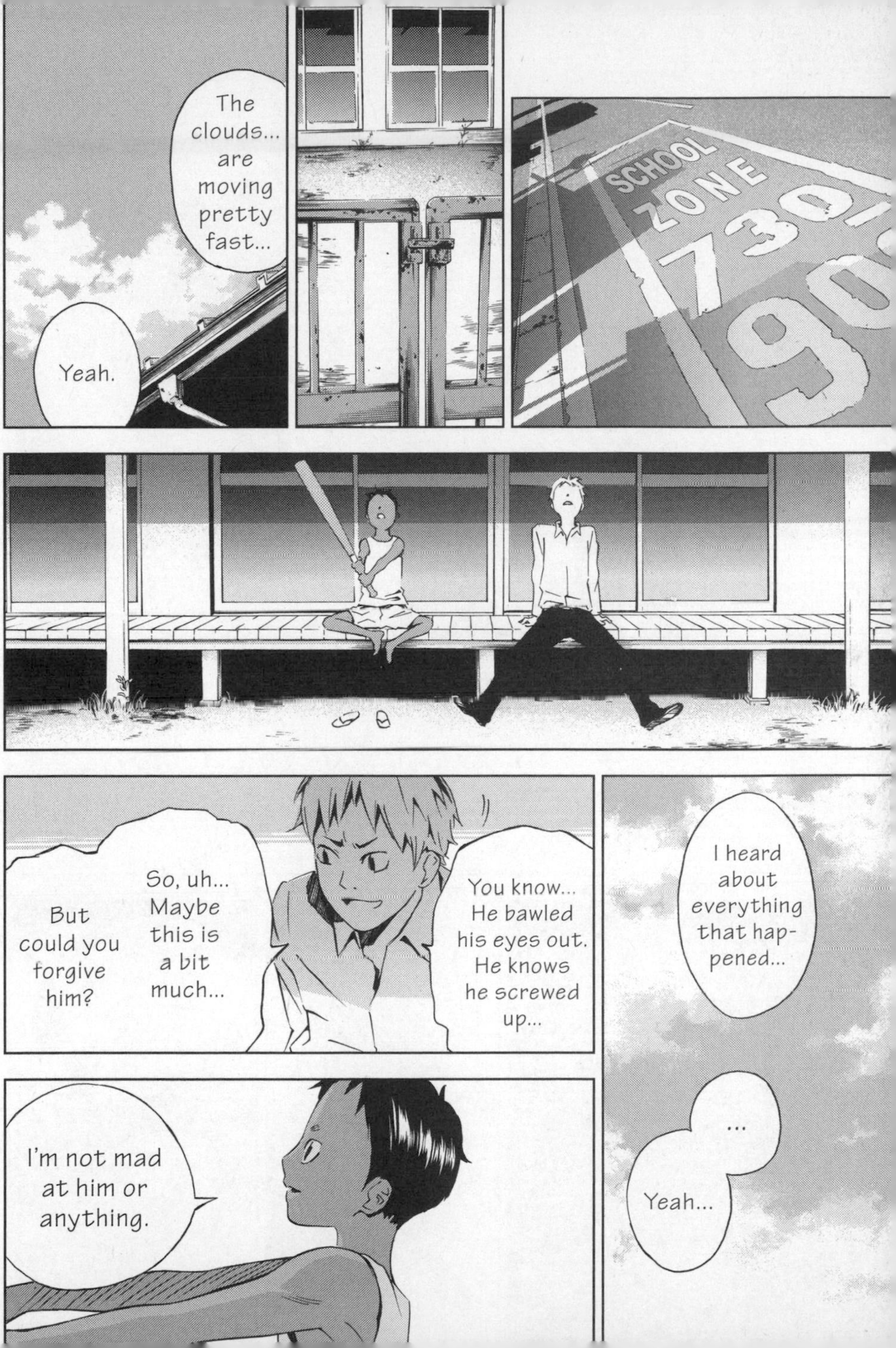
SCHOOL ZONE
The clouds... are moving pretty fast...
Yeah.
I heard about everything that hap-pened...
...
Yeah...
You know... He bawled his eyes out. He knows he screwed up...
So, uh... Maybe this is a bit much...
But could you forgive him?
I'm not mad at him or anything.

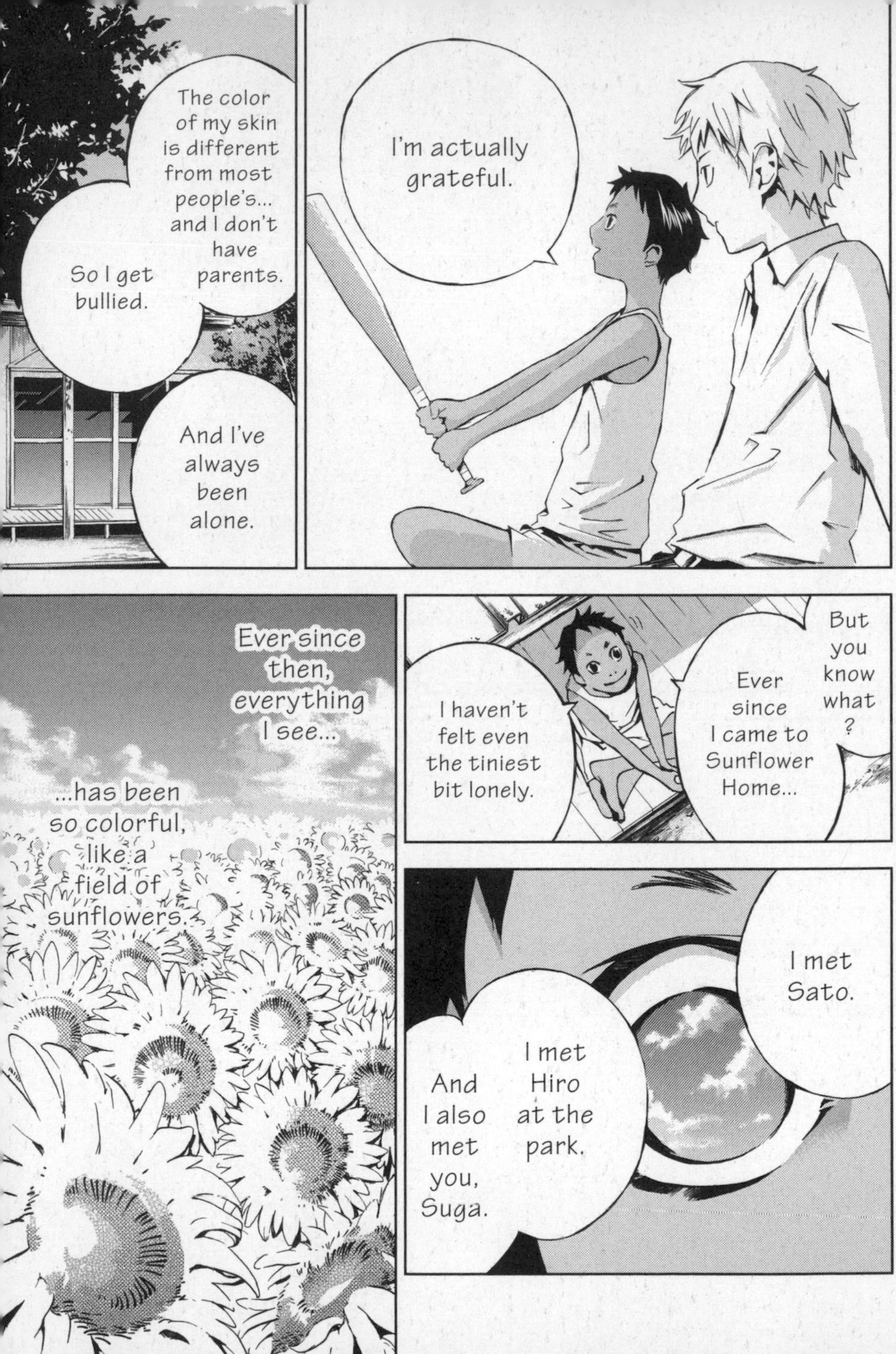
I'm actually grateful.
The color of my skin is different from most people's... and I don't have parents.
So I get bullied.
And I've always been alone.
But you know what?
Ever since I came to Sunflower Home...
I haven't felt even the tiniest bit lonely.
I met Sato.
I met Hiro at the park.
And I also met you, Suga.
Ever since then, everything I see...
...has been so colorful, like a field of sunflowers.

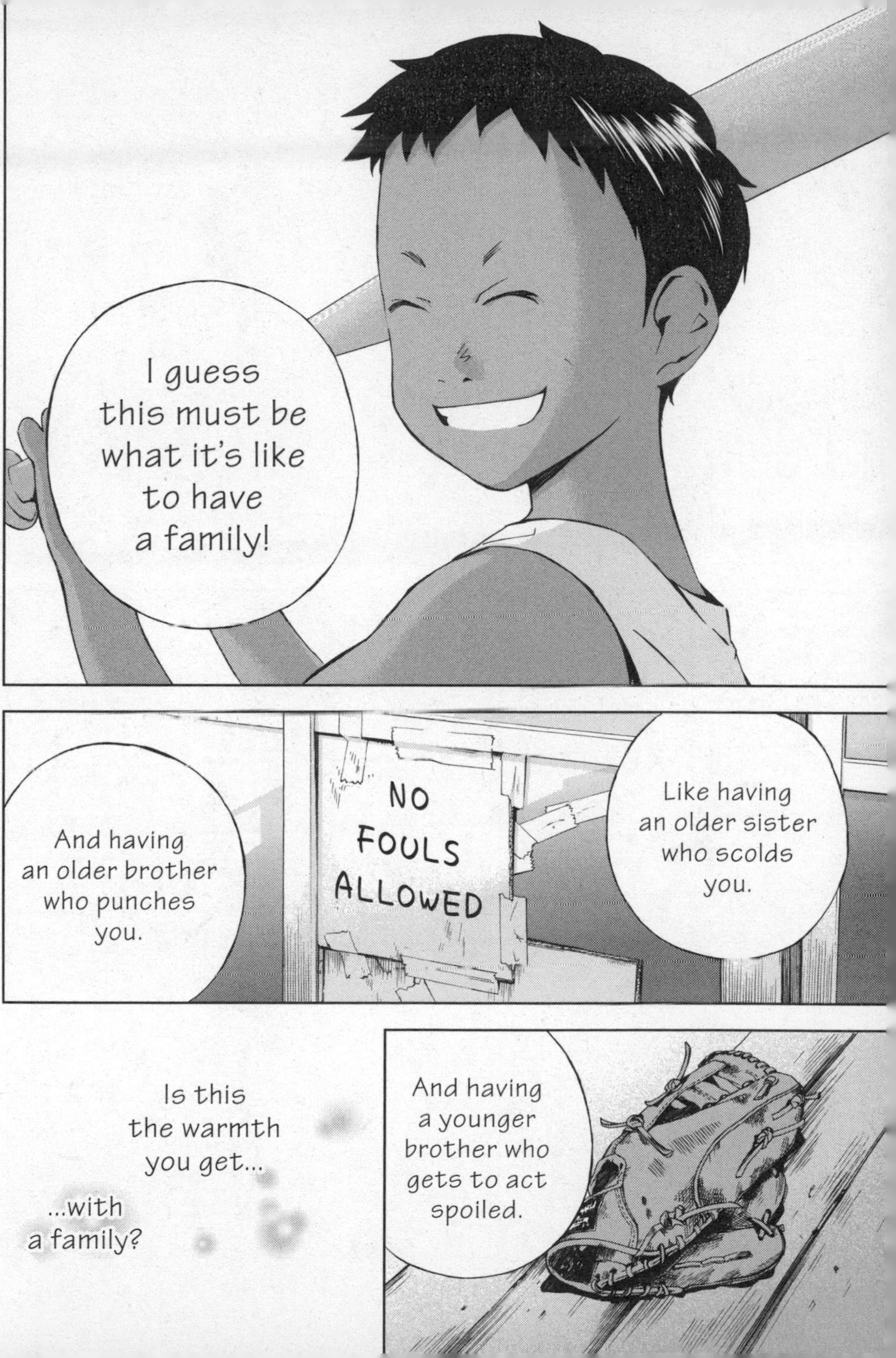
I guess this must be what it's like to have a family!
Like having an older sister who scolds you.
And having an older brother who punches you.
NO FOULS ALLOWED
And having a younger brother who gets to act spoiled.
Is this the warmth you get...
...with a family?

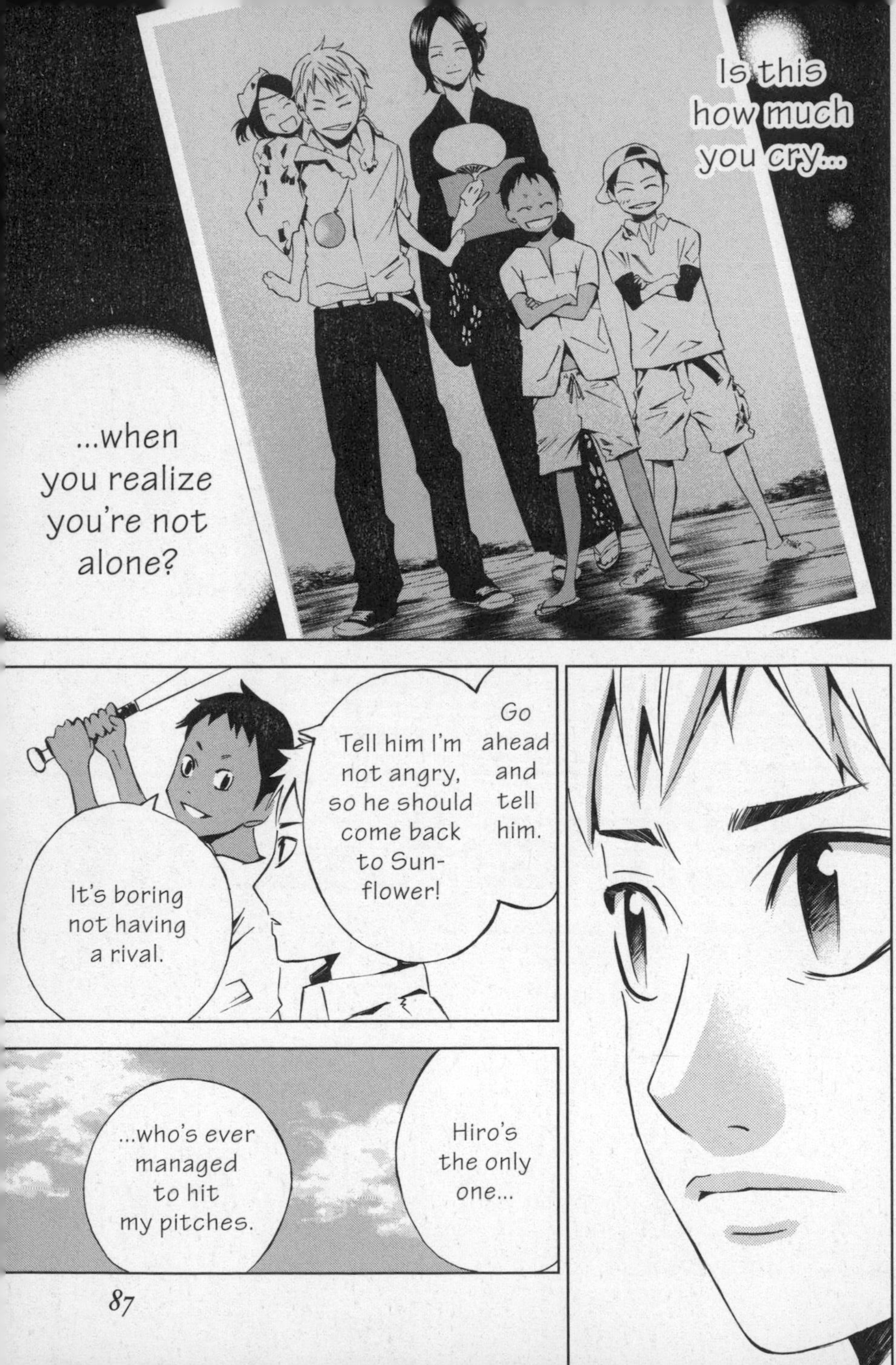
Is this how much you cry...
...when you realize you're not alone?
Go ahead and tell him.
Tell him I'm not angry, so he should come back to Sun-flower!
It's boring not having a rival.
Hiro's the only one...
...who's ever managed to hit my pitches.

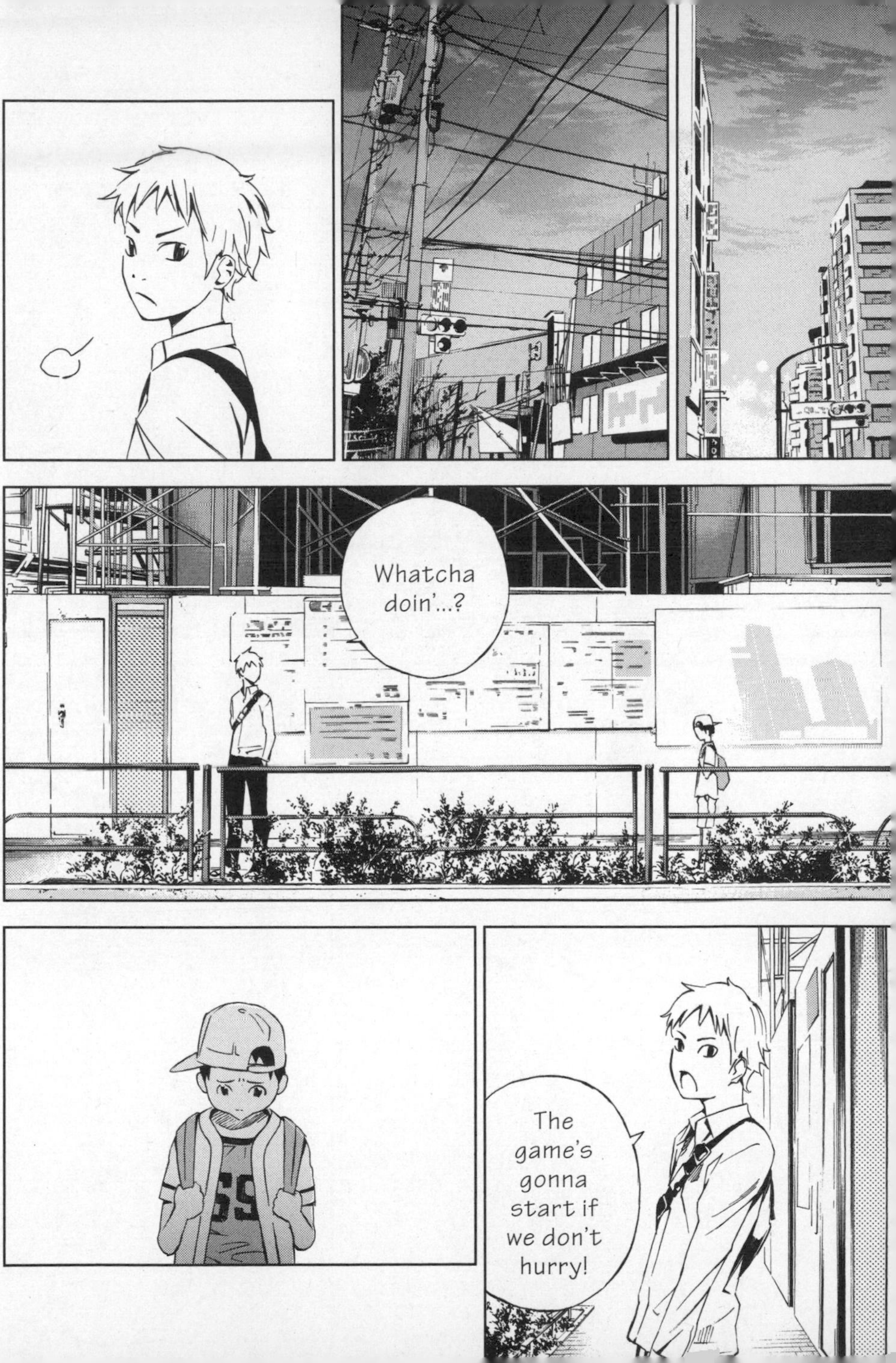

Whatcha doin'...?
The game's gonna start if we don't hurry!

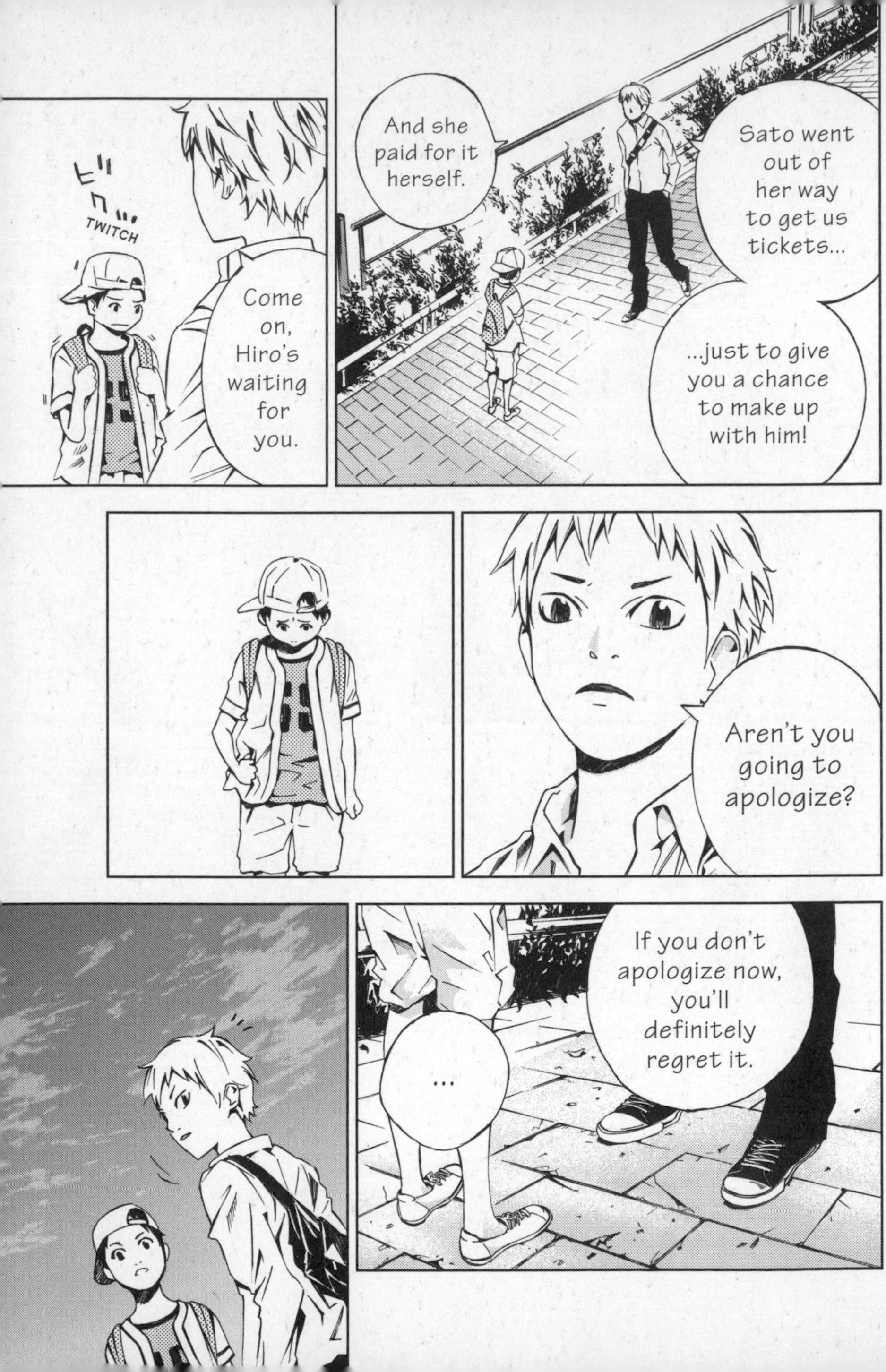
Sato went out of her way to get us tickets...
And she paid for it herself.
...just to give you a chance to make up with him!
ビクッ
TWITCH
Come on, Hiro's waiting for you.
Aren't you going to apologize?
If you don't apologize now, you'll definitely regret it.
...

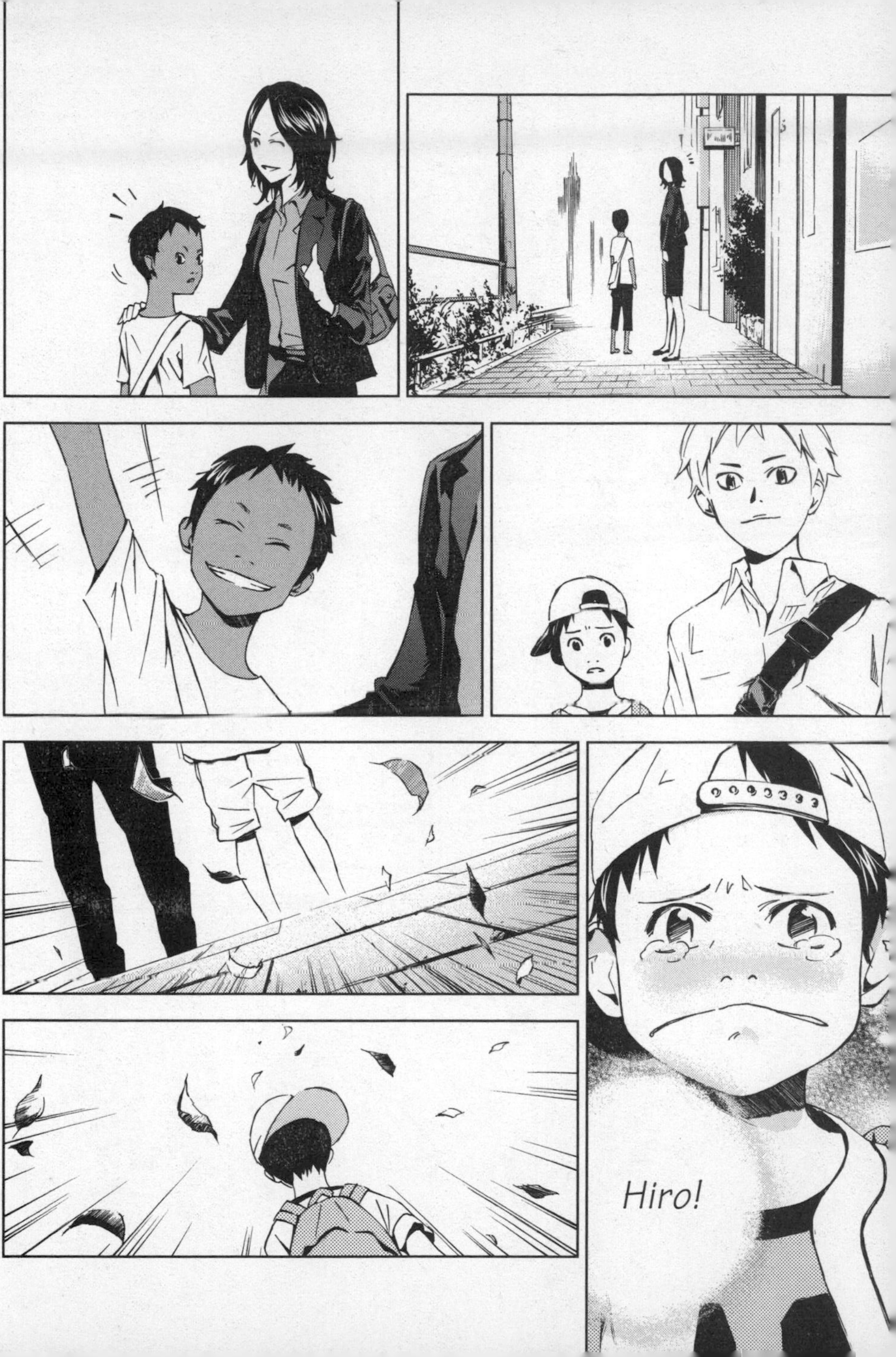
Hiro!

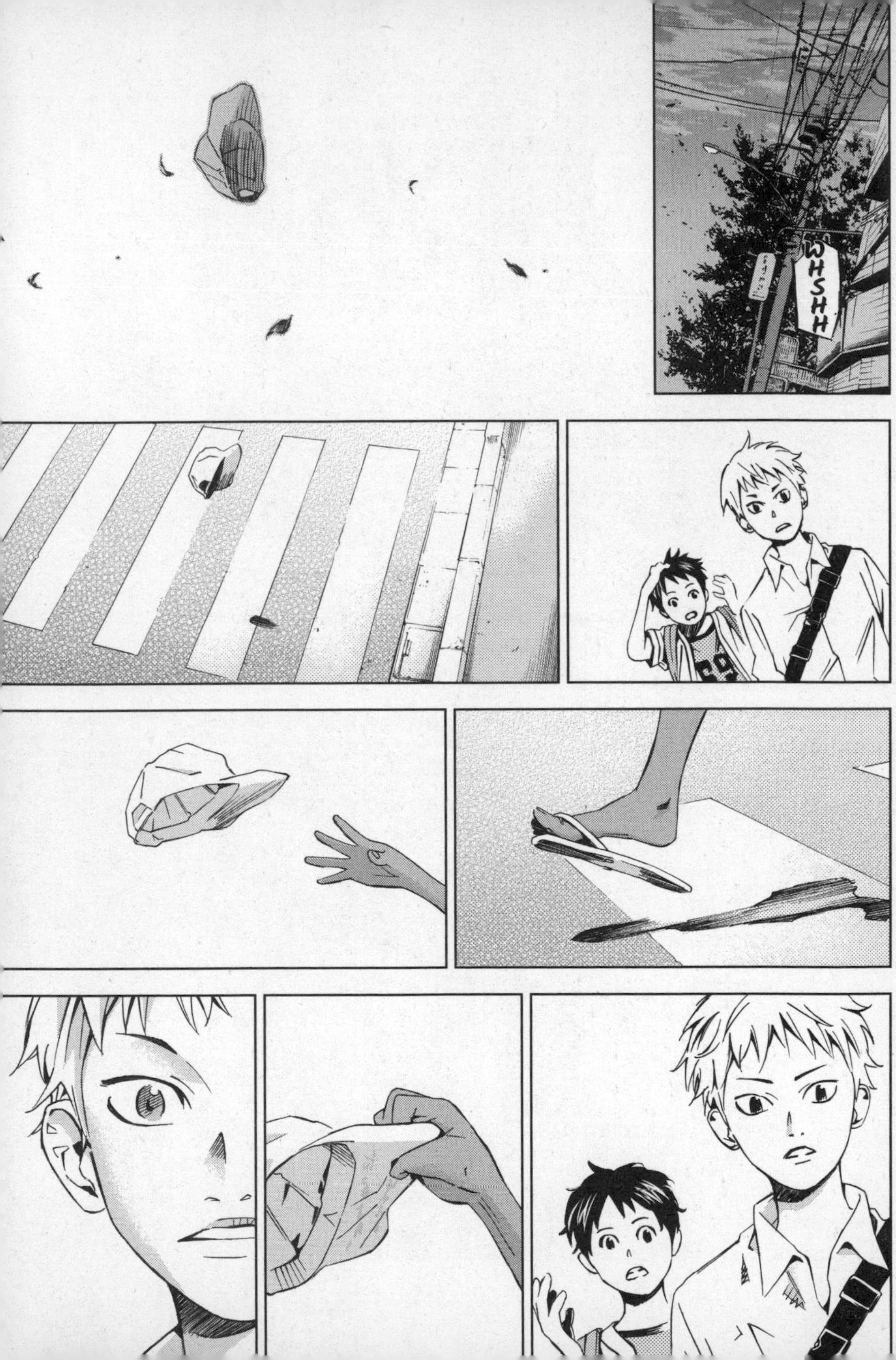
WHSHH

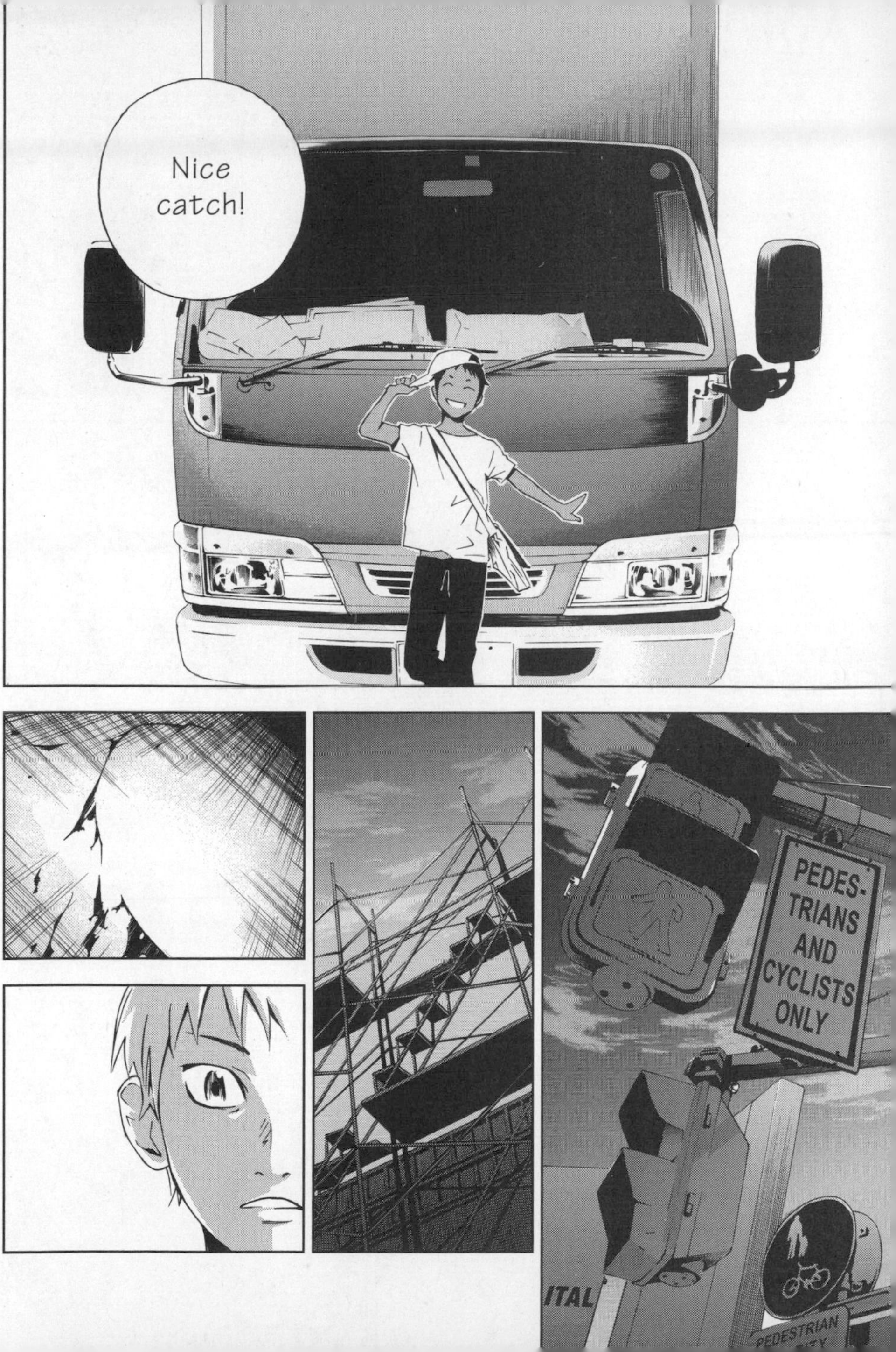
Nice catch!
PEDES-TRIANS AND CYCLISTS ONLY
ITAL
PEDESTRIAN

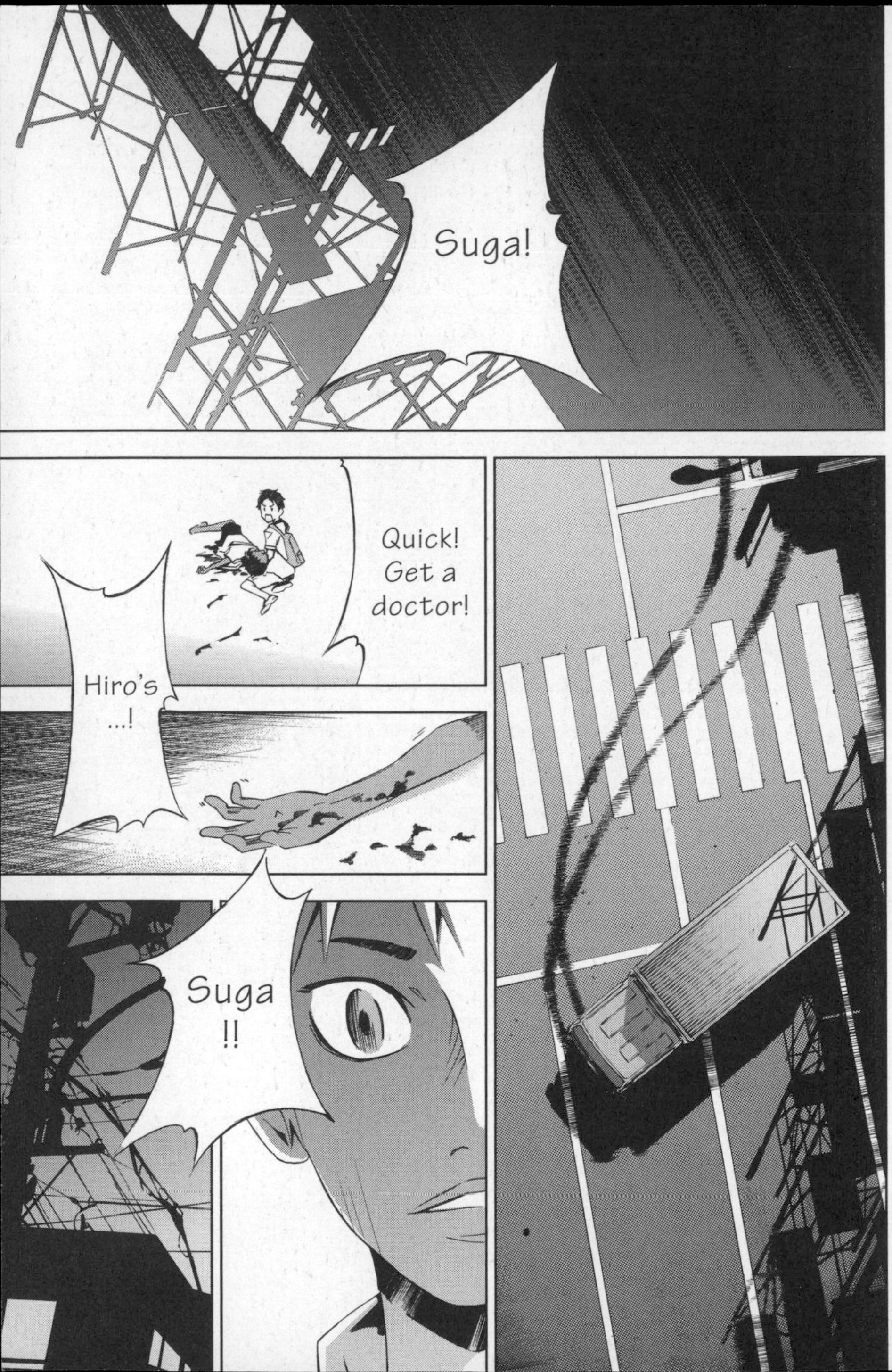
Suga!
Quick! Get a doctor!
Hiro's ...!
Suga !!

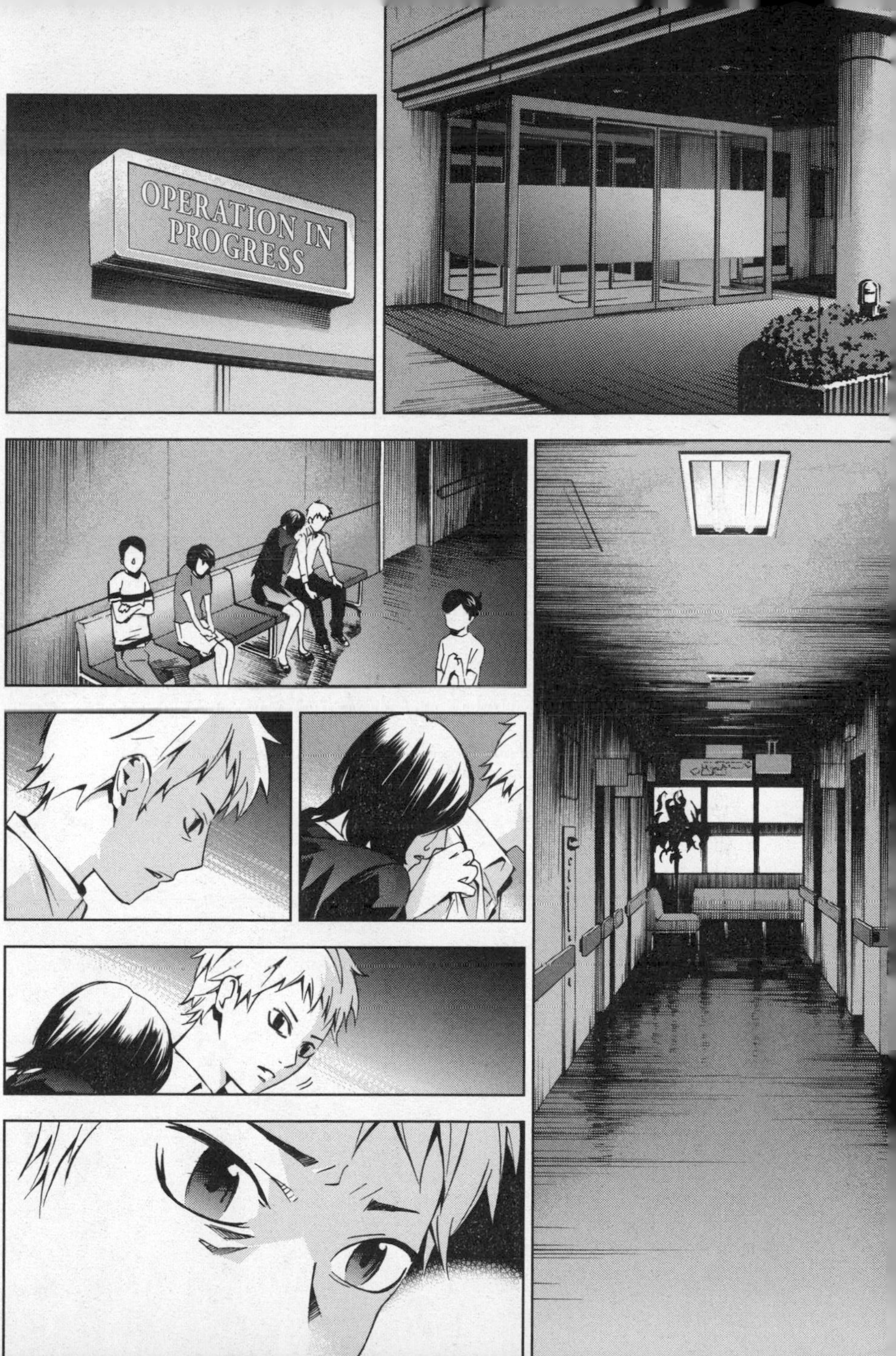
OPERATION IN PROGRESS

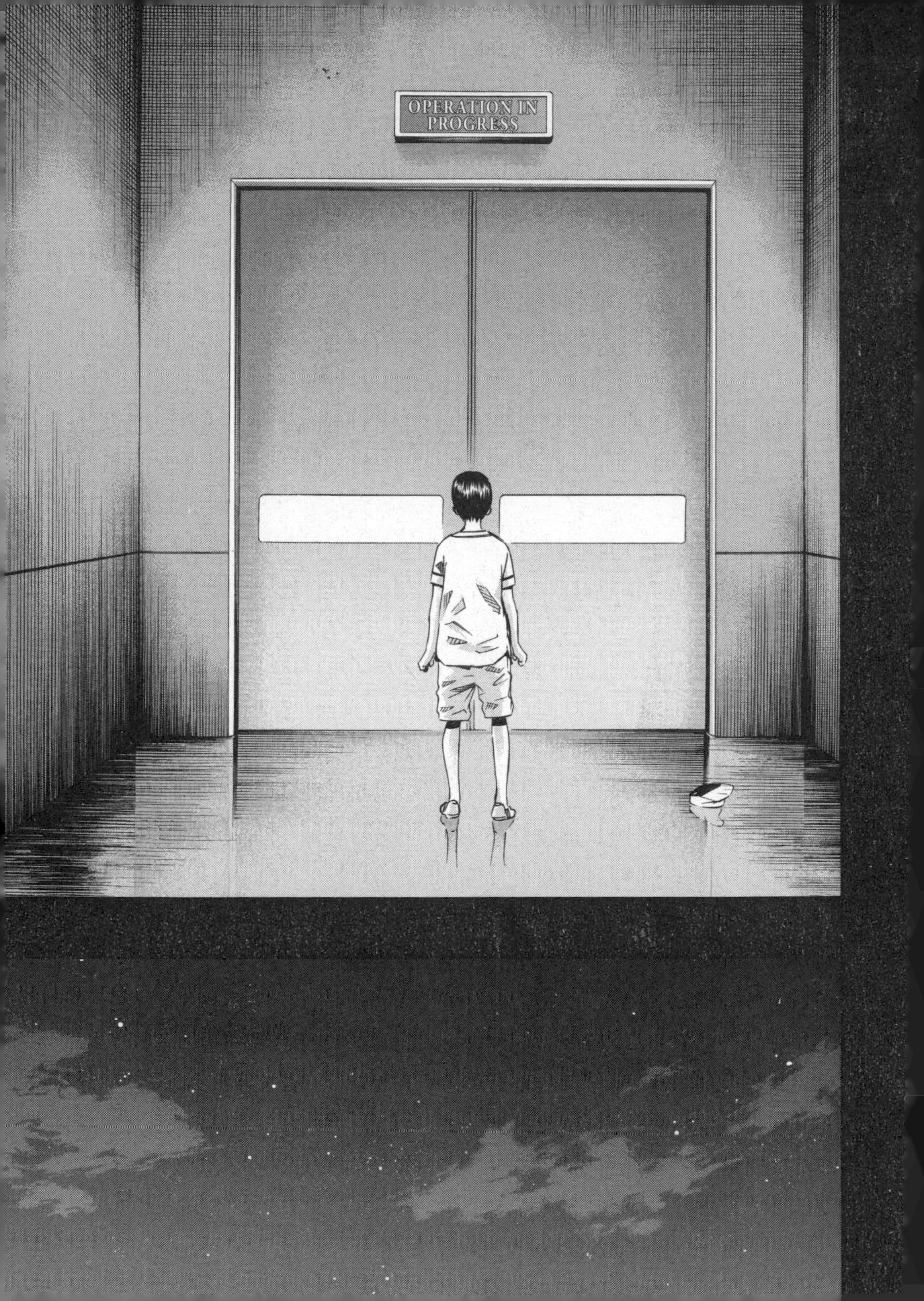
OPERATION IN PROGRESS

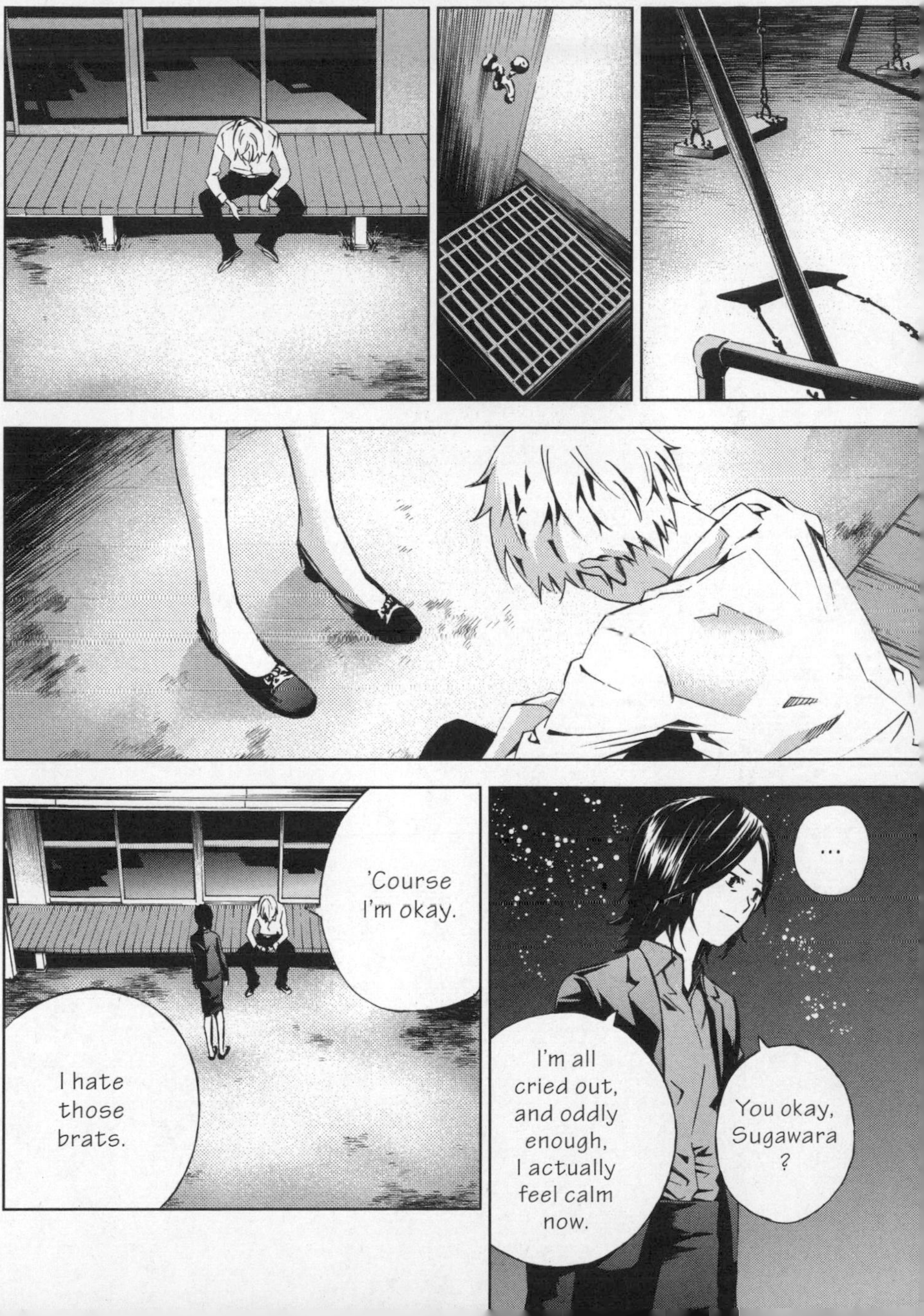
...
You okay, Sugawara ?
I'm all cried out, and oddly enough, I actually feel calm now.
'Course I'm okay.
I hate those brats.

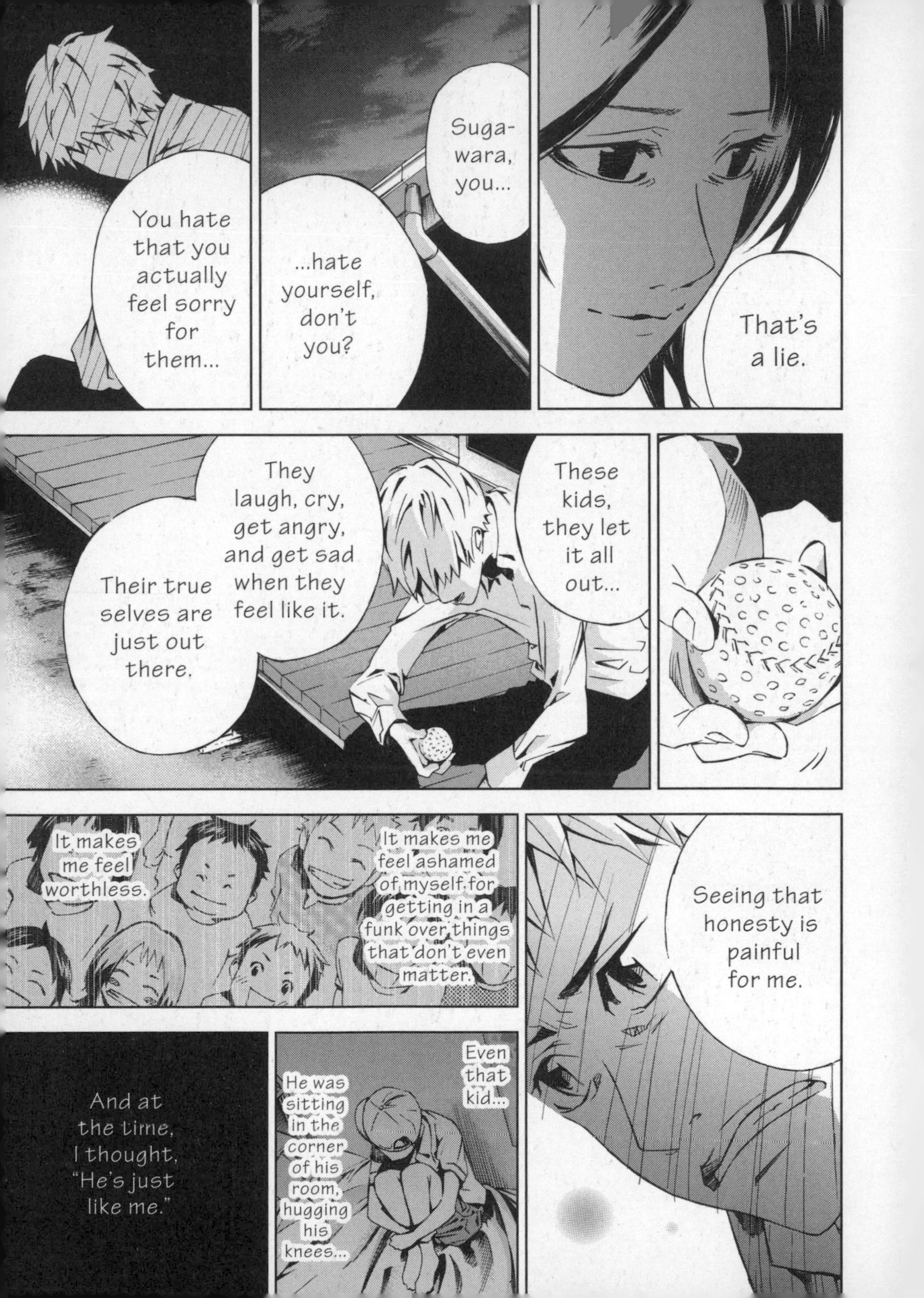
Suga-wara, you...
That's a lie.
...hate yourself, don't you?
You hate that you actually feel sorry for them...
These kids, they let it all out...
They laugh, cry, get angry, and get sad when they feel like it.
Their true selves are just out there.
Seeing that honesty is painful for me.
It makes me feel ashamed of myself for getting in a funk over things that don't even matter.
It makes me feel worthless.
Even that kid...
He was sitting in the corner of his room, hugging his knees...
And at the time, I thought, "He's just like me."

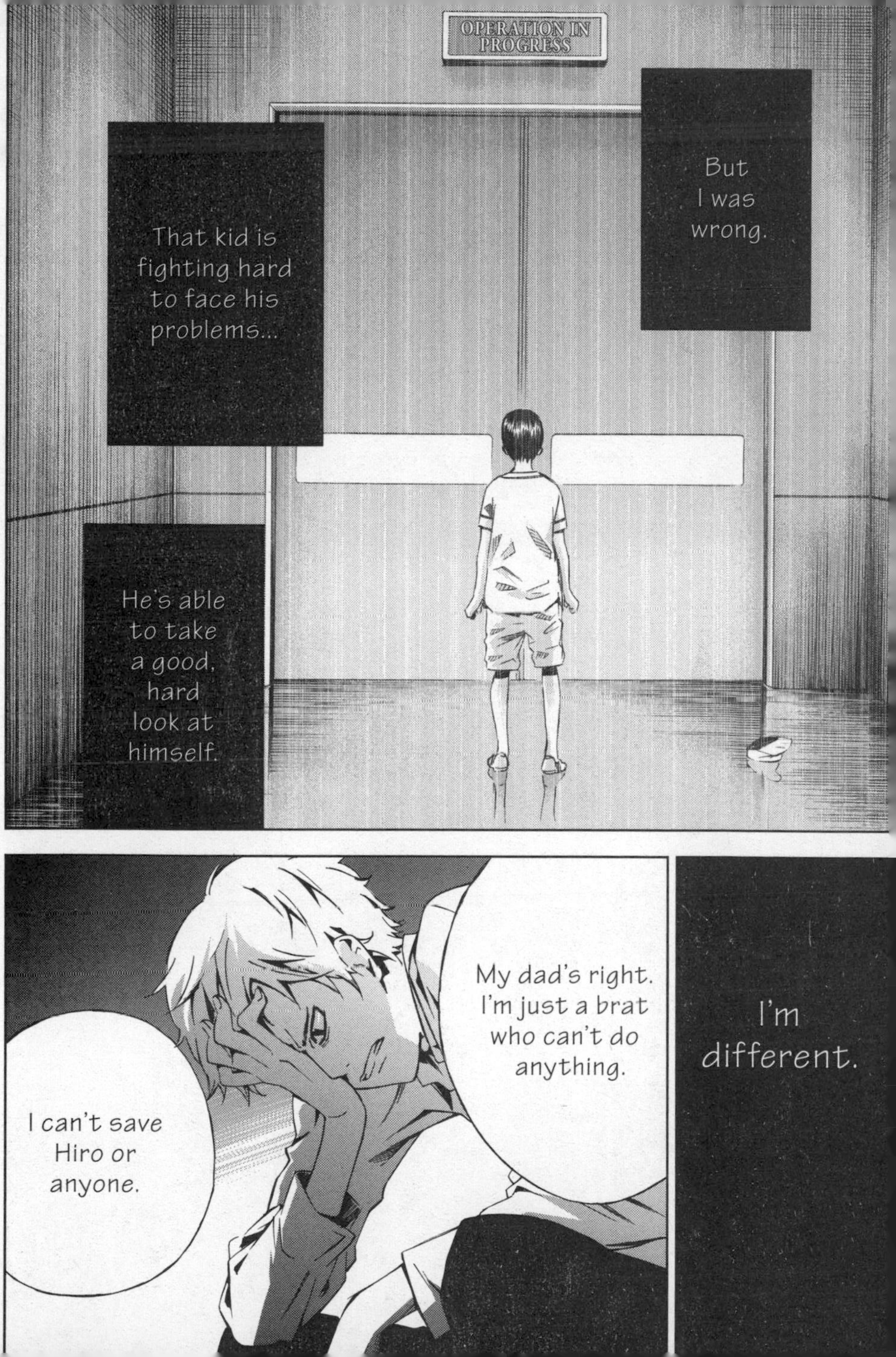
OPERATION IN PROGRESS
But I was wrong.
That kid is fighting hard to face his problems...
He's able to take a good, hard look at himself.
I'm different.
My dad's right. I'm just a brat who can't do anything.
I can't save Hiro or anyone.

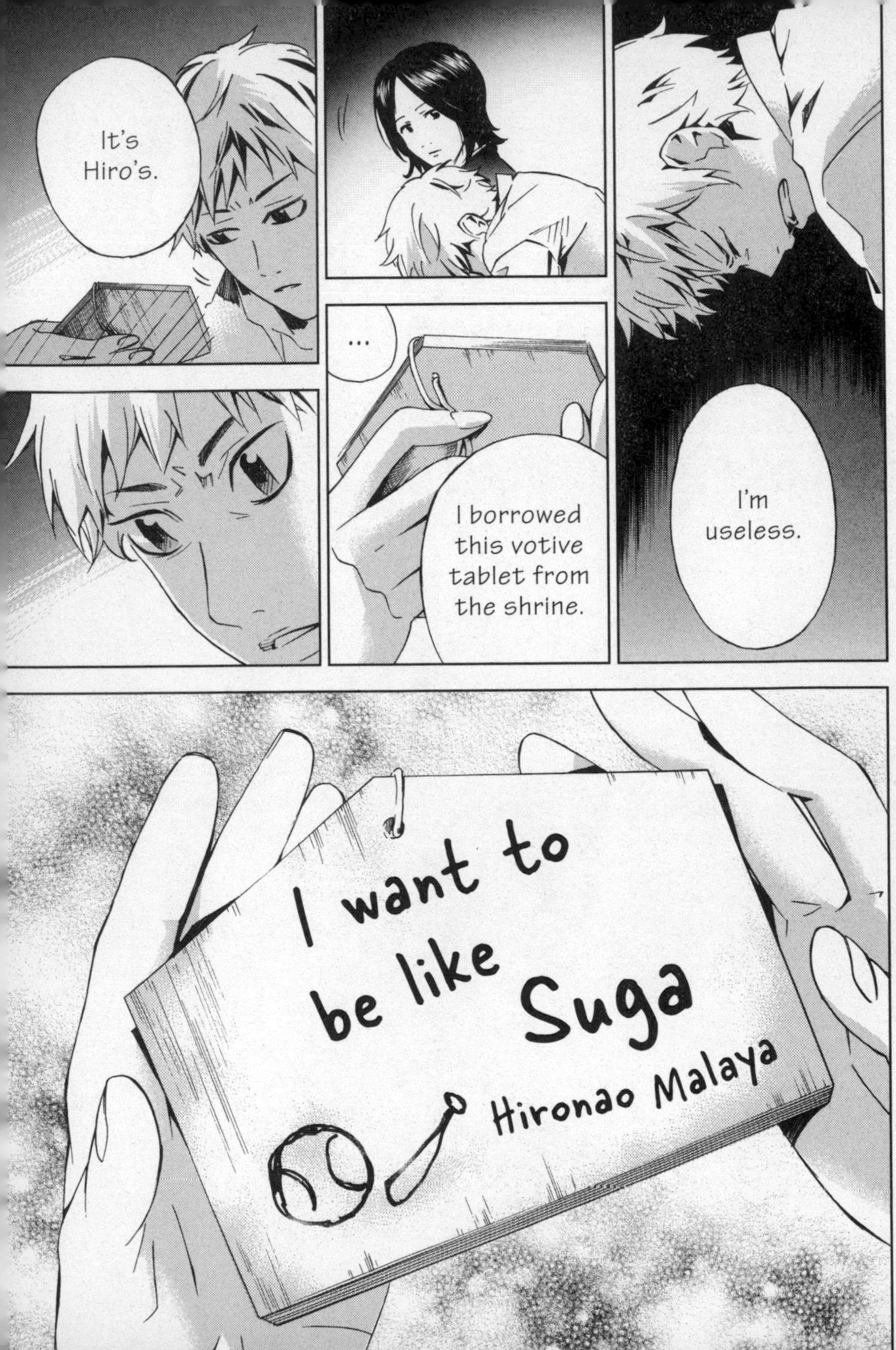
I'm useless.
It's Hiro's.
...
I borrowed this votive tablet from the shrine.
I want to be like Suga
Hironao Malaya

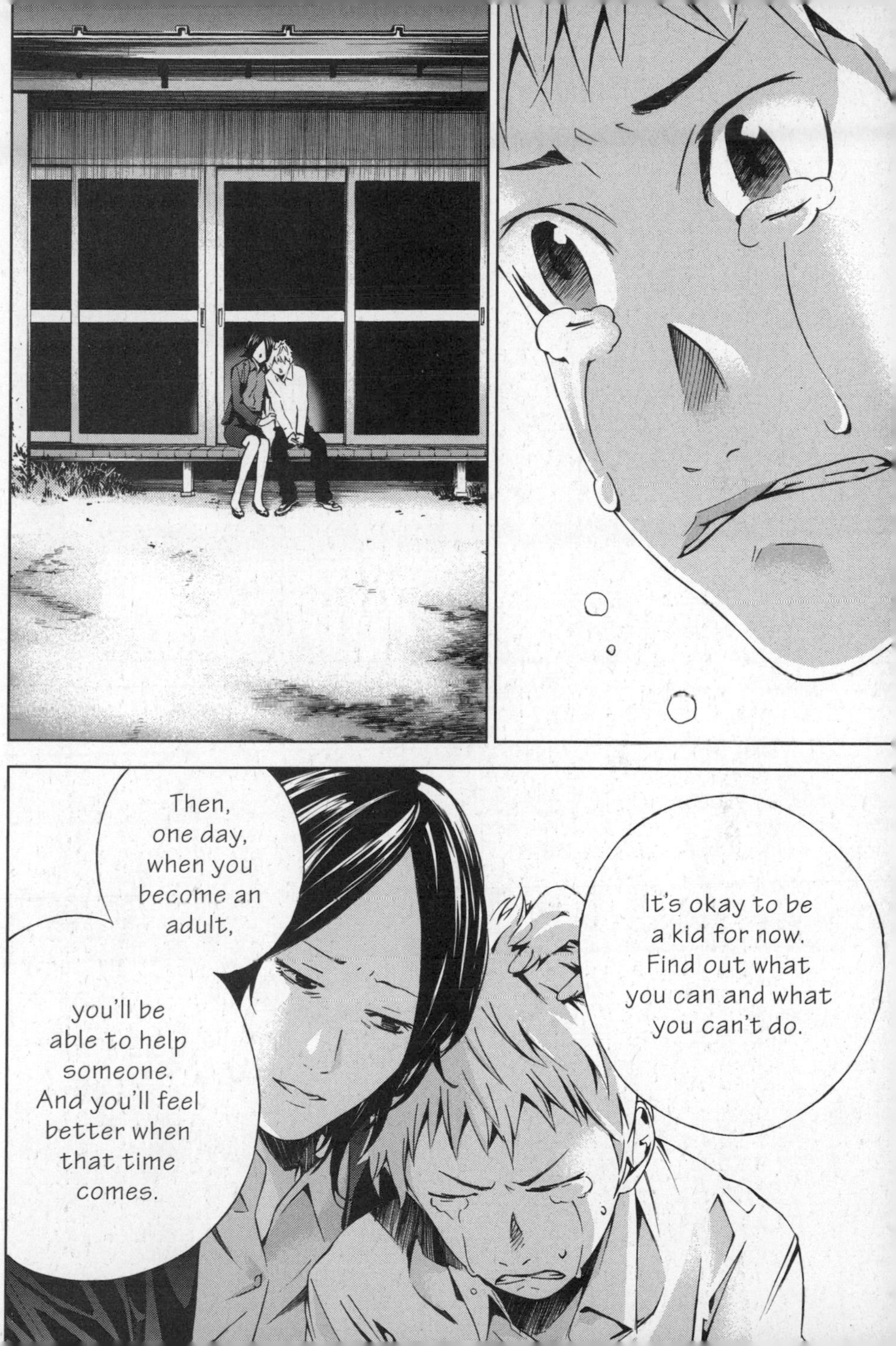
It's okay to be a kid for now. Find out what you can and what you can't do.
Then, one day, when you become an adult,
you'll be able to help someone. And you'll feel better when that time comes.

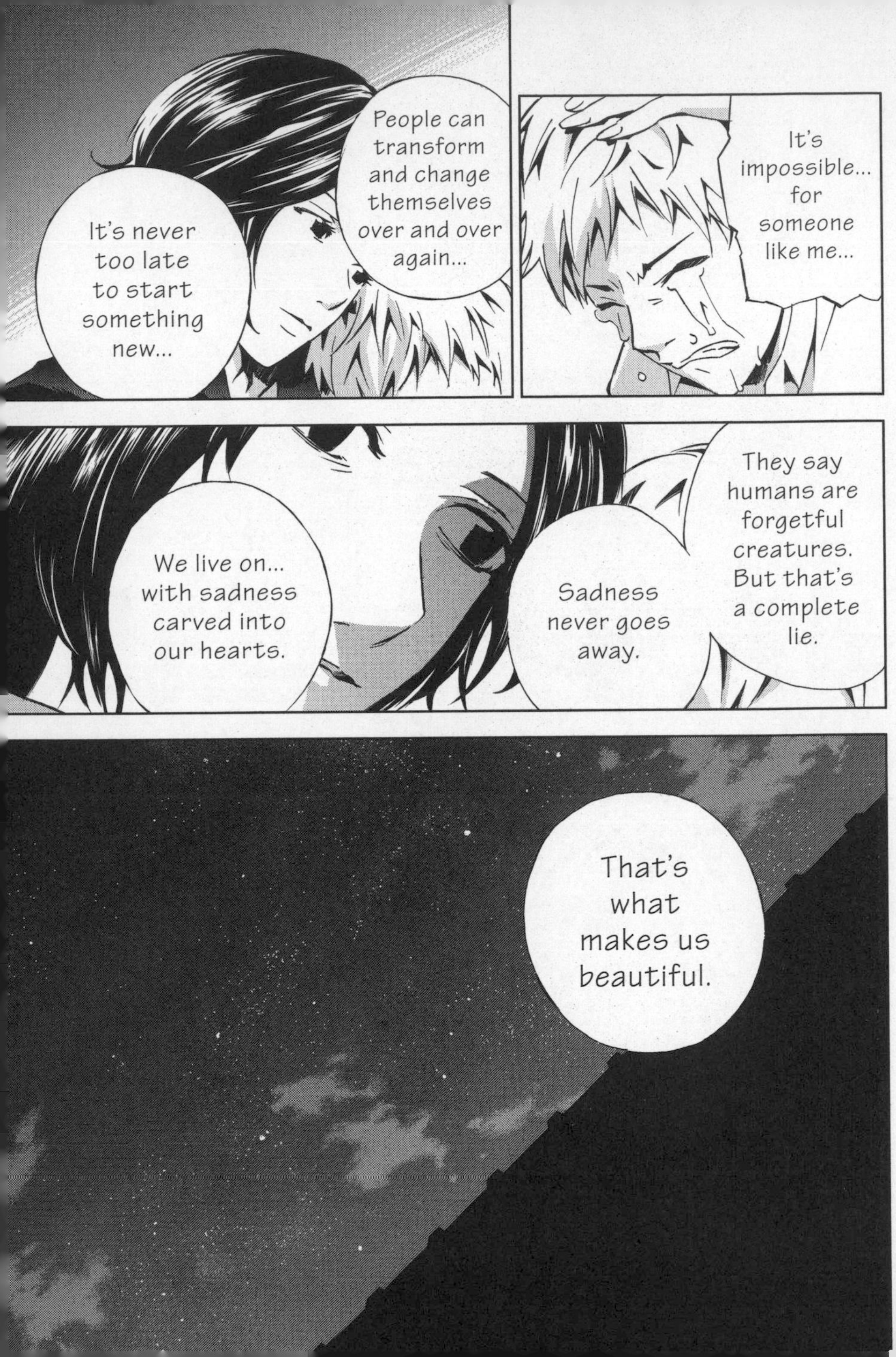
It's impossible... for someone like me...
People can transform and change themselves over and over again...
It's never too late to start something new...
They say humans are forgetful creatures. But that's a complete lie.
Sadness never goes away.
We live on... with sadness carved into our hearts.
That's what makes us beautiful.

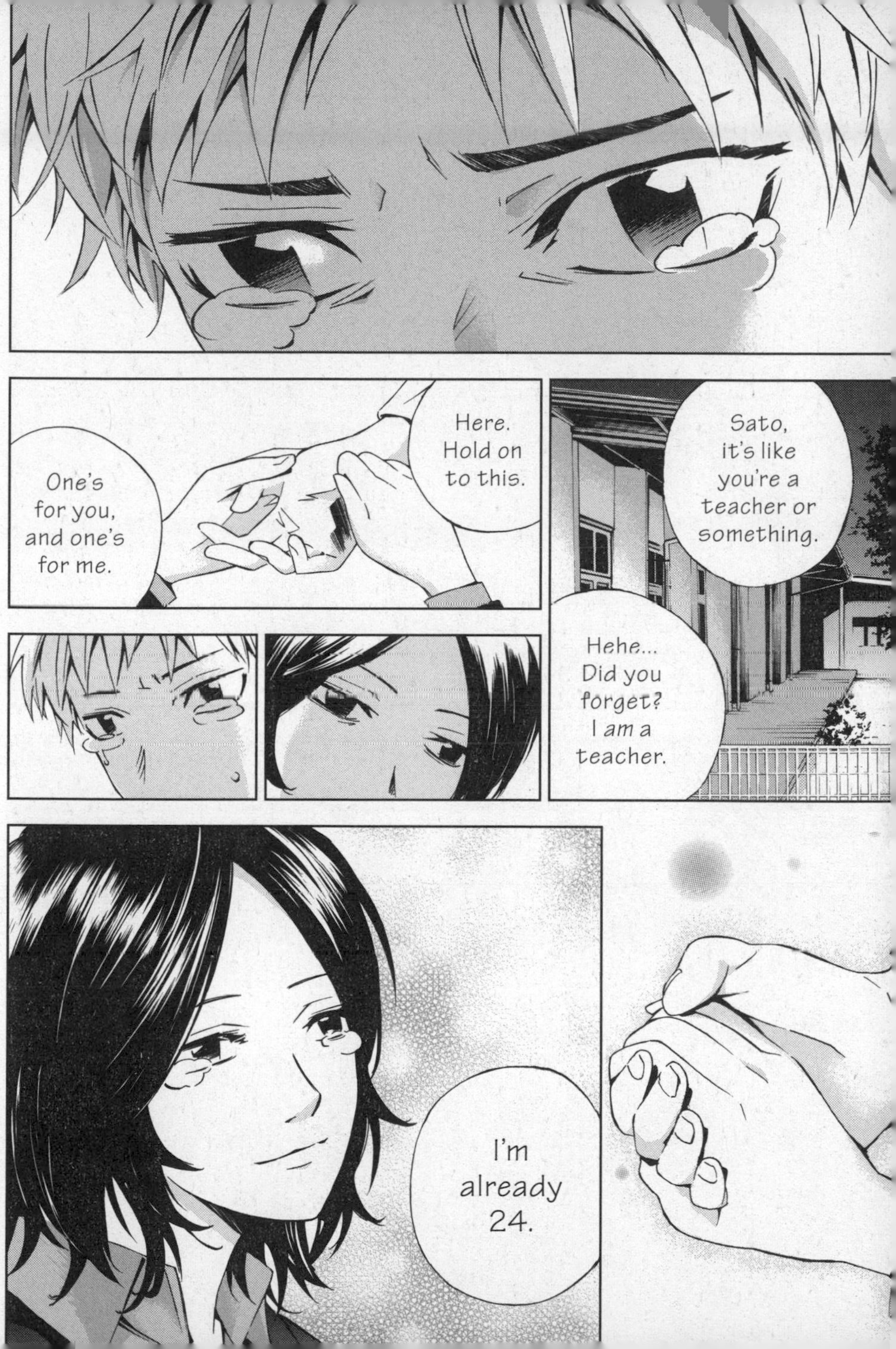
Sato, it's like you're a teacher or something.
Hehe... Did you forget? I *am* a teacher.
Here. Hold on to this.
One's for you, and one's for me.
I'm already 24.

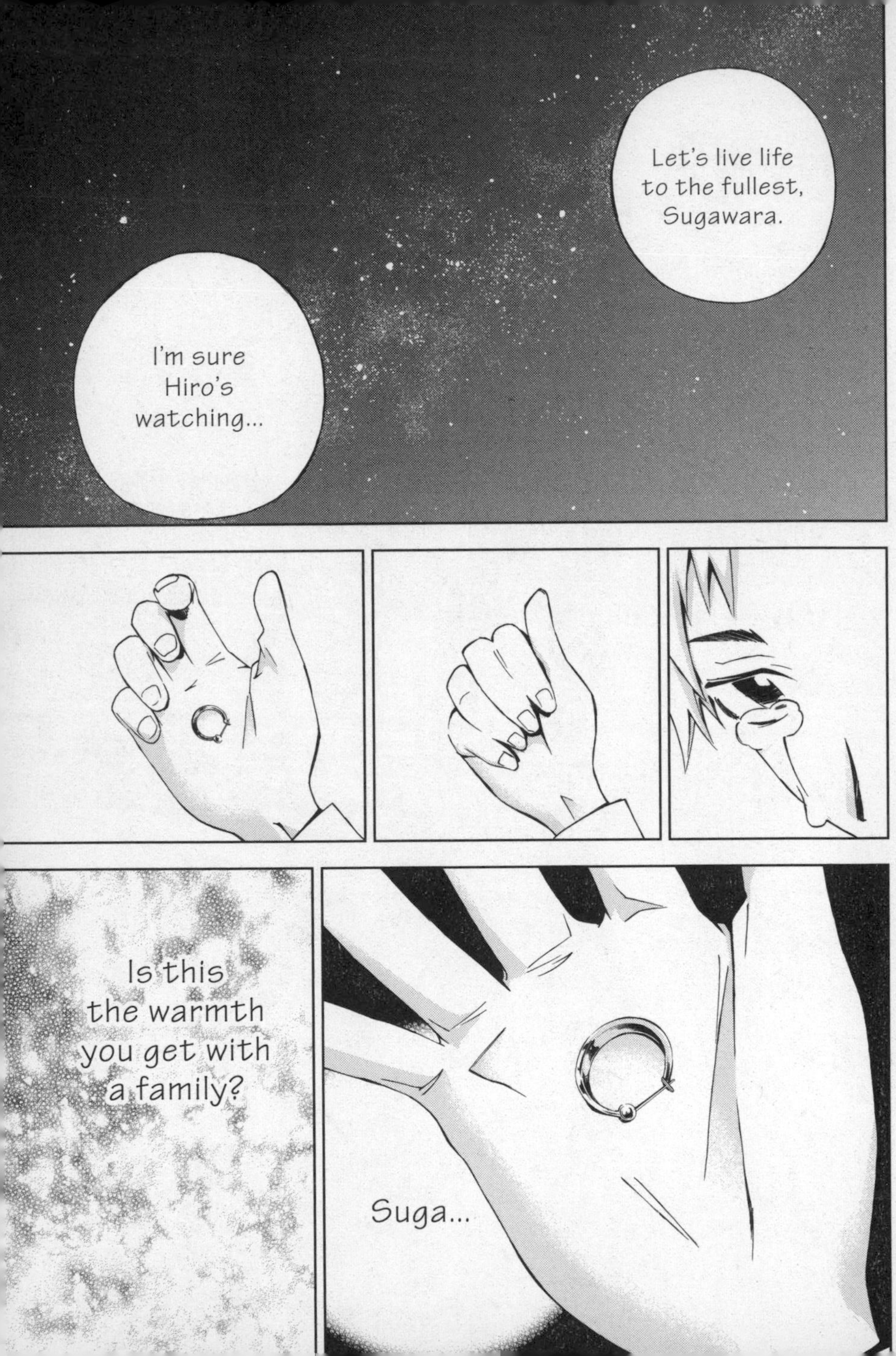

Let's live life to the fullest, Sugawara.

I'm sure Hiro's watching...

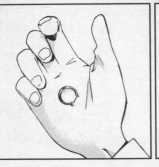

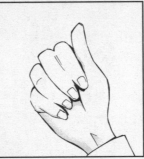

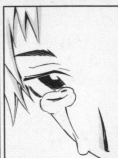

Is this the warmth you get with a family?

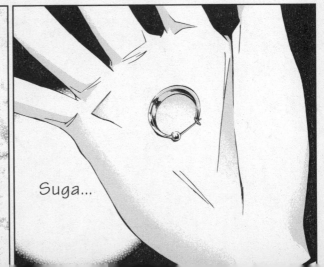

Suga...

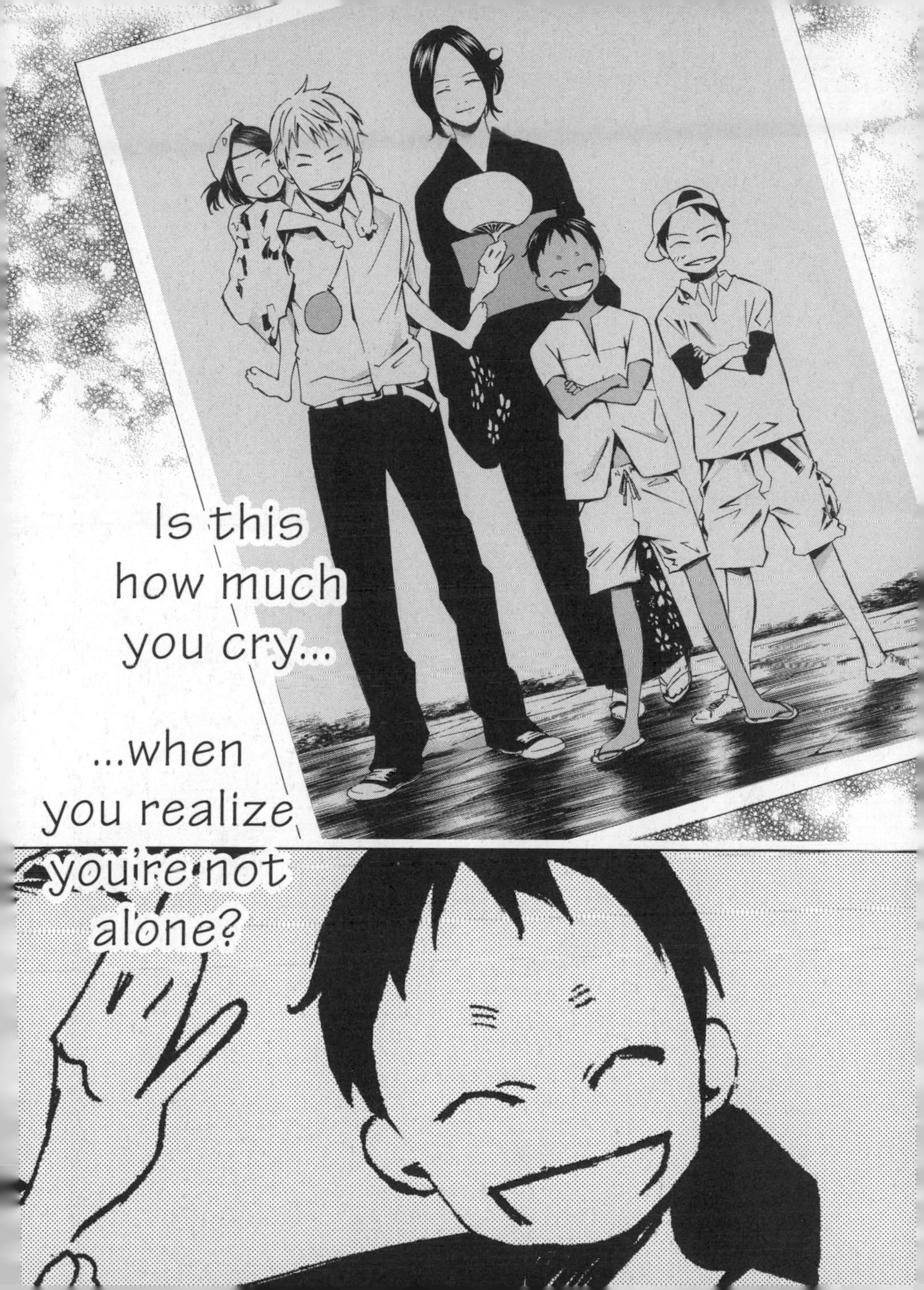
Is this how much you cry...
...when you realize you're not alone?

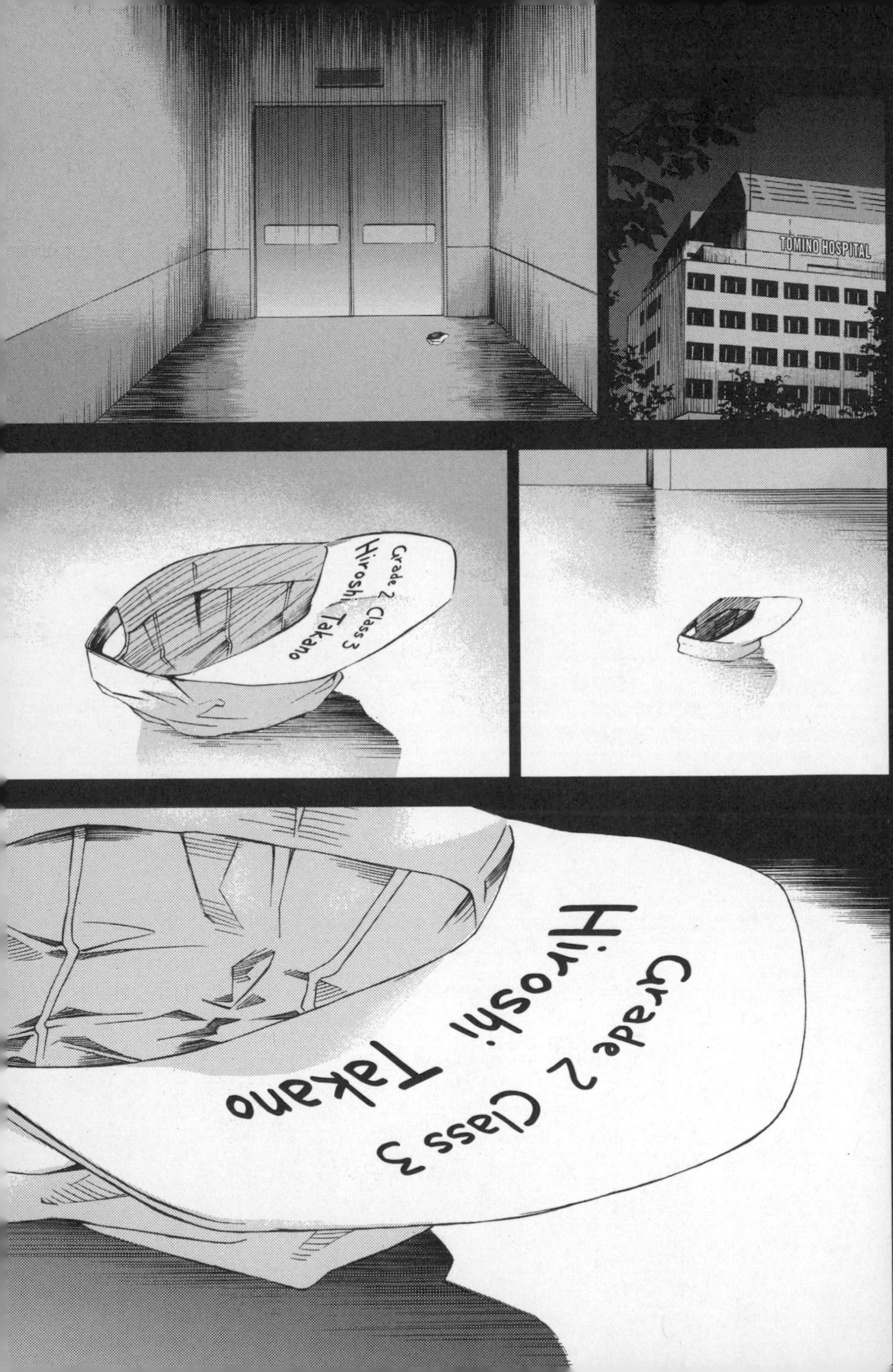
TOMINO HOSPITAL
Grade 2 Class 3
Hiroshi Takano
Grade 2 Class 3
Hiroshi Takano

A School Frozen in Time

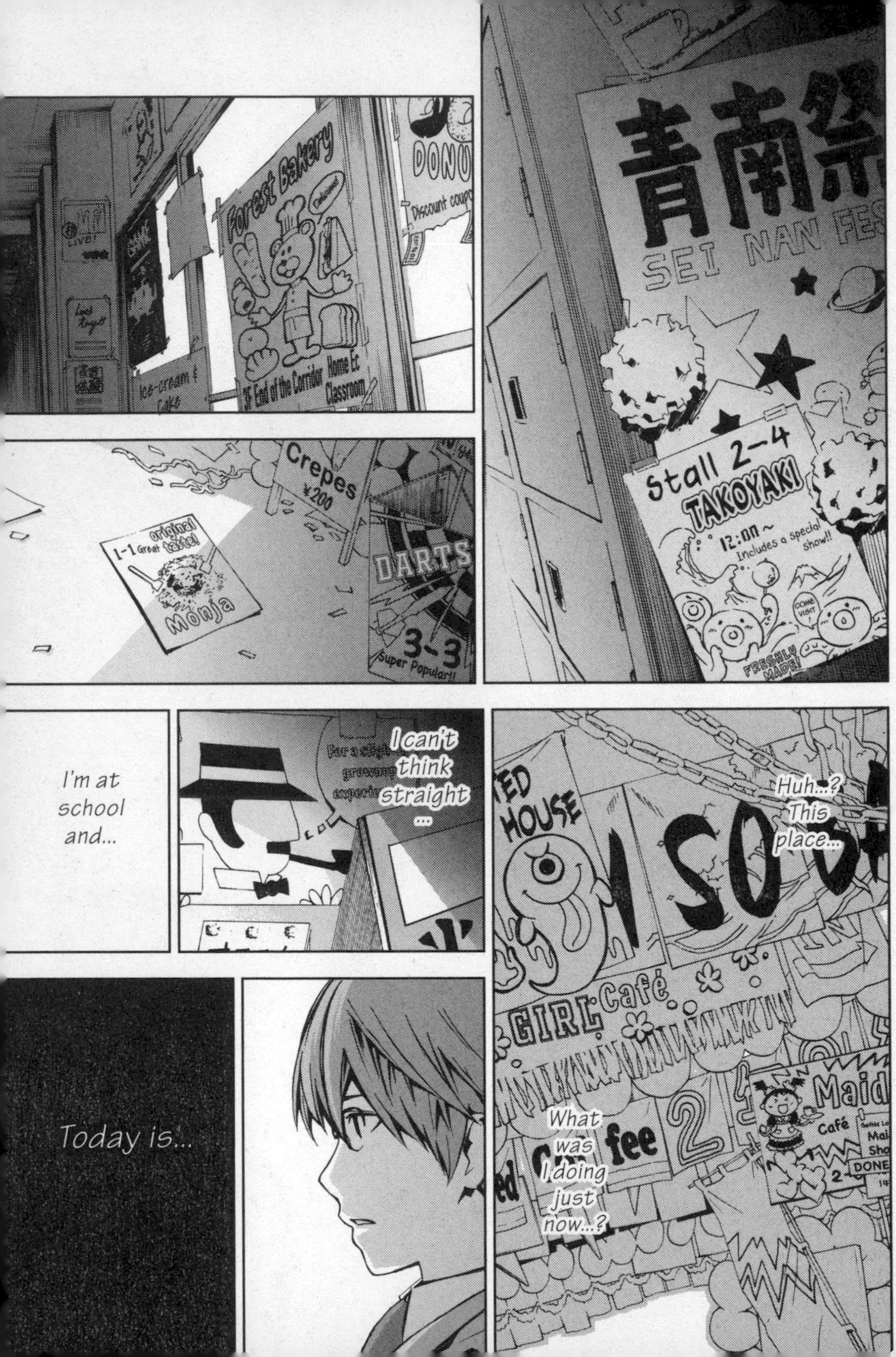

青南祭
SEI NAN FES
Stall 2-4
TAKOYAKI
12:00 ~
Includes a special show!!
COME VISIT!
FRESHLY MADE!
Forest Bakery
DONU
Discount coupo
Ice-cream & Cake
End of the Corridor Home Ec Classroom
Crepes
¥200
1-1 Great original taste!
Monja
DARTS
3-3
Super Popular!!
Huh...? This place...
GIRL Café
Maid Café
What was I doing just now...?
I can't think straight...
I'm at school and...
Today is...

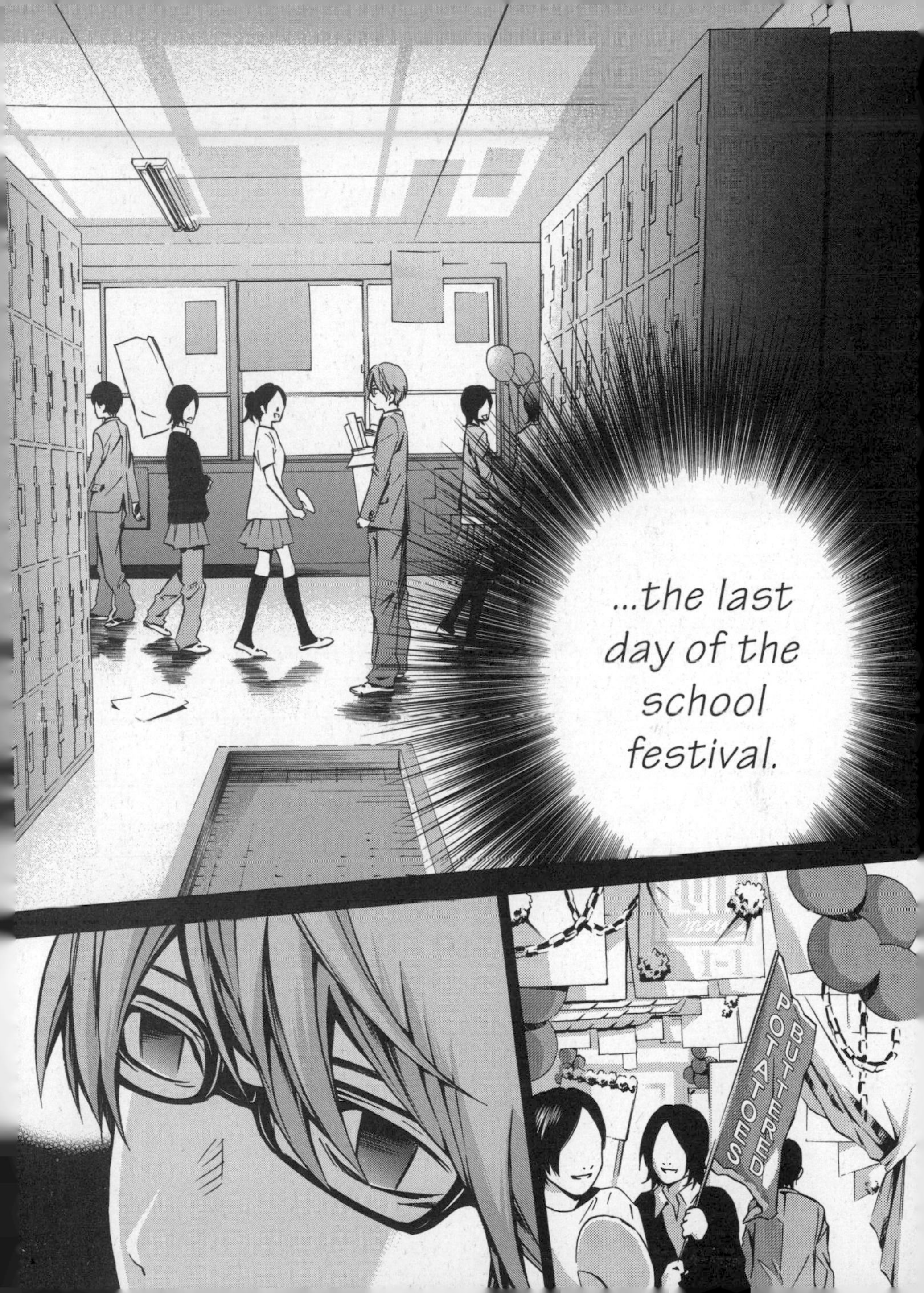
...the last day of the school festival.
BUTTERED POTATOES

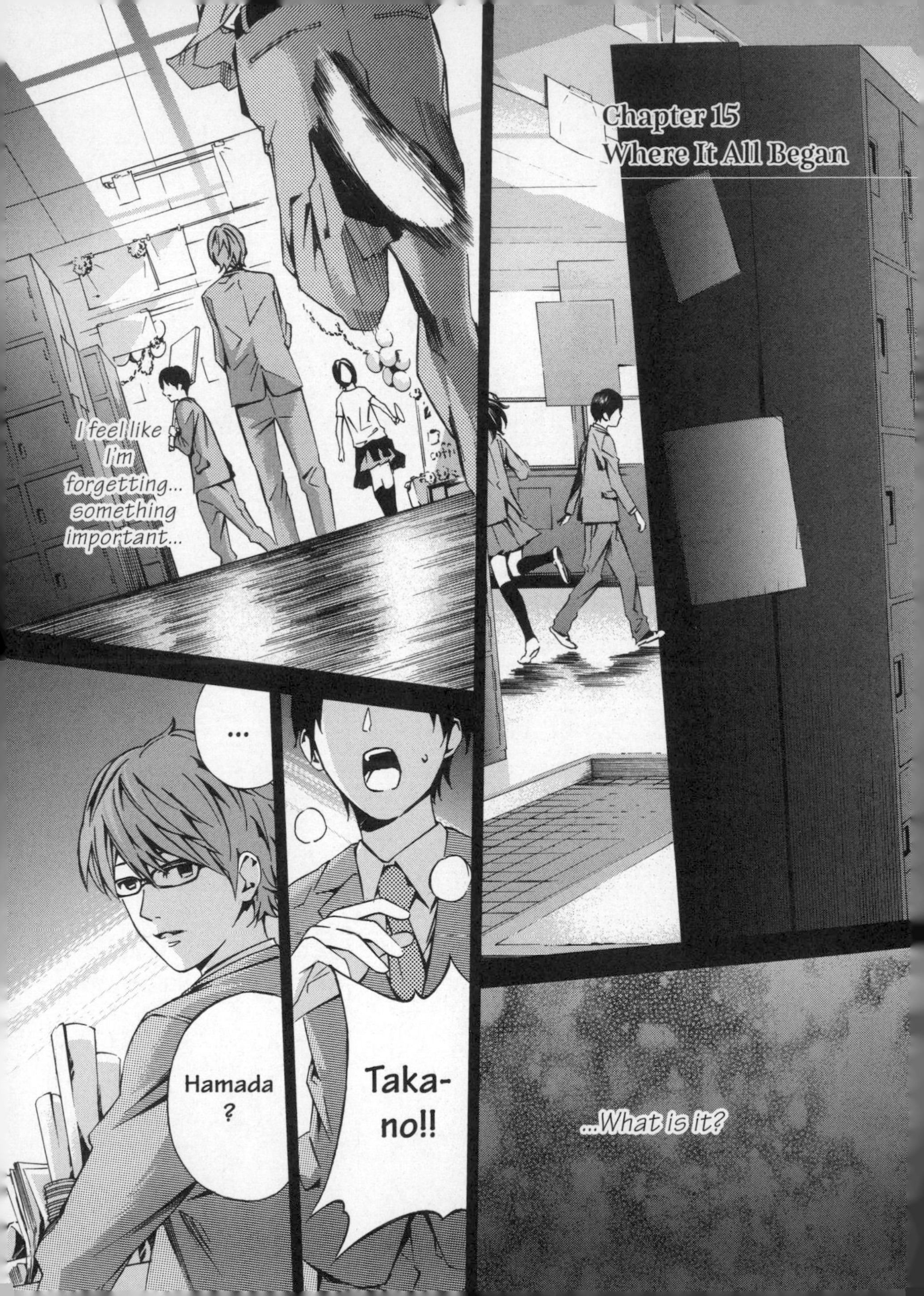
Chapter 15
Where It All Began
I feel like I'm forgetting... something important...
...What is it?
Taka-no!!
...
Hamada?

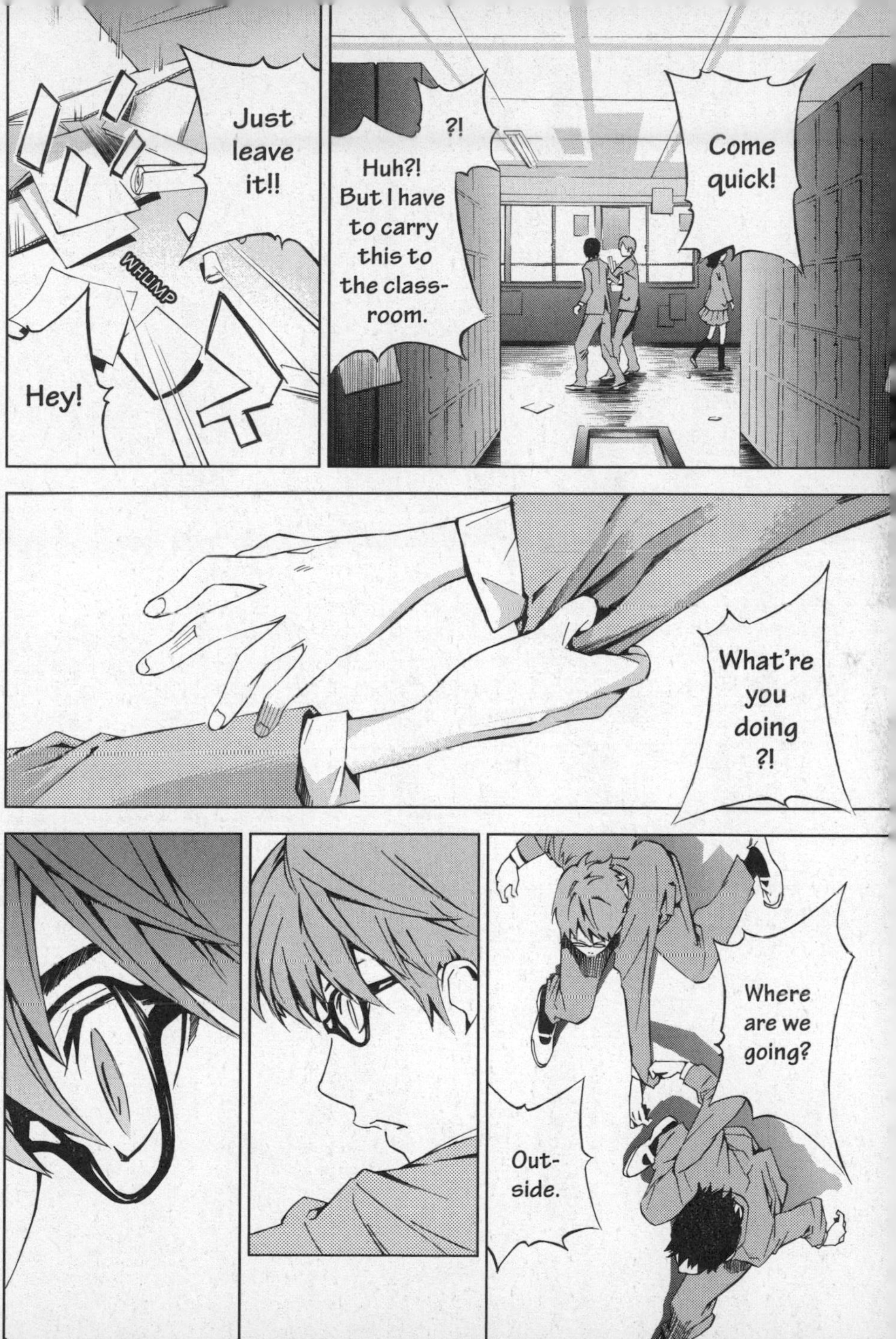
Come quick!
?!
Huh?! But I have to carry this to the class-room.
Just leave it!!
WHUMP
Hey!
What're you doing ?!
Where are we going?
Out-side.

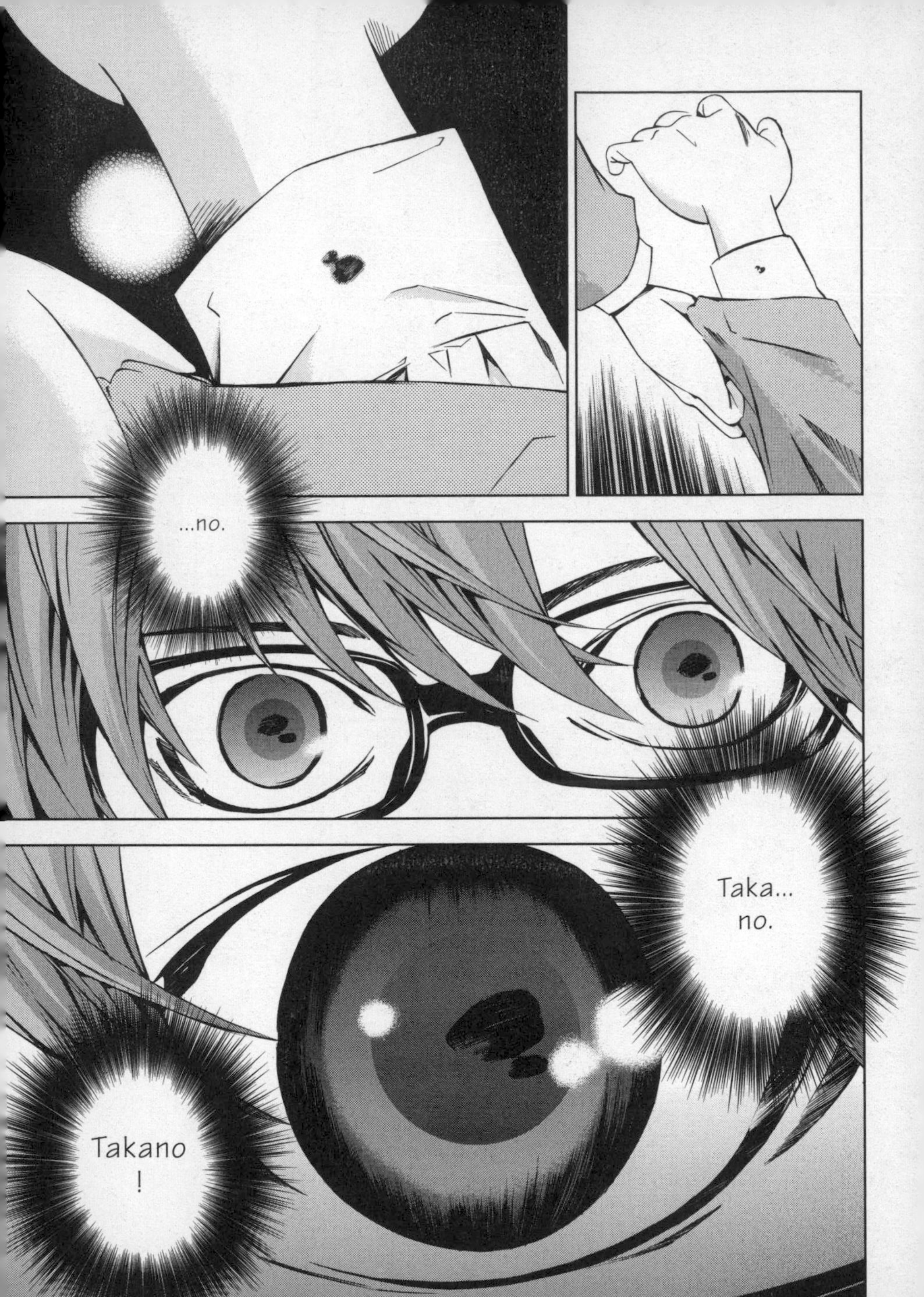
...no.
Taka...
no.
Takano
!

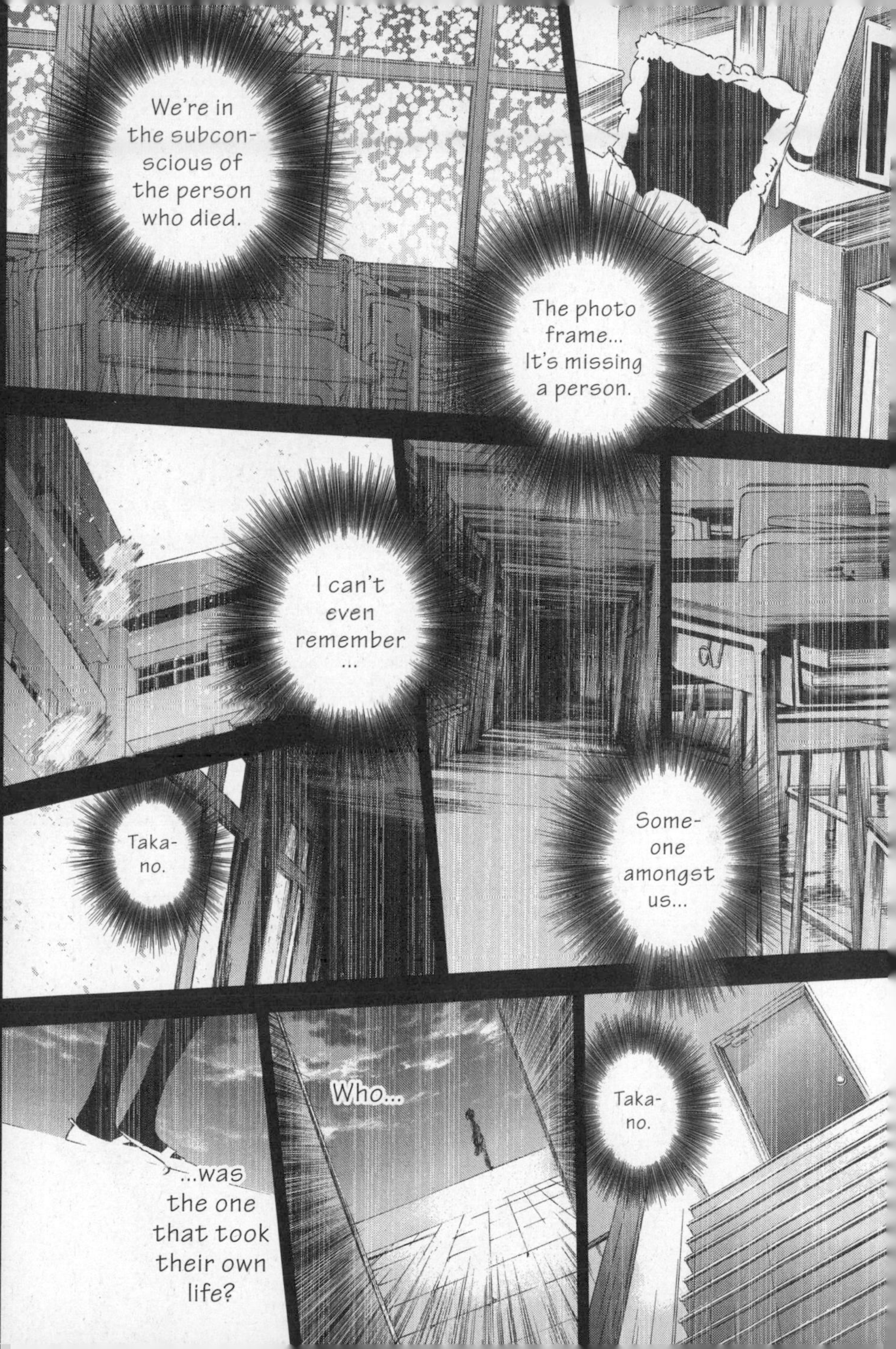
The photo frame... It's missing a person.
We're in the subconscious of the person who died.
Some-one amongst us...
I can't even remember ...
Taka-no.
Taka-no.
Who...
...was the one that took their own life?

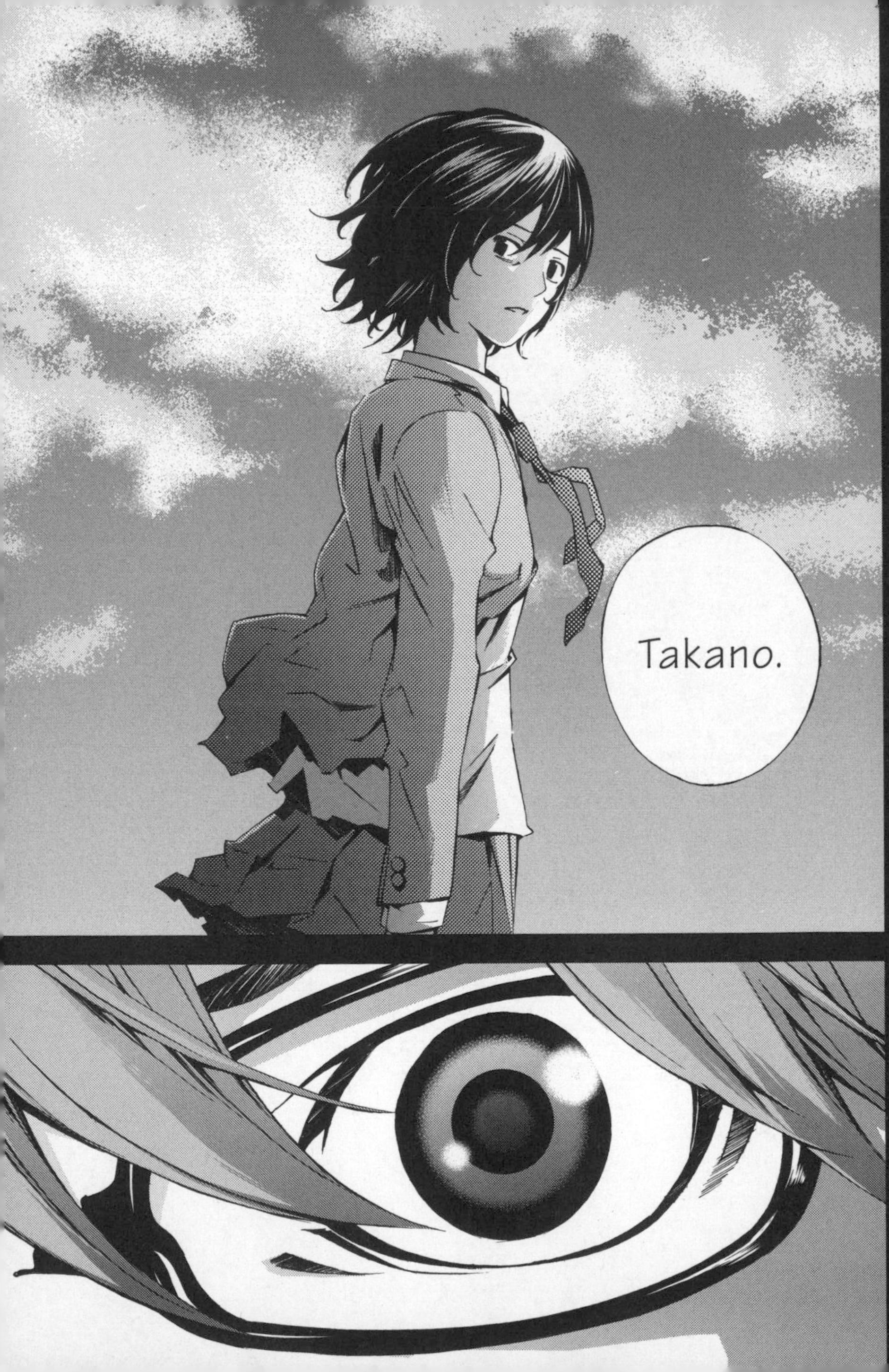
Takano.

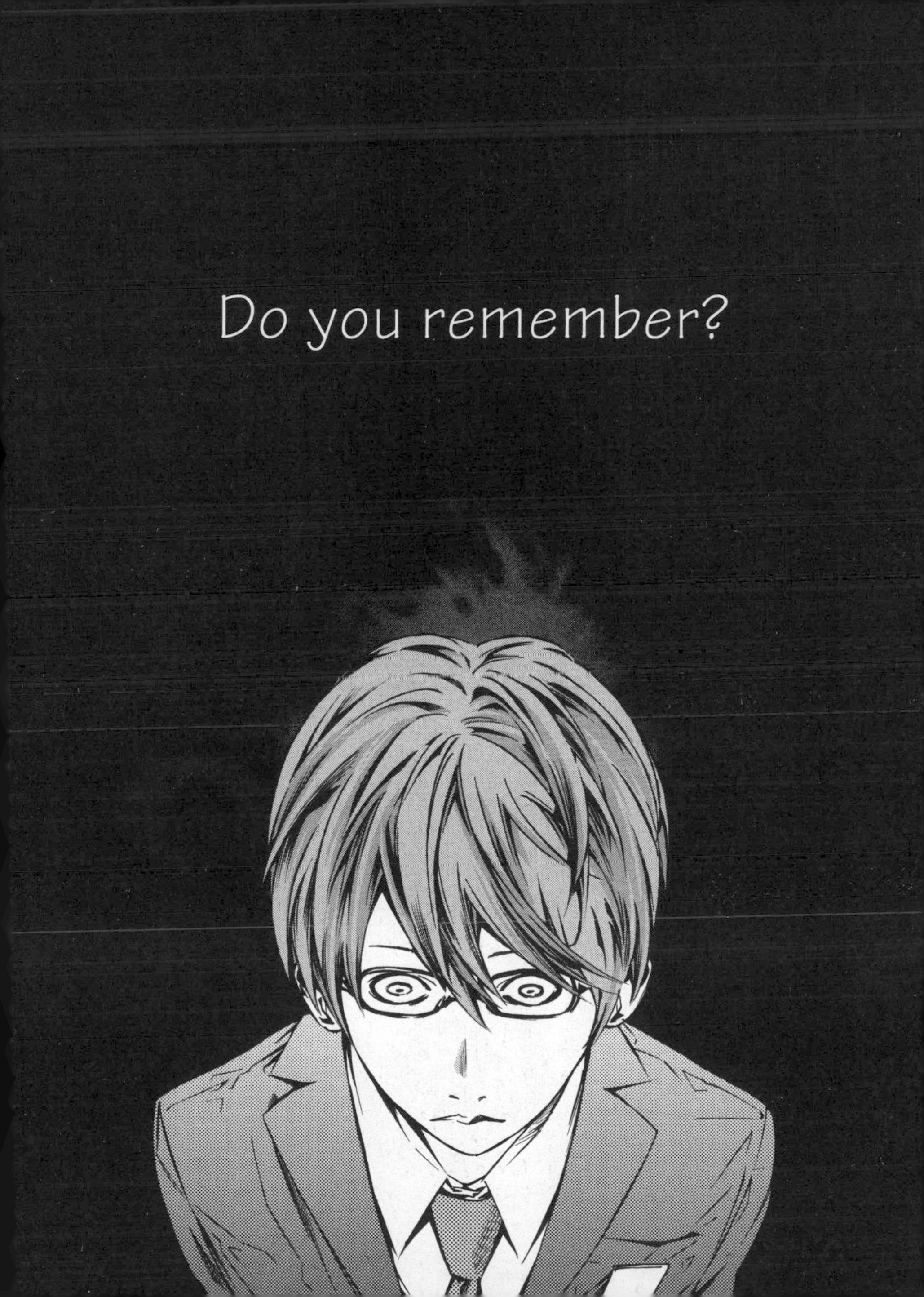
Do you remember?

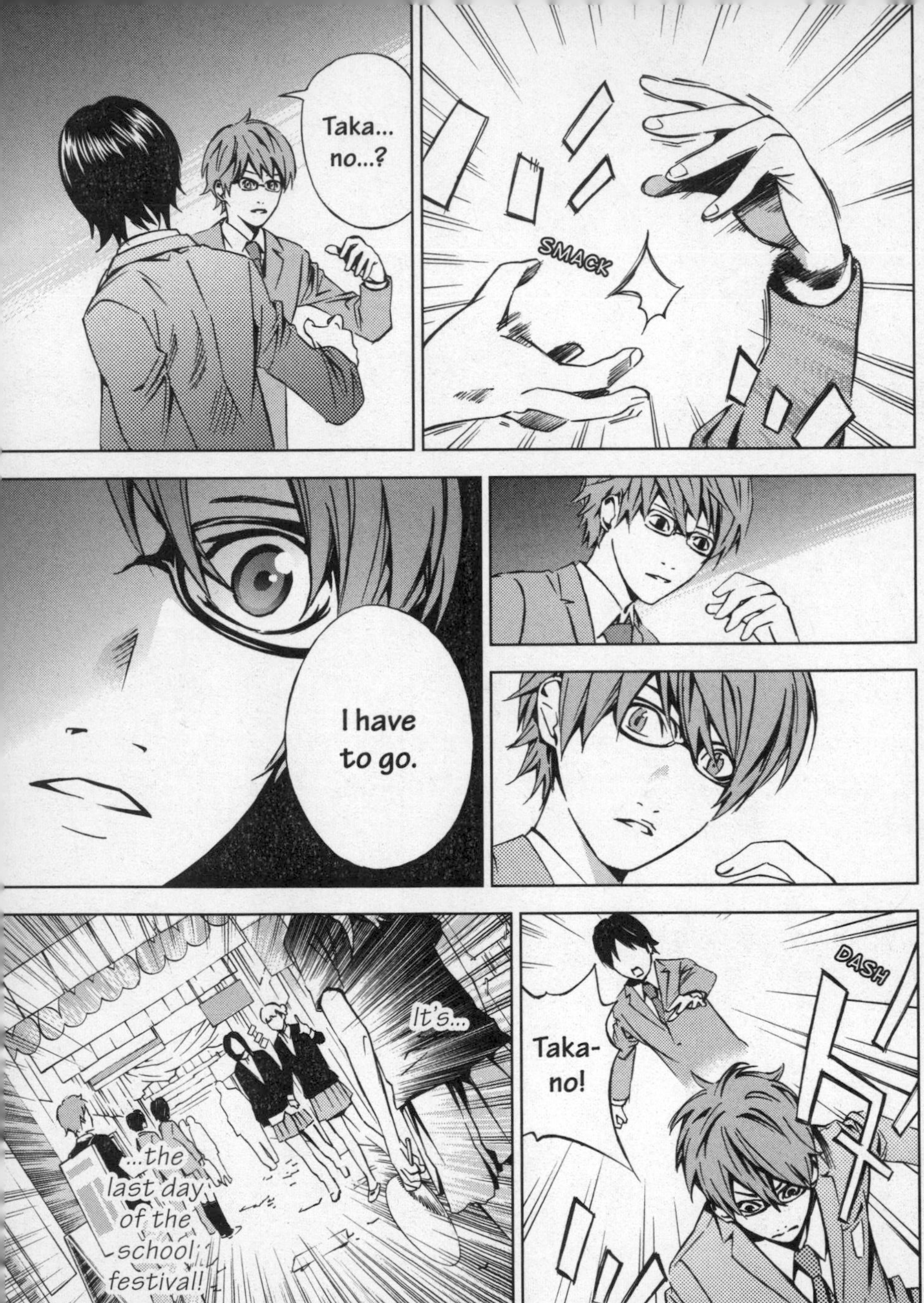
SMACK
Taka... no...?
I have to go.
DASH
Taka- no!
It's...
...the last day of the school festival!

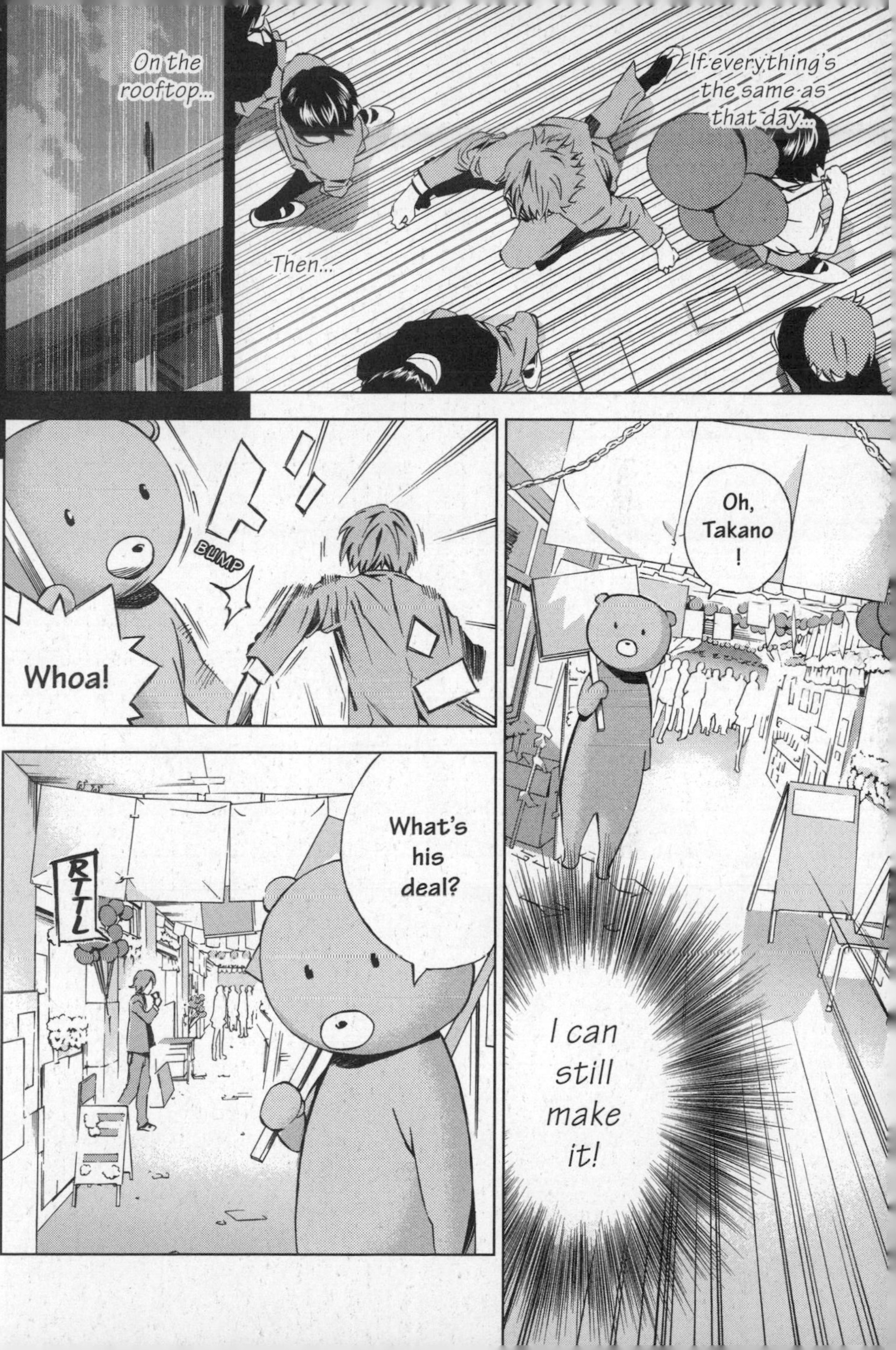
If everything's the same as that day...
Then...
On the rooftop...
Oh, Takano!
I can still make it!
BLUMP
Whoa!
What's his deal?
RTTL

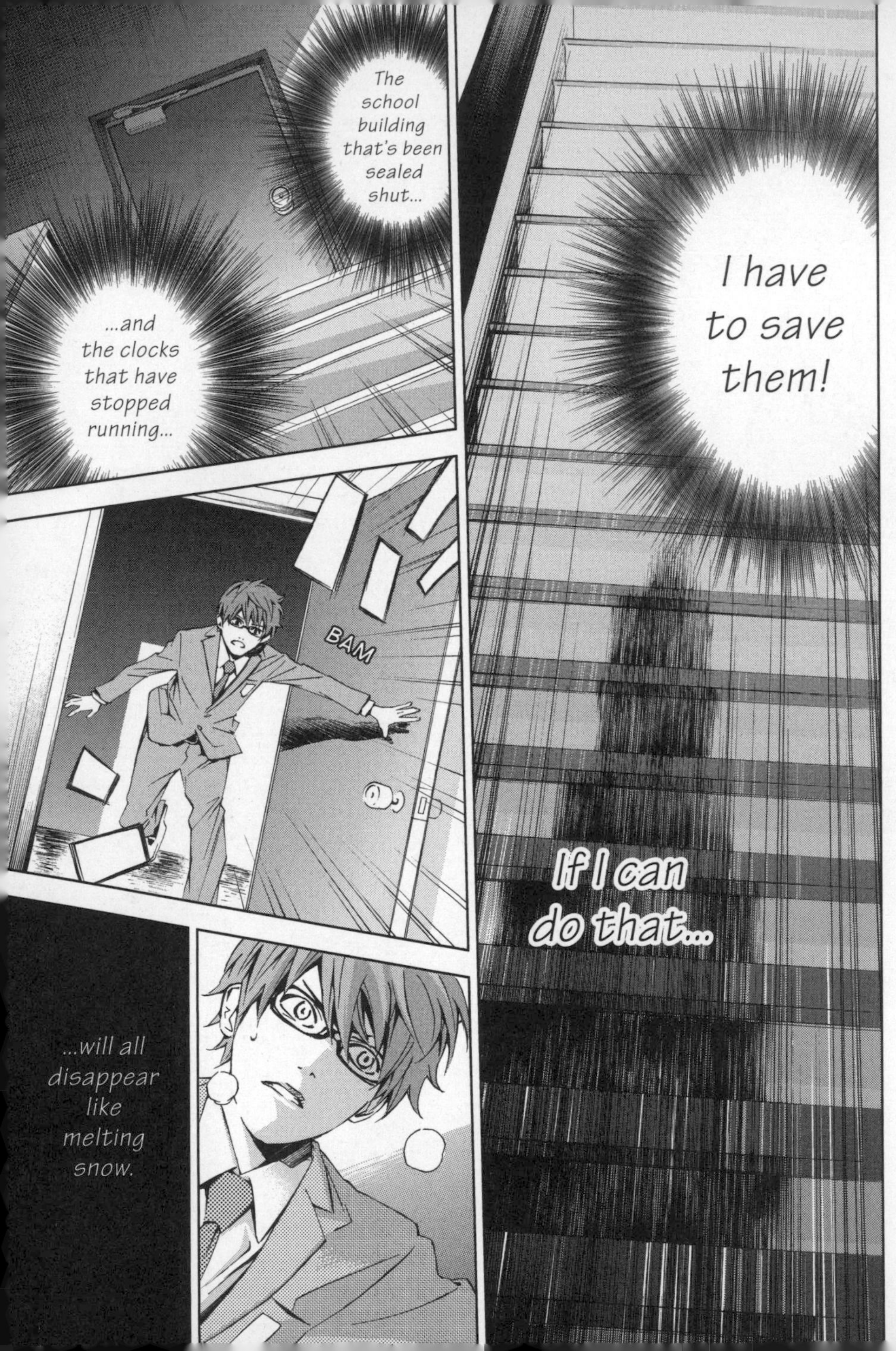

I have to save them!
If I can do that...
The school building that's been sealed shut...
...and the clocks that have stopped running...
BAM
...will all disappear like melting snow.

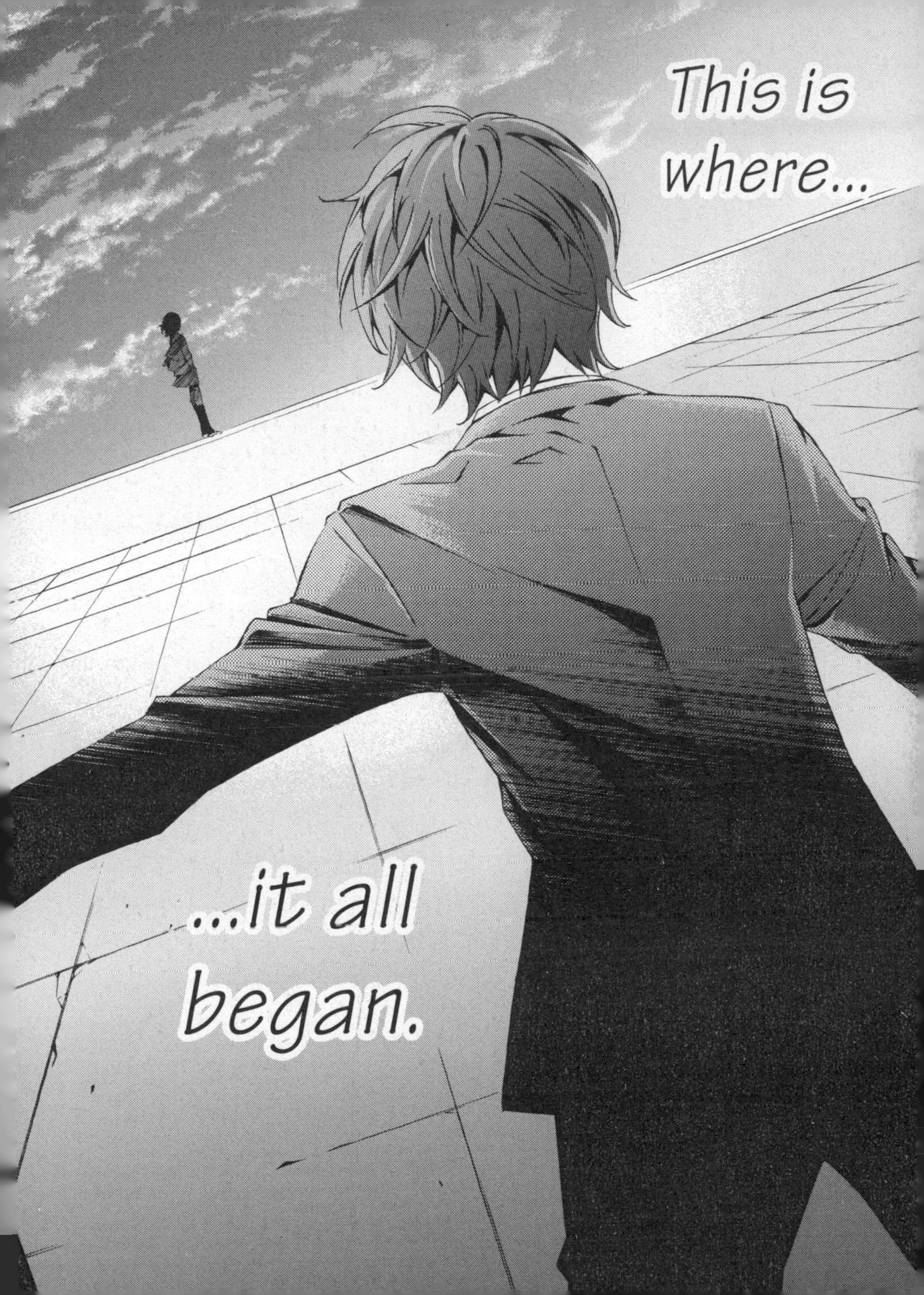
This is where...
...it all began.

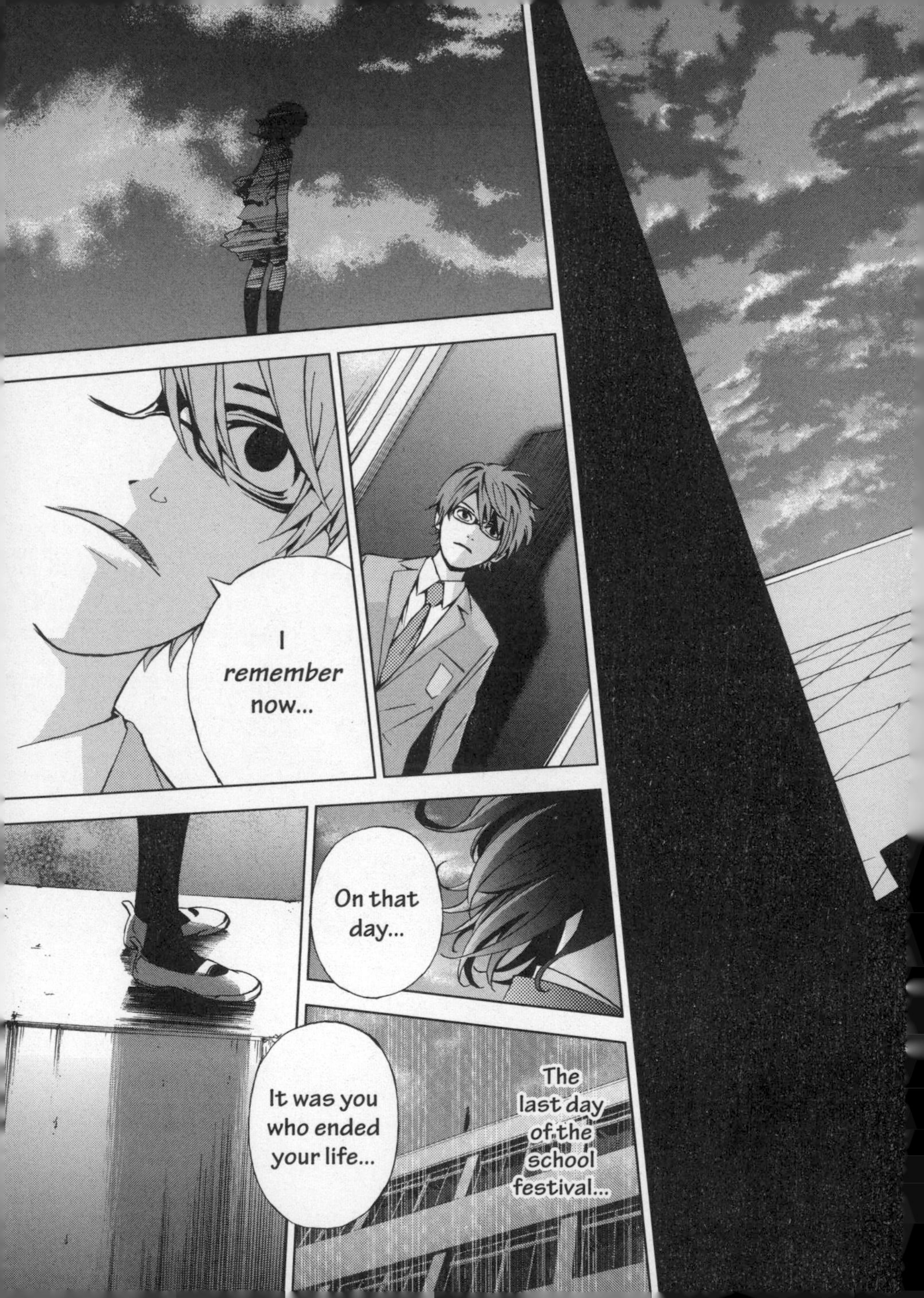
I remember now...
On that day...
The last day of the school festival...
It was you who ended your life...

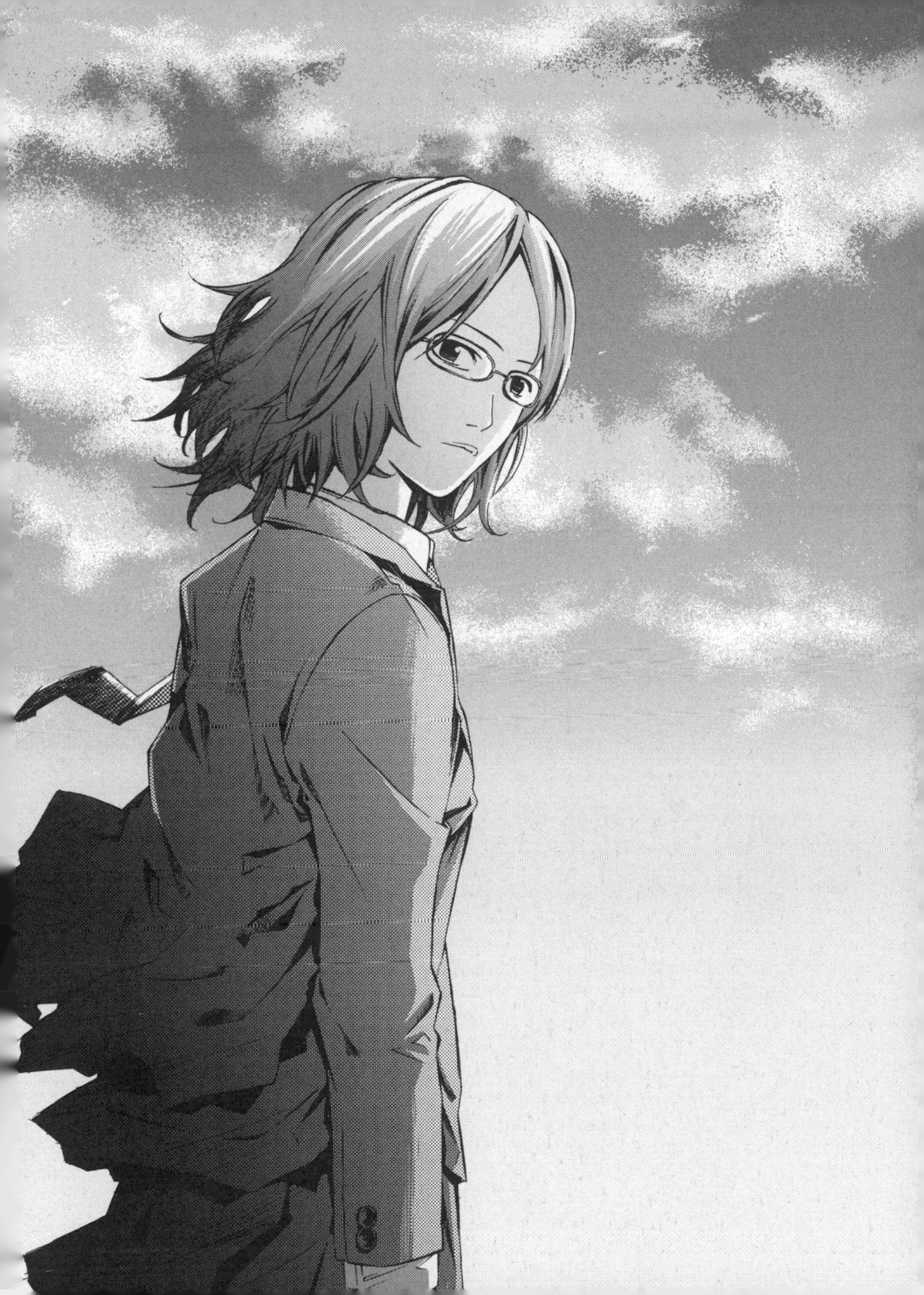

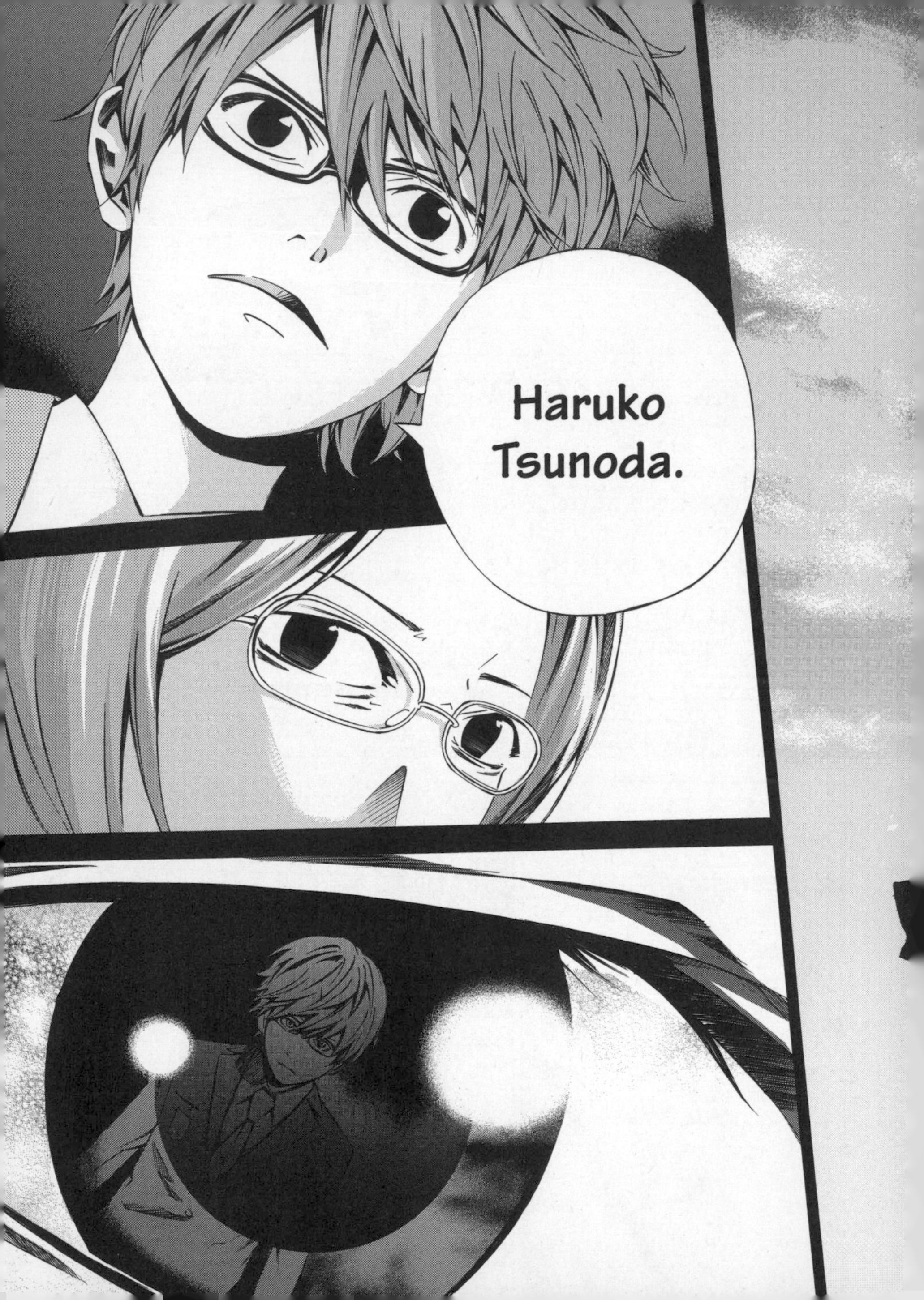
Haruko Tsunoda.

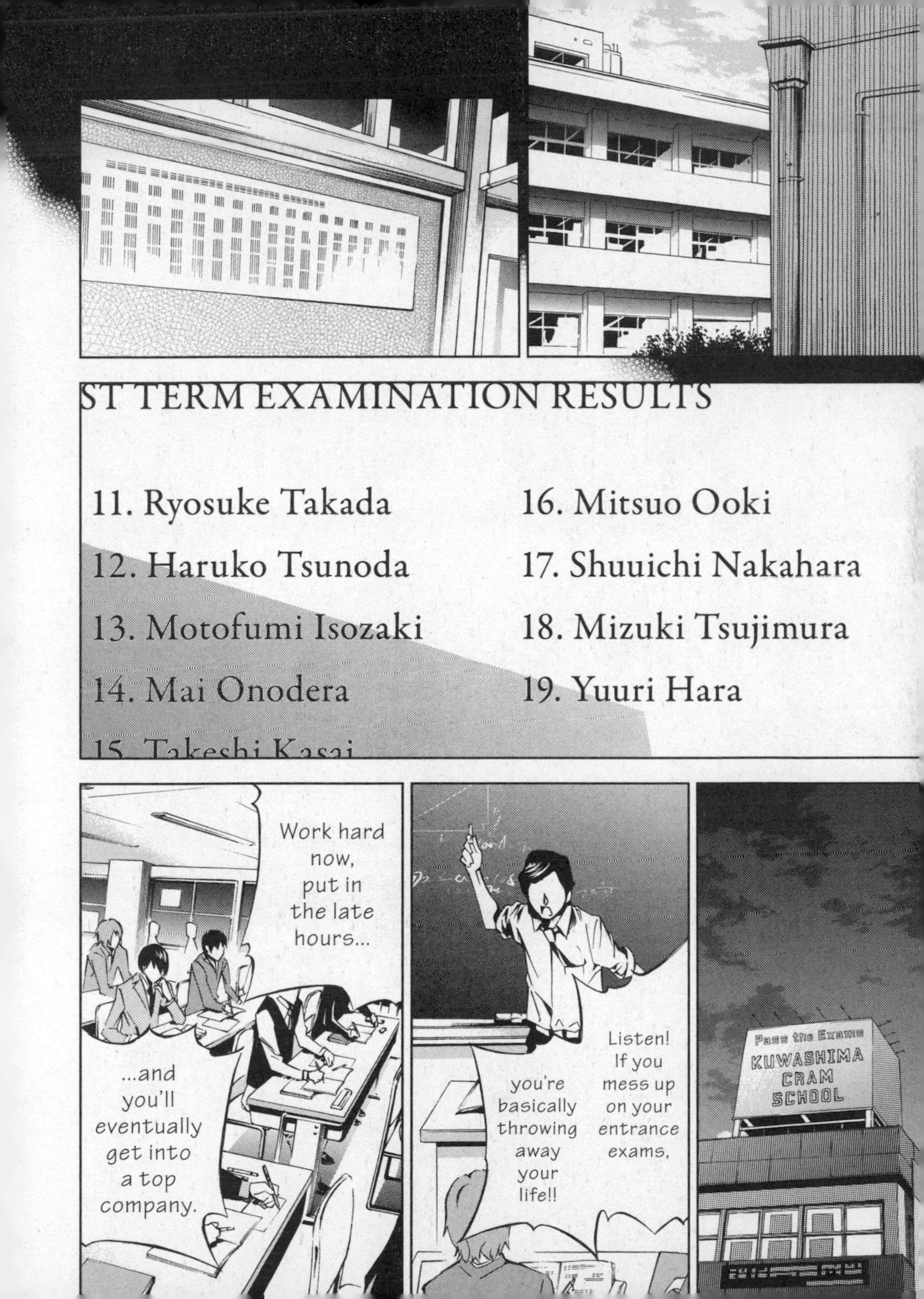
ST TERM EXAMINATION RESULTS
11. Ryosuke Takada
12. Haruko Tsunoda
13. Motofumi Isozaki
14. Mai Onodera
15. Takeshi Kasai
16. Mitsuo Ooki
17. Shuuichi Nakahara
18. Mizuki Tsujimura
19. Yuuri Hara
Pass the Exams
KUWASHIMA CRAM SCHOOL
Listen! If you mess up on your entrance exams,
you're basically throwing away your life!!
Work hard now, put in the late hours...
...and you'll eventually get into a top company.

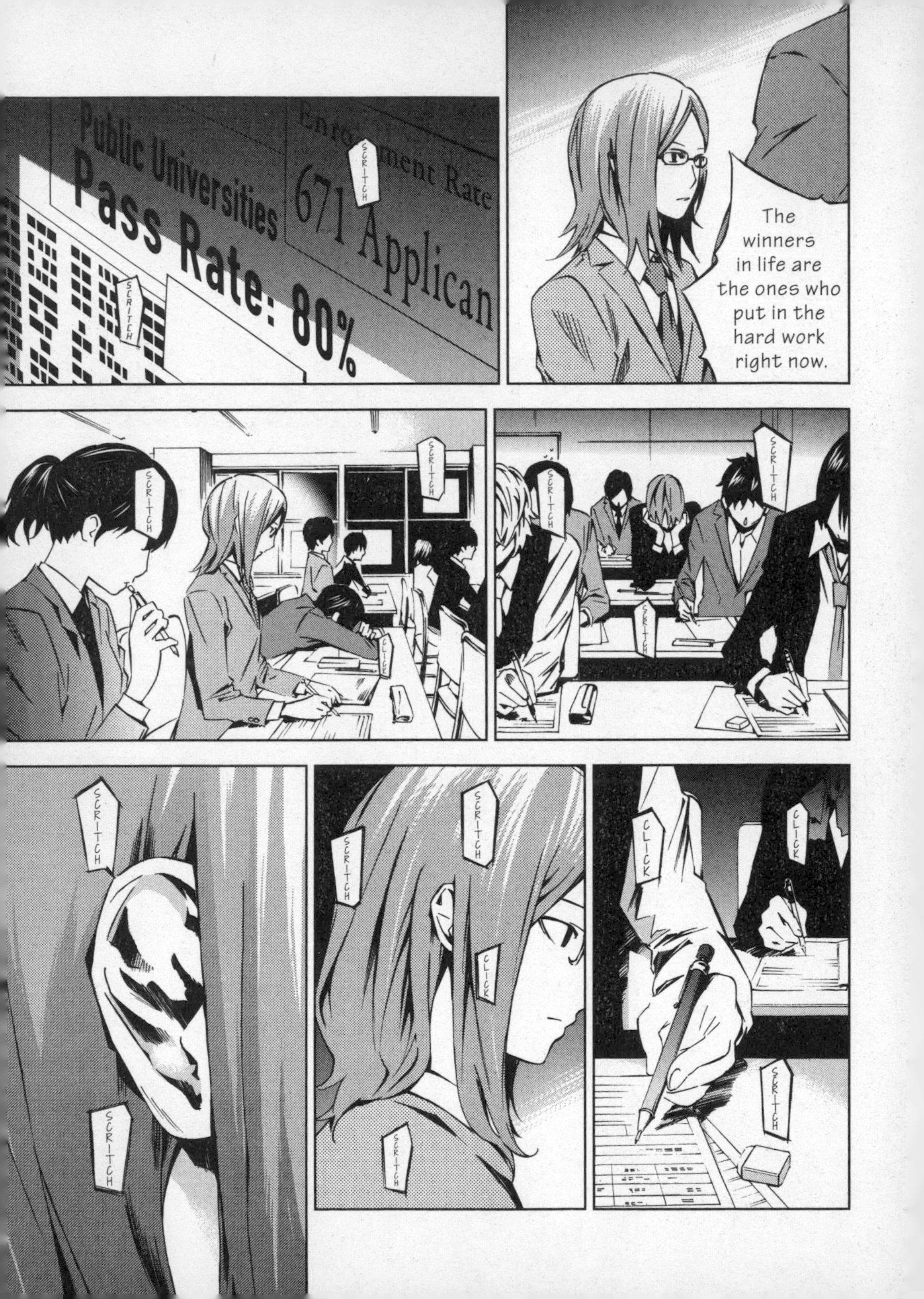

The winners in life are the ones who put in the hard work right now.
Enro
ment Rate
671 Applican
SCRITCH
Public Universities
Pass Rate: 80%
SCRITCH
SCRITCH
SCRITCH
SCRITCH
SCRITCH
SCRITCH
CLICK
CLICK
CLICK
SCRITCH
SCRITCH
SCRITCH
CLICK
SCRITCH
SCRITCH
SCRITCH

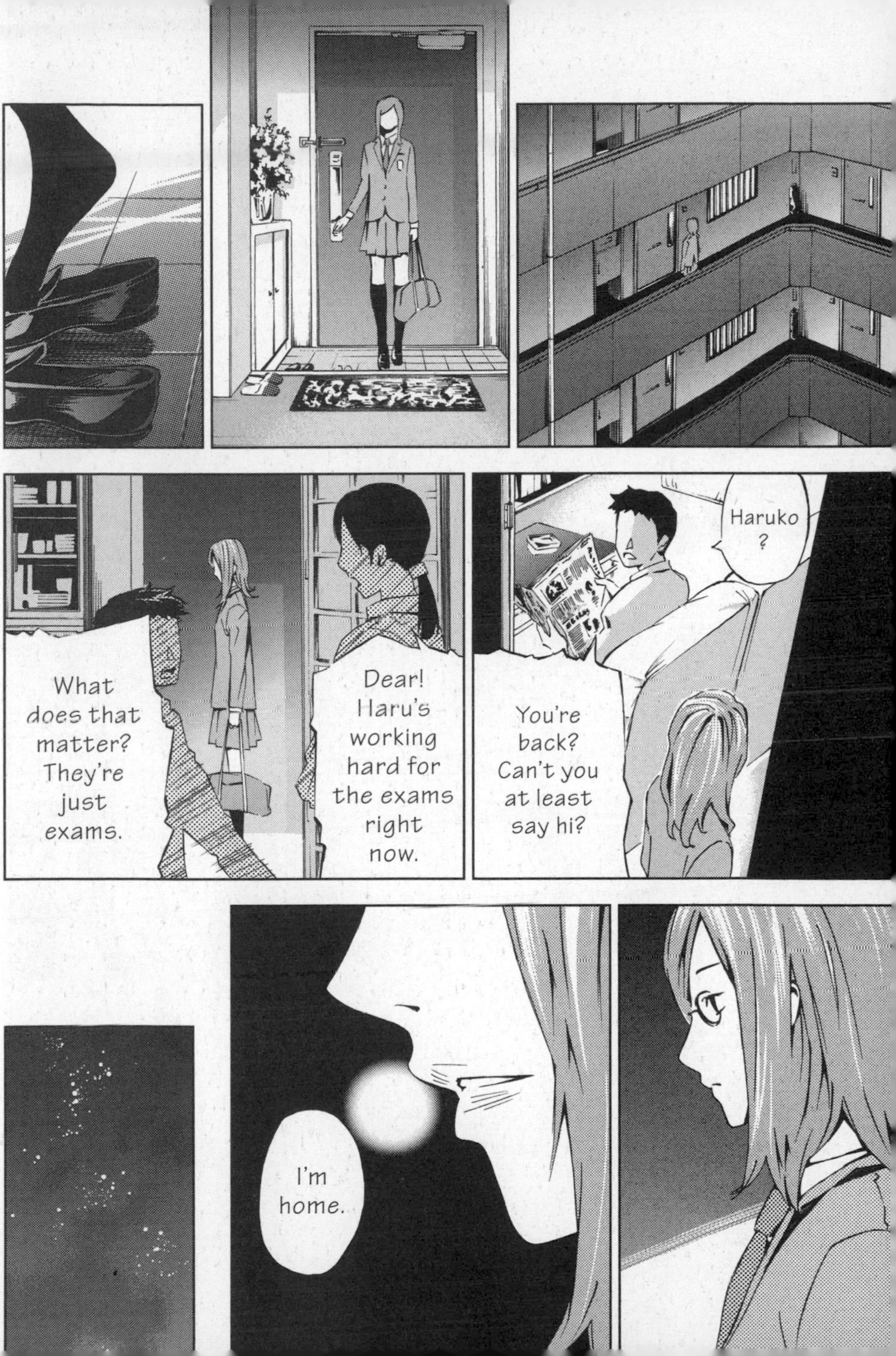
Haruko?
You're back? Can't you at least say hi?
Dear! Haru's working hard for the exams right now.
What does that matter? They're just exams.
I'm home.

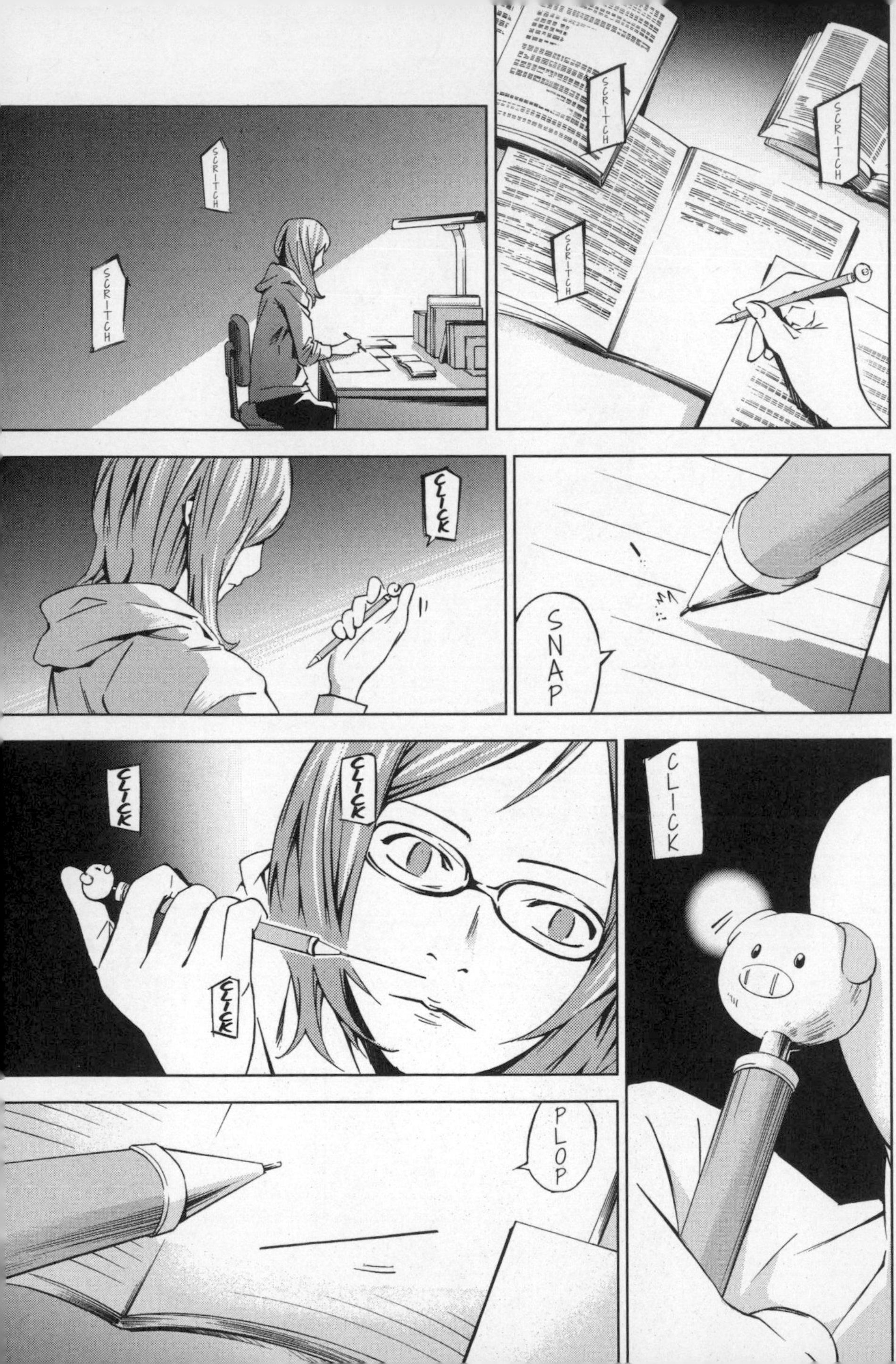
SCRITCH
SCRITCH
SCRITCH
SCRITCH
SCRITCH
SNAP
CLICK
CLICK
CLICK
CLICK
CLICK
PLOP

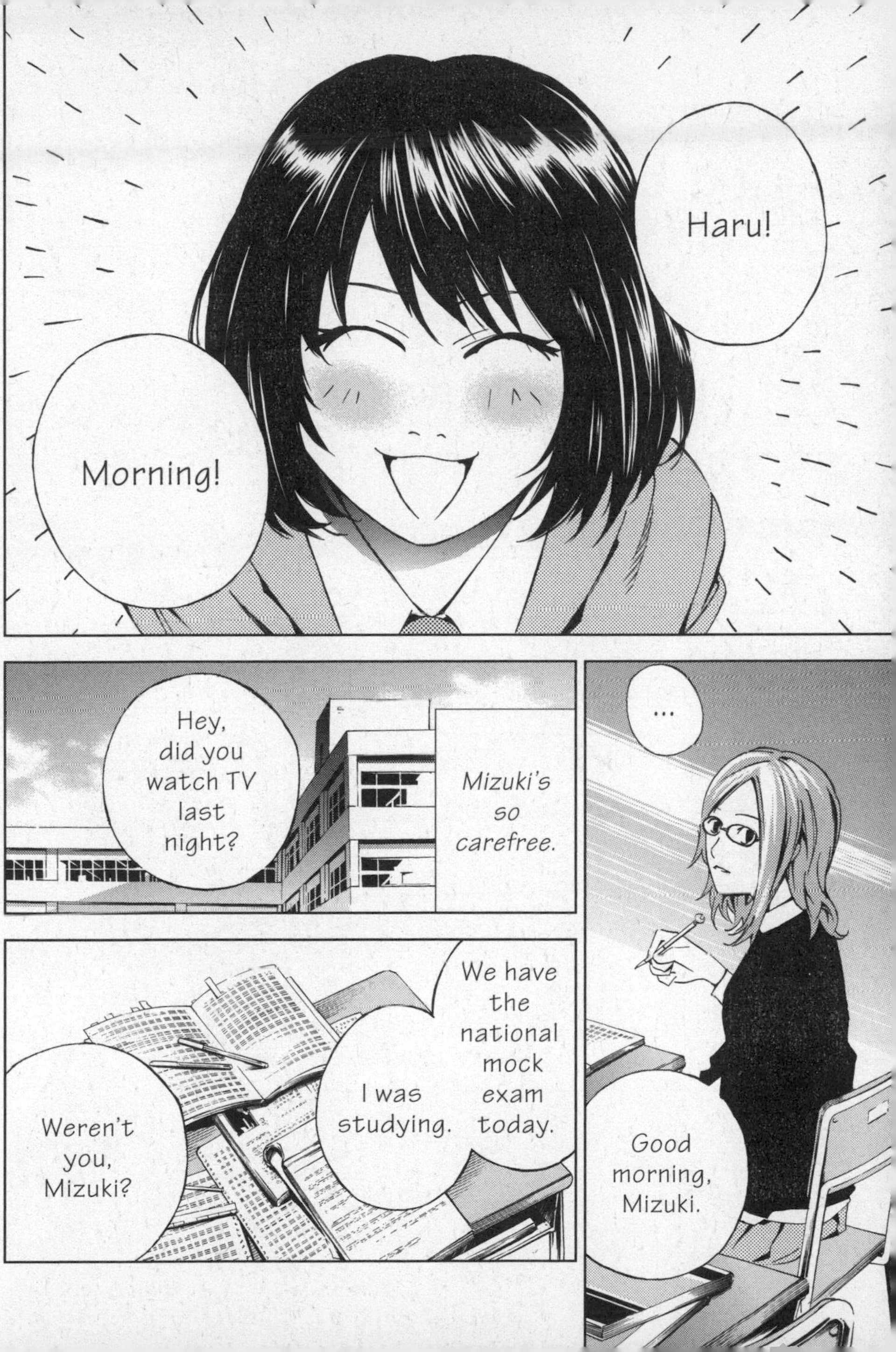

Haru!
Morning!
...
Good morning, Mizuki.
Mizuki's so carefree.
Hey, did you watch TV last night?
We have the national mock exam today.
I was studying.
Weren't you, Mizuki?

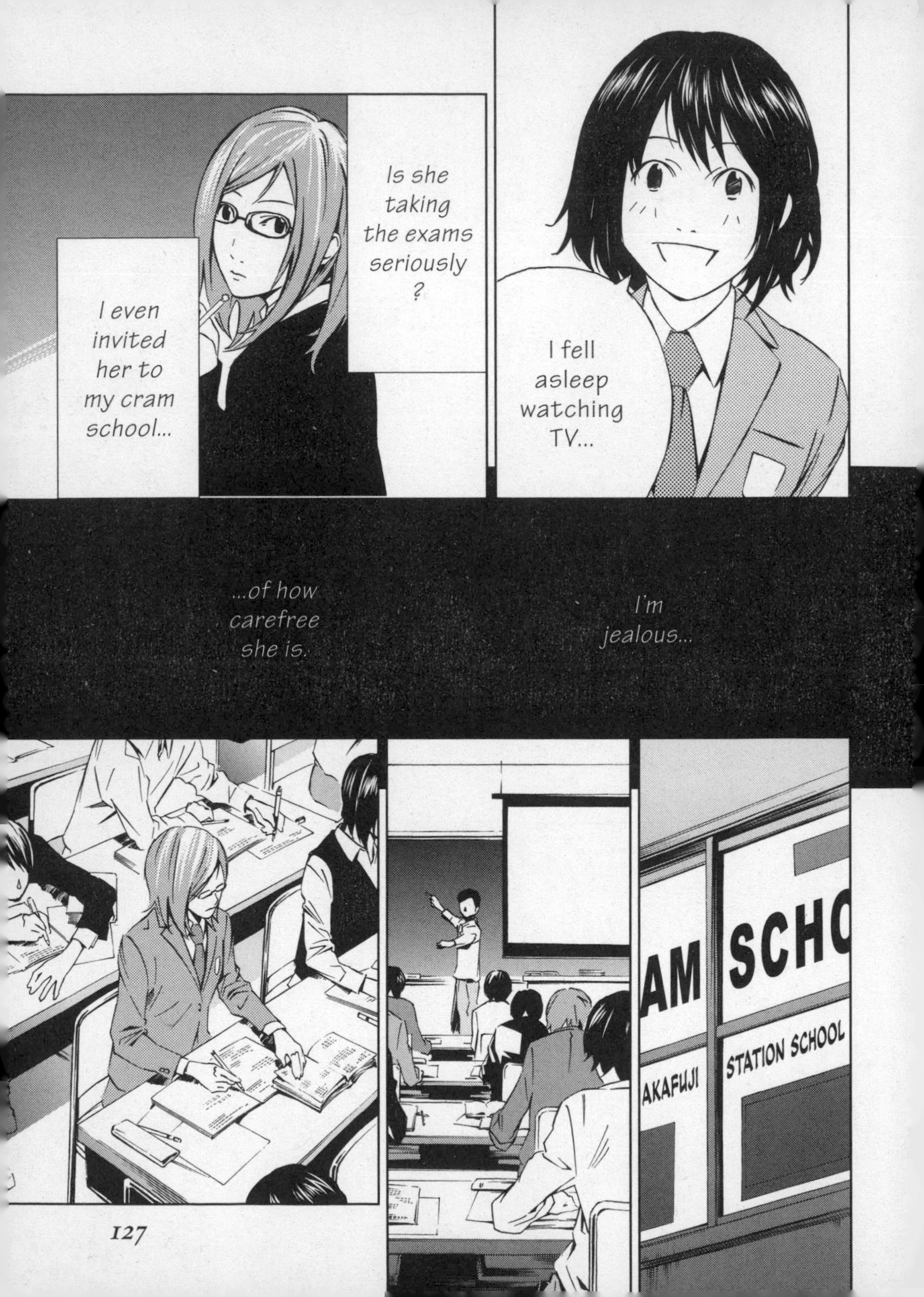
I fell asleep watching TV...
Is she taking the exams seriously?
I even invited her to my cram school...
I'm jealous...
...of how carefree she is.
AM SCHO
AKAFUJI
STATION SCHOOL

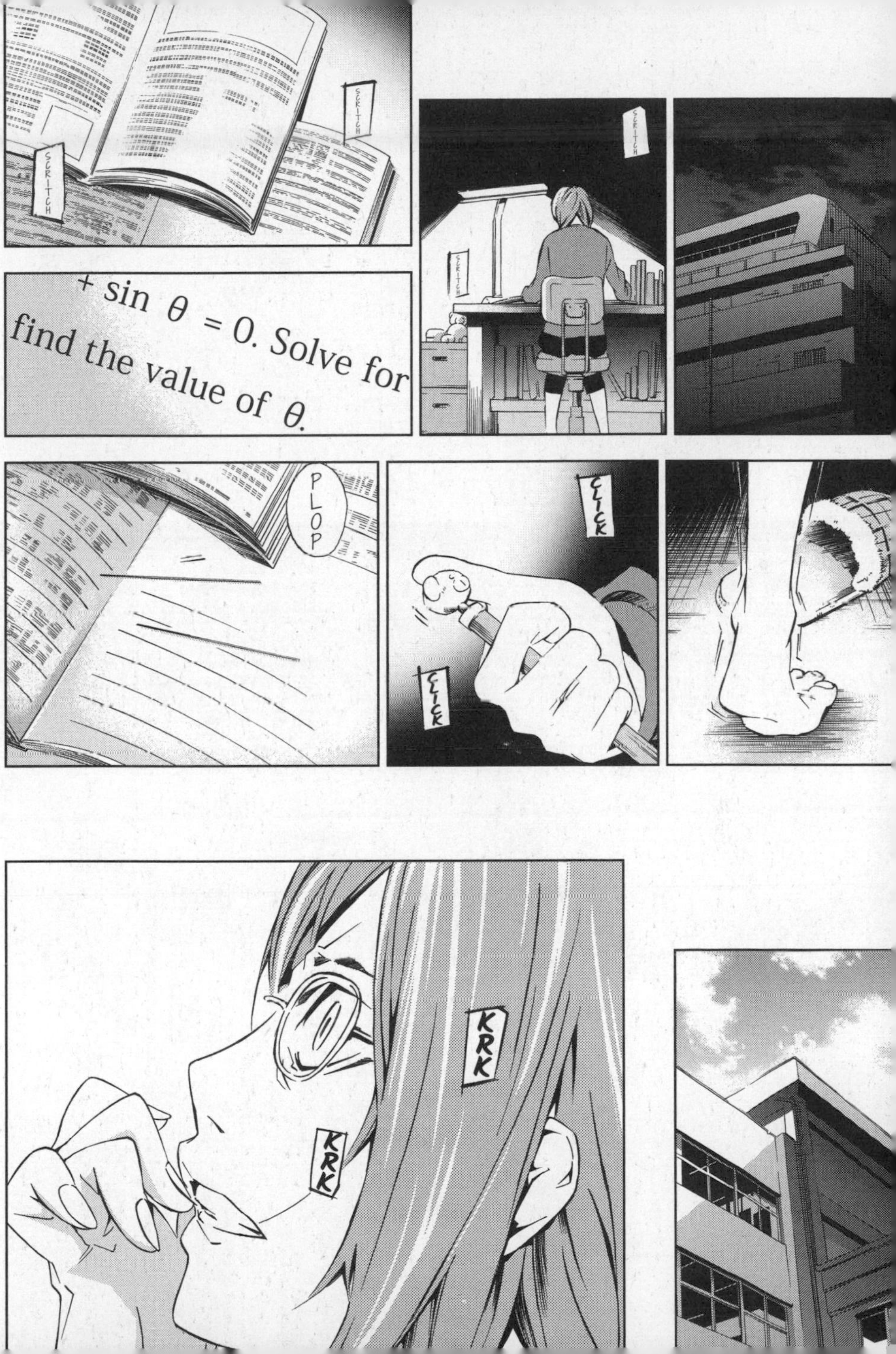
SCRITCH
SCRITCH
SCRITCH
SCRITCH
+ sin θ = 0. Solve for
find the value of θ.
CLICK
CLICK
PLOP
KRK
KRK

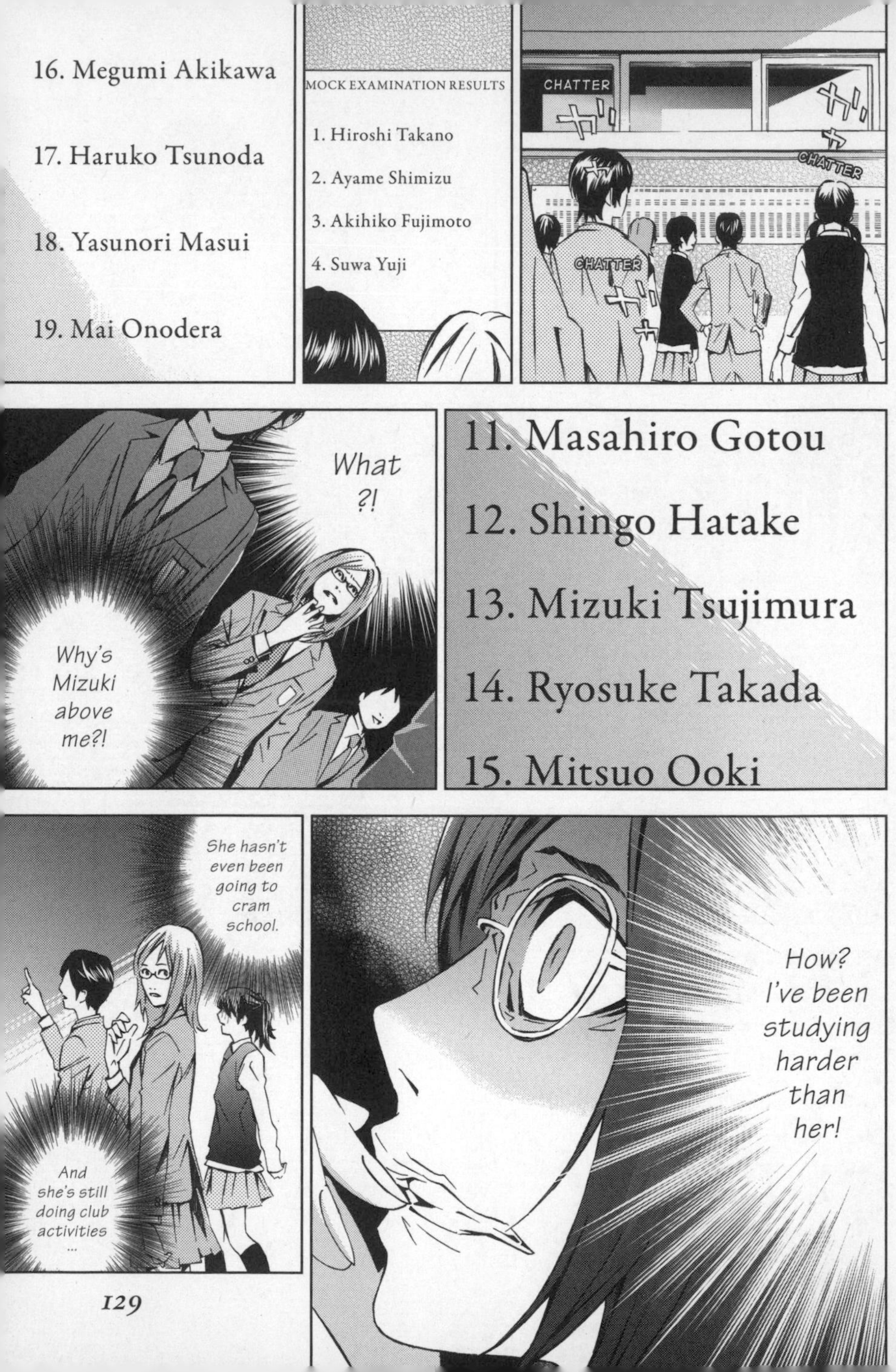
CHATTER
CHATTER
CHATTER
MOCK EXAMINATION RESULTS
1. Hiroshi Takano
2. Ayame Shimizu
3. Akihiko Fujimoto
4. Suwa Yuji
16. Megumi Akikawa
17. Haruko Tsunoda
18. Yasunori Masui
19. Mai Onodera
11. Masahiro Gotou
12. Shingo Hatake
13. Mizuki Tsujimura
14. Ryosuke Takada
15. Mitsuo Ooki
What ?!
Why's Mizuki above me?!
How? I've been studying harder than her!
She hasn't even been going to cram school.
And she's still doing club activities ...

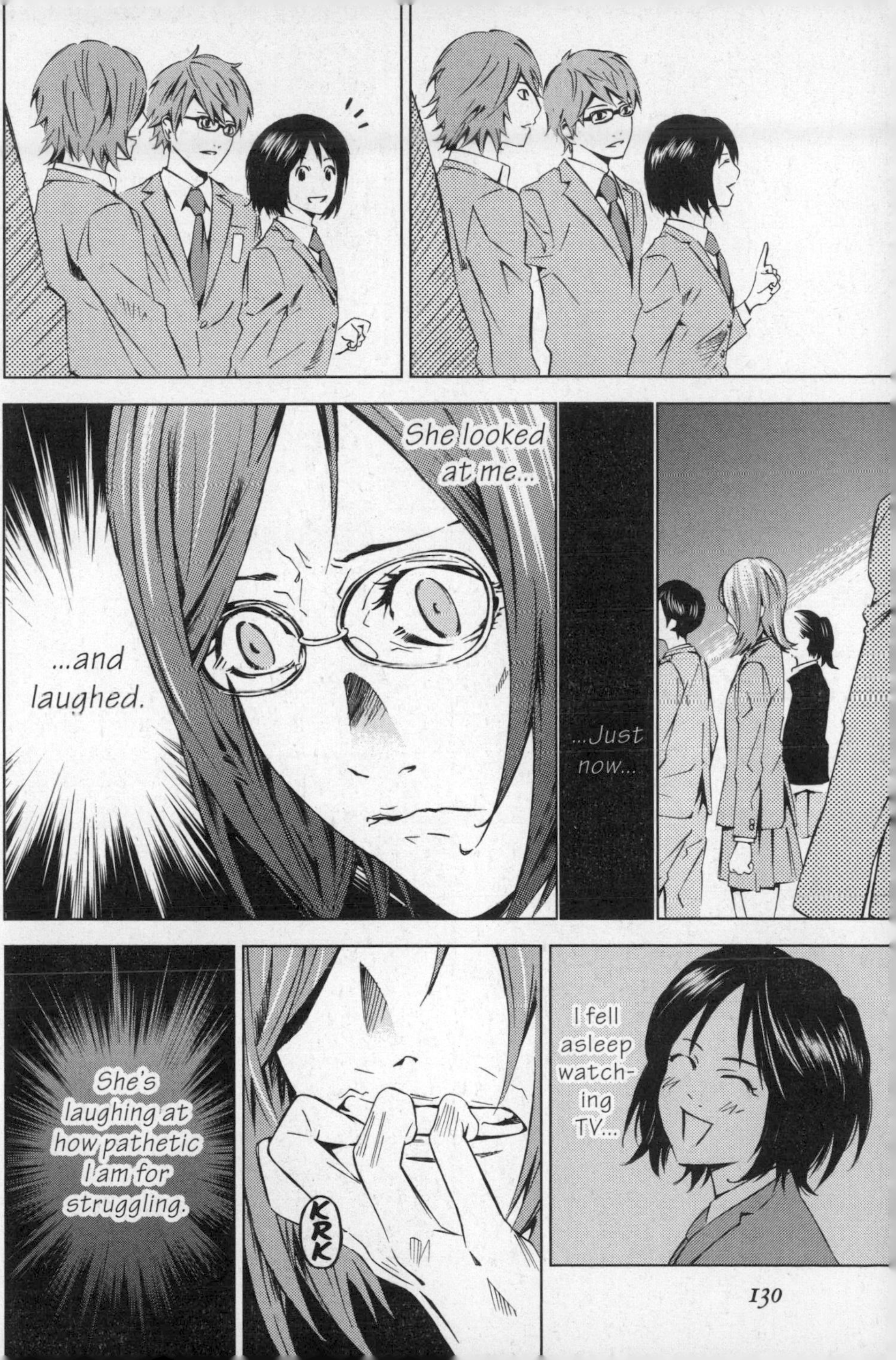
...Just now...
She looked at me...
...and laughed.
I fell asleep watching TV...
KRK
She's laughing at how pathetic I am for struggling.

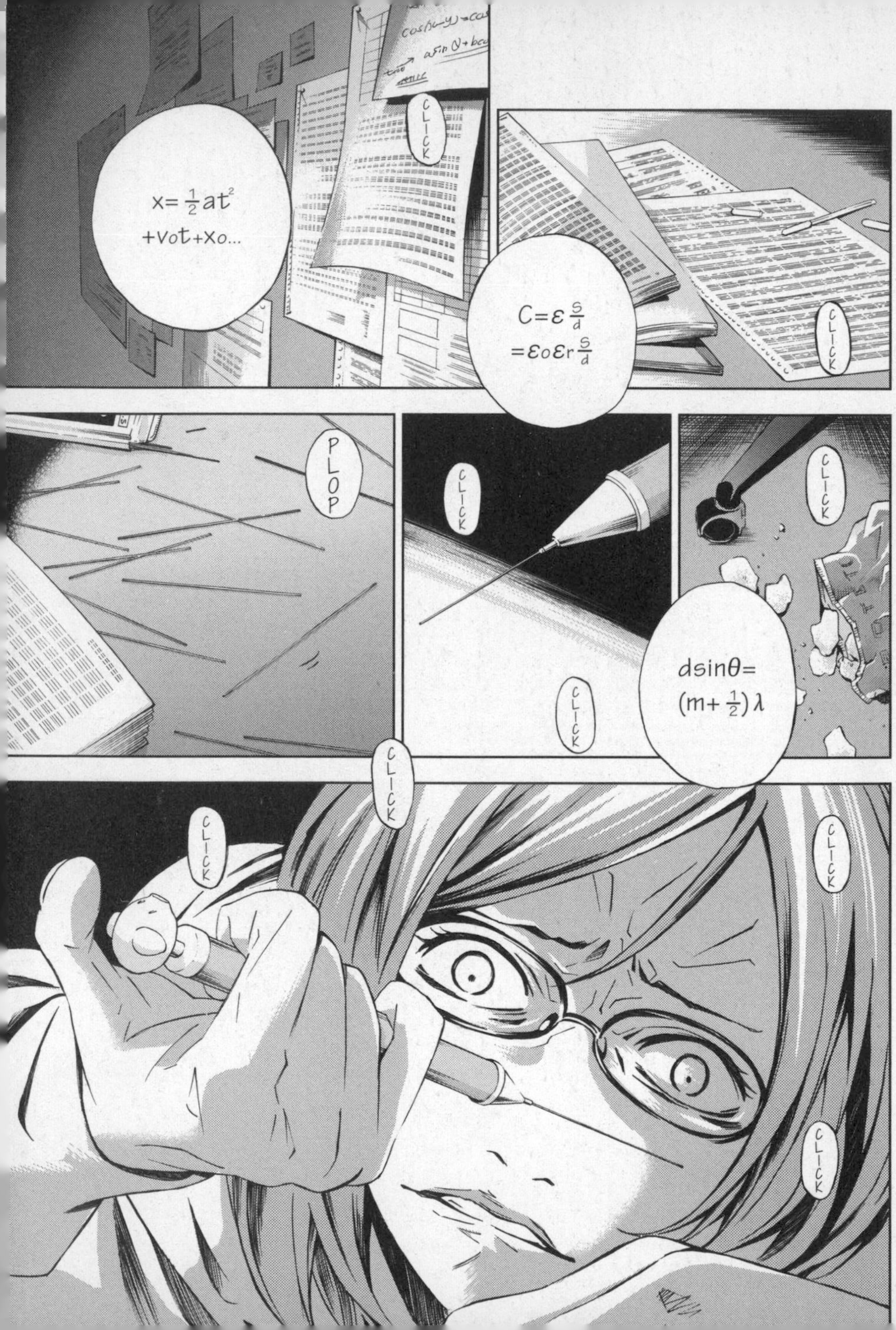

$C=\varepsilon\frac{S}{d}$ $=\varepsilon_0\varepsilon_r\frac{S}{d}$
CLICK
CLICK
$x=\frac{1}{2}at^2$ $+v_0t+x_0$...
CLICK
$d\sin\theta=$ $(m+\frac{1}{2})\lambda$
CLICK
CLICK
PLOP
CLICK
CLICK
CLICK
CLICK

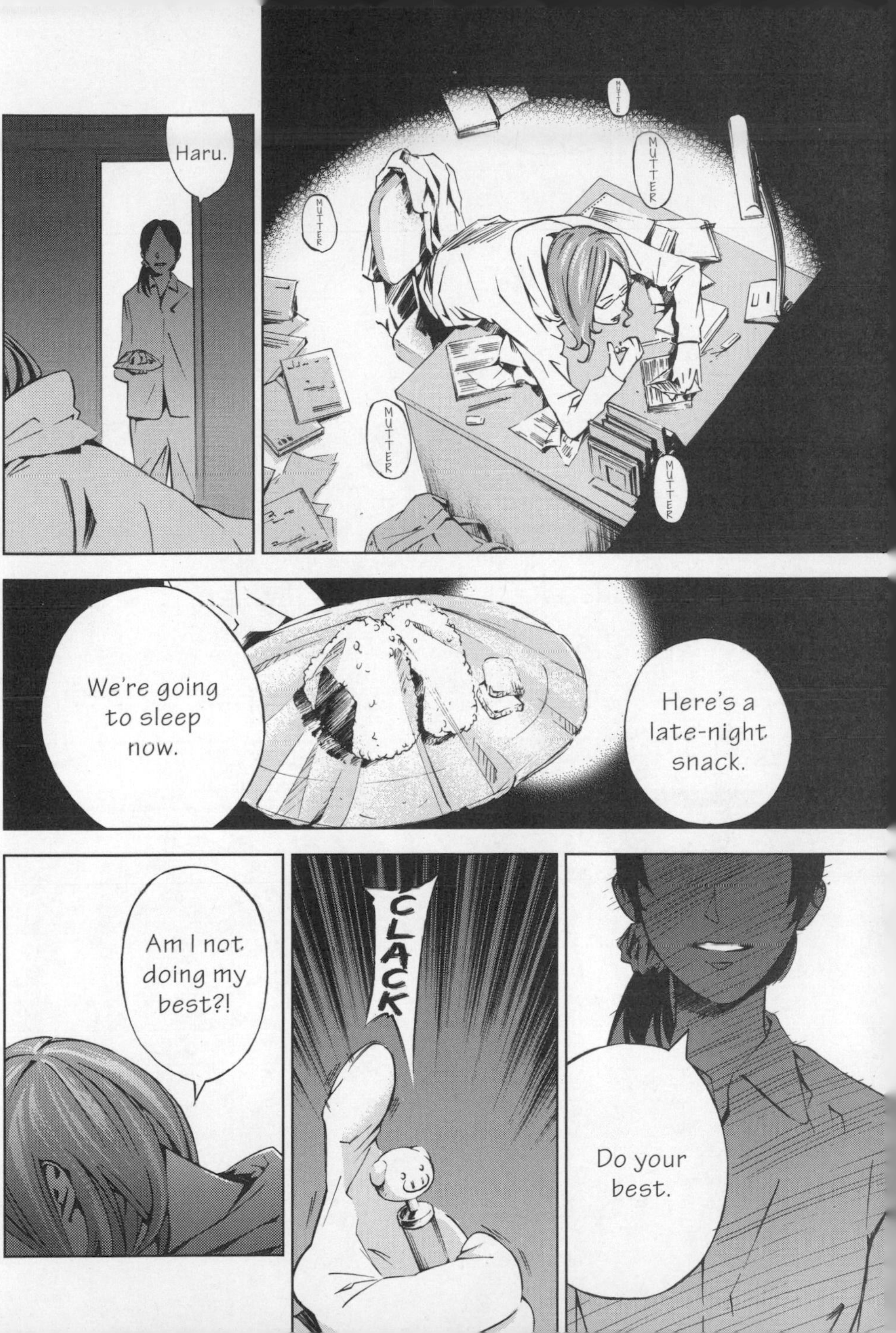
MUTTER
MUTTER
MUTTER
MUTTER
MUTTER
Haru.
Here's a late-night snack.
We're going to sleep now.
Do your best.
CLACK
Am I not doing my best?!

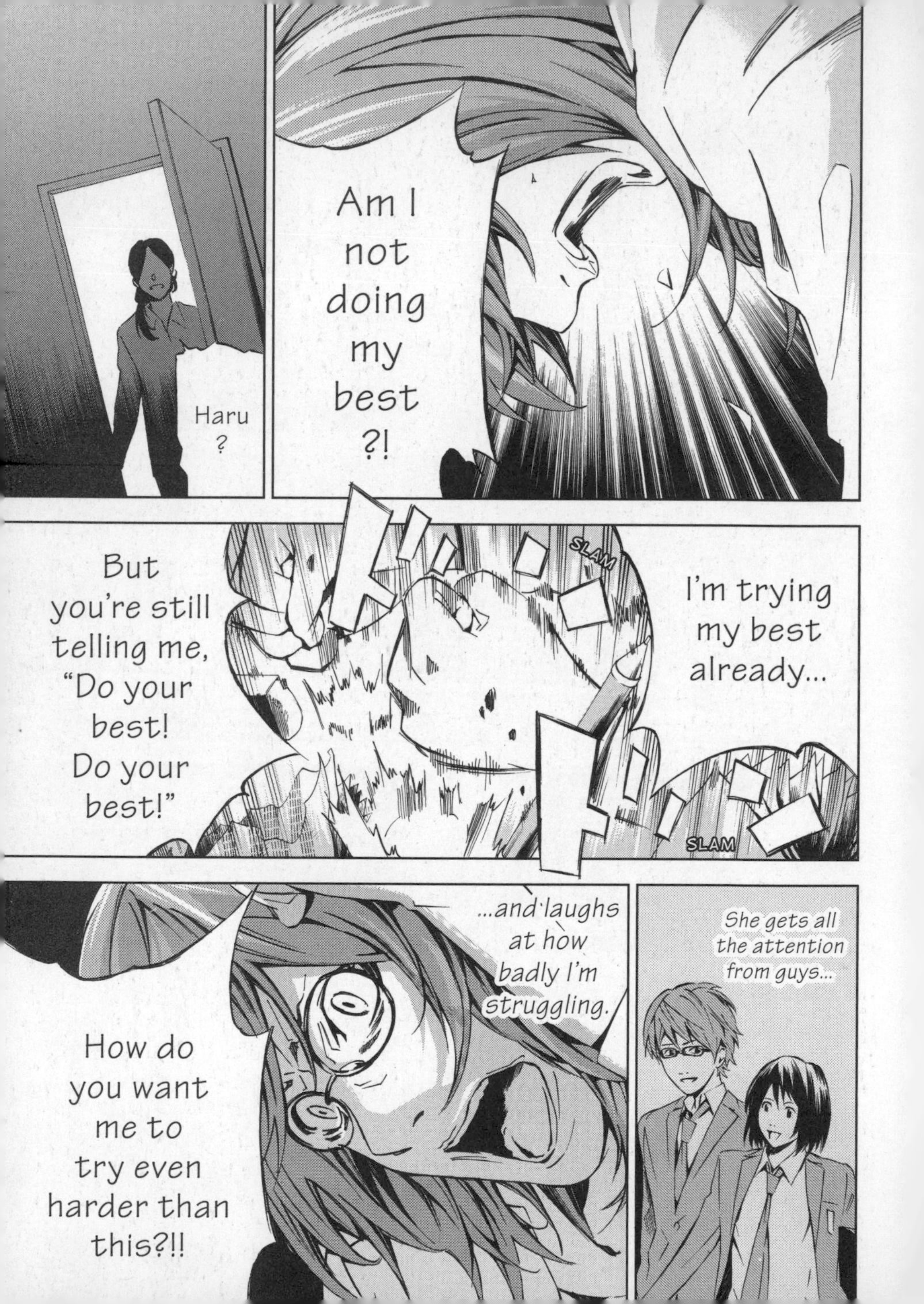
Am I not doing my best ?!
Haru ?
I'm trying my best already...
SLAM
But you're still telling me, "Do your best! Do your best!"
SLAM
She gets all the attention from guys...
...and laughs at how badly I'm struggling.
How do you want me to try even harder than this?!!

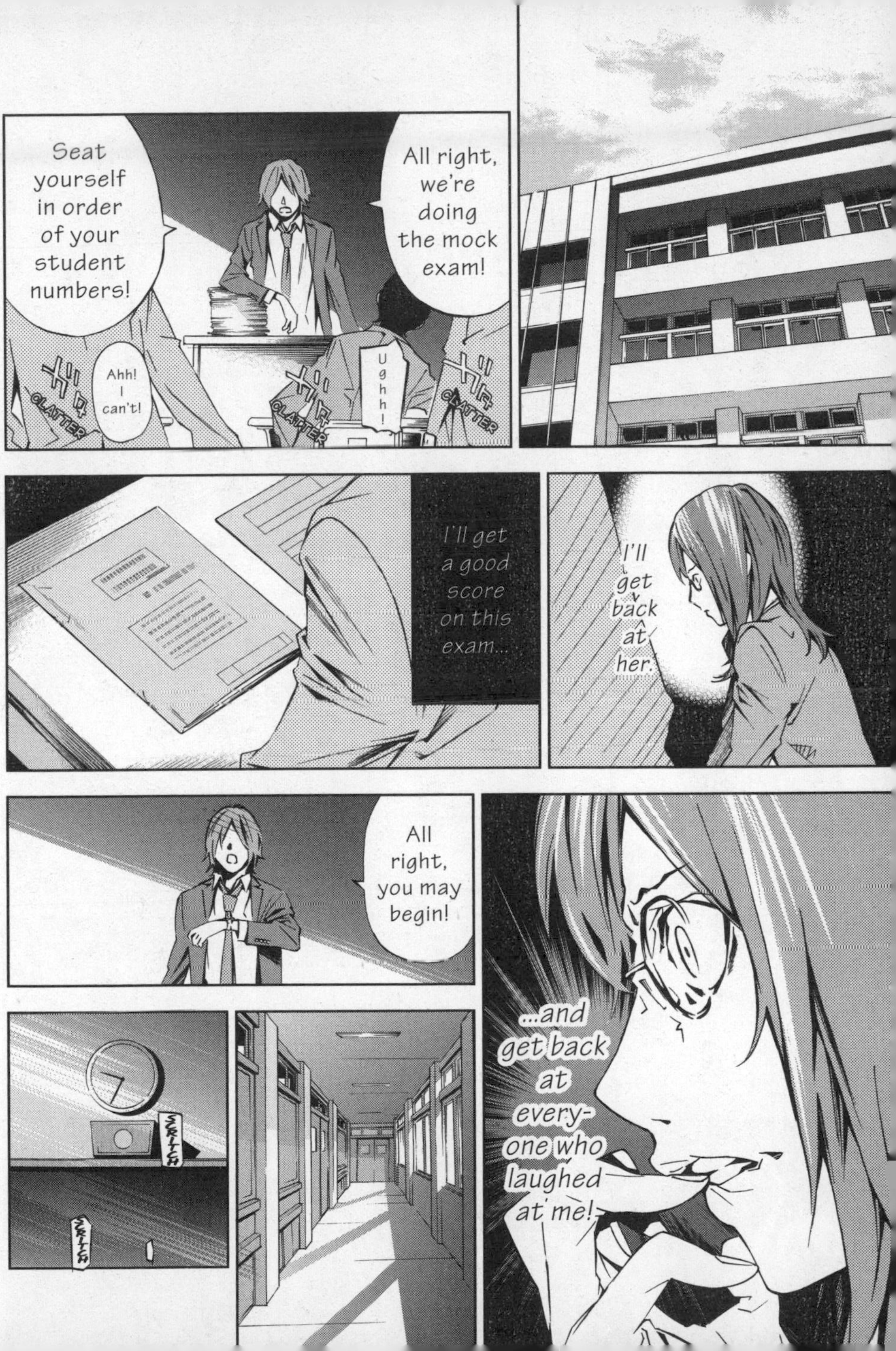
All right, we're doing the mock exam!
Seat yourself in order of your student numbers!
CLATTER
Ughhh!
CLATTER
Ahh! I can't!
CLATTER
I'll get back at her.
I'll get a good score on this exam...
...and get back at everyone who laughed at me!
All right, you may begin!
SKRITCH
SKRITCH

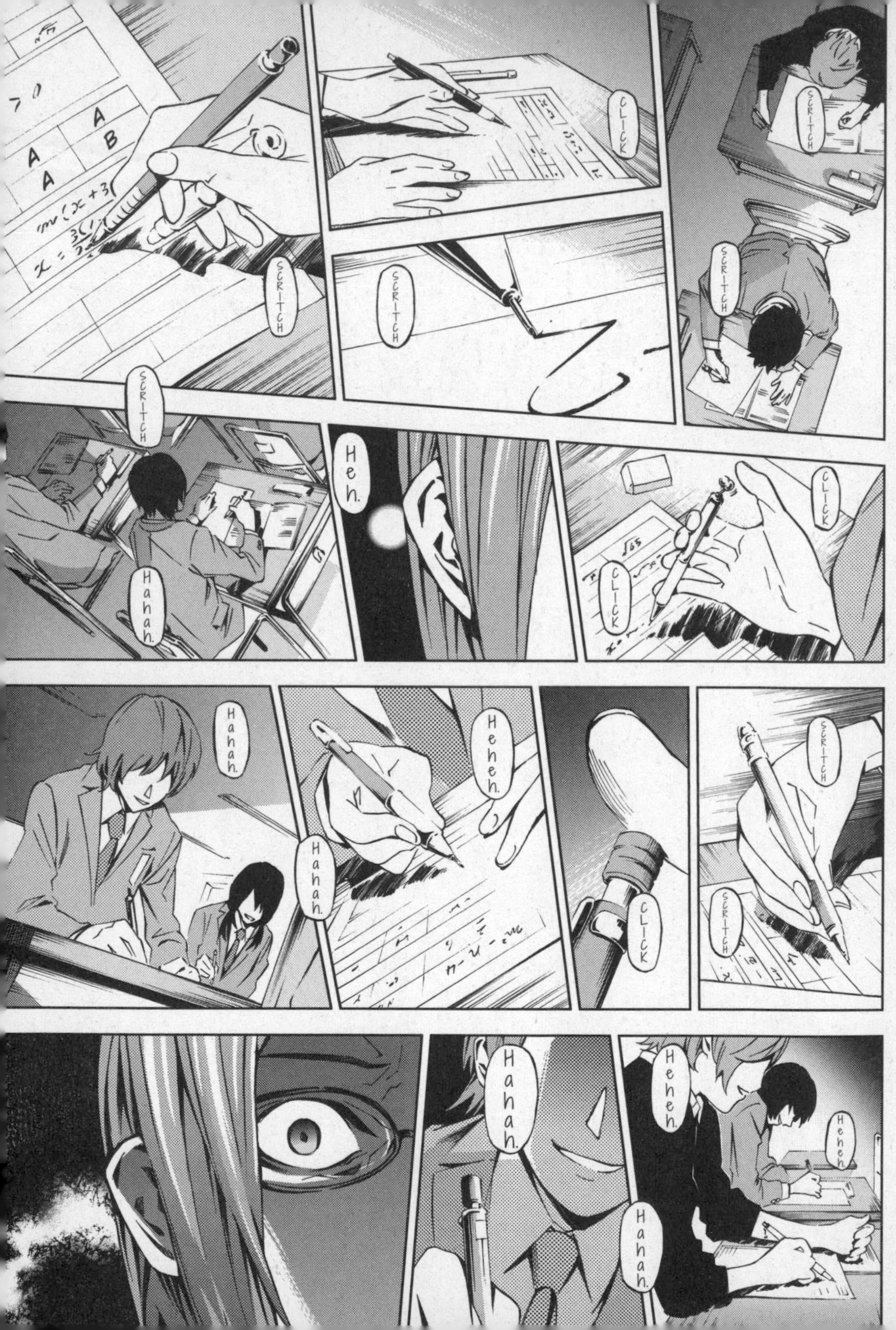
SCRITCH
SCRITCH
CLICK
SCRITCH
SCRITCH
CLICK
CLICK
Heh.
SCRITCH
Hahah.
SCRITCH
SCRITCH
CLICK
Heheh.
Hahah.
Hahah.
Heheh.
Heheh
Hahah.
Hahah.

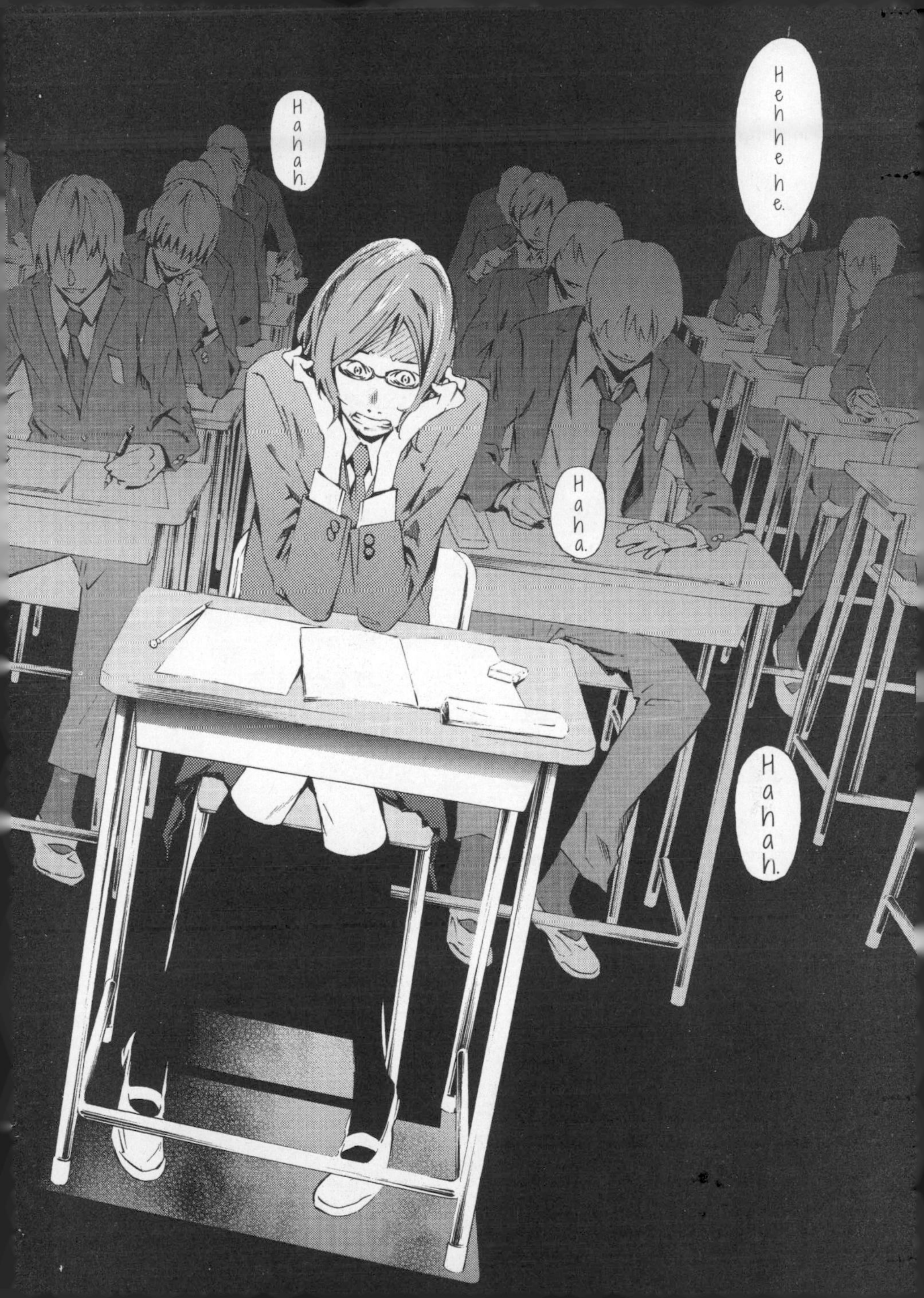
Hehhehe.
Hahah.
Haha.
Hahah.

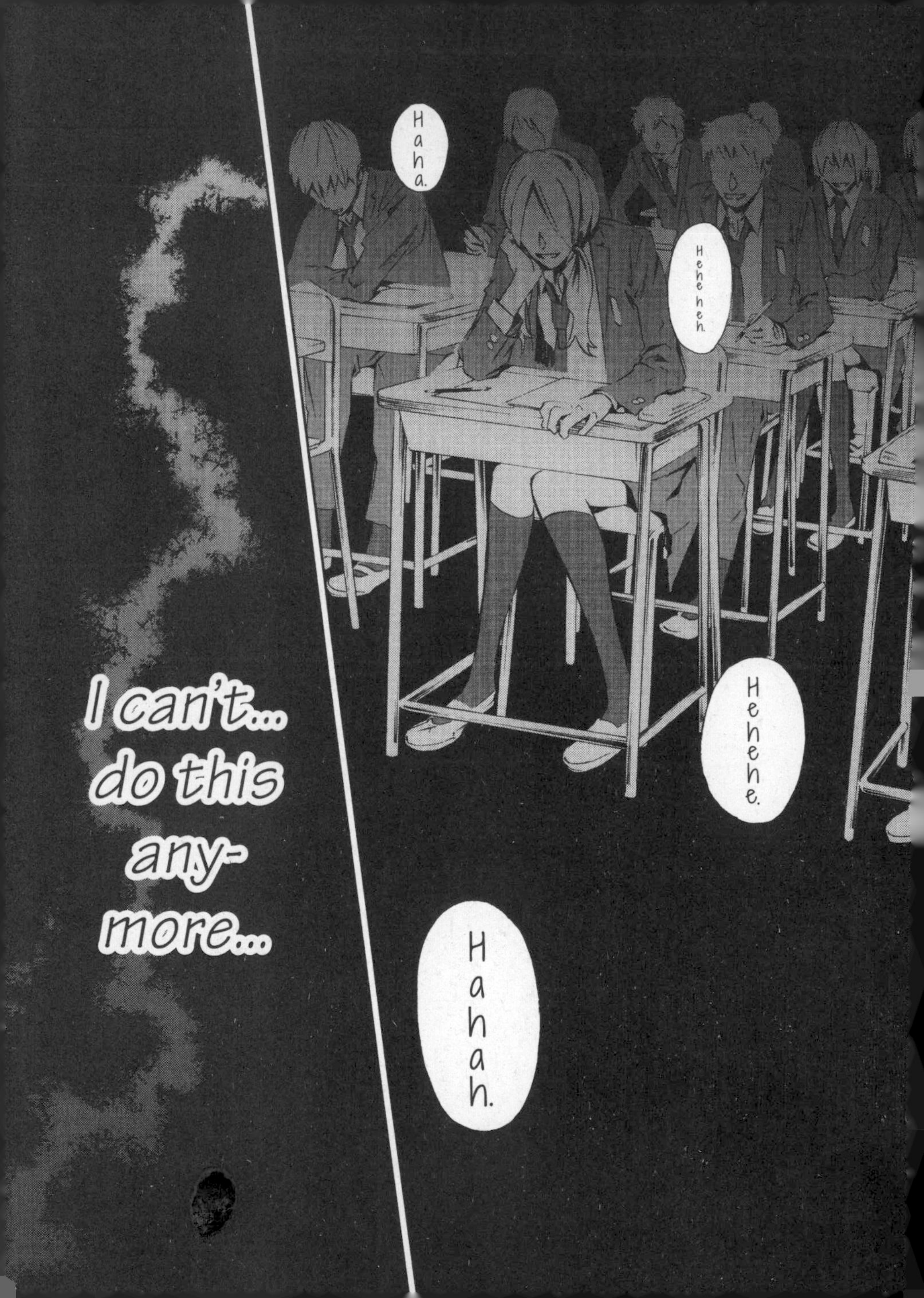
Haha.
Hehe heh.
Hehehe.
Hahah.
I can't... do this any-more...

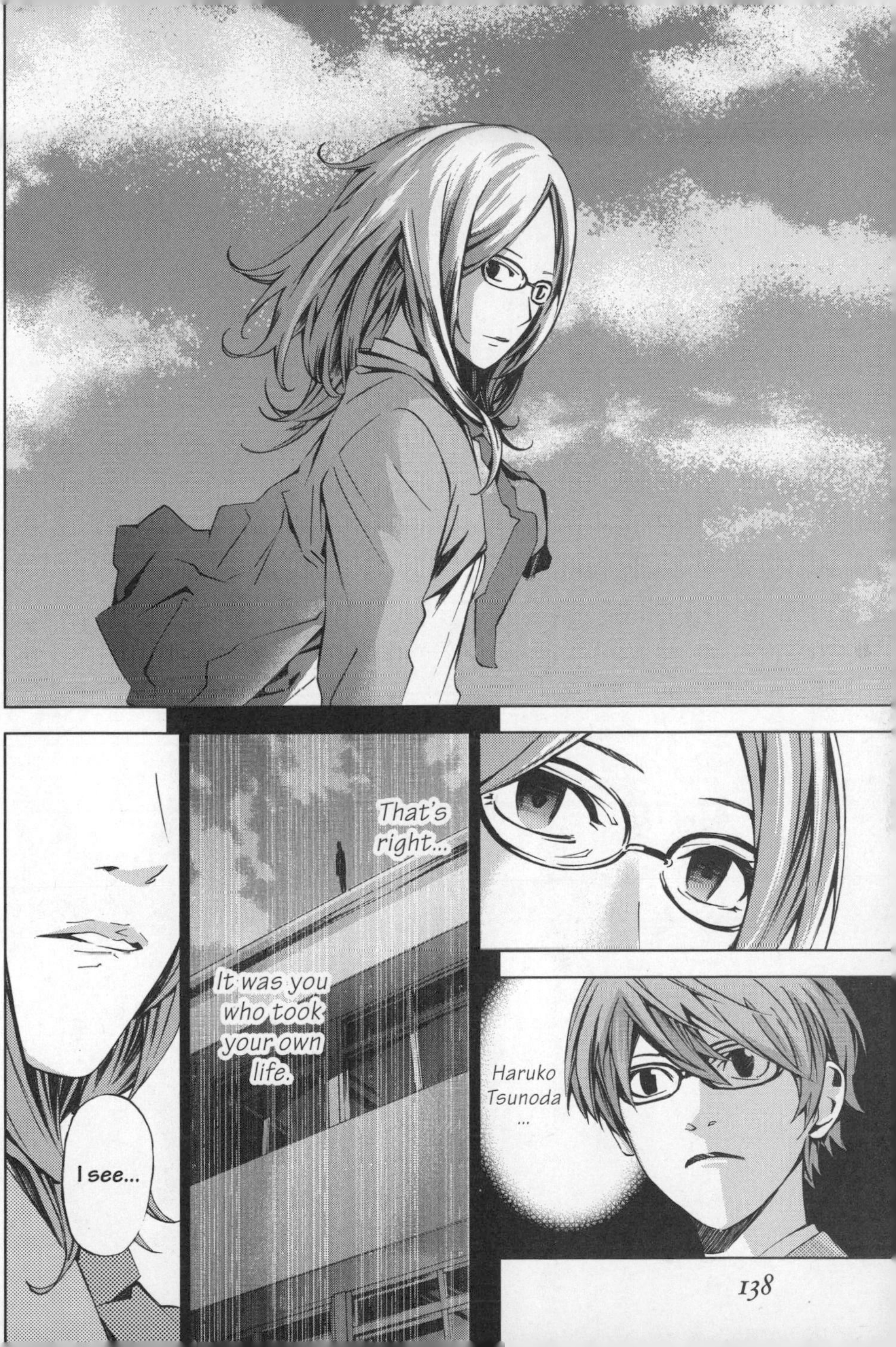
Haruko Tsunoda ...
That's right...
It was you who took your own life.
I see...

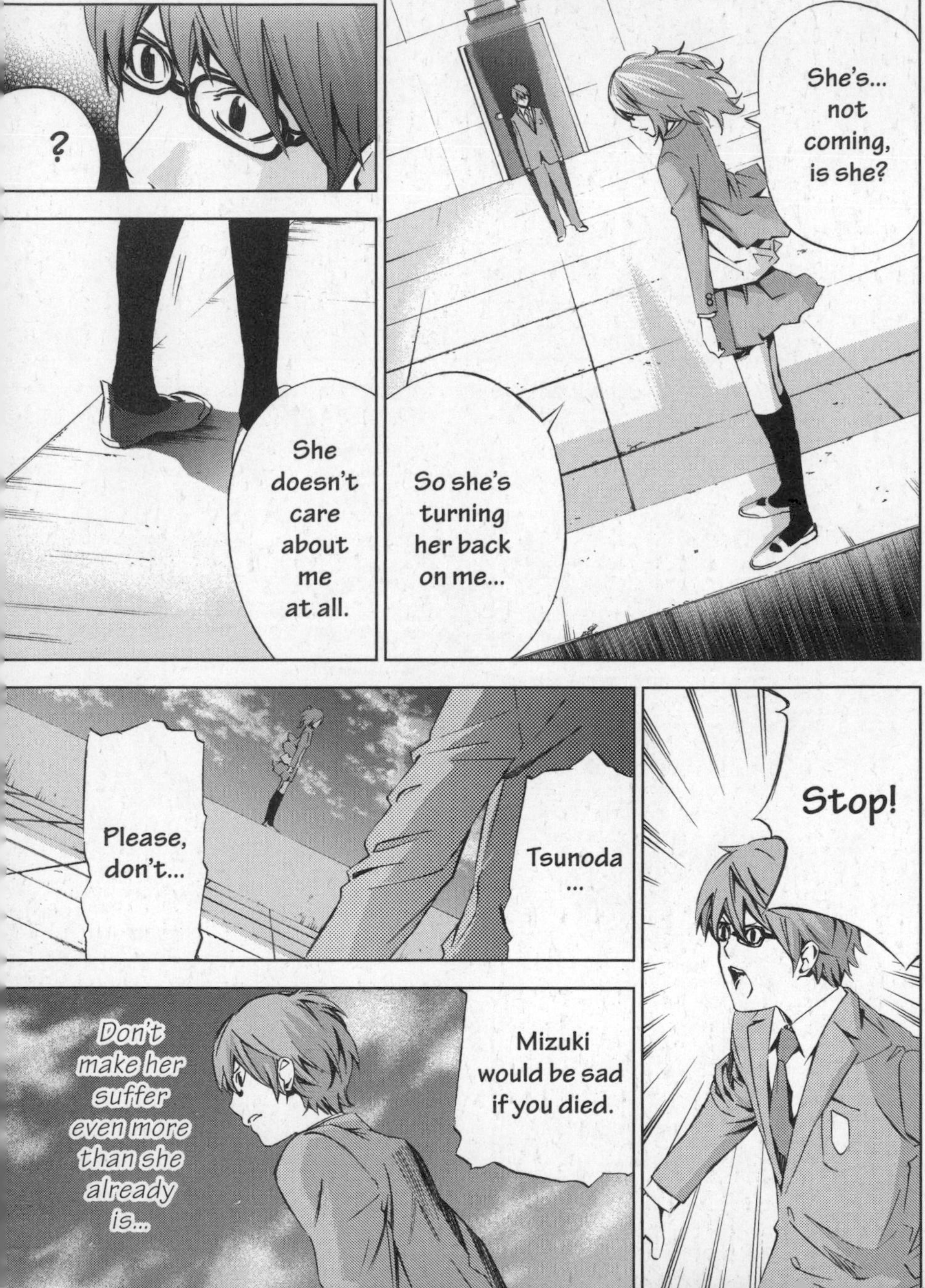

She's... not coming, is she?
So she's turning her back on me...
?
She doesn't care about me at all.
Stop!
Tsunoda...
Please, don't...
Mizuki would be sad if you died.
Don't make her suffer even more than she already is...

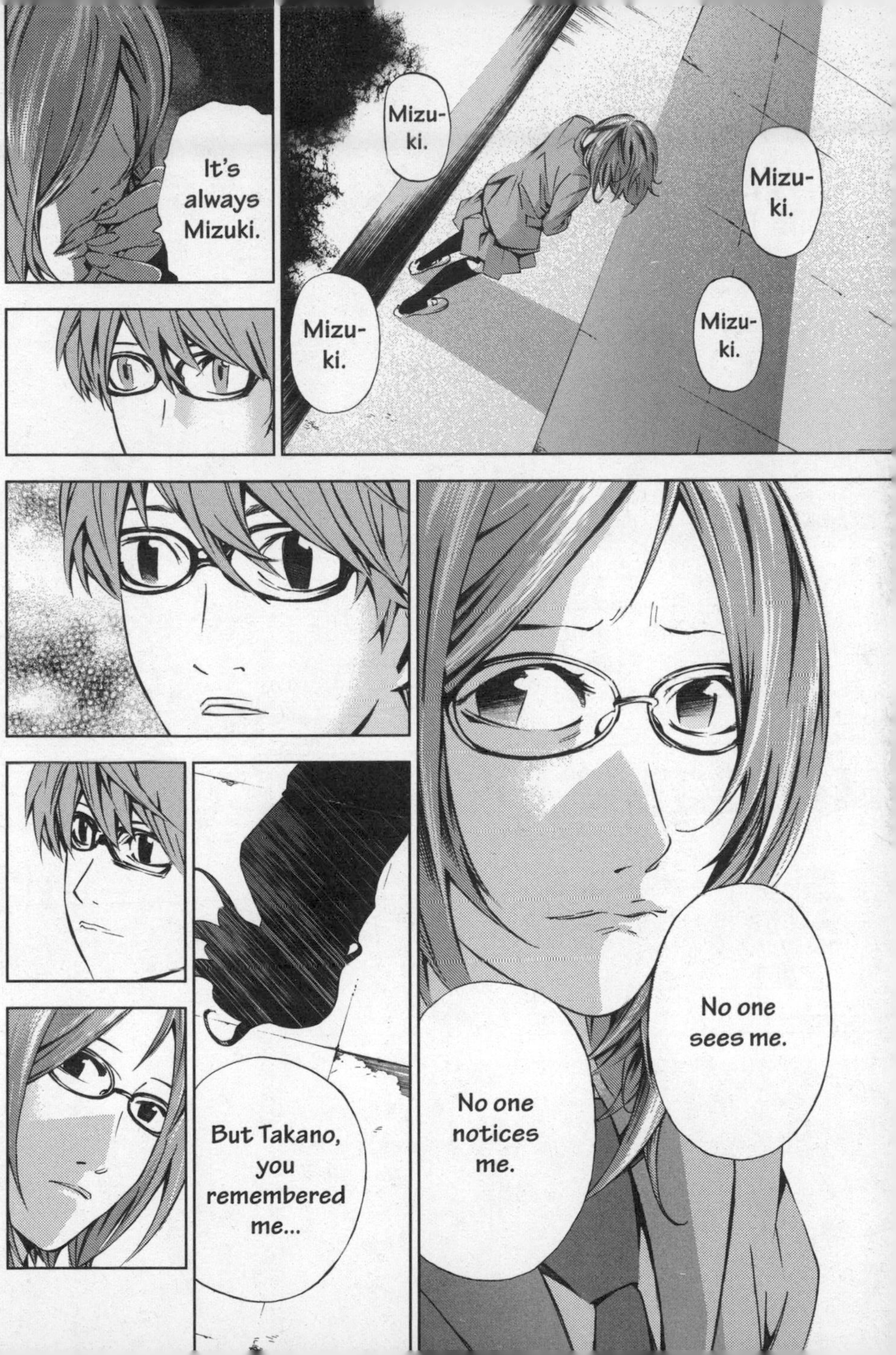

Mizu-ki.
Mizu-ki.
Mizu-ki.
Mizu-ki.
It's always Mizuki.
No one sees me.
No one notices me.
But Takano, you remembered me...

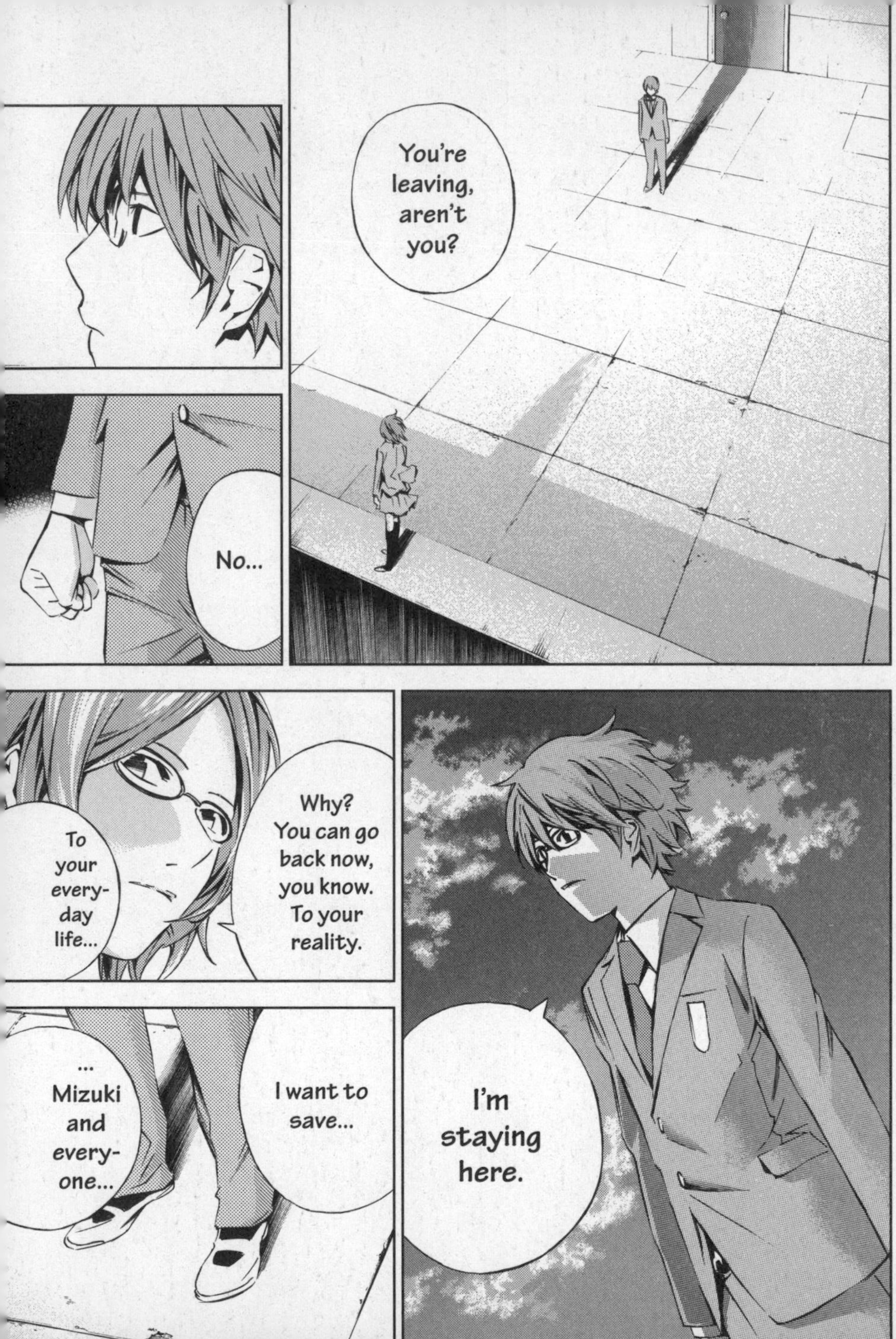
You're leaving, aren't you?
No...
I'm staying here.
Why? You can go back now, you know. To your reality.
To your every-day life...
I want to save...
... Mizuki and every-one...

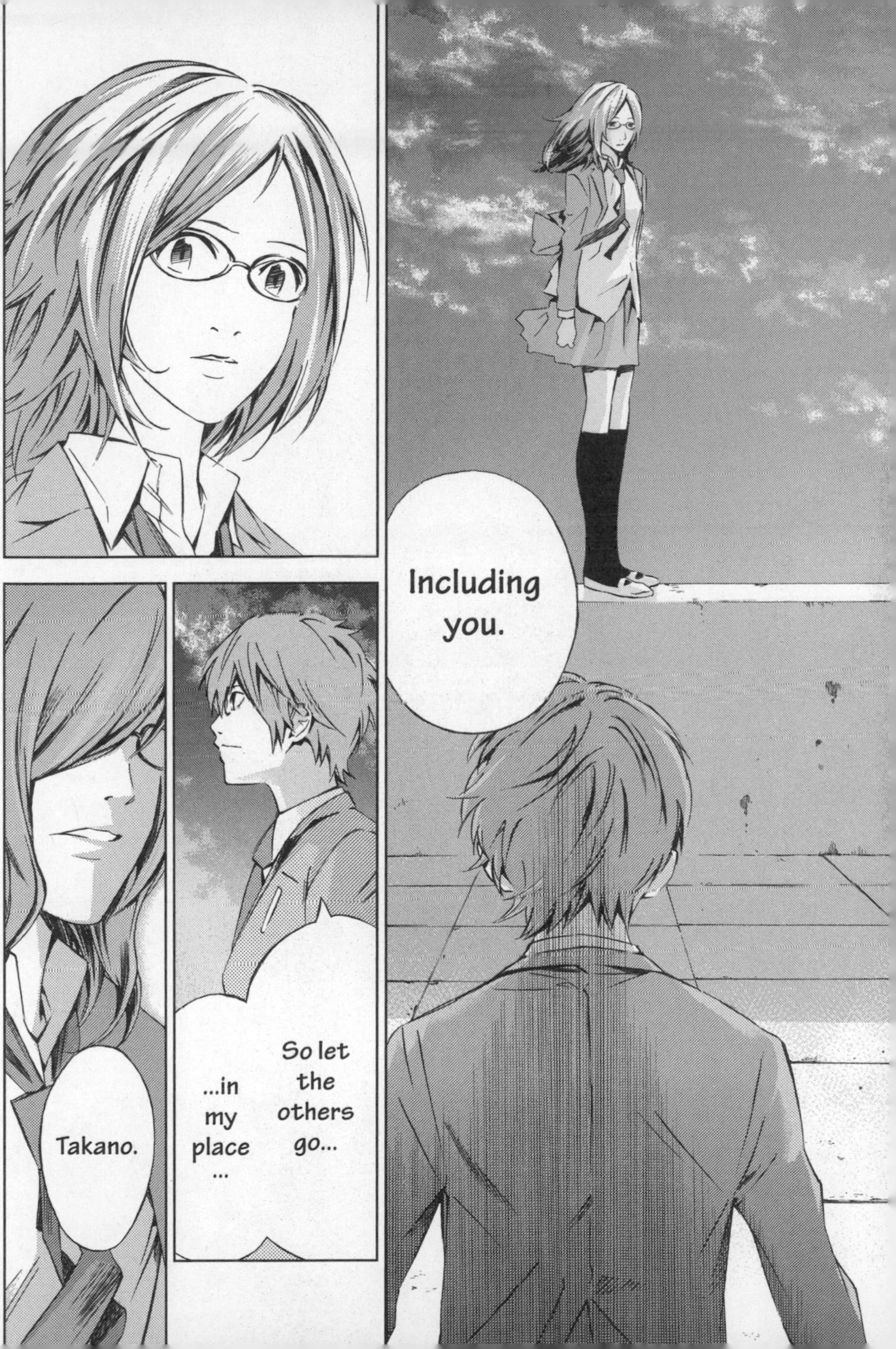
Including you.
So let the others go...
...in my place ...
Takano.

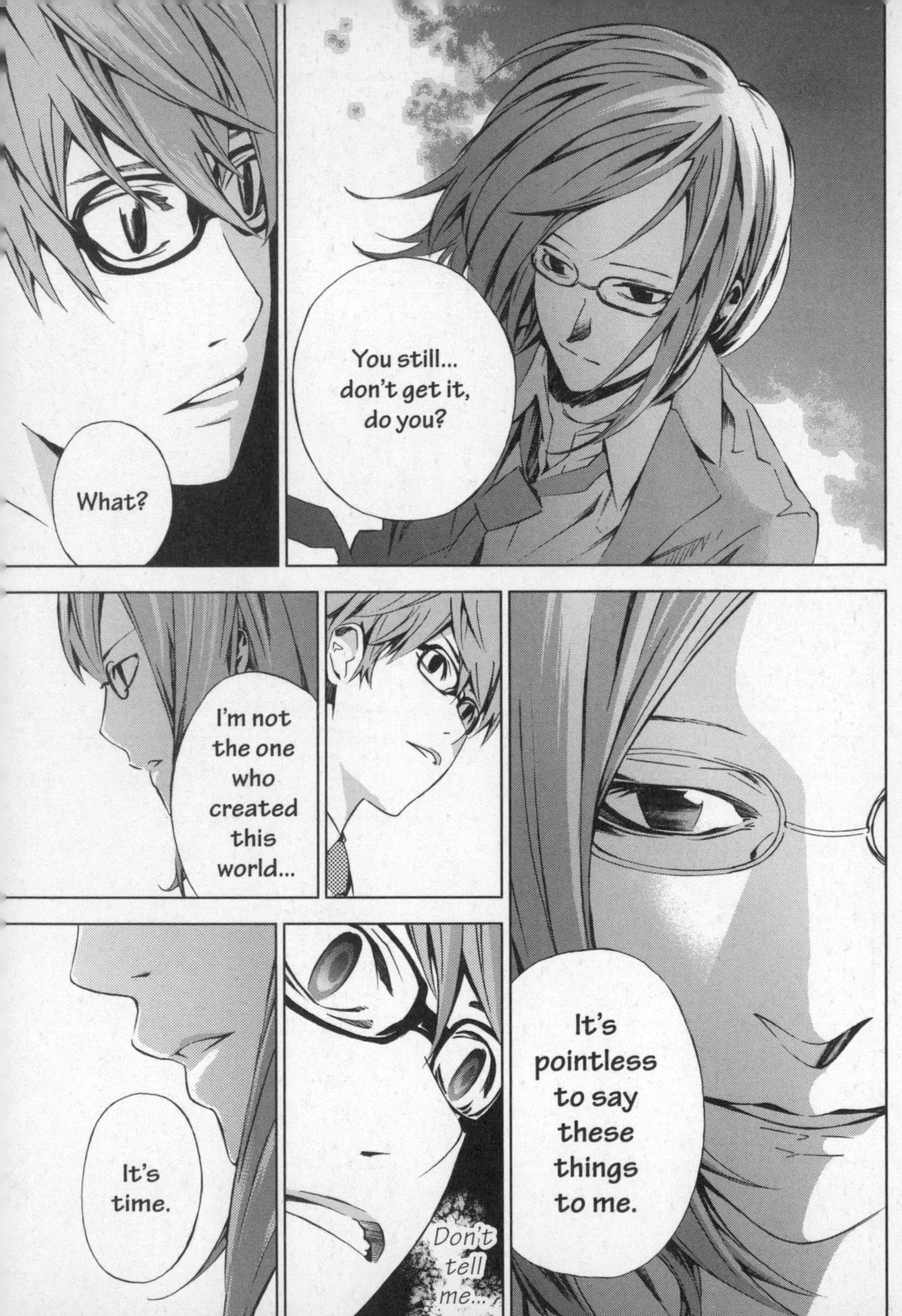
You still... don't get it, do you?
What?
It's pointless to say these things to me.
I'm not the one who created this world...
Don't tell me...
It's time.

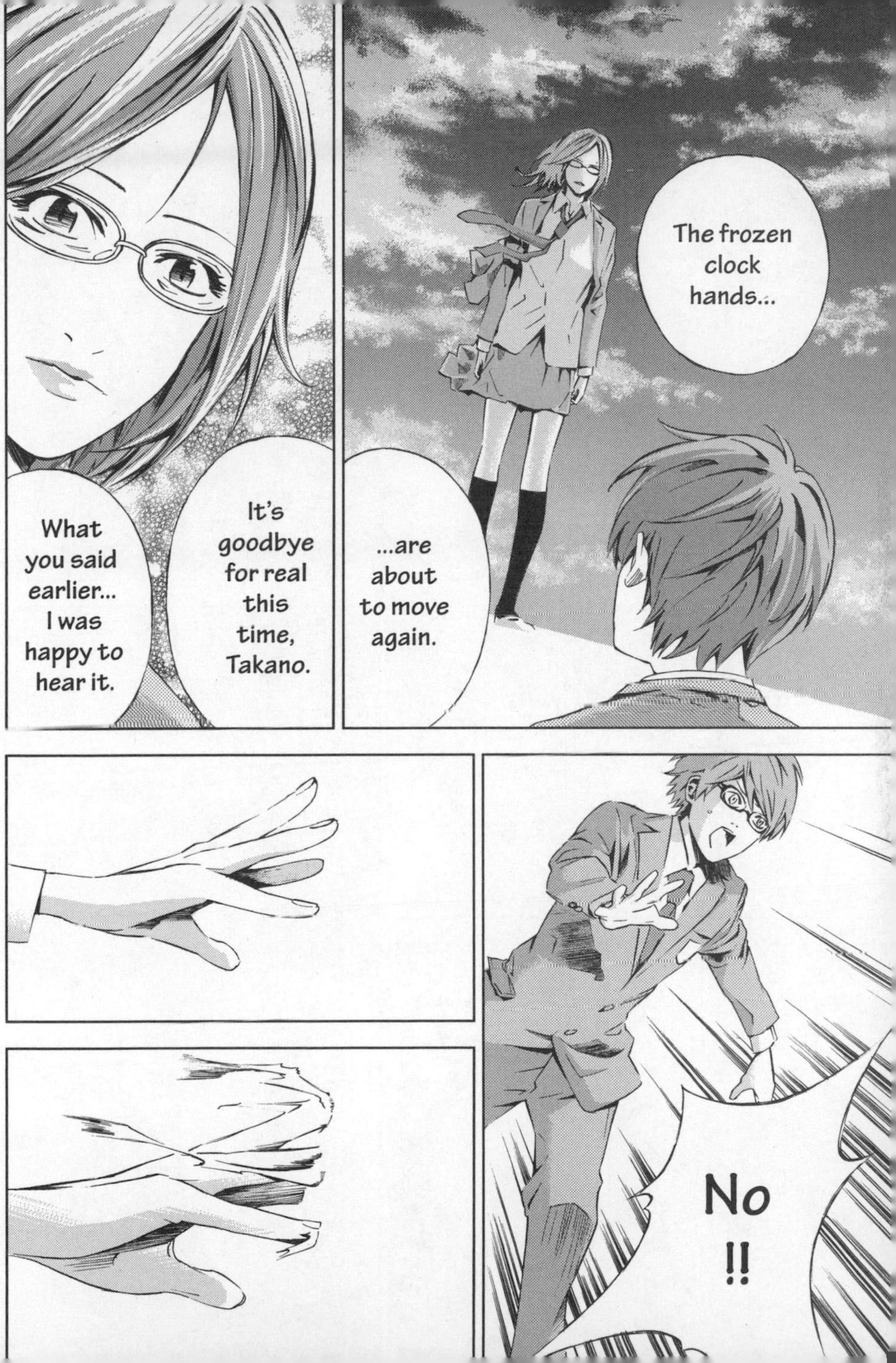
The frozen clock hands...
...are about to move again.
It's goodbye for real this time, Takano.
What you said earlier... I was happy to hear it.
No !!

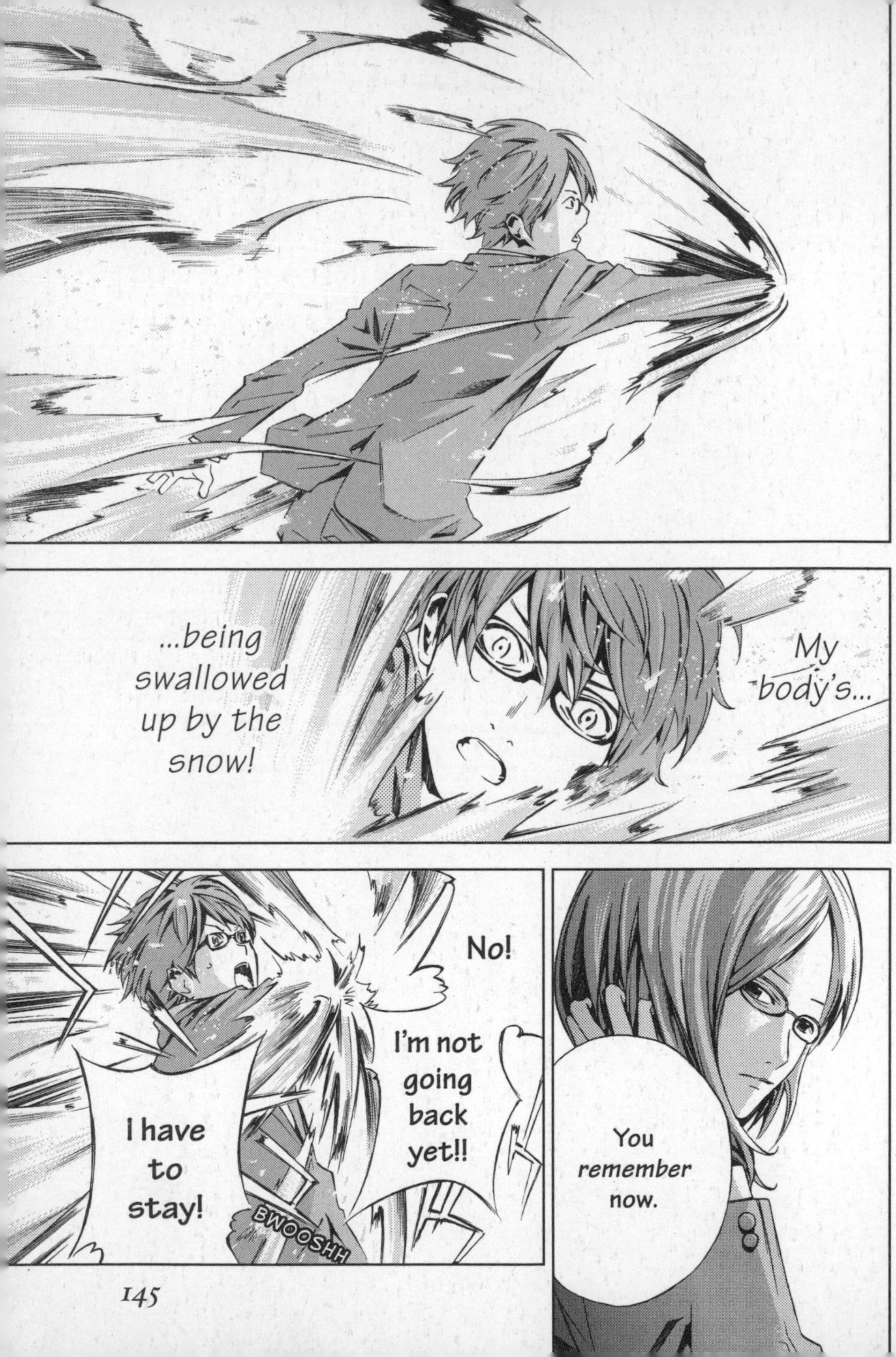
My body's...
...being swallowed up by the snow!
You remember now.
No!
I'm not going back yet!!
I have to stay!
BWOOSHH

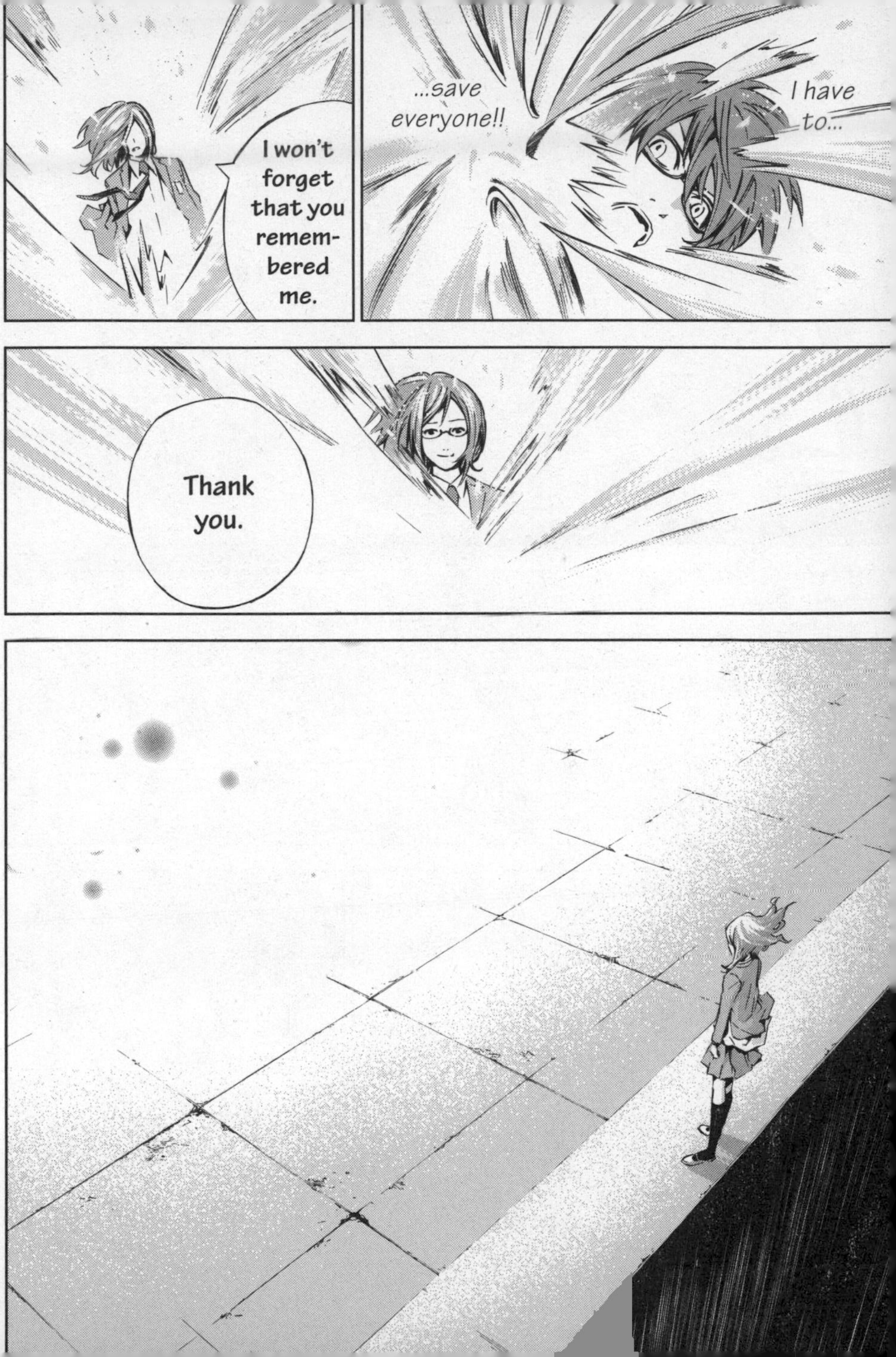
I have to...
...save everyone!!
I won't forget that you remem-bered me.
Thank you.

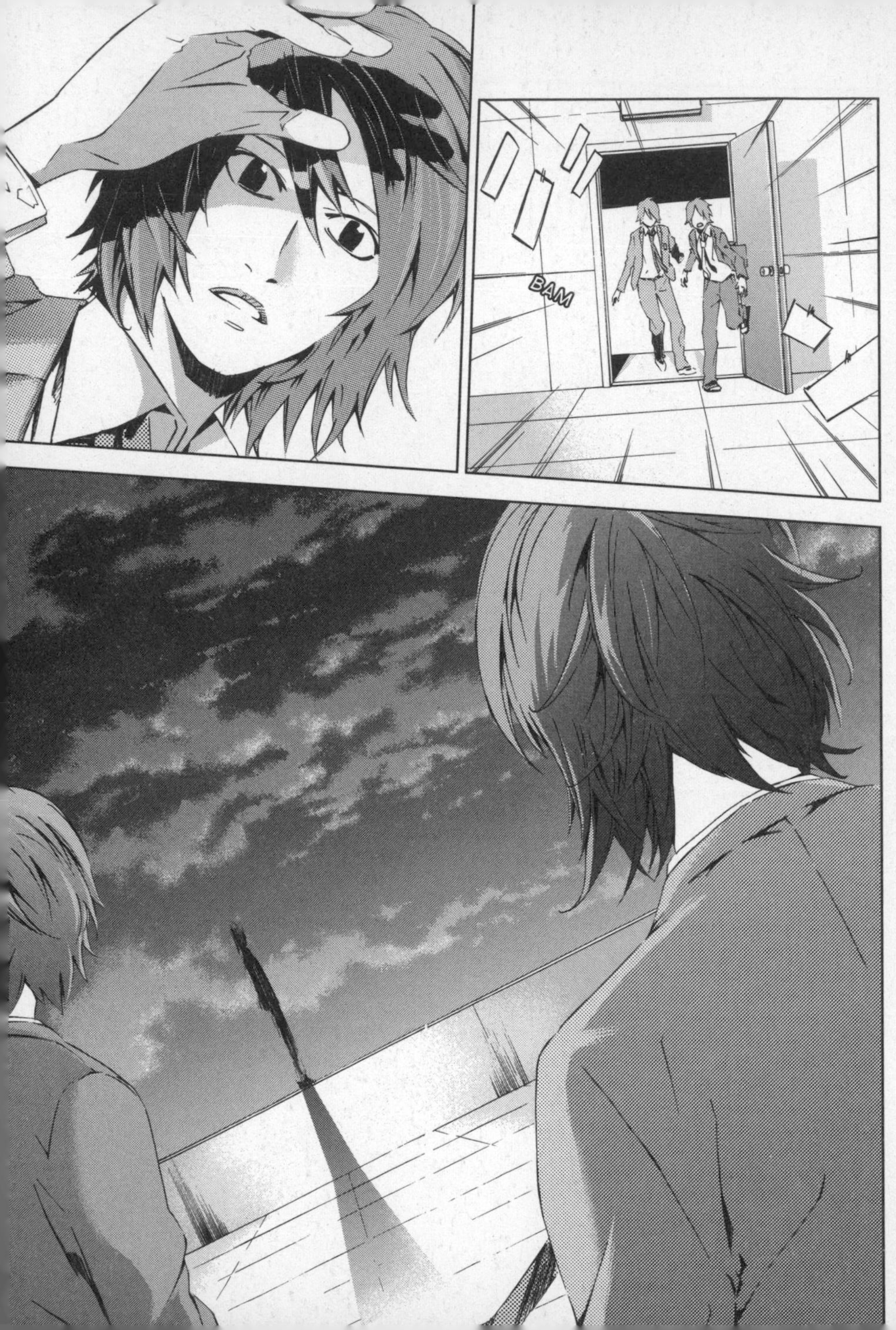
BAM

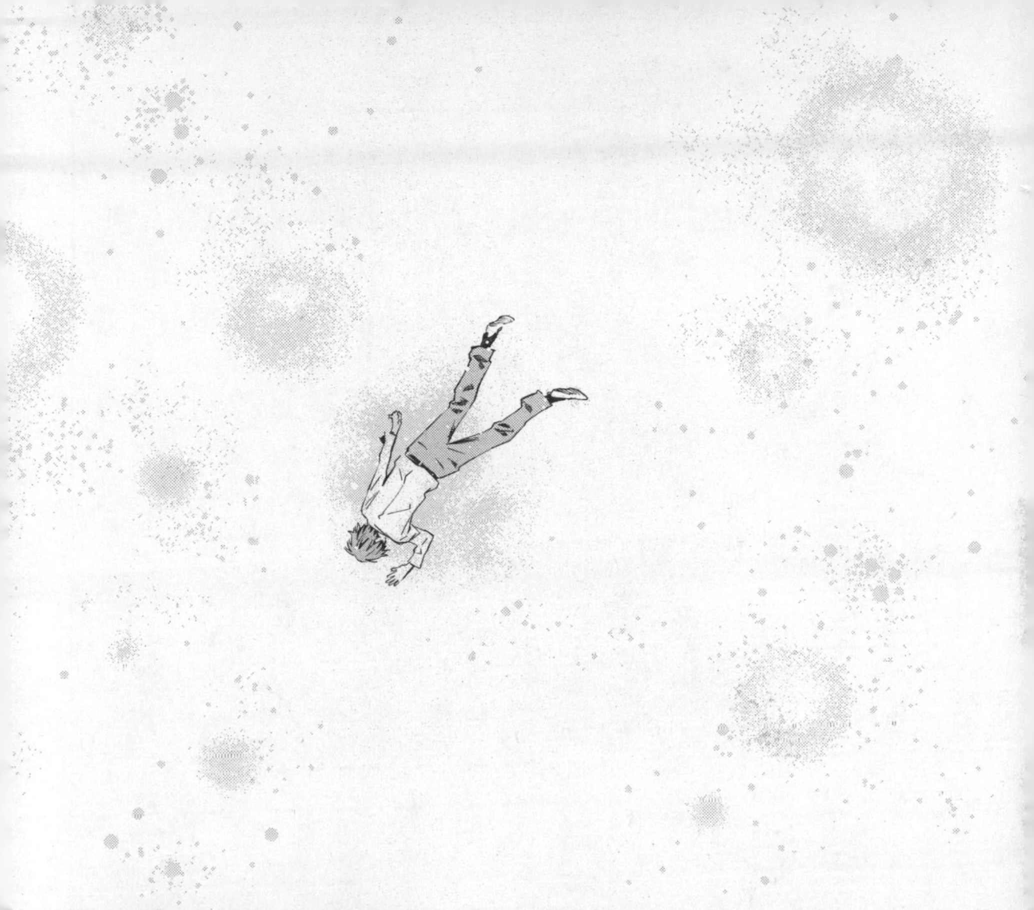
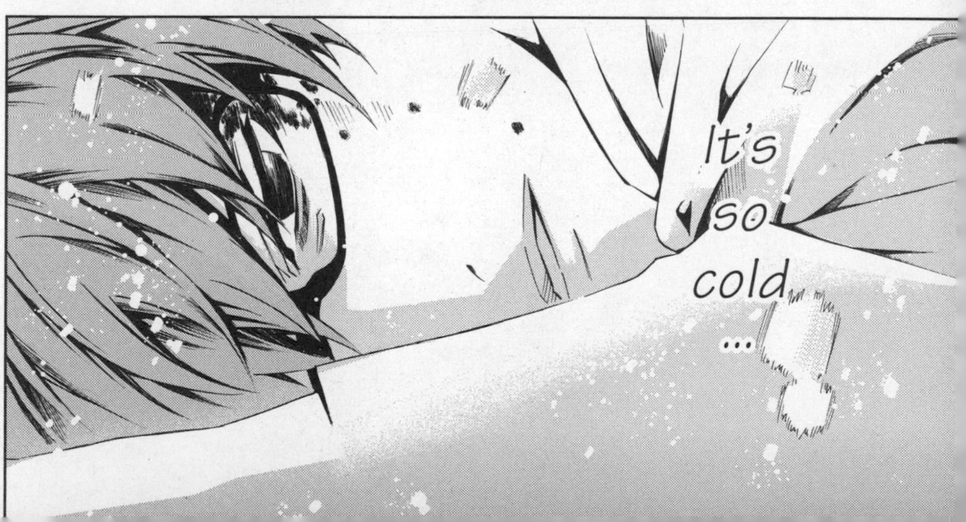
It's so cold...

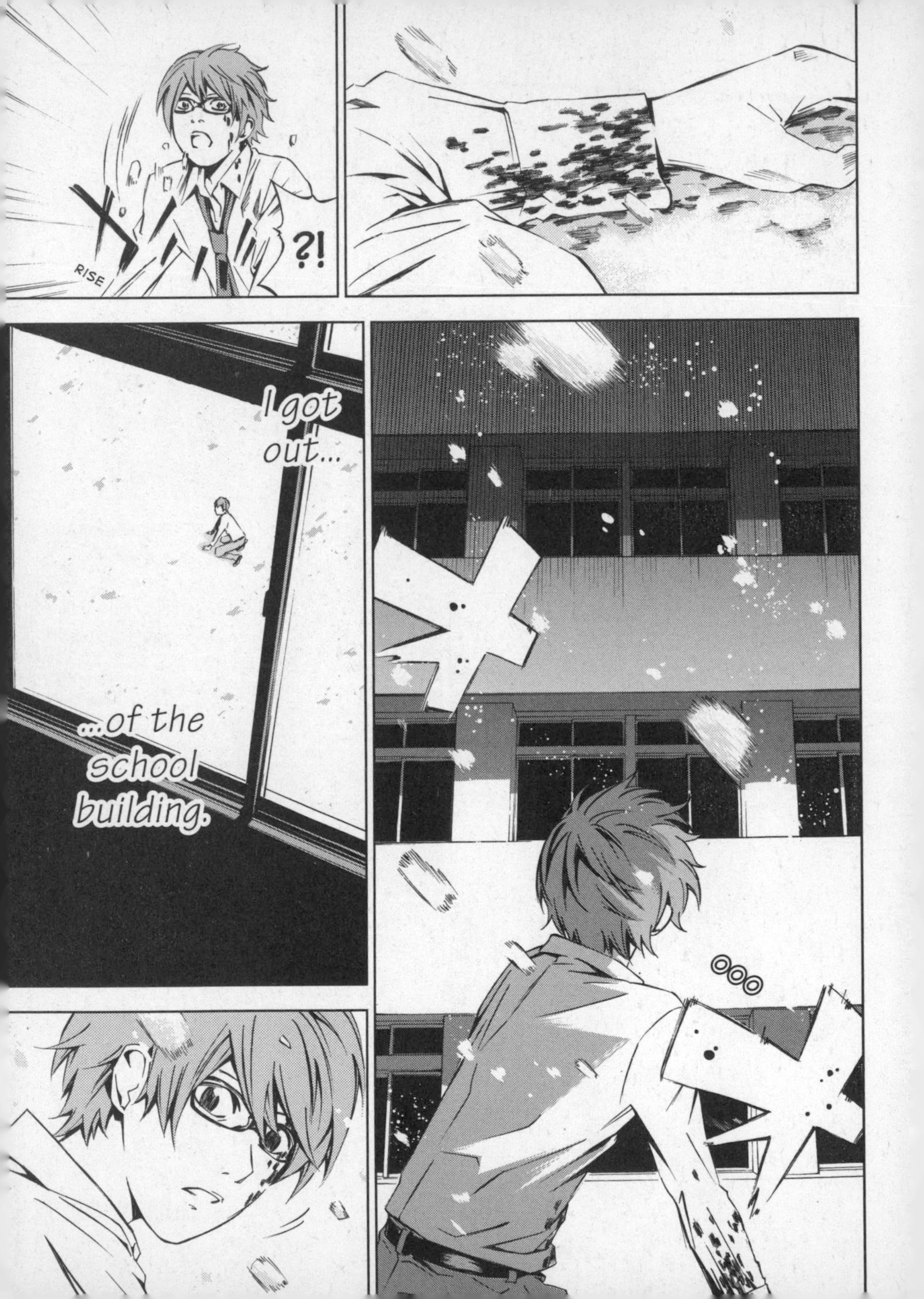

?!
RISE
I got out...
...of the school building.
OOO

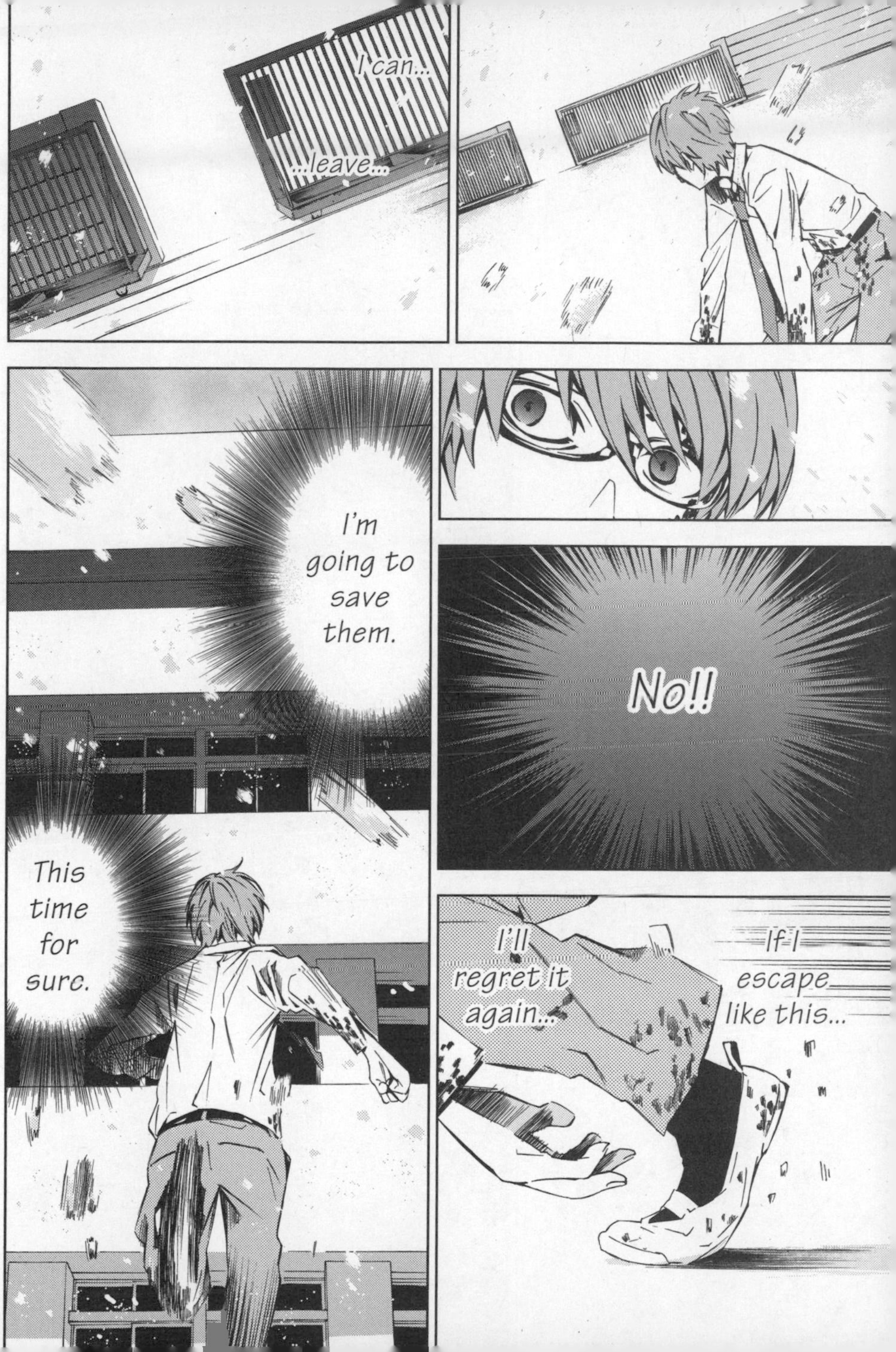
I can...
...leave...
No!!
If I escape like this...
I'll regret it again...
I'm going to save them.
This time for sure.

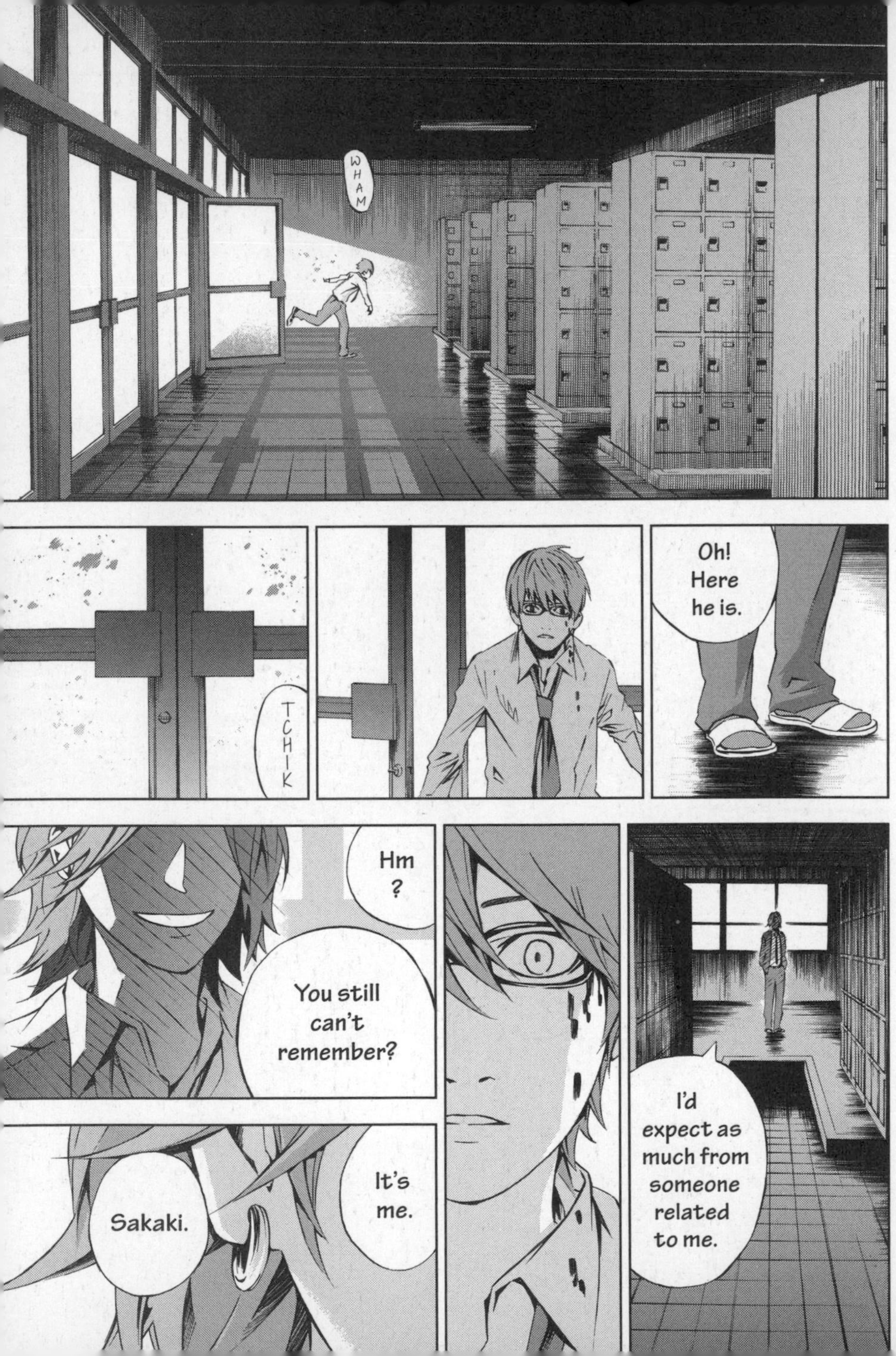
WHAM
Oh! Here he is.
TCHIK
I'd expect as much from someone related to me.
Hm?
You still can't remember?
It's me.
Sakaki.

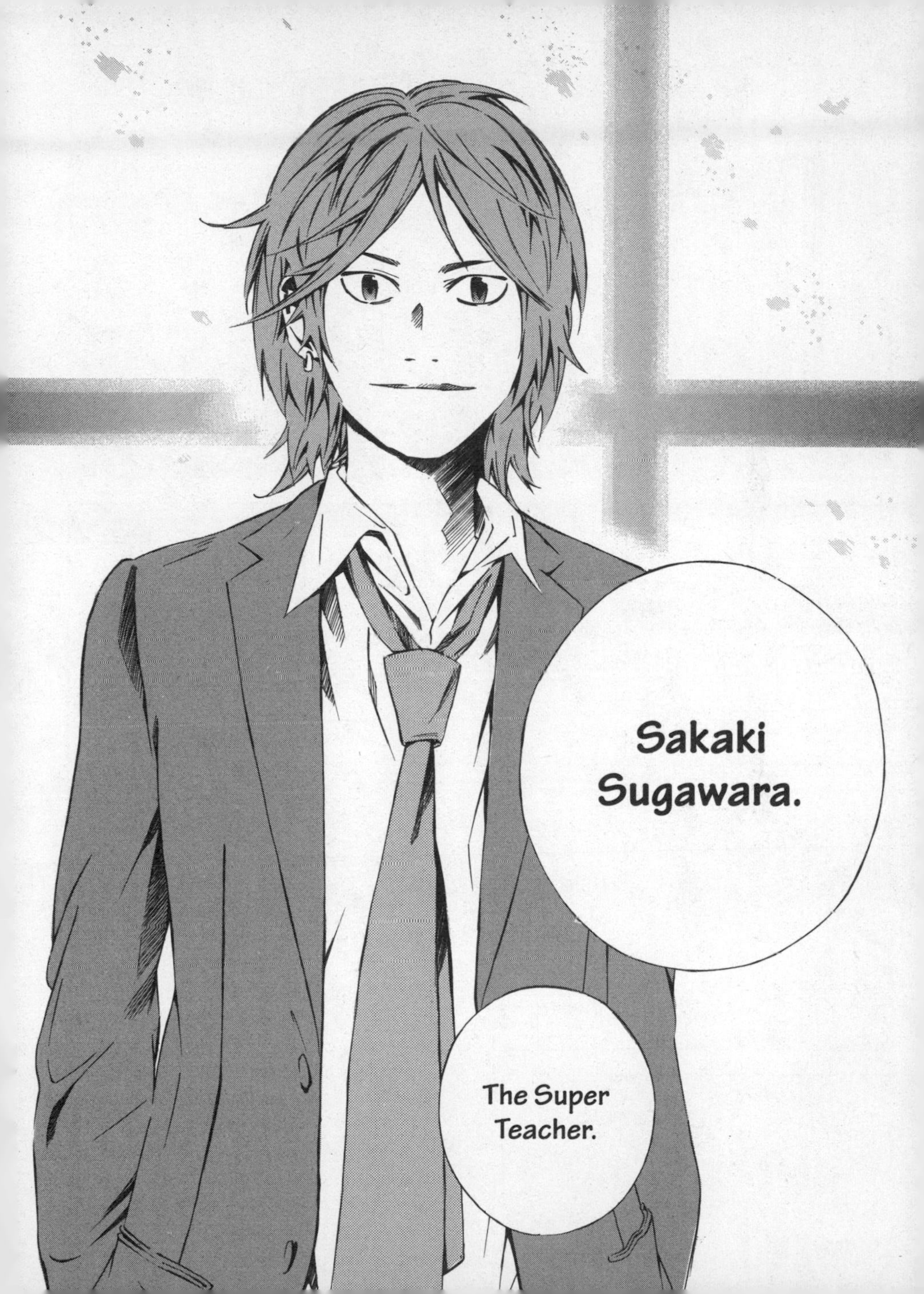
Sakaki Sugawara.
The Super Teacher.

A School
Frozen
in Time

A School
Frozen
in Time

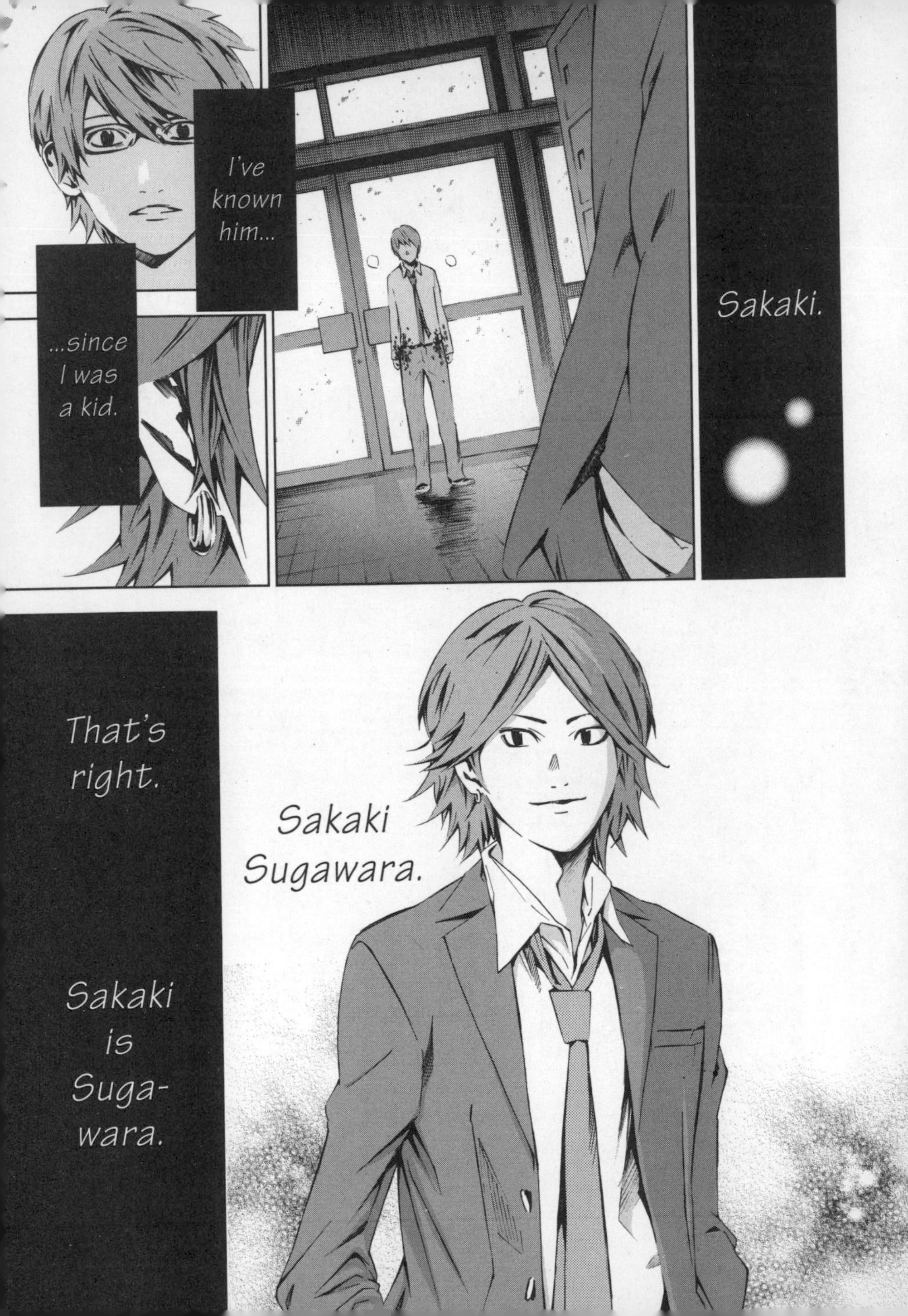
Sakaki.
I've known him...
...since I was a kid.
Sakaki Sugawara.
That's right.
Sakaki is Suga-wara.

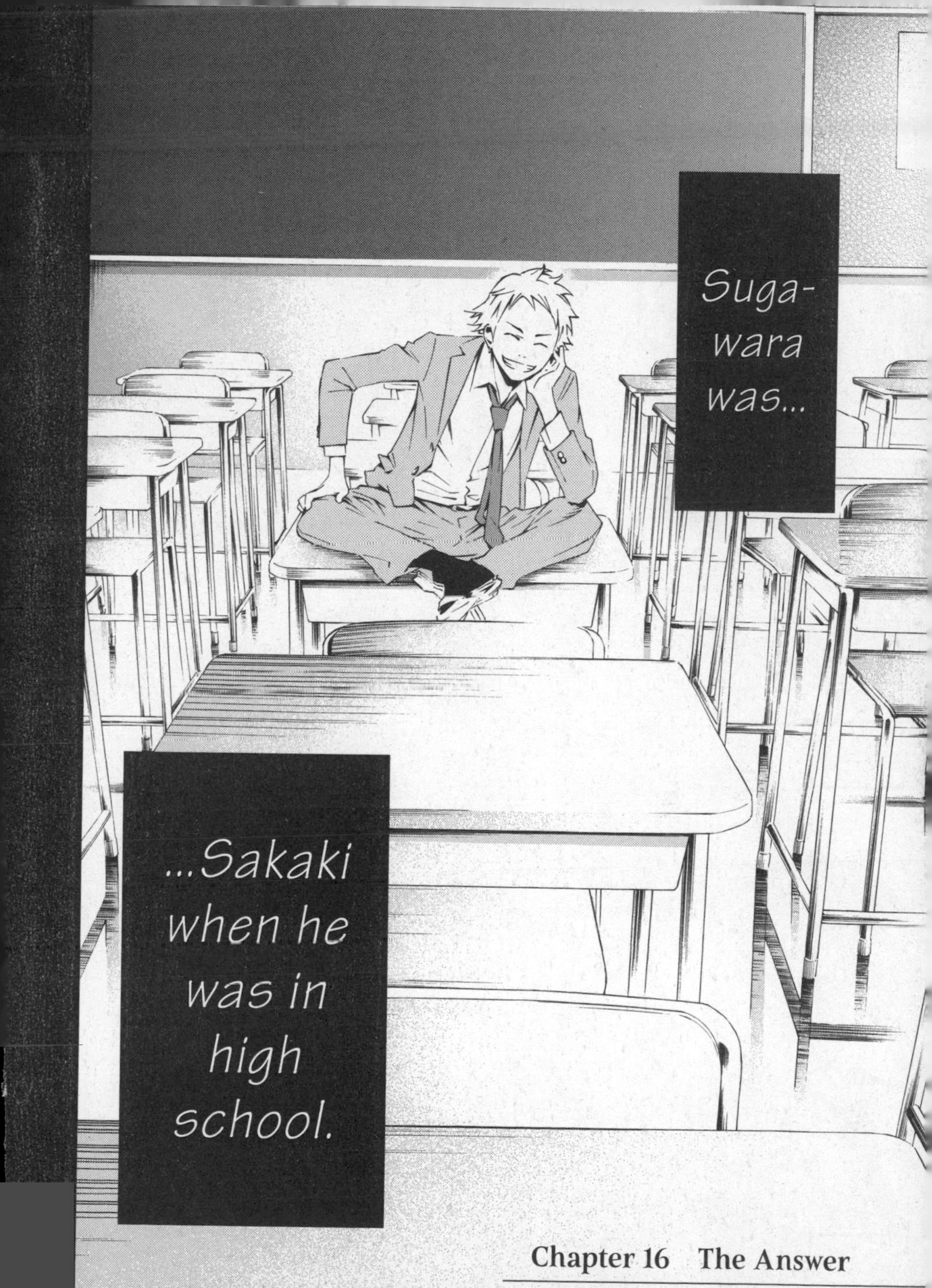
Suga-wara was...
...Sakaki when he was in high school.

Chapter 16 The Answer

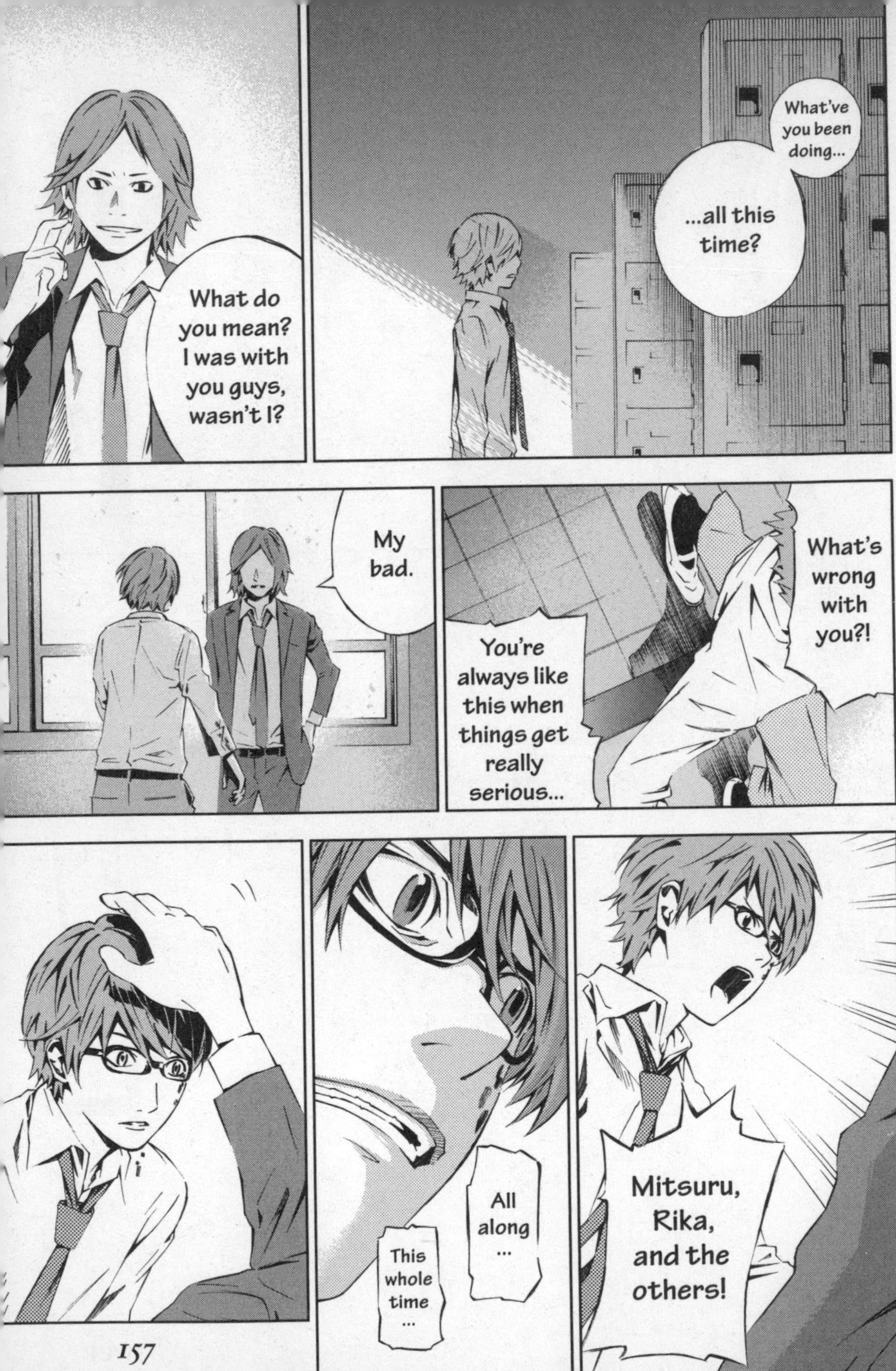
What've you been doing...
...all this time?
What do you mean? I was with you guys, wasn't I?
What's wrong with you?!
You're always like this when things get really serious...
My bad.
Mitsuru, Rika, and the others!
All along...
This whole time...

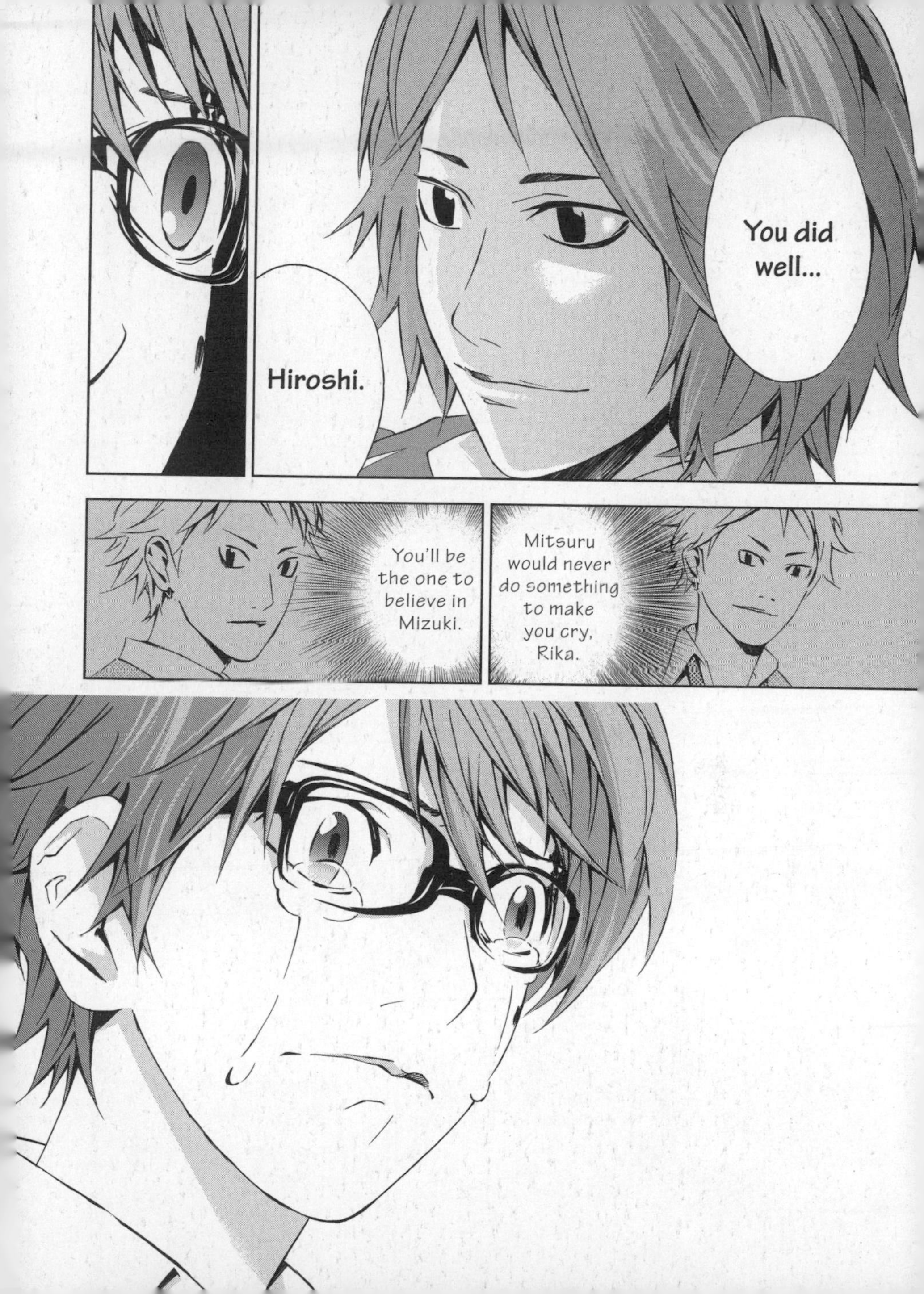
You did well...
Hiroshi.
Mitsuru would never do something to make you cry, Rika.
You'll be the one to believe in Mizuki.

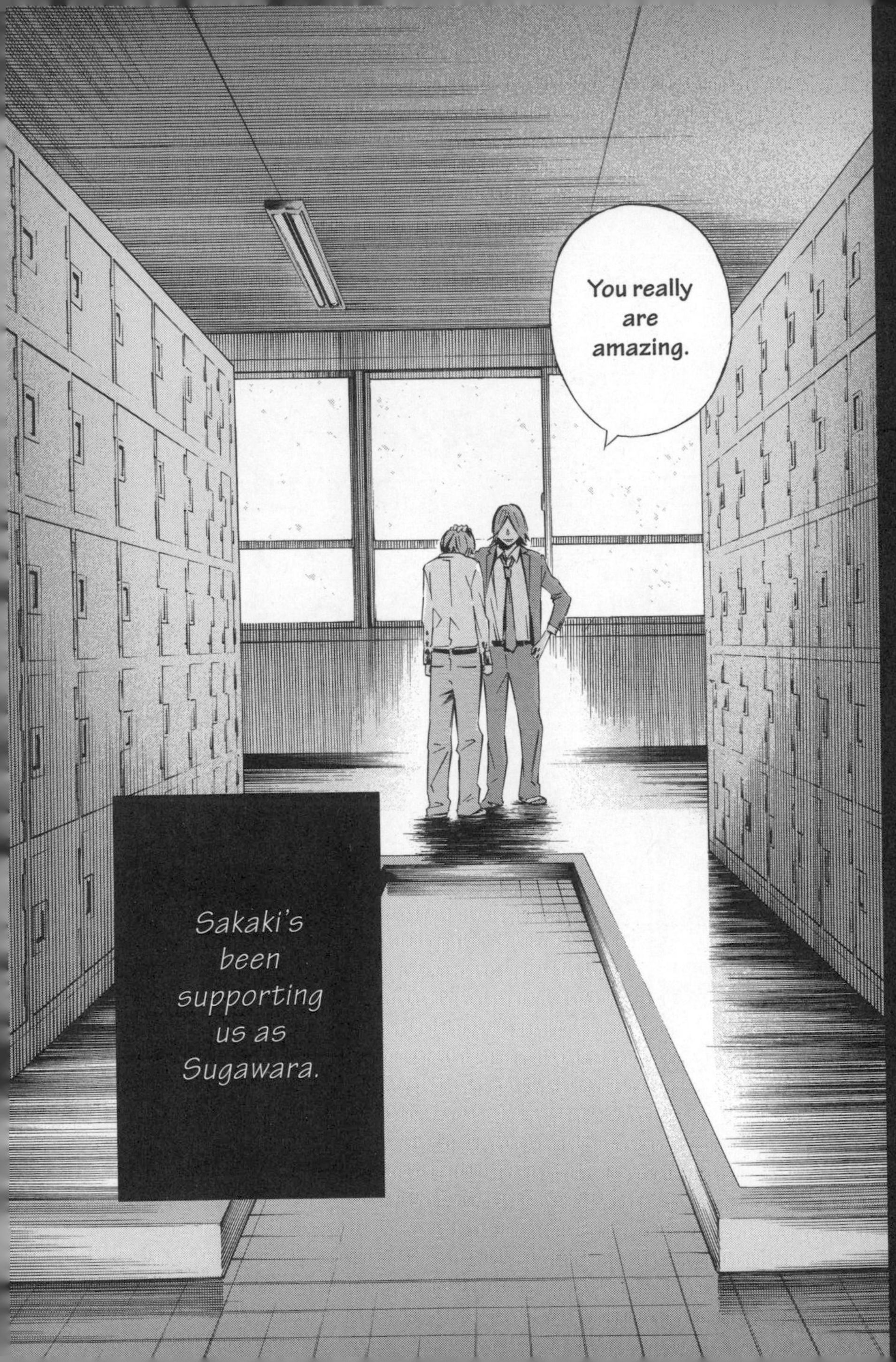
You really are amazing.
Sakaki's been supporting us as Sugawara.

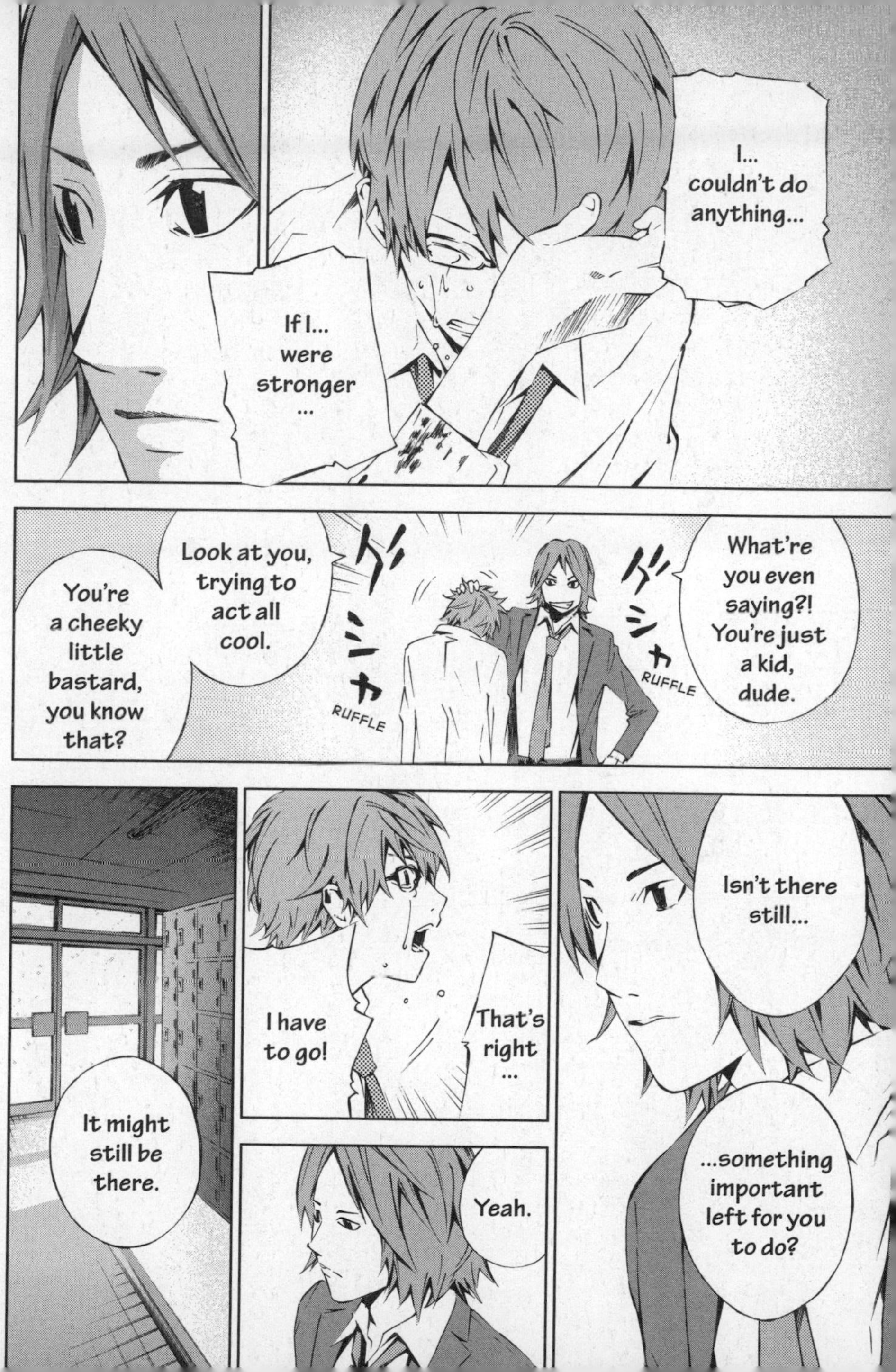
I... couldn't do anything...
If I... were stronger ...
What're you even saying?! You're just a kid, dude.
グシャ
RUFFLE
グシャ
RUFFLE
Look at you, trying to act all cool.
You're a cheeky little bastard, you know that?
Isn't there still...
...something important left for you to do?
That's right ...
I have to go!
Yeah.
It might still be there.

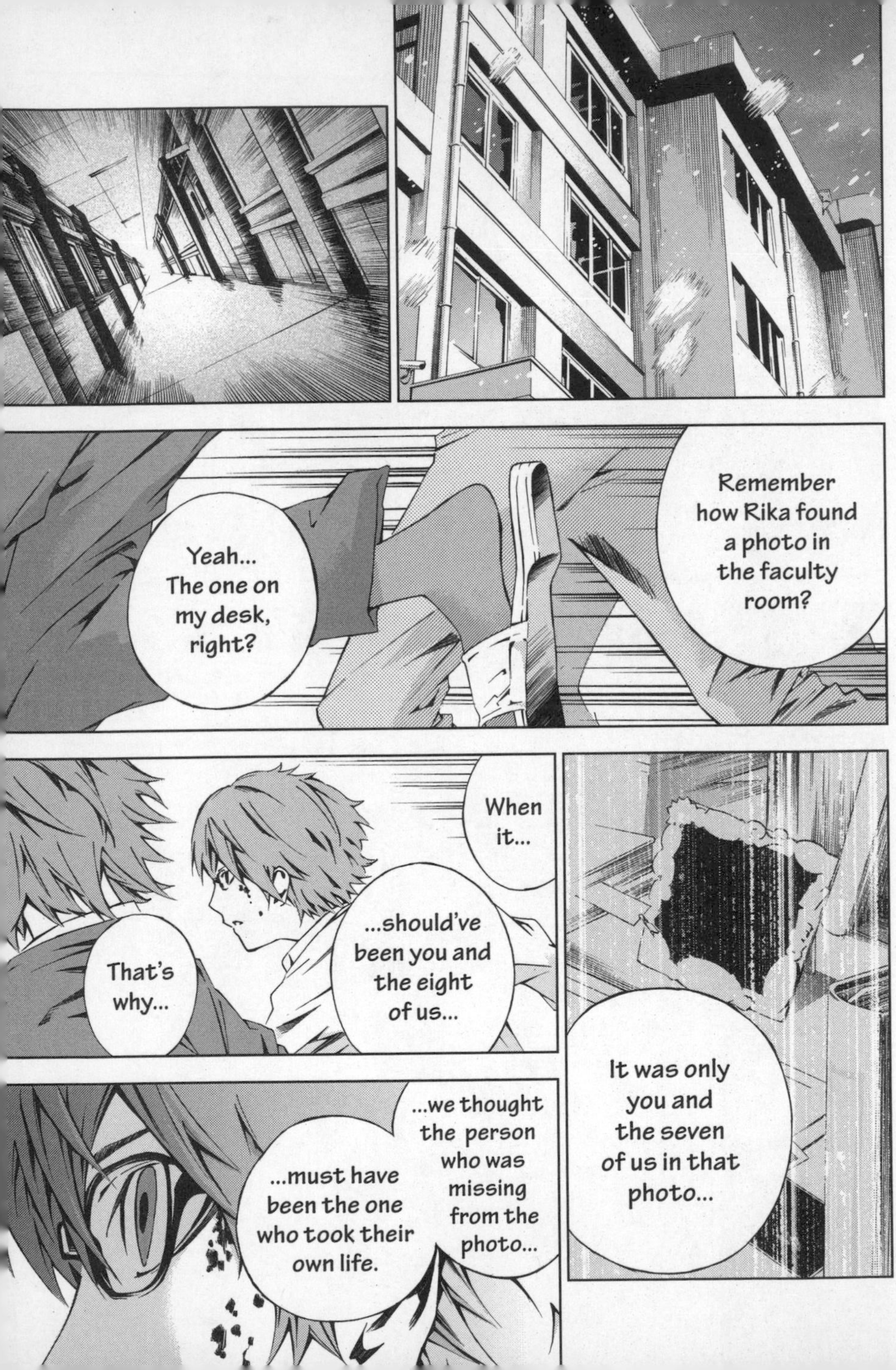

Remember how Rika found a photo in the faculty room?
Yeah... The one on my desk, right?
It was only you and the seven of us in that photo...
When it...
...should've been you and the eight of us...
That's why...
...we thought the person who was missing from the photo...
...must have been the one who took their own life.

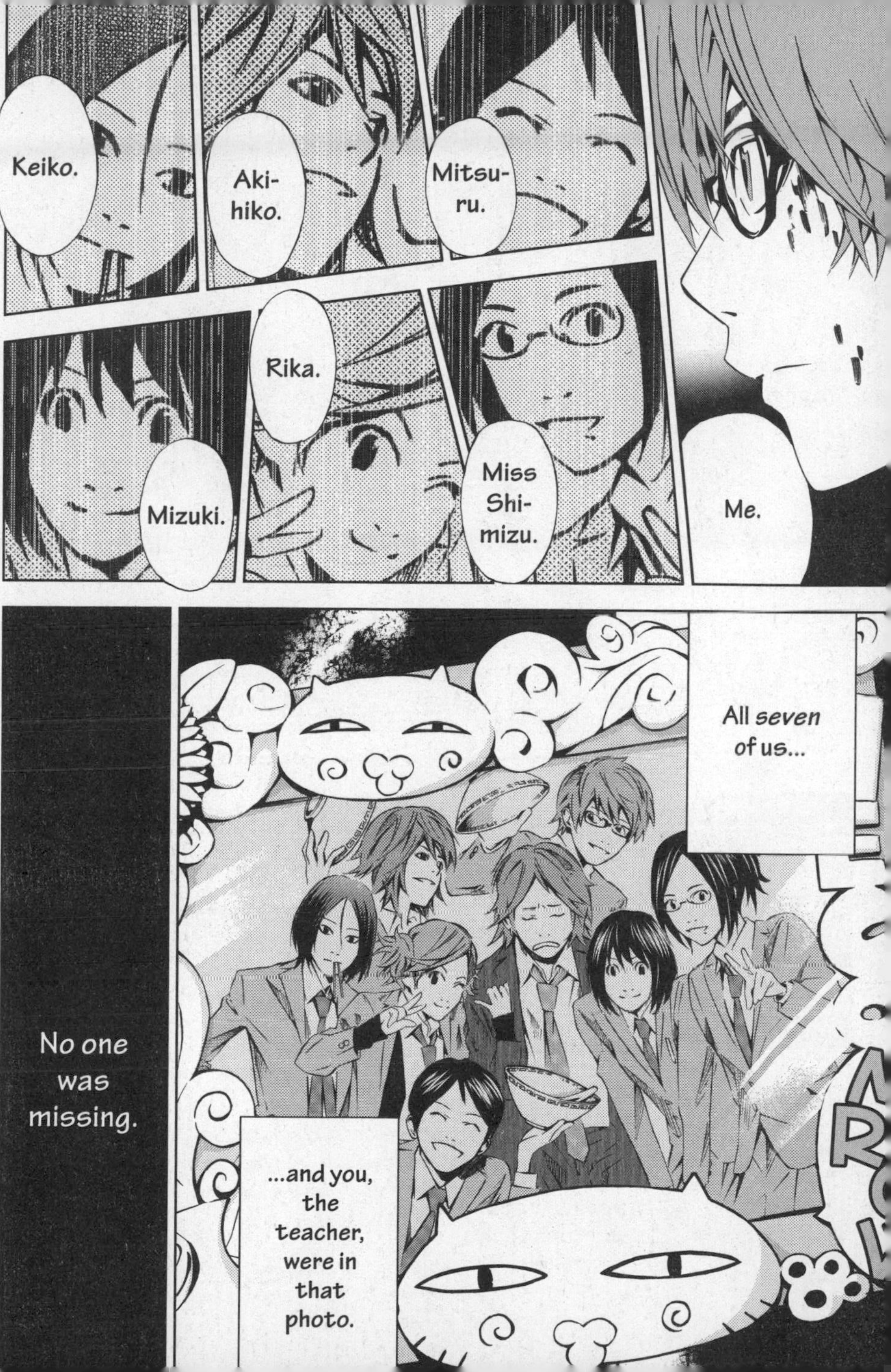
Me.
Mitsu-
ru.
Aki-
hiko.
Keiko.
Miss
Shi-
mizu.
Rika.
Mizuki.
All seven
of us...
...and you,
the
teacher,
were in
that
photo.
No one
was
missing.

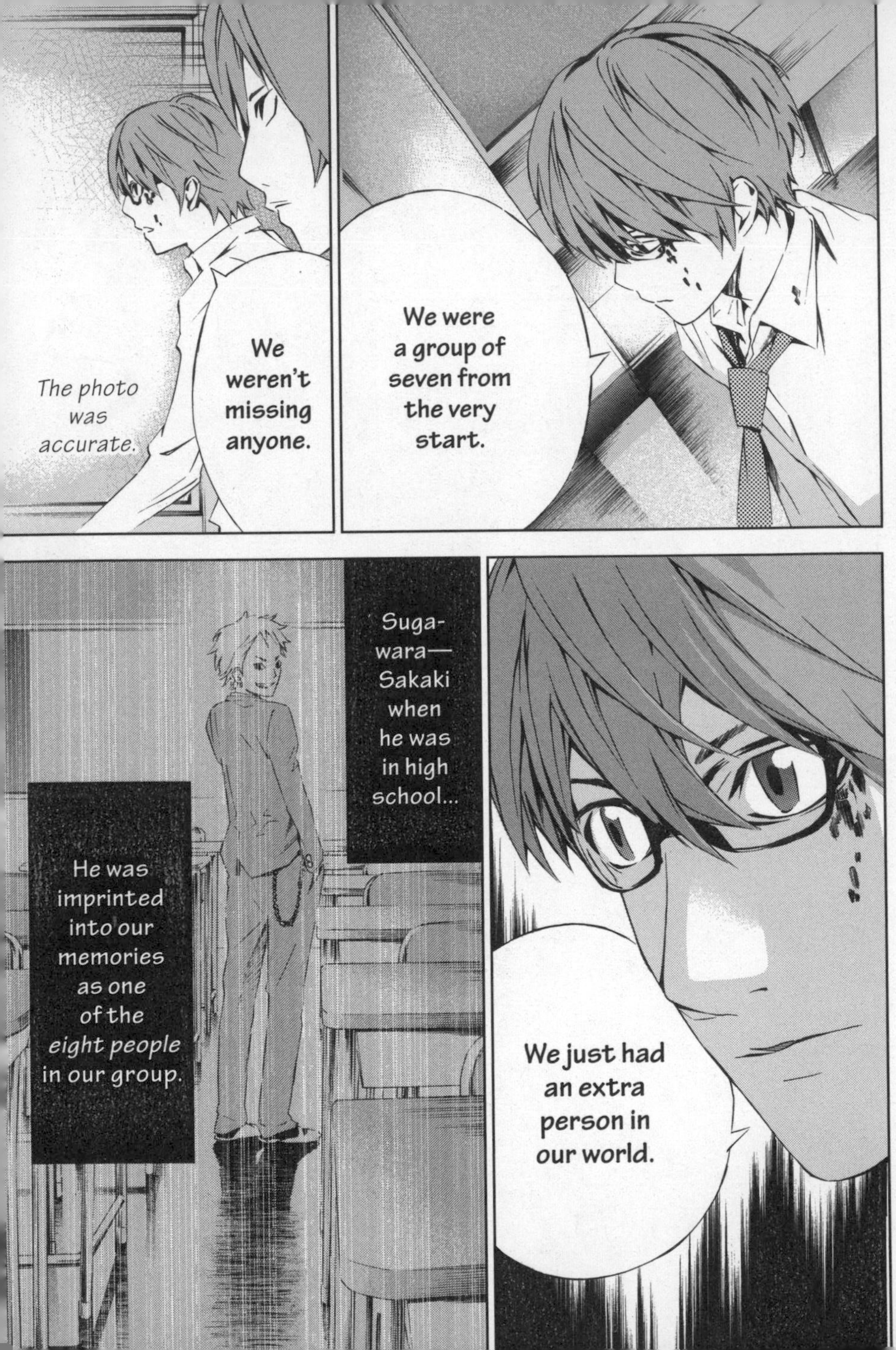
We were a group of seven from the very start.
We weren't missing anyone.
The photo was accurate.
We just had an extra person in our world.
Sugawara—Sakaki when he was in high school...
He was imprinted into our memories as one of the *eight people* in our group.

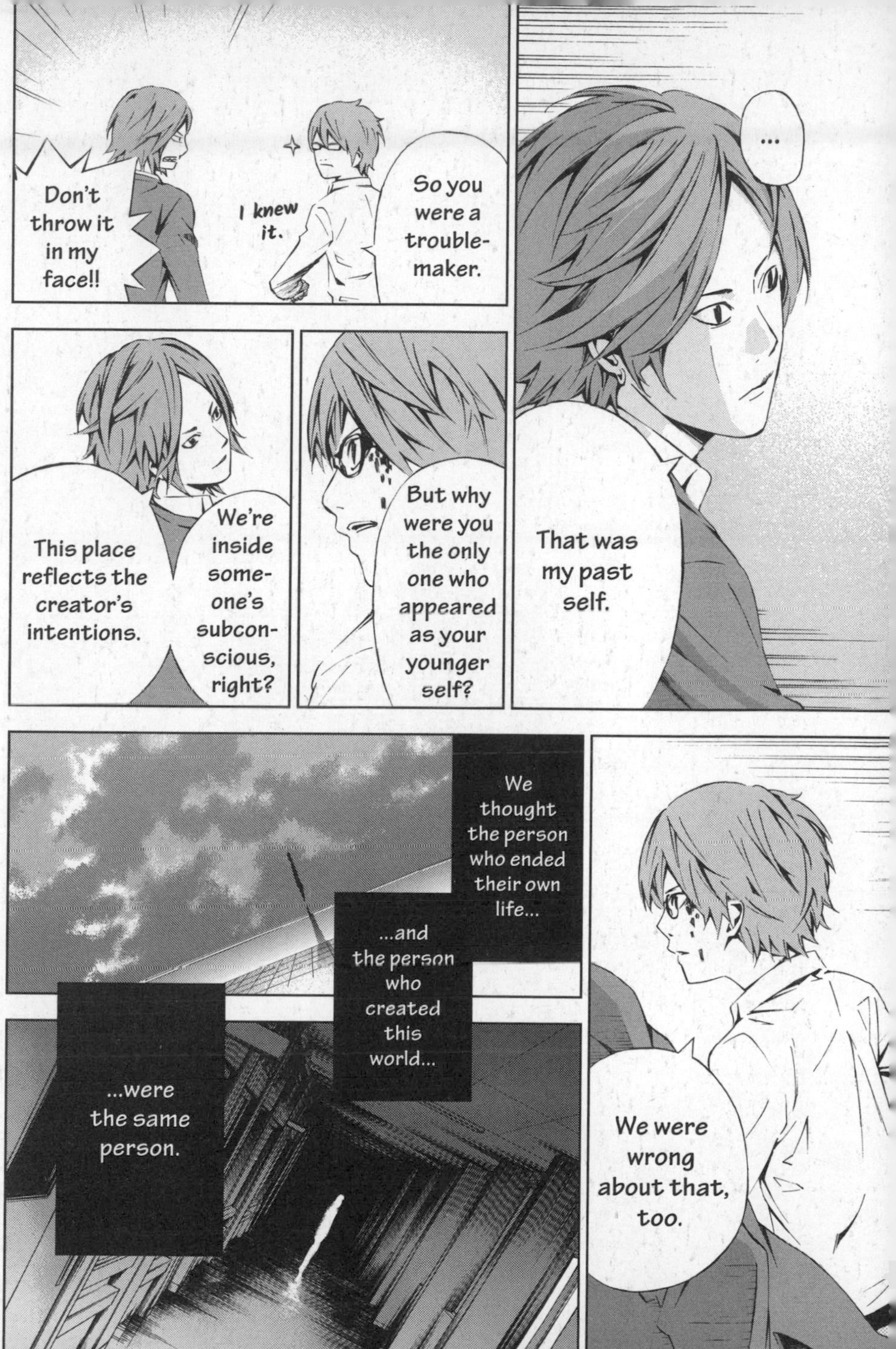
...
That was my past self.
So you were a trouble-maker.
I knew it.
Don't throw it in my face!!
But why were you the only one who appeared as your younger self?
We're inside some-one's subcon-scious, right?
This place reflects the creator's intentions.
We were wrong about that, too.
We thought the person who ended their own life...
...and the person who created this world...
...were the same person.

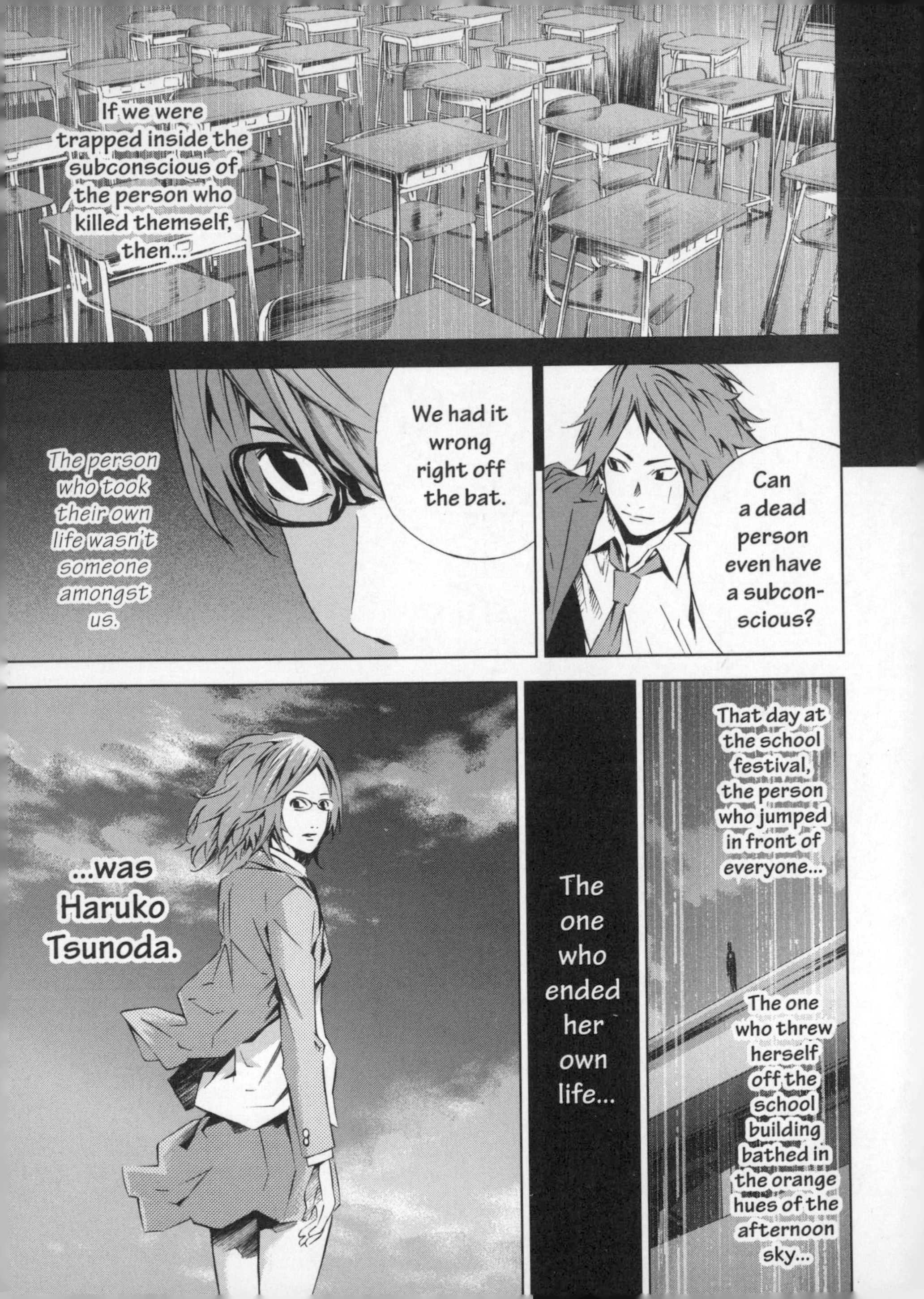
If we were trapped inside the subconscious of the person who killed themself, then...
Can a dead person even have a subconscious?
We had it wrong right off the bat.
The person who took their own life wasn't someone amongst us.
That day at the school festival, the person who jumped in front of everyone...
The one who threw herself off the school building bathed in the orange hues of the afternoon sky...
The one who ended her own life...
...was Haruko Tsunoda.

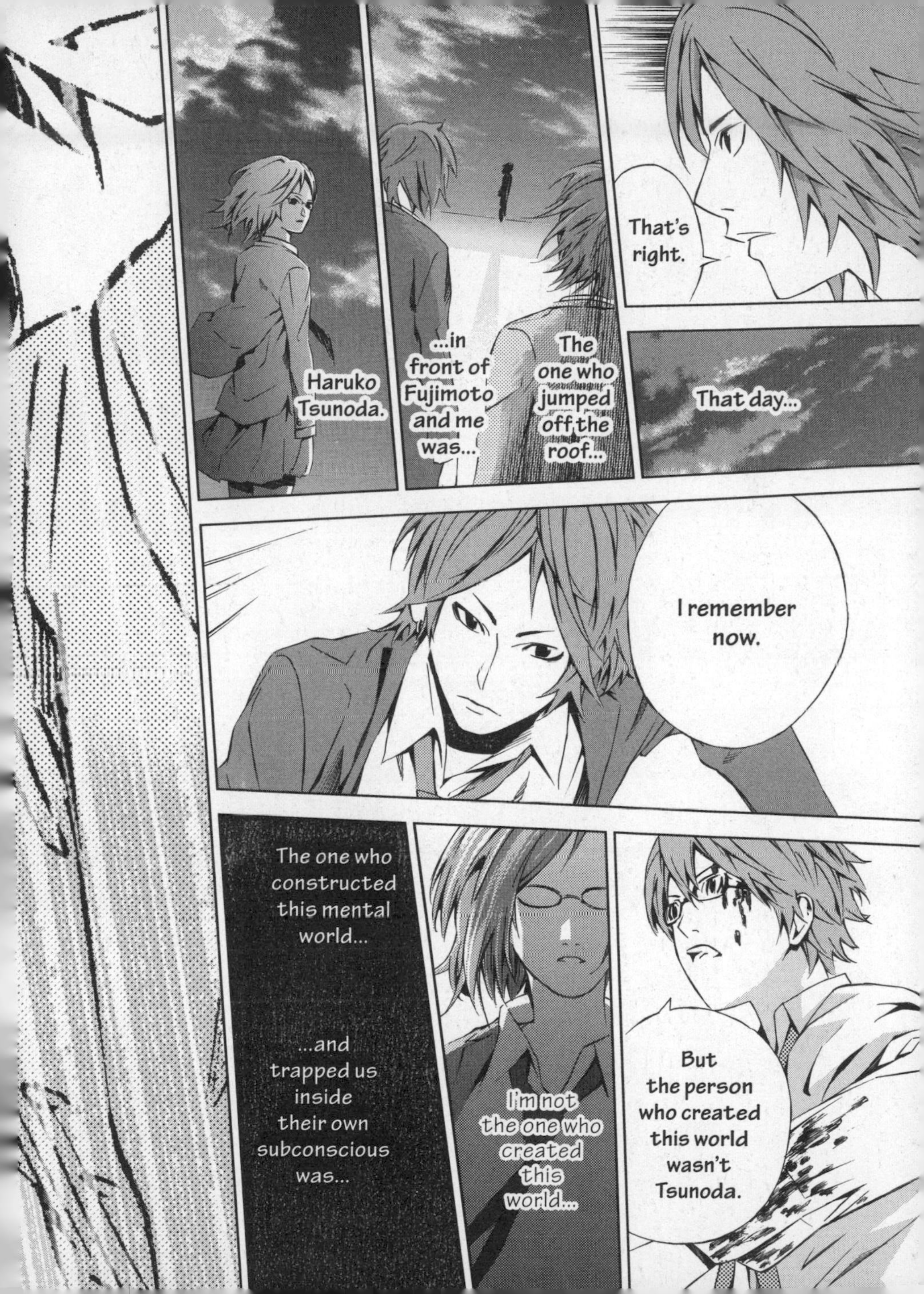
That's right.
That day...
The one who jumped off the roof...
...in front of Fujimoto and me was...
Haruko Tsunoda.
I remember now.
But the person who created this world wasn't Tsunoda.
I'm not the one who created this world...
The one who constructed this mental world...
...and trapped us inside their own subconscious was...

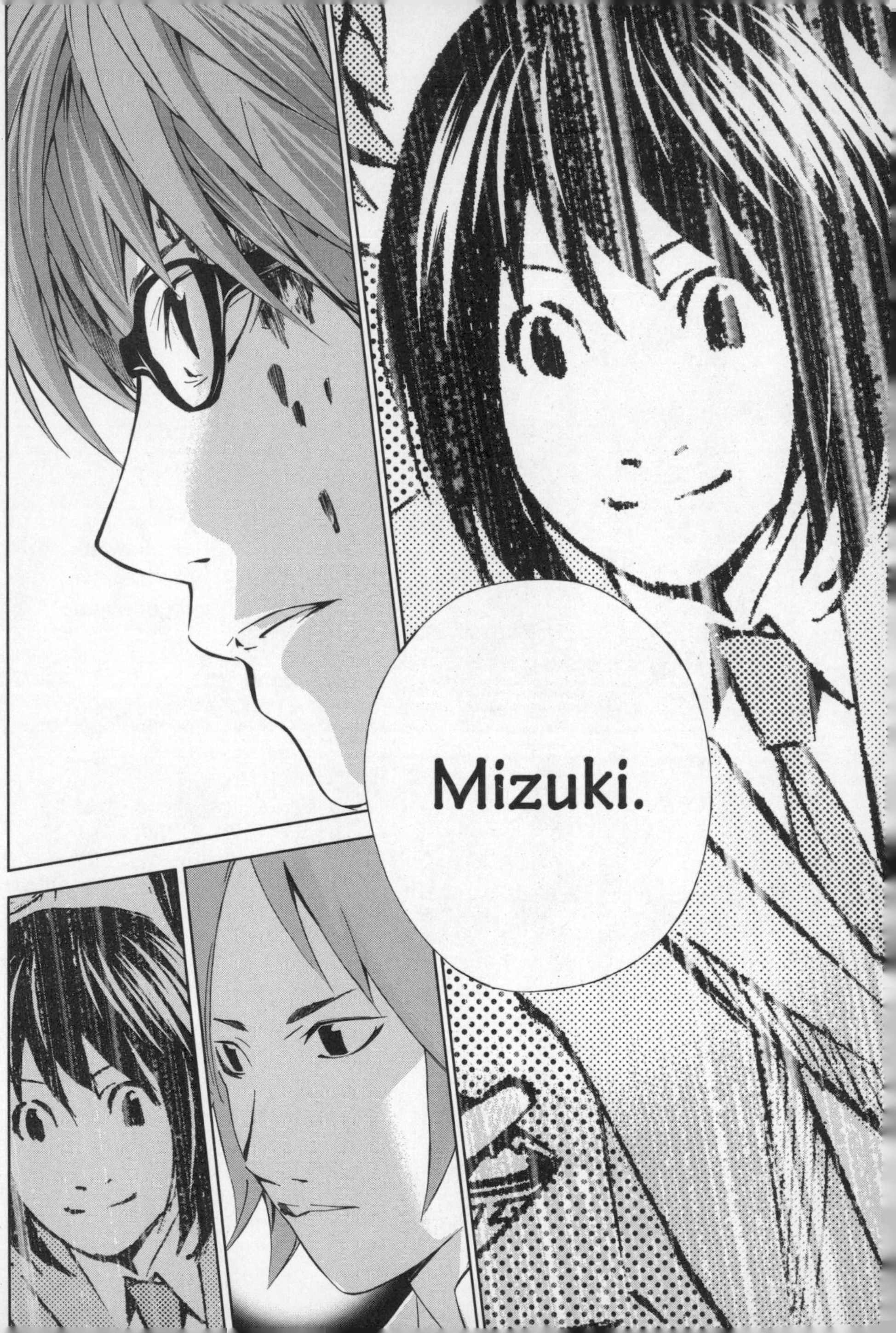
Mizuki.

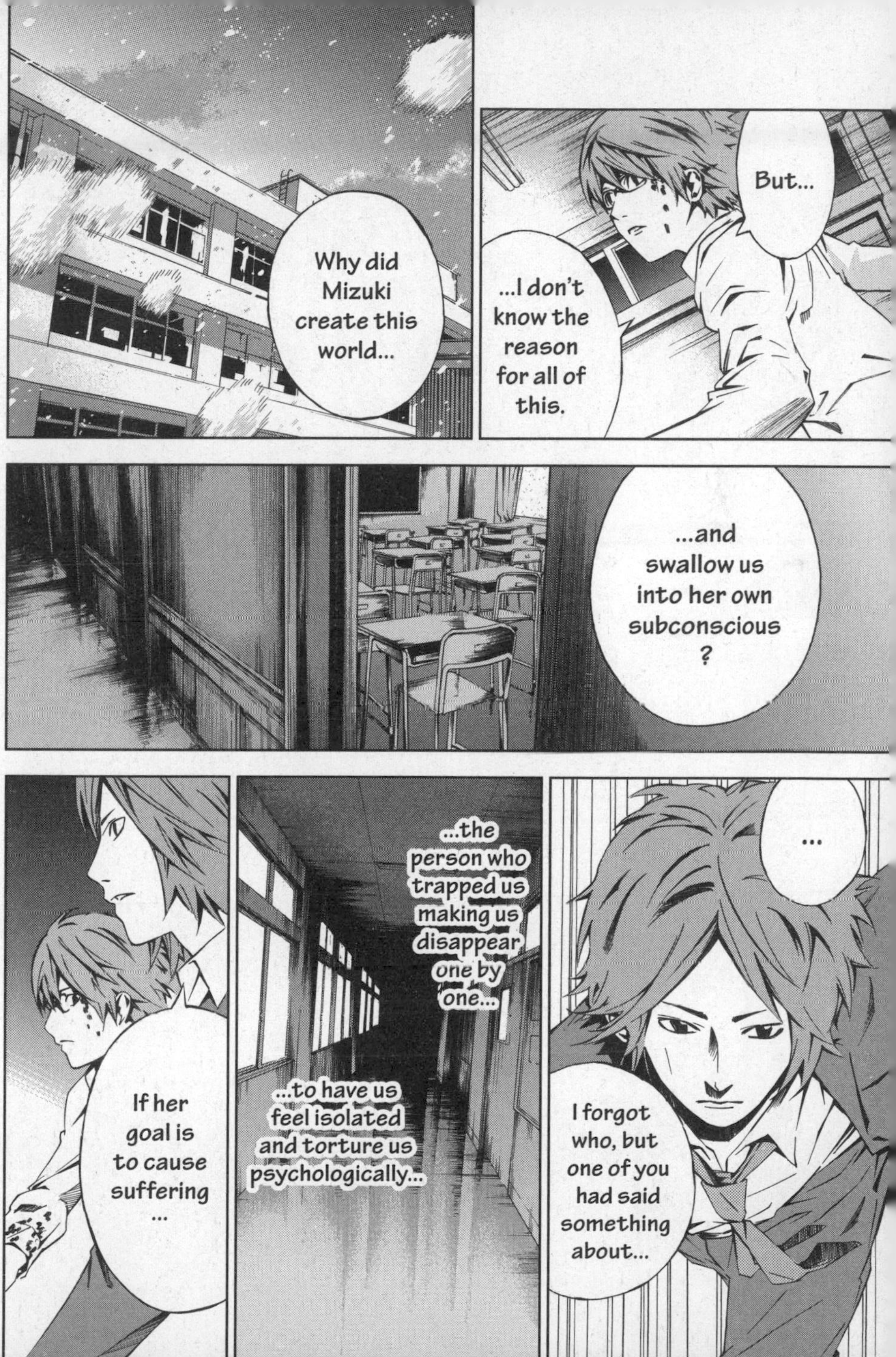
But...
...I don't know the reason for all of this.
Why did Mizuki create this world...
...and swallow us into her own subconscious ?
...
I forgot who, but one of you had said something about...
...the person who trapped us making us disappear one by one...
...to have us feel isolated and torture us psychologically...
If her goal is to cause suffering ...

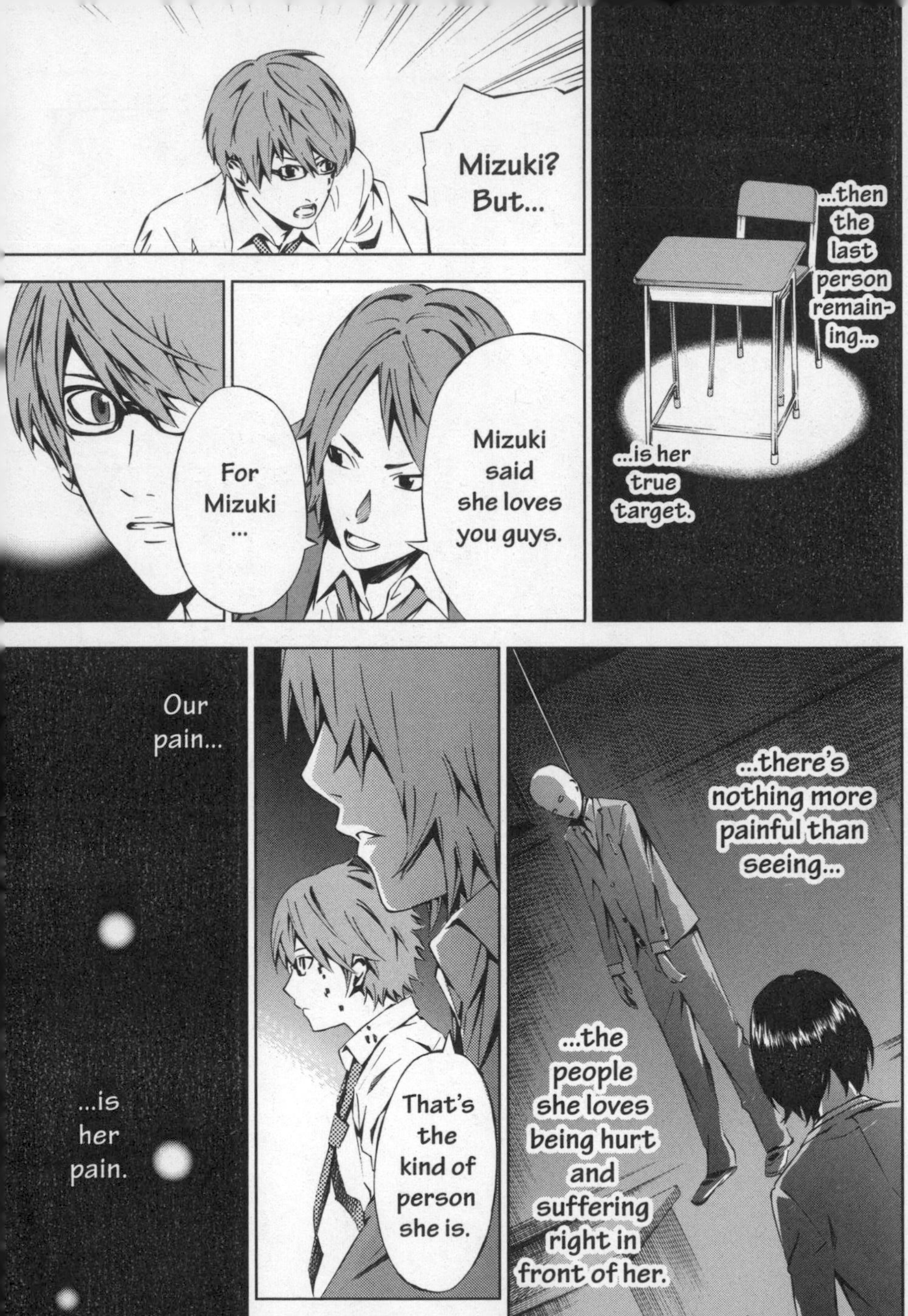
...then the last person remaining...
...is her true target.
Mizuki? But...
Mizuki said she loves you guys.
For Mizuki ...
...there's nothing more painful than seeing...
...the people she loves being hurt and suffering right in front of her.
That's the kind of person she is.
Our pain...
...is her pain.

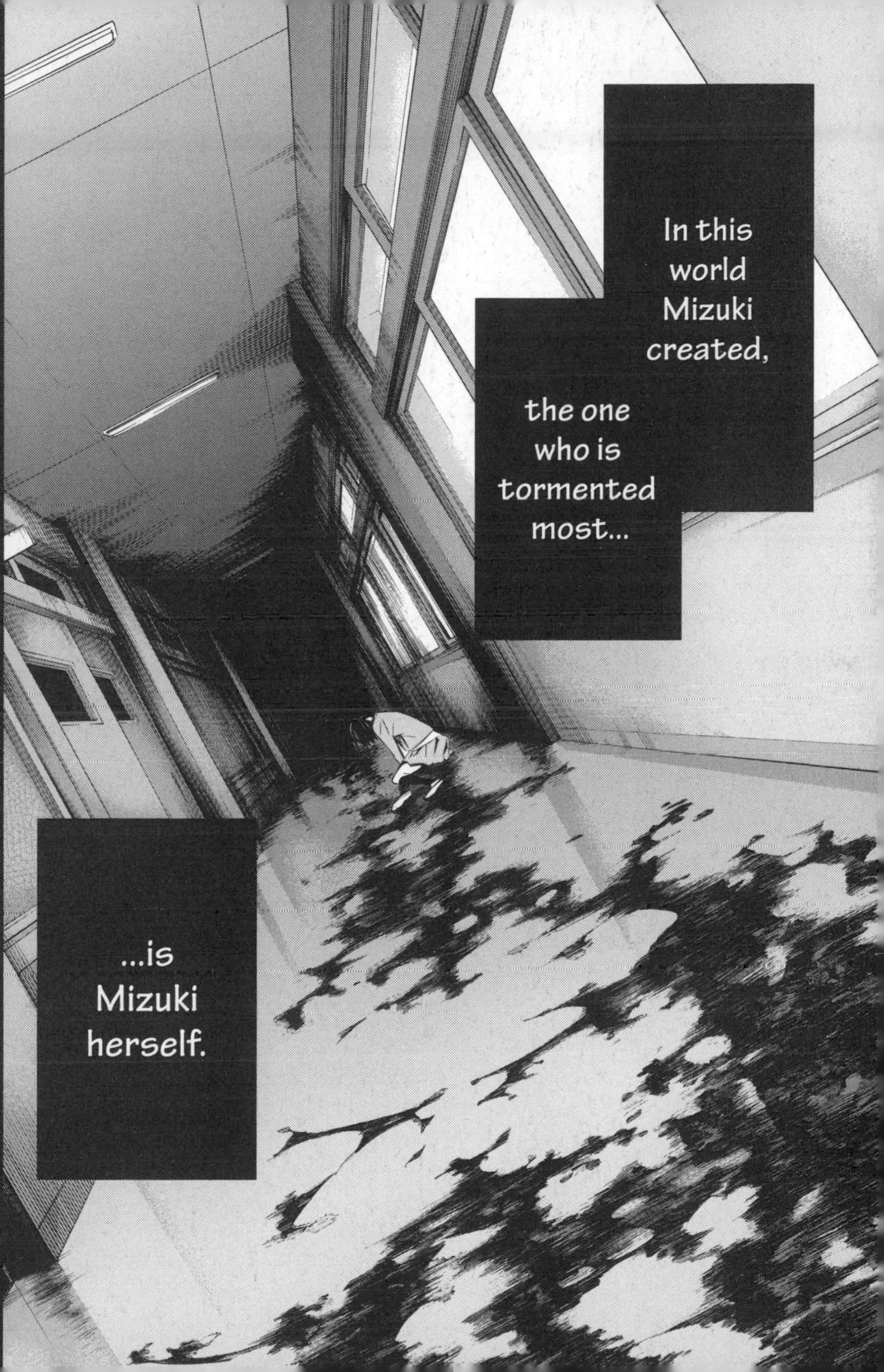
In this world Mizuki created,
the one who is tormented most...
...is Mizuki herself.

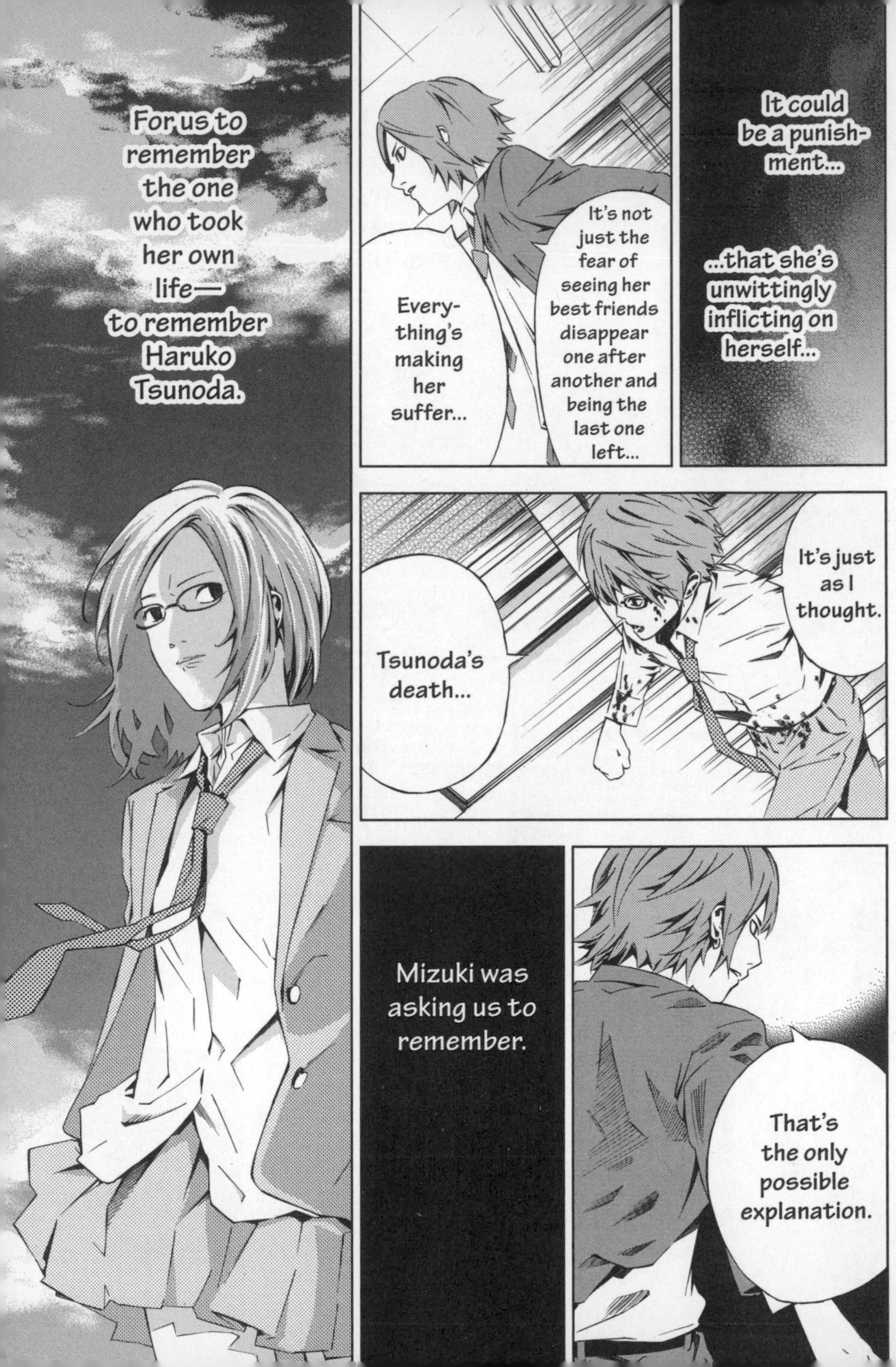
It could be a punishment...
...that she's unwittingly inflicting on herself...
It's not just the fear of seeing her best friends disappear one after another and being the last one left...
Everything's making her suffer...
It's just as I thought.
Tsunoda's death...
That's the only possible explanation.
Mizuki was asking us to remember.
For us to remember the one who took her own life—to remember Haruko Tsunoda.

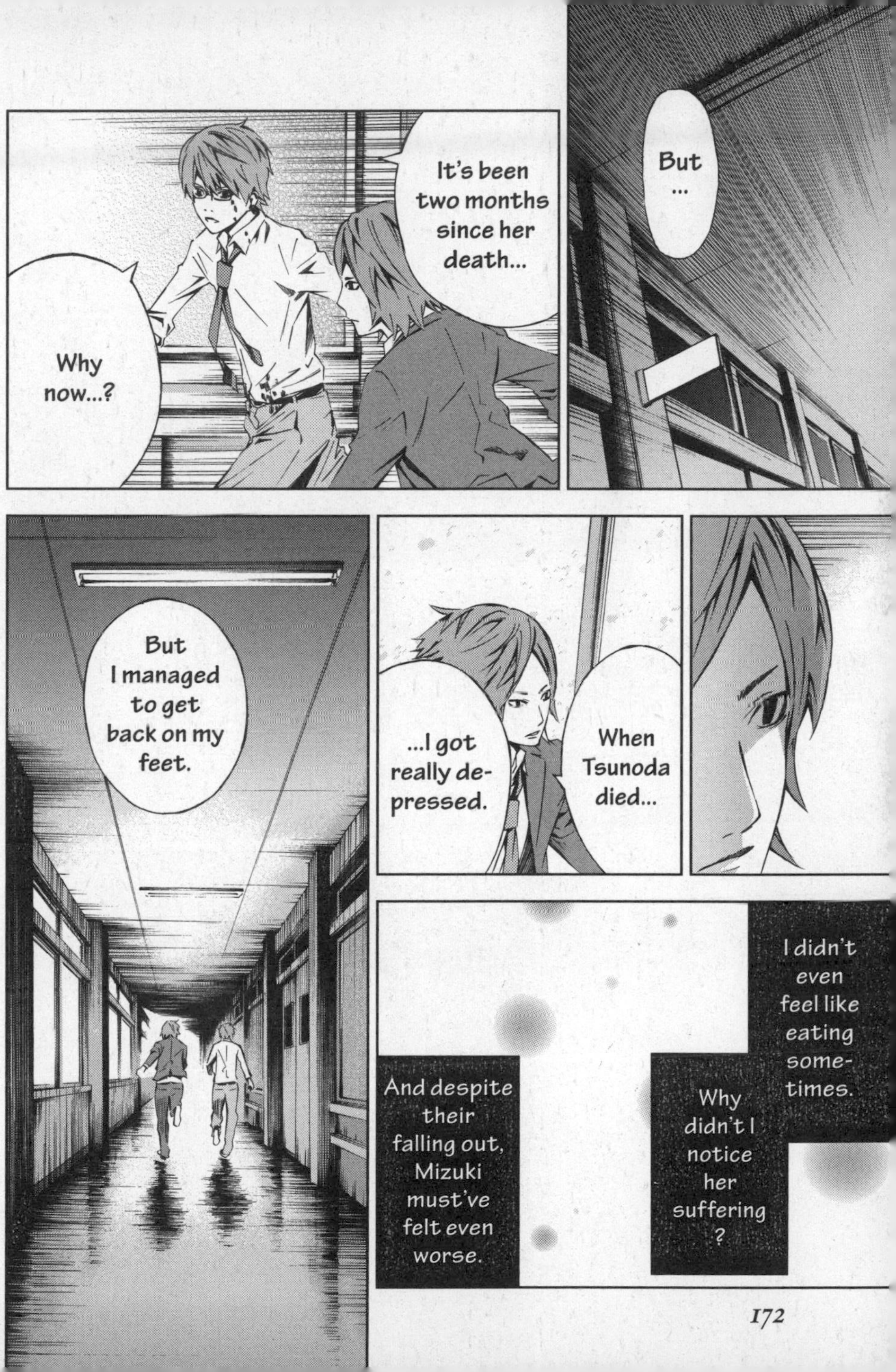
But ...
It's been two months since her death...
Why now...?
When Tsunoda died...
...I got really de-pressed.
I didn't even feel like eating some-times.
Why didn't I notice her suffering?
And despite their falling out, Mizuki must've felt even worse.
But I managed to get back on my feet.

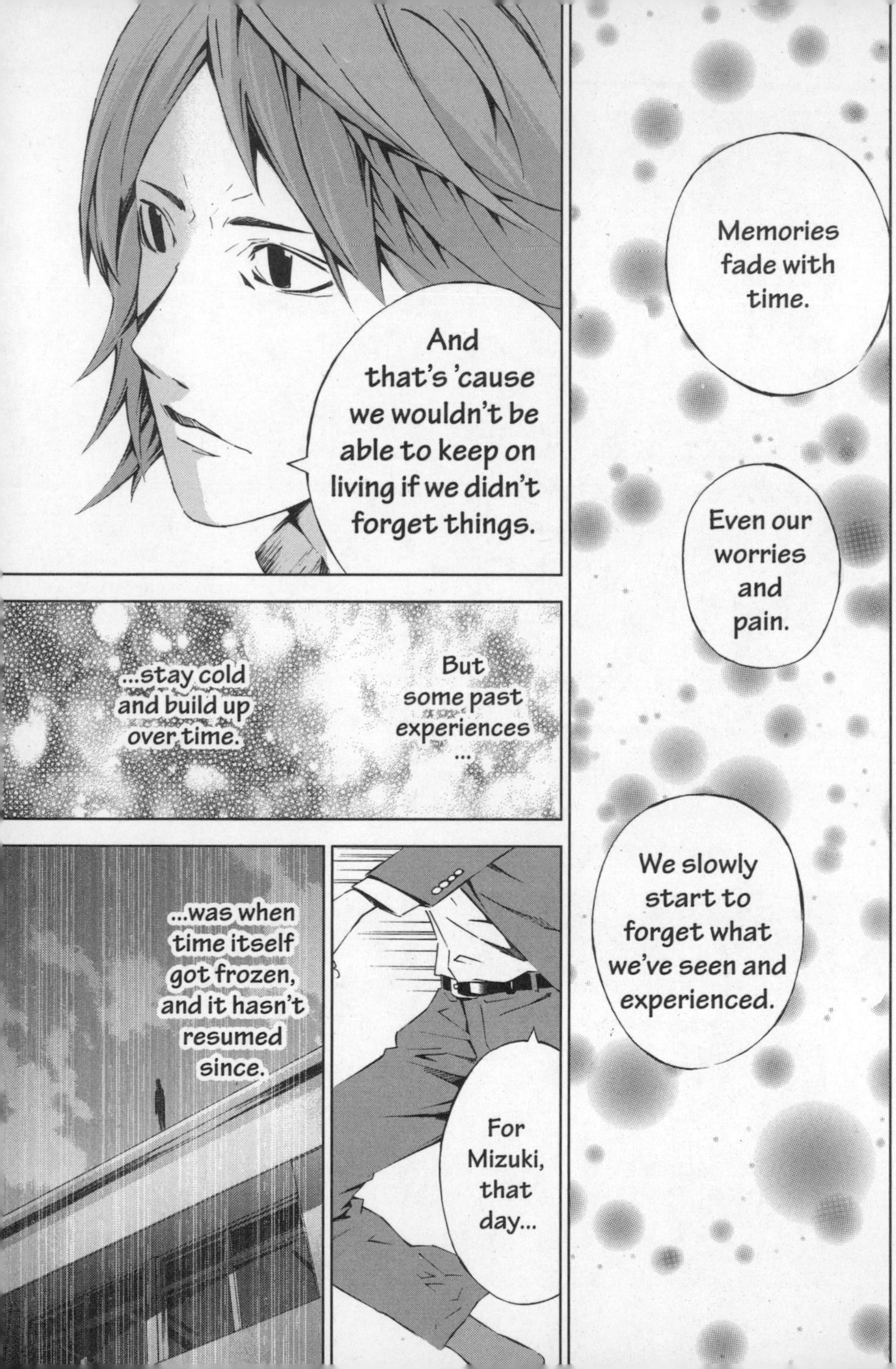
Memories fade with time.
Even our worries and pain.
We slowly start to forget what we've seen and experienced.
And that's 'cause we wouldn't be able to keep on living if we didn't forget things.
But some past experiences ...
...stay cold and build up over time.
For Mizuki, that day...
...was when time itself got frozen, and it hasn't resumed since.

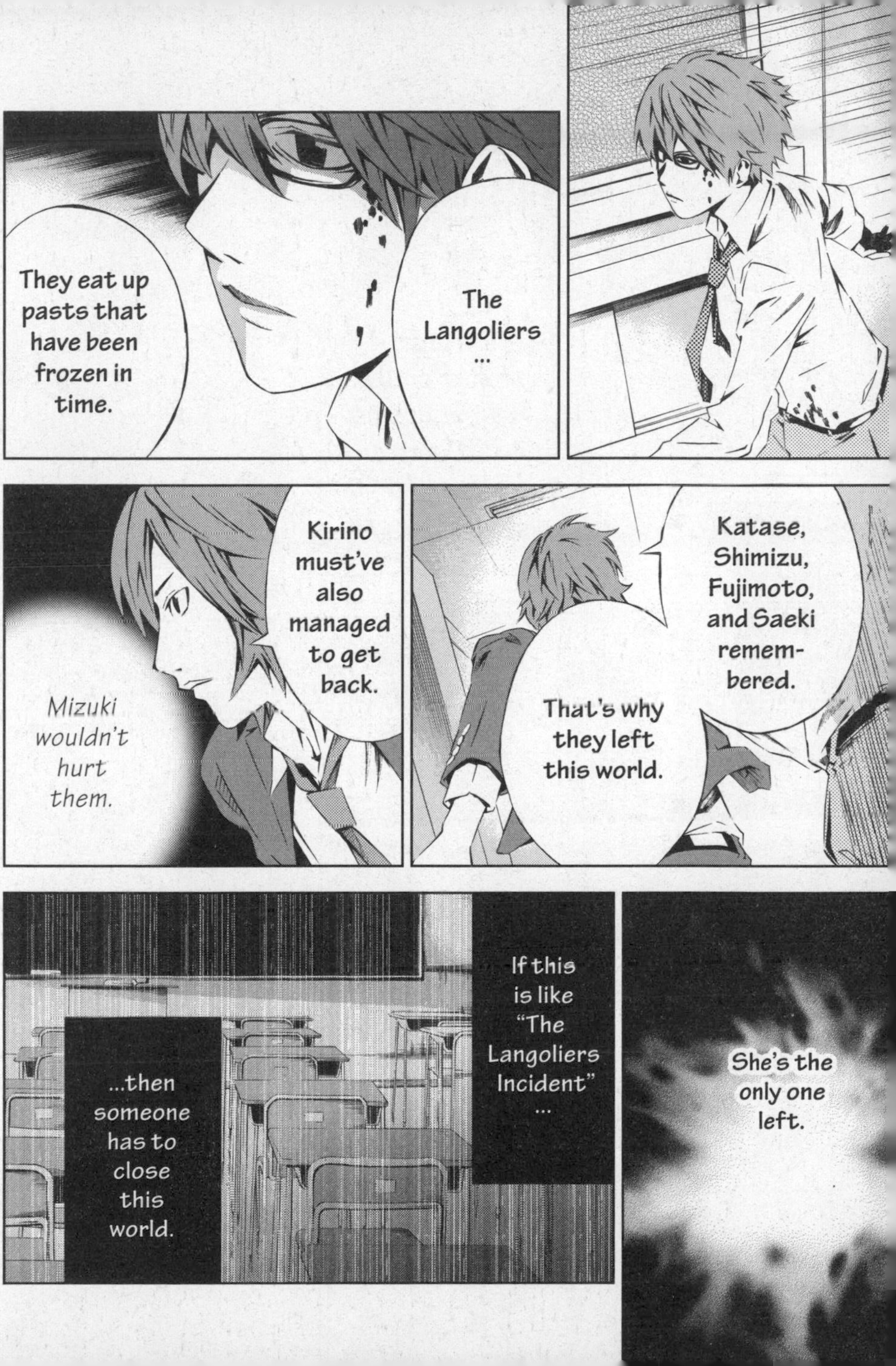
The Langoliers ...
They eat up pasts that have been frozen in time.
Katase, Shimizu, Fujimoto, and Saeki remembered.
That's why they left this world.
Kirino must've also managed to get back.
Mizuki wouldn't hurt them.
She's the only one left.
If this is like "The Langoliers Incident" ...
...then someone has to close this world.

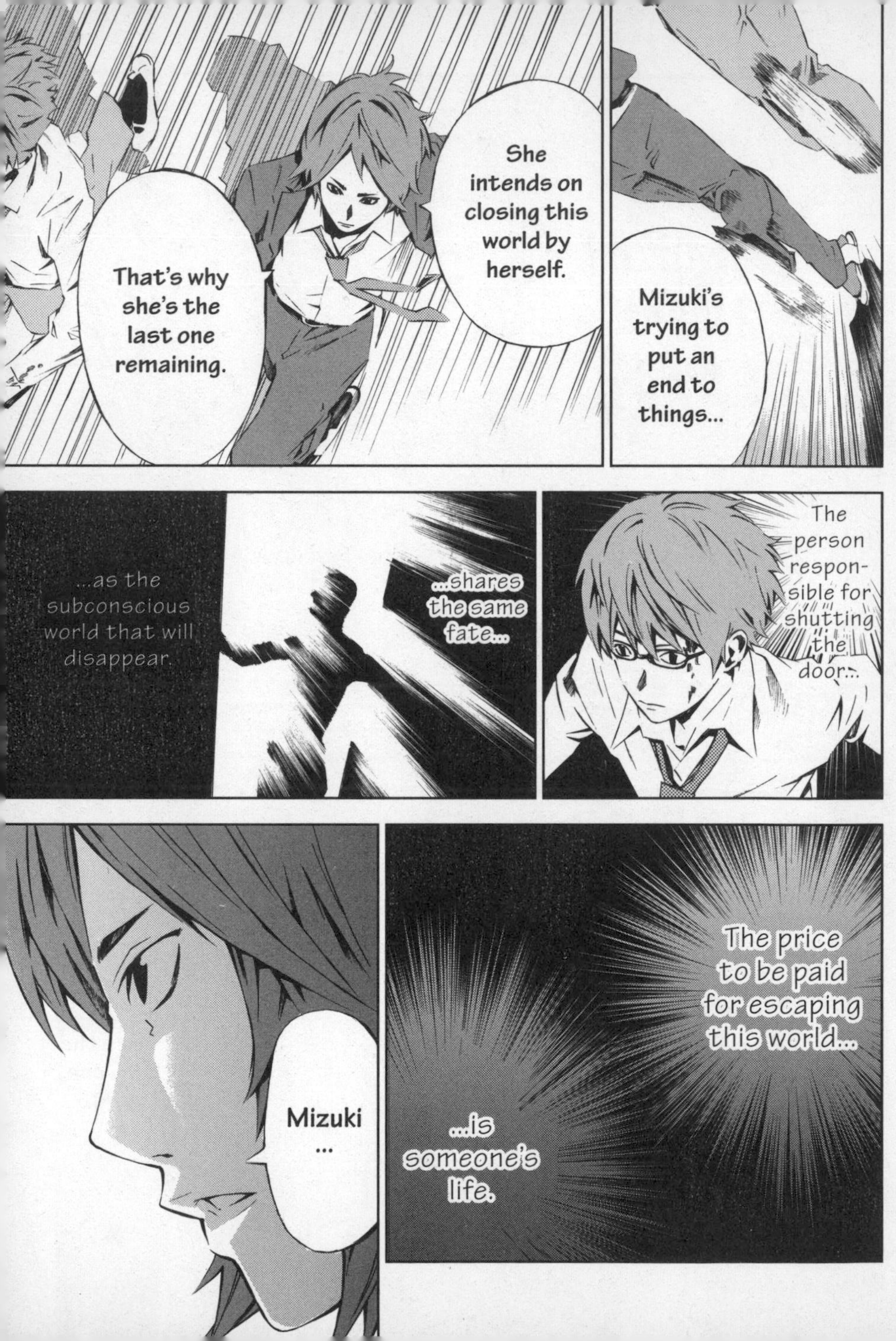
Mizuki's trying to put an end to things...
She intends on closing this world by herself.
That's why she's the last one remaining.
The person responsible for shutting the door...
...shares the same fate...
...as the subconscious world that will disappear.
The price to be paid for escaping this world...
...is someone's life.
Mizuki ...

Mizuki
wants
to die.

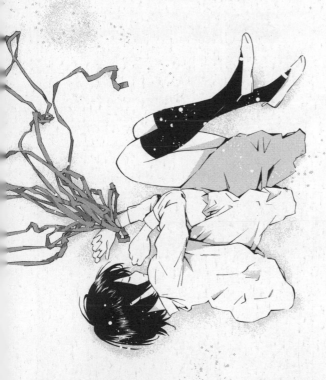

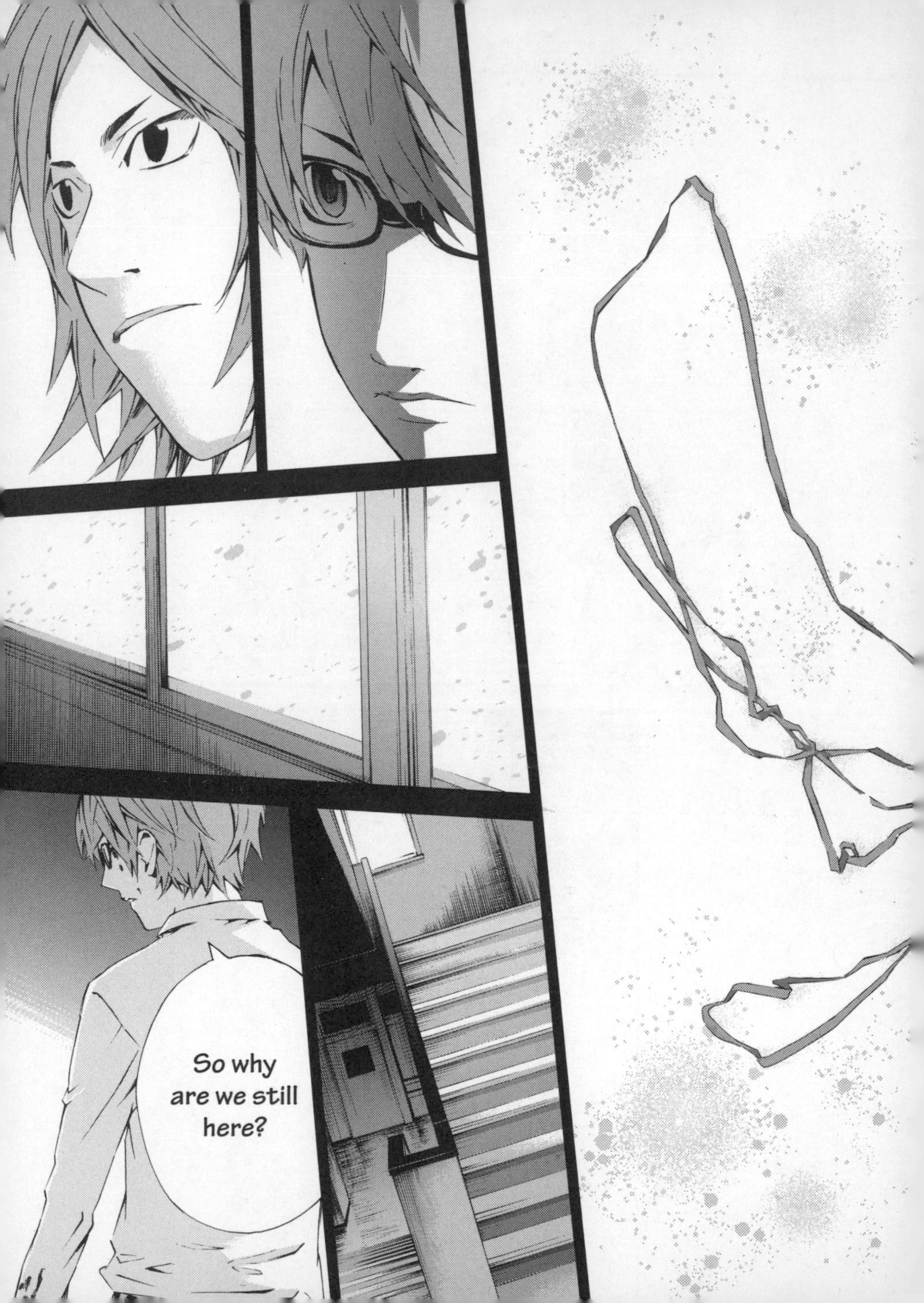
So why are we still here?

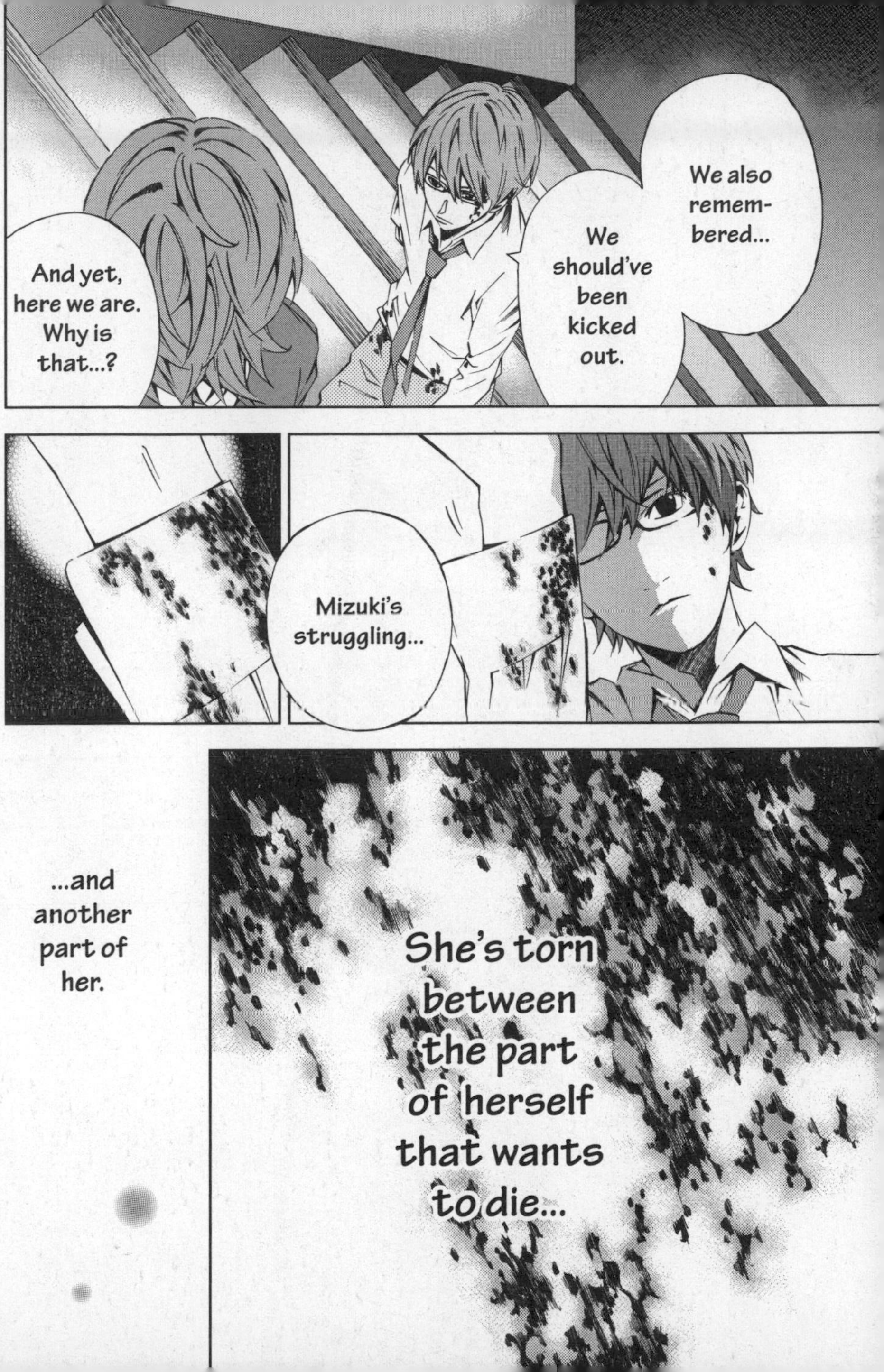
We also remem-bered...
We should've been kicked out.
And yet, here we are. Why is that...?
Mizuki's struggling...
She's torn between the part of herself that wants to die...
...and another part of her.

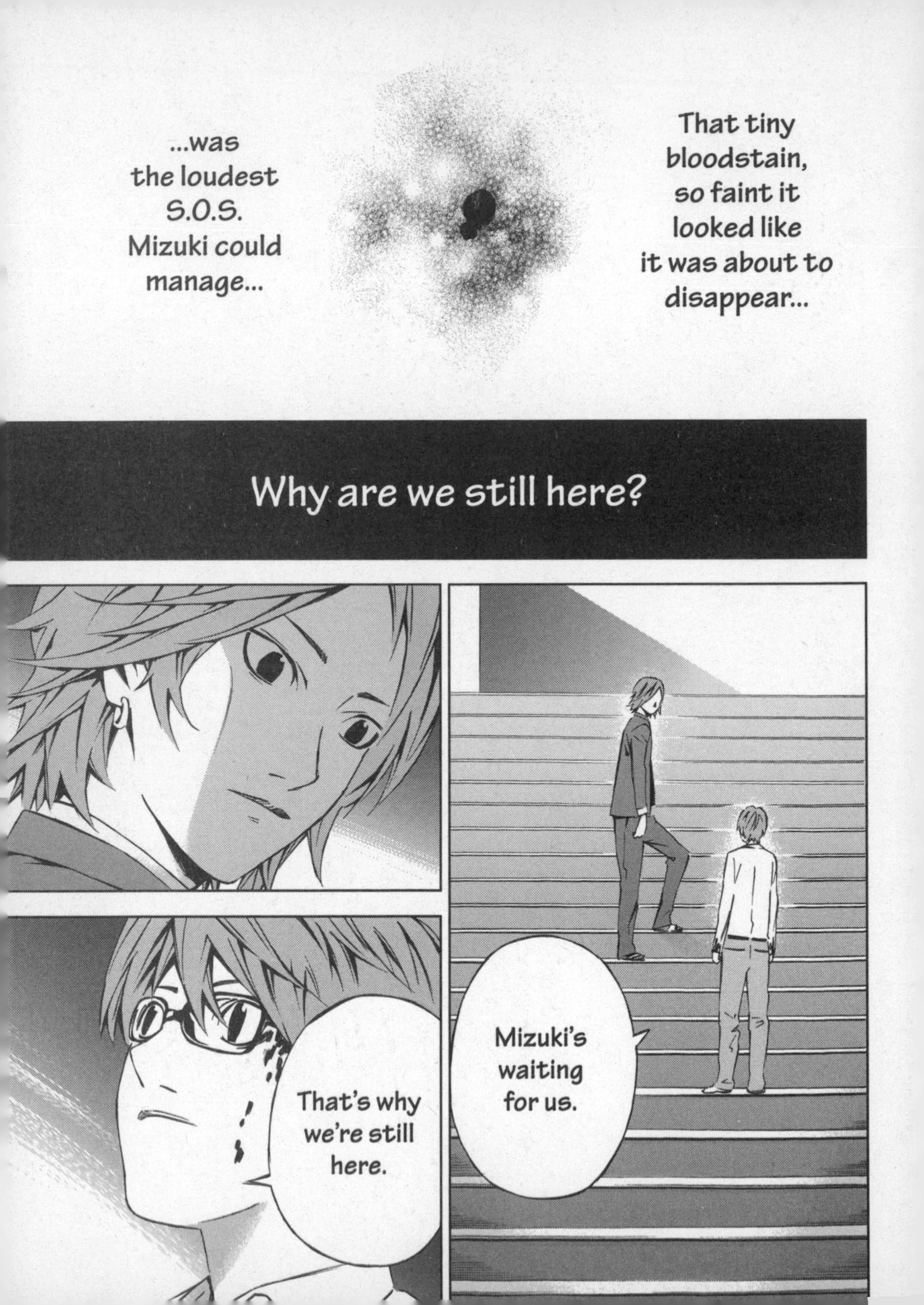
That tiny bloodstain, so faint it looked like it was about to disappear...
...was the loudest S.O.S. Mizuki could manage...
Why are we still here?
Mizuki's waiting for us.
That's why we're still here.

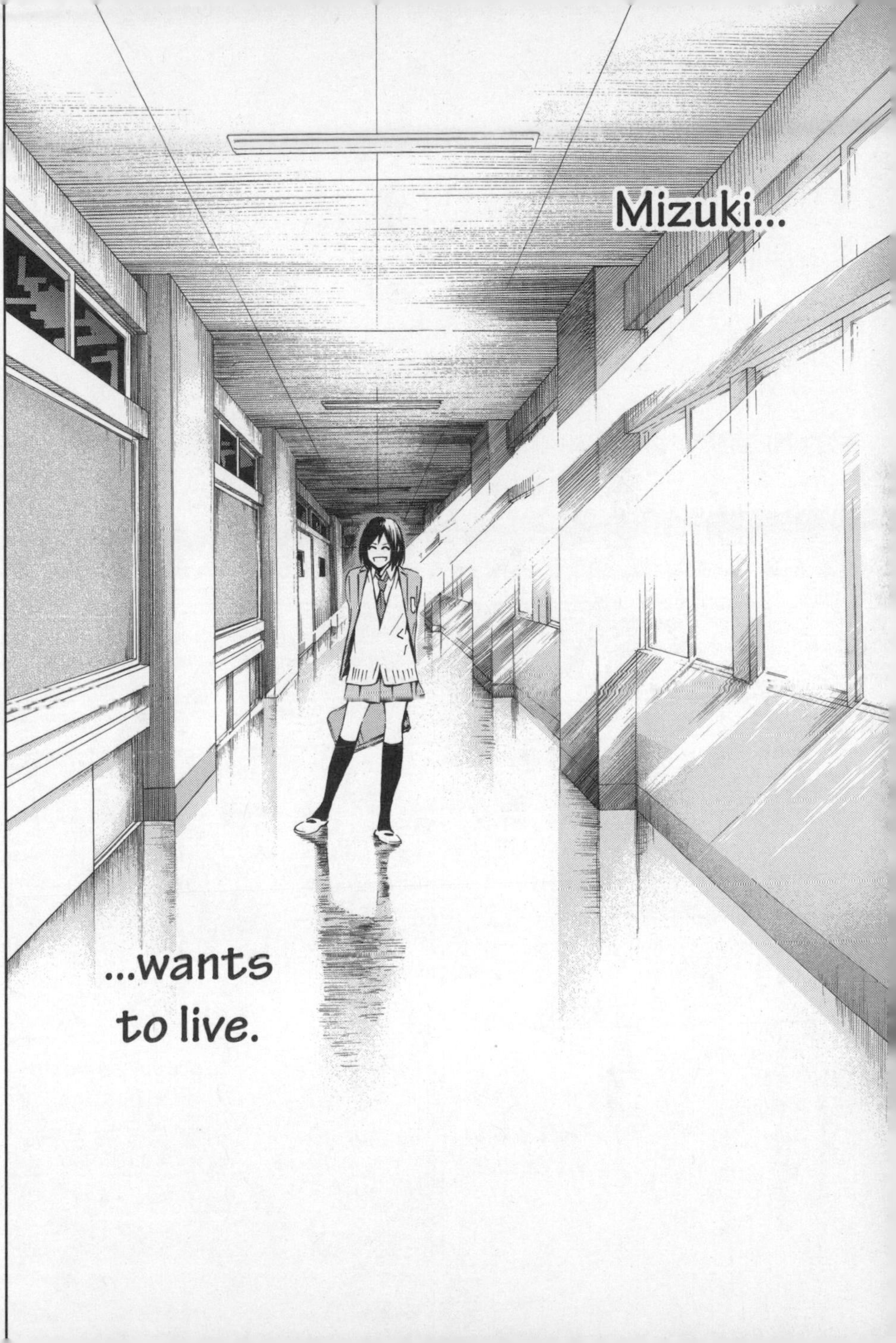
Mizuki...
...wants to live.

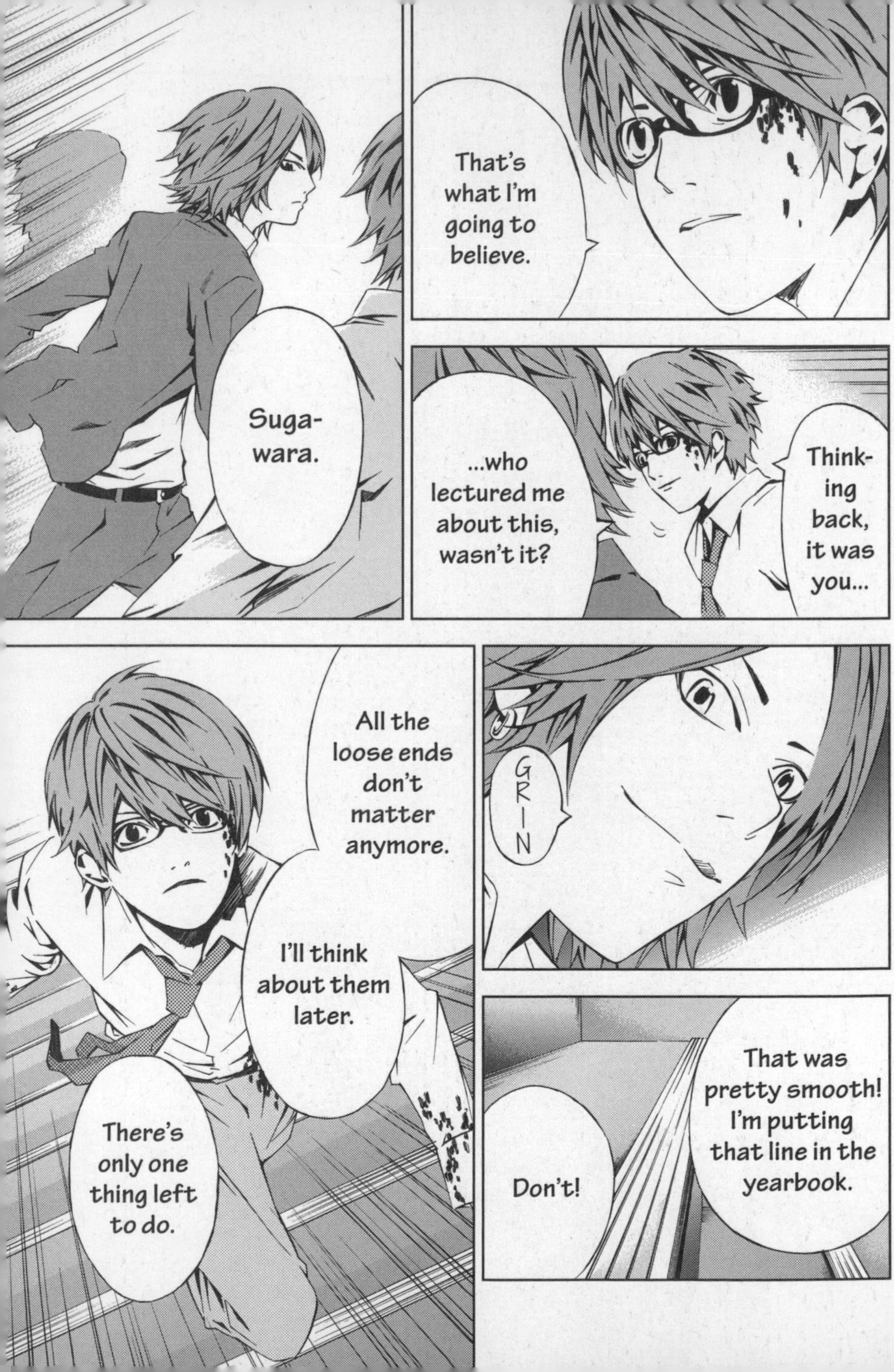
That's what I'm going to believe.
Thinking back, it was you...
...who lectured me about this, wasn't it?
Sugawara.
GRIN
That was pretty smooth! I'm putting that line in the yearbook.
Don't!
All the loose ends don't matter anymore.
I'll think about them later.
There's only one thing left to do.

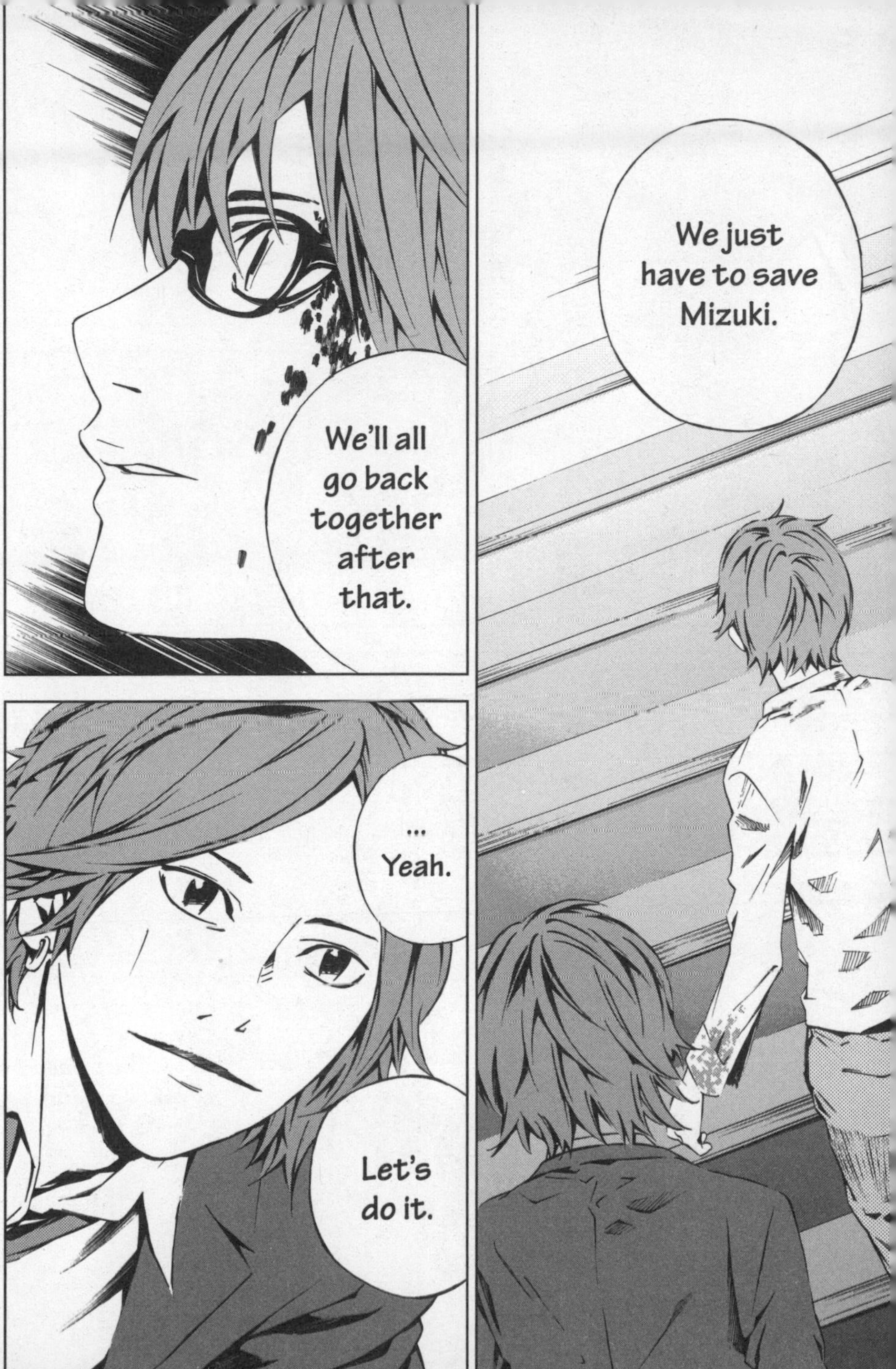
We just have to save Mizuki.
We'll all go back together after that.
... Yeah.
Let's do it.

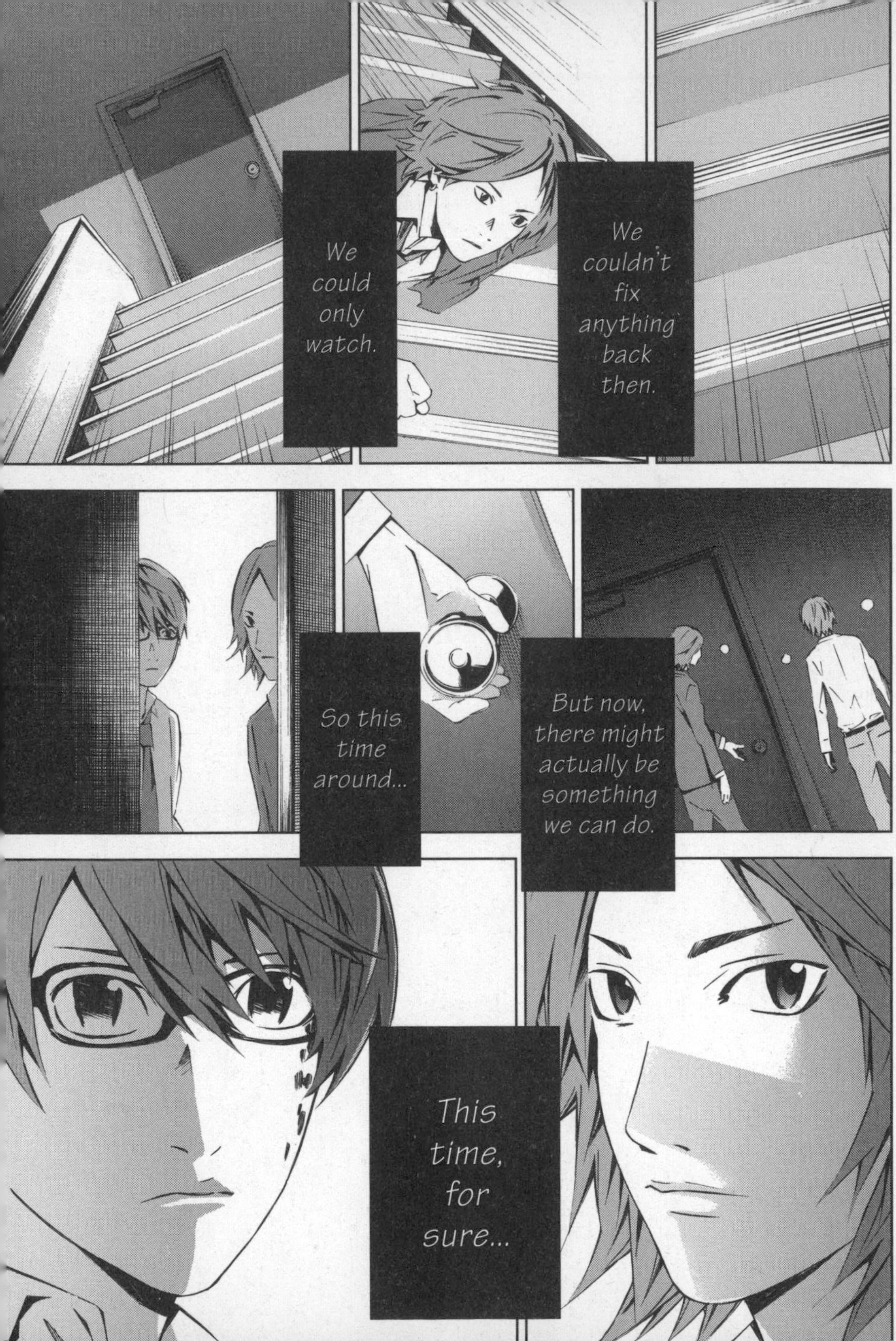
We couldn't fix anything back then.
We could only watch.
But now, there might actually be something we can do.
So this time around...
This time, for sure...

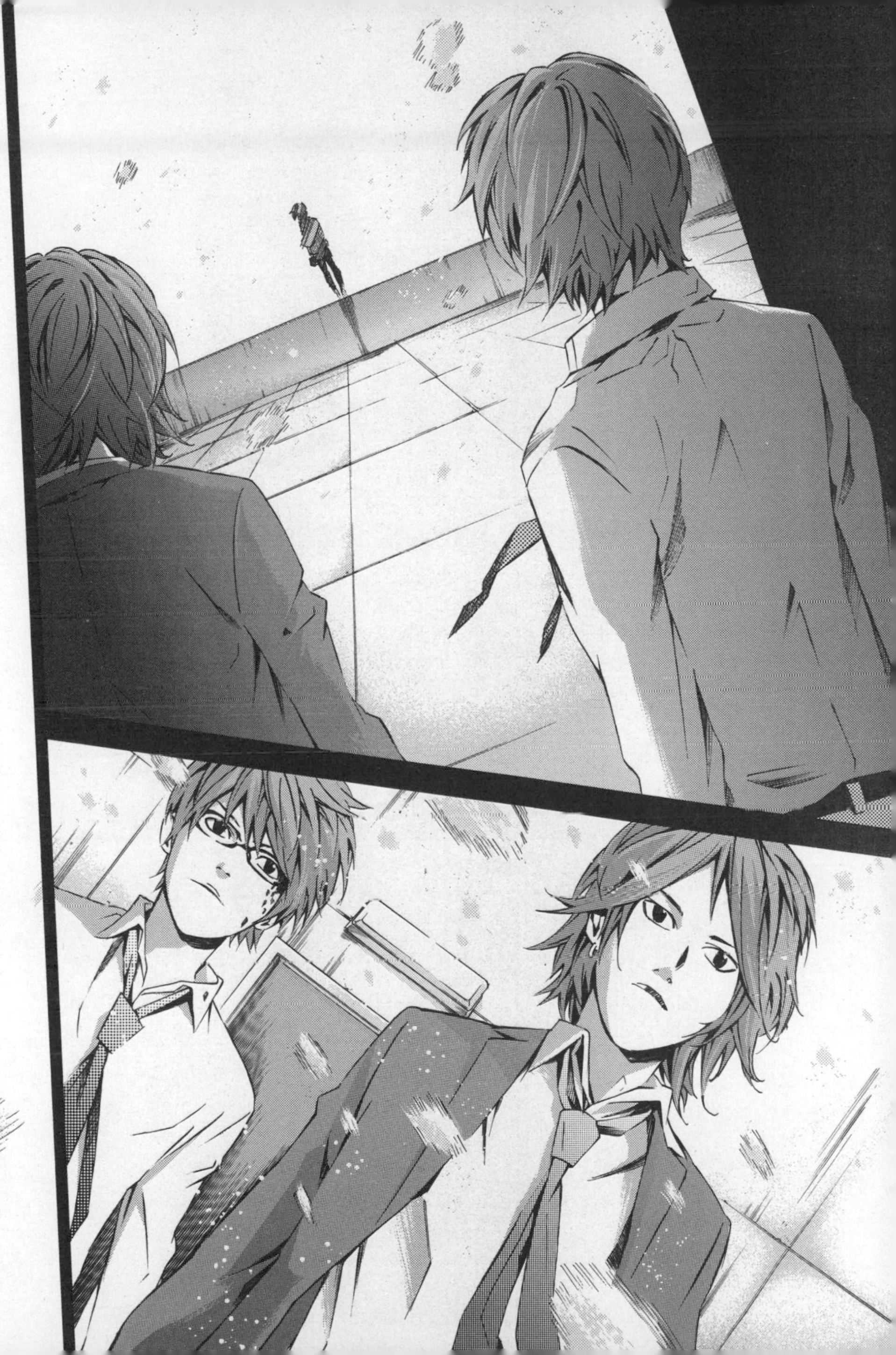

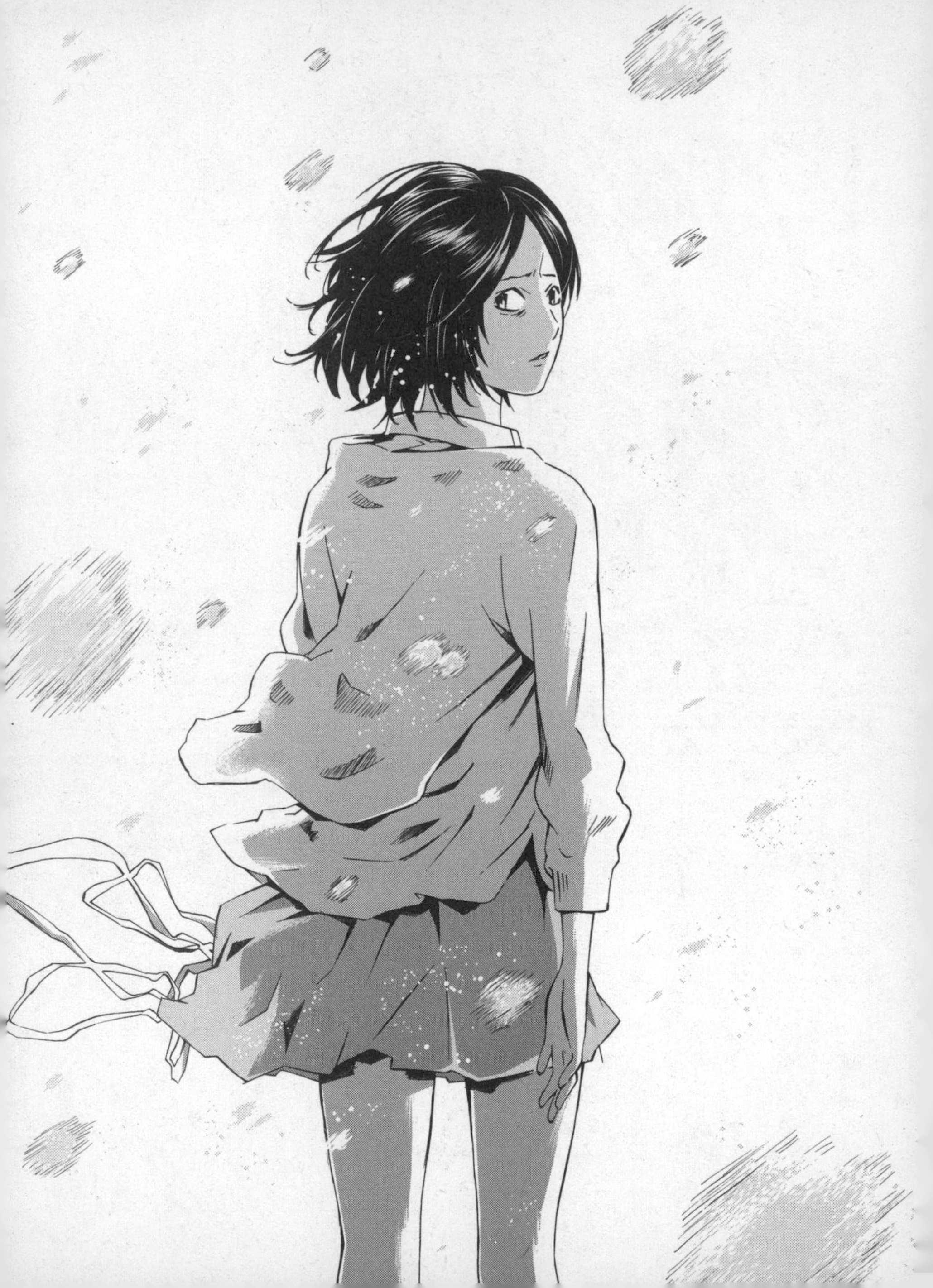

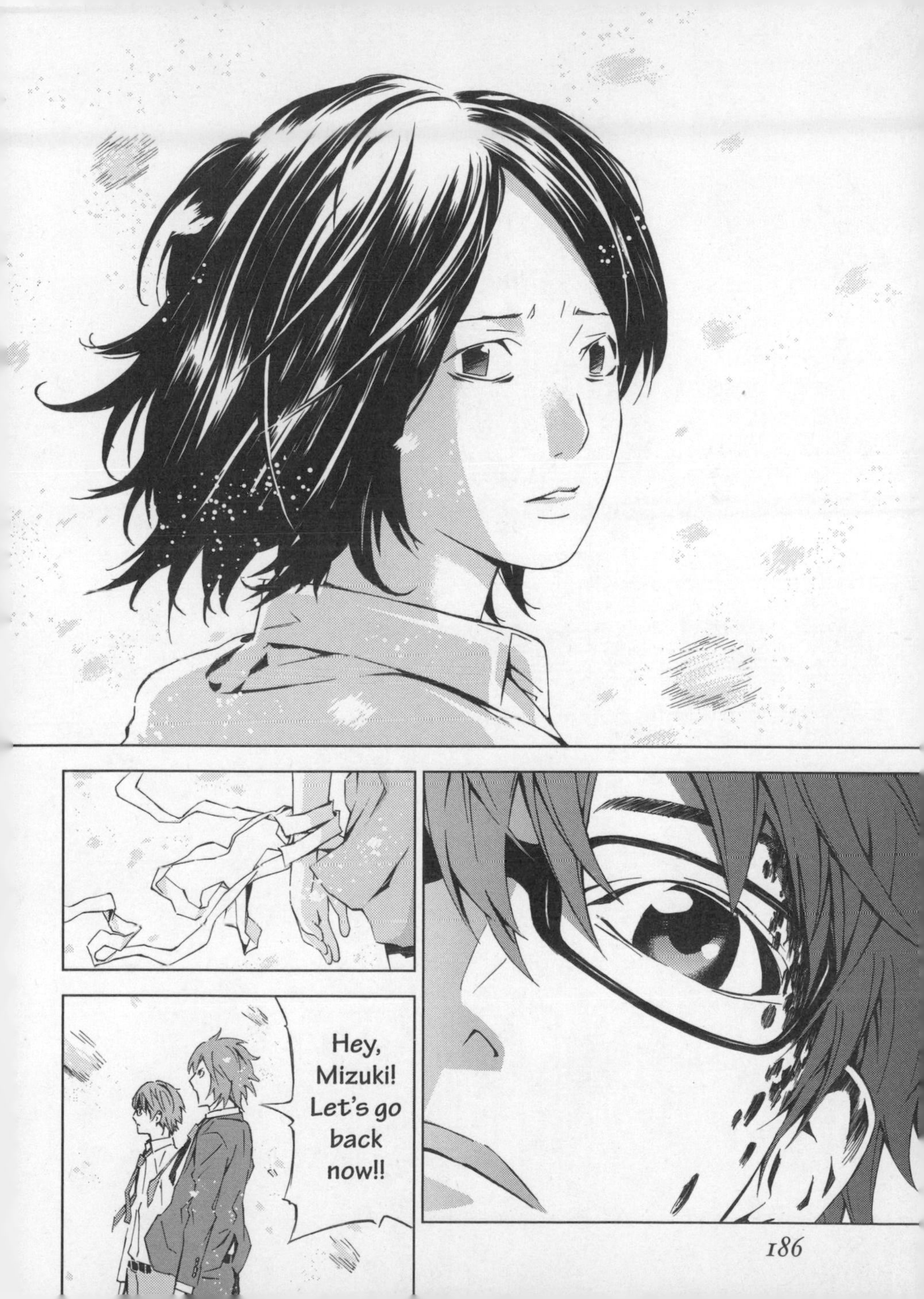
Hey, Mizuki! Let's go back now!!

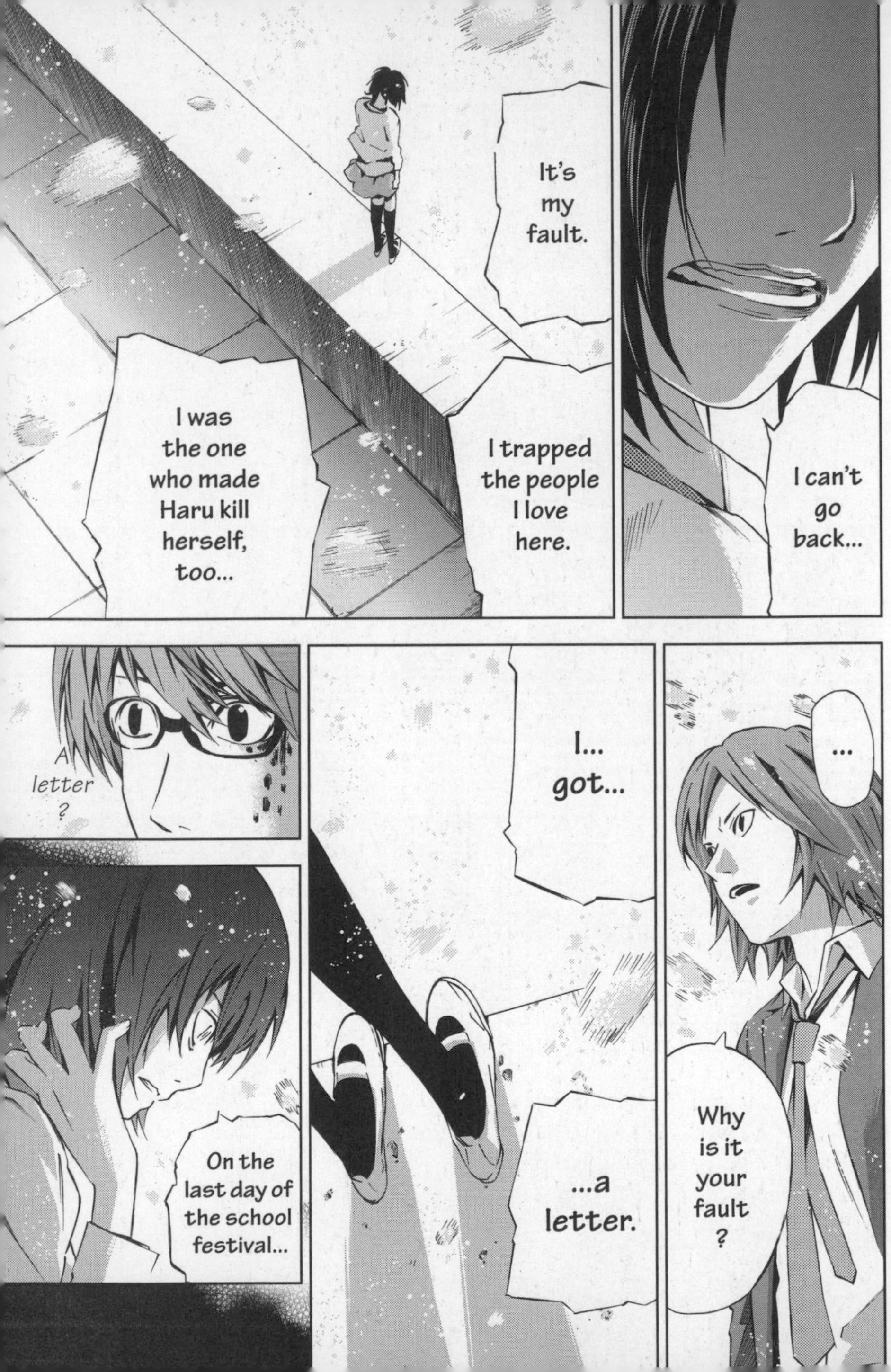
I can't go back...
It's my fault.
I trapped the people I love here.
I was the one who made Haru kill herself, too...
...
Why is it your fault?
I... got...
...a letter.
A letter?
On the last day of the school festival...

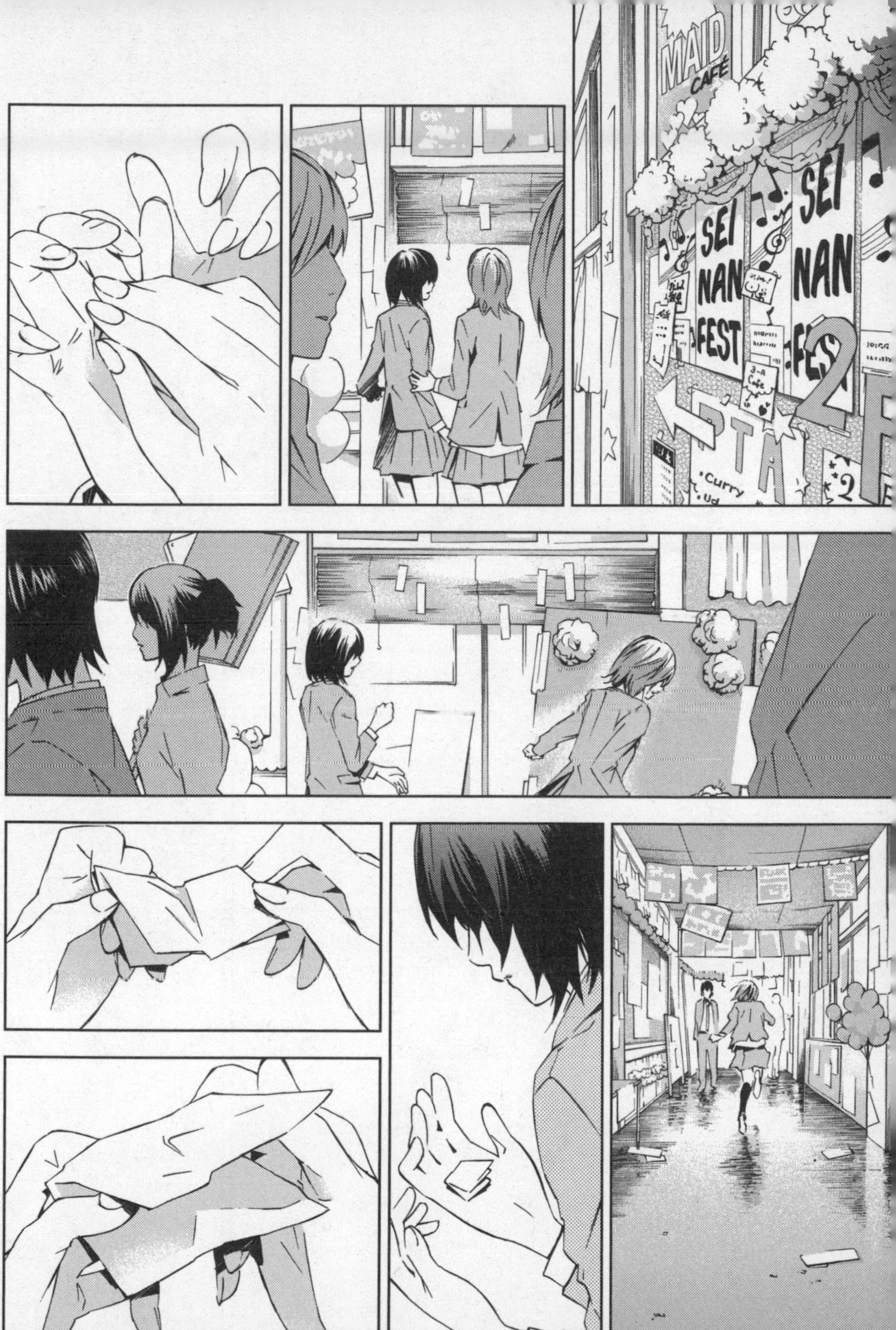
MAID
CAFÉ
SEI NAN FEST
SEI NAN
2F
PTA
3-A Cafe
•Curry

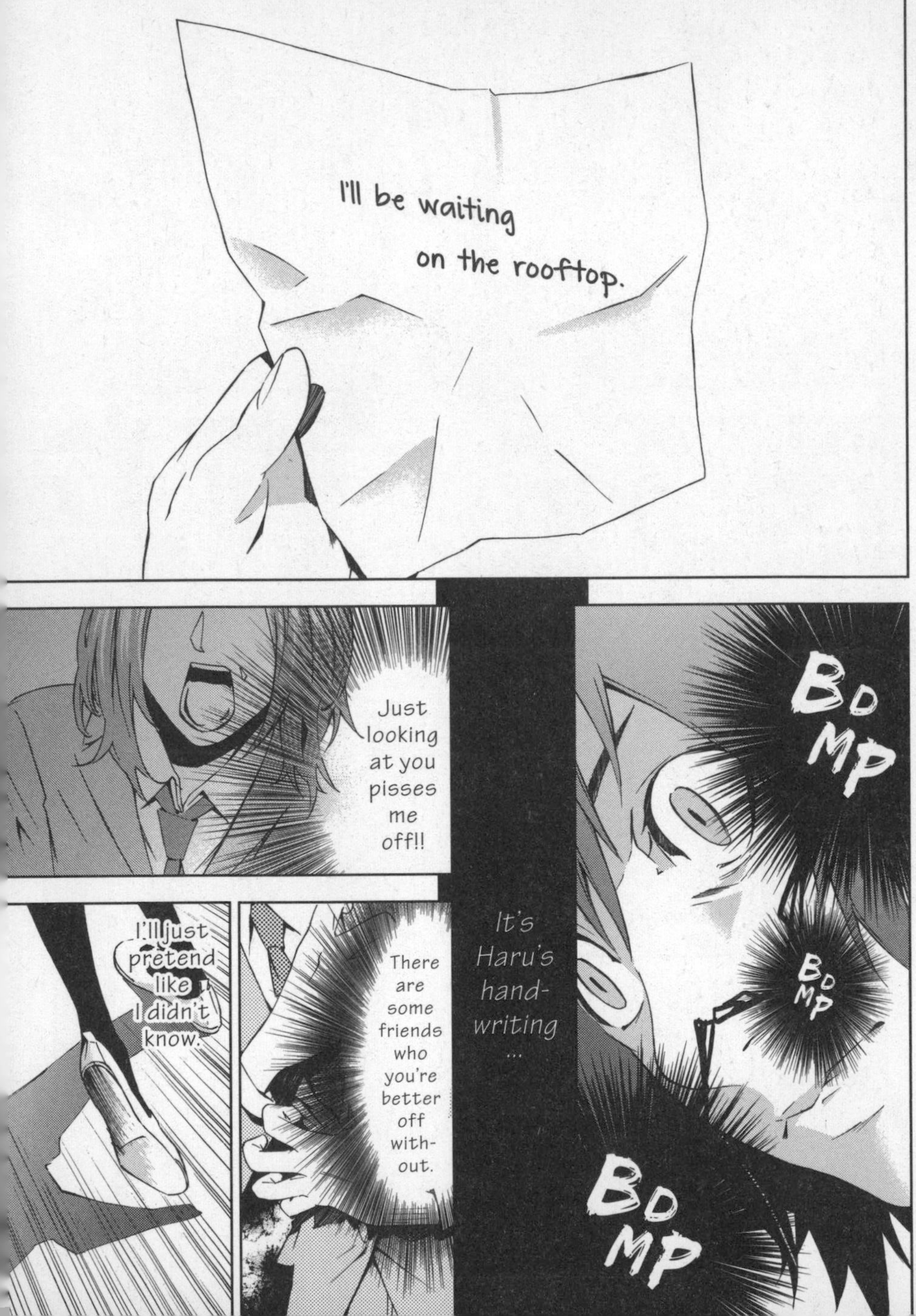
I'll be waiting on the rooftop.
BDMP
It's Haru's handwriting...
BDMP
BDMP
Just looking at you pisses me off!!
There are some friends who you're better off with-out.
I'll just pretend like I didn't know.

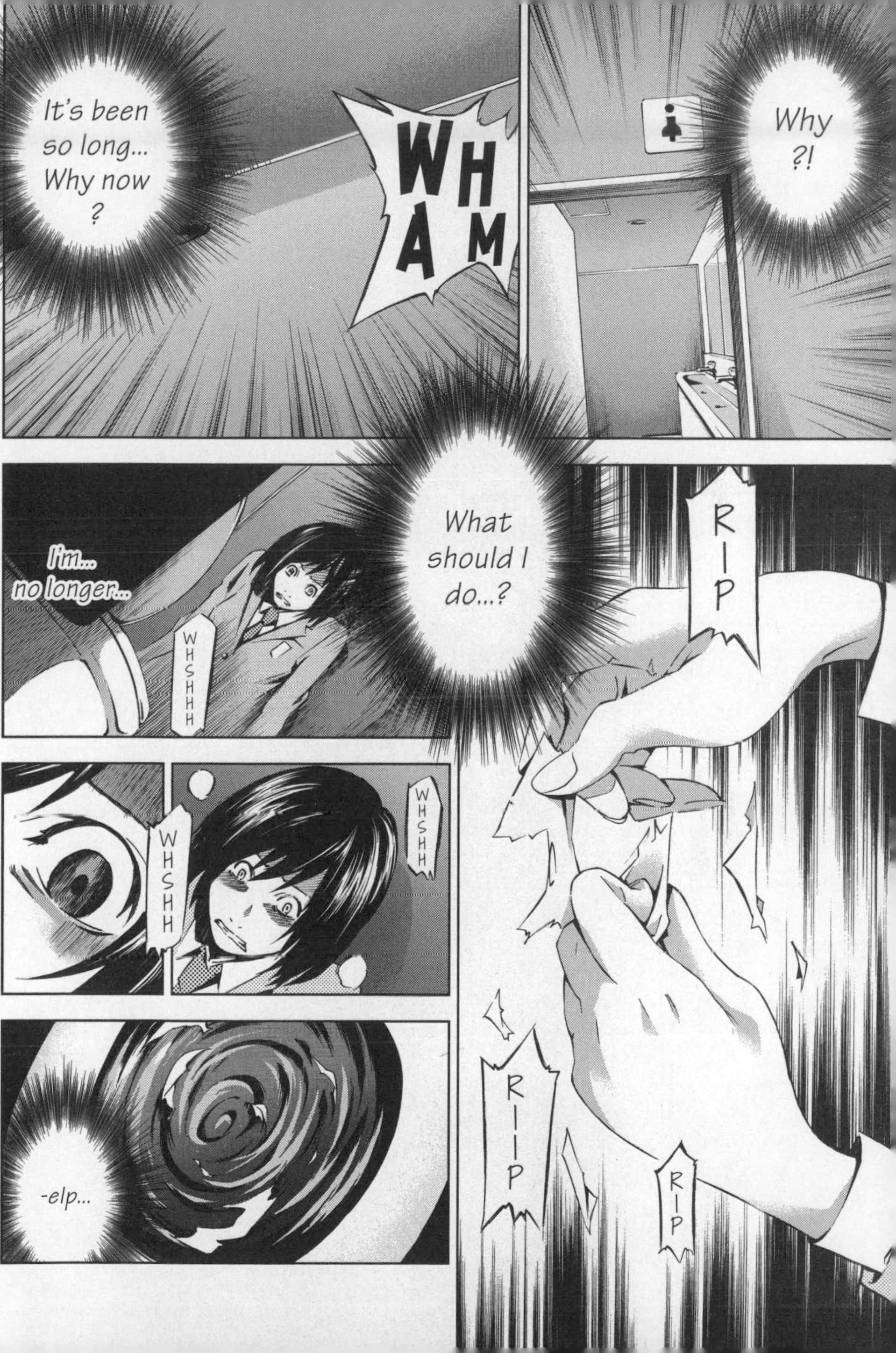
Why ?!
WHAM
It's been so long... Why now ?
RIP
RIIP
RIP
What should I do...?
I'm... no longer...
WHSHHH
WHSHH
WHSHH
-elp...

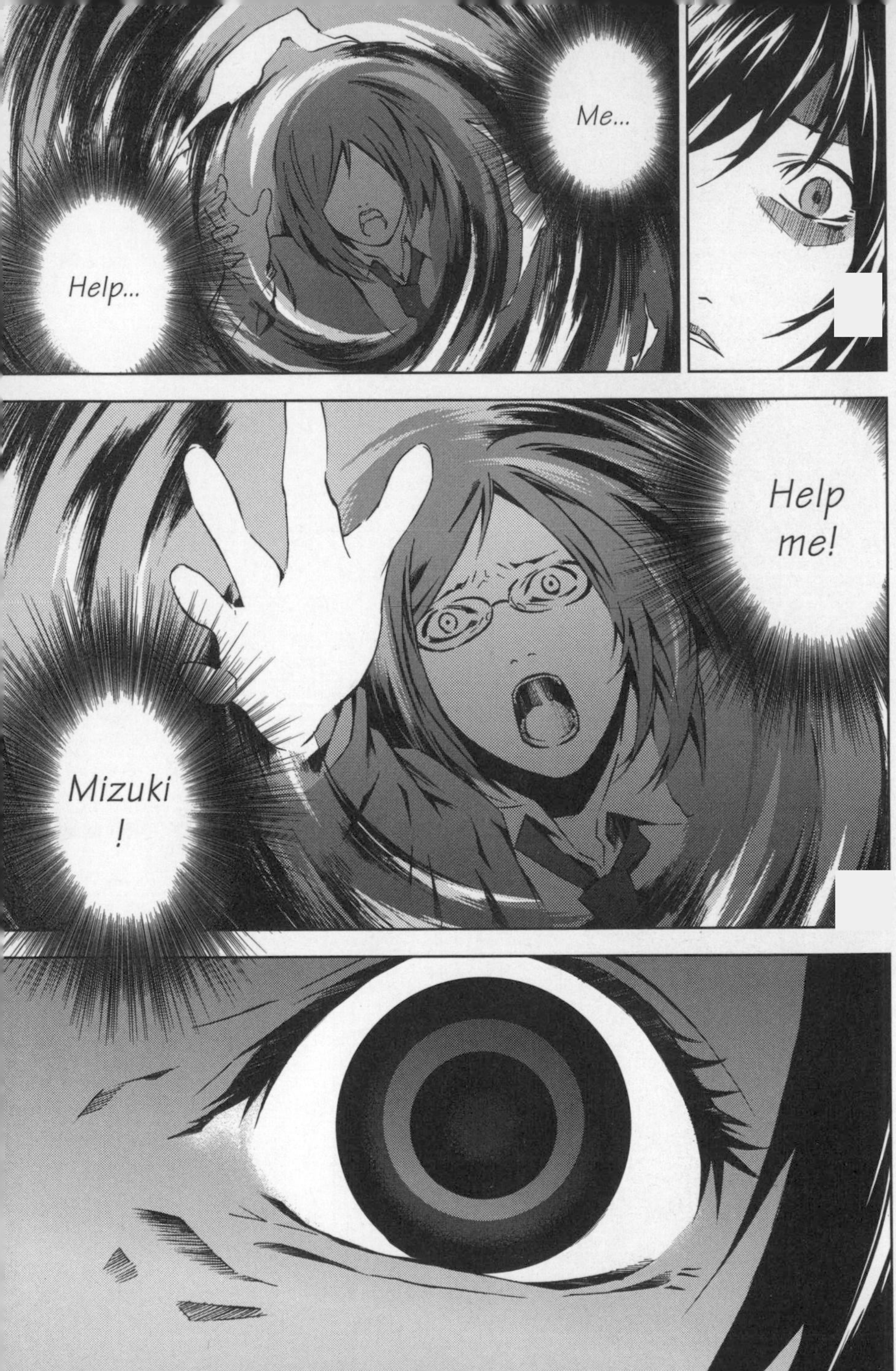
Me...
Help...
Help me!
Mizuki !

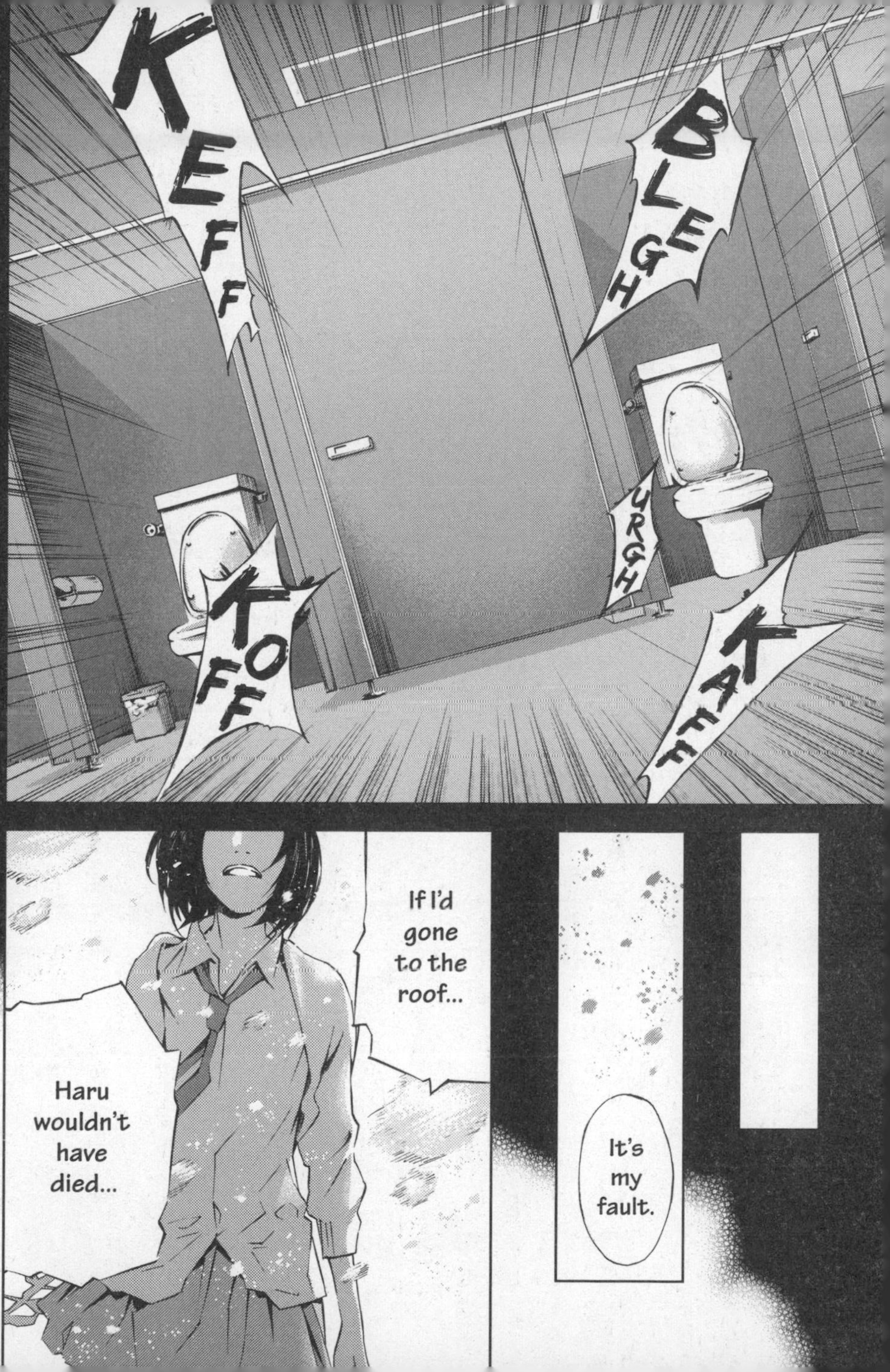
BLEGH
URGH
KAFF
KEFF
KOFF
It's my fault.
If I'd gone to the roof...
Haru wouldn't have died...

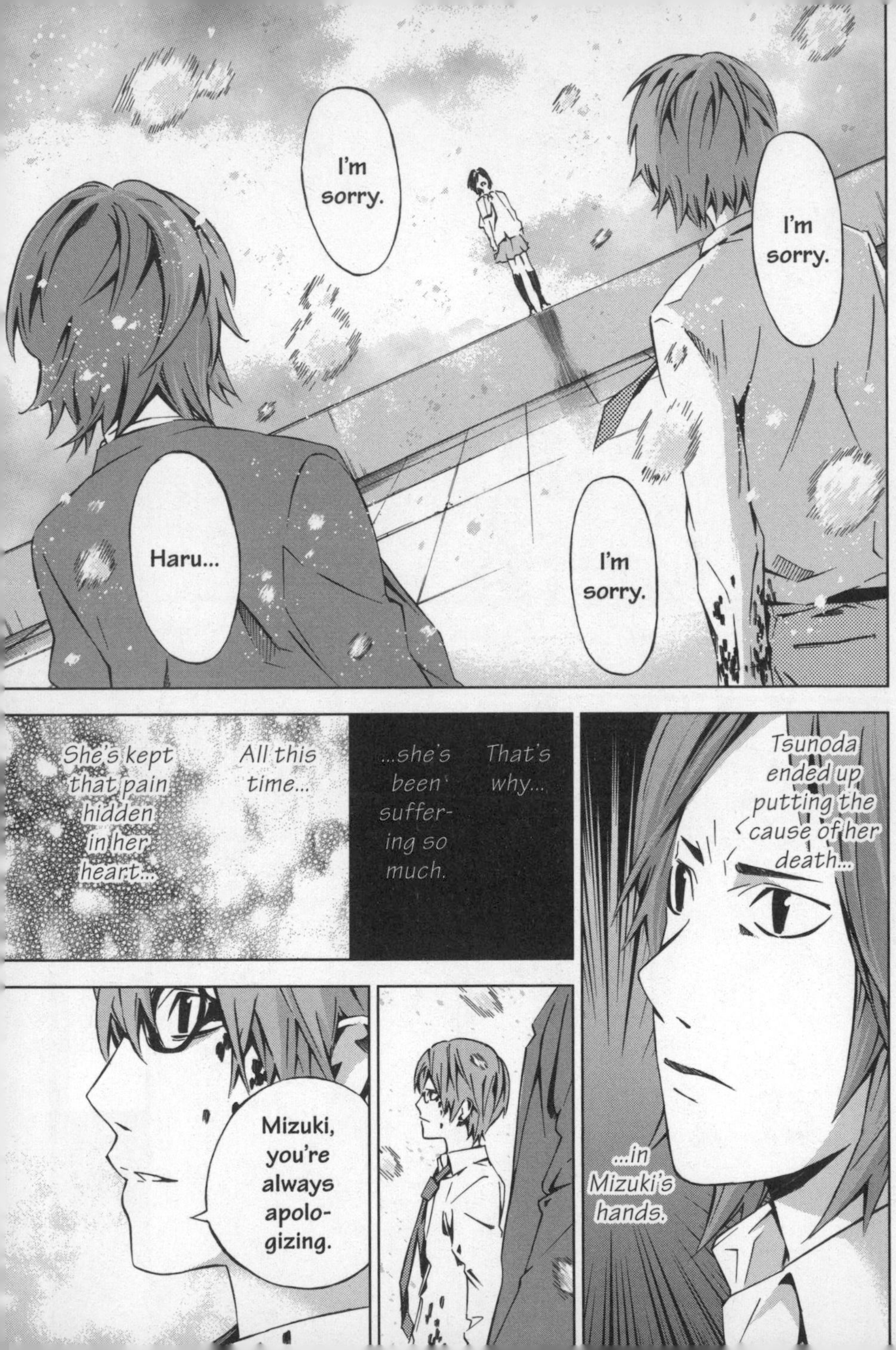
I'm sorry.
I'm sorry.
I'm sorry.
Haru...
Tsunoda ended up putting the cause of her death...
...in Mizuki's hands.
That's why...
...she's been suffer-ing so much.
All this time...
She's kept that pain hidden in her heart...
Mizuki, you're always apolo-gizing.

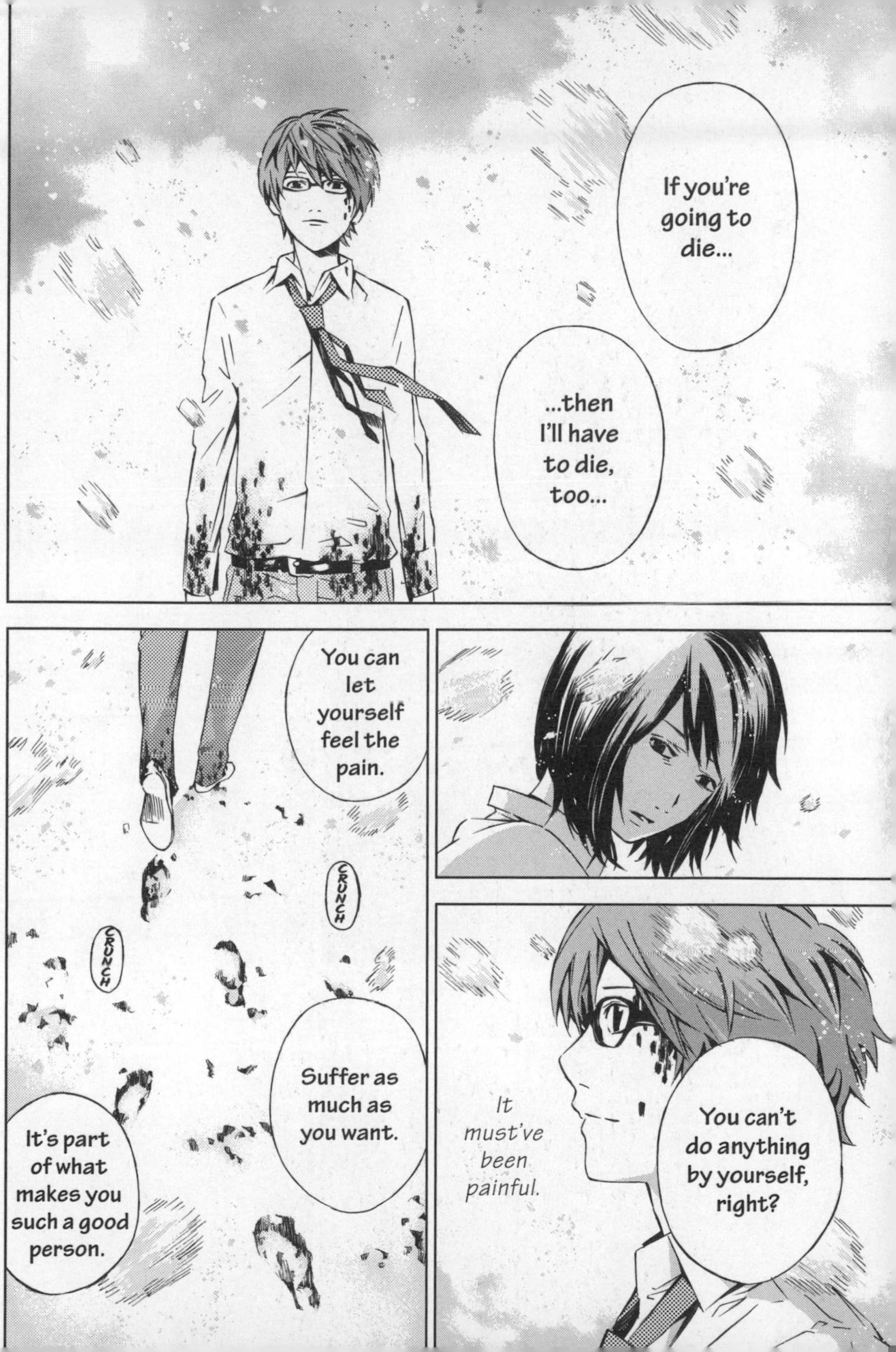
If you're going to die...
...then I'll have to die, too...
You can't do anything by yourself, right?
It must've been painful.
You can let yourself feel the pain.
CRUNCH
CRUNCH
Suffer as much as you want.
It's part of what makes you such a good person.

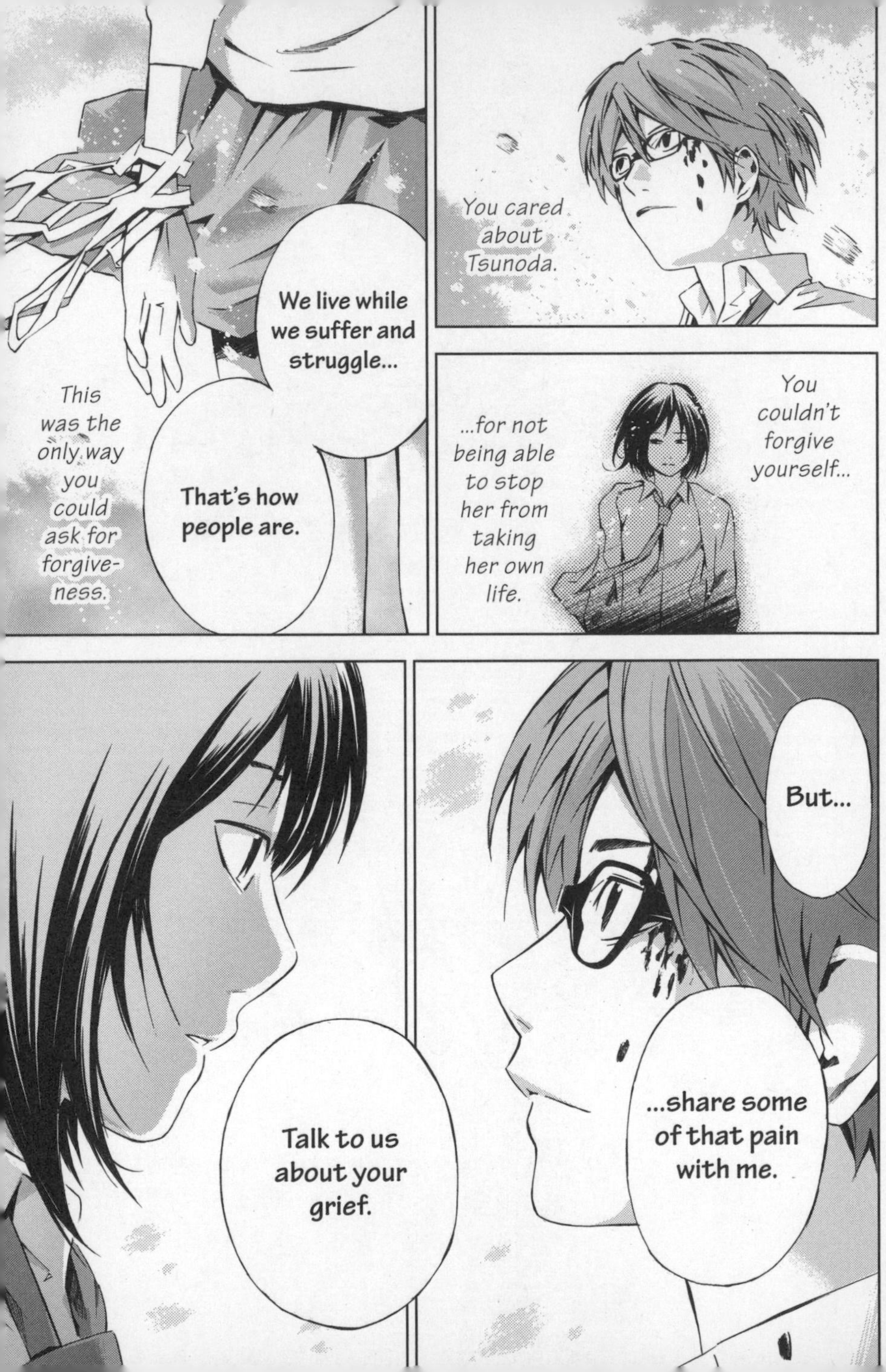
You cared about Tsunoda.
You couldn't forgive yourself...
...for not being able to stop her from taking her own life.
We live while we suffer and struggle...
That's how people are.
This was the only way you could ask for forgiveness.
But...
...share some of that pain with me.
Talk to us about your grief.

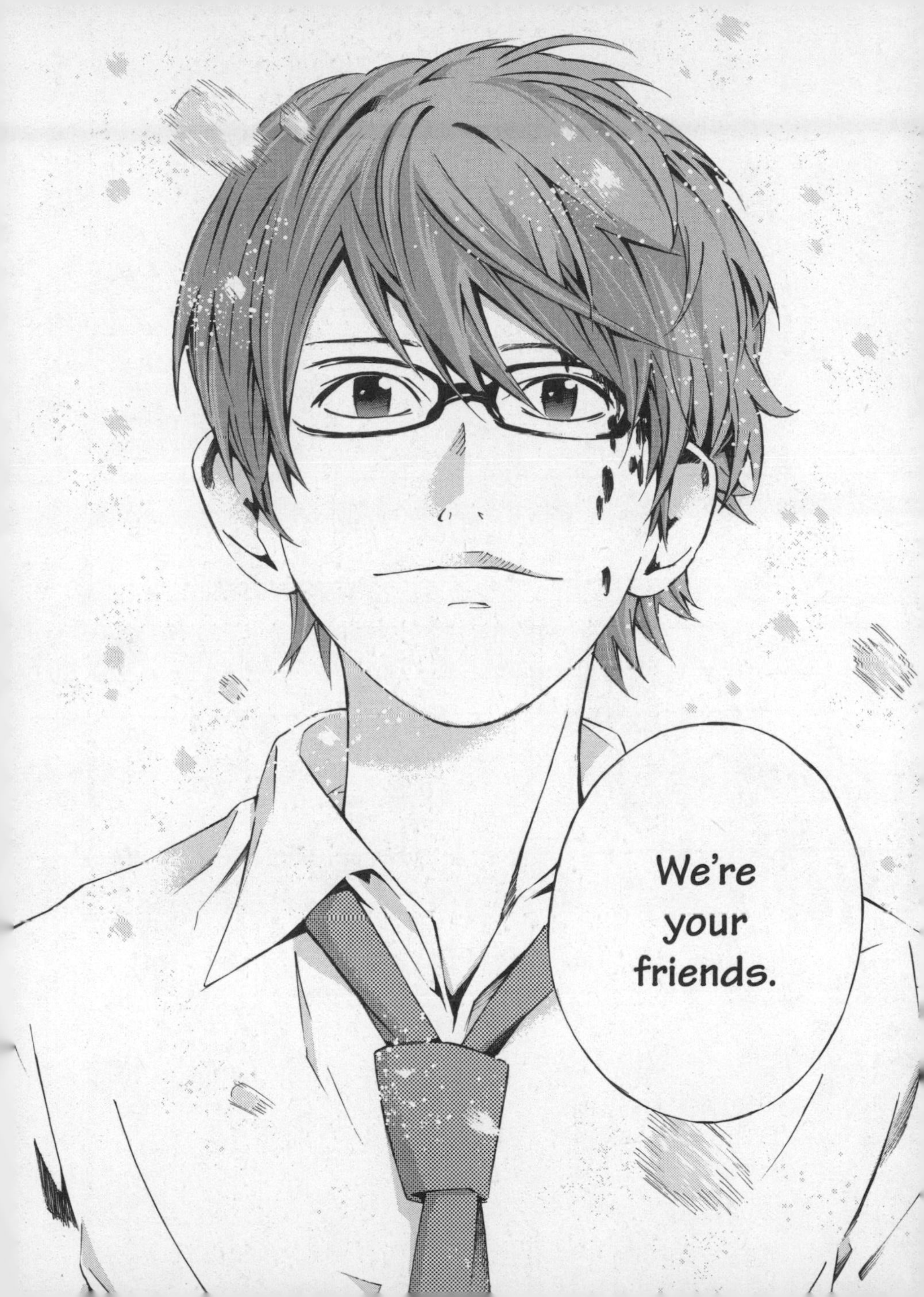
We're your friends.

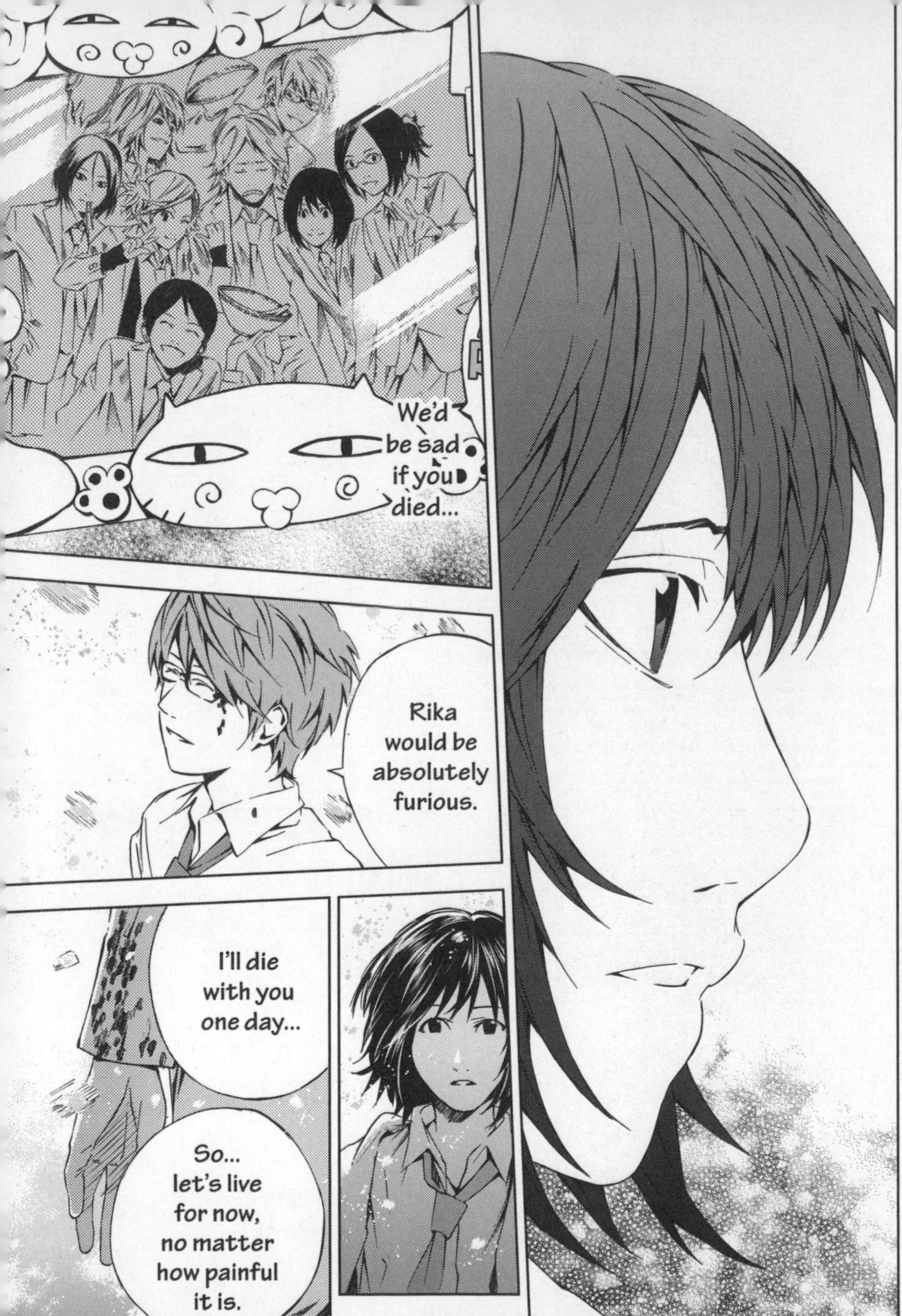
We'd be sad if you died...
Rika would be absolutely furious.
I'll die with you one day...
So... let's live for now, no matter how painful it is.

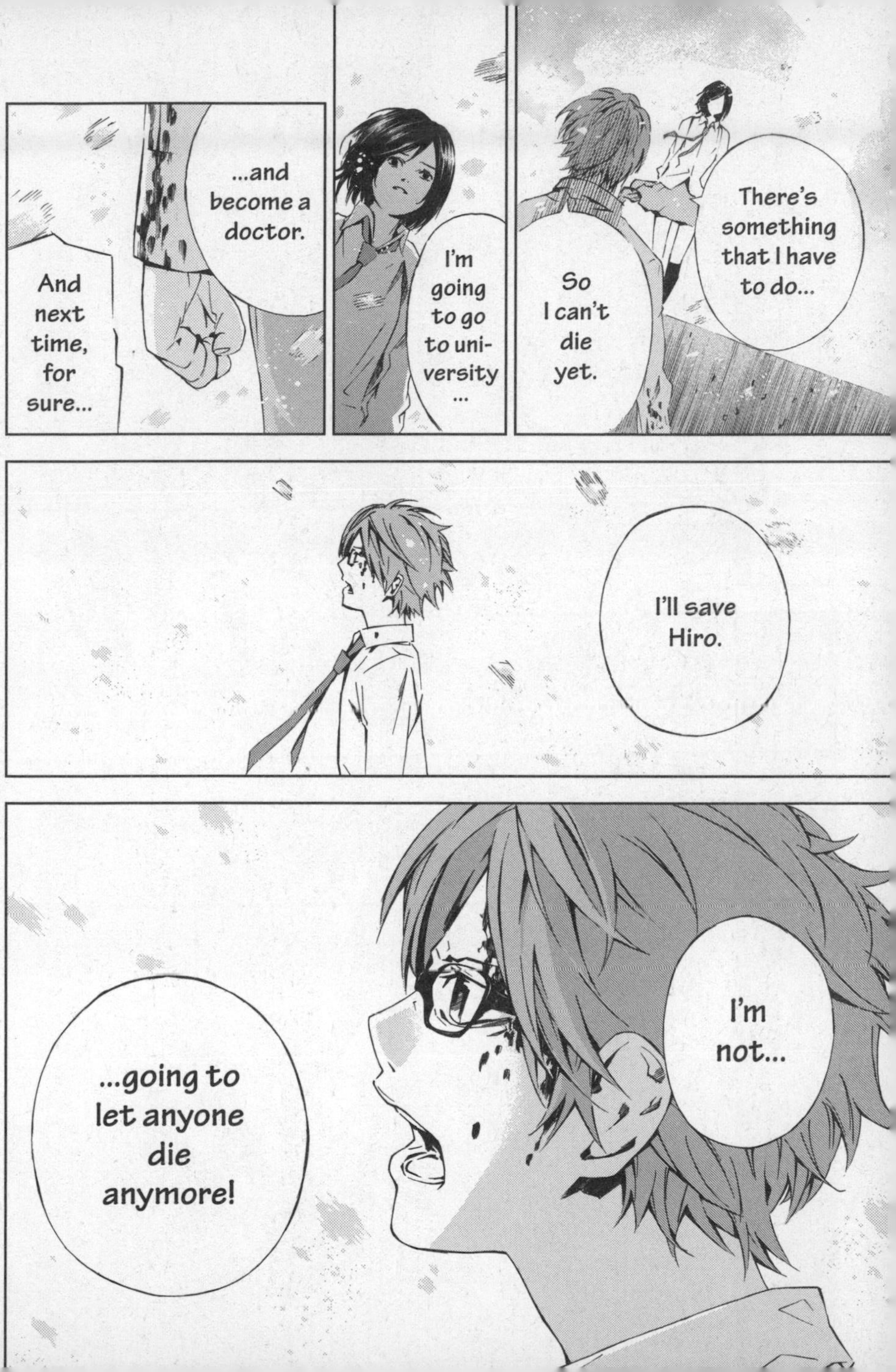
There's something that I have to do...
So I can't die yet.
I'm going to go to university...
...and become a doctor.
And next time, for sure...
I'll save Hiro.
I'm not...
...going to let anyone die anymore!

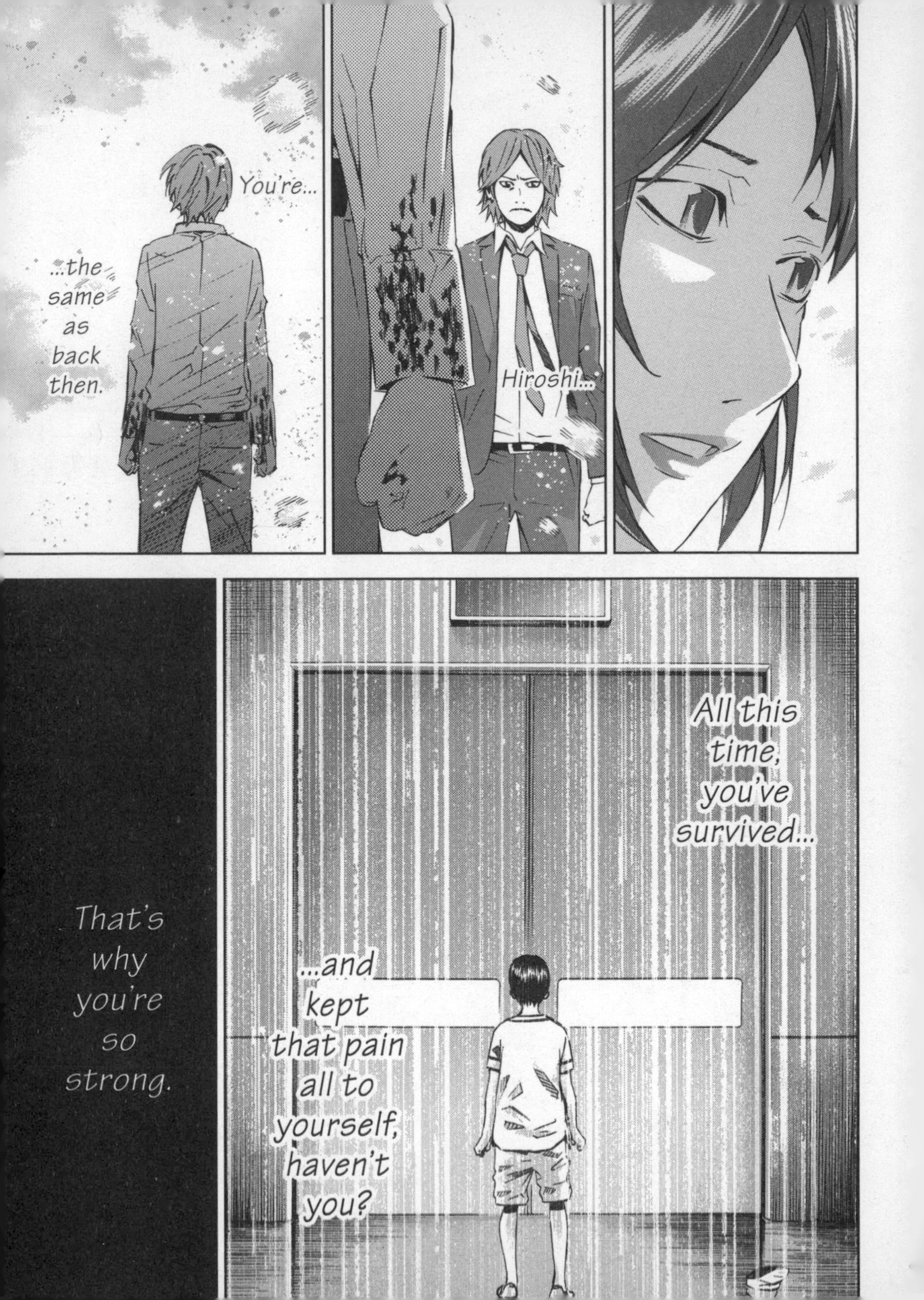
Hiroshi...
You're...
...the same as back then.
All this time, you've survived...
...and kept that pain all to yourself, haven't you?
That's why you're so strong.

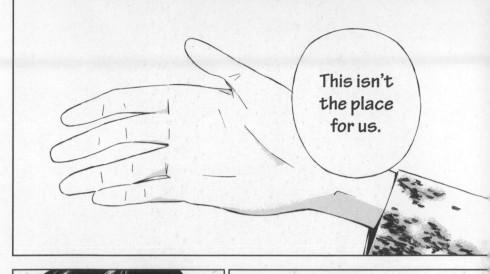

This isn't the place for us.

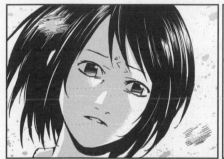

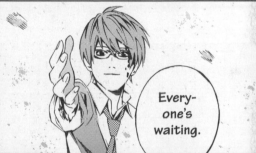

Every-one's waiting.

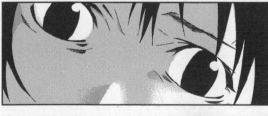

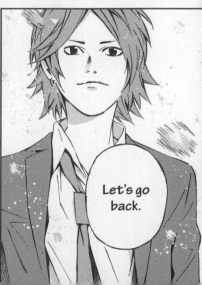

Let's go back.

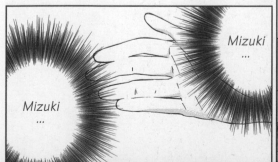

Mizuki
...

Mizuki
...

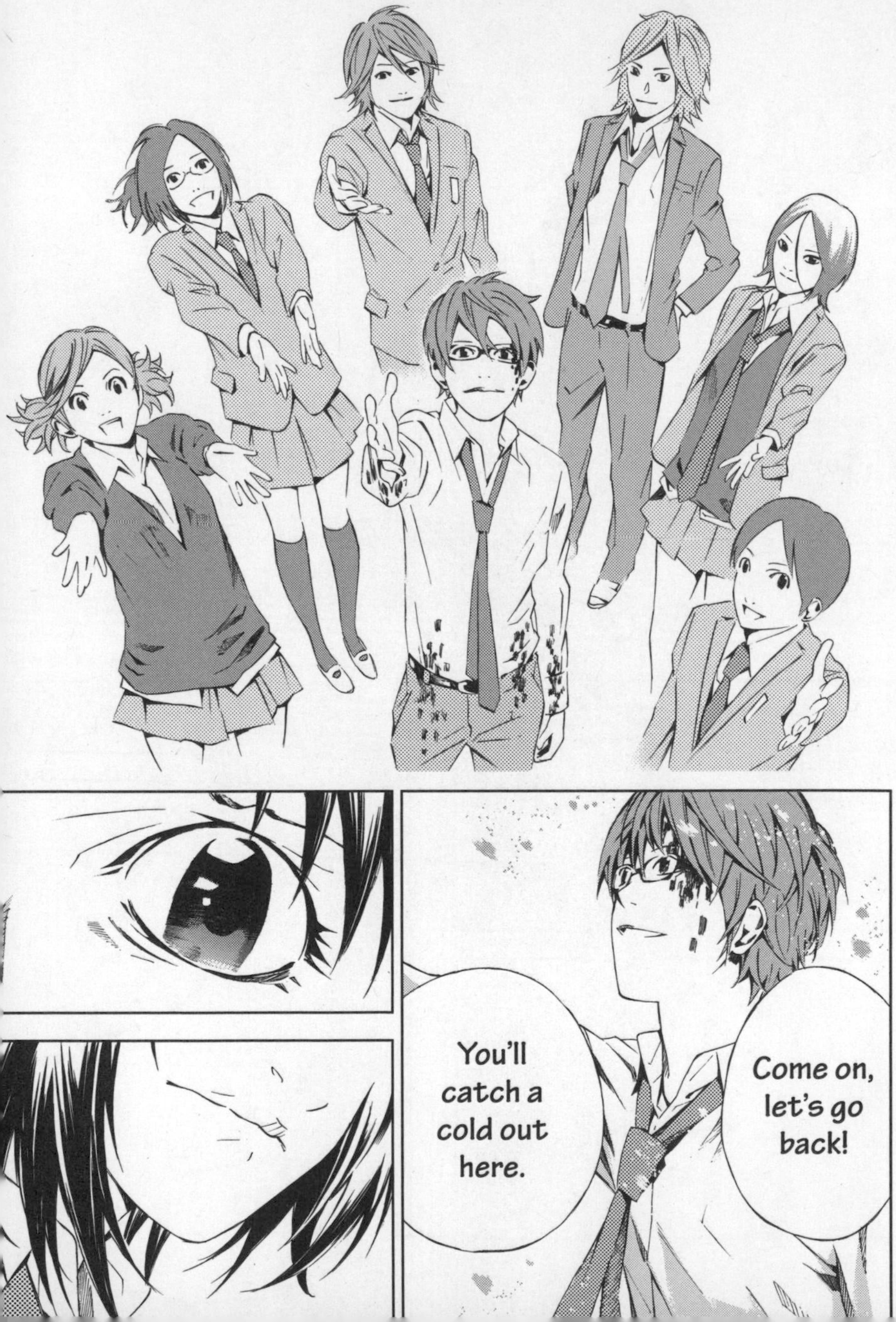
Come on, let's go back!
You'll catch a cold out here.

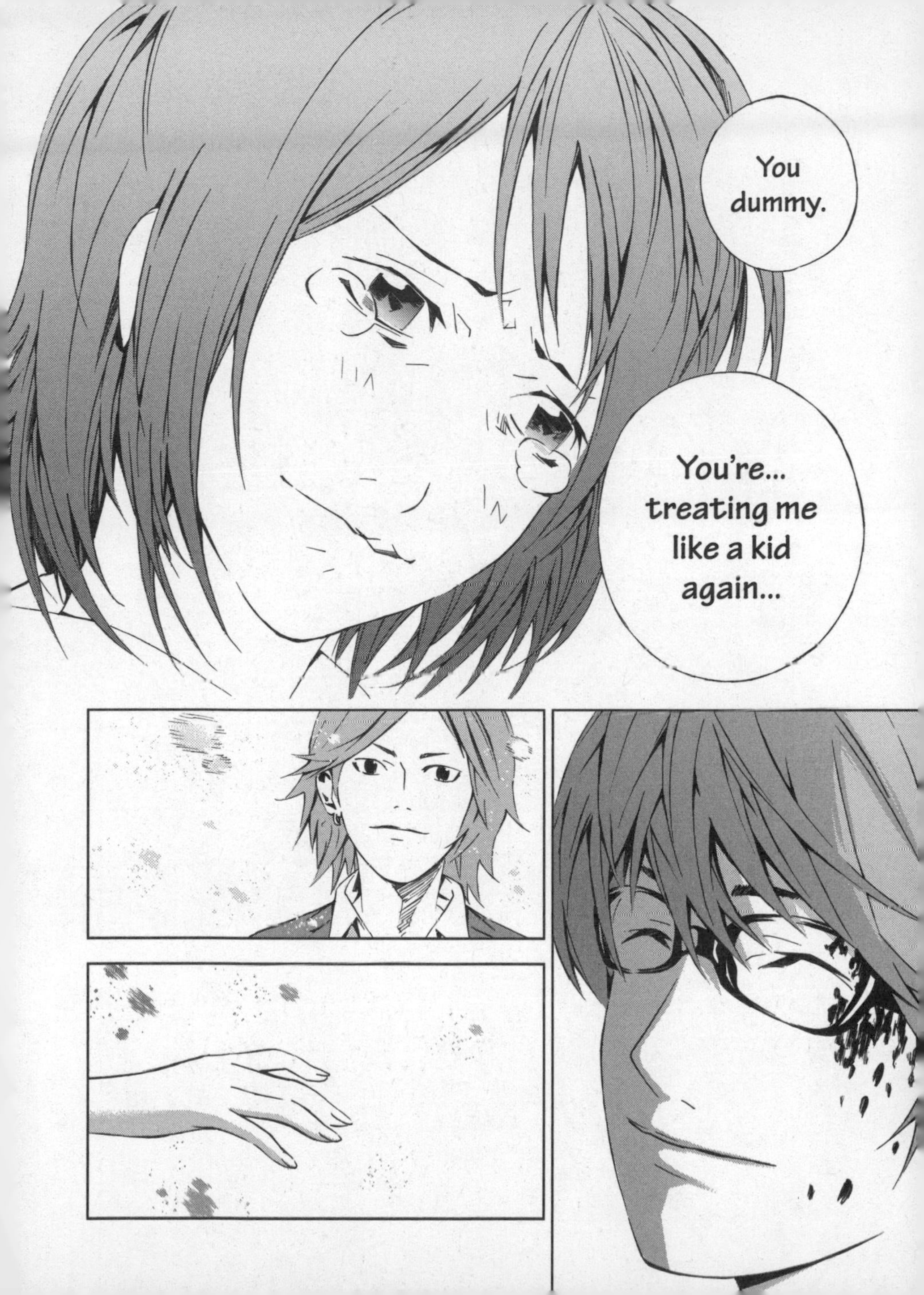
You dummy.
You're... treating me like a kid again...

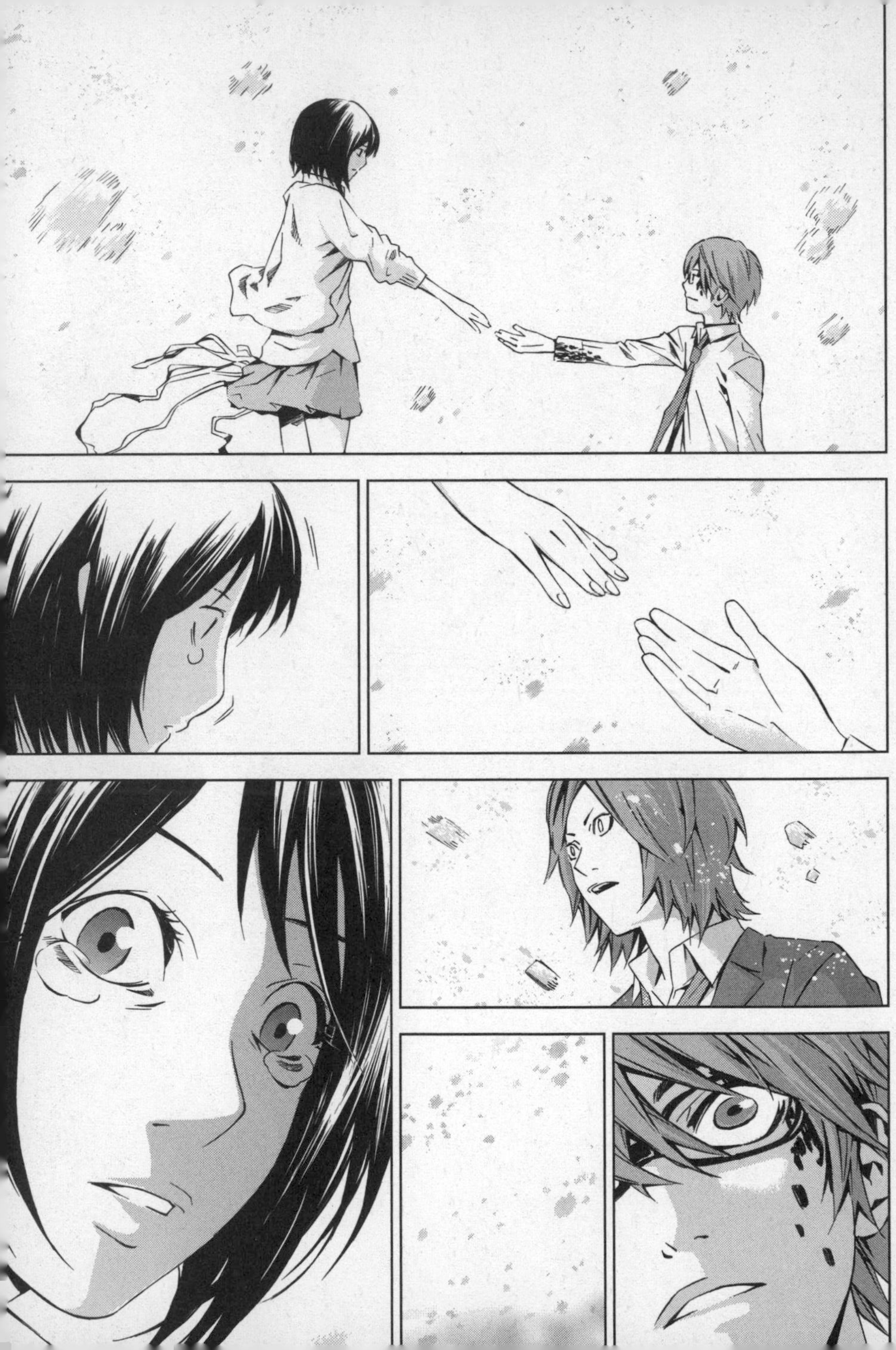

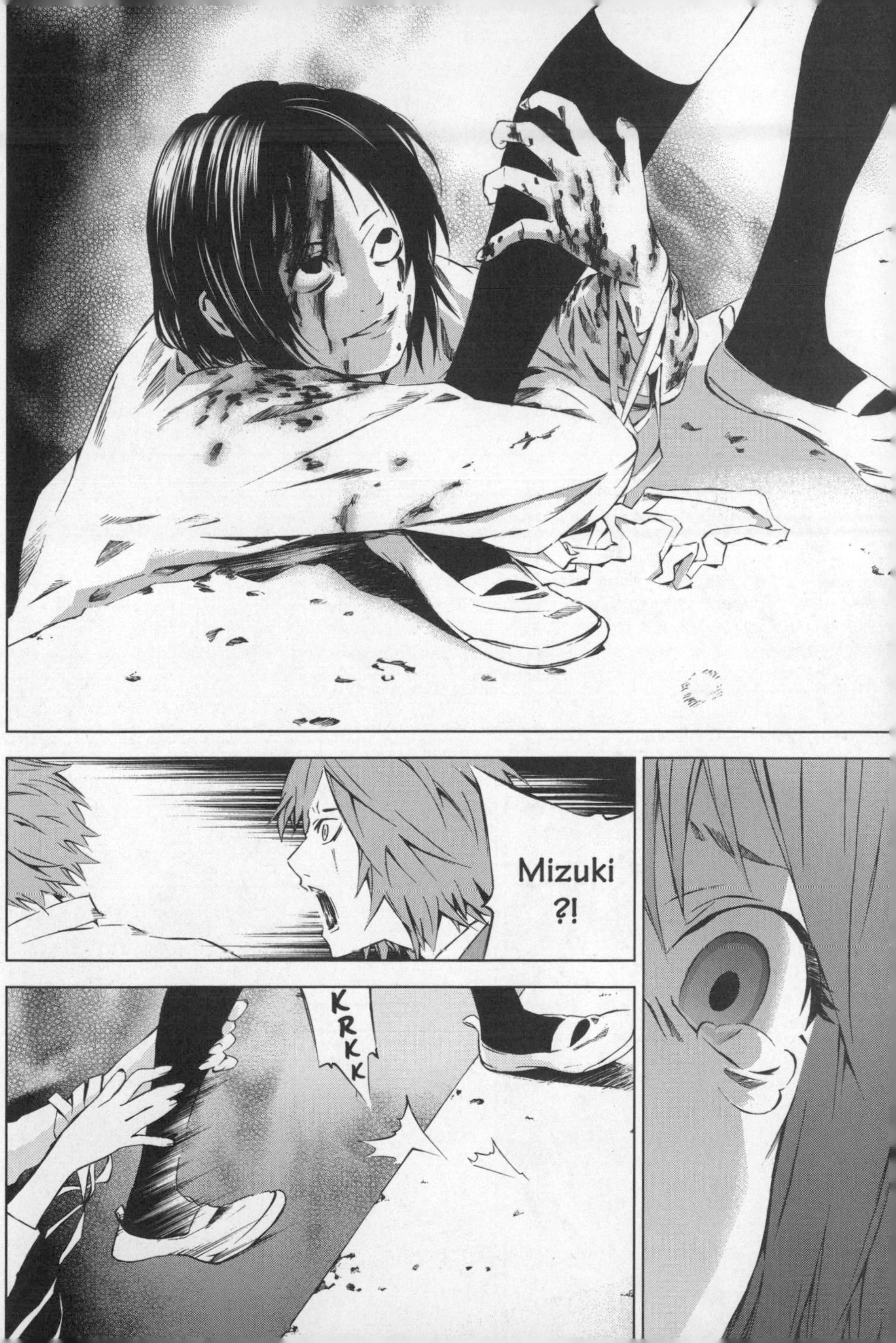
Mizuki
?!
KRKK

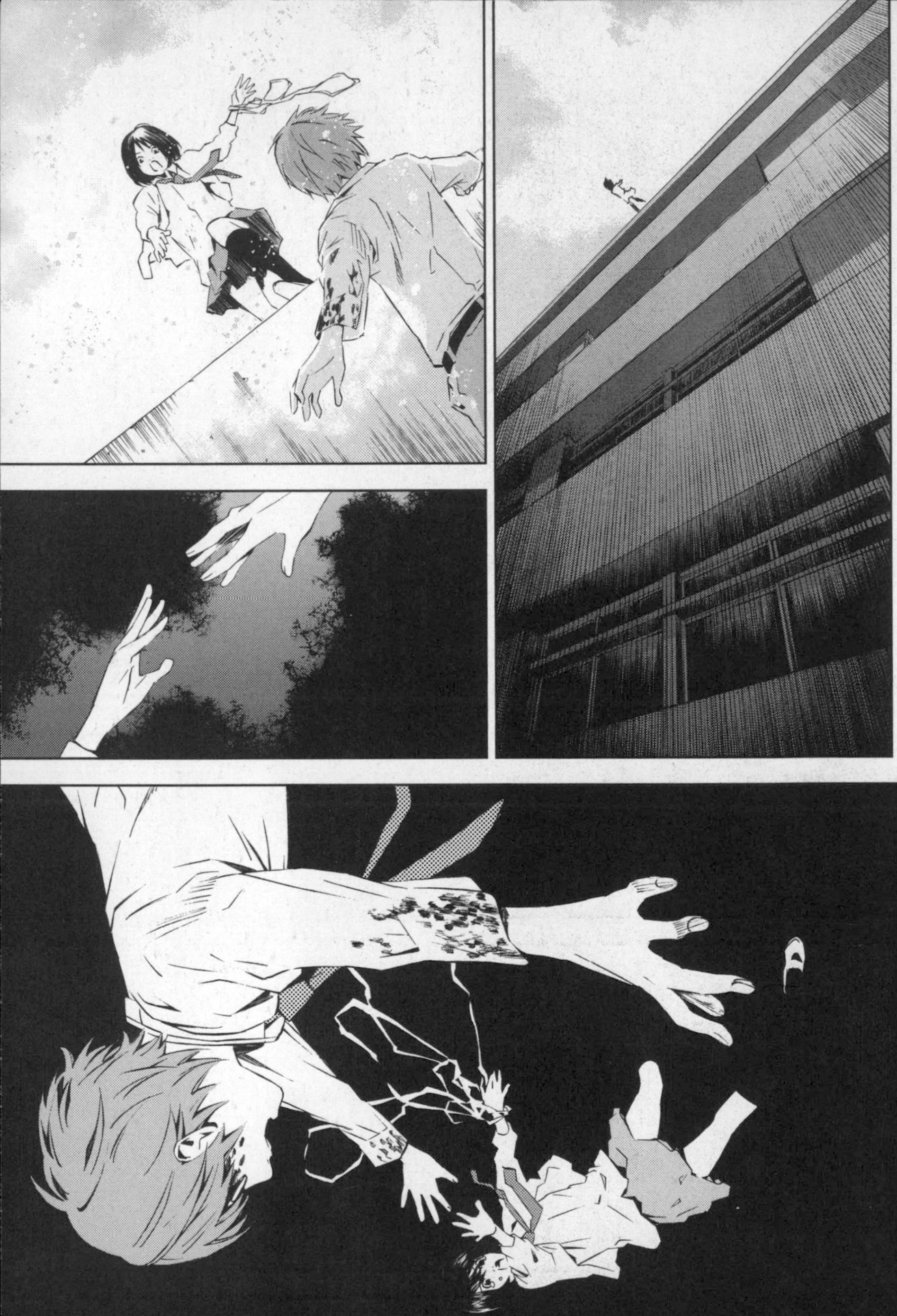

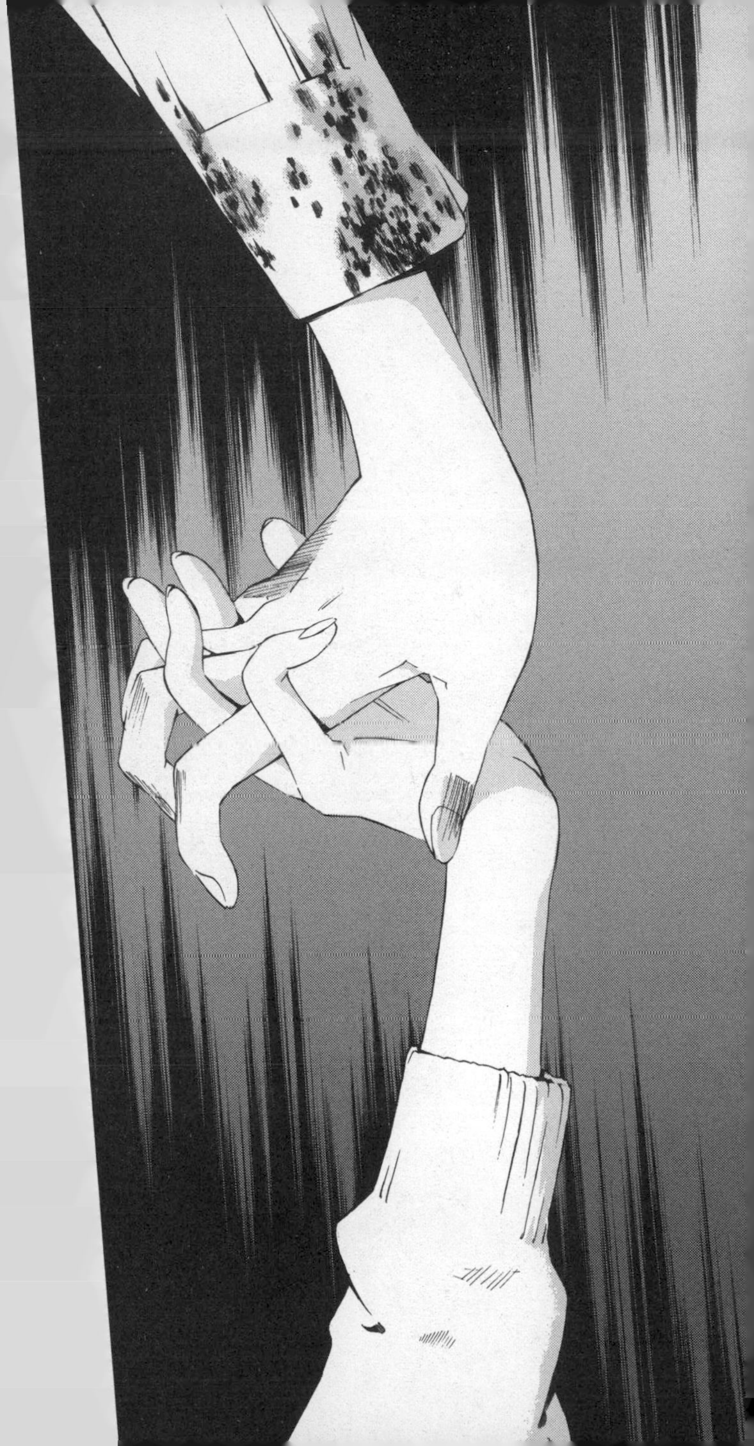

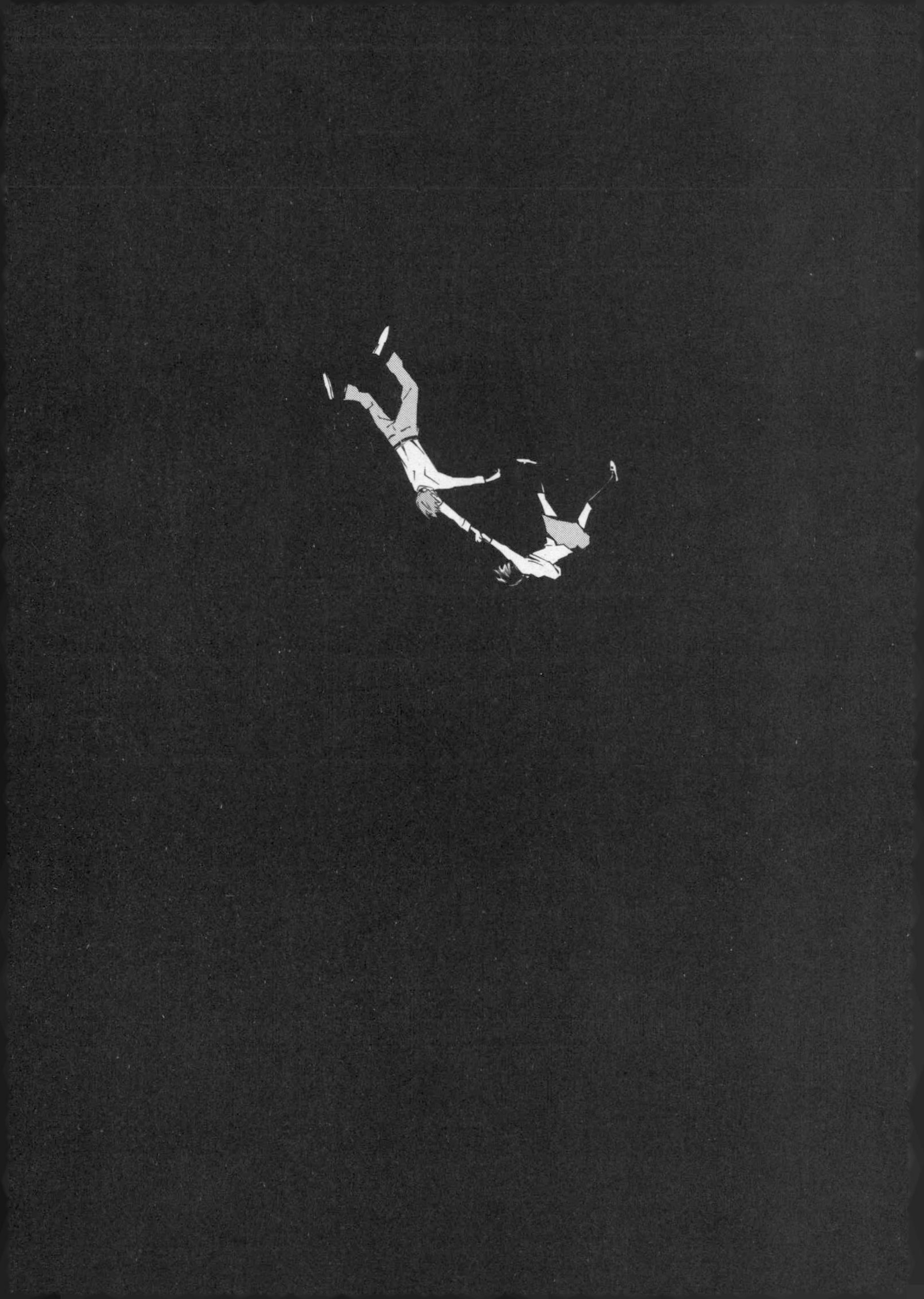

A School
Frozen
in Time

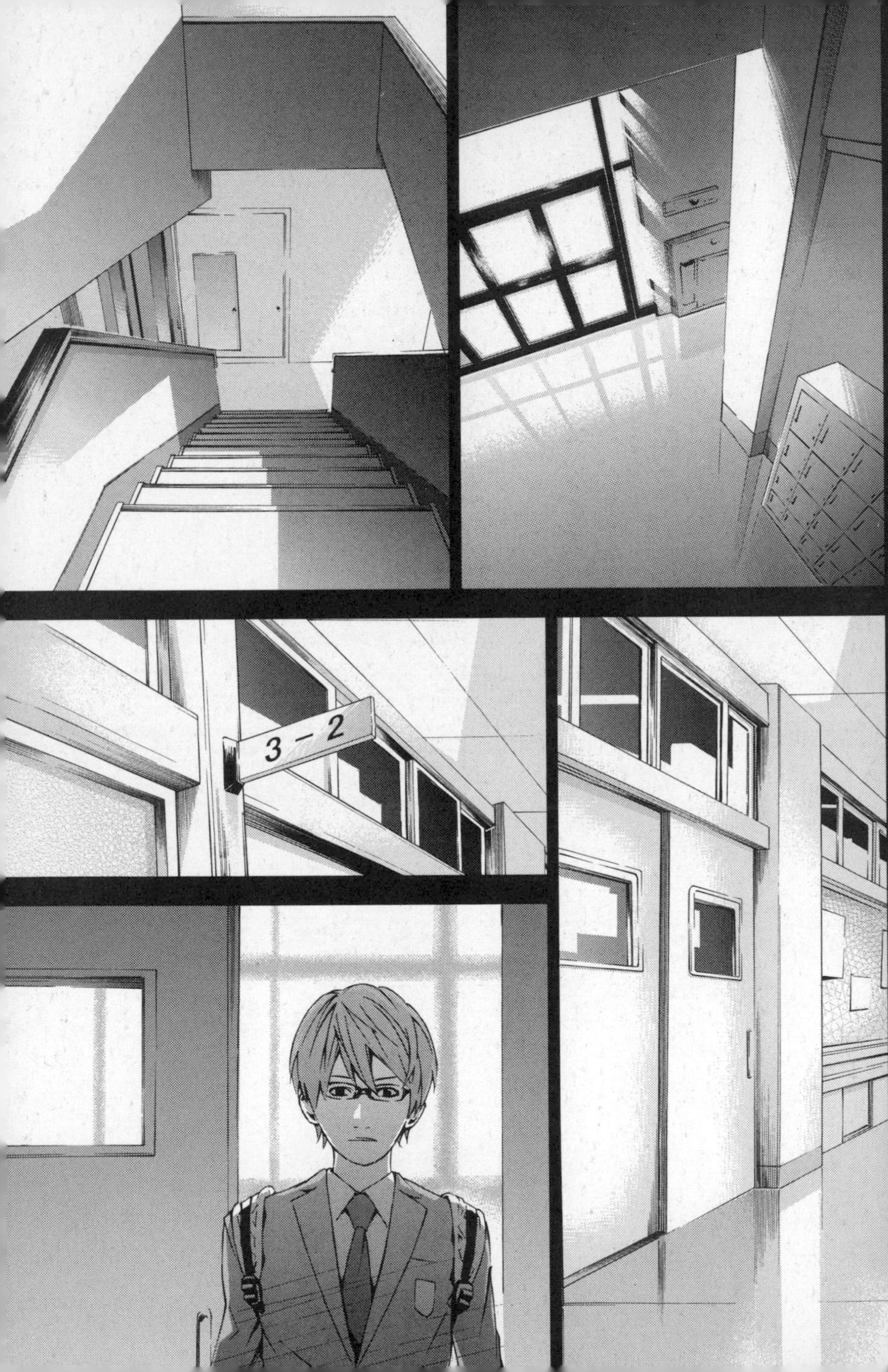
3－2

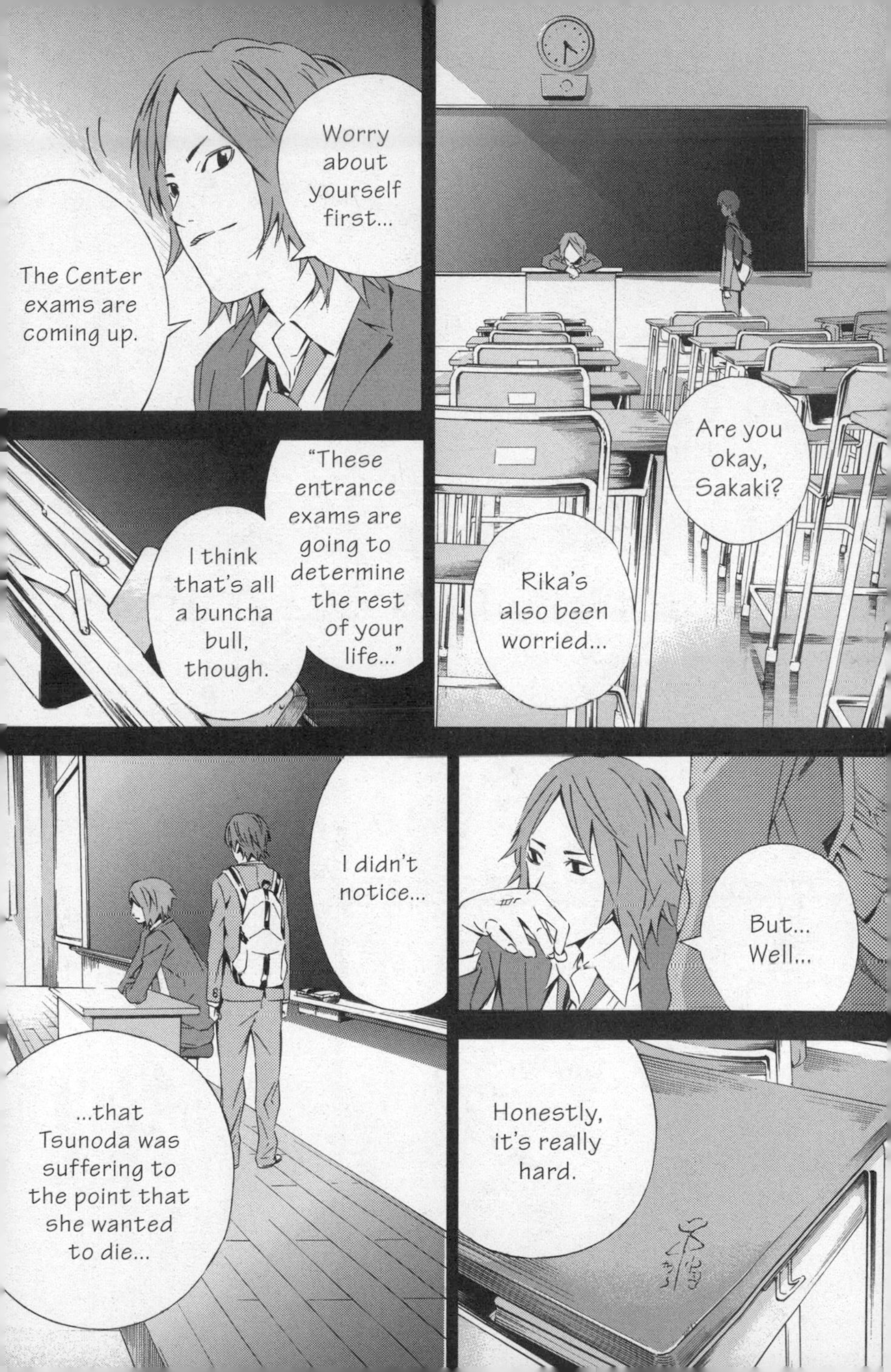
Are you okay, Sakaki?
Rika's also been worried...
Worry about yourself first...
The Center exams are coming up.
"These entrance exams are going to determine the rest of your life..."
I think that's all a buncha bull, though.
But... Well...
Honestly, it's really hard.
I didn't notice...
...that Tsunoda was suffering to the point that she wanted to die...

The Final Chapter
Graduation Ceremony

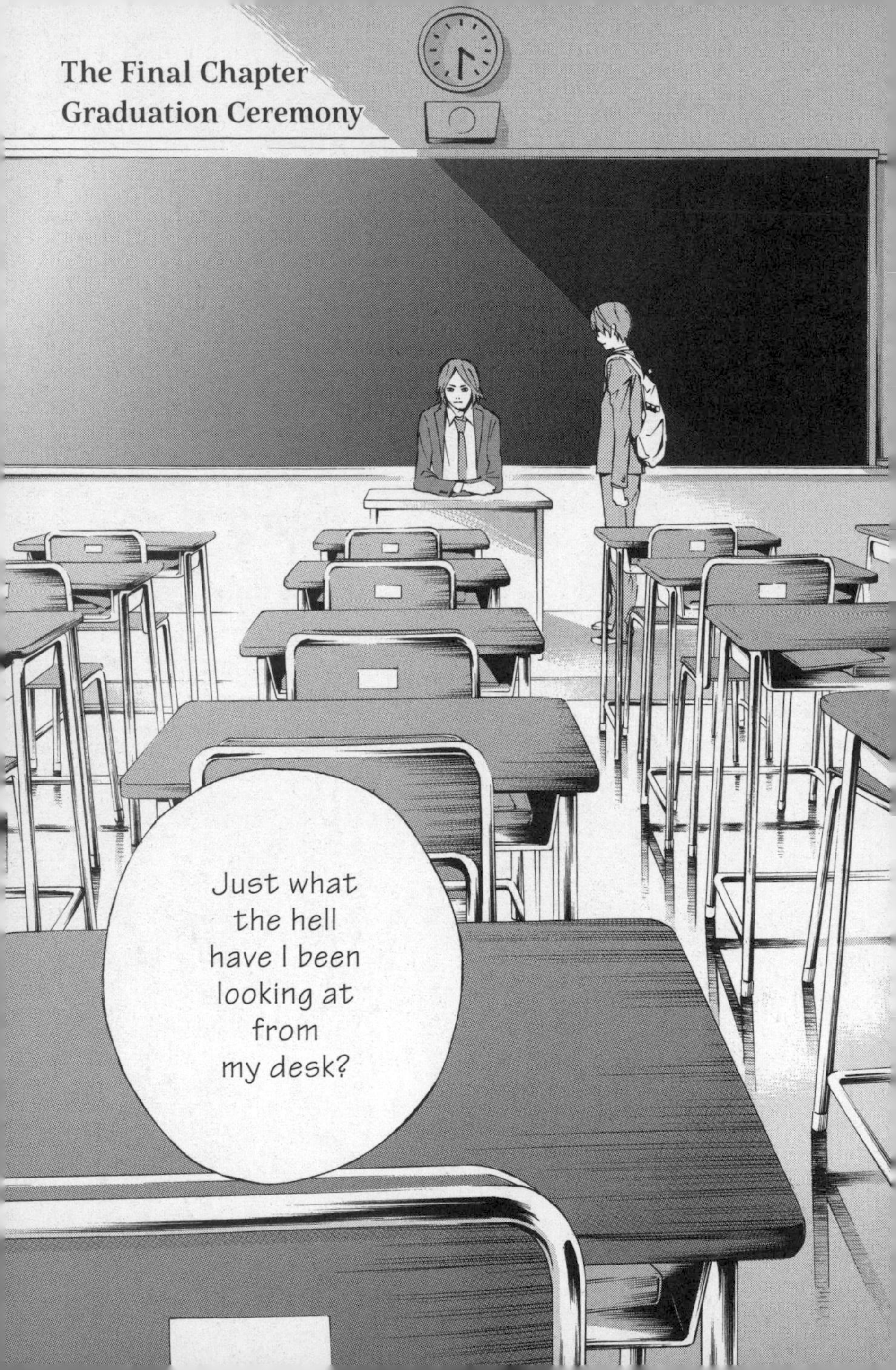
Just what the hell have I been looking at from my desk?

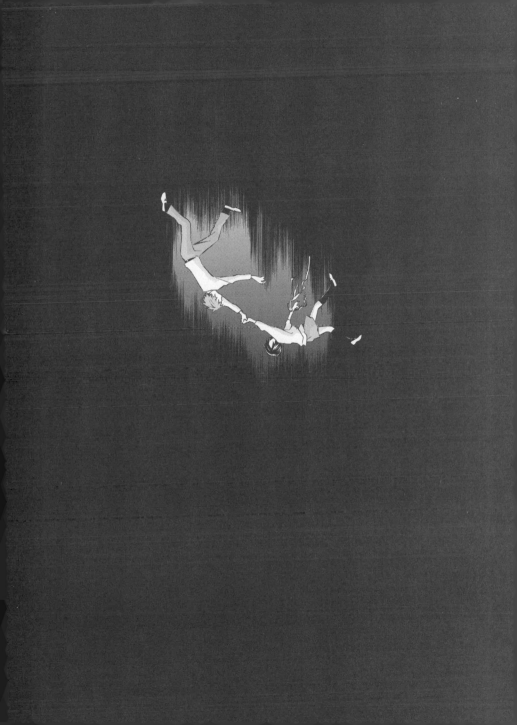

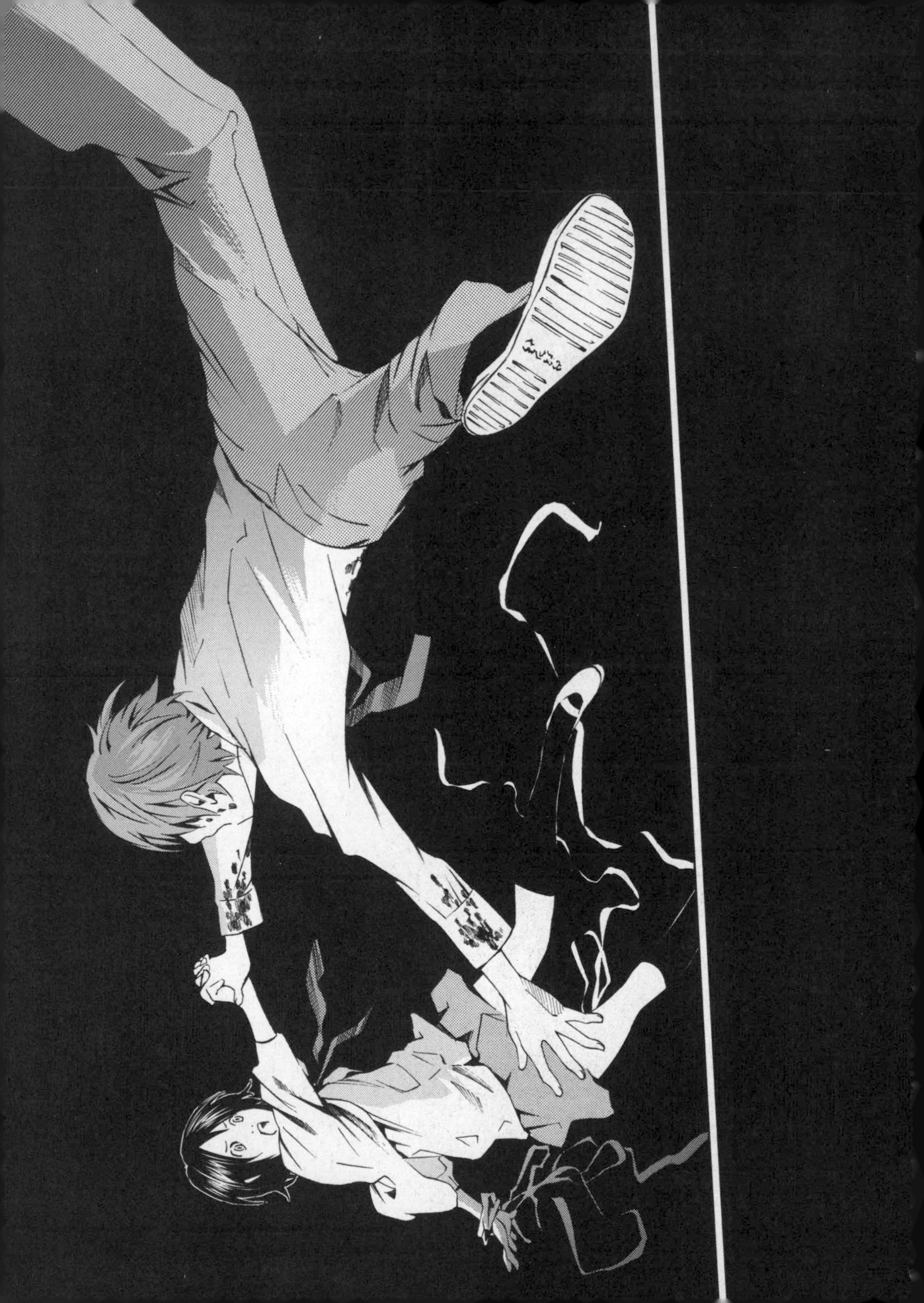

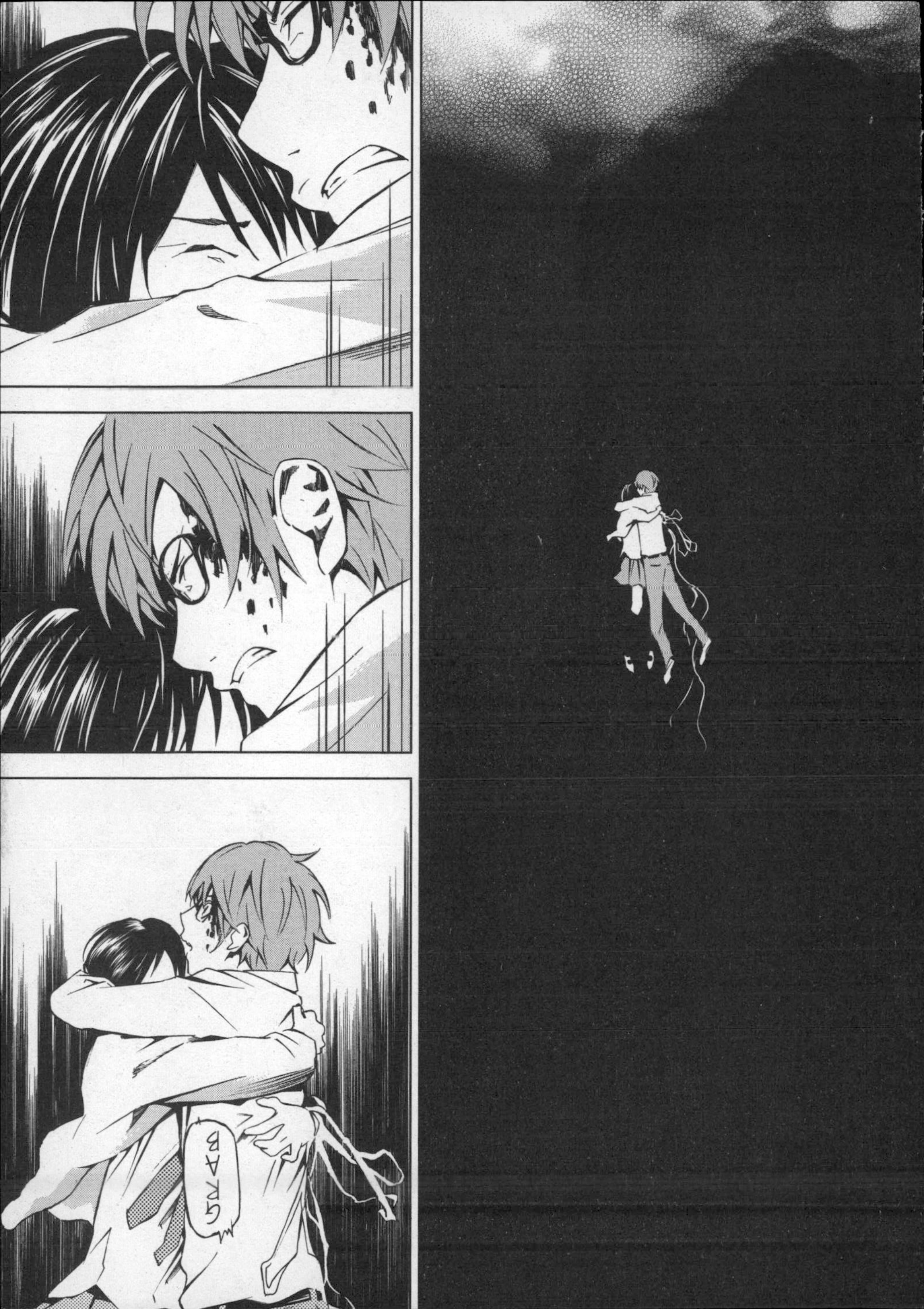
GRAB

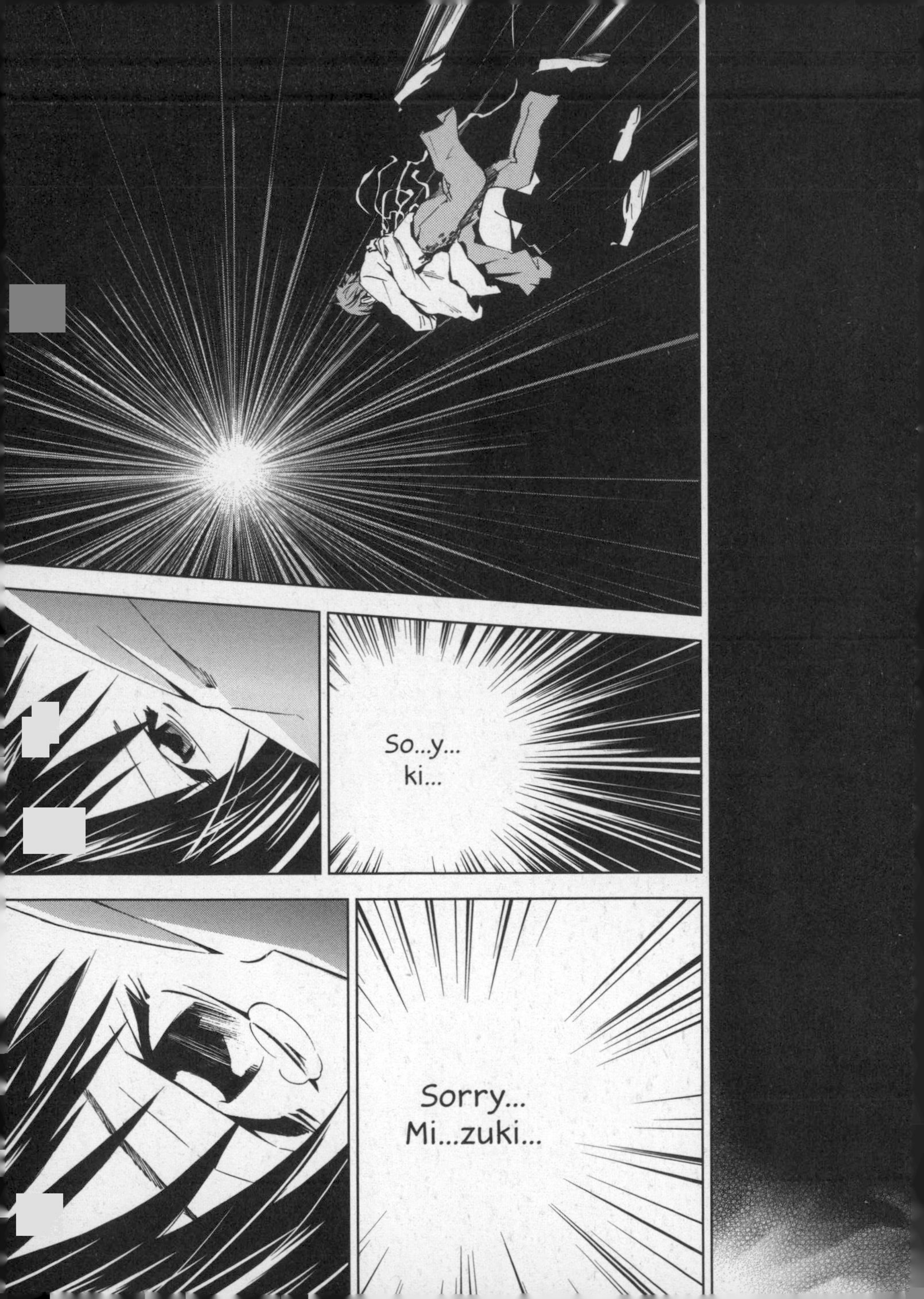

So...y... ki...
Sorry... Mi...zuki...

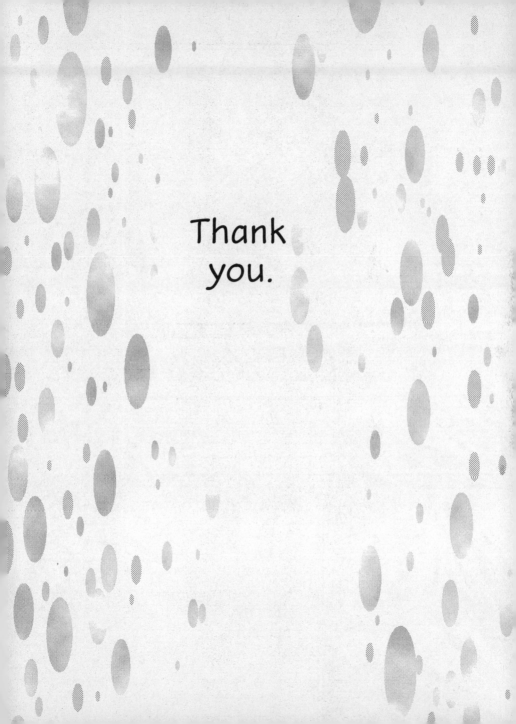

Thank
you.

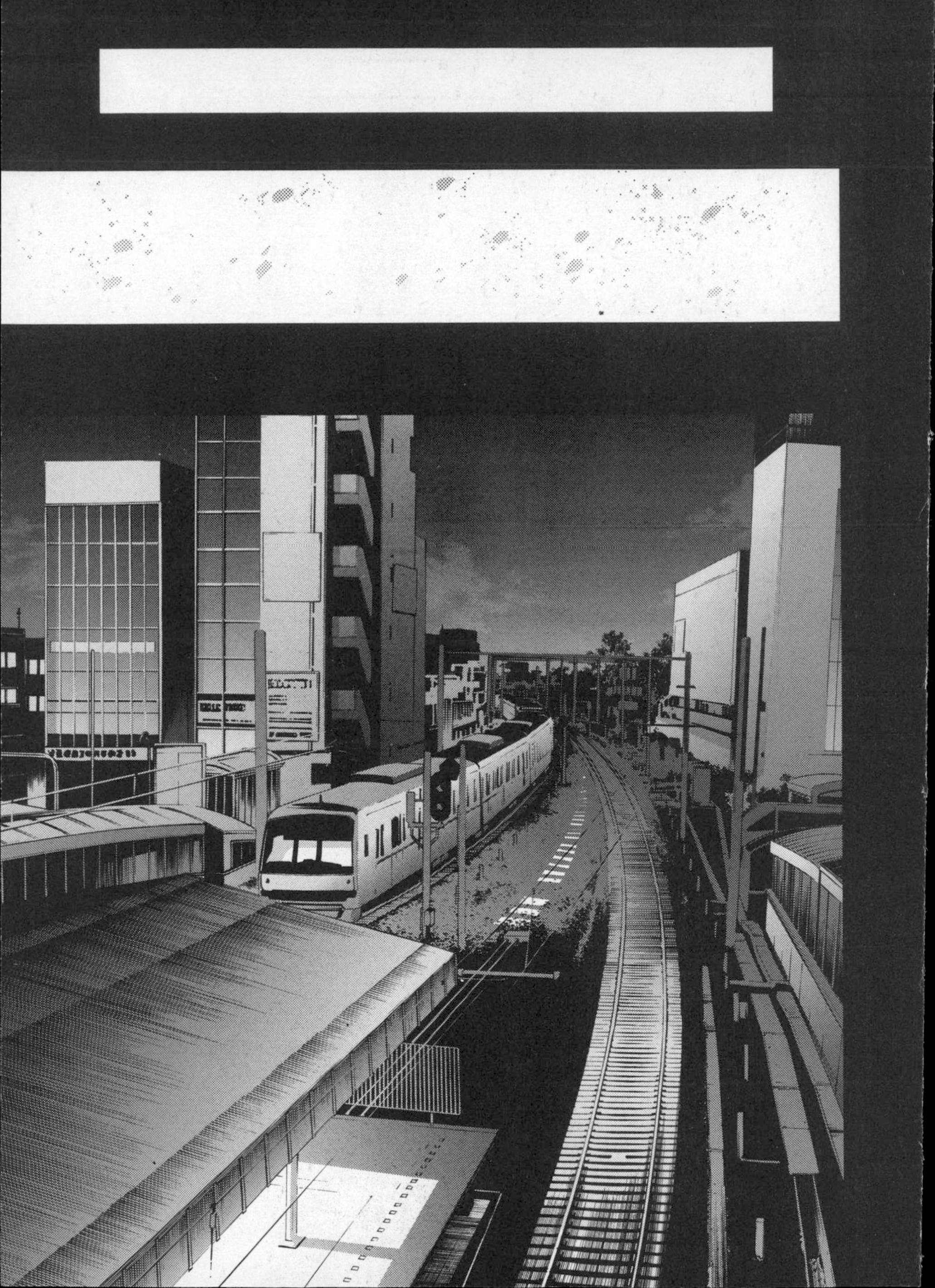

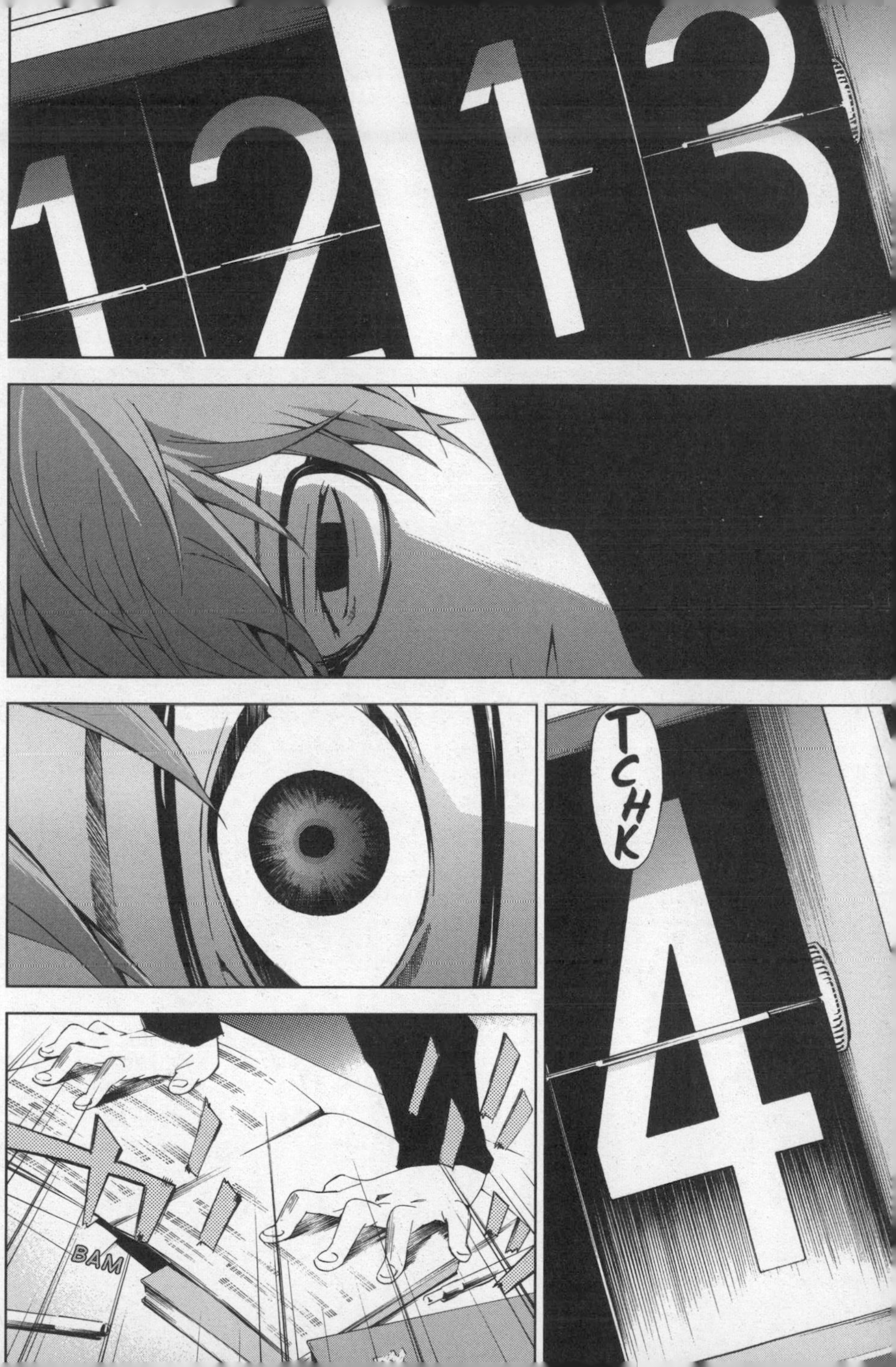
TCHK
BAM

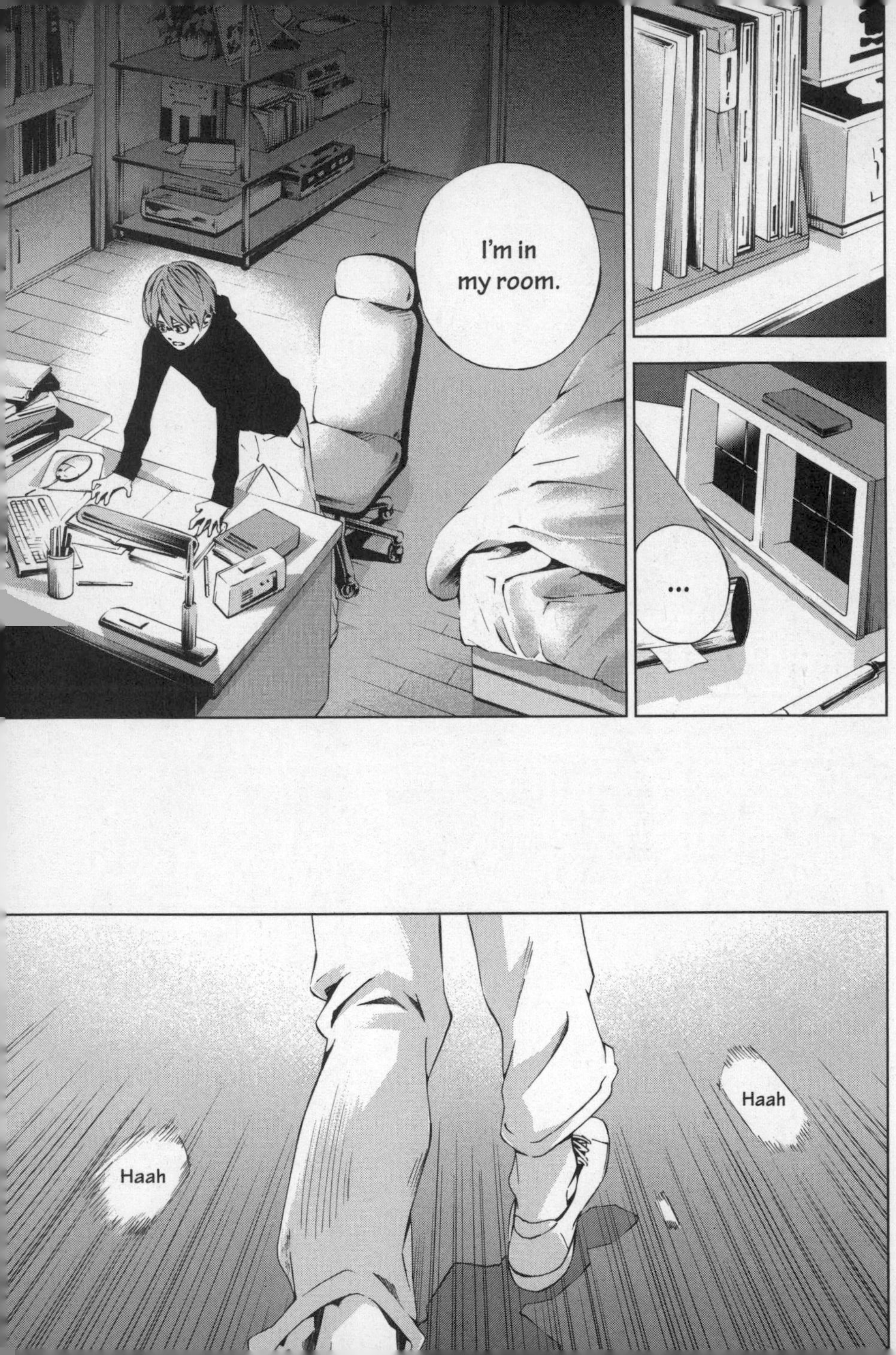
...
I'm in my room.
Haah
Haah

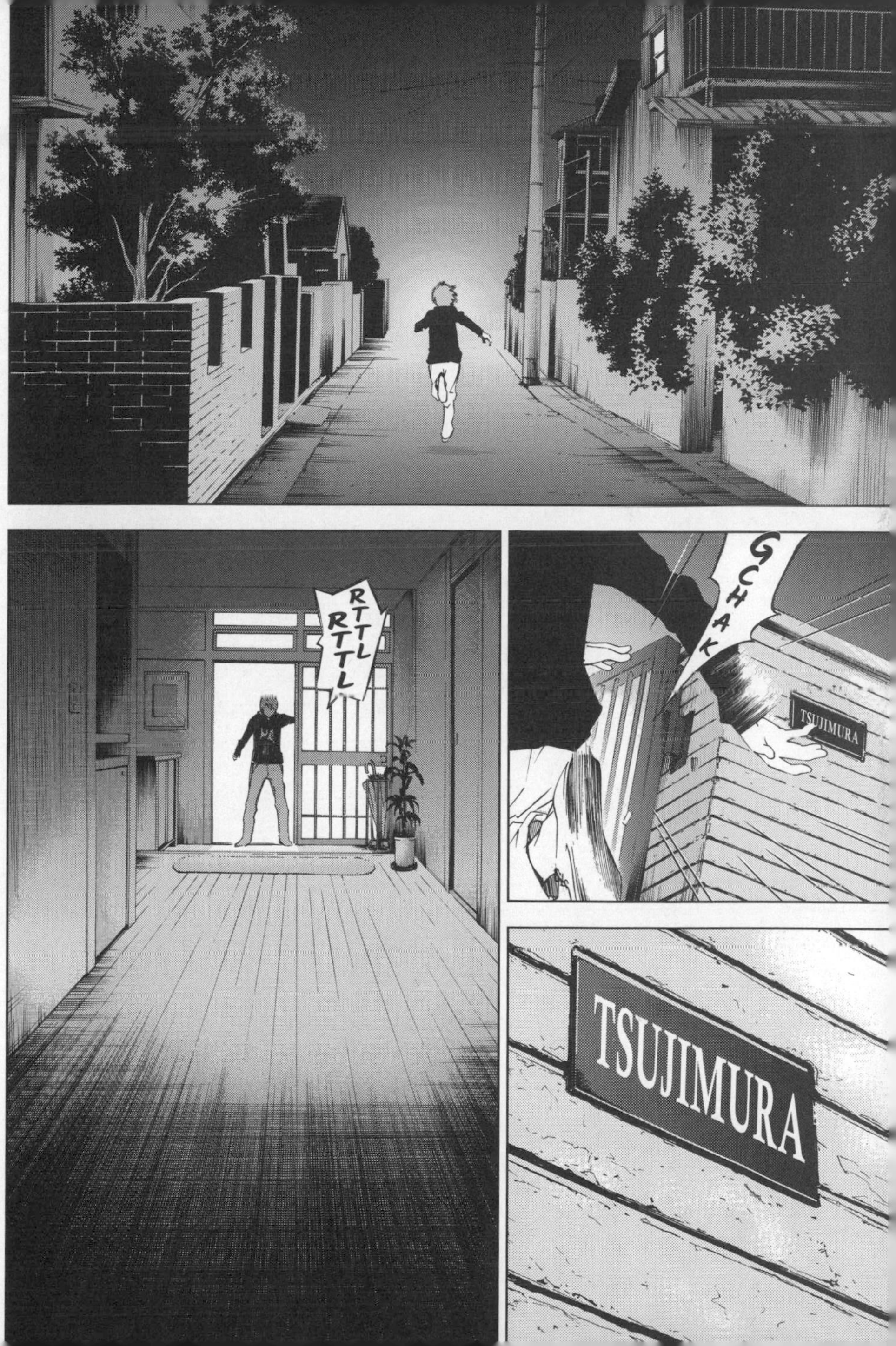
GCHAK
TSUJIMURA
TSUJIMURA
RTTL RTTL

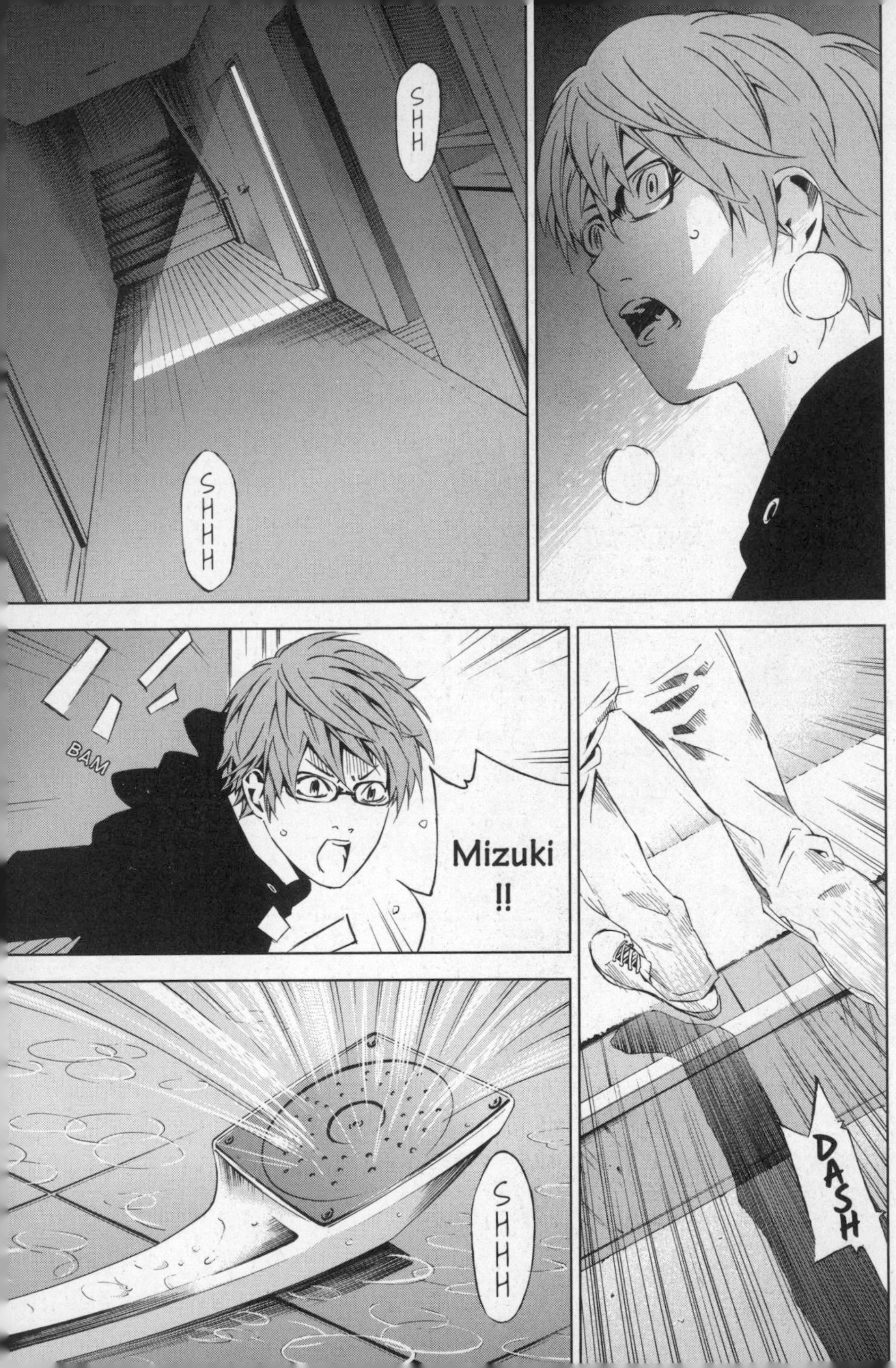
SHH
SHHH
DASH
BAM
Mizuki !!
SHHH

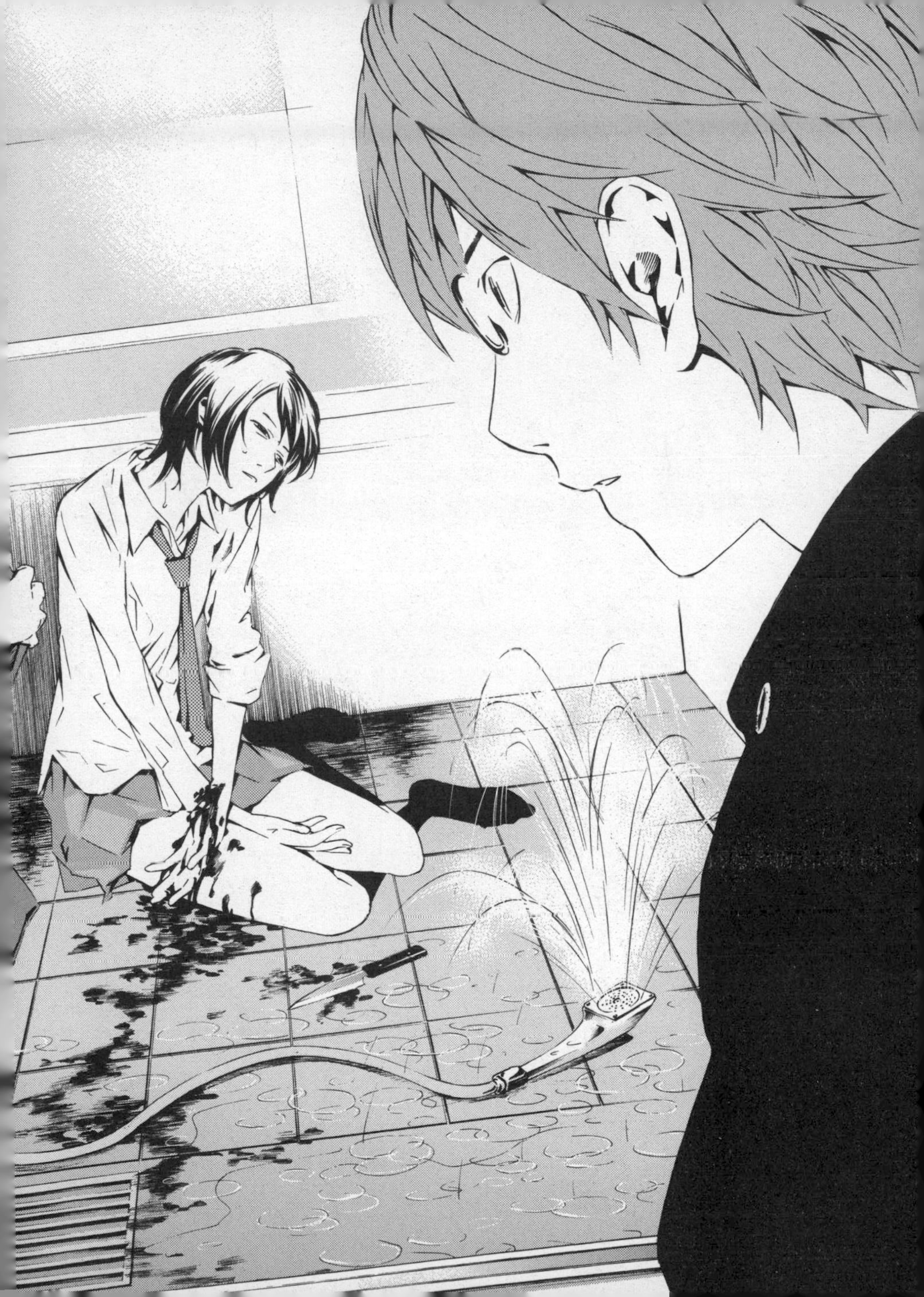

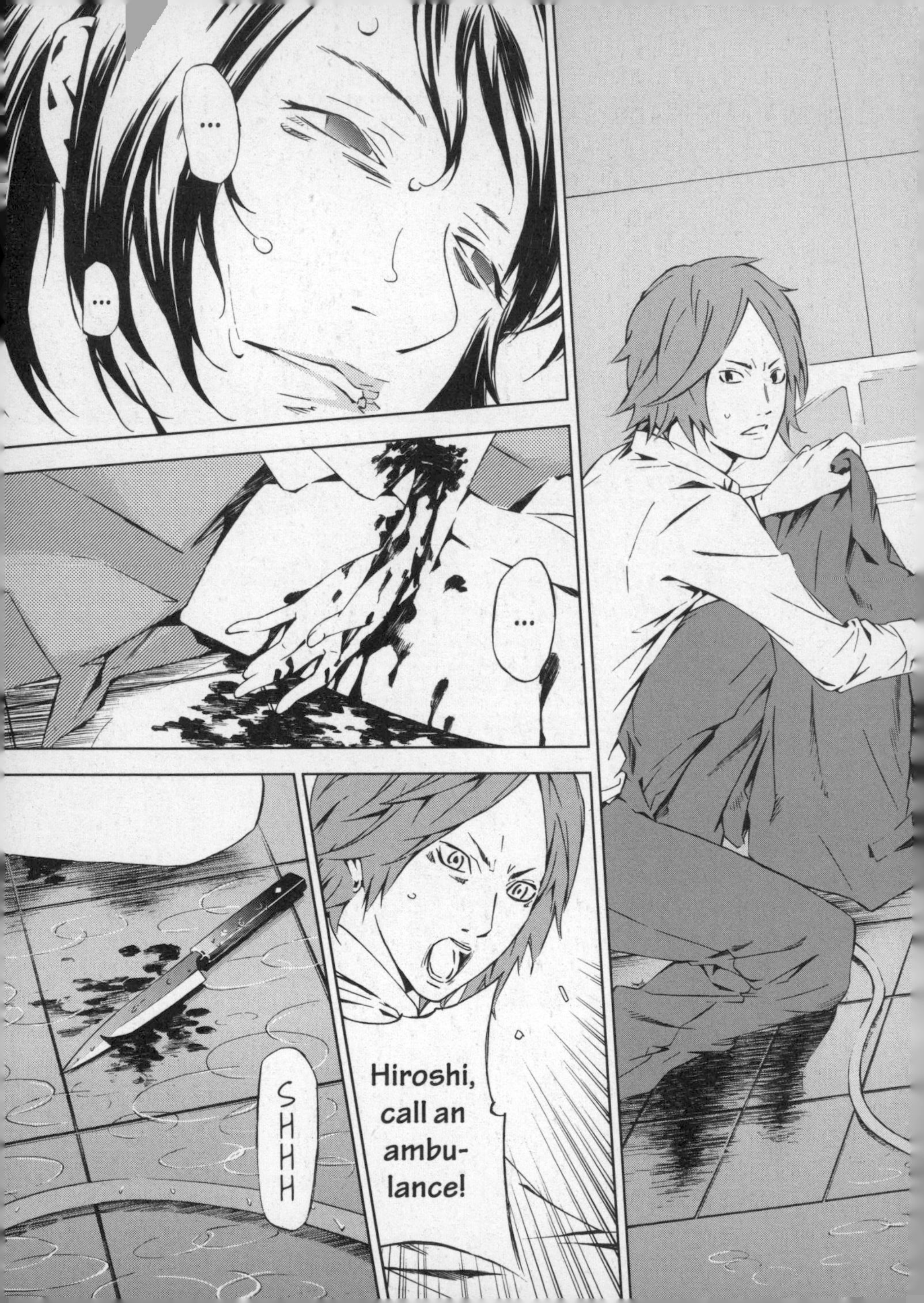
...
...
...
Hiroshi, call an ambulance!
SHHH

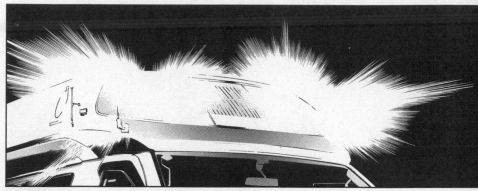

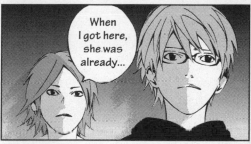

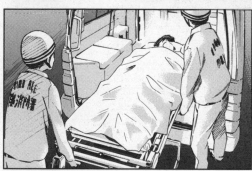

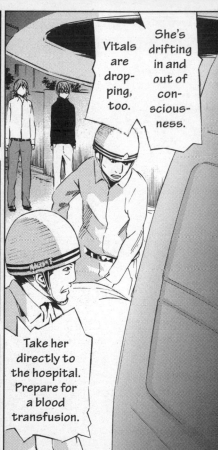

She's drifting in and out of consciousness.
Vitals are dropping, too.
Take her directly to the hospital. Prepare for a blood transfusion.
When I got here, she was already...

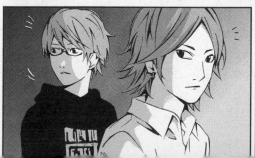

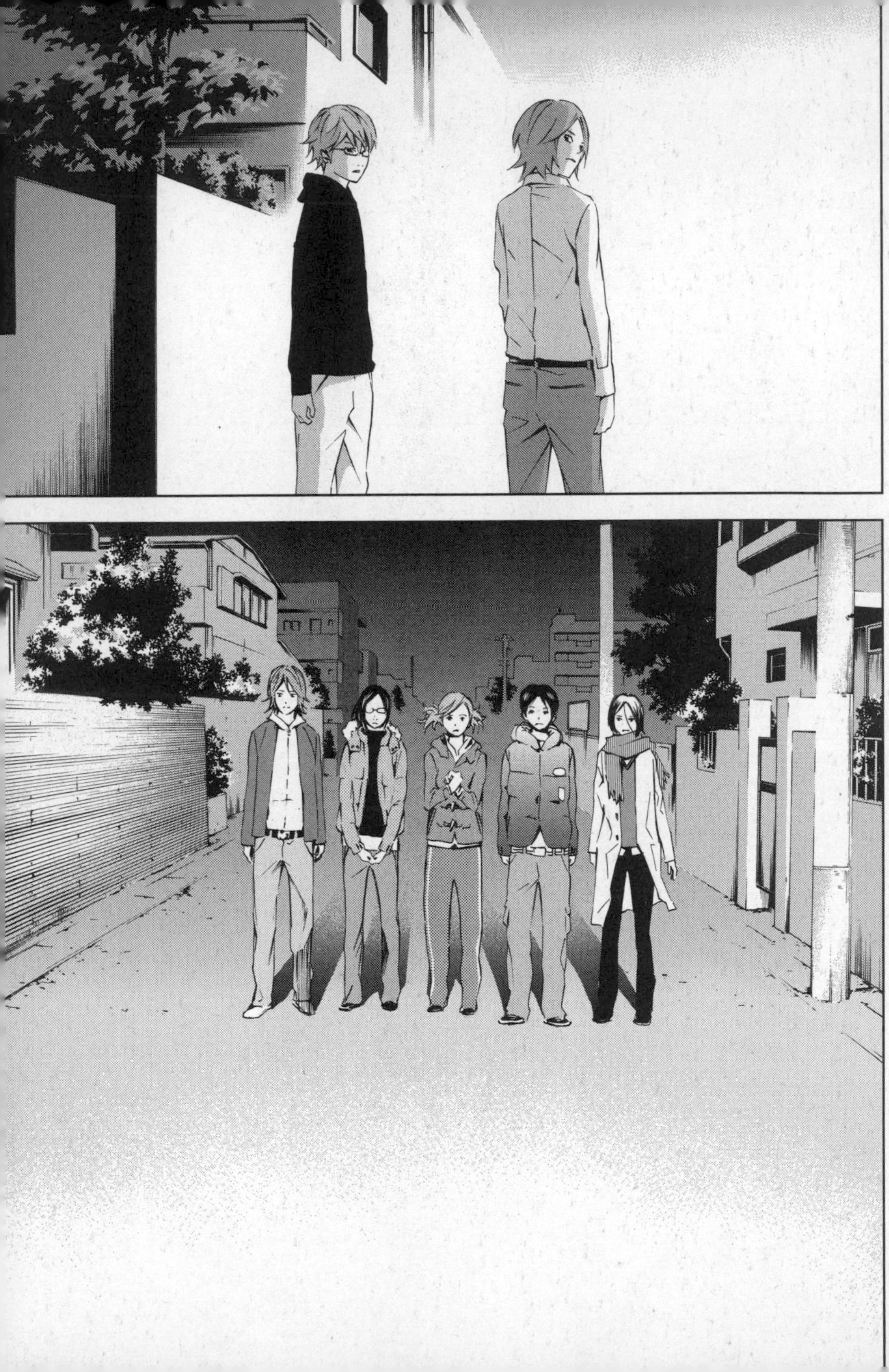

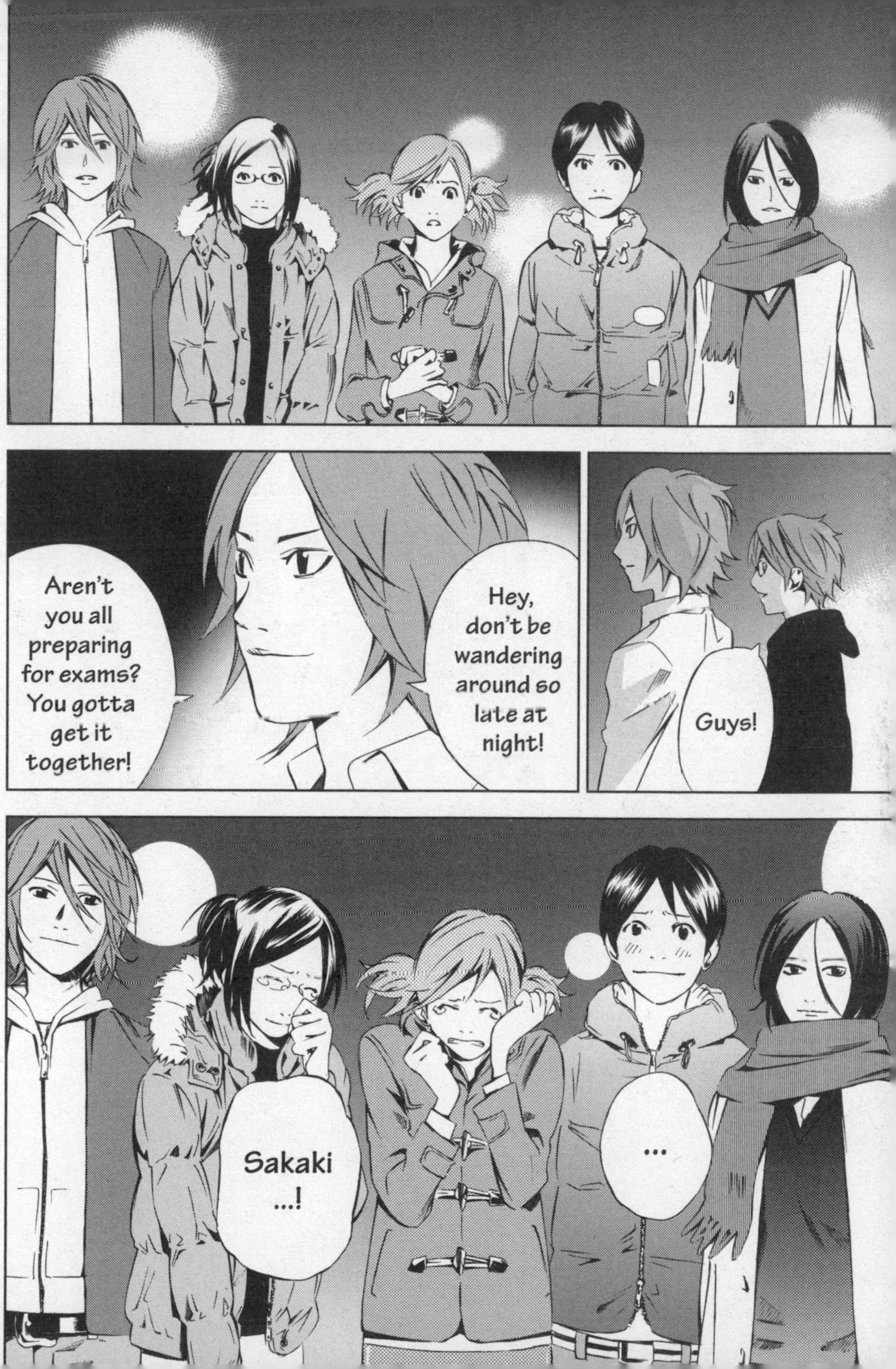
Guys!
Hey, don't be wandering around so late at night!
Aren't you all preparing for exams? You gotta get it together!
...
Sakaki ...!

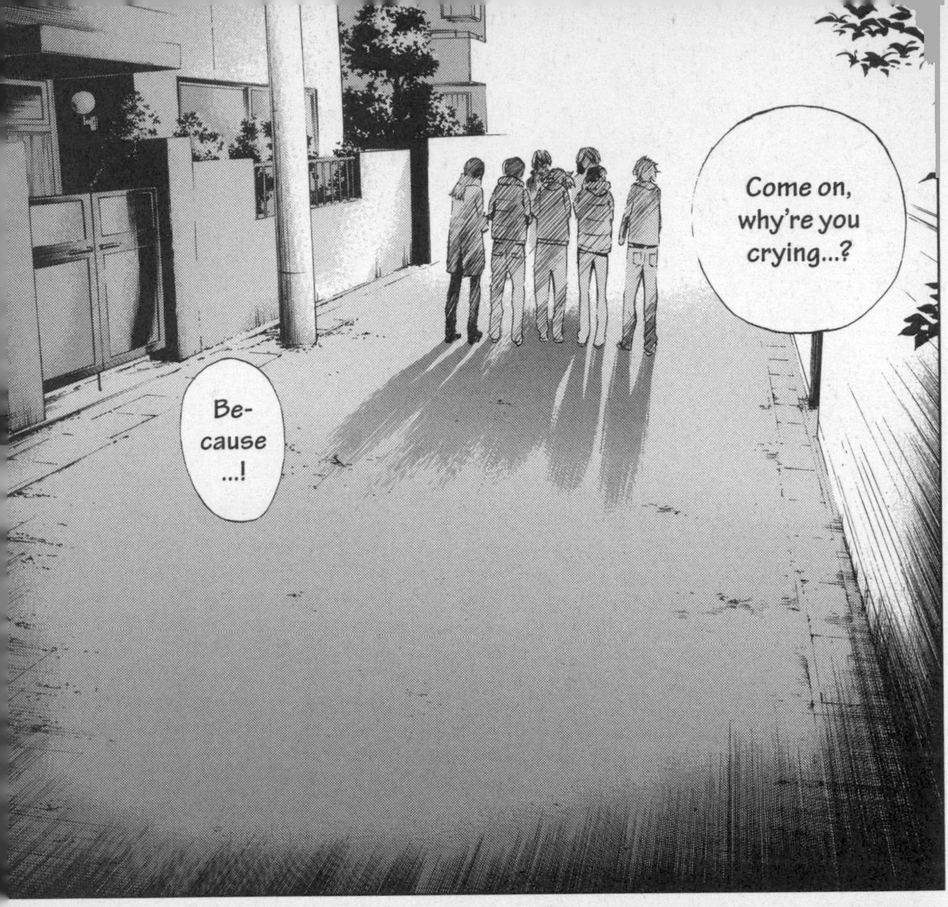
Come on, why're you crying...?
Be-cause ...!
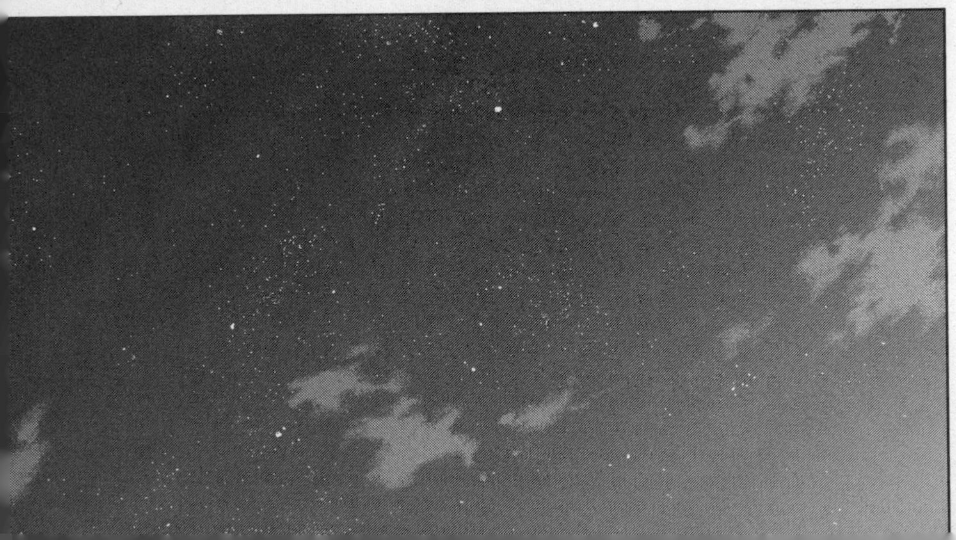

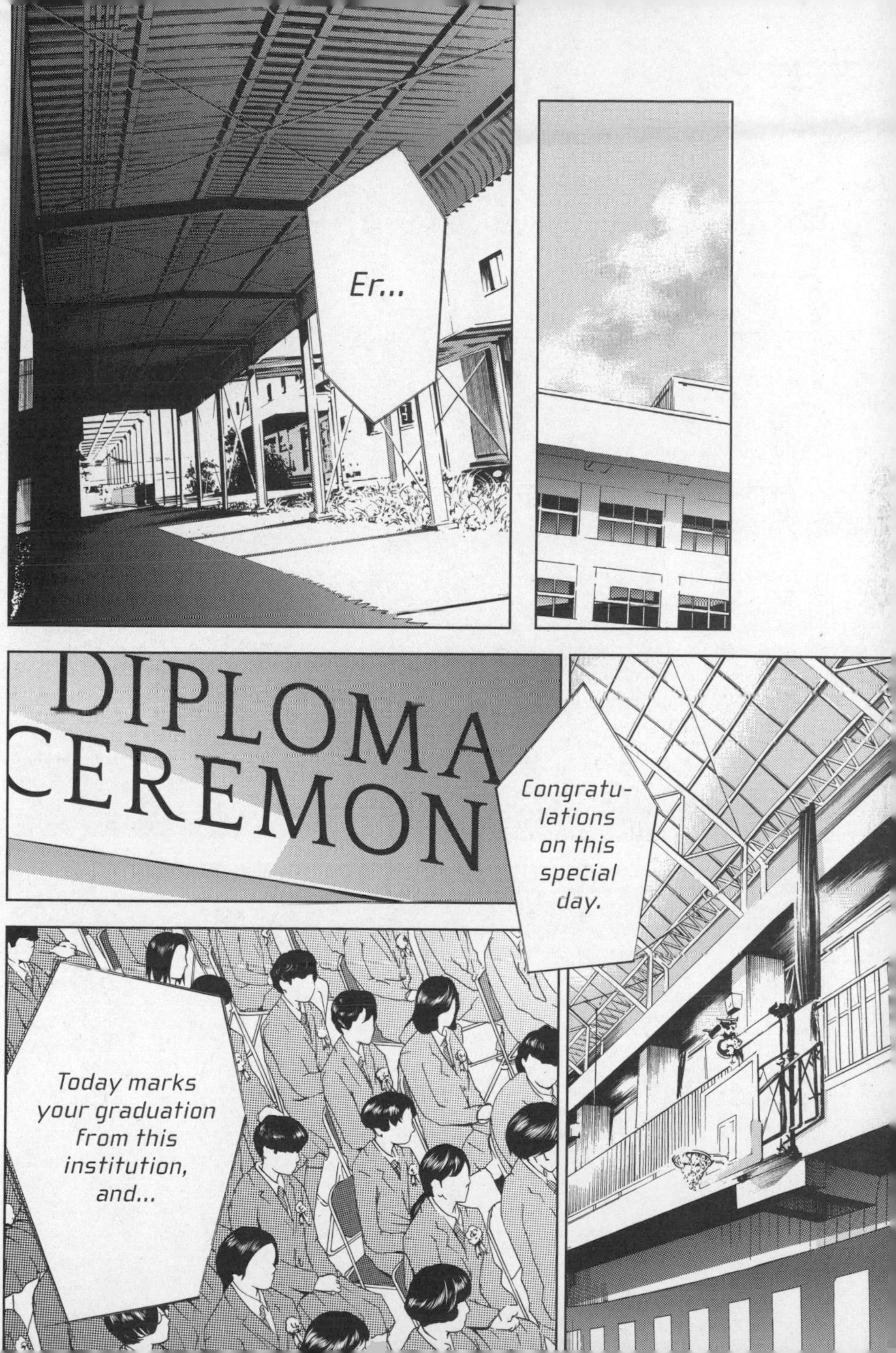

Er...
Congratulations on this special day.
DIPLOMA CEREMON
Today marks your graduation from this institution, and...

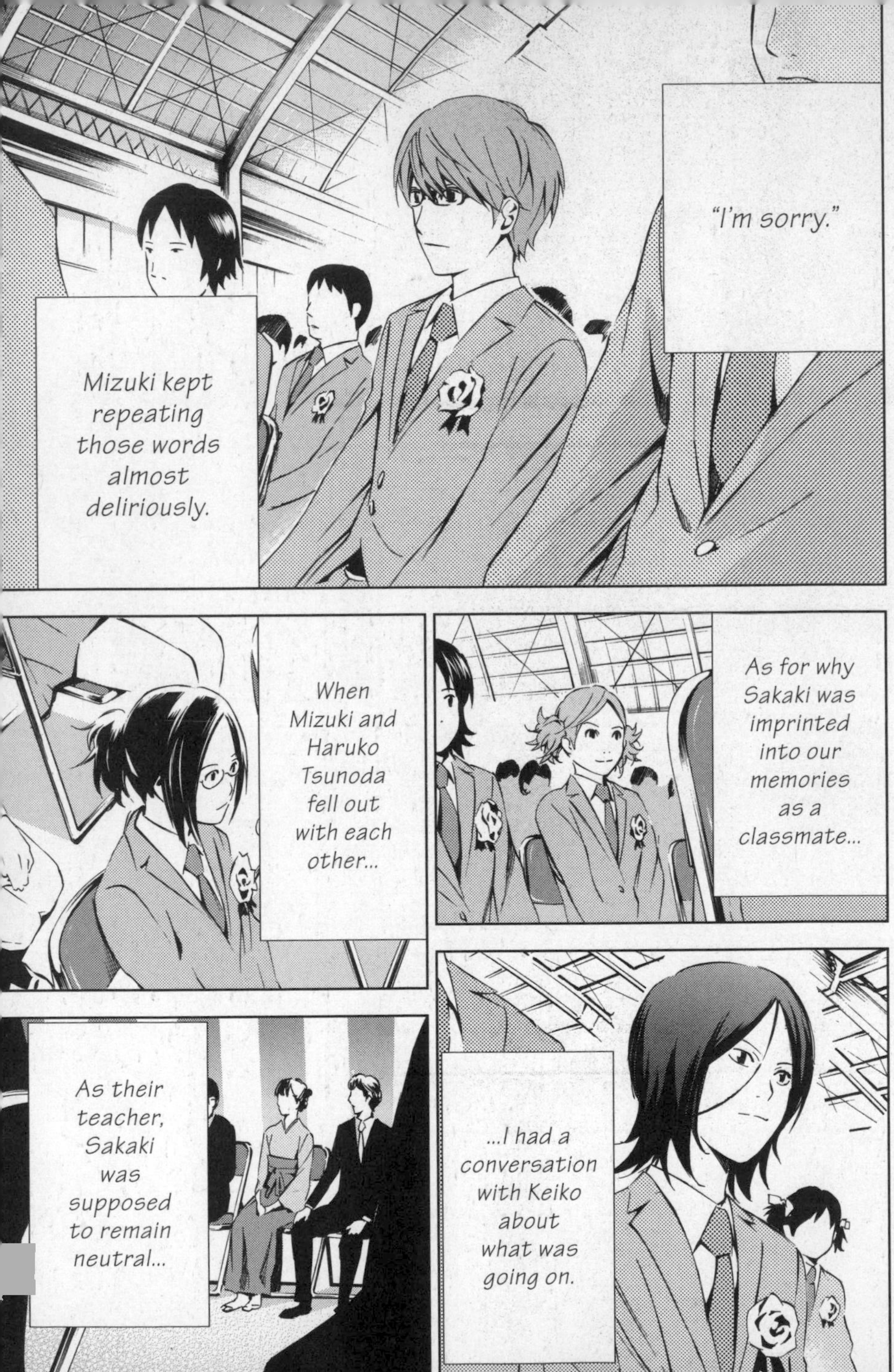
"I'm sorry."
Mizuki kept repeating those words almost deliriously.
As for why Sakaki was imprinted into our memories as a classmate...
When Mizuki and Haruko Tsunoda fell out with each other...
...I had a conversation with Keiko about what was going on.
As their teacher, Sakaki was supposed to remain neutral...

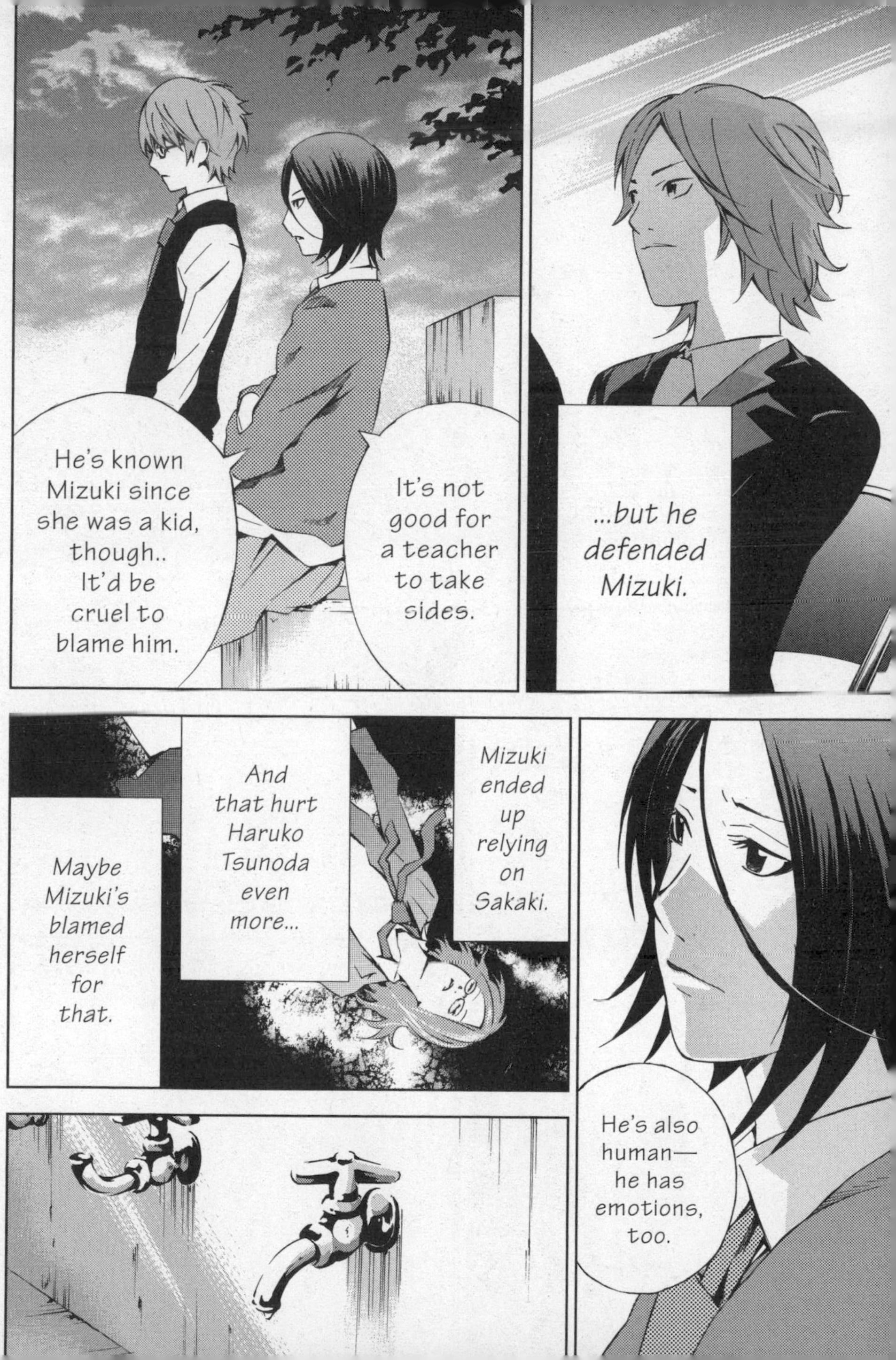
...but he defended Mizuki.
It's not good for a teacher to take sides.
He's known Mizuki since she was a kid, though.. It'd be cruel to blame him.
He's also human— he has emotions, too.
Mizuki ended up relying on Sakaki.
And that hurt Haruko Tsunoda even more...
Maybe Mizuki's blamed herself for that.

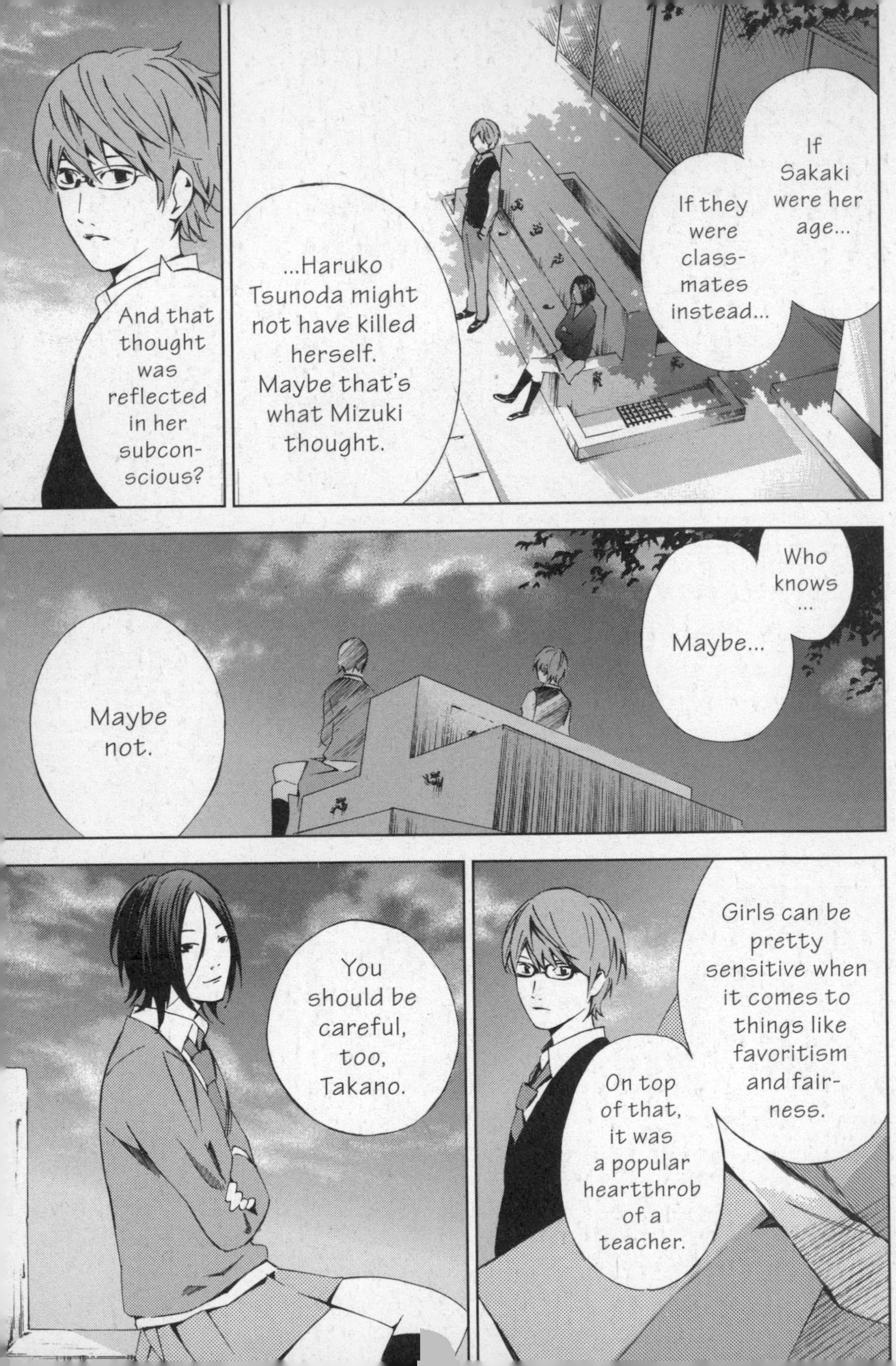
If Sakaki were her age...
If they were classmates instead...
...Haruko Tsunoda might not have killed herself. Maybe that's what Mizuki thought.
And that thought was reflected in her subconscious?
Who knows...
Maybe...
Maybe not.
Girls can be pretty sensitive when it comes to things like favoritism and fairness.
On top of that, it was a popular heartthrob of a teacher.
You should be careful, too, Takano.

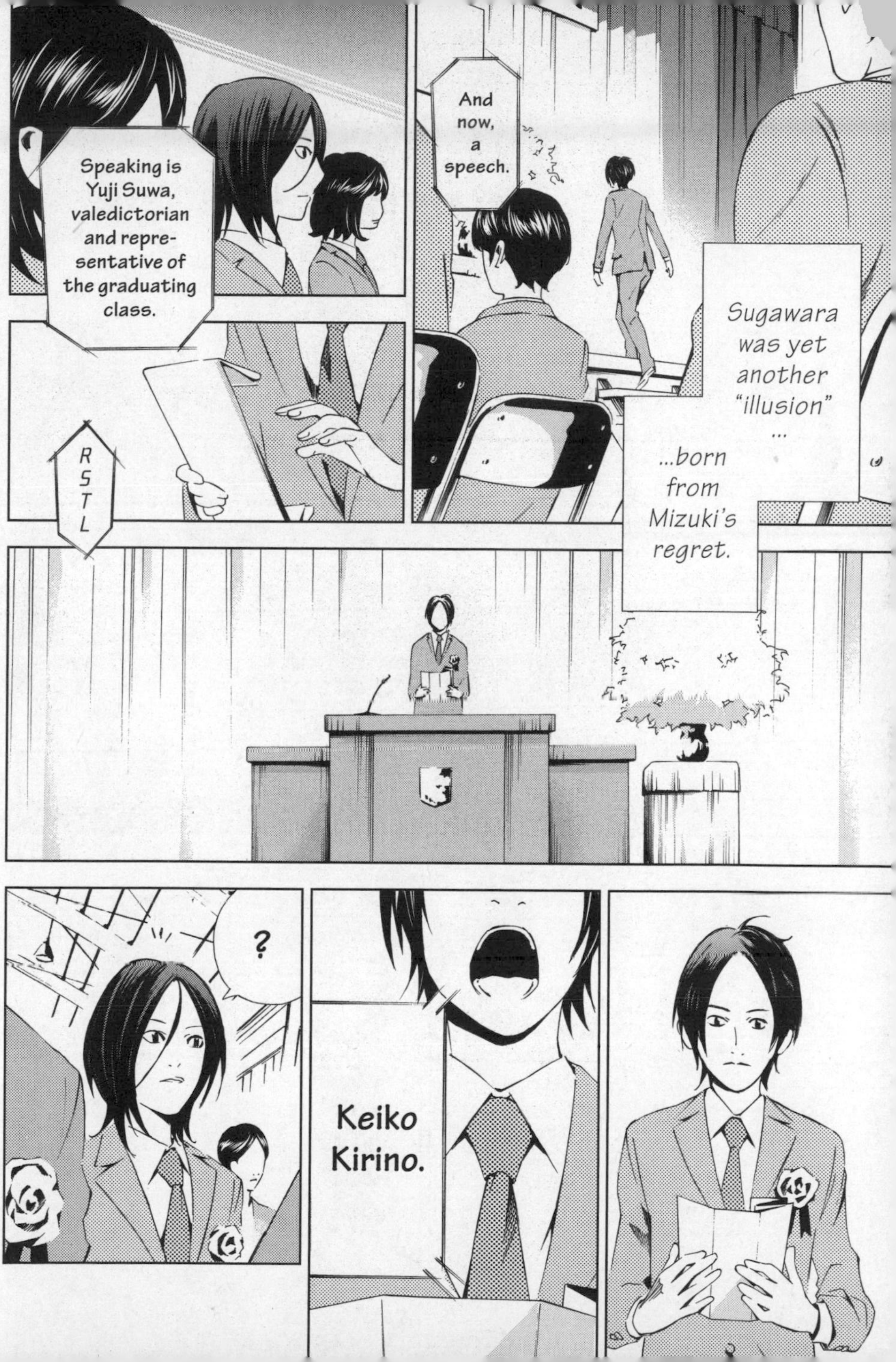

And now, a speech.
Sugawara was yet another "illusion"...
...born from Mizuki's regret.
Speaking is Yuji Suwa, valedictorian and representative of the graduating class.
RSTL
Keiko Kirino.
?

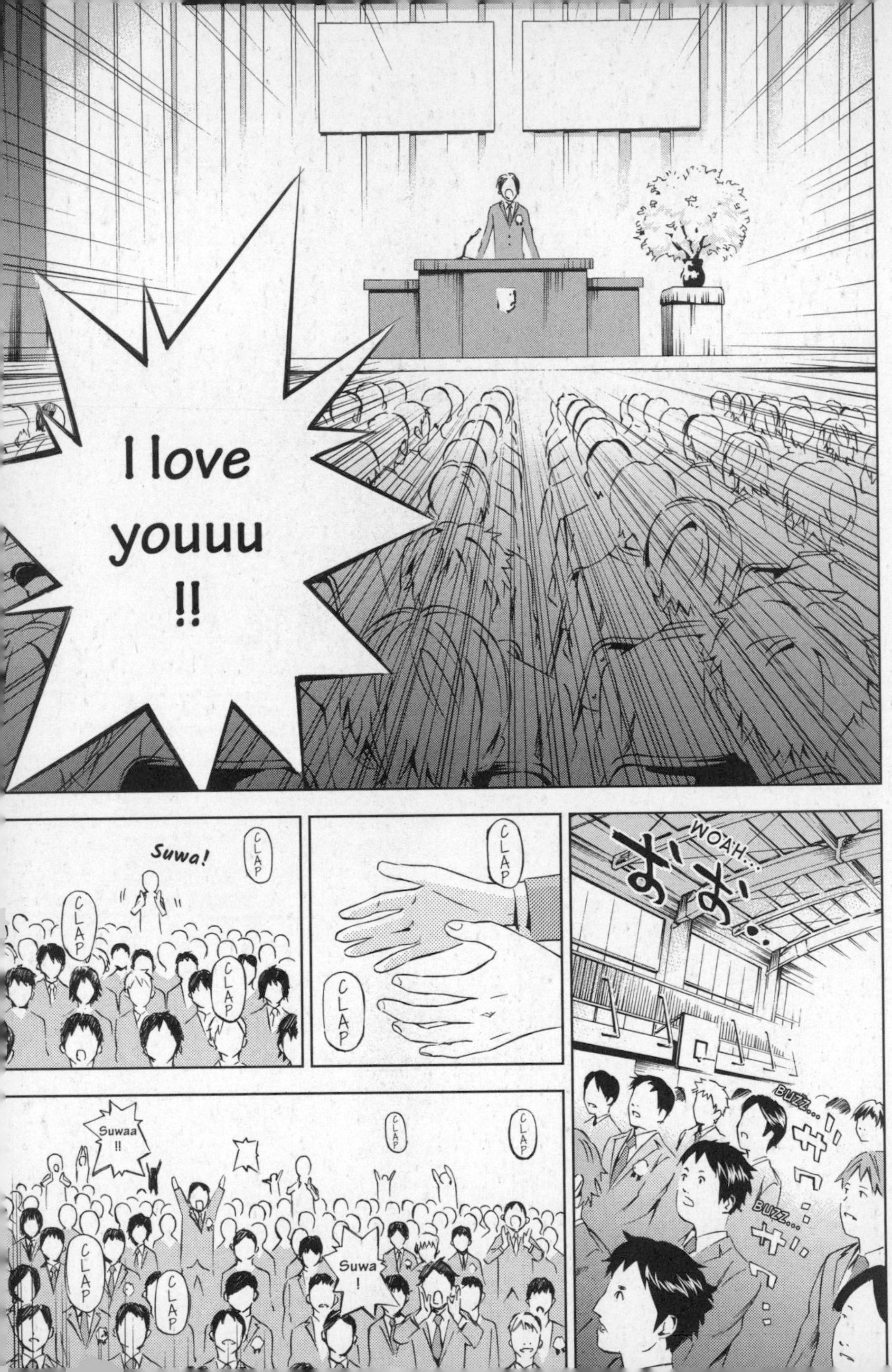
I love youuu !!
WOAH...
CLAP
CLAP
Suwa!
CLAP
CLAP
CLAP
BUZZ...
BUZZ...
CLAP
CLAP
Suwaa !!
Suwa !
CLAP
CLAP

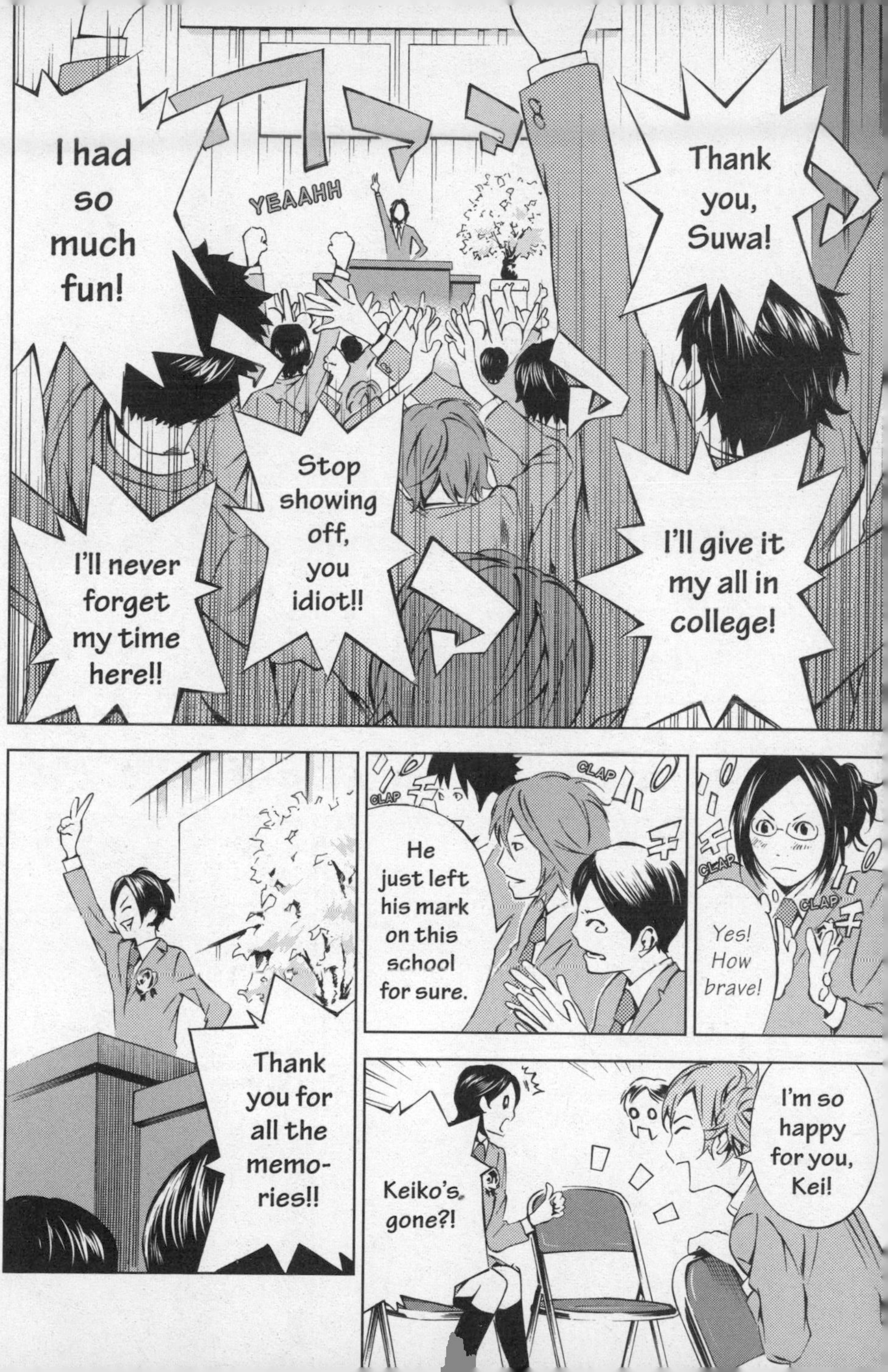
Thank you, Suwa!
I had so much fun!
YEAAHH
I'll give it my all in college!
Stop showing off, you idiot!!
I'll never forget my time here!!
CLAP
CLAP
Yes! How brave!
CLAP
CLAP
He just left his mark on this school for sure.
I'm so happy for you, Kei!
Keiko's gone?!
Thank you for all the memories!!

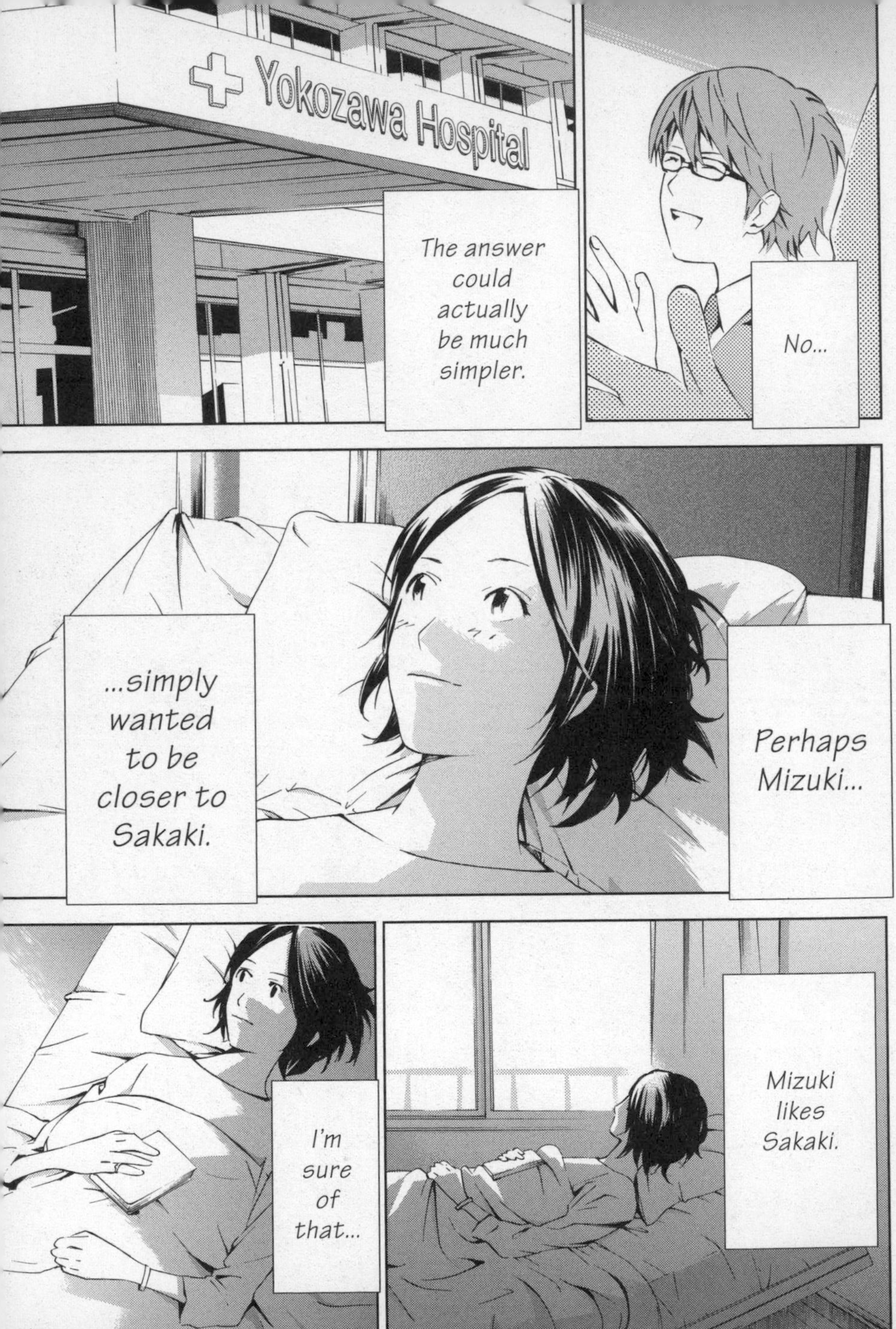
No...
Yokozawa Hospital
The answer could actually be much simpler.
Perhaps Mizuki...
...simply wanted to be closer to Sakaki.
Mizuki likes Sakaki.
I'm sure of that...

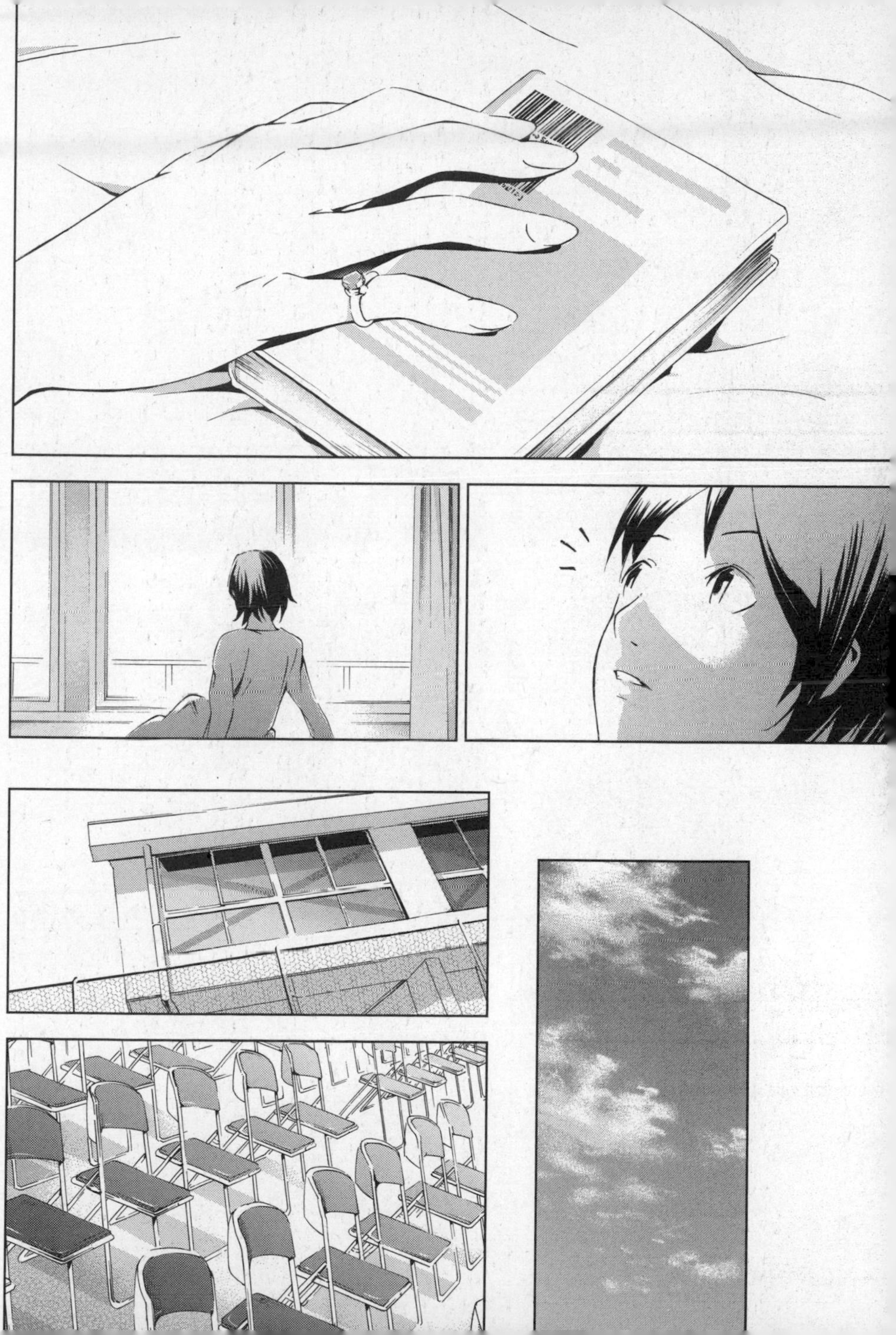

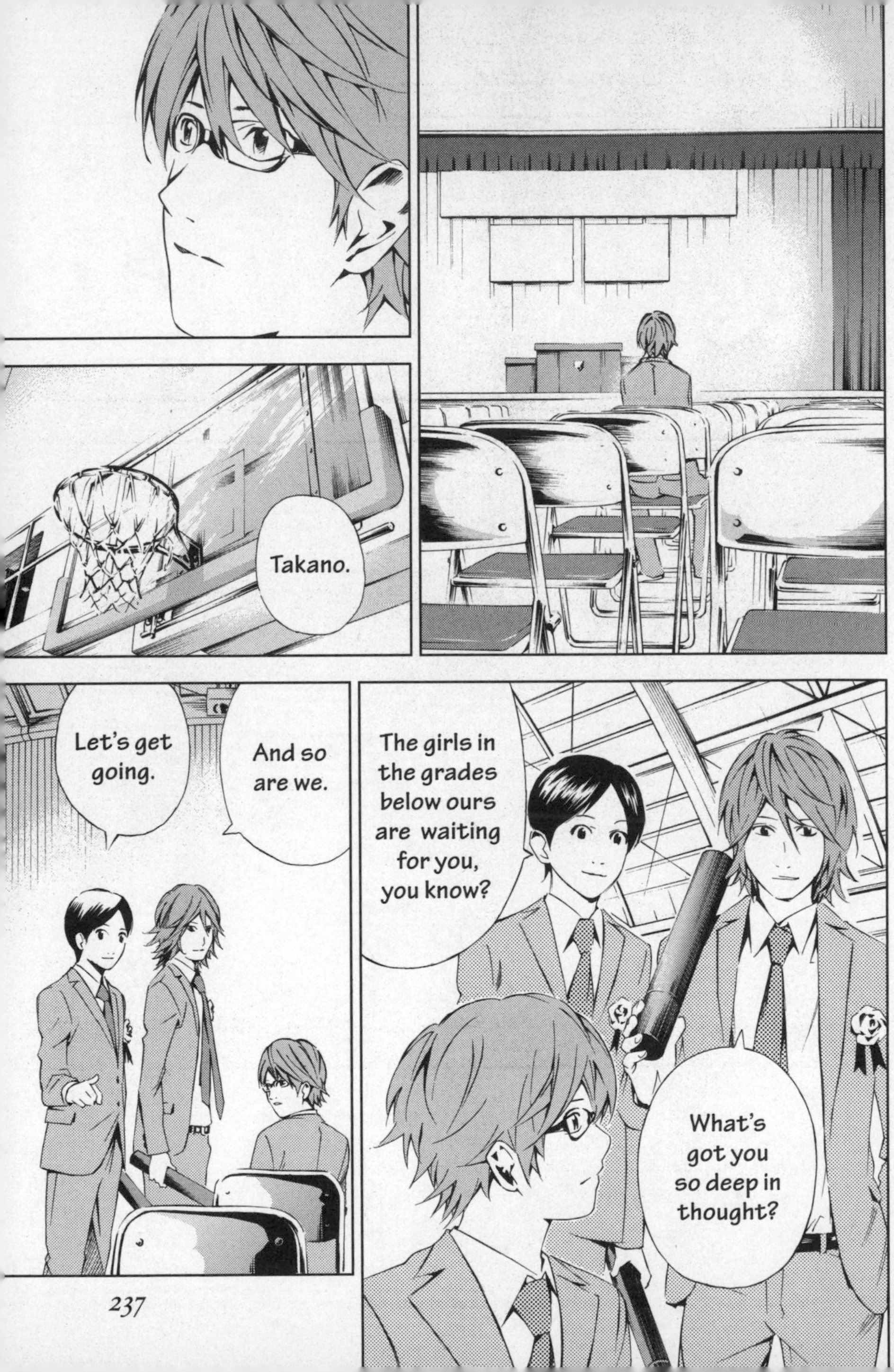
Takano.
The girls in the grades below ours are waiting for you, you know?
What's got you so deep in thought?
And so are we.
Let's get going.

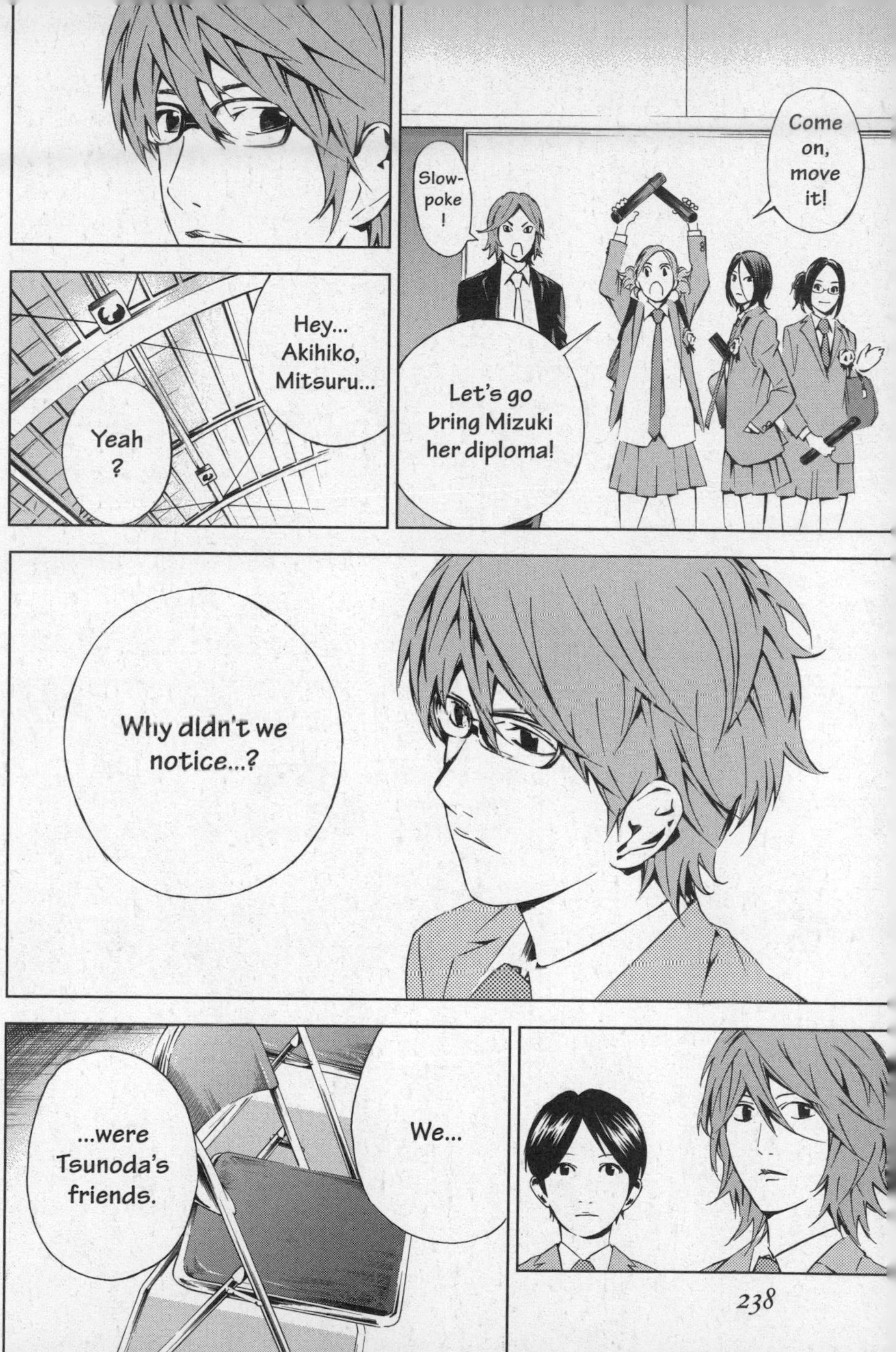
Come on, move it!
Slow-poke!
Let's go bring Mizuki her diploma!
Hey... Akihiko, Mitsuru...
Yeah?
Why didn't we notice...?
We...
...were Tsunoda's friends.

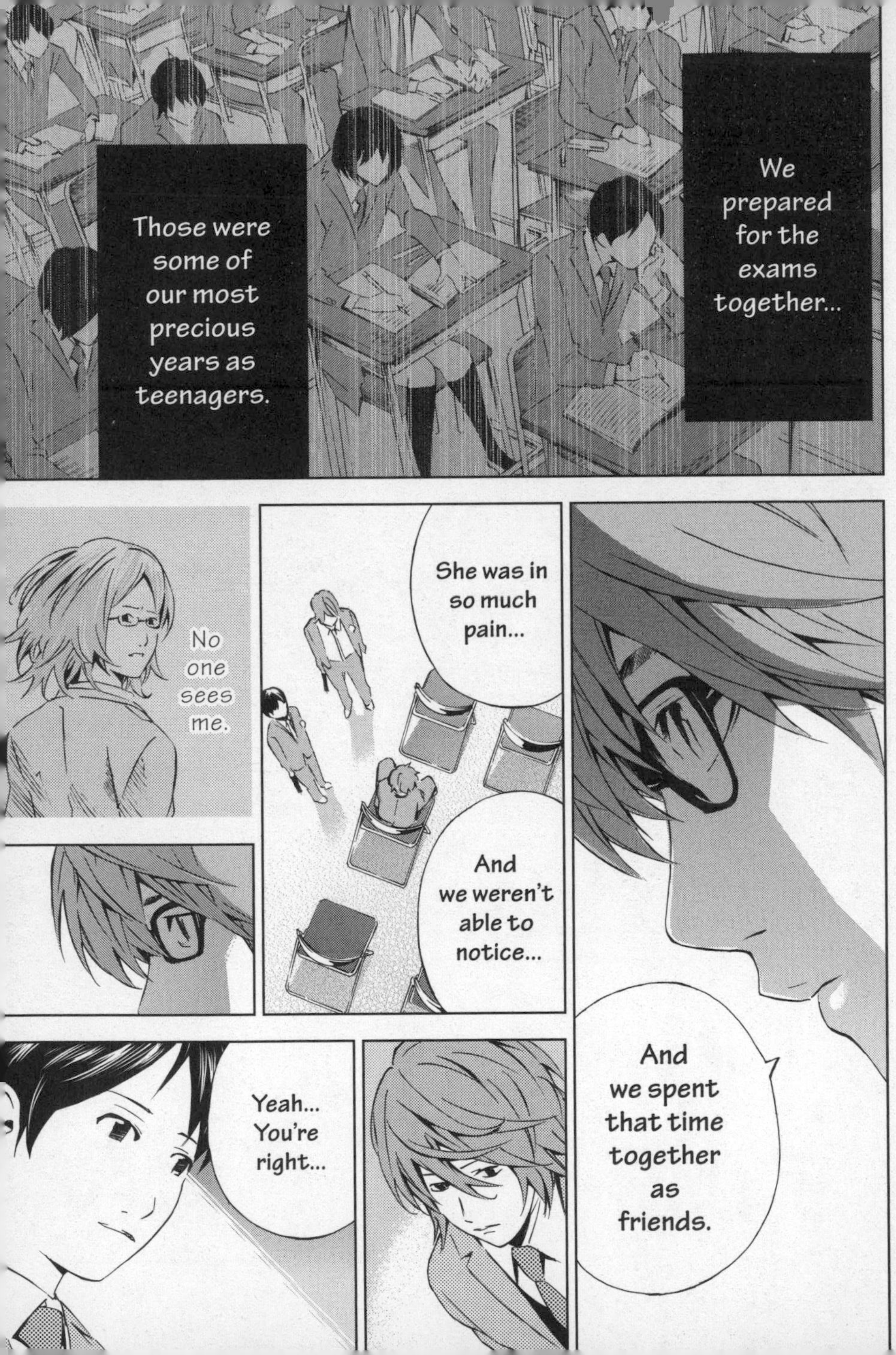
We prepared for the exams together...
Those were some of our most precious years as teenagers.
And we spent that time together as friends.
She was in so much pain...
And we weren't able to notice...
No one sees me.
Yeah... You're right...

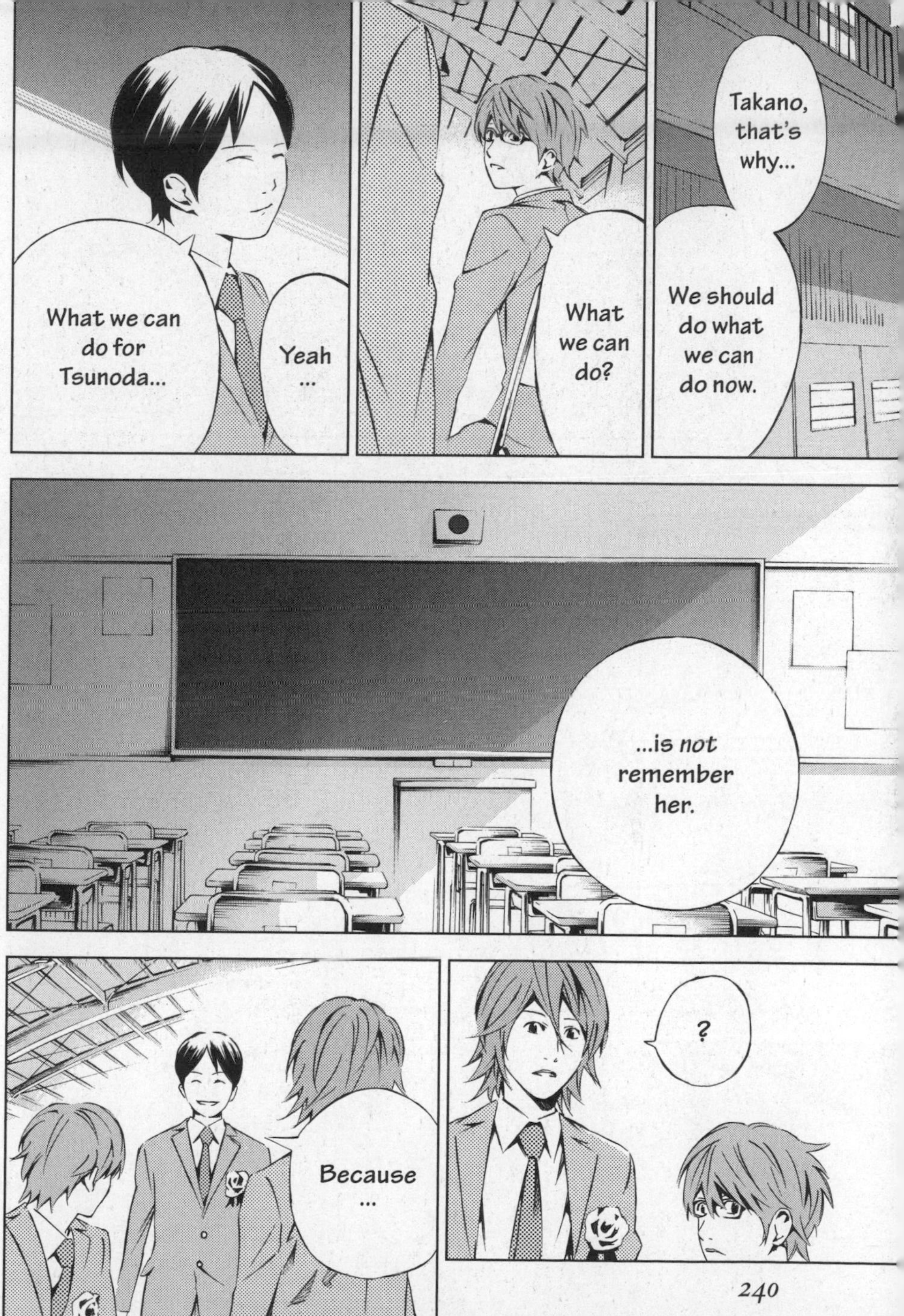
Takano, that's why...
We should do what we can do now.
What we can do?
Yeah ...
What we can do for Tsunoda...
...is *not* remember her.
?
Because ...

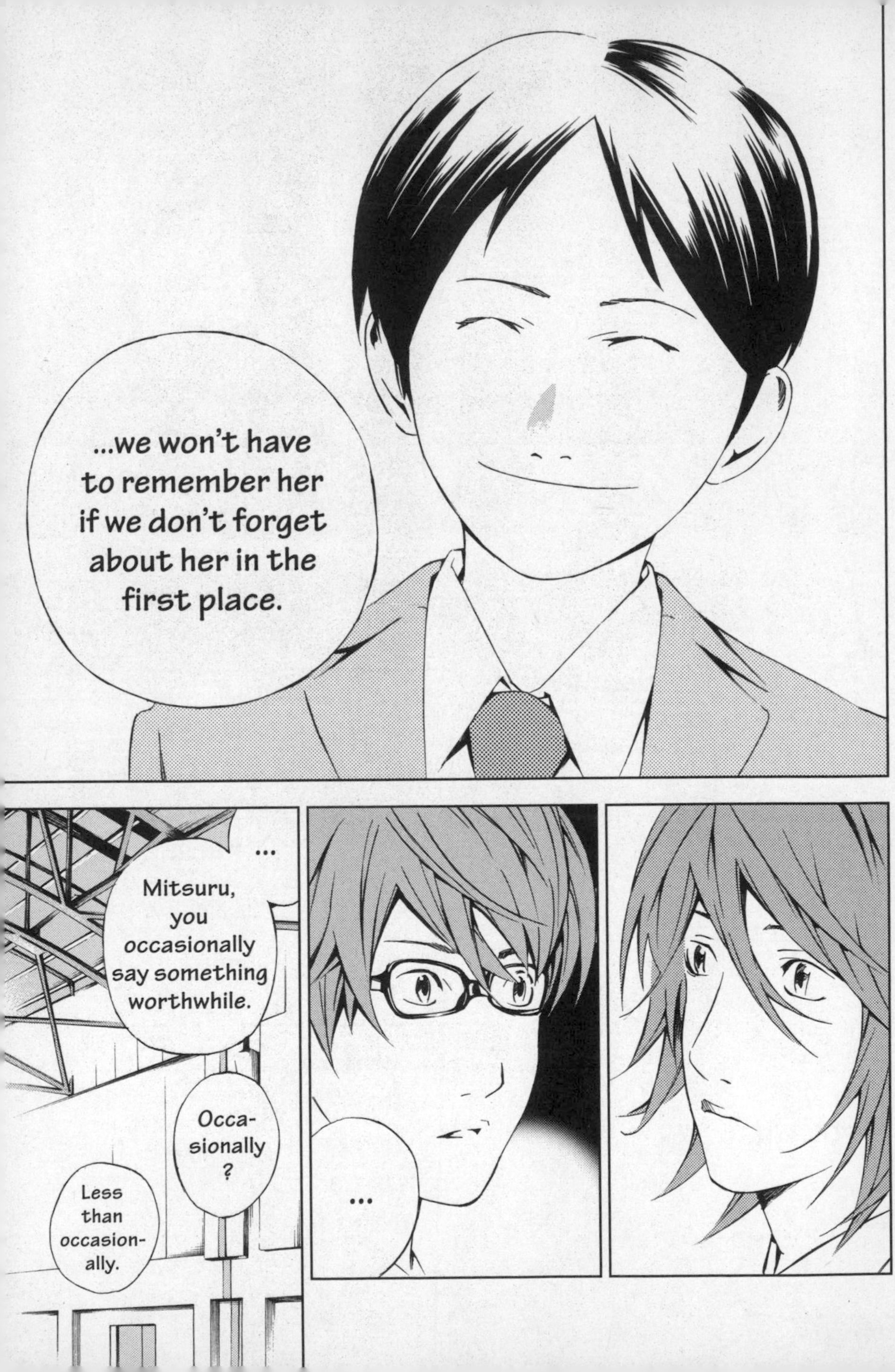
...we won't have to remember her if we don't forget about her in the first place.
...
...
Mitsuru, you occasionally say something worthwhile.
Occa-sionally?
Less than occasion-ally.

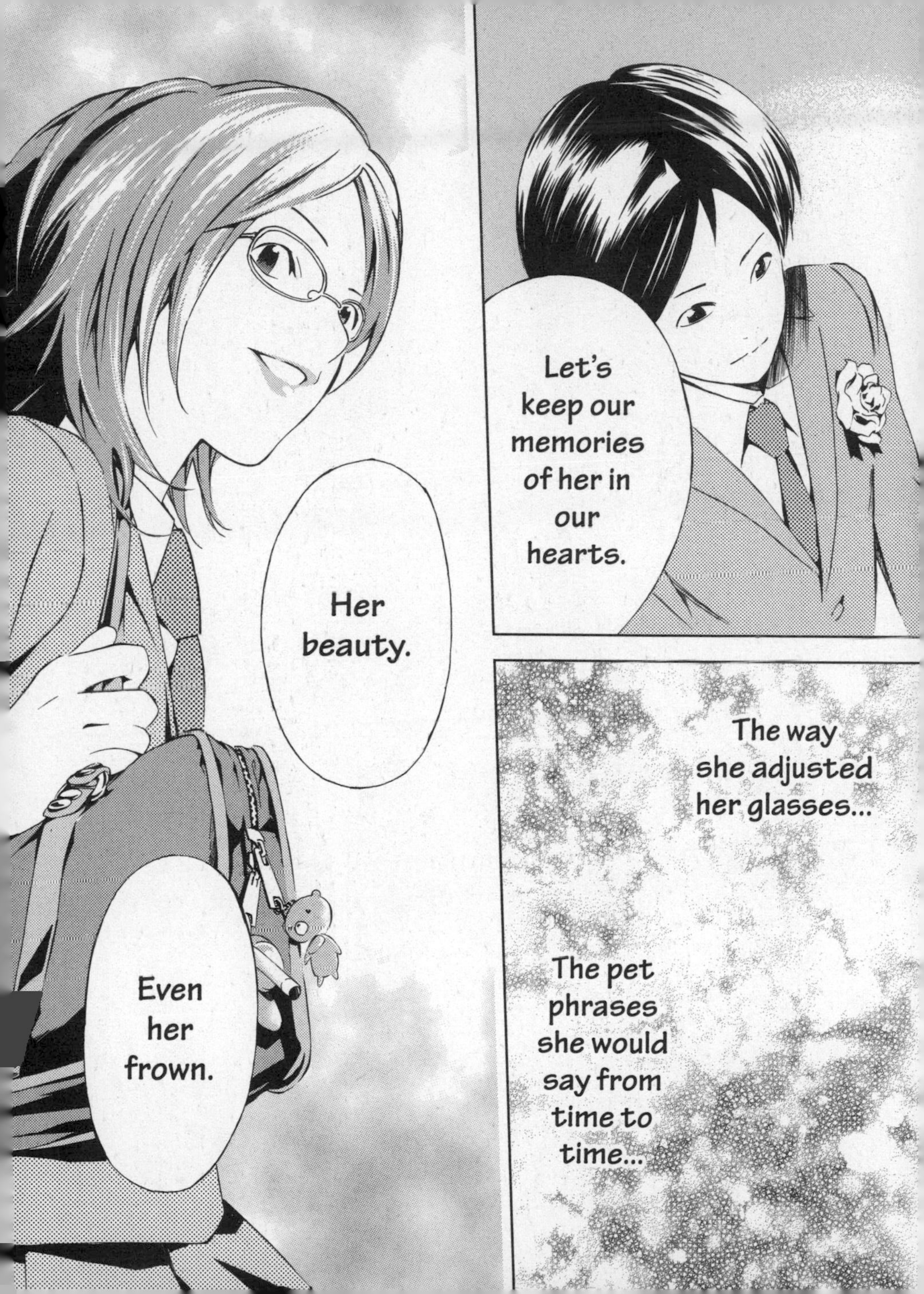
Let's keep our memories of her in our hearts.
The way she adjusted her glasses...
The pet phrases she would say from time to time...
Her beauty.
Even her frown.

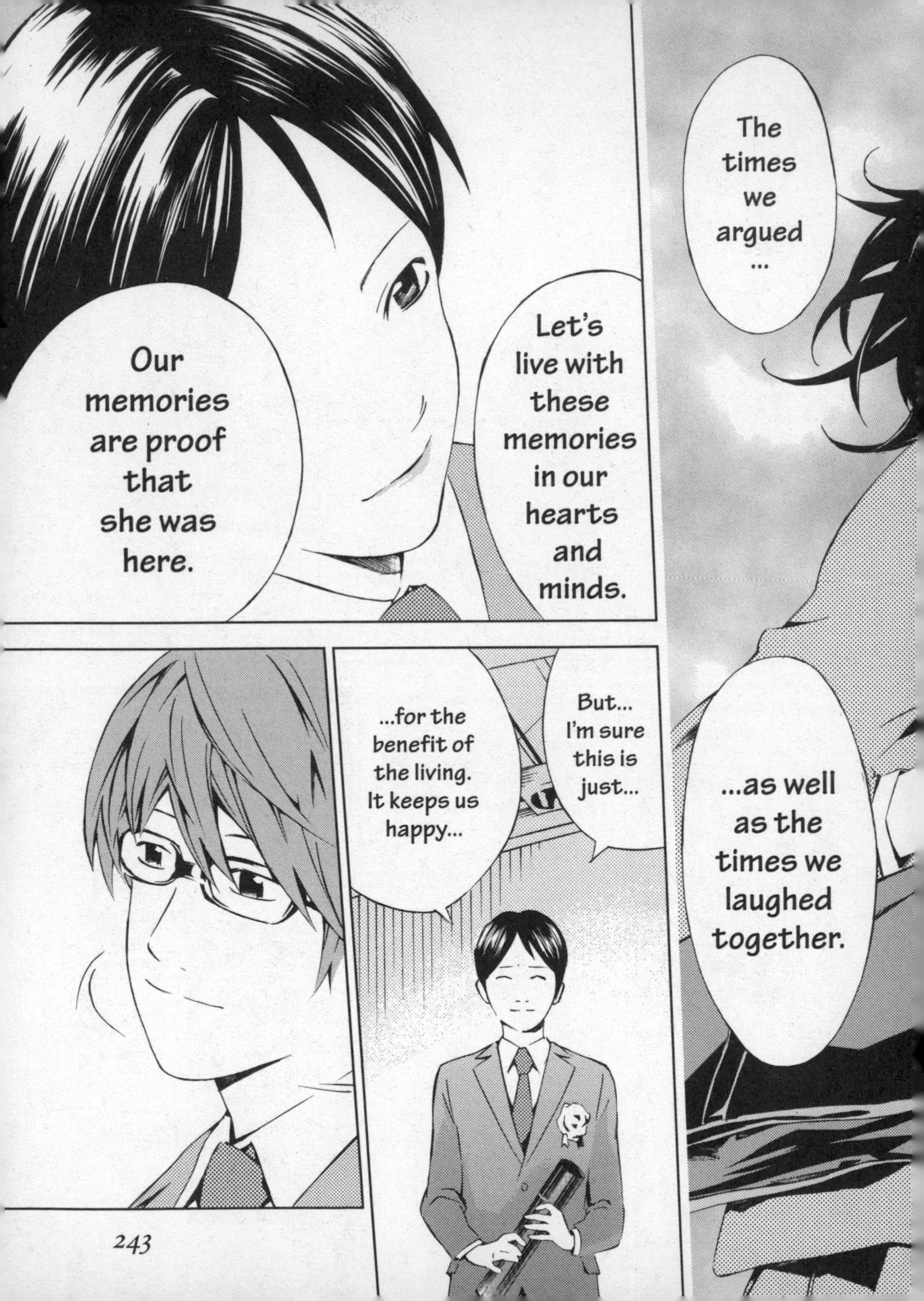

The times we argued ...
...as well as the times we laughed together.
Let's live with these memories in our hearts and minds.
Our memories are proof that she was here.
But... I'm sure this is just...
...for the benefit of the living. It keeps us happy...

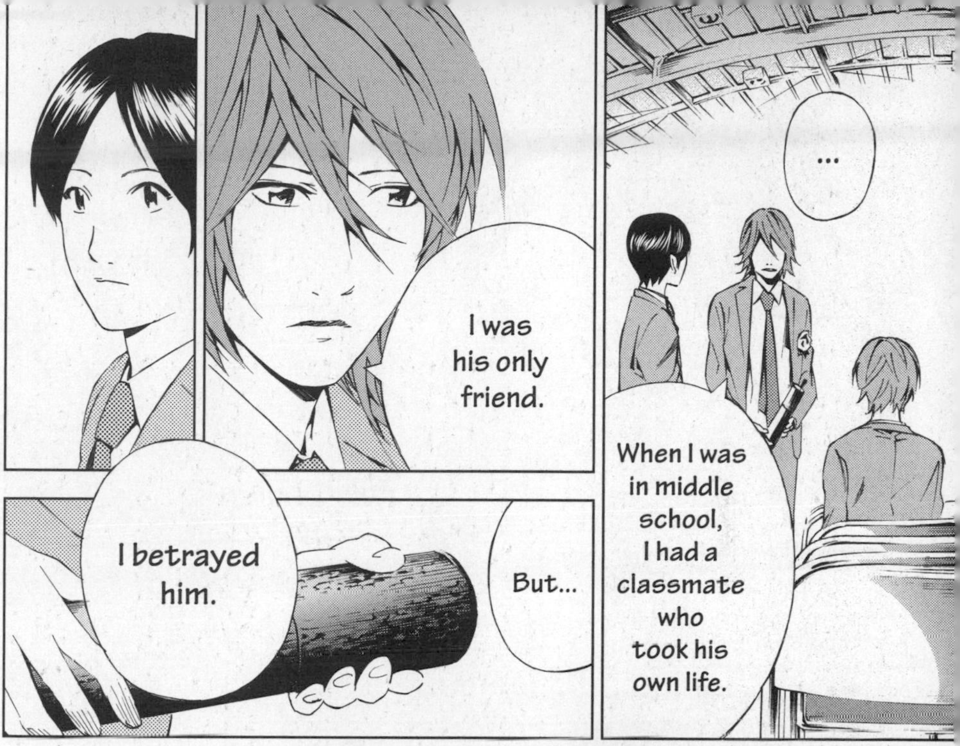
...
When I was in middle school, I had a classmate who took his own life.
I was his only friend.
But...
I betrayed him.

*Lantern (below): A memorial lantern used to send off and welcome the spirits of the dead.

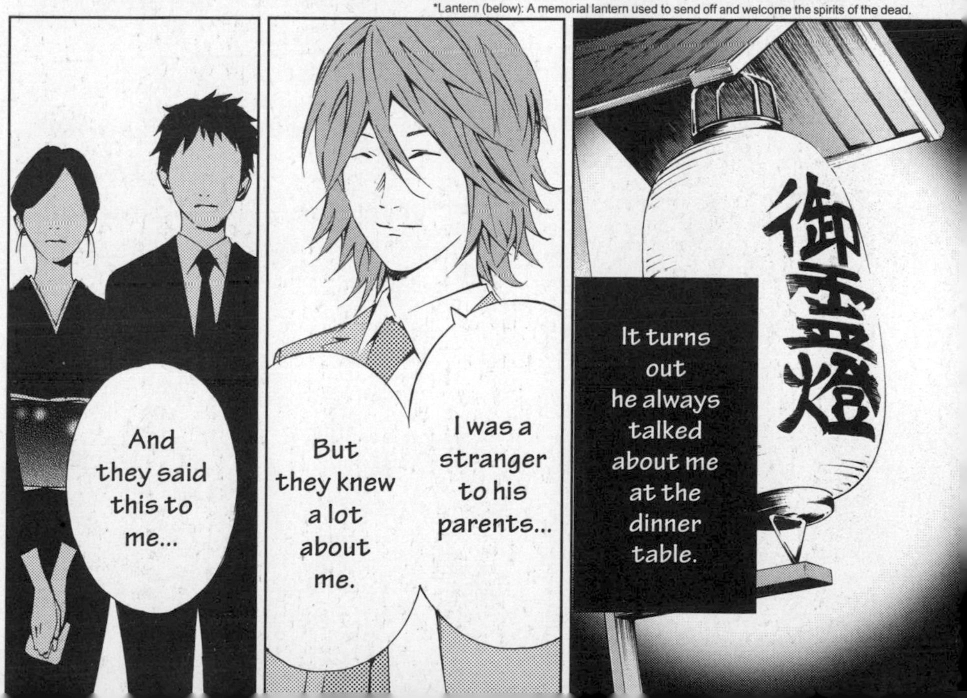
御霊燈
It turns out he always talked about me at the dinner table.
I was a stranger to his parents...
But they knew a lot about me.
And they said this to me...

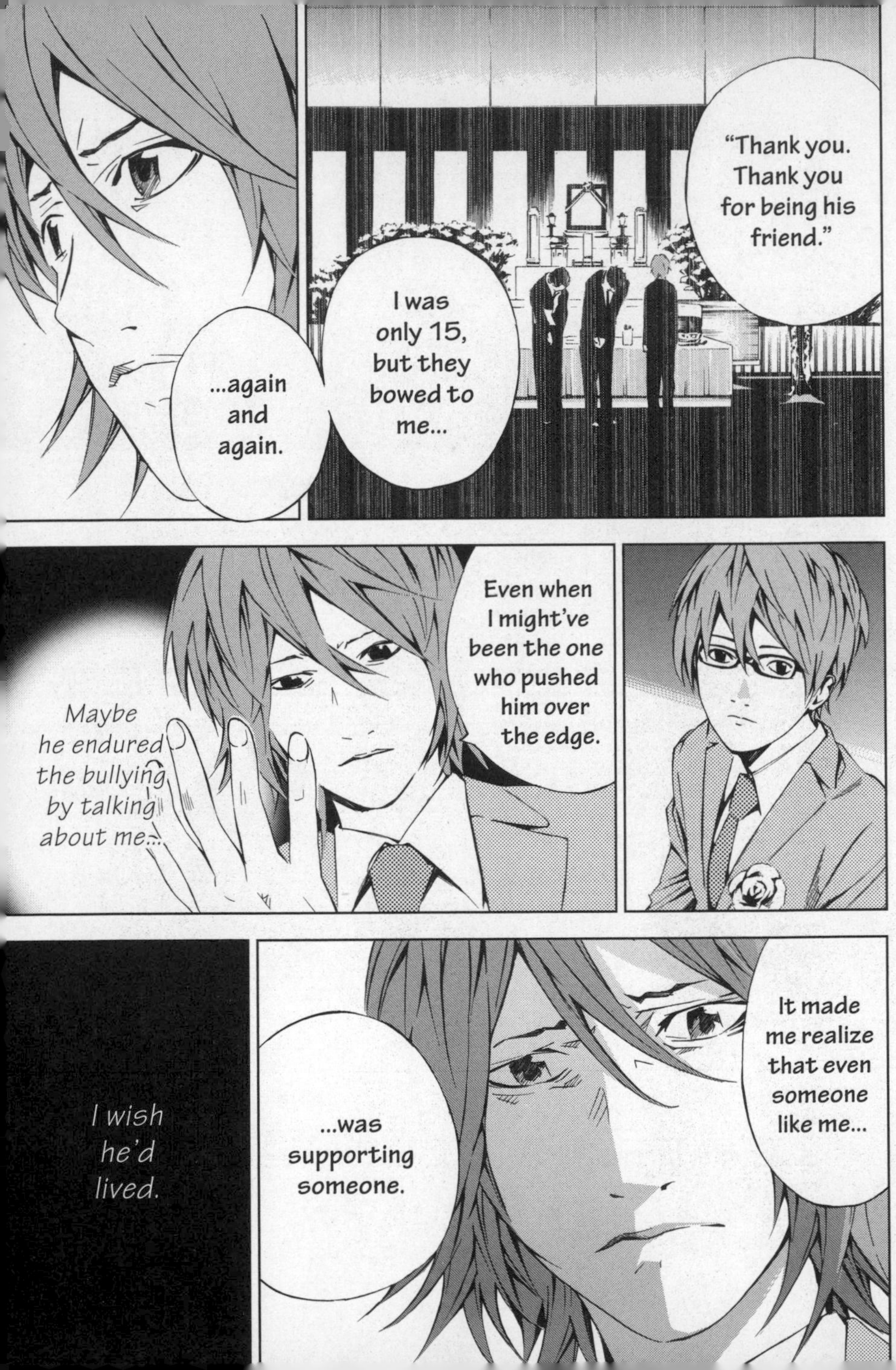
"Thank you. Thank you for being his friend."
I was only 15, but they bowed to me...
...again and again.
Even when I might've been the one who pushed him over the edge.
Maybe he endured the bullying by talking about me...
It made me realize that even someone like me...
...was supporting someone.
I wish he'd lived.

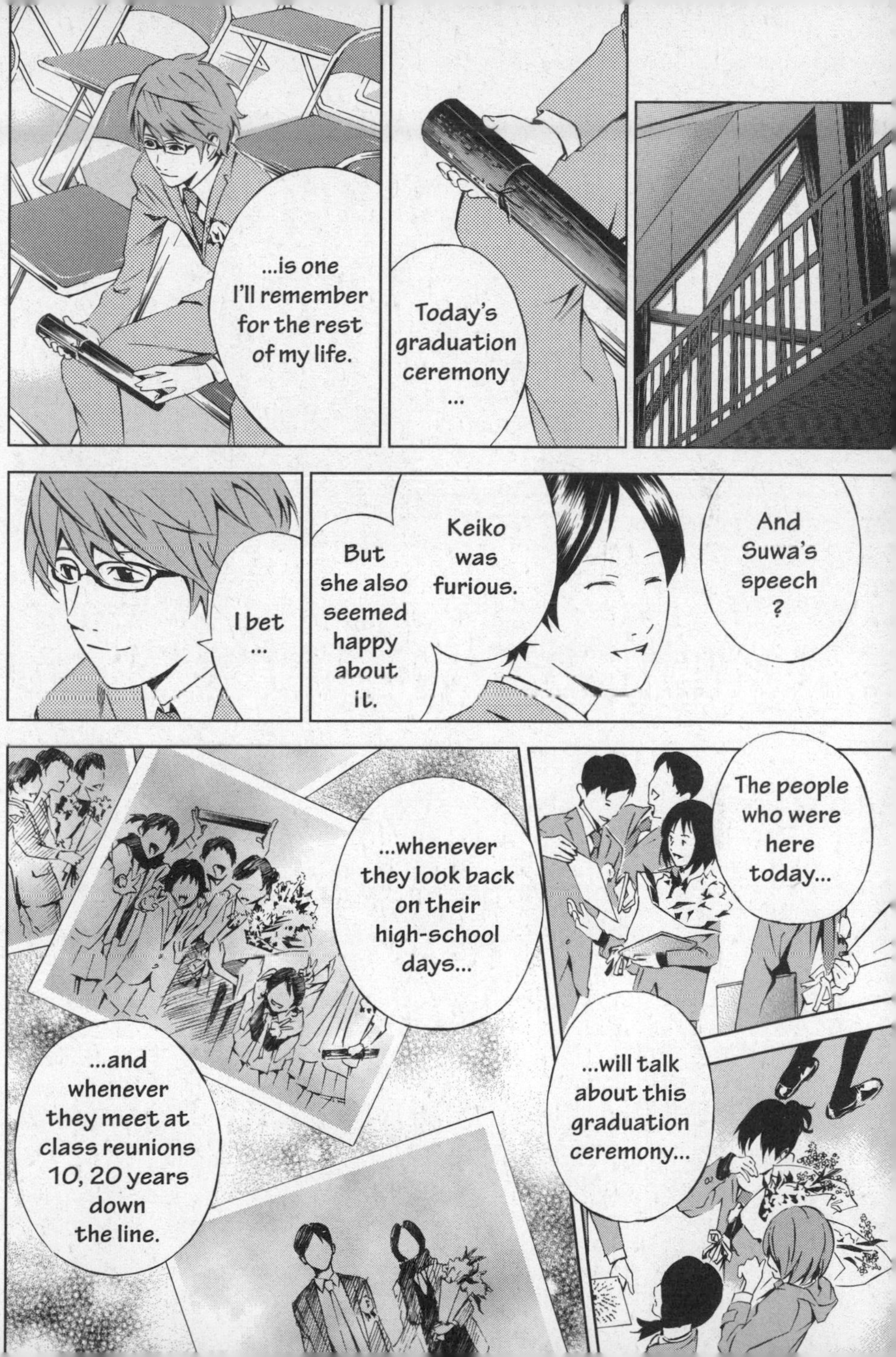
Today's graduation ceremony ...
...is one I'll remember for the rest of my life.
And Suwa's speech ?
Keiko was furious.
But she also seemed happy about it.
I bet ...
The people who were here today...
...will talk about this graduation ceremony...
...whenever they look back on their high-school days...
...and whenever they meet at class reunions 10, 20 years down the line.

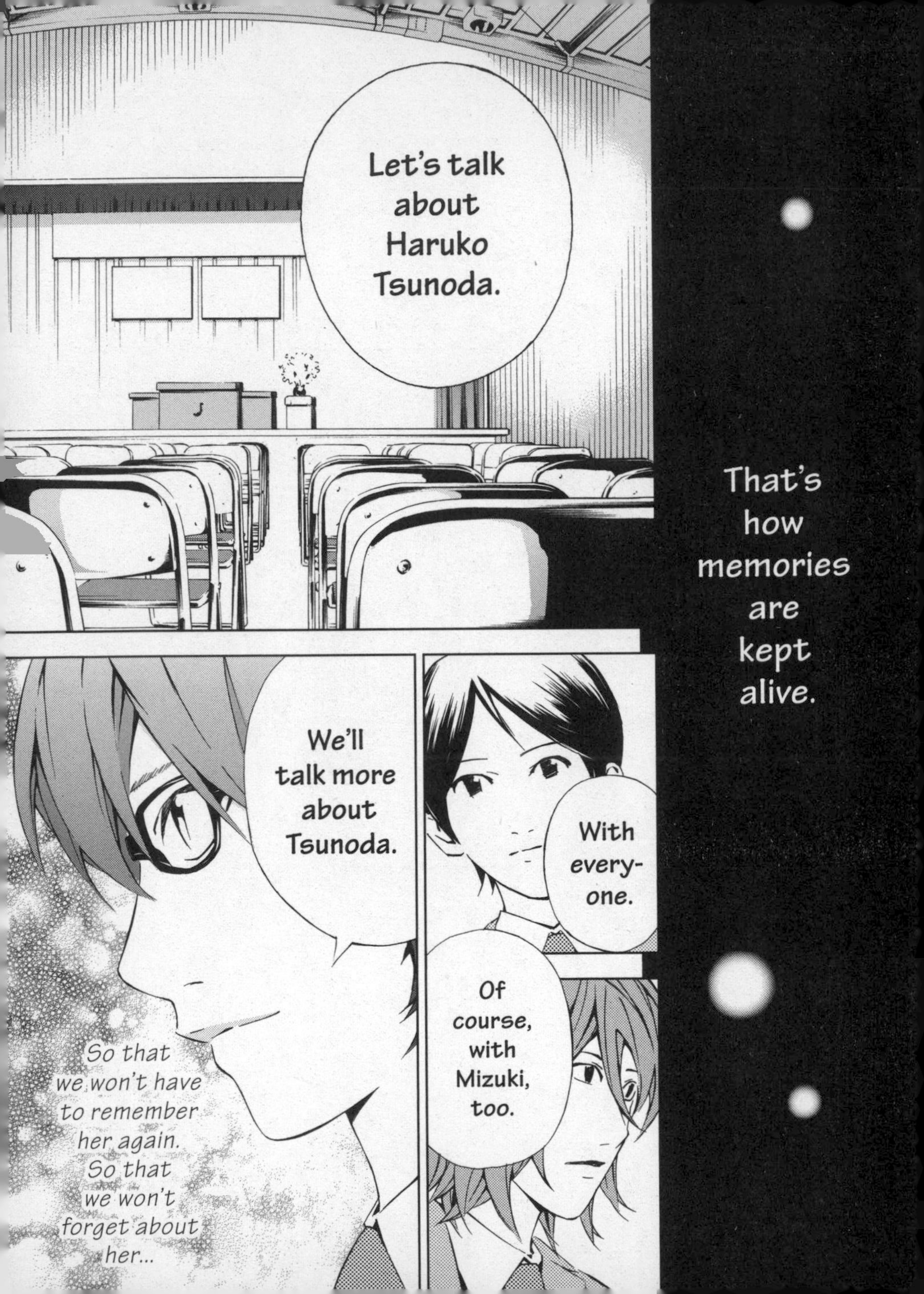
That's how memories are kept alive.
Let's talk about Haruko Tsunoda.
With every-one.
Of course, with Mizuki, too.
We'll talk more about Tsunoda.
So that we won't have to remember her again. So that we won't forget about her...

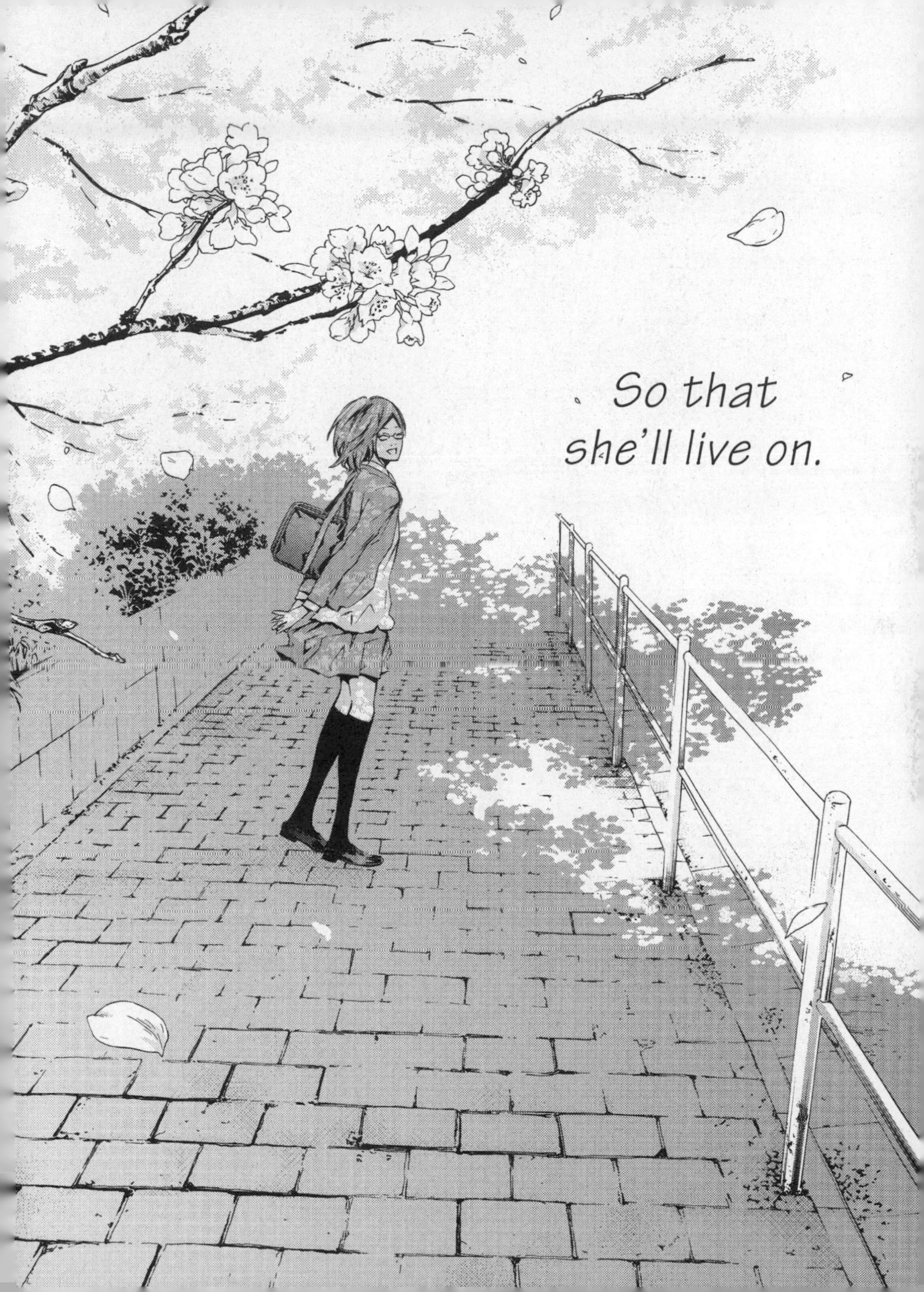
So that she'll live on.

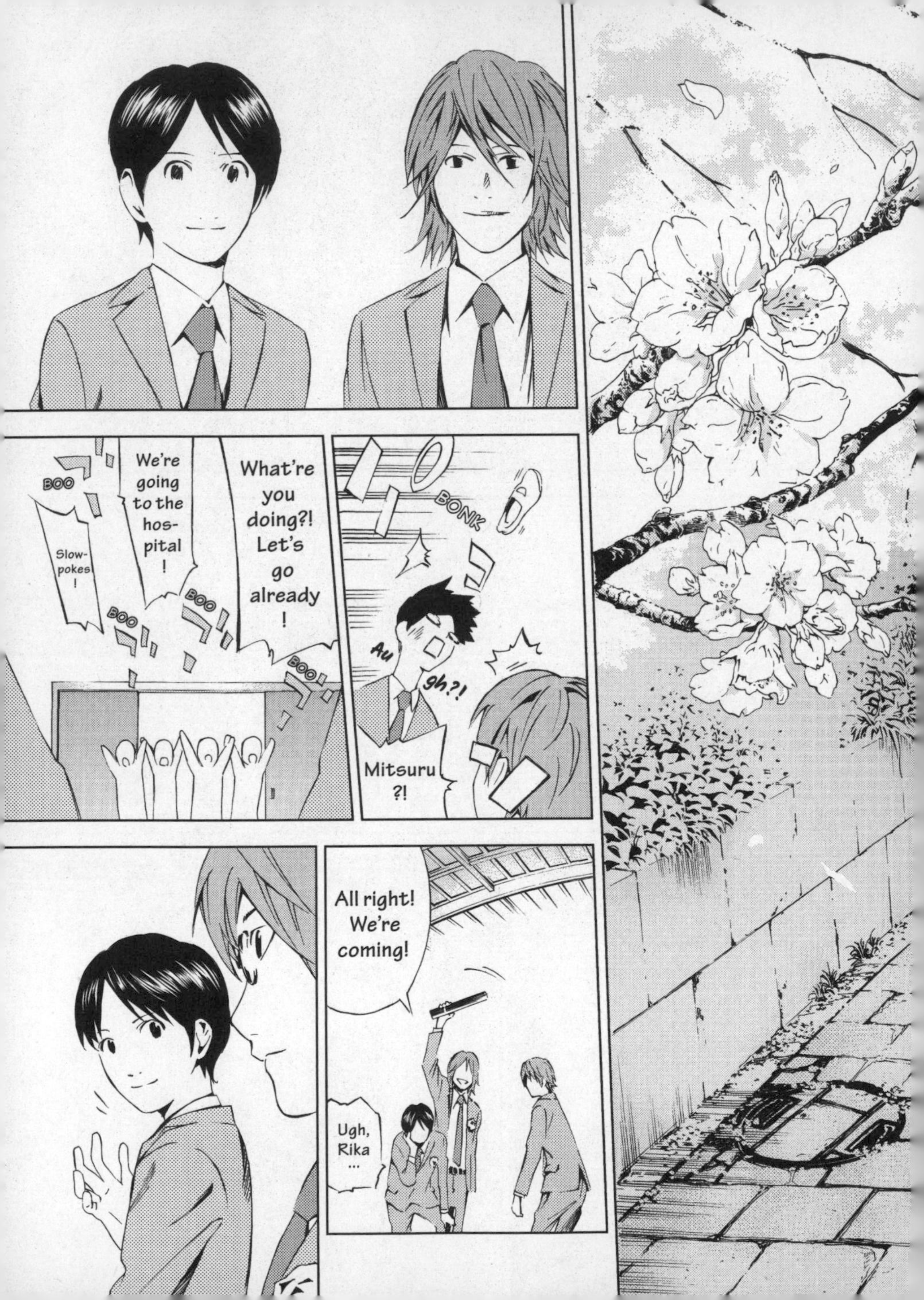
BONK
Augh?!
Mitsuru ?!
What're you doing?! Let's go already!
We're going to the hospital!
BOO
Slow-pokes!
BOO
BOO
BOO!
All right! We're coming!
Ugh, Rika ...

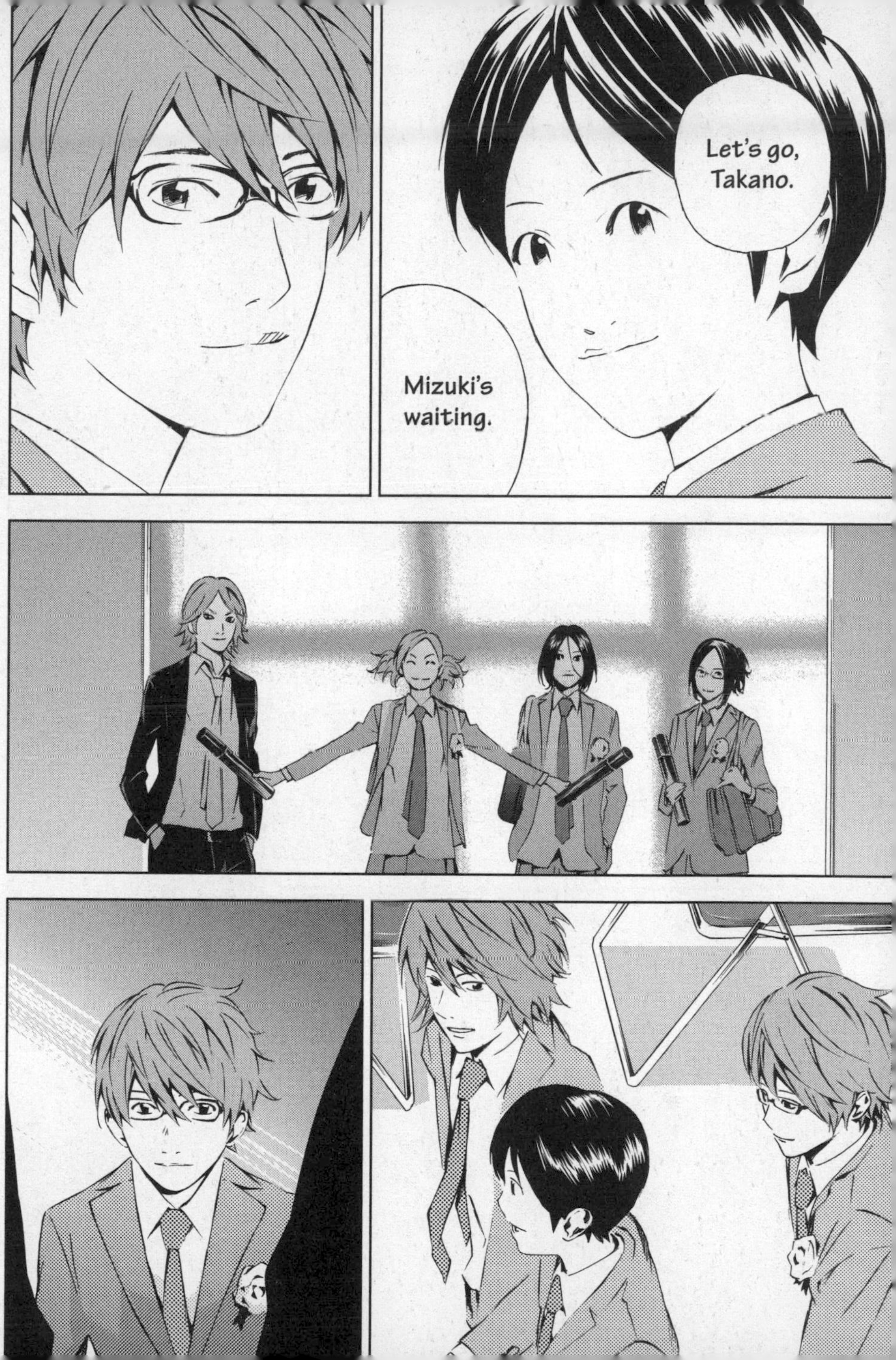
Let's go, Takano.
Mizuki's waiting.

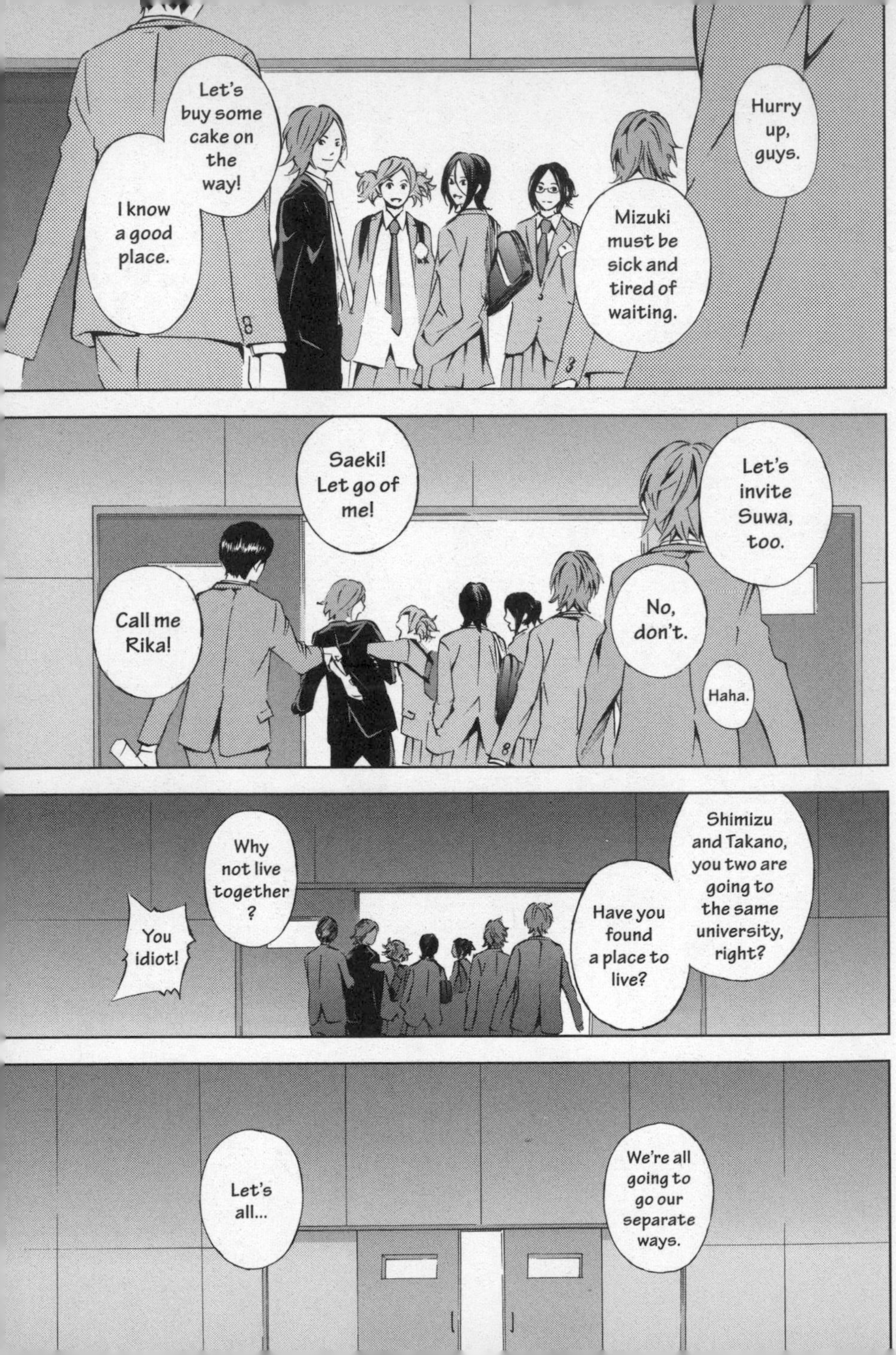
Hurry up, guys.
Mizuki must be sick and tired of waiting.
Let's buy some cake on the way!
I know a good place.
Let's invite Suwa, too.
No, don't.
Haha.
Saeki! Let go of me!
Call me Rika!
Shimizu and Takano, you two are going to the same university, right?
Have you found a place to live?
Why not live together?
You idiot!
We're all going to go our separate ways.
Let's all...

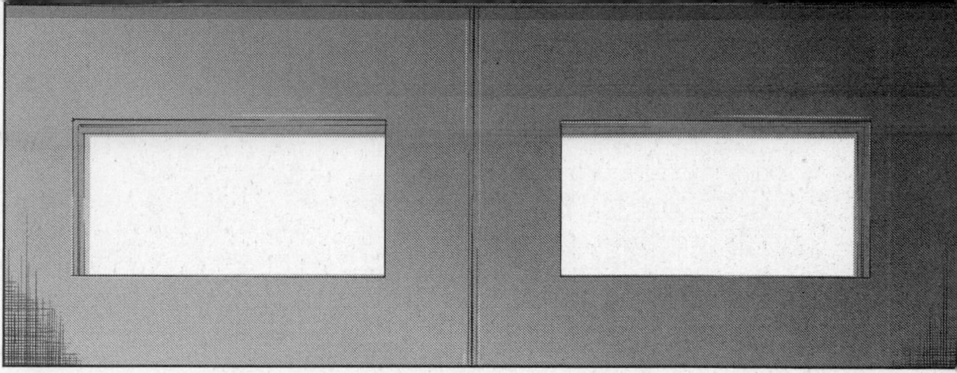
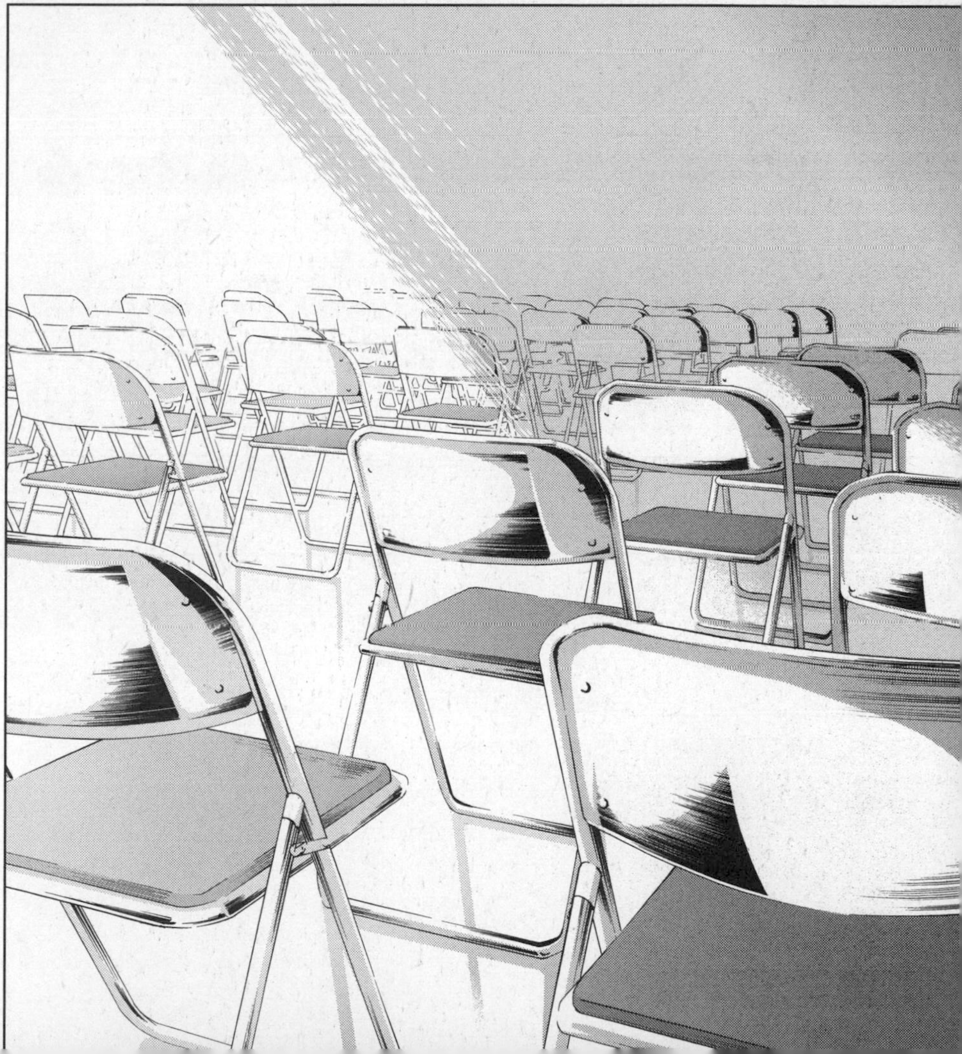

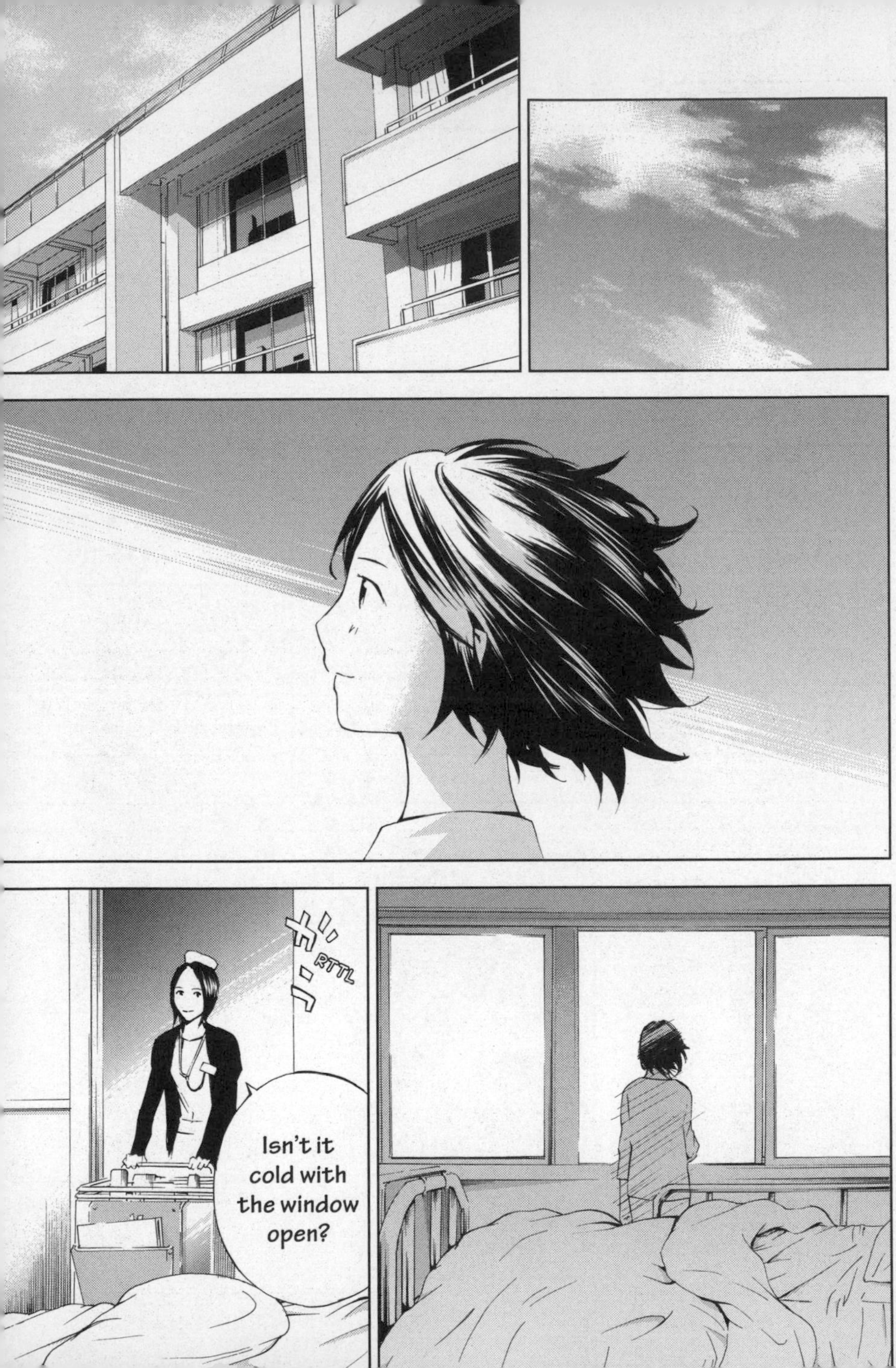
RTTL
Isn't it cold with the window open?

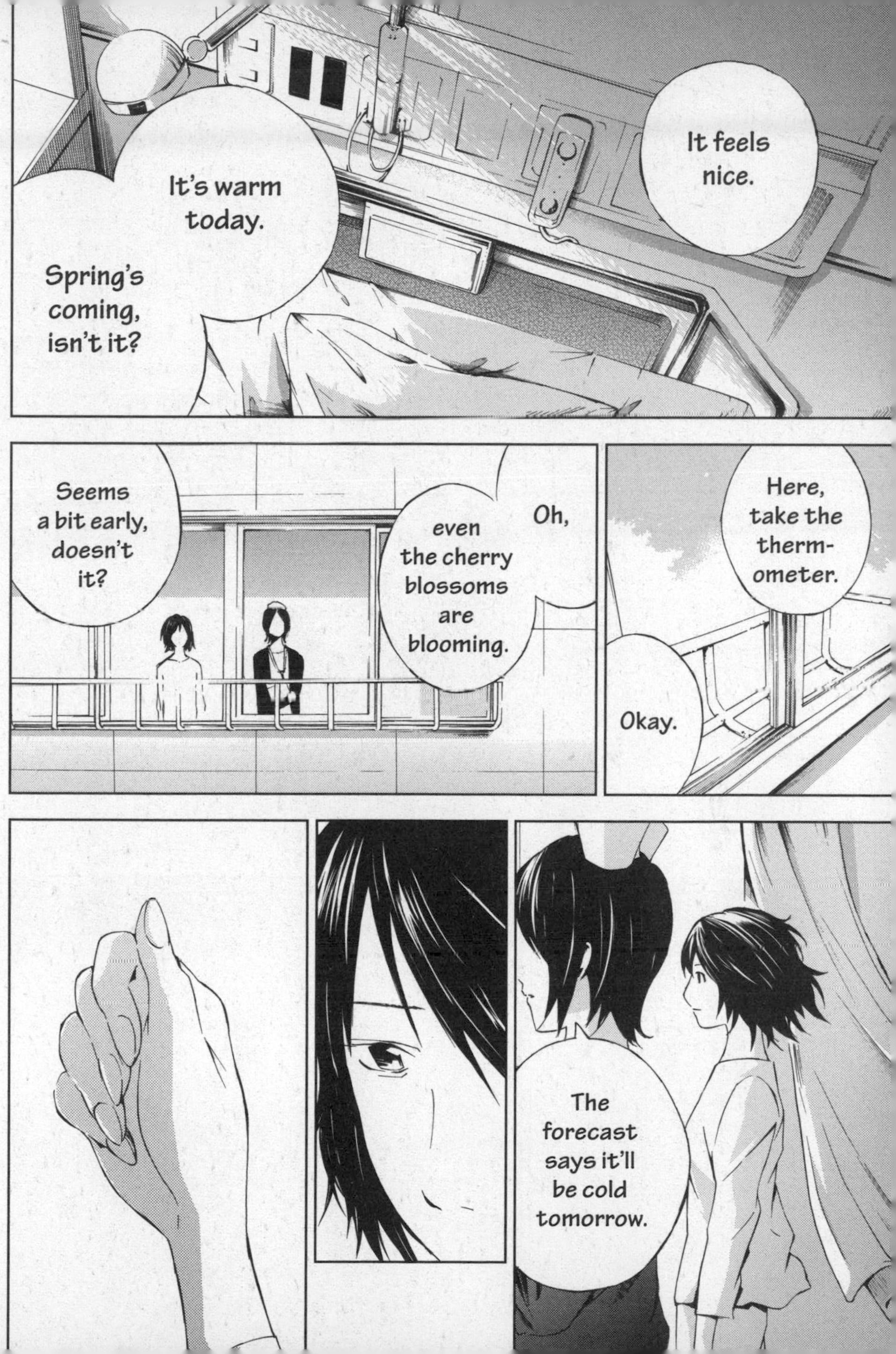
It feels nice.
It's warm today.
Spring's coming, isn't it?
Here, take the thermometer.
Okay.
Oh,
even the cherry blossoms are blooming.
Seems a bit early, doesn't it?
The forecast says it'll be cold tomorrow.

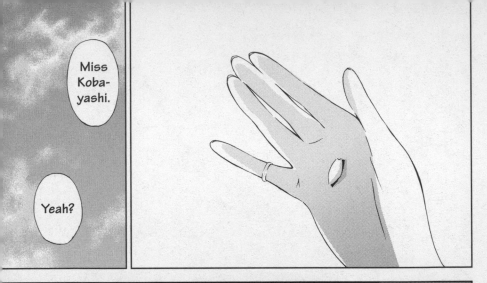

Miss Koba-yashi.

Yeah?

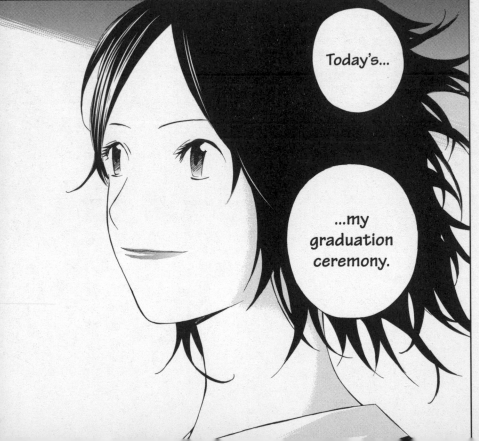

Today's...

...my graduation ceremony.

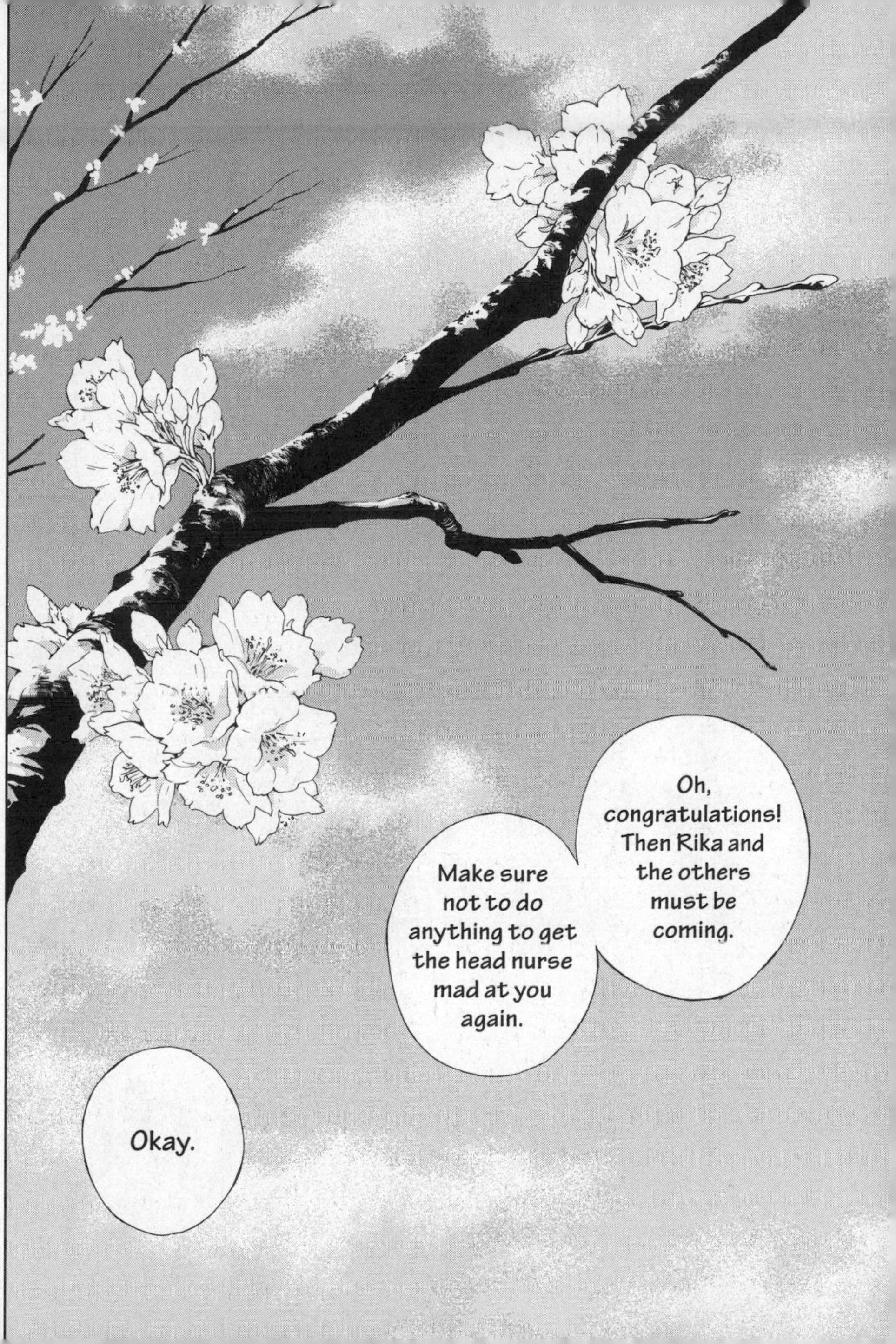
Oh, congratulations! Then Rika and the others must be coming.
Make sure not to do anything to get the head nurse mad at you again.
Okay.

A School Frozen in Time   *Fin.*

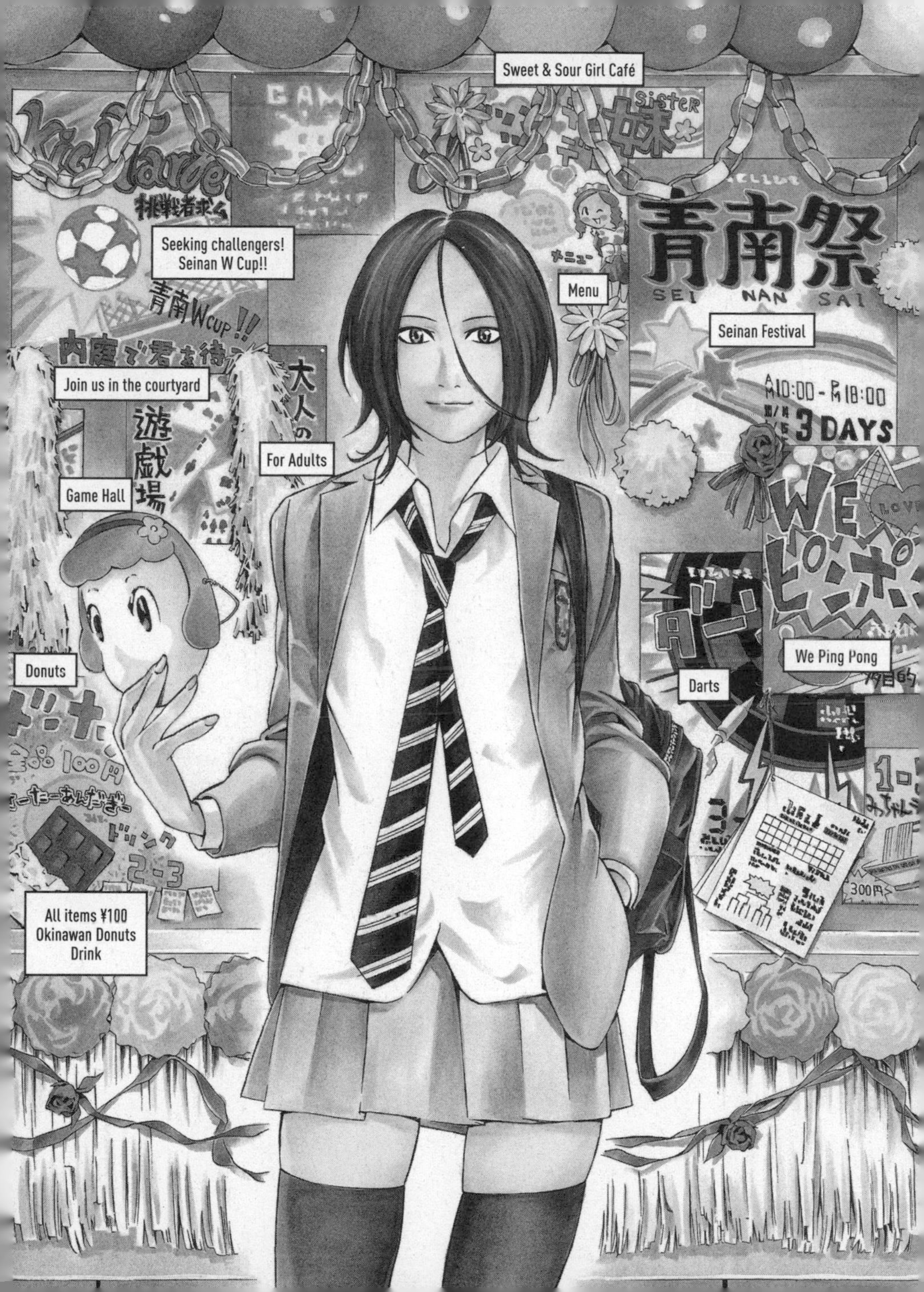

Sweet & Sour Girl Café
SISTER
青南祭
SEI NAN SAI
Seinan Festival
Menu
AM10:00 - PM18:00
3 DAYS
WE
LOVE
We Ping Pong
Darts
300円
Seeking challengers!
Seinan W Cup!!
青南Wcup!!
Join us in the courtyard
大人の
遊戯場
For Adults
Game Hall
Donuts
All items ¥100
Okinawan Donuts
Drink

TRANSLATION NOTES

p7 "Noh mask"
Noh is a traditional form of Japanese masked theater that has been performed since the fourteenth century. There are various types of Noh masks, each representing a different age, gender, and social ranking. Despite the different categories, however, Noh masks are all made to be expressionless. Actors portray their characters' emotions through subtle movements that alter the orientation and lighting of their masks.

p66 "Die-cut candy"
Die-cut candy, or *katanuki*, is a small and flat piece of colored candy commonly sold at Japanese festivals. These are sold not so much for eating, but for die-cutting. At festivals, children enjoy carving molded shapes out of these candies with a needle or toothpick, and a prize is awarded to those who carve the best shapes.

p99 "Votive tablet"
Votive tablets, or *ema*, are rectangular wooden plaques that can be found at Shinto shrines and Buddhist temples in Japan. Visitors can purchase and write their personal prayers or wishes on them. These tablets are then hung up on a special frame for the deities to receive them.

Stories by Yui Tokiumi
Created by Naoshi Arakawa

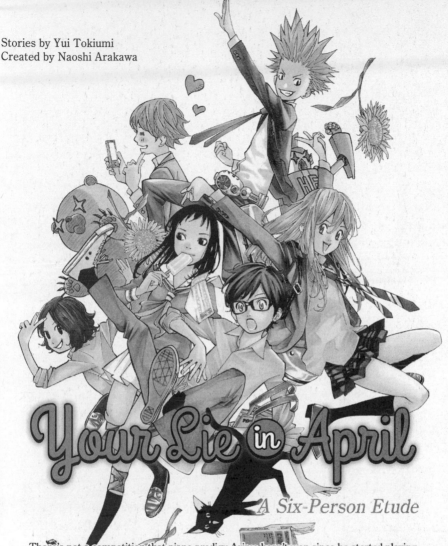

Your Lie in April

A Six-Person Etude

There's not a competition that piano prodigy Arima hasn't won since he started playing. His renditions are matchless in their precision. When he's only eleven, however, his peerless fingers fall silent—right up there on stage.

Exploring the shock of the incident and its aftermath from his friends' and rivals' perspectives, *A Six-Person Etude* accompanies the boy's halting efforts to pick himself up as an adolescent. Based on the hit series, these prose chapters expand on the original but form a coherent and hard-hitting tale of its own.

AVAILABLE NOW!

As three women—a producer, a director, and an animator—survive in a business infamous for its murderous schedules, demoralizing compromises, and incorrigible men, moments of uplift emerge against all odds. More than just a window into an entertainment niche, here's a kickass ode to work.

ANIME SUPREMACY!

MIZUKI TSUJIMURA

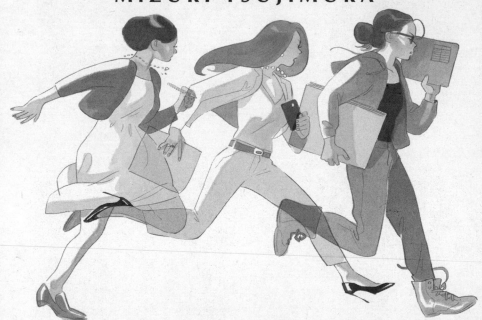

Paperback • 416 Pages • $16.95 US/$18.95 CAN
ON SALE NOW!

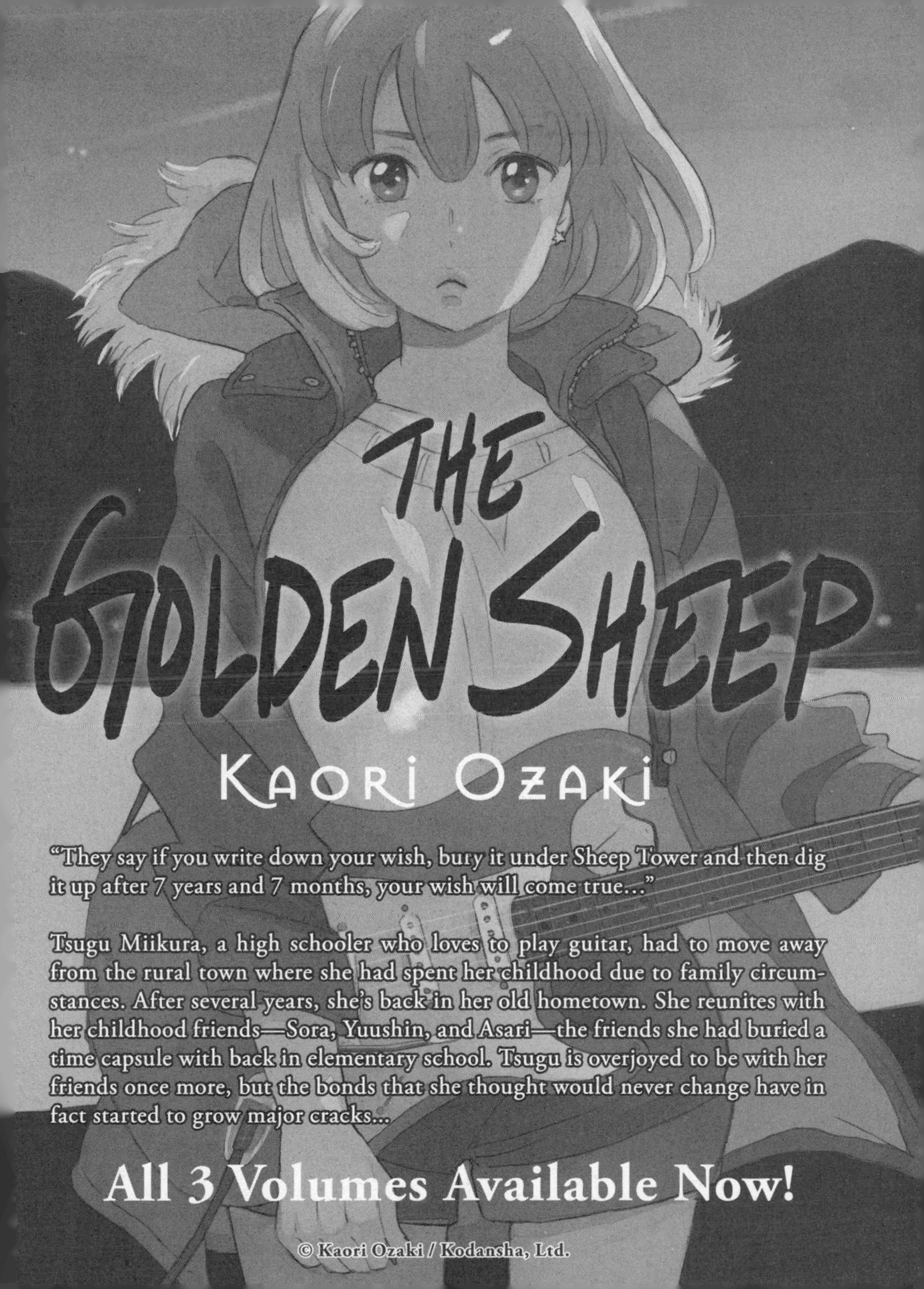
THE GOLDEN SHEEP
KAORI OZAKI
"They say if you write down your wish, bury it under Sheep Tower and then dig it up after 7 years and 7 months, your wish will come true..."
Tsugu Miikura, a high schooler who loves to play guitar, had to move away from the rural town where she had spent her childhood due to family circumstances. After several years, she's back in her old hometown. She reunites with her childhood friends—Sora, Yuushin, and Asari—the friends she had buried a time capsule with back in elementary school. Tsugu is overjoyed to be with her friends once more, but the bonds that she thought would never change have in fact started to grow major cracks...
All 3 Volumes Available Now!
© Kaori Ozaki / Kodansha, Ltd.

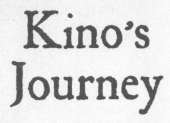

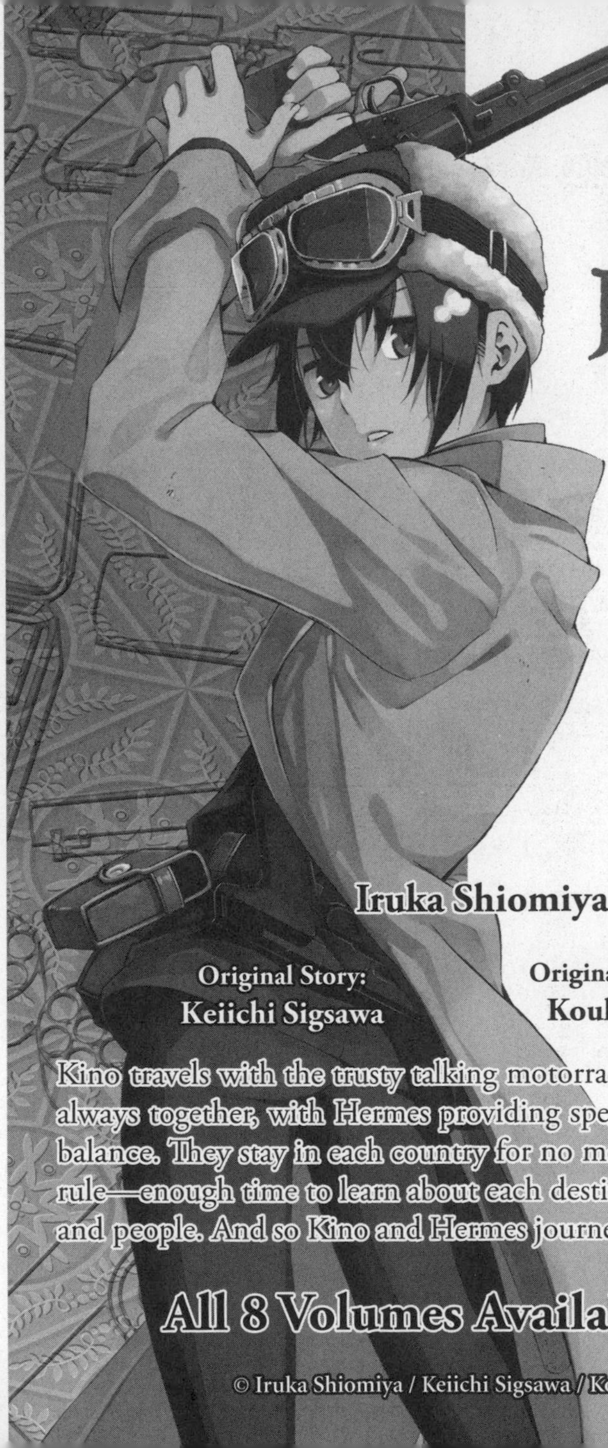

Kino's Journey

The Beautiful World

Iruka Shiomiya

Original Story:
Keiichi Sigsawa

Original Character Design:
Kouhaku Kuroboshi

Kino travels with the trusty talking motorrad, Hermes. The duo are always together, with Hermes providing speed, and Kino providing balance. They stay in each country for no more than three days, as a rule—enough time to learn about each destination's unique customs and people. And so Kino and Hermes journey ever onward…

All 8 Volumes Available Now!

A School Frozen in Time
volume 4

A Vertical Comics Edition

Editing: Ajani Oloye
Translation: Michelle Lin
Production: Grace Lu
           Tomoe Tsutsumi
Proofreading: Micah Q. Allen

First published in Japan in 2009 by Kodansha, Ltd., Tokyo
Publication for this English edition arranged through Kodansha, Ltd., Tokyo
English language version produced by Vertical Comics,
an imprint of Kodansha USA Publishing, LLC

Translation provided by Vertical Comics, 2021
Published by Kodansha USA Publishing, LLC, New York

Originally published in Japanese as *Tsumetai Kousha no Toki wa Tomaru 4*
by Kodansha, Ltd.
Tsumetai Kousha no Toki wa Tomaru first serialized in *Gekkan Shounen Magazine*,
Kodansha, Ltd., 2008

This is a work of fiction.

ISBN: 978-1-64729-073-3

Manufactured in the United States of America

First Edition

Kodansha USA Publishing, LLC
451 Park Avenue South
7th Floor
New York, NY 10016
www.kodansha.us

Vertical books are distributed through Penguin-Random House Publisher Services.

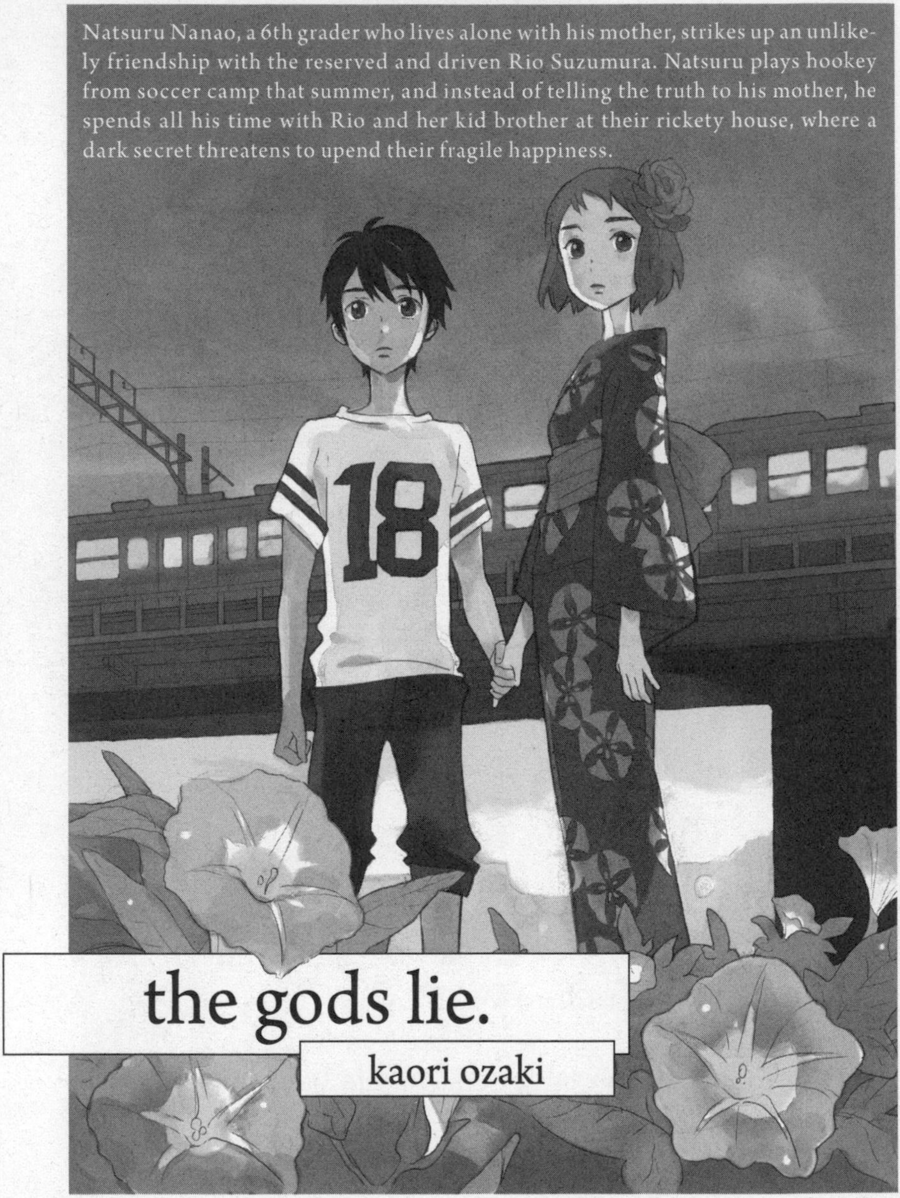
Natsuru Nanao, a 6th grader who lives alone with his mother, strikes up an unlikely friendship with the reserved and driven Rio Suzumura. Natsuru plays hookey from soccer camp that summer, and instead of telling the truth to his mother, he spends all his time with Rio and her kid brother at their rickety house, where a dark secret threatens to upend their fragile happiness.
18
the gods lie.
kaori ozaki

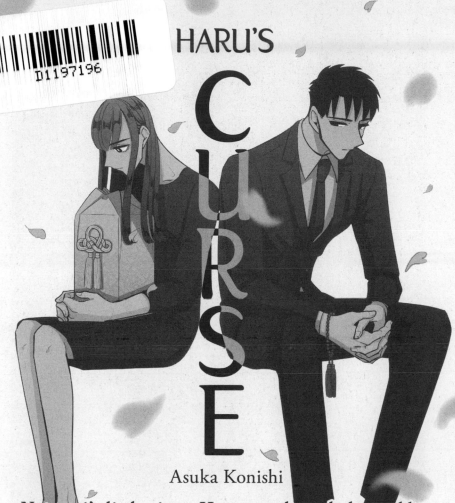

HARU'S CURSE

Asuka Konishi

Natsumi's little sister Haru was her whole world—and now she's gone.

After the funeral, Natsumi reluctantly agrees to date her sister's fiancé Togo. But as their relationship develops with the passing seasons, Haru's memory lingers over them like a curse.

Asuka Konishi's English-language debut is a nuanced and affecting portrait of the conflict between romantic and familial love, and of the hard choices that face us all in making our lives our own.

Available Now!